Anaphora and Language Design

Linguistic Inquiry Monographs
Samuel Jay Keyser, general editor

A complete list of books published in the Linguistic Inquiry Monographs series appears at the back of this book.

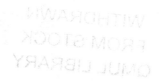

Anaphora and Language Design

Eric Reuland

The MIT Press
Cambridge, Massachusetts
London, England

For information about special quantity discounts, please e-mail special_sales @mitpress.mit.edu

This book was set in Times New Roman and Syntax on 3B2 by Asco Typesetters, Hong Kong. Printed and bound in the United States of America.

Library of Congress Cataloging-in-Publication Data

Reuland, Eric
Anaphora and language design / Eric Reuland.
    p.   cm. — (Linguistic inquiry monographs)
Includes bibliographical references and index.
ISBN 978-0-262-01505-9 (hardcover : alk. paper) — ISBN 978-0-262-51564-1 (pbk. : alk. paper) 1. Anaphora (Linguistics) 2. Grammar, Comparative and general—Syntax. I. Title.
P299.A5R48   2011
401'.456—dc22   2010020909

10 9 8 7 6 5 4 3 2 1

For Wimke

Contents

Series Foreword   xi

Preface   xiii

1   Introduction   1

1.1   Goals   1

1.2   Background   4

1.3   Variation in Binding   7

1.4   Toward Explanation in Linguistics   9

    1.4.1   Linguistics as a Cognitive Science   9

    1.4.2   A Minimalist Perspective on Natural Language Grammar   10

    1.4.3   What Would Make C_{HL} Trivial?   14

1.5   Unity and Diversity in Anaphoric Dependencies   19

    1.5.1   Universals and Sources of Invariance   19

    1.5.2   Toward Explaining the Binding Conditions   22

1.6   Interpretive Dependencies   25

    1.6.1   Binding and Coreference   27

    1.6.2   A Definition of A-Binding   30

    1.6.3   A-Binding: Logical Syntax and Semantics   34

1.7   The Canonical Binding Theory   38

    1.7.1   An Overview of the CBT   38

    1.7.2   Locality   40

    1.7.3   BT Compatibility   42

    1.7.4   Some Further Challenges to the CBT   43

1.8   Beyond the CBT   44

    1.8.1   Types of Nominal Expressions   44

    1.8.2   Parameters of Variation   46

1.9   Indices and Their Demise   53

1.10   Binding and Coreference Revisited   56

1.11   Summary and Structure of the Book   58

2   Structural Conditions on A-Binding   69

2.1   Background   69

2.2   The Status of C-Command in Binding   70

2.3 Pronominals versus Anaphors   79
2.4 Conclusions   80

3   A Modular Approach to Binding: Reflexivity, Chains, and Exemption   81
3.1 Defining Reflexivity   81
3.2 Condition B: Main Facts   83
3.3 Condition A: Main Facts   88
3.4 Semantic and Syntactic Predicates   95
3.5 The Structure of SE Anaphors and SELF Anaphors   96
3.6 An Independent Factor: Syntactic Chain Formation   100
     3.6.1 Dutch versus Frisian   100
     3.6.2 Chains and the Chain Condition   102
     3.6.3 Where Neither the Chain Condition nor Condition B
           Applies   105
     3.6.4 Chains and Hierarchy   107
3.7 Condition B in N- and P-Predicates   109
     3.7.1 N-Predicates   109
     3.7.2 P-Predicates   110
3.8 Toward Explaining the Binding Conditions: Reflexivity and
    Chains   115
3.9 Conclusion   120

4   Representing Anaphoric Dependencies: Issues of Economy   123
4.1 Introduction   123
4.2 The Nature of Economy: Its Rationales   126
4.3 Competition in Brazilian Portuguese   130
4.4 A Synthesis: The Competition between *Hem* and *Zich* Revisited   131
4.5 Conclusions   136

5   Binding by Chains: The Syntactic Encoding of Interpretive
     Dependencies   137
5.1 Introduction   137
5.2 Underspecification   138
5.3 Index-Free Binding   140
5.4 The Binding Requirement on Anaphors   144
5.5 Encoding Dependencies within C_{HL} 145
     5.5.1 Dependencies in the Framework of Chomsky (1995)   146
     5.5.2 Overt V-to-T   149
     5.5.3 Checking *Zich*'s Features   151
     5.5.4 Linking   151
     5.5.5 Features and Feature Bundles   153
     5.5.6 CHAINs and Chains   155
     5.5.7 Covert V-to-T   156
5.6 Conditions on the Tail: What Blocks Chain Formation?   159
     5.6.1 Recoverable Features   159
     5.6.2 A Nonrecoverable Property: Number   162

5.6.3   A Further Perspective: The Role of D   164
5.6.4   Definiteness and POSS Anaphors   166
5.7   Binding versus Logophoricity   169
5.7.1   Subjunctive   170
5.7.2   Nonmatching Antecedents   171
5.8   Maximality of Chains and Conditions on Chain Heads   173
5.8.1   The Issue   173
5.8.2   SE as a Subject   173
5.9   Agreeing to Bind   174
5.9.1   Background   174
5.9.2   Implementation   176
5.9.3   An Empirical Consequence   178
5.10   Conclusion   179

6   Deriving the Binding Conditions: Encoding and Sources of Invariance   181
6.1   Introduction   181
6.2   Deriving the Binding Conditions: Why Conditions A and B?   185
6.2.1   Why is Reflexivity Marked?   185
6.2.2   Condition B and the IDI   186
6.3   Licensing Reflexivity   189
6.3.1   Operations on Argument Structure: The θ-System   192
6.3.2   From Lexical Reflexivity to Structural Case and Pronouns in English   202
6.3.3   Protecting a Variable   206
6.4   A Note on Binding and an Interim Summary   209
6.4.1   A Note on Binding   209
6.4.2   An Interim Summary   211
6.5   Deriving Condition A   214
6.5.1   The Syntax of Reflexive-Marking   215
6.5.2   Reference by Proxy and the Functional Semantics of Pronominals   219
6.5.3   How SELF Movement Is Enforced   222
6.6   Remaining Questions and Summary of Results   237
6.6.1   Revisiting Faltz's Typology   237
6.6.2   The Notion "Anaphor": Its Theoretical Significance   239
6.7   From Invariants to Variation: Masking   240
6.8   Conclusions   245

7   Reflexive-Marking by SELF Movement: A Case Study   247
7.1   Introduction   247
7.2   The Internal Structure of SELF Anaphors   247
7.3   Further Consequences of SELF Movement   249
7.4   The Definition of Syntactic Predicates: Which Property Attracts SELF?   253
7.5   Local Binding of 1st- and 2nd-Person Pronominals   255

7.6   Maximality of Chains and Conditions on Chain Heads   259
    7.6.1   The Issue   259
    7.6.2   Nominative Complex Anaphors   260
7.7   Summary and Conclusions   266

8   Variation in Anaphoric Systems within Germanic   267
8.1   Introduction   267
8.2   Local Binding of Pronouns in Frisian   268
8.3   German *Sich*   273
    8.3.1   German *Sich* and Reflexivity   273
    8.3.2   Case and Case Distinctions   279
    8.3.3   Concluding the Discussion of Case and Chains   283
8.4   Long-Distance Anaphors in Germanic   285
    8.4.1   Introduction   285
    8.4.2   Anaphors across Germanic Languages   286
    8.4.3   Capturing the Variation in Binding Domains   295
    8.4.4   Discussion from Current Perspectives: Long-Distance Binding and Minimalism   302
    8.4.5   Long-Distance Binding of Direct Object SE   311
8.5   Logophoricity: Icelandic Logophoric Anaphora   314
    8.5.1   Introduction   314
    8.5.2   Subjunctives   316
    8.5.3   Infinitives   319
    8.5.4   Summary of the Facts   320
    8.5.5   The Interpretation of *Sig*: Binding versus Coreference   321
    8.5.6   Conclusions and Open Issues   322
8.6   Summary and Conclusions   323

9   Discussion, Summary, and Conclusions   325
9.1   Introduction   325
9.2   How to Encode Anaphoric Dependencies: Theoretical and Crosslinguistic Variation   326
    9.2.1   Kayne 2002   327
    9.2.2   Zwart 2002   330
    9.2.3   Boeckx, Hornstein, and Nunes 2007   331
    9.2.4   Safir 2004a and 2004b   335
    9.2.5   Hicks 2009   336
9.3   Overview and Summary of Results   337
9.4   General Conclusions   341

Notes   345
References   393
Author Index   419
Subject Index   425

Series Foreword

We are pleased to present the sixty-third in the series *Linguistic Inquiry Monographs*. These monographs present new and original research beyond the scope of the article. We hope they will benefit our field by bringing to it perspectives that will stimulate further research and insight.

Originally published in limited edition, the *Linguistic Inquiry Monographs* are now more widely available. This change is due to the great interest engendered by the series and by the needs of a growing readership. The editors thank the readers for their support and welcome suggestions about future directions for the series.

Samuel Jay Keyser
for the Editorial Board

Preface

Finishing this book marks the end of the first stage of a project that essentially started with a workshop on long-distance anaphora in Groningen on June 18–20, 1987. Before that workshop I always told myself that I was never going to work on binding theory, since the canonical binding conditions were just too boring. It did not help that the crosslinguistic facts obviously did not fit, since I did not see how they could be made to fit without all kinds of ad hoc solutions. Most crucial, however, was the fact that it kept eluding me why something like the binding conditions would hold. The workshop, and especially the decision to edit a volume together with Jan Koster on the basis of that workshop and to include Tanya Reinhart in the process, changed that. (See Koster and Reuland 1991.)

In my work with Jan Koster on the introduction to the book I learned that the apparent variation in the binding domains of long-distance anaphors reflected very simple binding principles interacting with independently varying properties of the syntactic structure, a discovery that for the most part had been made earlier by Martin Everaert (Everaert 1986) but that somehow had not received sufficient attention. Given a distinction between structural binding and logophoricity, much of the variation fell into place.

My work with Tanya Reinhart on the material that ended up as chapter 14 of that volume (Reinhart and Reuland 1991) really got me hooked on the subject. The modular approach to binding that came out of that work helped me understand a range of initially puzzling facts, from anaphors in English that do not obey the canonical condition A, to the contrast between *zich* and *zichzelf* in Dutch (and similar contrasts in other languages) and the existence of locally bound pronominals in Frisian, discussed earlier by Martin Everaert. After finishing this article we decided to work on a journal article, which after the most intense series of working sessions I have ever experienced, was published as Reinhart and Reuland 1993. The results convinced us that we had discovered fundamental principles of the organization of the anaphoric system in natural language, but on the other hand, we were faced with the challenges posed by crosslinguistic variation, and, of course, the even more fundamental question of why there would be special conditions on binding at all.

Some decisions are not made consciously, but in retrospect I can say that subsequently Tanya Reinhart and I started working on different pieces of the puzzle that in the end all came together. Tanya first resumed her work on the division of labor between the semantics and discourse components of the language system, resulting in her 2006 book, and I started thinking about issues of crosslinguistic variation and about why there would be conditions on binding. My decision to take up the latter question was heavily influenced by what I thought was one of the most challenging and attractive features of the Minimalist Program, namely the inclusiveness condition, eliminating the use of indices from the syntax. For me, the result, reported in my 1995 GLOW talk (Reuland 1995)— that syntactic conditions on binding (the chain condition of Reflexivity) could be derived without recourse to indices—was a breakthrough. That this particular way of encoding dependencies accounted for their variability in a natural way provided an incentive to continue this line of inquiry. So, I became more and more intrigued by anaphora and convinced that our approach led to an understanding of the basic mechanisms. This feeling was strengthened by my chance to work with Sigga Sigurjónsdóttir on long-distance anaphora in Icelandic, where again important pieces of a puzzle all of a sudden turned out to fit. In a nutshell, that is the reason I pursued that area of linguistics.

Between 1995 and 2004 most of my time was taken up by administrative duties, hence it was not for several years that my ideas from 1995 were published (as Reuland 2001b). So, although I kept doing some work on anaphora, it was not nearly enough to satisfy my own curiosity. Luckily, Tanya had meanwhile taken up another issue from reflexivity that we had had to leave open at the time, namely lexical reflexivity, and embedded it in θ-theory, a more general theory of operations on argument structure. An initial version of her work on this subject was accepted as a *Linguistic Inquiry* monograph. Because of her sad and untimely death this monograph has not come out yet, but Martin Everaert, Marijana Marelj, Tal Siloni, and I are working on that. In the meantime, her insights are available, for instance, in Reinhart 2002, Reinhart and

Siloni 2005, and Marelj 2004, a dissertation Tanya and I jointly supervised. In that period Tanya, Tal, Marijana, and I had extensive discussions about reflexivity, operations on argument structure, and Case, which played an essential role in further shaping my ideas.

Around the same time I became involved in discussions about the relation between grammatical architecture and language processing. Sergey Avrutin, Frank Wijnen, and I had converging ideas on the role of economy in the processing of anaphoric relations, which Sergey elaborated with Esther Ruigendijk and Nada Vasić, whereas Frank and I worked on these ideas with Arnout Koornneef. In the present book I show how a synthesis can be found between these results and Tanya's view on economy.

Combining these various angles, we found that the conditions on anaphoric dependencies are the result of the interaction of many factors, some independent of language (as I showed in Reuland 2005a), others irreducibly linguistic. Small differences in structure, entirely independent of binding, may give rise to what appear to be major differences in the way anaphoric dependencies manifest themselves. The following conclusion is unavoidable: there is no dedicated "binding theory," and the superficial constraints on anaphoric dependencies tell us very little in isolation of other properties of a language. This means that in order to understand patterns of anaphora in one language—or language in general—one has to take into account a great many factors from different parts of the grammar. This has far-reaching methodological implications. On the one hand, one can no longer "falsify" an analysis on the basis of a simple isolated observation about anaphors in language x, y, or z, as is often attempted; but on the other hand, the exposure to falsification is increased, since data from many components of the grammar can be brought to bear on a particular analysis. Another implication is that it is important to seriously study languages that show patterns that are prima facie different.

My experience with discussions in the field convinced me that all the factors that played a role in my understanding of anaphoric relations should be brought together in one book. In 2004 I received a grant from the Netherlands Organization for Scientific Research (NWO) (grant number 365-70-014) to write up a synthesis of my previous research. I spent part of that period at MIT, which gave me an opportunity to work on the Agree-based encoding of anaphoric dependencies. I am very much indebted to Noam Chomsky for stimulating discussion and for pointing out an interesting implication of my approach, which turned out to be correct. My thanks go also to David Pesetsky for discussion of his approach to chain formation, which I adopted.

While at MIT I consulted with Jay Keyser about a possible venue for publication, and he suggested that I submit a book proposal on the basis of a collection of articles. When I was preparing it, I found that quite a bit of text was needed to connect the articles because of the time lapse and overall changes in theory between them. So, the manuscript I first submitted contained Reinhart and Reuland 1993 and Reuland 2001b as separate chapters, with quite a bit of connecting text, together with some more recent material. I received very stimulating and helpful reviews from three MIT Press reviewers, and I revised the manuscript along the lines they suggested, also incorporating the very helpful comments I had received from friends and colleagues. It circulated in that form for some time.

This final version, however, differs substantially from the intermediate version. This is largely because of the extensive comments on content and presentation that I received from Natasha Slioussar. She recommended a further integration and reorganization of the material; moreover, she convinced me to try to make the discussion as accessible as possible to a broader audience than the community of generative linguists. This, then, is what I have tried to do. I feel that in order to further our understanding it is essential that linguists with very different types of expertise work together. And I hope that this book contributes to this goal, although I realize that in its present form it gets only halfway there. It contains sections where basic issues of generative theory are explained, but it also has parts that in all probability are not accessible to readers without previous knowledge. So, in that sense it is not self-contained. On the other hand I have tried to present the material in such a way that the more technical parts can be skipped without making it impossible to understand what comes next, and the more elementary material can be skipped by readers who already know it.

Currently another project is underway that carries the research forward, a systematic investigation of universals and the typology of reflexives, a project that I am collaborating on with Martin Everaert, Alexis Dimitriadis, Dagmar Schadler, and Anna Volkova. This project, also funded by a grant from the NWO (360-70-330), is intended to result in a monograph that systematically investigates crosslinguistic variation, and hence will complement the present book.

The ideas in this book have been presented to a variety of audiences over time, and I have benefited enormously from the feedback I have received. Space limitations only allow me to list a few audiences. Clearly, the audience in the original workshop was important; so was the GLOW audience in Tromsø in 1995, as well as audiences at various NELS conferences, as can be seen from the reference section. An all-too-short stay at the Netherlands Institute for Advanced Studies (NIAS) in the fall of 2006 (as a participant in Martin Everaert and Henk van Riemsdijk's Syncom project) allowed me to work on a synthesis of long-distance anaphora and related issues in Germanic. Somewhat later, I was able to participate in the Symposium on Reflexives and Reciprocals organized by Zygmunt Frajzyngier and Traci Curl in Boulder, Colorado, in 1997, which was also very important in shaping my ideas. I taught parts of this material on two occasions at a LOT school (together with Martin Everaert), and in 2001 at the Department of Linguistics at UCLA. The Workshop on Reciprocity and Reflexivity organized by Ekkehard König and Volker Gast at the Free University of Berlin in 2004 also turned out to be extremely stimulating, as was the Workshop on Asymmetry and Interface Conditions organized by Anna Maria Di Sciullo in memory of Tanya Reinhart (July 21–22, 2008, as part of CIL 18, in Seoul). Especially fruitful for the eventual organization of the book were the courses I was invited to teach in spring 2007 at Rutgers University (thanks go to Ken Safir), fall 2007 in Rochester (special thanks to Jeff Runner and Greg Carlson), and spring 2008 at St. Petersburg University. The NORMS Workshop Relating to Reflexives (Reykjavik, April 2009; thanks to Tania Strahan) stimulated me to make precise the status of the assumptions needed, as did the Conference on Minimalist Approaches to Syntactic Locality (Budapest, August 2009; organized by Balázs Surányi). A formalization of the notion of reflexive marking, recently developed together with Yoad Winter, was presented in the Eighth Tbilisi Symposium on Language, Logic and Computation in September 2009, and in the Discourse Anaphora and Anaphor Resolution Colloquium (Goa, November 2009).

Virtually every page of this book shows my indebtedness to Tanya, and our years of intense discussion, although she never saw the first draft. This book is written in fond memory of her.

When I moved from Groningen to Utrecht I was extremely lucky to find Martin Everaert as a colleague and friend who shared my interest in anaphors (and who, as an associate director, enabled me to find just enough relief from my directorship to keep my research alive). Over the years he has served as a constant source of inspiration, and I am extremely happy to continue working with him on our universals project (which is now drawing him away from the daily chores of his director-ship). If the introduction to this book is readable at all, it is due to his advice.

I have had the privilege of working with a large number of great doctoral students. Let me only mention a few whose influence on the present work is substantial. Taka Hara showed how reflexivity plays a role in Japanese, despite his original goal of showing that it doesn't. Marijana Marelj greatly contributed to developing θ-theory, providing crucial tools to distinguish between "syntax" and "lexicon" languages (not all of which made it into this book for reasons of space). Nadya Vinokurova convinced me that apparently complex binding patterns in Sakha become simple once approached in the proper way. Nino Amiridze showed me that Georgian has the most beautiful pattern of complex versus simplex reflexives I have come across so far. Anca Sevcenco provided evidence that even Romanian is simple after all, if one takes into account that certain anaphors require A′-antecedents. Arnout Koornneef produced crucial experimental evidence for a systematic division of labor between syntax, logical syntax/semantics, and discourse in the processing of anaphoric dependencies, which influenced the way I ended up thinking about economy.

I would also like to thank my friends and colleagues who commented on various versions of this book. As I mentioned earlier, Natasha Slioussar went over the whole manuscript and gave me important suggestions on how to optimally present my ideas. Her contribution was invaluable. Ken Safir gave me detailed comments on content and exposition, as well as challenging facts to account for. I know how hard it is to find the time to do this and am very grateful to him for his time and effort. Ken Safir, like Martin Everaert, strongly advised me to kill a lot of my darlings. I did, but if I did not kill enough of them it is not their fault. I am also very grateful to Denis Delfitto for his many stimulating comments. Alexis Dimitriadis gave me very valuable feedback on some of the more formal parts of the analysis. In addition, I am very much indebted to Yoad Winter. While we were going through the book in detail, we got stuck on the workings of reflexive marking in what was chapter 3 at that time. His suggestions led to a whole new line of research, only part of which is covered in chapter 6 of this book; the rest will hopefully lead to a new, joint, project. Thanks also to Dagmar Schadler and Anna Volkova for reading and commenting on a previous version.

What was intended to be a yearlong project (the period covered by the original NWO grant) turned out to last more than five years. Bad plan-

ning, an efficiency manager would say. Well, that's what it takes to get
something done would be my answer.

But even so, writing a book is a task that weighs on you and on those
around you. Wimke, Merijn, Ascelijn, Marike, and Michiel, thanks for
making it so abundantly clear that there is a life out there. I would also
like to thank Suus and Jane for their continuing interest in the project. I
am extremely lucky that Wimke knows what one has to go through if one
really wants to solve a question (her work involves immune responses,
genetics, and our dentition rather than language). Nevertheless, she has
been looking forward to a time when playing tennis, taking a nice long
walk in the snow, or watching a good movie is not an irresponsible dis-
traction from a "more important" goal. Wimke, thanks a lot for your
love and support during all these years. As a minimal token of love and
gratitude, this book is for you!

1 Introduction

Alice laughed. "There's no use trying," she said: "one can't believe impossible things."

"I daresay you haven't had much practice," said the Queen. "When I was your age, I always did it for half-an-hour a day. Why, sometimes I've believed as many as six impossible things before breakfast."

—Lewis Carroll, *Through the Looking-Glass*, 153

1.1 Goals

The use of language comes as naturally to us as breathing. This is why it is so tempting to take its properties at face value. A scientific enterprise, however, requires distance from the object of interest, and departing from one's everyday perspective. It starts with curiosity about what appears obvious and natural, and an open mind.

What the Queen is telling Alice is that impossible things are perhaps not so impossible after all, if you try hard enough (and perhaps that believing impossible things is fun, although we cannot be so sure in the case of the Queen). Turning around what she said, it surely is fun to think of familiar things every day (and perhaps six and before breakfast), to discover how curious they actually are. This is what we should do with language.

I begin this book with a simple fact of language that only reveals how curious it is if we are open to what small things may tell us. Let me put it in the context of Alice's world. The story of *Alice's Adventures in Wonderland* begins as follows:

(1) Alice was beginning to get very tired of sitting by her sister on the bank.

This fragment contains an occurrence of the pronoun *her* in *her sister*, and it is pretty clear that *her* can only be Alice. As we know, after this the story introduces the White Rabbit, how the Rabbit popped down the rabbit hole, and how Alice went after it. The story goes on as in (2):

(2) The rabbit-hole went straight on like a tunnel for some way, and then dipped suddenly down, so suddenly that Alice had not a moment to think about stopping herself before she found herself falling down a very deep well.

This fragment has two occurrences of the word *herself*. *Herself* is an anaphor, and all speakers of English will without hesitation give these occurrences of *herself* the value Alice as well. So, in the context of this part of the story both *her* and *herself* receive the same value. What happens if we replace *herself* with *her* in (2')?

(2') The rabbit-hole went straight on like a tunnel for some way, and then dipped suddenly down, so suddenly that Alice had not a moment to think about stopping her before she found her falling down a very deep well.

Here, for some reason, *her* cannot be Alice, and since the text did not introduce any other suitable female character, this change makes the fragment unacceptable. The puzzle is, then, the following:

(3) Why can't the pronoun have the value *Alice* in (2'), although it can have the value *Alice* in other environments?

As illustrated in (4), freely improvising on other parts of the tale, there is another puzzle, and it relates to anaphors such as *herself*.

(4) a.   *Alice* found *herself* falling.
    b.   *Alice expected the Mad Hatter to invite *herself* for tea.
    c.   *The Mad Hatter invited *herself*.

In (4a) *herself* receives the value of *Alice* but in (4b) this is impossible. (In (4) and elsewhere, italicized expressions have the same values.) Whereas in (2') our interpretive system can value *her* with any female individual other than Alice—if contextually available—and the sentence will be grammatical, in (4b) there is no escape, and the same holds true for (4c). No interpretation is available for *herself* in these environments. Summarizing, we have the puzzle in (3'):

(3') Why can't the anaphor *herself* have the value Alice in (4b,c), although it can have the value Alice in other environments?

These seem small questions, but as we pursue them, they will turn out to bear on the core design properties of language.

Even at this stage of our inquiries, this fragment teaches us one important point. Whatever lies behind the need for the use of *herself* in (2) instead of *her*, it cannot be a putative principle that natural language avoids ambiguity, or that we have to use the most informative form if the language has two or more options. When these paragraphs tell us how Alice is falling down the rabbit hole, it is abundantly clear that the only person she would think of stopping, or who she found falling, can be Alice. Thus whatever *herself* does, it is not there to restrict the pragmatically available interpretations, since there is only one to start with.

The pattern illustrated above is not specific to English. All languages have elements that *may* or *must* depend on another expression in the same sentence for their interpretation. Pronouns may depend on another element in the sentence for their interpretation, but need not. For instance, in an alternative story line in which Alice and her sister both ran toward the rabbit hole, *her* could easily be valued as Alice's sister in (2′). Expressions such as *herself* show a stronger requirement: they must depend on an antecedent. Since *the Mad Hatter* in (4b,c) is masculine it cannot provide the value the feminine *herself* requires, and unlike *her* the expression *herself* cannot simply be assigned a value from the context. The sentence is, therefore, ill-formed.

To understand such puzzles, it is essential to have precise descriptions of the facts. The canonical binding theory (henceforth CBT) outlined in Chomsky 1981 presents a good first approximation of the restrictions on the interpretation of pronouns and anaphors. I will discuss its structure in more detail in section 1.7.

Descriptions by themselves do not answer such *why*-questions, though. In this book I will be concerned with the basic mechanics of the grammatical system. The question driving our discussion is why these facts are the way they are. Are they just quirks of the language system, idiosyncrasies varying from one language to another, or do these facts reveal basic properties of the relation between form and interpretation?

As we will see, they do reveal such properties, which is the reason I chose to study this domain. Compared to "full" nominal expressions such as *Alice, the Cheshire cat, the white rabbit, the king of hearts*, or *the Mad Hatter*, pronominals and anaphors by themselves provide very few clues about their interpretation. Consequently, the study of their interpretation provides us with a probe into the basic mechanisms underlying linguistic computation, and, as we will see, ways to differentiate between the contributions the various components of the language system make.

As I will show, the puzzles in (3) and (3′) receive straightforward answers, in terms of the basic mechanisms of the grammar. And, in fact, the principles we need are not at all special to anaphora.[1]

My primary focus will be on the principles that (dis)allow anaphora where judgments are categorical (reflecting "grammar"), like in (2) and (4). I will have little to say about factors that choose between grammatically admissible options as illustrated in (5):

(5) Alice looked at the Queen. She was angry.

Here, grammatical principles allow both "Alice" and "the Queen" as values for *she*. It is our knowledge of the story that will determine which of the two options is realized. Such dependencies—pertaining to what one may broadly call the field of *anaphora resolution*—are addressed in centering theory (see, for instance, Walker, Joshi, and Prince 1998), and in the further vast computational literature on the subject (see, for instance, Mitkov 2002 for an overview). Many of the properties discussed there are gradient and involve plausibility judgments. These will have to stay outside the scope of the present book, if only for practical reasons.

The questions I started out with are linguistic, but language is part of our cognitive system. Exploring how language is rooted in the human cognitive system is among the most fascinating endeavors science has embarked on. What components of the cognitive system underlie language? What are their essential mechanisms and how do they interact? What in the systems underlying language is specific to language, and which of their properties follow from general cognitive mechanisms? These are among the core questions that need to be answered. Contributing to their answers is the main goal of this book, using our anaphora puzzles as a window.

1.2 Background

This enterprise finds its starting point in issues that were highlighted for the first time within the framework of "generative grammar." They are reflected in Chomsky's (1986b) basic questions: (i) *What constitutes knowledge of a language,* (ii) *How is this knowledge acquired,* and (iii) *How is it put to use?* To the extent that a theory answers (i), it is *descriptively adequate* (it provides adequate description of the knowledge native speakers have of their language). If it allows an answer to (ii), it is *explanatorily adequate* (it embodies a characterization of the properties all languages share, and accounts for the limits on crosslinguistic variation). In other words, it puts sufficient limits on the hypotheses the child would have to consider in acquiring some language, and thus explains the fact that language can be acquired under natural conditions of access to data (see Wexler and Culicover 1980). By (iii) the following is meant: How is the knowledge of language realized in our mind and how does it interface with other subsystems of our cognitive system (for instance, the conceptual system as well as the processing and inference systems). Thus, investigating (iii) leads *beyond explanatory adequacy*, along the lines discussed in Chomsky 2001, 2004, 2005, and into the main themes that will concern us in the present book.

A systematic investigation of (iii) with realistic prospects for progress has begun only recently. It has been made possible by the rapprochement between linguistics and the other cognitive sciences, stimulated by the advances made in these fields in recent years.

Note that the questions to be addressed are general, and have an interest independent of any particular theory of grammar or cognition. However, naturally, any attempt to answer such questions will require developing a precise theory within a theoretical framework.[2] Theories and frameworks change over time. Changes may involve the basic fabric of a theory, or just superficial issues of terminology. Yet, it is important to see that real insights should be maintained over theoretical changes, and that often it is possible to recast an insight in different terms. That is why in my exposition below I will distinguish between broader conceptual issues and specific issues of implementation, making the issues and their solution accessible to an audience that is as broad as reasonably possible.

To understand the main motivation behind this book, let us come back to examples (1), (2), and (4). In relatively theory-neutral terms, one can say that an element such as *herself* must be valued by an antecedent that is sufficiently close, that an element such as *her* cannot be valued by an antecedent that is too close, and that *Alice* cannot be valued by an antecedent at all. Any theory must provide a precise characterization of what distinguishes elements like *her*, *herself*, and *Alice*, of how antecedency is represented, and of what it means to be "sufficiently close" or "too close."

As is well known, (1), (2), and (4) reflect a pattern that is crosslinguistically pervasive. Many languages from a range of different families have elements that must have a local antecedent, and elements that may not. A widely adopted view is that nominal expressions in natural language are divided into three categories: anaphors (elements like *herself*),[3] pronominals (like *her*),[4] and R-expressions (i.e., referential expressions, like

Alice, the king, no cat, etc.).[5] R-expressions have a lexical specification and must be valued independently. Pronominals lack a specification for lexical features—they typically carry only grammatical features, such as person, gender, and number (*φ-features*)—and they may, but need not, obtain their value from an antecedent. Otherwise, their value is established deictically (for instance, we can establish a referent for *her* in (1) or (2′) by pointing to a female individual other than Alice). Anaphors are referentially deficient, and must obtain their value from a linguistic antecedent.

This division forms the basis of the canonical binding theory presented in Chomsky 1981, henceforth CBT. In this theory and the subsequent work inspired by it, the informal notion of getting *valued by an antecedent* is reflected in the more technical notion of *binding*. The CBT is summarized in (6); see section 1.7 for a more detailed discussion.

(6) (A) An anaphor is bound in its local domain.
   (B) A pronominal is free in its local domain.
   (C) An R-expression is free.
   Free means *not bound*.

Conditions A and B exemplify *locality conditions* on binding. The *local domain* of an anaphor or pronominal can be approximated as the *minimal clause* containing it, and conditions A and B together yield that bound pronominals and anaphors are in complementary distribution.[6] The CBT is attractive in its simplicity: structures like (2′) are ill-formed since they violate condition B. Examples (4b,c) and their equivalents in other languages violate condition A.

From an empirical perspective, my approach is inspired by the fact that work on binding in recent decades has led to the discovery of an ever-increasing range of exceptions to the CBT, but on the other hand has shown that core patterns are stable. To put it succinctly, the CBT is *too bad to be true*, but *too good to be false*. To give the reader a first impression of the type of facts I have in mind, I present some of them in section 1.3.

From a theoretical perspective, an important question that remained open in the CBT is the issue of explanation. *Why* would the principles in (6) hold—to the extent to which they do? Or, why would there be special conditions on binding at all? What are the sources of invariance or variability? The main goal of this book is to answer such *why*-questions. Its main claim is that the facts that appear to motivate special conditions on binding, all follow from general properties of the language system, so in the end no special binding conditions are needed.

The main focus of the discussion will be on the domain roughly covered by binding conditions A and B. For practical reasons discussion of condition C effects will be limited to cases where they directly bear on the issues at hand.

1.3 Variation in Binding

In this section I discuss some of the facts that are puzzling for the CBT, adding clarification where necessary. All these facts are discussed extensively later; at this point they should simply serve as a first tableau of orientation for the reader.

First of all, crosslinguistically, one finds a considerable variety of anaphoric systems. English just has pronominals versus anaphors. Dutch and the Scandinavian languages provide good illustrations of more complex systems. These languages have *simplex anaphors* and *complex anaphors*, in addition to pronominals. Simplex anaphors are essentially pronominal elements that lack a specification for certain features (typically, number and gender, but occasionally also person). Complex anaphors are made up of combinations of a pronoun or simplex anaphor with another morpheme (elements like *self* or their cognates, body-part nouns, or occasionally another pronoun).[7]

Dutch, for instance has a simplex anaphor *zich*—which is only specified for person, not for number and gender—together with a complex anaphor *zichzelf*, which differ in distribution. Henceforth, I will refer to elements such as Dutch *zich* and cognates such as Norwegian *seg*, Icelandic *sig*, and so on as simplex-element anaphors, or briefly SE anaphors.

Contrasts between simplex and complex anaphors/anaphoric markers can be found in numerous other languages, as typologically diverse as Georgian (Kartvelian), Sakha (Turkic), Mandarin Chinese, Japanese, Erzja (Uralic), Mohawk (Iroquoian), or Fijian (Austronesian).

Just as there is variation in anaphoric forms, cognates of one form may differ in their binding domain, even within one language family. This is illustrated by the variation in the binding domains of SE anaphors in Germanic. For instance, in Dutch and German simplex anaphors can be bound by an antecedent in a higher clause in causative and perception verb constructions (with bare infinitives), but not as objects of *to*-infinitives. For instance, the equivalent of ***Alice** heard [the queen against SE argue]* is well formed, but not ***Alice** asked the king [to save SE]*. In Scandinavian, binding is allowed in both cases.

Also, properties of predicates have been found to play a role in determining binding possibilities. For example, in English *John washed* (without an object) has a reflexive interpretation, but *John hated does not. Dutch has Jan waste zich (a SE anaphor), but with the verb haten 'hate' a complex anaphor is required, as in Jan haatte zich*(zelf).[8] Norwegian and Danish have the same pattern as Dutch. In Russian, verbs like myt' 'wash' can be reflexivized with the reflexivizing affix s'a, but verbs such as nenavidet' 'hate' cannot; these require the anaphor seb'a. Again, these are just a few examples—more will be discussed in the course of the present book—but such effects are widespread crosslinguistically.

Contrary to condition B in (6), many languages allow local binding of 1st- and 2nd-person pronominals. German ich wasche mich, Dutch jij wast je, French nous nous lavons, etc., are all fine, unlike their English counterparts: I wash myself/*me, you wash yourself/*you, and so on. Although none of these languages allows local binding of 3rd-person pronominals, closely related Frisian does, as in **Jan** waske **him** 'John washed himself', as did Old English. Note that as a matter of principle I will take these facts seriously. I will not attempt to accommodate them by stipulating that such pronouns are in some sense anaphors in disguise. And, as we will see in detail in chapters 5 and 8, there is also no need to make such an assumption. The facts will follow directly from the feature composition these elements have.

There is also a range of facts that appear to be problematic for condition A, as stated in (6). Certain anaphoric forms in some languages need not be bound in their local domain, or may even lack a linguistic antecedent altogether. Well-studied cases are the locally free ("logophoric") use of English himself, as in **John** was hoping that Mary would support *(no one but) **himself**, or Icelandic sig in (69) below.

The languages mentioned constitute only a tiny fraction of the 6,000—8,000 or so languages or major dialects assumed to exist. Yet these facts alone require rethinking of the CBT. In fact, to motivate reassessing the basic properties of the CBT just three languages are enough. For instance, the existence of free anaphors as in English and Icelandic or locally bound pronominals as in Frisian shows that it is impossible to provide an independent characterization of anaphors versus pronominals in terms of an intrinsic obligation to be locally bound or free.

I come back in more detail to the problems the CBT faces in sections 1.7 and 1.8. Many of the issues raised are extensively discussed in subsequent chapters. As we will see, there is, nevertheless, unity in this diversity. However, showing this requires a finely grained conception of linguistic mechanisms, of the type provided by the Minimalist Program (henceforth occasionally referred to as MP) as presented in Chomsky 1995 and subsequent work.

1.4   Toward Explanation in Linguistics

1.4.1   Linguistics as a Cognitive Science

During the 1950s and 1960s we find a divide between linguistic research oriented toward description and research looking for explanation. Much of the latter focused on the properties of just a few natural languages—in fact, primarily English, based on the insight that a thorough study of the structure of even one language can provide us with important information about the language faculty, since it tells us what the language faculty must minimally be able to do.

In the 1970s, but in particular through the 1980s and 1990s, this divide was bridged. An increasing amount of research was devoted to detailed study of individual languages and the types of variation they exhibit; see, for instance, Keenan and Comrie 1977 or Faltz 1977. This line of research led to a great deal of insight into the structure of natural language and the restrictions on crosslinguistic variation (see Everaert and Van Riemsdijk 2005 for a fascinating collection of results). This development led to a systematic "generative" typology as exemplified by detailed work on morphology, word-order variation, and the effects of word order on interpretation (see, for instance, Baker 1988; Rizzi 1997; Cinque 1999).

Crucial is the conception of language as a biological system, forcefully expressed in Lenneberg 1967. In the 1980s this led to a boost in experimental and formal studies of the acquisition of language, as exemplified by Wexler and Culicover's influential 1980 work on formal principles of language acquisition, which for the first time enabled the requirement of explanatory adequacy to serve as an effective constraint on theory development. Issues of learnability became a standard item in the assessment of theoretical proposals.

Subsequently, we see a strengthening of the connections between linguistics and cognitive science in other domains. Work on language disorders showed convincingly that linguistically motivated structures provide the instruments for understanding language deficits and their manifestations.[9] The study of language processing showed how linguistically motivated processes of structure building provide insight in the time course of the interpretative process and the resources it uses.[10] As observed in Chomsky 2004, 2005, for the first time it has become feasible to move beyond explanatory adequacy, thus bringing within the scope of systematic inquiry the question of how language is embedded in our cognitive system.

As always when progress occurs in a field, this is brought about by a variety of factors. There were advances internal to linguistics, advances in the cognitive sciences broadly conceived, and perhaps also challenges posed by alternative approaches. But in any case, in order for a common framework effectively covering linguistics and the other fields within cognitive science to develop, one must be able to match linguistic operations and components of linguistic representations with processes and representations at the neurocognitive level. This is indeed the essence of the course established during the 1980s.

My own position on the relation between linguistics and neurocognition is best reflected in the following quote from Marantz 2000b:

> The split between linguistics and psycholinguistics in the 1970's has been interpreted as being a retreat by linguists from the notion that every operation of the grammar is a mental operation that a speaker must perform in speaking and understanding language. But, putting history aside for the moment, we as linguists cannot take the position that there is another way to construct mental representations of sentences other than the machinery of grammar.... There is no retreat from the strictest possible interpretation of grammatical operations as the only way to construct linguistic representations.

Clearly, this thesis holds independently from how successful we are in finding the neurocognitive processes matching the linguistic operations. But it is precisely an understanding of the microstructure of grammatical operations that enables us to pursue its consequences empirically, and actually match linguistic and neurocognitive architecture.

In my view, the Minimalist Program provides a crucial step forward. It provides a perspective on the microstructure of grammatical operations that is fine grained enough to be related to at least the macrophenomena at the neurocognitive level.

As we will see, the MP provides the instruments needed to fruitfully address the *why*-questions I am interested in, due to its attention to the details of the computational system underlying human language, its principled approach to demarcating the subsystems involved in language, and its systematic conceptual parsimony. In the next section I discuss its relevant properties in more detail. This section can be skipped by anyone who has a basic knowledge of the program.

1.4.2 A Minimalist Perspective on Natural Language Grammar

Natural language embodies a systematic mapping between form and interpretation. It seems to me that this position is essentially shared by all linguistic theories. Forms can be realized in a (possibly) external physical medium (sound, gestures); interpretations are ultimately changes in the state of certain internal subsystems of the human mind. This should be uncontroversial as well. A schematic representation of the "language system" is given in (7). In line with the usage in Chomsky 1995, C_{HL} will be used for the Computational System of Human Language, also referred to as Narrow Syntax. The terms *PF interface* (Phonetic Form) and *C-I interface* (Conceptual-Intentional) stand for the interfaces with the sound (or gesture) system and the interpretation system respectively. The lexicon is an inventory of minimal form-meaning combinations (*tree, -s, do, -able, the, of,* etc.). Lexical elements contain instructions for realization, instructions for interpretation, and instructions for how they may be combined. These systems are taken to be embedded in the human cognitive system (HCS), informally, the human mind. Unless sparked by the choice of terms, I submit there should again be no controversy here.

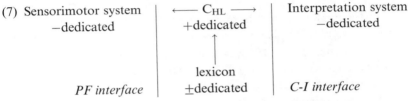

(7) Sensorimotor system $\longleftarrow C_{HL} \longrightarrow$ Interpretation system
    −dedicated   +dedicated   −dedicated

                       lexicon
       PF interface   ±dedicated   *C-I interface*

Our capacity for language obviously relies on many processes that are not dedicated to language (expressed as −*dedicated* in (7)). Our articulatory system is used for functions varying from eating to respiration. Our auditory system can process sounds irrespective of whether they pertain to language. Our thought system can process a variety of information types that reach us through the different channels provided by our senses.

    Our lexicon is closely related to our conceptual system, the system that allows us to organize our internal representation of the world around us.[11] Concepts like that of elephant, lion, trout, poison ivy, fear, running, and hunting are independently important to have for any being evolving in something like our niche in the world. Concepts, therefore, are not dedicated to language. Having them is presumably not even specific to humans. Hence, insofar as a concept is part of the lexical entry—which represents the mapping between these concepts and the arbitrary sound sequence indicated by the italics—such an entry cannot be completely dedicated to language either.

    However, certain formal aspects of the lexicon are dedicated to language, such as the fact that word forms are combinable, that they contain properties that are just there to drive the computation. Similarly, the lexicon contains a rich variety of elements that are not directly linked to our conceptual system. These are the elements of the functional system such as articles, Case or agreement markers, auxiliaries, prepositions such as *of* in *the destruction of Rome*, and so forth. These elements must be dedicated to language, like the mental capacity to represent them presumably is. Hence the characterization ±*dedicated* holds for the lexicon as a whole.

Thus, C_{HL} is the computational system connecting the form and interpretation systems. A minimal requirement is that C_{HL} provide expressions that are "readable" at the PF and C-I interfaces. C_{HL} is by assumption that component of the language system that is dedicated to language. Note that this assumption does not prejudge any empirical questions. It is logically possible that C_{HL} is a highly impoverished system, or even empty.

One of the core questions in the study of language is, then, how rich this system actually is. The MP explores the idea that the syntactic system is intrinsically very simple. As a strategy this again should be uncontroversial. A minimally complex system will easily show its limits if the reality it sets out to model is more complex than it can handle. Subsequently, it can be stepwise enriched as new discoveries require. This is essentially what minimalism stands for. A model that is overly rich from the start, will much less easily reveal where and how it can be appropriately trimmed down.

As Chomsky (1995) notes, as the descriptive breadth of linguistic research in the 1980s increased, a variety of elements and devices were introduced that appeared to be useful but that had not been shown to be indispensable. What minimalism comes down to is a heuristic strategy to ensure that no types of elements and operations are included in linguistic theory other than those absolutely necessary for the system to work. It expresses a commitment to conceptual parsimony, and to reassess what we really need in order to explain linguistic phenomena. Examples illustrating this point will come up as our discussion proceeds.

In this vein, Chomsky (2005, 2008) proposes that C_{HL} only contains the operations in (8):

(8) i. *Merge*

    a. Combine two expressions into a composite expression.

    b. Specify which of the two determines the further combinatorial properties of the result (the "head").

  ii. *Agree*

    a. Check whether two expressions match in features (such as category, person, number, gender).

    b. Share feature values.

A sequence of applications of the *Merge* operation builds complex expressions from elementary lexical elements.[12] The elements each application of *Merge* combines are either copies of elements retrieved from the lexicon, or they are (composite) expressions already in the workspace. As stated, *Merge* goes only a little (namely in the *ib*-clause) beyond an operation that any computational system must have by necessity, namely in that its expressions result from combining (minimal) expressions. The *ib*-clause expresses a property that may well be specific to language, namely the endocentricity of its expressions: every natural language expression has a head (note that it is even hard to see how such a notion can be applied to objects outside language). The matching requirement expressed by Agree typically obtains with subject-verb agreement, as we can see (rudimentarily) in English, where one has *Alice$_{SING}$ was$_{SING}$ in the garden* but not *Alice$_{SING}$ were$_{PLUR}$ in the garden*. It also obtains, generalizing the traditional notion, with Case dependencies as in *The cat was watching$_{ACCassigner}$ her$_{ACC}$* but not *The cat was watching$_{ACCassigner}$ she$_{NOM}$*. *Check* does not go beyond the power that any computational system must have that contains an identity predicate (in order to see whether $exp_1 = exp_2$ holds, the system must be able to inspect expressions and *check* whether they are identical).

Like Chomsky (1995 and subsequent work), I will take as a working hypothesis that C_{HL} is a perfect system:[13]

(9) C_{HL} is the optimal solution to letting the PF and C-I systems read each other.

The heuristic strategy is that (9) is to be abandoned only in the face of compelling evidence. In line with (9) the following methodological guideline will be employed in this book:

(10) *Uniformity*
   - The formal properties of the computational system are uniform across languages.
   - The formal properties of the conceptual system are uniform across languages.

The same holds true for the formal properties of the realization and interpretation systems. Together these entail that the locus of crosslinguistic variation is in the functional system, the system for marking Case, Agreement, and so on. This is a generally adopted working hypothesis in current generative theory. This does not mean it is unfalsifiable. However, in actual practice, this does mean that these assumptions will only be dropped as a last resort. As I will show in this book, there is no indication that they have to be dropped. In fact, as we will see, maintaining them will allow us to explain a range of puzzling phenomena from the interaction of simple factors. To give one example at this point, consider pronoun binding in Frisian.

As was mentioned in section 1.3, 3rd-person pronominals in Frisian can be locally bound, unlike their counterparts in many other languages. The question is, then, whether this means that Frisian requires a different binding theory, or that Frisian pronominals are conceptually different, and so forth. The uniformity principle in (10) tells us to make such assumptions only as a last resort. To understand what is going on in Frisian, we should look for peculiarities in its functional system, rather than decide that Frisian has different concepts or different *principles* for the encoding of anaphoric dependencies. Given the theory to be presented here, one of the components of the functional system one may expect to be involved is the Case system. As we will see in chapters 3 and 8, this strategy gives us what we want. The Frisian binding facts will be seen to be reducible to a simple property of the Case system of Frisian. Similar results will be obtained for the other examples of variation.

As noted earlier in this section, it is logically possible that C_{HL} is trivial. In the next section I briefly present some considerations bearing on this issue.

1.4.3 What Would Make C_{HL} Trivial?

In fact, there are two possible states of affairs that would make C_{HL} as described here trivial (see Chomsky 1995 and subsequent work for a discussion along the lines sketched below): (i) the PF and C-I interfaces can read each other directly, or (ii) C_{HL} is parasitic on other cognitive systems.

Taking (i) first, there are pervasive word-order effects in natural language that challenge an overly simplistic view of the relation between the C-I and PF interfaces. Computing the interpretation of a complex expression (sentence) standardly requires relating parts of the expression that occupy different positions in the PF representation. Chomsky (1995) refers to it as the *dislocation property* of natural language. Question formation as in (11) is a canonical illustration.

(11) What do you think that Alice saw?

What in initial position plays two roles: it signals that (11) is a question, and it represents the direct object of *saw* that is being questioned. The object position has to be empty, witness the ill-formedness of *What did you think that Alice saw the white rabbit*. So, essentially, *what* satisfies the direct object requirements of *saw*—that is, it *saturates* the position.

Note that this observation is not dependent on any particular theory of language. Any theory of language must account for this dual role of *what*. Doing so requires a representation in which *what* is related both to the initial position and to the object position of *saw*. One among several possibilities is to represent this as in (11′):

(11′) What did you think that Alice saw (what)?

In this representation, the dual role of *what* is captured by having two copies of *what* in the structure. In theories building on Chomsky 1995, this is achieved by having the operation Merge apply to the expression *what* in *did you think that Alice saw what*. Instead of copying an element from the mental lexicon, in this case Merge applies to an element that is already part of the structure being built. That is, we have a case of *Internal Merge* in the sense of Chomsky's approach. In (11′) the leftmost occurrence of *what* has been copied from the one in brackets, and merged in the initial position. The pair ⟨*what*, *what*⟩ forms one composite syntactic object, a *chain*.

A standard effect of copying is that only the copy is pronounced, here the leftmost occurrence of *what*. This is informally indicated by putting the unpronounced copy in brackets. One may either assume this to be implemented as an effect of the copying operation itself, or attempt to derive this from more basic properties of the syntactic system. An intriguing proposal as to how this can be derived is provided in Nunes 2004. Further discussion would lead us beyond the scope of this book.

The rightmost occurrence of *what* in (11′) is in a position where the verb *saw* can assign it a semantic role. (For the moment the traditional understanding of semantic roles as reflecting notions such as agent, patient, goal, etc., suffices.) A general term for the positions to which semantic roles can be assigned or where Cases can be checked is *A-position* (for *argument position*).[14] The leftmost occurrence is in a non-A-position, or A′-position. In this position its role as a question marker is realized. The former position is also called the *source* position, the latter position the *target*. In the framework of Chomsky 1981, *what* was taken to *Move* from the source position to the target, leaving an empty element, its *trace* in the source position. In line with current practice, I will still informally refer to this process of dual role assignment as *movement*, and to unpronounced copies as traces, marking them in representations with *t*.

Copying and movement are not the only proposals found in the literature. Regardless of how precisely this dual role is expressed, however, on the basis of phenomena as in (11) one cannot escape the conclusion that option (i) has to be discarded.

In terms of (7), option (ii) would mean that the role of C_{HL} is performed by processes that are all involved in other tasks within our cognitive system. The idea that there is no "innate" dedicated language system seems attractive to many philosophers and cognitive scientists. But consider what this claim involves.

We humans have a motor system, input systems (visual, tactile, olfactory, auditory), and memory systems (organized along dimensions such as long-term/short-term, phonological/visual, procedural/declarative, and so on; see, for instance, Baddeley 2007, Ullman 2004). A moment's reflection shows that regardless of their role in language, whatever these systems do must be orthogonal to C_{HL}. Input systems allow us to construct a mental representation of the world as it is at a particular time and place. (Note that such a representation in fact constitutes an interpretation of the world, since surely we actively shape this representation.) Memory systems allow us to retain a version of that mental representation through time (without prejudging the trustworthiness of such representations). None of these give us the unbounded variety of new language forms that C_{HL} must be able to give us (or of any courses of action, for that matter). So, regardless of one's pet theory of whether unboundedness resides at the syntactic level, the semantic level, or the discourse level, one has to assume some generative engine that goes beyond input systems and memory systems. Hence, we have to look elsewhere.

Uncontroversially, human cognition allows us to escape from the here and now. This ability rests on systems involved in imagination, reasoning, and planning. Imagination, since we are able to create mental representations of a world that differs from the world as we perceive it to be; reasoning, since we have to analyze how to go from one state of affairs to another; and planning, since we must be able to perform sequences of actions to bring about the state of affairs that we imagined (see Reuland 2005c).

Are imagination, reasoning, and planning enough to give us C_{HL}? This would be an interesting claim. There is no escape, though, from actually assessing in detail what C_{HL} has to be able to do, and what imagination, reasoning, and planning can do. One also has to assess to what extent these are really independent of language, since, clearly, much of our actual reasoning and planning depends on language. The same holds true for any attempt to reduce language to domain-general properties of our cognitive system. One must avoid introducing by the back door what one is attempting to explain.

In such an endeavor it is the detail that counts, since one would have to explain linguistic phenomena without any recourse to linguistic notions, such as head, category, lexical item (or template/construction), argument, and so on. It would be a major result if it could be shown that for instance locality conditions on movement operations (such as the island constraints discussed in Ross 1967) can be derived in toto from properties of other cognitive systems. But no viable proposals have been made for how this could be done.[15] This is not to say that the effort is a priori futile or misguided. But the only way to fruitfully investigate the issue is without philosophical preconceptions, instead treating it as a straightforward empirical problem, taking seriously all the intriguing properties languages have been shown to have.

As I explain in detail in this book, there are indeed nontrivial properties of language that can be derived from general principles, but there is no indication that this applies to language as a whole.

Note that Hauser, Chomsky, and Fitch (2002) (HCF) propose a line of thought that comes very close to a marginalization of the dedicated component of language, not in the form of a preconception, but in the form of an empirical hypothesis. They suggest that the sole evolutionary innovation that gave rise to natural language is recursion. The notion of 'recursion' used in HCF occasionally generates discussion. Which of the uses of the term found in the literature is intended? If put into the perspective of Chomsky 2008, it is enough to say that Merge can apply to an expression resulting from an application of Merge. That is, Merge can apply to its own output.[16] Recursion is found in language but also outside it, in mathematics, and, arguably, music. Mathematics and music can be argued to be derivative of language. However, we also find recursion in planning and navigation (see HCF). These cannot be derivative of language. If so, it is not recursion per se that is unique to language, but rather the particular way recursion is made available for language.

The core question, then, is how the recursive property of language is mentally encoded. For instance, is there a specific rule expressing recursion? Chomsky (2008) proposes that recursion itself is solely encoded in what is called the *edge feature* of lexical items. The edge feature of lexical items encodes the property that they can be combined (Merged) to form a composite expression. Thus, if *a* and *b* are lexical items that are combined into the composite expression *ab*, *ab* is an element of the same general kind, which in turn can be merged with a further lexical item c, or complex expression e, and so on. Thus, Merge is the property that gives rise to the discrete infinity of natural language and its concomitant expressive power.

In a nutshell, then, what is special to language is the specific format of its lexical items. Lexical items are objects of the following kind (Chomsky 2008):

(12) $\langle f, g, i \rangle$

where f is an instruction to create a form in a medium (sound, gesture), i an instruction for interpretation, and g a set of formal instructions driving the computation

The recursive capacity of language is encoded among the instructions in g. So what is specific to language is a particular way of encoding recursivity.

As noted, the other component of C_{HL} is Agree. In its barest form, Agree is just *making a comparison*, and comparing is just a very general property of our cognitive system. What is specific to language, though, is the use of Agree as an operation asymmetrically checking and filling in values, as in the *share* clause in (8iib). For instance, in subject-verb agreement as in *Alice is watching the cat*, there is a sense in which the 3rd-person singular value of *is* depends on *Alice* rather than the other way around. So it is in the context of C_{HL}, where it operates on natural language expressions, that Agree gets a role that it could not have outside this context—a role, therefore, that is specific to language.

Be this as it may, general considerations as given above make the language specificity of C_{HL} quite marginal indeed. The question is whether the operations in (8) are indeed all there is to C_{HL}. As Chomsky notes, if option (ii) can be demonstrated to be correct, that would be a highly significant finding. Proving such a claim, however, requires a detailed understanding of the nature of the operations involved in the mapping between the sensorimotor and interpretation systems. Crucially, a demonstration should involve no operations that depend on language for their justification.

Therefore, a systematic and serious quest for evidence that C_{HL} is trivial is deemed fruitful even if (ii) turns out to be incorrect. Paradoxically, it may well be the method of choice to find out what are ultimately irreducible properties of C_{HL}.

Note that, even if all deep properties of language can be traced back to more general systems, this does not necessarily mean that a dedicated language system does not exist at some level of organization. For the moment, therefore, I will confine my discussion of dedication to these remarks. For a more than programmatic attempt one should first have a clear understanding of the phenomena themselves, which is what I set out to achieve in this book.

So, I will take my starting point in models of C_{HL} that are as trivial as possible, in the expectation that such models will allow us to see sharply what is universal in the language system and why. This idea is further explored in the next section.

1.5   Unity and Diversity in Anaphoric Dependencies

In section 1.3 we ended up with questions about unity and diversity in the domain of anaphoric dependencies. Why is the CBT such a good approximation crosslinguistically? Why do the binding conditions look the way they do? In the present section we will find that exploring the basic properties of C_{HL} to see how trivial they can be gives us a novel perspective on language universals.

1.5.1   Universals and Sources of Invariance

One of the central foci of linguistic research over the last sixty years or so has been the investigation of language universals. In a sense the result has been somewhat paradoxical. If one considers the range of universals that have been proposed, from Greenberg's (1963) word-order universals to Chomky's (1981) binding conditions, they all are at least very good approximations. It seems that they must reflect some true insight into the structure of language. Yet, as we saw, once we consider the binding conditions in detail, they meet too many empirical challenges to ignore. Moreover, the structure of the canonical universals cannot easily accommodate the attested variation without becoming empirically vacuous (imagine what one must do to make locally bound 3rd-person Frisian pronominals compatible with condition B).

In response to this problem, one may say, as is often the case in descriptive typology, that linguistic universals are statistical rather than unconditional. However, this move does nothing to explain why and how the relevant tendencies arose.

In any case, what is universal cannot be the macrouniversals of the Greenberg and Chomsky 1981 type. This warrants closer scrutiny of what language universals could come from.

If one considers natural language grammar as a computational system effecting a systematic mapping between forms and interpretations, one can expect the following sources of invariance on general grounds (putting aside lexical-conceptual or, possibly, more general cognitive—for instance, pragmatic—sources of invariance) (see Chomsky 1995, 2005):[17]

(13) *Sources of invariance* (Reuland 2005b)

> *Type 1*: Necessary properties of computations, modulo a medium in which they take place
>
> *Type 2*: Economy of computation, modulo resource types and restrictions
>
> *Type 3*: General properties of computations specific to language

Type 1 invariants reflect properties that any computational system must have. For instance, the fact that all languages have a vocabulary, combinatory principles, and a space in which the computations take place is a type 1 universal.[18] A less obvious example is discussed below in connection with binding. If computations with identical elements are carried out and the medium in which computations take place does not allow distinguishing between these (i.e., the workspace has no ordering or other structure), any system must develop some means to tell identicals apart.

Type 2 invariants reflect the fact that any physical computational system has spatial and temporal limitations and must be engineered around them. For example, because the size of the workspace is finite, the computation of different options in the case of dependencies must be limited so as to avoid "combinatorial explosions"; similarly, there might be a conflict between the speed of computations and requirements on when the output must be available. (See for instance Chomsky 1995 and subsequent work on how to avoid combinatorial explosion. Also see Grodzinsky and Reinhart 1993 and Reinhart 2006 for a discussion of restrictions inspired by processing considerations; see Vasić 2006 and Koornneef 2008 as well. To give an example, Grodzinsky and Reinhart argue that in certain environments applying condition B of the CBT requires a comparison between two alternative derivations. This is resource-demanding, hence explains why children and agrammatic aphasics have trouble with condition B under those conditions; see section 1.10 and chapter 4 for discussion.)

Type 3 invariants are potentially exemplified by locality conditions on movement (recall the locality conditions on binding discussed in section 1.1). Whereas locality by itself may well reflect type 2 invariance, there are also locality conditions that have been stated in terms of intrinsically linguistic categories. Take for instance a universal stating that *no expression can be moved out of a coordinate structure* (the *coordinate structure constraint*), thus blocking a question like *Who did Alice see [the rabbit and t]* modeled on *Alice saw the rabbit and the cat.* In this version this universal has been stated using the intrinsically linguistic notion of *coordination.* Suppose that there is no way to derive the effects of this constraint without reference to the notion of coordination. If so, and assuming it holds, it is a type 3 invariant. The same holds true for other constraints found in the literature, such as the *adjunct island condition* or the *head-movement constraint.* Let me, for sake of concreteness, also illustrate the former. Consider the contrast in (14):

(14) a.   *What* did Alice fear that the queen would say *t*
      b. **What* was Alice weeping after the queen said *t*

In (14a) *what* questions the object of *say,* and *that the queen would say* is itself an *argument* of *fear.* In (14b) *after the queen said* is an adverbial clause, or *adjunct.* Adjuncts are generally "islands" for question formation and other dislocations. The notion of an adjunct is an intrinsically linguistic notion. The possibility that we will find a way to characterize the notion of an adjunct in nonlinguistic terms cannot be excluded. But unless we succeed in doing so, the adjunct island condition—which is in fact quite a good candidate for holding universally—is a type 3 invariant.

To the extent to which one finds invariant properties of natural language that are demonstrably of type 1 or type 2, a parsimonious view of the computational system of human language C_{HL} gains credibility, all the more so if the invariants come close to "acknowledged" linguistic universals. Macrouniversals are like the tips of an iceberg, where conspiracies of more basic—low-level—operations become visible.

Among the main theses I put forward in this book is that what is general in the conditions on binding finds its source in invariance of the types indicated above: (i) a significant part of condition B phenomena reflects type 1 invariance; (ii) its residue and much of condition A reflect type 2 invariance; (iii) there is a residue of condition A that may reflect type 3 invariance, although ultimately a reduction to type 2 invariance may be possible here as well.

What is variable reflects differences in the way lexical elements—specifically pronominals and anaphors—are built up and interact with the properties of the structure containing them, along lines to be made precise. This implies that we have to give up the idea that an understanding of the core linguistic principles can be achieved by limiting our investigation to the macrolevel. Progress toward explanation can only be expected if we shift our perspective toward the fine structure of the grammatical system (though based on the insights the study of the macro-phenomena provides).

1.5.2 Toward Explaining the Binding Conditions

Nothing in (8) or (13) is specific to binding. Since parsimony is the basis for explanation, our theory should contain no statements specific to binding, except for a definition of binding itself, given in section 1.6.2. Throughout, we are striving for a theory in which all the properties of anaphors and pronominals can be explained in terms of their feature content, and in terms of the way these features allow them to interact with their environment.

As we saw in section 1.2, and will see in more detail in chapter 5, pronominals such as English *him*, Dutch *hem*, and so on entirely consist of ϕ-features. SE anaphors, such as Dutch *zich*, typically consist of a subset of the features pronominals have. In the end we wish to fully understand the behavior of SE anaphors (and other simplex anaphors) in terms of their ϕ-features and in terms of how their feature composition differs from that of full pronominals. Complex anaphors such as *himself* or *zichzelf* consist of a pronoun and another morpheme. Again, the goal is to explain their behavior entirely in terms of their ϕ-features and whatever the self-morpheme (or the element corresponding to it in other languages) contributes. For the sake of concreteness I will formulate this in the form of what I call the *Feature Determinacy Thesis* (FDT):

(15) *Feature Determinacy Thesis*
Syntactic binding of pronominal elements (including anaphors) in a particular environment is determined by their morphosyntactic features and the way these enter into the syntactic operations available in that environment.[19]

Before embarking on our enterprise in detail, as I do in the subsequent chapters of this book, let's take a brief look at the task facing us.

As we saw in section 1.3, certain patterns the CBT expresses are surprisingly pervasive and stable. Many languages have anaphoric elements that do behave as condition A of the CBT would lead one to expect. A similar observation can be made about the core of condition B. As is observed, for instance, in Schladt 2000, languages go to great lengths to avoid simple reflexive instantiations of transitive predicates as in (16), where the Pronoun in object position is bound by the SUBJECT:

(16) SUBJECT   V   Pronoun

(16) illustrates the notion of a *reflexive predicate*, one of the patterns I will extensively discuss. Informally, a predicate is reflexive iff one of its arguments binds another of its arguments. **The caterpillar** admired **himself** is a well-formed instantiation; **the caterpillar** admired **him** with *him* bound by *the caterpillar* is also a reflexive predicate, but ill-formed.

The pattern we saw reflected in (16) is widespread. Schladt gives an overview of over 140 languages from many different language families that all require a special marking of reflexive predicates instead of simply having a locally bound simplex anaphor or pronominal. Heine and Miyashita (2008, 172, 175) state that "reflexivity and reciprocity are universal concepts in so far as all languages can be expected to have some grammaticalized expression for both." As these authors note, especially among pidgins and creoles one tends to find exceptions; the same has been claimed to hold true of the group of Malayo-Polynesian languages, especially the Oceanic languages. Yet, Moyse-Faurie (2008, 107) argues that Oceanic languages are in fact no exception to Heine and Miyashita's statement and "offer a large spectrum of morpho-syntactic devices to mark coreference." In short, this amounts to (17):

(17) Reflexivity of predicates must be licensed.[20]

The means languages employ to license reflexive predicates are varied (reflexive clitics, doubling, verbal affixes, body-part expressions, and so on, as well as putting the reflexive in a prepositional phrase), but the need to do so is general enough. These phenomena are too pervasive to be accidental. They must reflect a deep property of natural language.[21] Chapter 6 provides an in-depth discussion and an explanation of why this is so.

Note, however, that the amount of potential material bearing on this issue is daunting. The question is to what extent we will be able to maintain (17) as more facts become available. Only a few languages have been described in the detail necessary to understand the interplay between morphological, syntactic, and semantic factors relevant for binding. In section 1.3 I sketched some of the patterns observed in relatively well-studied languages. The remainder of the 6,000–8,000 languages that constitute our potential material have been described in only the most fragmentary or superficial ways, or even if they have received more extensive analyses, these analyses are still insufficient for real insight. Given this, we have no choice but to proceed in the usual scientific manner: *Formulate clear hypotheses and test them against the empirical material as it becomes available.* If the hypotheses are minimal, it is equally important not to succumb too easily to prima facie problematic facts and propose solutions that in fact hide stipulations. As always, the best strategy is to investigate how far independently motivated principles lead us, determine the empirical residue, and look for an explanation for this residue. Since the feature composition of pronouns is easily accessible, the FDT in (15) is optimally suited as a starting point.

So far, we have essentially adopted the dichotomy between anaphors and pronominals assumed by the CBT. However, given the variation we have observed, one might even ask whether there is a strict dichotomy between anaphors and pronominals, or why there would be anaphors at all. But in fact this question has a trivial answer. Part of the feature inventory of natural language are categorial features and ϕ-features (minimally, person, number, gender—putting aside the question of whether some of these features have a finer articulation).

The null hypothesis is that any combination of values for these features can in principle exist as a vocabulary item, in particular, the set of bundles of ϕ-features [αperson, βnumber, τgender] with a category feature (the category feature of pronouns will be discussed in more detail in chapter 5), which characterizes the set of pronominals, and, in the absence of motivated restrictions, also any element characterized by a subset of these features. SE anaphors in Dutch, Icelandic, and so forth precisely fit that bill. They are neither marked for gender nor for number, but are marked for person. So, according to the null hypothesis their existence comes at no cost, which of course does not mean that they have to be present in every language.[22]

Complex anaphors are made up of combinations of morphemes (pronouns, elements like *self* or their cognates, body-part nouns, etc.) that exist independently.[23] Again, such combinations cannot be prevented without stipulation. Hence, the existence of the various pronominal and anaphor forms comes for free. The core question we have to solve is why they behave and contrast the way they do, on the basis of properties that are independently motivated.

The only way to understand complex phenomena is by disentangling the component parts, analyzing the individual pieces, and then putting them back together again. This leads us to a modular approach to "binding theory." This book's basic claim is that, given a general definition of binding (provided in section 1.6.2), the prima facie diversity in the conditions on binding will not require any statement in the grammar that is specific to binding. This can be put succinctly as (18):

(18) There is no dedicated binding theory.

As I will show in this book, what is constant and variable in the behavior of anaphoric elements follows from the interaction between independent factors such as the following: general properties of computational systems, Agree-based operations on morphosyntactic features (agreement, Case-checking—leading to feature chains), operations on the argument structure of predicates, general principles of interpretation, economy principles, general operations on linguistic structures, and so on, complemented with specific lexical properties of individual morphemes.

Our discussion so far covers the conceptual foundations of the approach I pursue in the book. A more detailed discussion of the notion of binding and patterns of variation is given in the subsequent sections. To make this book as self-contained as possible I also present a recapitulation of the main features of the CBT.

Some of what I will say is elementary and may be familiar to many readers, but I also include a number of conceptual remarks that may be less trivial. I include these sections to make my perspective explicit against the background of the canonical theory.

1.6   Interpretive Dependencies

To begin, consider a simple system of Saussurean signs, of the type often assumed as a model for (proto-)languages in discussions of the evolution of language (see, for instance, Deacon 1997 and Arbib 2005). In such a system, it will be impossible to prevent—except by stipulation—different expressions from receiving identical values in some actual or virtual world without any particular formal encoding. For celestial objects this may be true without the community being aware of it, but nothing changes in the linguistic system if—to use a venerable example—it is discovered that the expressions for *morning star* and *evening star* both have the same entity as their value. That is, the expressions are coreferential, referring to the planet Venus.

Coreference may hold on the basis of an empirical fact, as in the Venus case, but speakers' intentions may also suffice to establish coreference. In English, a pronominal such as *he* can be used to refer to any object linguistically classified as masculine and singular. Consider the example *John's mother thought he was guilty*. Here, *he* may refer to John but also to some other masculine individual. Note that coreference is not linguistically encoded. No formal property of *morning star* or *evening star* indicates that they are coreferential; no formal property of *he* reveals whether its value is John or another masculine individual.[24]

The following conclusion is inescapable: *The possibility for (co)refer-ence is a deep-rooted property of any symbolic system with referring expressions.*[25]

In natural language it is easy to find restrictions on coreference apart from canonical binding effects. For instance, if one of the individuals in a story is a white rabbit, we may refer to him as *the white rabbit*, or even *this intriguing white rabbit who keeps looking at his watch*, but also more simply as *the rabbit*, *the animal*, or even just *he*. The following two versions of a story show that their order of occurrence is not exactly free:

(19) a. The white rabbit jumped from behind the bushes. The animal looked around and then he ran away to avoid the angry queen.
    b. The animal jumped from behind the bushes. The rabbit looked around and then the white rabbit ran away to avoid the angry queen.

In (19a), the expressions *the white rabbit*, *the animal*, and *he* easily receive the same value. For *he*, for instance, a reading where it gets the same value as *the animal/the white rabbit* is highly preferred. Not so in the b-case. Here *the rabbit* is preferred to have a value different from *the animal*. For the second sentence a felicitous interpretation is hard to construe.

Such facts are addressed in accessibility theory as developed in Ariel 1990. Informally, the idea is that expressions differ in the amount of descriptive information they contain. According to this theory, one will use an expression with relatively rich descriptive content—such as *the white rabbit*—to refer to an individual that is not very salient. Conversely, when an individual is salient enough, expressions such as *the animal* or *he* or *she* will be used. They are so-called high accessibility markers since they are low in descriptive content (pronominals even lack real descriptive content—think of what "feminine" stands for in a language allowing ships to be feminine).

Depending on shared knowledge and expectations, there may be variation from one exchange to another in the amount of information participants actually need to converge in their identification of a discourse referent, but in general the information provided must be commensurate with the information needed. In (19b), *the animal* introduces a discourse referent. *The rabbit* provides more specific information than *the animal*, hence general principles of conversational parsimony and cooperation (do not provide more information than you need to) entail that it should not have been used to identify the same referent, hence should be taken to introduce a new discourse referent. In (19a), *he* hardly provides any descriptive information, hence is highly preferred to receive an existing discourse entity as its value.

Note that in (19a) the relevant referring expressions are given from left to right in descending order of specificity; in (19b) the order is reversed. So, one might wonder whether that is not all there is to these facts. However, as one can see from sentences like *after she had seen the rabbit, Alice fell into the well*, which is perfectly well formed, a simple order-based approach will not work.

Further questions arise, such as why in (19b) *the rabbit* can easily update the discourse by introducing a further individual in addition to the one introduced by *the animal*, but *the white rabbit* cannot easily introduce a further individual in addition to the rabbit. I will not pursue these here. The considerations so far suffice to illustrate the existence of general strategies of anaphora resolution.

1.6.1 Binding and Coreference

Two questions arise. First, how *linguistic* the restrictions of the type discussed in the previous section are, and second whether more is needed than such general strategies to account for anaphoric dependencies in natural language. Both are related to a more general debate on how much of the structure of language is to be explained by mechanisms dedicated to language, rather than by general reasoning strategies. An extreme position is taken by Tomasello (2003), who claims that binding theory is just an artifact, and that all that matters is "communicative intentions" and "communication" (without presenting any evidence, though). The only serious attempt to date to derive binding theory from pragmatic principles is Levinson 2000. However, even in his own terms this derivation is not complete (see section 1.6.7 for more discussion and criticism of Levinson's assumptions).

In evaluating such claims, note that all the information conveyed by natural language expressions is encoded in grammatical and lexical features. These represent atomic elements of information content. Any measure of descriptive content must be made in terms of such features. Hence, even apart from the role of structure in anaphoric relations, which is discussed below, the very status of being a higher or lower *accessibility marker* itself rests on fundamentally linguistic notions. Therefore, despite what one may think, facts about relative prominence and accessibility do not follow from external functional considerations alone. Anyone who has paid serious attention to the facts should be able to see that there is much in anaphoric relations that is impossible to capture in terms of relative prominence, communicative function, and similar notions.

Although much of the present book is devoted to facts challenging overly simplistic approaches to language, like the range of facts given in section 1.1, I feel that contrasts of the type in (20)—discussed in chapter 3—should be sufficiently baffling to show anyone that syntax plays a crucial role in this domain.

(20) a. ^{ok}*Max* expected the queen to invite Mary and *himself* for a drink.

b. **Max* expected the queen to invite *himself* for a drink.

In the well-formed (20a) *himself* is even farther removed from its antecedent than in the ill-formed (20b). So the main task that I will take up in this subsection is to identify the types of processes involved in establishing anaphoric dependencies.

There is an extensive literature, starting with Keenan 1971, on the issue of *variable binding* versus *coreference* (see in particular Evans 1980, Heim 1982, Reinhart 1983, Wexler and Chien 1985, Grodzinsky and Reinhart 1993, Chierchia 1995, and Fiengo and May 1994). Here, I focus on the approach outlined by Heim 1982 and Reinhart 1983. As they argue, the pattern in (21) and (22) shows that, in addition to coreference, there is another fundamentally different type of anaphoric dependency:

(21) a. *John* has a gun. Will *he* attack?

b. *Everyone/No one* has a gun. *Will *he* attack?

(22) a. *John* was convinced that *he* would be welcome.

b. *Everyone/No one* was convinced that *he* would be welcome.

Although coreference is possible across sentences, as in (21a), where *John* and *he* can be independently used to refer to the same individual, *everyone* and *no one* in (21b) are expressions that cannot be assigned an individual as a discourse referent; hence, an interpretive dependency between *he* and these expressions cannot be established through coreference. If (co)reference were all there is, a pronominal could never depend on a quantificational expression. However, the well-formedness of (22a,b) shows that this is incorrect. Hence, there must be another route that is available for quantificational antecedents. This is the route that involves *binding* in a strict sense. These patterns show that the notion of *getting a value from an antecedent* as it was introduced in section 1.1 is indeed just a first informal approximation of a more complex state of affairs.

Binding is subject to a structural condition; more specifically, it requires that the antecedent c-command the element that depends on it.

(23) *a* c-commands *b* iff *a* is a sister to a category γ containing *b*.
    Schematically: [a [γ ... b ...]], or

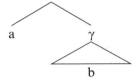

According to this definition and common syntactic assumptions, the subject of a clause will c-command the object, but not vice versa. Hence in *I expected himself to admire John*, *John* cannot bind *himself*. The c-command requirement cannot be satisfied cross-sententially: *no one* in (21b) does not c-command *he*. Hence the sequel in (21b) is not felicitous. But it is in (22b), where *he* is indeed c-commanded and *bound* by the quantificational antecedent (see chapter 2 for discussion of apparent exceptions to the c-command requirement).

The inevitability of a model with minimally two routes is interesting from the general perspective of language evolution and language design. A way of understanding the contrast between coreference and binding is that coreference need involve no more than assigning two (or more) expressions a value that happens to be the same. Binding, on the other hand, represents a fundamentally different type of process. Binding does not interpret an expression by assigning it a value directly. It computes its interpretation by linking it to another expression and determining the interpretation of the latter, as informally indicated by the arrow in (24).

(24) Exp .... exp
    ↑_____|

Binding is therefore also interesting from an evolutionary perspective. As noted in section 1.4, Hauser, Chomsky, and Fitch (2002) argue that the crucial innovation that gave rise to language is recursion applying to vocabulary items, making it possible to form complex expressions from simple ones. Binding, however, represents an innovation in the interpretive system that goes beyond mere recursion, by allowing an indirect mode of interpretation, which is based on a two- (or more-) step process (see Reuland 2008b, 2009a, and 2010a for further discussion).

The system thus entails that we have two ways of deriving the relevant interpretation of (22a), one by binding, the other by coreference. As we will see in the next section, there is indeed evidence for both (and as our discussion proceeds we will see that in fact even more processes are involved in the encoding of binding relations).

It is occasionally felt that such a dual route goes against the idea of optimal design, and that, hence, coreference should ideally be reduced to binding (as in Kayne 2002). Note, however, that the possibility of coreference follows independently of any operation of the grammatical system. So, optimality and parsimony of the latter are not at all affected by its existence. Hence, there is no conceptual need for reducing coreference to binding, if this were possible at all without brute-force stipulation. However, as will be extensively discussed in chapter 4, there is a division of labor between these options where they overlap, with a preference for the evolutionary innovative process.

1.6.2   A Definition of A-Binding

Much of our discussion will focus on the question of how binding relations are encoded in language. Hence we need a conception of binding independent of particular grammatical notations. Reinhart (2000, 2006) presents a definition of binding in which the *linguistic* notion of Argument binding is explained in terms of the *logical* notion of binding. This is important since it makes available for linguistic discussions about binding the rigor provided by logic. It is also important since it enables one to make a principled distinction between those interpretive dependencies that involve binding in the relevant sense, and those that do not.

Reinhart's position on the relation between linguistic and logical structure is based on the view that natural language expressions feed the human inference system, and, as Reinhart (2006, 4) puts it, "The inference system is essentially logic, and its inventory includes, for example, logical relations, functions, abstract predicates and variables. . . . The outputs of the CS (the linguistic computational system, ER) are representations that are legible to the inference system, which can read them as propositions fit for its computations." Thus, given that inference rules are formal— that is, operate on expressions—natural language expressions must be translated into a proper format in order to be readable to the inference system. A minimal requirement on this format is that it makes explicit quantifier-variable relations and scope. Also, distributive versus collective readings of predicate-argument structures must be structurally represented for the inference system to operate on. Rules of the inference system must see instantiations of predicates—for instance, they must see that (25a) has (25b) as one of its entailments, since *vote for* is distributive, and that (26a) does not entail (26b), *elect* being collective.

(25) a. We voted for me.
      b. x voted for x, with x=I

(26) a. We elected me.
      b. x elected x, with x=I

Similarly, the inference system must represent that (27a) entails (27b):

(27) a. John hated everybody but himself.
      b. It is not the case that John has the property of self-hatred (where
         some x has the property of self-hatred if *x hates x*).

Reinhart refers to representations meeting the requirements inherent in
this format as *logical syntax* (LS), hence the name *logical syntax binding*
for the binding relation as defined for these representations.

   In Reinhart's approach, binding is analyzed as the procedure of closing
a property. This is reflected in the following definition, which I adopt in
the present work:

(28) *Logical syntax binding*
      Binding is the procedure of closing a property. (Reinhart 2006, 171)
      A-binding
      α A-binds β iff α is the sister of a λ-predicate whose operator binds
      β.[26]

This definition introduces the notion of a *λ-predicate*. For current purposes we need only the intuition behind the λ-formalism.

   Consider, to this end, a sentence such as *Alice likes the garden* and the
VP *likes the garden* that it contains. This VP has the semantic status of a
property, which we can also represent using a free variable as in *x likes
the garden*. Intuitively we would like to have an operation in which adding an argument to the VP gives a proposition with the property denoted
by the VP (being in the garden) being predicated of that argument,
here the subject *Alice*. The formal means is supplied by λ-*calculus*. The
required interpretive effect is obtained by prefixing a λ-*operator* to the VP
with its free variable, yielding λx *(x likes the garden)*. Assigning *Alice* as
an argument to the expression λx *(x likes the garden)* yields the proposition *Alice likes the garden*.[27]

   This carries over to A-binding in the following way. Consider the sentence *Alice likes her garden*, and its VP *x likes her garden*. As we know *her*
can either remain free, and refer, for instance, to the queen, or it can end
up being bound by *Alice*. To obtain the latter interpretation, *her* should
be translated as a variable identical to the subject variable as in the open
expression *x likes x's garden*. Prefixing the λ-operator yields λx *(x likes*

x's garden), in which the subject variable and the possessive pronoun are bound by the same operator. Adding *Alice* yields *Alice (λx (x likes x's garden))*, which has the required interpretation. So, in order for an expression to be bound under (28) it should be translated as a variable. A working hypothesis will be that only pure φ-feature expressions are translated as variables. In my discussion of complex anaphors I will come back to this issue.

Note that the expression *λx* as such has no status other than satisfying a convention handling open expressions, and keeping track of which binder relates to which variable. There is no need to assume this element is part of the linguistic (mental) vocabulary, but the notion of an open expression and operations to close it must be available to our mental computations.[28]

As discussed in section 1.4.3, there can be several copies of an expression in a sentence. For instance, in a sentence with dislocation, such as (29a), the syntactic representation has a copy of *himself* in the initial position, but in the object position of *admire* as well; see (29b).

(29) a. *Himself, John admired.*
    b. himself *John* admired (*himself*)

Putting certain complications aside, it is always the source position (an A-position) that counts for the application of the definition of binding. Thus, as we will see in more detail in the next section, it is *John* that binds the copy of *himself* in A-position. Hence the term *A-binding*.[29]

A similar positional restriction applies to the binder. As we saw, operations such as question formation (*wh-movement*) and *topicalization* move a phrase from an A-position to a A'-position.

Pronominals can be bound by *wh*-phrases and by quantifiers like *everyone* (using the trace notation for movement):

(30) a. Who *t* complained that Mary damaged *his* car
    b. *Everyone* complained that Mary damaged *his* car.

When A'-movement crosses a pronominal, two cases are to be considered. In (31) the pronominal c-commands the trace of the moved element:

(31) a. ____ he saw who
    b. *Who* did *he* see *t*

(31) instantiates *strong crossover*. The *wh*-trace is an R-expression. In the representation indicated here *he* binds the trace; this is a condition C violation (6C), which is strongly ungrammatical, as illustrated in (31b).

In (32b) the pronoun does not c-command the base position of the *wh*-phrase that crossed over it (it is contained in the expression *his mother*):

(32) a. ____ *his* mother loves *who*
     b. ??*Who* does *his* mother love *t*

(32b) is not felicitous, but it is also not as ungrammatical as (31b). Hence this phenomenon is called *weak crossover*. What we see is that the *who* that originates in a position where it is not a possible binder for *his*—because of the lack of c-command—moves to a position where it does c-command *his*. Yet the latter step is not sufficient to make binding felicitous. Reinhart (1983) argues that weak crossover violates the requirement that the antecedent c-command the bound element from an A-position. That is, the position that *who* moved to does not count for purposes of A-binding.[30]

A similar phenomenon obtains in the case of *scope*. For illustration of the phenomenon in general consider (33).

(33) A guard was standing in front of every building.

The most prominent reading is one in which for each building there was a guard standing in front of it. In this reading, *every building* has scope over *a guard*; it has *wide scope*. The alternative—the *narrow-scope* reading—is the one in which one guard was standing in front of the whole group of buildings.

A widely adopted way of handling scope assignment is by having the element with wide scope move to a position where it c-commands the expression it has scope over, as in (34).

(34) (*Every building*) [a guard was standing in front of *every building*]

The position the wide scope element moves to is again an A′-position. The only difference is that for reasons that do not concern us here, in the case of scope assignment only the lower copy is pronounced. (Hence this movement is said to be *covert*.) Consider from this perspective sentence (35a), with the scope indicated in (35b):

(35) a. ??Its guard was standing in front of every building.
     b. ??(*Every building*) [*its* guard was standing in front of *every building*]

Sentence (35a) is as infelicitous as (32b). To see why, consider (35b) where the wide scope of *every building* is configurationally represented.

(35) violates the condition that the envisaged binder (*every building*) must be in a c-commanding A-position to felicitously bind the pronoun *its*.

Note that (28) generalizes over quantificational and nonquantificational antecedents as is independently needed. The way it captures binding in contrast to coreference is illustrated by the two readings of (36) and (37). (36) illustrates the case of VP-ellipsis. The variable binding option for the interpretation of *his* gives the sloppy reading; the option where *his* corefers with *John* (*his* is valued as some individual who happens to be John) produces the strict reading:

(36) a. John loves his cat and Peter does too.
 b. John (λx (x loves x's cat)) and Peter (λx (x loves x's cat))
 c. John (λx (x loves a's cat & a=John)) and Peter (λx (x loves a's cat & a=John))

(37) illustrates the effect of the focus particle *only*. In (37b) the property ascribed only to Lucie is that of respecting a certain individual (Mr. X), who happens to be her or somebody else's husband. All other women do not respect this person, but they may well respect their own husbands. In (37c) the property ascribed only to Lucie is that of respecting her own husband. By implication, all other women do not respect their own husbands. Thus, in order for binding to obtain, it is necessary that the dependent element be translated as a variable, and that its antecedent be a sister to the λ-expression.

(37) a. Only Lucie respects her husband.
 b. Only Lucie (λx (x respects y's husband)) (y can be valued as any female individual)
 c. Only Lucie (λx (x respects x's husband))

The fact that (36) and (37) have the interpretations indicated shows that the computational system must have access to representations with variables (or to notions of binding in other semantic systems, such as Jacobson's 1999 variable-free semantics).

One may wonder whether *logical syntax* is an additional level of representation that one should try to get rid of when striving for parsimony. In my view logical syntax is not controversial, however. It is just a formal representation of the output of the computational system with the degree of detail required by the inference system (and independently justified because of the requirements of the inference system). Essentially, it is syntax with an extended vocabulary.

1.6.3 A-Binding: Logical Syntax and Semantics

To demarcate the scope of the present book, I should make clear that there are interpretive dependencies that do not fall under the notion of binding captured by the canonical binding theory, nor under the binding definition of (28). Hence, they will not be discussed here.

In current syntactic theory, for instance, *dislocation* is a dependency, but it does not involve binding as conceived here.[31] Other well-known types of interpretive dependencies, perhaps closer to binding than dislocation, are given in (38):

(38) a. *Donkey anaphora*
Every man who owns *a donkey* beats *it*.
   b. *Scopal dependencies*
Three men lifted *a* table.

In (38a) *it* depends for its interpretation on *a donkey*, with the actual interpretation a bit more complex than this statement suggests, since the dependency is limited to donkeys owned by donkey owners.[32] In the relevant reading of (38b) the number of tables lifted is not just one, but three. In this book I primarily address dependencies that involve *A-binding*, and its relation to coreference/covaluation.

The definition of A-binding in (28) is essentially syntactic, although not pertaining to narrow syntax. It applies to expressions containing variables. Such variables are the translations of designated lexical items—pronouns (pronominals and anaphors consisting solely of φ-features)—and not others. These elements, then, end up bound in an environment in which the configurational requirements are satisfied. Note that complex anaphors such as English *himself*, or body-part reflexives in other languages, contain more than just φ-features. Consequently, the definition in (28) only applies to the pronoun part. This has nontrivial consequences, to be discussed in chapters 5 and 6.

The semantics of binding can be understood in the standard way by *assignment functions* for the variables restricted by the relevant properties of the antecedent. (See, for instance, Heim and Kratzer 1998.) Keeping things informal, the basis of any interpretation system for a language is the assigment of values from a domain of discourse to its expressions. An expression like *he* in *he arrived* is semantically a variable since its value depends on the assignment: under one assignment it may get the value John, under other assignments the values Bill, Charles, Randy, and so forth. Under the bound reading of *John$_1$ thought he$_1$ arrived*—binding indicated by subscripts—things are different, though. Here the value assignment to *he* is restricted, namely to the assignment function giving it the value John. This is essentially how Heim and Kratzer explain the semantic basis of binding: any semantic operation that induces a dependency in value assignment.

However, restricting assignment functions is a powerful tool, and easily generalizable to cases beyond the canonical binding environments, hence restrictions on assignment functions cannot take over the role of the syntactic definition in (28). To see this consider sentences like (39) (discussed by Evans 1980 and Hara 2002):

(39) Every boy wonders what that boy's friend will become in the future.

Informally, one can easily imagine an instruction for obtaining a dependent interpretation of *that boy* along the lines in (40):

(40) Take any member of the set of boys you wish, and call it *a*; *a* wonders what *a*'s friend will become in the future.

For many speakers, such structures are felicitous even when we have *no boy* instead of *every boy*. In (41) the instruction "Take any member of the set of boys you wish, and call it *a*; *a* will not recommend *a*'s best friend for the class monitor" will yield the required interpretation.[33]

(41) No boy recommended that boy's best friend for the class monitor.

Prima facie (39) seems parallel to (42) with a bound pronominal:

(42) Every boy wonders what his friend will become in the future.

But, as the contrast between (44) and (46) shows, pronominals and *that N* do not behave identically:

(43) *Every student/no student* turned in an assignment before *he* went home.

(44) Before *he* went home, *every student/no student* turned in an assignment.

(45) *Every student/no student* turned in an assignment before *that student* went home.

(46) #Before *that student* went home, *every student/no student* turned in an assignment.

In (43) and (44) with a pronoun, a dependent reading is available irrespective of the position of the adverbial clause. In (45) and (46), however, with the *that N*-expression, the dependent reading requires a canonical configuration. These and related facts are extensively discussed and explained in Reuland and Avrutin 2005, 2010, which the reader is referred to.[34] For current purposes it suffices that this pattern shows that a distinction between canonical bound variables and other dependent argument expressions must be maintained.[35]

The availability of split antecedents for pronominal binding is another indication that purely semantic dependencies exist, as for instance in (47):

(47) a. Every man told Mary that they should get married.

b. Each woman said that every man that dated her said that they should get married.[36]

Such sentences do not directly fall under the scope of (28). Rather, they involve the formation of composite plural individuals—in (47a), for example, ⟨x, Mary⟩ pairs, where x ranges over the set of men, such that it is such pairs that determine the value of *they*. (For a formal treatment of pluralities that accommodates dependencies with split antecedents see for instance Landman 2000.) It is an empirical matter how the type of operation required for the formation of pluralities is best accommodated in the grammar. Given the conception of logical syntax in the sense of Reinhart 2006, it is in any case straightforward to apply such expressions to the λ-expression of (28) once they have been formed.

This result raises an issue of crosslinguistic variation. Do all languages have binding in the sense defined here? The definition of A-binding as given in (28) only applies to expressions containing variables in A-position. These in turn are the translation products of lexical items that consist only of φ-features. Above I defined pronouns as those elements that only consist of φ-features.

The question is, then, whether languages could exist that lack pronominals. It is standardly assumed that the inventory of lexical and functional features is universal. Hence, it follows that in every language φ-feature-only items are *possible* lexical items. However, since at any given stage each language need not realize every possible lexical item, it is conceivable that languages without true pronouns (and anaphors) exist. So, from the perspective of a systematic typology a language whose interpretive dependencies do not involve A-binding as defined here is an option. This bears on the question of whether there can be languages that really do not require any special marking of reflexivity as stated in (17).

Is it conceivable that some languages allow expressions of the form *DP V Pronoun* with DP and Pronoun covalued? From the perspective to be developed in subsequent chapters, it is at least conceivable that a language would have no binding alternative over coreference, depending on the feature makeup of the Pronoun. Given the strategy sketched above, such a language would not necessarily be lacking in expressive power. However, if the DP is an intrinsically quantificational expression like *everyone* or *no one*, coreference is not an option. This is also important from a methodological perspective. So, suppose some language is claimed to lack binding, or to lack any specific conditions on reflexives. Many language descriptions only present examples with referential binder DPs such as proper names or definite descriptions (*the man*), as in *John/the man washes him*. These however are insufficient to decide. Rather, information about dependencies with *quantificational* antecedents like *everyone* or *no one* is crucial.

So far, it seems that the necessary data about potentially relevant languages are lacking. I come back to this issue in section 6.7, where I discuss the notion of masking.

1.7   The Canonical Binding Theory

The key fact in binding theory is that certain binding dependencies are subject to further constraints, which cannot be explained on the basis of the logical properties of binding alone. The canonical approach to these constraints is the CBT, as indicated in section 1.1. It will be briefly reviewed in the next section, which can be skipped by readers familiar with the canonical binding theory.

1.7.1   An Overview of the CBT

The CBT, as developed in Chomsky 1981, captures the interpretive dependencies between phrases that can occur in argument positions, or A-positions, briefly *arguments*.

As we saw in section 1.2, arguments are classified as R-expressions, pronominals, or anaphors. This classification is based on two designated features: [+/−anaphoric] and [+/−pronominal]. Binding theory is concerned with relations of anaphors, pronominals, and R-expressions to possible antecedents (Chomsky 1981, 6).[37] R-expressions are referentially independent in the sense that they cannot be bound,[38] pronominals may but need not be bound, and anaphors cannot be interpreted independently, hence they must be bound. As noted in section 1.2, in the literature the term *reflexive* is often used as a synonym for anaphor. One also finds *pronoun* as an umbrella term for anaphors and pronominals. I will not be following this usage. In this book the term *reflexive* will be used for a subclass of anaphors, as will become clear in chapter 3.[39]

It is an important empirical question whether [+/−anaphoric] and [+/−pronominal] are primitive features, or whether the anaphoric or pronominal properties of an expression derive from its morphosyntactic feature composition. In fact, if the head of a phrase has lexical features (or certain grammatical features, such as *wh*), this phrase is most certainly an

R-expression. Thus *the merry linguist, the idiot, no one, everyone, who* (to give an example of a head with *wh*-features), *which man,* etc., are all R-expressions. In addition to lexical features, nouns—but finite verbs and adjectives and in some languages even prepositions as well—also carry φ-features. As noted earlier, the term *φ-feature* typically stands for the core features of the pronominal system: number, gender, and person (see Chomsky 1981). Pronominals (*I, you, he,* etc.), only specified for φ-features and grammatical category, can be accompanied by a pointing gesture (i.e., used deictically). Anaphors are referentially defective nominal elements (i.e., they cannot be used deictically). Anaphors often lack a specification for certain φ-features, such as Dutch *zich* 'himself', which is specified for person but not for gender and number, as we noted. Given this prima facie correlation between binding properties and morphosyntactic feature composition, in the optimal system the latter should be enough. As we saw in section 1.3 and will see in more detail later, the features [+/−anaphoric] and [+/−pronominal] are at best epiphenomenal.

Chomsky 1980a and 1981 as well as much of the subsequent literature use a system of indexing to mark anaphoric relations in the linguistic representation. Each argument is assigned a certain integer as its index. If two arguments are assigned the same integer they are coindexed. In practice one uses subscripts such as i, j, k, and so on as variable indices. Thus, in an expression $(a_i \ldots b_i)$ a and b are coindexed. In (48a) coindexing *Max* and *himself* represents an inadmissible interpretation but in (48b) coindexing *Max* and *him* is fine:

(48) a. Max$_i$ boasted that the king$_j$ had appointed himself$_{*i/j}$ as commander-in-chief
      b. Max$_i$ was shocked that the king$_j$ appointed him$_{i/*j}$ as commander-in-chief

Since indices are essentially linguistic markers in the structure, it is still possible for two expressions to be assigned the same object in some world if they are not coindexed (*morning star* and *evening star* are not necessarily coindexed in a sentence like *The morning star is the evening star*). Binding without coindexing is not possible, though. In order for a and b to be coindexed (49) must be satisfied:

(49) a and b are nondistinct in features for person, number, and gender.[40]

Nondistinctness rather than identity of features is required for coindexing, since in many languages one anaphoric element is compatible with masculine or feminine, singular or plural antecedents. This property is illustrated by, for instance, Dutch *zich* and Icelandic *sig*, which can have antecedents of any gender or number. On the other hand, both are specified as 3rd person, and cannot have 1st- or 2nd-person antecedents. In other languages (for instance Slavic languages like Russian) a person specification is lacking as well, and we find one anaphoric form for all persons.[41]

In order for binding to obtain the binder must *c-command* the element to be bound, as in (23). Putting the coindexing and c-command requirements together yields (50) as the canonical definition of binding:

(50) *a* binds *b* iff *a* and *b* are coindexed and *a* c-commands *b*.

1.7.2 Locality

One of the recurrent themes in binding theory is how precisely the locality conditions that anaphors and pronominals impose on their binders are captured. In the case of anaphors, the basic intuition is that they do not allow a binder that is beyond the nearest subject. In earlier stages of the theory (Chomsky 1973) this was expressed as the *Specified Subject Condition* (SSC), as in (51):

(51) No rule can involve X, Y in (i)
    (i) ...X...[ₐ...Z...-WYV...]...
    where Z is the specified subject of WYZ in *a*

A subject can be informally characterized as specified if it is lexical—with some provisos I will not discuss here. In Chomsky 1981 the local domain is made explicit by the notion of a *governing category*. (52) gives the binding conditions formulated in Chomsky 1981:

(52) *Binding conditions*
    (A) An anaphor is bound in its governing category.
    (B) A pronominal is free in its governing category.
    (C) An R-expression is free.

The notion of a governing category is defined as in (53):

(53) γ is a governing category for α if and only if γ is the minimal category containing α, a governor of α, and a SUBJECT (*accessible to α*).

In the framework of Chomsky 1981, a governor of α is an element assigning a semantic role (agent, theme, etc.) or Case to α. (54) illustrates the paradigm cases that are captured by (53). Binding is indicated by italics; [GC-α stands for the *governing category* of α.

(54) a. *John* expected [$_{\text{GC-himself/him}}$ the queen to invite *him/*himself* for a drink]

    b. [$_{\text{GC-himself/him}}$ *John* expected [$_{\text{IP}}$ *himself /*him* to be able to invite the queen]]

    c. **He* expected [$_{\text{GC-John}}$ the queen to invite *John* for a drink]

Ignoring for a moment the italicized condition from (53), (54a,b) directly exemplify the SSC: the governing category of α is the domain of the subject nearest α. For *him/himself* this subject is *the queen* in (54a) and *John* in (54b). Binding of *him* by *John* in (54a) satisfies condition B; binding of *himself* by *John* does not satisfy condition A. In (54b) it is the other way around. In (54c) *he* is outside the governing category of *John*. But since an R-expression must be free in the whole sentence, the construal in (54c) is nevertheless illicit.

Unlike what is seen in infinitives, a finite clause comes out as the governing category for its subject. In Chomsky 1981 this is captured by assuming that the finite inflection, which is a carrier of nominal features (agreeing for person, number), also counts as a subject for the computation of the governing category. As a result of the agreement process the inflection gets coindexed with the subject. The notion SUBJECT (in capitals) thus generalizes over the DP in canonical subject position and the Agreement on the tensed verb/auxiliary.

Under certain conditions, an anaphor can be appropriately bound by an antecedent that is outside the finite clause containing the anaphor. This is illustrated in (55):

(55) *The boys* were afraid [that [pictures of *themselves*] would be on sale]

This "domain extension" is captured by the italicized condition in (53). To count for the computation of the governing category of an anaphor, a SUBJECT must be accessible to the anaphor. Accessibility is defined in (56):

(56) *Accessibility*
    α is accessible to β if and only if β is in the c-command domain of α, and assignment to β of the index of α would not violate the *i-within-i condition.*

    i-within-i condition
    *[$_{\gamma}$ ... δ ...], where γ and δ bear the same index.

In the case of (55), coindexing *[pictures of themselves]* and *would* by "subject-verb" agreement (irrespective of the fact that the auxiliary *would* does not carry overt agreement in English), and subsequently coindexing *themselves* and *would* by the "test indexing" of (56), yields the indexing configuration of (57).

(57) *The boys* were afraid [that [$_\gamma$ pictures of *themselves*$_i$]$_i$ would$_i$ be on sale]

This configuration violates (56), hence is marked illicit, and therefore *would* does not count as an accessible SUBJECT for *himself*. Hence, γ is not a governing category for *himself*, which may therefore look for an antecedent in the next higher clause.

As is extensively discussed in chapter 3, the configuration in (57) is not the only case where an anaphor may be unexpectedly bound by a more distant antecedent. This is one of the reasons for developing alternatives to the CBT.

As noted earlier, arguments can be dislocated, ending up in a non-A-position—for instance, by topicalization as in (58a,b) or question formation as in (58c). Here, *t* indicates their source position.

(58) a. *Him*, I never believed the baron to have pulled out *t*
　　 b. *Himself*, the driver pulled *t* out immediately
　　 c. *Which man* did he think *t* fell off the bridge

The rules of A-binding apply to dislocated elements in their source position (for complex phrases this is an approximation; for the moment such complications can be disregarded). With the framework of Chomsky 1981 such dislocated elements showed *reconstruction*. In a minimalist conception, as we saw, we only have to say that the lower copy—the one in A-position—counts. For current purposes this summary suffices.

1.7.3　BT Compatibility

Although the Chomsky 1981 version of the binding theory combined simplicity with substantial factual coverage, right from the start the complementarity between bound pronominals and anaphors, which is one of its key features, faced empirical challenges. For instance, as noted by Huang (1982) the CBT does not capture the fact that in the possessor position of a DP bound pronominals and anaphors are not in complementary distribution, as illustrated in (59):

(59) a. *The girls* admired [$_\gamma$ *their* friends]
　　 b. *The girls* admired [$_\gamma$ *each other*'s friends]

On the basis of this and following Huang's (1982) proposals, Chomsky (1986a) developed an alternative procedure for computing the local domain. The core domain is that of a *Complete Functional Complex* (CFC), a domain in which all grammatical functions of a given predicate are realized. It is proposed, then, that the binding domain of some element α is the smallest CFC containing α for which there is an indexing *I* that is BT compatible, where BT compatibility reflects the following assumptions: (i) anaphors must be bound; (ii) pronominals need not be bound; (iii) any indexing to be taken into consideration must obey the i-within-i condition; and (iv) nominal heads may carry indices but are not possible antecedents just by themselves, since only full nominal phrases are. So, for an anaphor the binding domain is the smallest CFC in which it can be bound under some indexing *I*; for a pronominal the binding domain is the smallest CFC in which it can be free under *I*. Thus, for *their* in (59a) it is sufficient if it is free in γ, which it is. For *each other* in (59b) it is sufficient if it is bound in the next higher binding domain, which it is too.

In order for an anaphor in the subject position of a finite clause to be correctly ruled out, Chomsky adopts a proposal by Lebeaux (1983), who assumes that anaphors undergo so-called covert movement toward their antecedents—that is, in current terms, internal merge with only the lower copy spelled out.[42] Anaphor movement from the subject position of a finite clause creates a configuration just like the one that in the case of overt movement creates a so-called Comp-trace effect. The parallel is illustrated in (60):

(60) a. *Who$_i$ do you think [that [t$_i$ came]]
      b. *John [himself$_i$ T] thought [that [t$_i$ would come]]

Here, (60b) is ruled out, just like (60a) since the trace is not "properly governed," which was taken to be a general requirement for traces in that approach.[43] Subsequently, covert movement of anaphors became an important tool in the analysis of so-called long-distance anaphors in a range of languages varying from Icelandic to Chinese. Curiously enough, the BT based on BT compatibility never became as entrenched as the CBT. Perhaps developments took this turn because the discussion shifted to different ranges of facts that were beyond the scope of either.

1.7.4   Some Further Challenges to the CBT

The absence of complementarity between bound pronominals and anaphors in the possessor position was only one of the minor and major challenges for the CBT. Another fact, already observed in Chomsky 1981, 148, is that there is no clear complementarity between anaphors and pronominals in locative PPs such as (61) either.

(61) *He* pulled the table toward *him(self)*.

This was not captured by the revision discussed in the previous section. Furthermore, not only is there an occasional lack of complementarity, it also turned out that anaphors themselves are not always well behaved. As early as the 1970s, Ross (1970), Cantrall (1974), and Kuno (1972, 1975) observed that 1st- and 2nd-person anaphors in English can occur without a linguistic antecedent, as illustrated in (62):

(62) Physicists like *yourself* are a godsend. (Ross 1970)

In the same vein, Postal (1970) had noted that reflexives in picture NPs are not subject to the same constraints as reflexives in other positions (see chapters 3 and 7 for more discussion of picture NPs). For instance, *a picture of myself would look nice on that wall* is fine, although *myself* is not bound. In section 1.3 I referred to the observation that in (63) *himself* can be nonlocally bound:

(63) John was hoping that Mary would support no one but himself.

During the 1970s and early 1980s such facts were largely put aside for later investigation. In the late 1980s this changed, when different patterns from a variety of languages were brought together, enabling a picture of patterns of variation into which such facts could fit. In the next section I present an overview of a number of core phenomena whose investigation shaped subsequent developments.

The fact that binding relations and coreference relations occur in overlapping environments poses yet another challenge to the CBT. Its consequences will be briefly discussed in section 1.9. In the next section I discuss how the conceptual underpinning of the CBT changed.

1.8 Beyond the CBT

1.8.1 Types of Nominal Expressions

As discussed in section 1.7.1, the canonical binding theory distinguishes between anaphors, pronominals, and R-expressions. The original idea was that the existence of just these three classes was a direct consequence of an underlying feature system. This system consisted of two binary features: [+/−pronominal] and [+/−anaphoric]. The former reflects being subject to condition B, the latter being subject to condition A. So we have a neat dichotomy between the anaphoric and the pronominal property. These features yield a matrix with four possible combinations, realized in four phonological null elements and three lexical counterparts:

(64) a. *Lexical*

	+pronominal	−pronominal
+anaphoric	—	anaphor
−anaphoric	pronominal	R-expression

b. *Null*

	+pronominal	−pronominal
+anaphoric	PRO	NP-trace
−anaphoric	pro	*wh*-trace

The values in the lexical portion of the matrix are self-explanatory, except for the empty slot in the upper-left quadrant, to be discussed after discussing the null part of the matrix. Except for the element in the upper-left quadrant, the elements in the null section directly correspond to their correlates in the lexical matrix. *NP-trace* (+anaphoric, −pronominal) is the trace left by dislocation of the object in passives, relating *The queen forgot Alice* to *Alice was forgotten t by the queen*, where *Alice* in subject position retains the semantic role it received in object position. This movement is local, and its domain coincides with the domain in which anaphors are bound according to condition A. *Wh-trace* is the trace left by question formation, topicalization, and so on. *Wh*-movement is less strictly local than A-movement; it cannot be A-bound. *pro* is just a null version of standard pronominals, and for the binding theory it behaves like that. It occurs in the subject position of so-called pro-drop languages like Italian or Czech, where *sono arrivati* just means *they have arrived*. The subject position is taken to be syntactically represented as *pro* in *pro sono arrivati*.

This leaves PRO. PRO is the null element in the subject position of control structures, as in *The caterpillar asked Alice [PRO to go away]*. Since PRO represents the feature combination [+pronominal, +anaphoric], it is subject to both condition B and condition A. This means it must be both bound and free in its governing category. This requirement is contradictory unless PRO has no governing category. For a null element this condition can be met if it is in a position where it is not governed. This was taken to be the case in the subject position of *to*-infinitives. Lexical noun phrases, however, are required to have Case. Case is taken to require a governor. Therefore, a lexical counterpart of PRO cannot exist since it would need Case. Hence, the upper-left quadrant of the lexical matrix had to remain empty. This has come to be known as the *PRO-theorem*. Like the CBT itself, this provides a highly appealing picture.

Chomsky (1982, 1986a) revised this approach by introducing a functional/contextual definition of empty categories, essentially motivated by the existence of *parasitic gaps*.[44] Whether an element qualified as an NP-trace, *wh*-trace, and so forth was not determined by its intrinsic feature content, but by the nature of its binder (see Brody 1984 for criticisms). For current purposes it is important to note that the direct parallelism between A-binding and A-movement was lost by this step, hence the direct correspondence between null elements and their lexical counterparts had to be given up, undermining the attraction of the feature system.

However, as discussed in section 1.4.3, in current theory source positions are not occupied by special null elements, but by copies of the expressions "moved" (Chomsky 1995). This completes the elimination of any conceptual underpinning of the feature system underlying (64).

I will not discuss the interpretation of PRO in this book. (For a comprehensive analysis of PRO, see Landau 2003, 2006, 2008. For an alternative approach, see Hornstein 2000 and subsequent work.) Yet, one insight has turned out to be important: whether or not an element requires a binder is not only determined by its intrinsic properties. It may also depend on how these properties interact with the syntactic environment. This is relevant for an understanding of the phenomenon of *exemption*, discussed in detail in chapter 3, that is, cases where an anaphor escapes the requirement that it must be bound, as in (62).

1.8.2 Parameters of Variation

1.8.2.1 Types of Anaphoric Expressions   In our first sketch of exceptions to the CBT in section 1.3 Germanic languages are well represented. Now I return to them, discussing them in a bit more detail. That they are well represented is no accident, since they have been extensively studied. But there is no reason to expect that there aren't many other language groups with the same variability. Within Germanic, English with its two-way distinction between anaphors and pronominals is the exception rather than the rule. Most other languages have simplex anaphors and complex anaphors. Germanic complex anaphors are often formed with a cognate of English *self*. Since they share crucial properties, as discussed in chapter 3, I will refer to them with the general term *SELF anaphor*. It is important to note that not all complex anaphors behave as SELF anaphors. Chapter 3 specifically discusses the role of SELF-anaphors. In chapters 6 and 7 their properties are put in a more general perspective.

Dutch has a three-way distinction between SE anaphors, SELF anaphors, and pronominals (1st- and 2nd-person singular and plural, 3rd-person singular masculine, feminine, and neuter, 3rd-person plural common gender). Pronominals occur in a weak and a strong form. The SE anaphor is *zich*, which only occurs in 3rd person. It is underspecified for gender and number. That is, it is possible with masculine, feminine, and neuter antecedents, both singular and plural. In this respect SE anaphors are similar to reflexive clitics in Romance, such as Italian *si* and French *se*. However, as chapter 6 shows in more detail, in other respects they differ. Hence, Romance clitics will not be analyzed as SE anaphors. To make this clear, I will use the term *SE anaphor* as follows:

(65) A SE anaphor is a nonclitic pronominal that is underspecified in φ-features.[45]

Note that making the notion of underspecification precise is less trivial than it may seem. I discuss it in chapter 5 in the necessary detail. For now an informal understanding suffices.

In environments where *zich* would be used for 3rd person, 1st and 2nd person are realized by a canonical pronominal form (either the strong or the weak form *mij/me* in 1st-person singular, just the form *ons* in 1st-person plural, the weak form *je* in 2nd-person singular, and mostly *je* but sometimes *jullie* in 2nd-person plural). The 3rd-person complex anaphor has the form *zichzelf*. In 1st and 2nd person the SELF anaphor is realized as the corresponding pronominal with *zelf*. It was clear right from the beginning that the anaphoric system of Dutch and similar languages could not be straightforwardly captured in the CBT. Everaert (1984, 1986, 1991) presents an extensive discussion of the several anaphoric systems of the Germanic languages, putting them in a systematic comparative and crosslinguistic perspective. As I discuss in detail in chapter 3, *zich* and *zichzelf* and their cognates in the Scandinavian languages occur in distinct but structurally overlapping environments. This makes it impossible to capture their distribution in terms of governing categories as originally conceived.

Scandinavian languages (Icelandic, Faroese, Danish, Norwegian, and Swedish) have a four-way system: pronominals, SE anaphors, complex anaphors of the form SE-SELF, and Pronominal-SELF. SE(-SELF) is required if the antecedent is a local subject, Pronominal(-SELF) if it is not. Moreover, these languages have a possessive anaphor, in addition to a possessive pronominal. The possessive anaphor must be selected if the antecedent is a local subject.

Frisian has a two-way system, but different from English. As noted in section 1.3, its system is, in fact very important for our understanding of how binding works. It is like Dutch, but instead of a SE anaphor like *zich*, it uses the pronominal *him* 'him', *har* 'her', *har(ren)* 'them' (given in their strong forms). These are true pronominals, yet they can be locally bound. So, contra condition B of the CBT, Frisian has local binding of pronominals in all persons (see Everaert 1986, 1991). Consequently, a sentence like *Jan fielde him fuortglieden* 'John felt PRON slip away' is ambiguous between a reading in which John is the person slipping away and a reading in which someone else slips away. Its Dutch counterpart with *zich* only allows the former reading. This fact is not just problematic for the CBT; it undermines its very foundation. Frisian is discussed in detail in chapters 3, 5, and 8, where I evaluate the consequences of this fact.

German (especially the standard variant High German) prima facie has a two-way system, distinguishing between pronominals and anaphors. The canonical 3rd-person anaphor is a prima facie monomorphemic *sich*. Although German allows the morpheme *selbst* to be attached to *sich* and *pronominals*, there is little evidence that it is more than an emphatic element. In many current German dialects, *sich* is limited to accusative positions or even to just the direct object positions (Keller 1961), with a locally bound pronominal where *sich* does not occur. This is also true of Middle High German up to the fifteenth or sixteenth century (Keller 1978). The relation between the German system and the apparently more complex systems in other Germanic languages is discussed extensively in chapter 8.

Not only is there substantial variation in the number of distinctions between anaphoric expressions, there is also considerable variation in the domains in which SE anaphors must be bound. The initial facts about Icelandic long-distance anaphora were already brought up in Clements 1975; Thráinsson 1976a, 1976b; Hellan 1980; and Maling 1982, 1984. For extensive subsequent discussion of the possible factors involved in the variation, see Everaert 1986, 1991; Hellan 1988, 1991; and Thráinsson 1991. In all of Icelandic, Faroese, and mainland Scandinavian, SE anaphors may allow their antecedent to occur in a position considerably beyond the governing category as computed in the CBT. This is illustrated in (66) from Icelandic.

(66) Jón$_i$ sagði [Maríu$_j$ hafa$_{(inf.)}$ látið [mig þvo$_{(inf.)}$ sér$_{i,j}$]]
      John said   Mary   have   made me   wash   SE
      'John said that Mary had made me wash him.'

In Dutch and German this possibility is far more restricted, and the equivalent of (66) ill-formed. This raises the question of how such differences are encoded in the grammar. This will be the topic of discussion in chapter 8. There it will be shown that given the theory of encoding of anaphoric dependencies to be developed in the next few chapters, this contrast follows from an independent property of the grammars of these languages. I mention it here, since it is one of the contrasts that provided an important reason for developing alternatives to the CBT.

Turning from Germanic to languages of other families, we also find pronominals, simplex anaphors, and different types of complex anaphors. Crosslinguistically, anaphoric systems that show a contrast between complex anaphors and SE anaphors—sharing the requirement that they must be bound but with different distributions—are pervasive. Faltz (1977) provides an extensive survey of anaphoric systems of the languages of the world. He shows that complex reflexives are formed from pronominals and SE anaphors by adding elements such as body-part expressions, intensifiers, and so on. All the complex anaphors Faltz discusses are made up of morphemes that exist independently. According to him, complex reflexives are formed in two ways: head reflexives and adjunct reflexives.

Head reflexives are based on an element that occurs independently as a nominal head, generally with a pronominal specifier. The relation between head and specifier may be understood as one of inalienable possession (see Pica 1987, 1991; Everaert 2003).[46] Faltz discusses a few examples (including Basque, Fula, Malagasy, and Hebrew). (67) from Basque is given here for illustration:

(67) *Basque*
    a. Aitak   bere   burua   hil du.
       father+ERG 3SG.POSS head+NOM.DEF kill have+3SG+3SG
       'The father killed himself.'
    b. Bere   buruan   txapela   ipini du.
       3SG.POSS head+LOC.DEF cap+NOM put have+3SG+3SG
       'He put the cap on his head.'

The same stem that occurs as a lexical N meaning 'head' in (67b) is used as a reflexive in (67a).

Adjunct reflexives are construed of a pronominal or SE anaphor and an adjunct, marking emphasis or focus, which may also attach to lexical NPs. According to Jayaseelan (1997), Malayalam represents this option. One of the examples Faltz gives is Irish, repeated here:[47]

(68) *Irish*
   a. Ghortaigh Seán é.
      hurt   Sean him
      'Sean hurt him.'
   b. Ghortaigh Seán é   féin.
      hurt   Sean him EMPH
      'Sean hurt himself.'
   c. Bhí   an t-easpag féin i láthair.
      be+PAST the bishop EMPH present
      'The bishop himself was present.'

One of my goals in this book is to explain how rather different strategies apparently play the same role in the linguistic system.

1.8.2.2 Binding Requirements on Anaphors The assumption that anaphors must be (locally) bound constitutes one of the basic principles of the CBT. Yet many languages have anaphoric elements that need not be locally bound, or need not be bound at all in certain environments. This section introduces some of the main issues.

Anaphors that need not be bound constitute a major problem for the CBT. Moreover, the behavior of anaphors is not always clear-cut. As we have seen on the basis of English *himself*, languages may have forms that must be bound in one environment but not in another.[48] A further well-studied case is *sig* in Icelandic. It must have a binder in (69a), and failing this, due to a feature mismatch between *þú* and *sig*, the sentence is ill-formed, but not so in (69b).

(69) a. *Þú hefur svikið   sig.
      you have betrayed self
   b. María var alltaf svo andstyggileg. Þegar Olafur$_j$ kæmi segði
      hún sér$_{i/*j}$ áreiðanlega að fara. (Thráinsson 1991)
      'Mary was always so nasty. When Olaf would come, she would certainly tell himself [the person whose thoughts are being presented—not Olaf] to leave.'

In (69b) *sér* is without a linguistically expressed antecedent, and yet the sentence is well formed. Why this is so is discussed in chapter 5. Traditionally anaphors such as *sig* in (69b) were called *indirect reflexives* (Hagège 1974, 289). This use of reflexive-like forms is not limited to Icelandic or Latin (discussed by Hagège) but widespread over the languages of the world.[49]

Since Clements 1975, the term *logophor* has come to be used for such anaphors. It was introduced by Hagège (1974) to characterize a class of pronouns in languages from the Niger-Congo family that refer to the "auteur d'un discours" (the "source of a discourse" in the terms of Clements 1975). As Hagège puts it, "These pronouns distinguish the individual to which they refer from the speaker himself who uses them, in . . . 'indirect speech'" (Hagège 1974, 287; translation ER). They refer to the individual cited, the secondary speaker, as opposed to the primary speaker.

A formally distinct series of pronouns for this type of use is found in, for instance, Mundang, Tuburi, and Ewe from the Niger-Congo family. These pronouns bear no formal resemblance to reflexives, hence Hagège considers the term "indirect reflexive" inappropriate and calls them logophoric.[50] Yet, as Hagège and Clements note, the discourse function of such logophoric pronouns is similar to the indirect reflexive, which can be illustrated by the following example from Ewe (Clements 1975):

(70) Tsali gbl? na-e   be ye-e dyi   yè gake yè-kpe dyi.
     Tsali say to-Pron that Pron beget LOG but LOG be victor
     'Tsali$_i$ told him$_j$ (i.e., his father) that he$_j$ begot him$_i$ but he$_i$ was the victor.'

Here *LOG* is the gloss for the logophoric pronoun *yè*.[51] Only *Tsali*, the source of the reported discourse, can be the antecedent of *yè*. As Clements notes, the logophoric pronoun may occur at any depth of embedding. In fact, these pronouns do not require a cosentential antecedent— the antecedent can be several sentences back. The subsequent sentences of the discourse will continue to present the events described by the narrator from the point of view of the same individual or individuals (Clements 1975, 170).

The terminology of Hagège, and of most of the standard typological literature, explicitly distinguishes indirect reflexives from logophoric pronouns. Modern syntactic literature often follows the usage of Clements 1975, which extends Hagège's usage.

Clements (1975, 171–172) gives the following crosslinguistic characterization of logophoric pronouns in this broader sense:

i.   logophoric pronouns are restricted to *reportive contexts* transmitting the words or thoughts of an individual or individuals other than the speaker/narrator;
ii. the antecedent does not occur in the same reportive context as the logophoric pronoun;
iii. the antecedent designates the individual or individuals whose words or thoughts are transmitted in the reported context in which the logophoric pronoun occurs.

Clements observes that in some languages logophoric pronouns may occur in sentences that strictly speaking do not satisfy conditions (i)–(iii), but that are in some sense modeled on sentences in which these conditions are satisfied. He notes that these conditions are primarily semantic/pragmatic, but does not elaborate on this. Furthermore, he indicates that languages may impose varying idiosyncratic conditions on logophors. In Ewe, for instance, logophors are restricted to clauses introduced by the complementizer *be*.[52] They also show special agreement properties.[53] Icelandic logophoric anaphora requires a subjunctive, in Mandarin Chinese the antecedent must be a living human being, and so on.[54]

These results notwithstanding, many approaches to long-distance binding have rested on the assumption that the anaphoric dependencies we are discussing invariably reflect structural binding relations.

However, extensive investigation of the issue conducted on Icelandic (Thráinsson 1976a, 1976b, 1991; Maling 1982, 1986; Anderson 1986; Sells 1987; Hellan 1988, 1991; Sigurðsson 1990; Sigurjónsdóttir 1992) revealed systematic differences in Icelandic between long-distance "binding" into subjunctive clauses and long-distance binding into infinitival clauses. As will be discussed in detail in chapter 8, an important conclusion is that the antecedent possibilities of long distance *sig* in subjunctives are not constrained by structural conditions such as c-command but rather by discourse factors such as perspective and point of view. This constituted one more source of motivation to rethink the foundations of the binding theory.

While English *himself* and Icelandic *sig* must be locally bound in some positions and not in others, there are other languages with yet a different pattern. They require a special form to license a reflexive predicate—that is, when a pronominal form ends up locally bound—but that form does not have to be locally bound. A well-known example is Malayalam (Jayaseelan 1997):

(71) a. raaman$_i$ tan-ne$_i$ *(tanne) sneehikunnu
       Raman SE-acc self   loves
       'Raman loves him*(self).'
    b. raaman$_i$ wicaariccu [penkuttikal tan-ne$_i$ tanne sneehikkunnu
       Raman thought   girls   SE-acc self   love
       ennə]
       Comp
       '*Raman* thought that the girls love *himself*.'

As (71a) shows, the anaphor *tan-ne* must be accompanied by *tanne* in a local binding context, but as (71b) shows, in an embedded clause *tan-ne* _tanne_ may have a matrix antecedent. In the corresponding English sentence that construal is impossible.

Again, as in the previous subsection, what we have here is just a tiny sample of the existing languages, but it suffices to illustrate a range of variation that is unexpected from the perspective of the CBT.

This overview should give the reader a general idea of the issues a theory of binding has to deal with. In the subsequent chapters I return to all of them. In the next section I discuss another core notion of the CBT and show that it should be rethought.

1.9   Indices and Their Demise

The formulation of the CBT is based on the notion of an index, as reflected in the definition of binding in (50), repeated here:

(50) *a* binds *b* iff *a* and *b* are coindexed and *a* c-commands *b*.

Whereas the use of indices as descriptive devices is generally accepted, their precise status in the grammar has been the subject of considerable debate. In the canonical binding theory any DP in a sentence comes with an index; coindexing represents *intended coreference* (or *covaluation*, to use a more general term that I will quite often employ). This intended covaluation is assumed to be part of the meaning of a sentence (Fiengo and May 1994). Also, conversely, intended covaluation, under this assumption, should be linguistically expressed by coindexing. The only escape from this is if one lacks information about the relevant facts, such as the speaker's intentions, or if it is part of the meaning of a sentence that the values of two expressions are to be identified. Fiengo and May's position can be illustrated on the basis of the following text:

(72) The robber had entered the vault. John's accuser swore that he had taken the diamonds.

Suppose *he* is intended to refer to *the robber*. This is expressed by coindexing *the robber* and *he*. Suppose the speaker does not wish to take a stand on whether John's accuser is right and *John* and *he/the robber* are actually the same person. If so, the indexing should be as in (73):

(73) The robber$_i$ had entered the vault. John$_j$'s accuser swore that he$_i$ had taken the diamonds.

Yet criminal investigation can subsequently establish that *he* and *John* (and the robber) are one and the same person. This does not affect the propriety of the indexing in (73). On the other hand, if the speaker wants to take a stand on whether *John* and *he* are the same person, they can and should be coindexed. Similarly, given that some subsequent statement *John is the robber* is not a tautology, *John* and *the robber* should not be coindexed, even though they refer to the same individual if the sentence is true.

The canonical binding theory is thus stated in terms of coindexing and c-command. Debates about indices continue up to the present day, though the issues vary.

Within the canonical binding theory the indexing in (74) is a part of the syntactic structure that is semantically interpreted, although, since there is no c-command, *John* does not bind *him*:

(74) Pictures of John$_1$'s father belong to him$_1$

Reinhart (1983 and subsequent work) argues that the linguistic status of coindexing is strictly determined by the binding theory. C-command and coindexing determine whether the relation between an antecedent and an anaphor or pronominal is one of *variable binding*. It is variable binding that is governed by the binding theory; coindexing is an annotation of the structure that is only interpreted in the context of the binding theory—that is, in the context of a theory that only "sees" bound variable readings. Hence, in Reinhart's approach indices as in (74) are not part of the syntactic structure. It is entirely proper to represent the sentence as in (75a) without indices. The syntactic structure does not prescribe whether (75a) is assigned the interpretation (75b), (75c), and so on.

(75) a. Pictures of John's father belong to him.
     b. Pictures of John's father belong to him & him=John
     c. Pictures of John's father belong to him & him=Peter, etc.

That is, assigning *him* and *John* the same individual as their value has the same status in the theory as assigning *him* any other male individual as a value. What value is actually assigned is fully determined by the interpretive component. In Reinhart's approach the interpretation represented by (74)/(75b) typically instantiates what has been called "accidental coreference." In a Fiengo-and-May type approach "accidental coreference" is limited to cases like (73), where to the relevant parties involved it is not known whether *John* is actually identical to *he/the robber*.

Clearly, the two approaches embody a different view of cutting the pie of anaphoric dependencies. In a Fiengo-and-May type approach the bulk of the work is done in the syntax by indexing, and only a marginal part of it is left to an interpretive component. In a Reinhart type of approach the work is rather equally divided over the interpretive component and the computational system (syntax and logical form, governing binding relations), leading to a modular approach to binding in which indices are not part of the syntactic structure. Apart from various technical and empirical considerations (discussed in Reinhart 2006) that I will not go over here, theoretical parsimony should lead one toward a Reinhart type of approach anyway. Indices are theoretical tools to capture dependencies in a particular way. Processes assigning values to natural language expressions are part of the language system by necessity. Hence, in case of redundancy parsimony entails that what is contingent has to be dropped, and as we will see shortly, this is the next step.

In the context of the Minimalist Program the issue was sharpened. One of the prerequisites for attaining its goals is to draw the boundaries between syntax and other components of the language system in a principled way. The MP proposes that the computational system of human language reflects the combinatorial properties of a purely morpholexical vocabulary. Furthermore, its guiding hypothesis is that C_{HL} is an optimal solution for a system pairing form and interpretation that is to meet the specific conditions imposed by the human systems of thought and perception/articulation. Such an optimal system should meet the condition of *inclusiveness*: any structure formed by the computation is constituted of elements already present in the lexical items selected. No new objects such as indices are added in the course of the derivation. Hence, indices, the core ingredient of the canonical binding theory, have no place in syntax, unless coindexing is really morphosyntactically expressed, which is not the case in any language we know of.[55] This line is incompatible with a Fiengo-and-May type of approach. In Reinhart's approach syntactic indices are dispensable in the definition of binding, since their work can be taken over by variable binding at the relevant level.[56]

In preminimalist versions of the theory indices also played a role for expressing syntactic dependencies. As noted in section 1.4, dislocation can be expressed by trace notation. If so, the dependency between *what* and its trace *t* is expressed by coindexing, as in (76a). In a copy-based approach this type of dependency can be represented without indices. In line with Chomsky 2005, 2008, copies in (76b) by definition stand in an equivalence relation. In fact, as shown in Frampton 2004, copying can be further reduced to reusing (remerging) the same element. If so, copying/reusing is the canonical syntactic operation to represent identity of different occurrences of an element.

Consider next the Agree operation. Agree typically leads to the presence of two occurrences of the same feature bundle, as in (76c):

(76) a. What$_i$ did you think that Alice saw t$_i$
   b. What did you think that Alice saw (what)
   c. Alice$_\phi$ was$_\phi$ standing in the garden

Again this effect can be obtained by copying/reusing a feature bundle, along the lines proposed by Frampton and Gutmann 2000. Pursuing this proposal, we may draw the following conclusion:

(77) The Agree relation represents identity of feature bundles in syntax.

For the moment this is a simple conclusion, but it will have far-reaching consequences for our perspective on anaphor binding. It will provide the basis for the systematic investigation of binding without indices that will be carried out in this book.

1.10 Binding and Coreference Revisited

The demise of indices also bears on the following issue. As we saw in section 1.6.2, a pronoun is either interpreted as a bound variable or referentially. One of the environments where this shows up is VP-ellipsis. So we had the pattern in (36), repeated as (78), where binding is reflected in the sloppy reading, and coreference in the strict reading:

(78) a. John loves his cat and Peter does too.
   b. John (λx (x loves x's cat)) and Peter (λx (x loves x's cat))
   c. John (λx (x loves a's cat & a=John)) and Peter (λx (x loves a's cat & a=John))

In CBT-based approaches, the indexing in the syntax determines whether a strict or a sloppy reading is assigned. From the current perspective this is impossible, since the expressions on which C$_{HL}$ operates contain no indices. Therefore, the choice between (78b) and (78c) as the translation of (78a) cannot be syntactically encoded. Hence, up to the C-I interface, pronouns are only characterized by their ϕ-features. This leads to (79):

(79) At the C-I interface pronouns can be translated either as expressions receiving a value directly from a discourse storage, or as variables to be bound by an antecedent.

This choice must be intrinsically free. This has an important consequence, which can be illustrated on the basis of (80), with *him* identical to *Bill*.

(80) *Bill adores *him*.

Given (79), (80) has two representations at the interface, one with *him* a variable bound by *Bill*, the other with *him* referential:

(81) a. Bill (λx (x adores x))
     b. Bill (λx (x adores a))

Since the value of *a* can be freely chosen, one interpretation of (81b) is (82):

(82) Bill (λx (x adores Bill))

Reading (81a) for (80) is ruled out under the standard binding condition B (whatever its proper formulation), but (82) is not, despite the fact that (80) does not obviously allow this reading.

As is well known, ruling out this interpretation under all circumstances would be wrong, since this would incorrectly also rule out (83) under the intended interpretation.

(83) I know what Mary and *Bill* have in common. Mary adores *him* and
     Bill adores *him* too. (Reinhart 1983)

Here, *him* must admit Bill as its value, yielding coreference between *Bill* and *him*. Any theory must represent the fact that coreference is allowed in (83), but impossible in (80).

Instead of formulating a rule that exceptionally allows the coreference option, Reinhart (1983) and Grodzinsky and Reinhart (1993) (henceforth, G&R) formulate an interpretive condition expressing when the coreference option is blocked:

(84) *Rule I: Intrasentential Coreference*
     NP A cannot corefer with NP B if replacing A with C, C a variable
     A-bound by B, yields an indistinguishable interpretation.

Applied to (80), (84) only lets through the bound variable structure represented in (81a). (81a) in turn is ruled out by condition B. Hence, (80) under the intended interpretation will end up being ruled out altogether.

Although it is possible to simply stipulate the *cannot corefer* part of (84), Reinhart (1983) proposes a rationale. Coreference is not "impossible" in (80), but the option is not used given the availability of a process that is preferred for independent reasons ("early closure" of an open expression; see the discussion in Reinhart 1983).[57] Applying Rule I requires comparing two different derivations. Grodzinsky and Reinhart propose that the demand on processing resources that this requires exceeds what is available to the child. This explains the fact that children master condition B at a substantially later age than condition A (the "delayed condition B effect").[58]

I will use Rule I as a model for other cases of division of labor between components to be discussed in chapters 4 and 5.[59] The status of economy principles of this kind in general will be extensively discussed in chapter 4.

The issue of "accidental coreference" has been taken up again by Kayne (2002) in a movement approach to binding. I come back to Kayne's approach in chapter 9. As we will see, there is a syntactic residue in certain binding relations but not others (essentially reflected in the locality conditions on binding discussed in section 1.7). How to represent this residue will be one of the main concerns of chapter 5.

1.11 Summary and Structure of the Book

Let me summarize what we did in this chapter—in particular, what goals were set for the book—and outline how we will arrive at these goals in subsequent chapters. It will be important to keep in mind throughout that we are striving for a theory in which all the properties of anaphors and pronominals can be explained in terms of their feature content and the way independent properties of the grammar allow these features to interact with the syntactic environment.

We discussed two ways to establish interpretative dependencies: binding and coreference. We adopted a perspective on binding developed in Reinhart 2000, 2006:

(85) *A-binding*
     α A-binds β iff α is the sister of a λ-predicate whose operator binds β.

A-binding applies at the level of logical syntax, where syntactic structures are read into the inference system. In particular, pronouns (pronominals and anaphors) are translated as variables that can be bound by λ-operators. A-binding is subject to the c-command/sisterhood requirement. Coreference is established in the discourse, and hence is not subject to any structural constraints and is not limited to pronouns.

In (86a), both binding and coreference can be used, leading to different interpretations: 'only Lucie respects her husband, and other women do not respect their husbands' or 'only Lucie respects her husband, and no-

body else respects this person'. (86b) can be interpreted only by coreference, and (87a) only by binding, since in this case, no discourse referent
is established for *no one* that *he* could refer back to. That coreference is
indeed impossible in such cases is illustrated by the ungrammaticality of
(87b).

(86) a. Only Lucie respects her husband.

   b. John has a gun. Will he/this man attack?

(87) a. No one was convinced that he would be welcome.

   b. *No one has a gun. Will he/this man attack?

The key fact that any binding theory strives to capture is that certain
binding dependencies are subject to *additional constraints*, other than the
c-command requirement that rules out binding in (86) and (87). Let us
come back to the examples at the very beginning of this book:

(88) a. *Alice$_1$ stopped her$_1$

   b. Alice$_1$ was beginning to get very tired of sitting by her$_1$ sister
      on the bank

(89) a. Alice$_1$ stopped herself$_1$

   b. *Alice$_1$ expected the Mad Hatter to invite herself$_1$ for a drink

In the canonical binding theory of Chomsky 1981, or CBT, these additional constraints were accounted for by principles A and B, repeated in
(90):

(90) (A) An anaphor is bound in its local domain.

   (B) A pronominal is free in its local domain.

Our short survey of binding patterns showed that these principles are too
good to be false and too bad to be true. The CBT definitely points to
some deep generalizations, since the core patterns are stable across languages, but has to be reformulated to accommodate an ever-increasing
number of exceptions. The solution I offer in this book has the following
properties:

(i) My account will rely only on independently motivated rules used in
     other components of grammar and on the morphosyntactic features
     of different pronominal elements. Arriving at a more parsimonious
     system becomes essential if the minimalist perspective on natural lan-
     guage is adopted.

     It is especially important to note that grammatical rules employed
     in my account are universal, while all crosslinguistic variation comes

from the lexicon, in particular from a different featural composition of pronominal elements that defines their behavior in various syntactic environments. This is reflected in the Feature Determinacy Thesis (FDT), introduced as (15) in section 1.5.2 and repeated here as (91).

(91) *Feature Determinacy Thesis*
Syntactic binding of pronominal elements (including anaphors) in a particular environment is determined by their morphosyntactic features and the way these enter into the syntactic operations available in that environment.

(ii) Another step toward conceptual parsimony will be dispensing with indices, which were used in the CBT and elsewhere to express identity. Indices are problematic anyway, and in the Minimalist Program have no status. The definition of A-binding in (85) no longer relies on indices. Thus, any principles describing additional constraints on binding should not employ indices either. As a result of (i) and (ii), the binding theory as we know it will disappear—the new account will not contain any statements specific to binding.

(iii) Given the way principles A and B are formulated, it is unclear *why* any restrictions of this sort exist in the grammar. In my account, the core generalizations will be traced back to the general sources of invariance that characterize language as a computational system, which were discussed in section 1.5.1. Thus, we will go beyond explanatory adequacy in Chomsky's (2004) sense, approaching the question of how the knowledge of language is realized in our mind, interfacing with other subsystems of our cognitive system—the central question of linguistics.

Apart from explaining and reducing principles A and B of the CBT, I will address several other problems, such as the role of c-command in binding (and, again, *why* it plays any role) and the nature of economy constraints in the encoding of anaphoric dependencies. Reinhart (Reinhart 1983, 2006; Grodzinsky and Reinhart 1993) shows that Rule I can be explained by economy considerations. I will pursue this line of thought, investigating whether there are other similar constraints in the grammar and comparing different ways of implementing them.

The FDT will play a crucial role in subsequent discussions together with the logical syntax perspective on binding, as formulated in (28)/(94).

One of the main claims of this book is that the key to a proper understanding of the conditions governing the interpretation of anaphoric expressions is the division of labor between three major components of the language system: narrow syntax, the C-I interface, and the discourse component. As stated earlier, narrow syntax is the component only containing elementary operations on morphosyntactic objects. At the C-I interface, as a first step toward interpretation and access by the inferential system, the logical syntax properties of the output of the narrow syntax are made explicit, specifically their operator variable structure as discussed in Reinhart 2000 and 2006. For our discourse component any system with file cards along the lines of Heim 1982 will do.

It is claimed that the division of labor between these components is governed by an economy principle to the effect that, where the choice exists, first encoding a dependency in narrow syntax is preferred over first encoding it at the C-I interface as an operator variable dependency in logical syntax. This in turn is preferred over first encoding it as covaluation in the discourse component. In short: narrow syntax < logical syntax < discourse. As is well known, such an economy hierarchy raises many questions (Reinhart 2000, 2006). Chapter 4 contains an extensive discussion of ways to justify this hierarchy, and to address the questions it raises.

Now let me show how we will arrive at these goals step by step in subsequent chapters.

1.11.1 Chapter 2

As noted above, A-binding per se is subject to one structural condition: it is limited by c-command. This is illustrated by (92), where *every student* cannot bind *him*.

(92) *The professor who failed every student$_i$ thought Mary liked him$_i$

Before I move on to derive additional restrictions reflected by principles A and B of the CBT, and to determine what will replace them, in chapter 2 I address the question of why this core restriction holds, relating it to the systematic bottom-up compositional interpretation procedure, and discuss what to do with some apparent exceptions. Prima facie in cases like (93a,b), the c-command requirement applies less strictly to pronominal binding.

(93) a. Every girl$_i$'s father loves her$_i$
     b. *Every girl$_i$'s father loves herself$_i$

The ill-formedness of (93b) can be accounted for by independent principles, namely by conditions on reflexivity marking that will first be formulated in chapter 3 and then elaborated on in subsequent chapters. So the main task of chapter 2 is to explain why (93a) is good. That it is follows from the definition of A-binding in (28), repeated here as (94), and the structural properties of specifiers/adjuncts:

(94) α A-binds β iff α is the sister of a λ-predicate whose operator binds β

Taking into account how the compositional interpretation proceeds, it is demonstrated that α can be the sister of the relevant λ-predicate when it is a specifier or an adjunct of a constituent γ that c-commands β. Consequently, binding out of specifiers and adjuncts is possible.

1.11.2 Chapter 3

At the beginning of this chapter, I sketch the first steps toward rethinking principles A and B along the lines of my previous joint work with Tanya Reinhart: Reinhart and Reuland 1989, 1991, and 1993. These principles are reinterpreted as being about reflexivity of predicates, as in (95).

(95) (A) A reflexive-marked syntactic predicate is reflexive.
    (B) A reflexive semantic predicate is reflexive-marked.

A predicate is reflexive iff two of its arguments are coindexed or, dispensing with indices, are bound by the same λ-operator.

Thus, (88a) and (89a), but not (88b) and (89b), contain reflexive predicates. The element *self* is a reflexive marker. Why exactly this is the case and what other types of reflexive markers exist crosslinguistically is discussed in chapter 6. Thus, (88a) is bad because the reflexive predicate *stopped* is not marked, while (89b) is bad because, despite the presence of a reflexive marker, the predicate *invite* cannot be made reflexive owing to a feature mismatch between its arguments.

Putting all the details aside for a moment (including the distinction between semantic and syntactic predicates), let us see the main advantages. First, some predicates are marked as reflexive in the lexicon. So, in line with the new condition B, SELF-marking becomes unnecessary, as demonstrated by Dutch (96a) as opposed to (96b).

(96) a. Willem$_1$ schaamt ??zichzelf$_1$/zich$_1$
        William shames   SEself/SE
    b. Willem$_1$ bewondert zichzelf$_1$/*zich$_1$
        William admires   SEself/SE

Second, as follows from the new condition A, reflexive-marking of a predicate depends on a SELF anaphor being its syntactic argument.

Thus, in (89b) *herself* reflexive-marks *invite*, while in (97) it does not, so the sentence is grammatical.

(97) Alice$_1$ expected the king to invite everybody but herself$_1$ for a drink

The sentence in (93b) is ungrammatical because the predicate *loves* is not reflexive. The differences between predicate classes, as in (96a,b), the behavior of so-called exempt anaphors, as in (97), the pattern in (93a,b), and many other facts discussed in chapter 3 remained unaccounted for in the CBT.

In the second part of chapter 3, I turn to facts that the new conditions A and B or the c-command requirement from chapter 2 have nothing to say about. For example, why is (98) bad, as opposed to (96a)?

(98) *Willem$_1$ schaamt hem$_1$
 William shames him

As noted above, the predicate *schamen* is lexically reflexive, which explains why *zichzelf* is ruled out, but an independent principle is needed to account for the choice between *zich* and *hem*. Ideally, this principle should also explain why the pronominal is fine in Frisian (99):

(99) Willem$_1$ skammet him$_1$
 William shames him

The same contrast between Dutch and Frisian can be seen in so-called ECM (exceptional case-marking) constructions in (100a,b):

(100) a. Willem$_1$ voelde [zich$_1$/*hem$_1$ wegglijden]
 William felt SE/him slip-away
 b. Willem$_1$ fielde [him$_1$ fuortglieden]
 William felt him slip-away

In Reinhart and Reuland's work (1989, 1991, 1993), a condition on the well-formedness of syntactic chains in (101) is responsible.

(101) *The chain condition*
 A maximal A-chain $(\alpha_1, \ldots, \alpha_n)$ contains exactly one link—α_1— which is fully specified for the (relevant) ϕ-features and for structural Case.[60]

At that stage, the notion of syntactic chain relied on c-command, coindexing, and the absence of syntactic barriers. In the minimalist framework adopted here, only c-command is retained. The second part of chapter 3 reviews how it worked and what facts it accounted for in Reinhart and Reuland's theory (1989, 1991, 1993).

Unlike pronominals and R-expressions, simplex anaphors are under-specified for ɸ-features (most notably for number; sometimes also for gender and person). By the definition of chain formulated in chapter 3, ⟨Willem₁, hem₁⟩ in (98) and (100a) is a chain but violates the chain condition in (101), since both *Willem* and *hem* are fully specified for ɸ-features and structural Case. The final part of chapter 3 paves the way for the transition to an approach in which ɸ-feature sharing takes over the role of coindexing in syntax. It shows that structural Case plays an important role in establishing syntactic dependencies, and indicates that pronominals cannot enter chains since they are not ɸ-feature deficient.

A detailed analysis of the Frisian Case system in chapter 8 explains the grammaticality of (99) and (100b): the Case that pronouns like *him* bear in Frisian is not structural, but inherent.

1.11.3   Chapter 4

In chapter 4 I further explore why 3rd-person pronominals cannot enter a syntactic chain with their antecedent. I show that feature sharing involves overwriting feature values, and that a general principle that requires *recoverability of deletions* guarantees that certain features of pronominals cannot be overwritten. However, if pronominals cannot enter into a syntactic dependency with their antecedent in a local environment such as (100a), the question remains why they cannot be interpreted as variables that are simply bound by the antecedent. It is argued that this follows from the economy hierarchy in (102):

(102) *Economy of encoding*

Narrow syntax < logical syntax (C-I interface) < discourse

If a dependency is blocked by a fundamental principle in a component that is lower on the hierarchy, the system cannot bypass this by resorting to an operation in a component higher in this hierarchy. Thus, in (100a), the syntactic encoding of the dependency between *zich* and its antecedent wins from the alternative in which *hem* is just a variable bound by its antecedent (see Reuland 2001b). In its initial form this economy principle faces a number of empirical problems (Reinhart 2006). It also faces a theoretical problem since the system compares two derivations with different lexical items, which goes against the standard view of economy. I review a number of perspectives on economy, including results from experimental research on processing economy. The chapter ends with a synthesis between the approaches in Reuland 2001b and Reinhart 2006. This synthesis resolves the empirical problems, and allows us to derive the contrast between the two options in (100a) without a direct comparison between their derivations.

1.11.4 Chapter 5

In this chapter I provide an explicit account of the syntactic encoding of anaphoric dependencies in the form of chains. We can do so on the basis of feature-matching operations that are indispensable in the grammar. No means are involved that are not independently necessary in a minimalist syntax. The chapter starts with a discussion of feature deficiency. SE anaphors such as Dutch *zich* are deficient in the sense that a cell in their feature matrix is present but lacks content. Subsequently, we will see in detail how a dependency between a simplex anaphor and its antecedent can be encoded in an index-free syntax on the basis of feature checking. Third-person pronominals cannot enter a syntactic chain without violating the principle of *recoverability of deletions*. This fact about 3rd-person pronominals is due to the structure of their left periphery, specifically in grammatical number and definiteness. This helps explain a correlation between definiteness marking and POSS anaphors. If a language has obligatory definiteness marking on D, it does not have a POSS anaphor, since D blocks chain formation between the anaphor and an antecedent in the verbal domain.

This prohibition against local binding of 3rd-person pronominals does not extend to 1st- and 2nd-person pronouns. So, whereas binding of the 3rd-person pronominal (98) is ill-formed, (103) with a locally bound 1st-person pronoun is fine.

(103) Ik schaam mij.
     I shame me

We will see that this difference follows from a difference in their semantics. All occurrences of 1st-person pronouns in the same reportive context receive dependent values. The same holds true for 2nd-person pronouns, but not for 3rd-person pronominals.

Since SE anaphors are feature deficient, they can enter a chain in order to be interpreted, and economy will force them to if they can. However, if chain formation is blocked, nothing prevents them from being interpreted on the basis of the feature content they have. We will see how the subjunctive in languages such as Icelandic blocks the formation of a chain between a SE anaphor and its antecedent, hence opens the possibility of an unbound, logophoric, interpretation.

Finally, we will see how an account based on feature checking can be reinterpreted in terms of Agree and feature valuation. This makes explicit that the syntactic encoding of the dependency between a SE anaphor and its antecedent crucially depends on the intervening functional system. In fact the SE anaphor need not be c-commanded by its antecedent, provided it is c-commanded by the functional element the antecedent agrees with.

1.11.5 Chapter 6

The role of this chapter can best be sketched on the basis of the diagram in (104), which puts the issues we deal with in chapter 6 in the context of the discussion in the preceding chapters.

First, we previously identified the main *modules* of the language system involved in anaphora. As a next step we focused on the grammatical *encoding* of interpretive dependencies. As the diagram shows, there is a split between SE anaphors and pronominals here. As we saw, pronominals, especially 3rd-person pronominals, cannot enter a syntactically encoded (Agree-based) dependency with an antecedent since this would violate the principle of recoverability of deletions (indicated by the * prefixed to *pronominals*). When different ways of encoding "compete," the outcome is regulated by economy.

(104) *Structure of the argumentation*

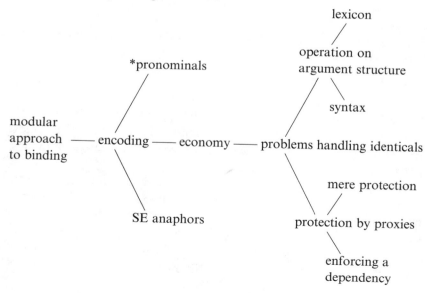

Chapter 6 discusses the last part of the diagram. It addresses the question of how binding patterns crosslinguistically reflect the sources of invariance introduced in section 1.5.1. If the anaphor and its antecedent are arguments of the same predicate, their dependency interacts with lexical properties of that predicate. Informally speaking, one can say that our computational system has a fundamental *problem with handling identicals*, a consequence of the inability to distinguish indistinguishables (IDI) in a way to be made precise. We will see that the need to license reflexivity—condition B as introduced in section 1.5.2, and further discussed in chapter 3—is a type 1 invariant, since it leads to a mismatch between grammatical structure and argument structure. The claim is that this problem is so deep that languages have to be "engineered" around it.

There are two general ways—reflected in the branching in the diagram—in which this problem is circumvented.

One option is to achieve this by an operation on the argument structure of the predicate involved in such a way that the targeted meaning can be expressed by an alternative path. This operation takes place either in the syntax or in the lexicon (see Reinhart 2002; Reinhart and Siloni 2005).

Another option, realized in many languages, is to use a complex element—for instance, a body-part reflexive like 'his head' or 'his bones'—as a proxy for the targeted interpretation, thus also avoiding the handling of identicals. Such proxy elements again come in two types: some require a local antecedent (*enforce a dependency*) like English *himself* except where it is exempt as we saw, while others do not (such anaphors occur in languages like Malayalam and Peranakan Javanese, as we will discuss in chapter 6). Again, this is represented by a branch in the diagram. Many of these processes are marked in the grammar, morphologically or otherwise. It is this marking that has been subject to extensive investigation in the typological literature. I will present a framework that explains existing puzzles and provides more precision.

Thus, reflexivity can be licensed either by a "protection" strategy with SELF (or another morpheme yielding complexity), or by an operation on argument structure (either in the lexicon or in the syntax). We will see how condition A involves a purely syntactic operation, covertly moving the SELF morpheme onto the head of the predicate. This requires no stipulation specific to binding, in line with the general aim to eliminate from the grammar all conditions specific to binding. Its further properties derive from general processes of interpretation and economy and manifest type 2 invariance. Finally, this chapter introduces the notion of

68   Chapter 1

masking as a way to understand why, crosslinguistically, anaphoric dependencies may show up so differently.

Chapters 7 and 8 present a number of case studies. The approach outlined in the preceding chapters is applied to a range of issues in particular languages.

1.11.6 Chapter 7

This chapter discusses the consequences of the analysis of SELF marking as covert movement. It shows how the dissociation between protection and reflexivization it entails yields a straightforward account of the behavior of SELF anaphors as ECM subjects in English and Dutch. Furthermore, it addresses the puzzles posed by locally bound 1st- and 2nd-person pronominals in English. Our analysis accounts for the fact that quite generally 1st- and 2nd-person pronouns may be locally bound. But if so, why are (105a,b) not good in English?

(105) a. *I behaved me.
      b. *We expected us to be on time.

As we will see with respect to English as well, nothing intrinsic prohibits local binding—in fact in other environments such pronominals may be locally bound. Instead the syntactic structure of structural accusative Case assignment in English gives rise to an IDI violation and requires protection. This property is absent in language such as Dutch. The chapter ends with a discussion of subject anaphors crosslinguistically.

1.11.7 Chapter 8

This chapter is a case study of crosslinguistic variation in Germanic, focusing on the nature of the differences between English and other Germanic languages in the local binding of 1st- and 2nd-person pronominals, and on the differences in the domains in which SE anaphors can be bound in Dutch and German on the one hand and Scandinavian on the other, as pointed out in section 1.8.2. It concludes with a more extensive discussion of logophoricity in Icelandic.

1.11.8 Chapter 9

This chapter summarizes and assesses the results obtained, against the background of a number of recent alternative approaches to binding.

2 Structural Conditions on A-Binding

2.1 Background

The Minimalist Program leads to questions about binding that were previously taken for granted. One is the status of indices, as we have seen; another is the role of structure.

As discussed in chapter 1, the inclusiveness condition entails that indices, the core ingredient of the canonical binding theory, are not available within C_{HL}. Because of this, Chomsky (1995) proposed that binding conditions apply at the C-I interface.

On a conceptual level, we can easily see that referential dependence finds a natural expression, and so do semantic differences between anaphoric expressions. Binding at this level can be straightforwardly understood as logical syntax binding, as discussed in chapter 1. Variable binding thus conceived is intrinsically unbounded and not sensitive to syntactic islands. Sentences like (1) show that this is indeed correct:

(1) a. **Every** boy was afraid that Mary would inform Zelda as to why the attic in **his** house was such a mess
   b. **Every** boy (λx (x was afraid that Mary would inform Zelda as to why the attic in x's house was such a mess))

A minimal assumption about the interpretive system is that the interpretation of the syntactic (LF) structures proceeds compositionally: for any constituent $K = [_L \alpha \beta]$, where L is K's label reflecting the way α and β have been merged, $\|K\|$ is determined by $\|\alpha\|$, $\|\beta\|$, and $\|L\|$.

The issue is then what aspects of binding theory can be accommodated in a compositional interpretation procedure, and, more specifically, how to understand the locality conditions on binding. The canonical binding conditions find no natural expression in such a conception of binding. Of course, one has the option to build them into the interpretive procedure.

However, since locality cannot be a characteristic of interpretive dependencies per se—as shown in (1)—such a step would state the problem, rather than solve it.

The central status within C_{HL} of the locality conditions on dislocation and checking indicates that the locality conditions on binding should ideally be derived from these (or any of their components). This challenges the conjecture (Chomsky 1995) that all binding pertains to the conceptual-intentional interface.

Evidence for a syntactic residue in binding comes from the considerable microvariation in the conditions on binding (see sections 1.1 and 1.7). In Germanic there are differences in the binding possibilities of pronominals between Dutch, German dialects, and Frisian. As I show in detail in chapters 5 and 8, these differences follow from sometimes subtle differences in the Case systems. French and the Germanic languages differ considerably as to binding into PPs (see chapter 6). There is further variation within the Romance languages—for example between Italian on the one hand and French, Spanish, and Portuguese on the other (see, for instance, De Jong 1996 and Menuzzi 1999 for relevant facts and discussion). Even apart from particular explanations, the mere existence of such microvariation indicates that binding is sensitive to properties of the language system that are morphosyntactic. The question is, then, whether it is possible in principle to develop an approach to binding that is compatible with the inclusiveness condition, and yet is sensitive to syntactic factors. This is what I will do in chapters 3–6. Here I discuss the status of c-command in binding.

2.2 The Status of C-Command in Binding

Since Reinhart 1976, the c-command relation has been one of the central structural notions in linguistic theory. It served as an important ingredient in definitions of the core concept of government, and it received a central status of its own as the ever-recurring structural factor in conditions on movement and binding. In (23) in chapter 1 I gave a definition, repeated here as (2a), which leads to the question in (2b):

(2) a. *a* c-commands *b* iff *a* is a sister to a category γ containing *b*. Schematically: [a [γ ... b ...]]

    b. Why is the logical syntax notion of binding subject to a structural condition of c-command?

Note the qualification *logical syntax* in (2b). For the current discussion I put aside the syntactic residue, to be discussed later.

Interpretive dependencies of the variable binding type illustrated in (1) are not syntactically encoded. That is, a pronominal does not carry on its sleeve whether it is bound or free. (In chapter 5 I discuss this in more detail.) Therefore, even if we understood why c-command is a condition on syntactic dependencies, this would not explain why it is relevant for interpretation (see, e.g., Reinhart 1983 for a range of arguments that variable binding is subject to c-command). In the present chapter I will discuss what the c-command requirement stands for.

It seems fair to say that all proposals to derive the syntactic c-command requirement on movement and chain formation presented so far connect it to the workings of the derivational process of structure building (Chomsky 1995; Epstein 1994–1995, 1999; see also Reuland 1998). As briefly discussed in chapter 1, the basic operation of structure building is Merge. Essentially: take two elements, either retrieved from the (mental) lexicon or present in the "workspace," and combine them.

In general, the c-command condition is taken to follow from the *extension condition* on Merge, illustrated in (3). Given some element δ (simplex or complex), and a composite structure with root γ, δ can only be merged at the root γ, but not in a position internal to γ.

(3) a.

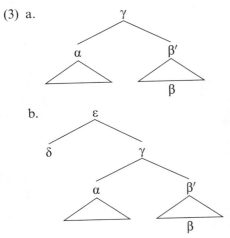

b.

This holds irrespective of whether δ comes from the lexicon, from the derivational "workspace," or from a position internal to γ. For current purposes it is immaterial how precisely the extension condition itself is derived (or even to what extent it always holds).[1] Let's just assume it holds for syntactic derivations. This makes it necessary to consider the role of c-command in semantic binding, since it is not obvious how it could be derived from anything like the extension condition directly.

The relevant insight has already been provided in Reinhart 1983, building on Kimball 1973. Consider (4):

(4)
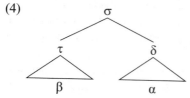

Here α is a pronominal element (an element just consisting of φ-features), which therefore semantically functions as a variable. Let's assume with Chierchia (1995) that a semantic variable may be either free or bound. If it ends up free, the context determines its interpretation. At any time, α may be construed as a bound variable, when it encounters a suitable antecedent. Note that as long as α has not been interpreted, it is "in storage." This is visible on the semantics of δ. Because the interpretation of δ has not been completed, δ is an open expression. Let's represent the semantically open character of δ in terms of a λ-expression. In order for the interpretation of δ to be completed, the λ-expression must receive an argument enabling α to receive a value. So, whatever the precise nature of representations at the relevant level, the status of δ will be equivalent to (5).

(5) λx (...x...)

As I said, I assume that interpretation proceeds compositionally. That is, for each step in the derivation resulting from Merge, an interpretive operation is defined representing the semantic counterpart of Merge; we may refer to this operation as Interpretive Merge (IM). In terms of (4), this means that the fact that δ is an open expression will be visible at δ's root. The open position can become saturated at the next interpretive step, namely the one composing δ with τ. If δ is represented as a λ-expression, the process can be viewed as the application of τ to δ. This comes down to using Reinhart's definition of A-binding discussed in chapter 1; (28) from chapter 1 is repeated here:

(6) β A-binds α iff β is the sister of a λ-predicate whose operator binds α.

The sisterhood condition just reflects a systematic bottom-up compositional interpretation procedure. Note that there is asymmetry between variables and their binders. A variable giving rise to a λ-expression intrinsically expresses nonsaturation. This must carry over to any expression containing it until an argument is found that saturates it. So, any composite expression carries the requirement to find a binder on its sleeve. There is no corresponding requirement to bind. Hence, a composite expression containing a number of DPs that are all potential binders does not inherit a requirement to bind from any of its component parts. The potential binders in natural language can always meet in their local environment any requirements they are subject to. Assuming that a determiner needs a variable to bind, that requirement is met by the variables in the set expression of the DP and the predicate. In a sentence like (7a) no pronoun needs to be introduced to yield a variable to be bound by *every duck*; instead the variable is provided from within the expression, as in (7b).

(7) a. Every duck swims.
    b. Every duck (λ x (x swims))

To put it differently, there is no "need to bind" for β that could be inherited by τ in (4), with β a DP binder and α a pronoun construed as a variable. However, there is a "need to get a value" for α, which will be inherited by δ. The relation between τ and δ can be represented as (8):

(8) τ (λx (...x...))

Therefore, whether β is able to provide the value of the open expression depends on the internal structure of τ, and its interaction with the compositional interpretation process. For instance, the expression *thought Mary liked him* in (9) must inherit the need to be bound of *him* construed as a variable, but the expression *the professor who failed every student* cannot inherit a need to bind from *every student*, since there is no need to bind that could be inherited to begin with. A simple economy perspective on meeting interpretive requirements then tells us that only the full expression *the professor who failed every student* will be available as a binder of *him*.

(9) [The professor who failed every student] [thought Mary liked him]

This is, then, what we see. *Him* can be bound by *the professor who liked every student*; it can remain free but cannot be bound by *every student* alone. The relevant logical structure of the bound reading is (10):

(10) [$_\tau$ The professor who failed every student] (λx (x thought Mary liked x))

The definition of binding in (6) correctly presents τ, and not *every student*, as the binder of *him/x*. The question is then how we can guarantee that no representation is derived where *every student* ends up binding *him*. One could think of all kinds of operations in which *every student* would be

stored in some sense, as in (11), with applying quantifier raising (QR) to
every student:

(11) a. [$_τ$ every student [$_τ$ a professor who saw ~~every student~~ swim]] (λx
(x thought Mary liked x))
    b. [$_τ$ every student [$_τ$ a professor who saw ~~every student~~ swim]] (λx
(λy (x thought Mary liked y)))

(11a) will not derive the impossible reading since, given current assumptions, such an operation will not turn *every student* into an argument of
the λ-expression: it is not a sister of the λ-expression. Rather, the relevant
argument will still be no other than τ. In (11b) we have separate subject
and object variables. Deriving the wrong reading would require first
"importing" *a professor...*, without the adjoined *every student* and then
importing *every student*. In fact what this would require is "splitting off"
every student from its adjoined position, and then treating it as a canonical sister of the λ-expression; the latter is an operation that would violate
our intuitive conception of economy since there is no intrinsic need of
every student that would be served by this operation. So far, then, the
c-command condition on variable binding appears to follow from very
general properties of the interpretive process. Thus, if "splitting off" is
generally impossible, nothing more needs to be said.

However, what I have said so far is not the full picture. There are
exceptions to the c-command requirement on variable binding as depicted
here. It is a long-standing observation that the c-command condition
applies less strictly to pronominal binding than to anaphor binding. Safir
(2004a,b) makes the problems it seems to raise for c-command into one of
the cornerstones of his criticism of extant versions of binding theory. The
contrast is illustrated in (12):

(12) [Every girl$_i$'s father] loves herself$_{*i}$/her$_i$

Every girl cannot bind *herself*, but it can bind *her*. From the perspective
of the CBT this was a highly puzzling fact. Any loosening of the c-
command requirement allowing *her* to be bound, appears to entail that
herself can be bound, contrary to fact.

I will take these points up in turn, first showing how a pronominal can
be bound, and then explaining in section 2.3 why this does not imply
binding of the anaphor.

The question is, then, how and why *every girl* can bind *her*. The relation between *every girl* and *her* must involve a real dependency as
expressed by variable binding, illustrated by VP-deletion contexts:

(13) [Every baby$_i$'s father] admires her$_i$ and every woman's (father) does too

Further examples like (14) are easily constructed:

(14) Every girl$_i$'s father wonders what will happen after she$_i$ goes to college

Such cases have not gone unnoticed (see Kayne 1994, to which I will return). Let, us see, then, how this exception to c-command can be accommodated. Again consider (4), repeated as (15):

(15)

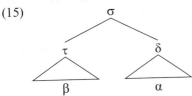

Note first that in the *professor/student* case, there was no sense in which the quantification over students induced a quantification over professors. In (12)–(14), however, the quantifier has a special effect on the interpretation of τ. We are talking of *father-girl pairs*, rather than the person who is the father of every girl. The occurrence of such an effect appears essential. This can be seen by constructing cases where its occurrence is optional and both readings are easily accessible:

(16) The owner of every car in the street should move it on Mondays.

The subject DP in (16) is ambiguous between a reading in which every car has a (possibly different) owner who moves it on Mondays, and a reading where the cars in the street all have the same owner. Binding of *it* by *every car* is only possible under the former, not under the latter reading. And the same contrast shows up in (12), although it is a bit harder to construe a pragmatically plausible case where *every girl's father* means the father of all the girls. But one can nevertheless observe that under that construal a bound reading of *her* becomes awkward.

Hence, a first intuition is that whether the quantificational properties of the embedded phrase are inherited by the DP as a whole determines whether non-c-command binding is possible. These are the cases that are known in the literature as inverse linking. Let's discuss this phenomenon in more detail.

Consider the buildup of the logical structure of (16). First the predicate:

(17) λx (λy (x moves y))

Its subject is *the owner of every car*. We could try to represent the inversely linked reading by having QR apply to *every car*, yielding (18):

(18) [every car [the owner of t]]

However, as we saw earlier, applying this structure as an argument to (17) only saturates one of the variables, let's say x (reflecting the subject θ-role). The other variable stays unsaturated, and no binding of y by *every car* follows. We thus appear to have obtained a reconstruction of c-command that rules out in a principled way the possibility of violating it. Given the need to use the closing element of an expression directly on availability, it seems that once we have put together *the owner* and *(of) every car*, there should no longer be a way of accessing *every car*.

To find out whether a principled solution is possible, let's go back to POSS phrases in specifier position:

(19) a. Every girl$_i$'s father loves her$_i$
    b. x loves y
    c. every girl (λy (y's father))

Note that if we could carry out our composition by first using *y's father* with y a free variable, the required interpretation would be derived:

(20) a. y's father (λx (x loves y))
    b. y's father loves y
    c. λy (y's father loves y)
    d. every girl (λy (y's father loves y))

In tree form, this would require an operation that would first take μ and δ, and then apply β to the result:

(21)

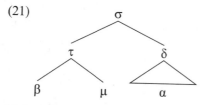

Note that we should be careful to derive the relevant condition from independent properties of the interpretation procedure (avoiding inadvertent stipulation of c-command). There is only one way μ and δ can be merged before β and μ, namely when τ is transparent in some independent sense. That is, it is syntactic properties of POSS phrases that will be decisive.

It is a well-known fact that a number of languages allow the POSS phrase to be detached from the DP by possessor raising (see, for instance,

Szabolcsi 1983 on Hungarian). In other languages, like Dutch, the most productive variant of the POSS construction is one in which a DP is combined with a possessive pronoun:

(22) a. Marie haar vader
       Mary her father
       'Mary's father'
     b. deze mannen hun vrienden
        these men   their friends
        'these men's friends'

A simple way of relating these forms to the 's-possessive is by postulating a null possessive pronoun in the latter cases, which is licensed by the possessive DP and the possessive 's jointly:

(23) a. ieder pro 's vader
     b. everybody pro 's father

This serves as an indication that POSS phrases of this type are adjuncts (without necessarily committing ourselves to the position that all specifiers are adjuncts, as argued by Kayne 1994). If so, the structure of τ in (21) is in fact as in (24):

(24)

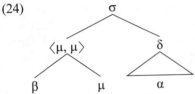

I will adopt the following position on adjunction structures, taking as a starting point Chomsky's (1995) notion of a term. According to Chomsky 1995, the syntactic node ⟨μ, μ⟩ is not a term visible to the interpretation process. That is, in line with Chomsky's proposal on intermediate projections, it is discarded for interpretation. If that is so, for purposes of interpretation we have a ternary structure. This will allow the merger of μ and δ to take place first, followed by the merger of (μ δ) with β. Thus, we arrive along a different path at the finding of Kayne 1994, and also Hornstein 1995, that adjuncts may c-command out of the category they belong to.[2]

Following the same approach, the inverse linking reading in (25a) and the impossibility of such a reading in (25b) rest on the same ground as in Hornstein 1995. Hornstein argues that adjuncts allow inverse linking, whereas complements do not.

(25) a. Some tourist in every city hates it.
  b. The protracted examination of every girl$_i$ tired her$_{*i}$[3]

Given that *in every city* is an adjunct, it will be able to merge after *some tourist*, hence bind *it*; *every girl*, being a complement, will not.[4] This approach to inverse linking brings us back to the issue of why *every student* in (11b), repeated here as (26), cannot be detached after having undergone QR and be imported after *the professor*.... Here *every student* would have originated as a complement. So, even apart from economy, detaching it would be ruled out:

(26) [$_τ$ every student [$_τ$ a professor who saw ~~every student~~ swim]] λx (λy
  (x thought Mary liked y))

What is interesting is that the merger of another adjunct on top of the adjunct containing *every* blocks inverse scope. This effect is illustrated by the contrast in (27).

(27) a. The owner of every car$_i$ washes it$_i$ regularly
  b. The owner of every car$_i$ in most cities washes it$_{*i}$ regularly

The possibility for *every car* to bind *it* has disappeared in (27b). The PP *in most cities* has been added as an adjunct on top of the constituent *every car*, such that it also must have scope over *the owner of every car*. Any theory preventing two adjuncts will now have the immediate effect that *(of) every car* cannot be an adjunct, but must be lower in the DP structure. Alternatively, even a weaker requirement that scope relations must be preserved has the same effect.

The relevant configuration for inverse linking is then simply the one in (28), slightly modifying (24) with the phrase "binding out" right-adjoined.

(28)

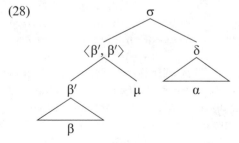

The relevant difference between constituents in the μ-position that do allow being split off, and adjuncts that do not, is that the former are base generated in the adjoined position, whereas the latter in fact head a chain formed by an overt or covert movement operation and connected to a lower base position in which they are interpreted, as in (29):

(29)

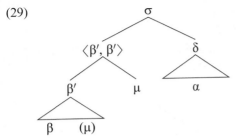

This is precisely the situation in (26). Here too the quantified expression has been raised from a position within the constituent it is adjoined to. The crucial difference between (28) and (29) is that μ in (28) is a sister of δ (and the λ-expression it is translated into) since it is not dominated by the full category β′, whereas the content of μ in (29) is spread out over two copies. The lower copy of μ is dominated by both segments of β′. Hence, the full content of μ is not a sister of δ, hence μ is not a possible argument of the λ-expression δ is translated into.

Although formulated in a rather different way, this account is intuitively quite similar to the ideas underlying accounts of weak crossover by Reinhart (1983, 1987) and Safir (1996). Since this issue is not central to our present endeavor, I refer to these works and to Reuland 1998 for more discussion.

2.3   Pronominals versus Anaphors

Let's now go back to the contrast in (12), repeated here as (30):

(30) [Every girl$_i$'s father] loves herself$_{*i}$/her$_i$

As noted, this contrast between variable binding and anaphor binding is puzzling for the CBT. To accommodate the difference, Kayne (1994) took the position of the quantificational element to be ambiguous. In fact, however, no special assumptions are necessary. The contrast follows immediately from analyses in which expressions such as *herself* and *himself* operate on predicates and mark them as reflexive (irrespective of whether reflexivization is analyzed as valency reduction, as in Keenan 1988 or Chierchia 1989, as a filter on the values of the arguments, as in Reinhart and Reuland 1991, or reflects cobinding as in Reuland and Winter 2009). Consider again the derivation of pronominal binding based on splitting off *every girl*, as in (20)—repeated as (31):

(31) a. y's father (λx (x loves y))
     b. y's father loves y

    c. λy (y's father loves y)
    d. every girl (λy (y's father loves y))

If *her* is replaced by *herself* the *love* predicate must be reflexive, as in (32), following the format of Reinhart and Reuland 1993.

(32) y's father (λx (x loves x))

Binding *y* by *every girl* as in (33), then, yields the correct interpretation and only that interpretation.

(33) every girl (λy (y's father (λx (x loves x))))

So, *every girl* cannot end up binding the object variable, hence the contrast is explained.

2.4 Conclusions

For our present purposes, the following conclusions are relevant:

- We have seen how the c-command requirement on binding follows from a general compositional interpretation procedure.
- I have explained the possibility of pronominal binding from a specifier and in general from adjuncts, on the basis of general differences between canonical merge (set-merge in the sense of Chomsky 1995), and adjunction, using Reinhart's definition of A-binding.
- We have seen how the asymmetry between binding of pronominals by a local specifier and the binding of anaphors such as *himself* follows from an approach in which such anaphors operate on predicates, marking them as reflexive.

In the next chapter I sketch the contours of my approach to binding and reflexivization. In chapters 4–6 I locate these issues in a broader context and discuss a specific implementation.

3   A Modular Approach to Binding: Reflexivity, Chains, and Exemption

As discussed in chapter 1, the CBT is based on a strict dichotomy between anaphors and pronominals. Yet, as we saw, many languages, including Dutch and the Scandinavian languages, have more complex systems of anaphora, with three- or four-way distinctions. Furthermore, contrary to what the canonical condition A leads us to expect, in English and Icelandic anaphors do not always need a linguistic antecedent, and Frisian allows pronominals to be locally bound in certain environments in violation of condition B.

In the present chapter I review the most important evidence that we must distinguish between conditions on reflexivity as a property of predicates, the syntactic encoding of dependencies between argument expressions, factors allowing exemption of the binding conditions, and discourse principles of interpretation applying where the binding conditions do not (see Reinhart and Reuland 1989, 1991; Reinhart and Reuland 1993 (henceforth R&R); and also Reuland 1990b). The task undertaken in this book is to show how conditions on reflexivity, syntactic encoding, and so on, and their interplay can be derived from basic properties of the grammatical system in a minimalist way that obeys the inclusiveness condition (and hence dispenses with indices). But I will be using indices where this helps exposition.

3.1 Defining Reflexivity

Intuitively a predicate is reflexive if one of its arguments is bound by another one. Reinhart's logical syntax definition of binding given in (28) in chapter 1 leads to the explicit definition in (1).

(1) *Reflexivity definition*
    A predicate (formed of a head P) is *reflexive* iff two of its arguments are bound by the same λ-operator.

The definition replaces the original definition from R&R in (1′), which I repeat here for convenience's sake.

(1′) *Reflexivity definition (R&R)*
A predicate (formed of a head P) is *reflexive* iff two of its arguments are coindexed.

So, in terms of (1′) both in *Alice$_1$ watched herself$_1$* and **Alice$_1$ watched her$_1$*, the predicate formed of *watch* qualifies as reflexive, the latter being ill-formed for reasons to be discussed. The representations with indices are easily translatable into representations with variables, but for expository reasons I use indices here.

Predicate is defined as in (2):

(2) *Definitions of predicate*
   a. The *syntactic predicate* formed of (a head) P is P, all its syntactic arguments, and an external argument of P (subject).
   The syntactic arguments of P are the projections assigned θ-role or Case by P.
   b. The *semantic predicate* formed of P is P and all its arguments at the level of logical syntax.[1]

This notion of a predicate has a morphosyntactic basis. *Alice, watched,* and *herself* in *Alice watched herself* form a syntactic predicate, but *Alice, put, the bottle,* and *her* in *Alice put the bottle behind her* do not, since here *her* is an argument of *behind*, which assigns the latter its Case and θ-role. Hence, in *Alice$_1$ put the bottle behind her$_1$* and *Alice$_1$ put the bottle behind herself$_1$*, the predicate formed of *put* does not qualify as reflexive. In *Alice depended on herself*, *herself* is part of the syntactic predicate of *depend*, since *on* does not assign Case and θ-role independently of the verb. (See section 3.7.2 for more discussion of PPs.)

The reflexivity conditions presented in R&R 1993 serve as descriptive generalizations that set the target for what has to be derived. Condition B in (4) reflects the need for reflexivity to be licensed. In chapter 6 I will explain the reasons in detail and discuss apparent exceptions. Condition A reflects the fact (one of our opening puzzles in chapter 1) that under certain conditions the licenser enforces reflexivity, even where ill-formedness results, as in **The Mad Hatter invited herself.* See (3):

(3) *Definition of reflexive marking*
A predicate (formed of P) is *reflexive-marked* iff either (i) P is lexically reflexive or (ii) one of P's arguments is a SELF anaphor.

So, switching to Dutch to exemplify the contrast, the predicate formed of *gedragen* 'behave' in *Alice gedroeg zich goed* 'Alice behaved well' is reflexive-marked by clause (i) and the predicate formed of *bewonderen* 'admire' in *Alice bewonderde zichzelf* 'Alice admired herself' is reflexive-marked by clause (ii). R&R's binding conditions are given in (4):

(4) *Conditions*
   (A) A reflexive-marked syntactic predicate is reflexive.
   (B) A reflexive semantic predicate is reflexive-marked.[2]

The claim that the analysis of reflexivity requires a distinction between syntactic and semantic predicates has generated considerable discussion. Note, however, that this distinction does no more than express that the obligation for a reflexive marker to actually make a predicate reflexive is subject to syntactic, not semantic conditions. It is therefore important to lay out the facts precisely. I will come back to this issue in section 3.4.

I first outline the main facts captured by condition B, then the main facts captured by condition A. Next I discuss the interaction between conditions on reflexivity and syntactic conditions, as well as the more complex issues. I conclude with an informal discussion of the way syntactic mechanisms relate SE anaphors to their antecedents.

3.2 Condition B: Main Facts

Starting out with Dutch and Frisian, we see the following pattern. Dutch has a three-way anaphoric system. In 3rd person it has a simplex anaphor *zich*, a complex anaphor *zichzelf* (neither shows contrasts for gender and number), and a pronominal form that does show such contrasts. Certain reflexive predicates occur with *zich* (glossing the simplex anaphor as SE, in line with our earlier usage):

(5) a. Willem$_1$ schaamt zich(??zelf)$_1$
     William shames SE
  b. Willem$_1$ wast   zich(zelf)$_1$
     William washes SE

Other reflexive predicates, with verbs such as *bewonderen* 'admire', *haten* 'hate', and so on, however, require *zichzelf* instead of *zich*:

(6) Willem$_1$ bewondert zichzelf$_1$/*zich$_1$
   William admires   SEself/SE

Frisian has a two-member anaphoric system in 3rd person; there is an anaphor *himsels*, and a pronominal *him*. However, unlike Dutch and

English, Frisian has locally bound 3rd-person pronominals. The paradigm is illustrated in (7) and (8).

(7) a. Willem₁ skammet him(??sels)₁
      William shames   him
  b. Willem₁ wasket him(sels)₁
      William washes him

(8) Willem₁ bewûnderet himsels₁/*him₁
    William admires   himself/him

Despite the possibility of having locally bound pronominals, the fact that verbs of the *admire/hate* class require a complex form with *sels* is unaffected in Frisian. What remains constant is that predicates of the latter class require an additional marking for reflexivity to be licensed.

The contrast between these verb classes can be characterized as follows: Verbs of the *shame* class cannot have an object with an independent value (**William schaamt Mary* is impossible). That is, they are obligatorily reflexive; verbs of the *wash* class allow a reflexive interpretation even without special marking (*wassen is gezond* 'washing is healthy' allows a reflexive interpretation, as washing oneself); verbs of the *hate/admire* class do not allow this (*haten is ongezond* 'hating is unhealthy' cannot be interpreted as 'hating oneself is unhealthy'). In R&R verbs of the *shame* and *wash* classes were classified as lexically reflexive (for *wash* optionally so). The generalization is that all reflexive predicates must be reflexive-marked, either lexically or by having an argument that is a SELF anaphor. Essentially the same verb classes are distinguished in many languages. (For discussion of the corresponding verb classes in Danish and Norwegian, see Vikner 1984, 1985, Hellan 1988, 1991, and Everaert 1986.) But such contrasts are also reflected in a language like Russian, where verbs of the *hate* class are incompatible with the reflexive clitic *s'a* (*myt's'a* 'wash oneself', but not **nenavidet's'a* 'hate onself') (see chapter 6 for discussion).[3]

This leads to the following initial typology of anaphoric expressions:

(9)   SELF   SE   PRONOMINAL
    Reflexivizing function   +   −   −
    R(eferential independence)   −   −   +

Both SE anaphors and SELF anaphors are referentially dependent as opposed to pronominals. They differ in their grammatical functions. SELF anaphors function as reflexivizers. This function is carried by the SELF-N, whose semantics is taken to impose cobinding on two arguments of a predicate, one of which is the pronoun determiner embedded in the SELF anaphor (see chapter 6 for more discussion). SE anaphors lack this function. Note that in much of the typological literature the SE anaphor is taken to be the reflexive marker. As will be discussed extensively in chapter 6, in many environments the SE anaphor, when it occurs in an argument position of a verb, is the side effect of a lexical reflexivization operation (see Reinhart and Siloni 2005). That a reflexivization operation can occur independently of any further marking is shown by lexical reflexives in English as in (10):

(10) John washed.

All this will be taken up in chapter 6 in a discussion of operations on argument structure.

As the range of languages investigated broadens, one sees that there are a variety of ways in which complex anaphors are formed in other languages (using intensifiers, body parts, etc.; see Faltz's (1977) overview discussed in section 1.8.2). This raises the question of whether morphologically complex anaphors of the type described by Faltz all have the properties of SELF anaphors. As will be shown in chapter 6, not all of them do.[4]

I will, therefore, distinguish between complex anaphors and SELF anaphors. *Complex anaphors* are elements that are referentially dependent in the sense discussed here (they cannot be used deictically), and that are morphosyntactically complex.[5] *SELF anaphors* are a subclass of complex anaphors, namely those based on a (functional) cognate of *self/zelf*. So, for any complex anaphor it is an empirical question whether or not it actually behaves as a SELF anaphor and is indeed a reflexivizer (and to the extent to which it does not, this has to be explained in terms of its feature composition and the syntactic environment). The discussion of complex anaphors in the present chapter will be limited to SELF anaphors. In chapter 6, I extend the scope.

According to the definition given, condition B effects are limited to coarguments of a predicate. It follows that in directional and locative PPs as in (11) no licensing is needed since the complement of the preposition and its binder are not arguments of the same predicate:[6]

(11) a. *John* put the book before *him*.
  b. *Jan* legde het boek voor *zich*. (Dutch)
  c. *Jan* lei it boek foar *him*. (Frisian)

None of the facts discussed so far bears on whether condition B applies to semantic or to syntactic predicates. However, the following facts do.

As discussed in Chomsky 1973, 1980a, and more extensively in Lasnik 1989, the canonical condition B is in fact a subcase of a more general effect, namely disjoint reference. The workings of disjoint reference are illustrated by the fact that (12a) is degraded:

(12) a. ??We voted for me.

Originally this was taken to follow from a generalization of the canonical condition B applied at the level of indices. Suppose the plural subject *we* is associated with an index set I and the object *me* with an index set J; if so, condition B could require that I and J are disjoint. This is consistent with what we see in cases like *They defended him* where *him* is interpreted as not being among the defenders. In the case of (12a), *me* cannot be interpreted as outside the *we* set—because of the semantics of *we* and *me*—hence the sentence is degraded. However, this conception of disjoint reference cannot work, since (12b) is well formed, despite the fact that here too *me* is among the members of *we*:

(12) b. We elected me. (Fiengo and May 1990)

Rather, the contrast correlates with the fact that *vote for* is distributive on its first argument, whereas *elect* is not. *Voting* is an individual action, but *elect* is a group action. Again, this contrast is witness to the fact that properties of predicates are involved in binding. The contrast follows from the difference in the way (12a) and (12b) are read by the inference system. Given the distributive character of *vote for*, (12a) gives rise to the inference *I vote for me*, which yields $I (\lambda x (x \text{ voted for } x))$, which is a reflexive predicate that is not reflexive-marked, hence violates condition B. (13), on the other hand, does not lead to the inference $I (\lambda x (x \text{ elected } x))$. Instead at all levels of representation to which condition B could apply the two arguments of *elect* are distinct.

Further evidence for the thesis that condition B applies to predicates that are reflexive at the level of logical syntax is provided by (13):

(13) a. In the end John convinced [Mary and him*(self)] [PRO to leave the country]

    b. In the end John expected [[Mary and him(self)] to leave the country]

In (13a) *him* cannot be bound by *John*. Instead, the SELF anaphor must be used. *Him* can be bound by *John* in (13b), and SELF-marking is optional. The essential difference between (13a) and (13b) is that (13a), being a control structure, entails a *convincing* relation between *John* and *him*, whereas there is no *expectation* relation between *John* and *him* in the ECM case (13b).

Examples like (14) show that referential disjointness cannot be the relevant factor, since (14a) is as bad as (14b), although the set of *Felix but not Lucie* in (14b) excludes Lucie—hence this NP and the pronoun are referentially disjoint.

(14) a. *[Felix and Lucie$_1$]$_2$ praised *her$_1$*
b. *Felix but not Lucie$_1$ praised *her$_1$*

In both cases the inference *(NOT) Lucie (λx (x praised x))* violates condition B, hence the ill-formedness.[7]

Note that, unlike (6) and (8), (12) and (14) cannot be saved by reflexive marking. *We voted for myself* is no better than (12), and, similarly, replacing *her* by *herself* saves neither (14a) nor (14b). Under the canonical condition A this is to be expected, since *myself* is an anaphor but cannot be coindexed with *we*; similarly *herself* in the position of *her* could not be coindexed with the subject in (14a,b). In the present theory this follows from the reformulated condition A, to which I turn in the next section.

First, some remarks on three-place predicates. In (15a) two of the arguments are coindexed, and since there is no reflexive marking, the sentence is ruled out by condition B. However, in (15b) (observed by Martin Everaert, personal communication), another coindexed argument of the predicate is a SELF anaphor, which therefore reflexive-marks the predicate. The predicate is 1-reflexive (with three arguments indexed 1), but as required by condition B, it is also 1-reflexive-marked. Hence, one reflexive marker is sufficient to license the reflexivization of more than two arguments. (In chapter 7 I will show precisely how it can do so.) In fact, choosing one marker is preferred here over the option of marking two arguments, as in (15e).[8] It does not matter which of the internal arguments is SELF-marked—(15b–d) illustrate this point with a different placement of the SE argument. (As in (5) and (6), a pronoun cannot replace *zich* in any of these examples for independent reasons to be discussed in section 3.6.)

(15) a. *Henk$_1$ wees   mij aan zich$_1$ toe[9]
Henk assigned me to SE PART
b. Henk$_1$ wees   zichzelf$_1$ aan zich$_1$ toe
Henk assigned himself to SE PART
c. *Henk$_1$ wees   zich$_1$ aan mij toe
Henk assigned SE to me PART

    d. Henk₁ wees   zich₁ aan zichzelf₁ toe
         Henk assigned SE   to   himself PART
    e. ?Henk₁ wees   zichzelf₁ aan zichzelf₁ toe
         Henk assigned himself to   himself PART

The facts of (5)–(8) and (15) show that condition B cannot be just a condition on specific lexical items (pronouns or SE anaphors), since it is sensitive to both anaphor types and predicate types. The generalization shared by all the cases discussed above is that reflexivization must be licensed either in the syntax or in the lexicon. Condition B, as stated, checks the reflexive marking of predicates, not just the properties of their arguments.

Let's now review the main issues concerning condition A.

3.3 Condition A: Main Facts

Condition A of the CBT requires anaphors to be locally bound, as in (16a) versus (16b,c):

(16) a. *Max* criticized *himself.*
     b. *I criticized himself.
     c. *Max* expected Lucie to criticize *himself.*

However, one of the problems for the CBT is that *himself* need not always be locally bound. Two minimal pairs are given in (17) (one of many examples given in Zribi-Hertz 1989) and (18) (from R&R):

(17) a. It angered him that she . . . tried to attract a man like himself.
     b. *It angered him that she tried to attract himself.

(18) a. Max boasted that the queen invited Lucie and himself for a drink.
     b. *Max boasted that the queen invited himself for a drink.

In the terms of Pollard and Sag 1992, the anaphors in (17b) and (18b) are exempt from the binding conditions. It is precisely this problem that is resolved by condition A as revised. This condition expresses that the SELF anaphor obligatorily contributes reflexive-marking only when it is an argument of a syntactic predicate.

So, in (18b) *himself* receives a θ-role and Case from *invite* (details depending on particular assumptions about Case-checking and the verbal projection that need not concern us here), hence it is a syntactic argument of *invite*. According to definition (2a) *the queen invited himself* qualifies as a syntactic predicate formed of *invite*, hence the SELF anaphor reflexive-marks it. Condition A then requires that it be reflexive. Due to the feature mismatch between *the queen* and *him*, they cannot be coindexed; hence binding cannot obtain and condition A is violated. The same reasoning applies to (16b,c). In (18a) the syntactic internal argument of *invite* is *Lucie and himself*. Thus, *himself* is not a syntactic argument of *invite*; it gets both Case and θ-role only indirectly. Therefore, *himself* does not reflexive-mark the syntactic predicate of *invite*, which entails that it need not be reflexive. In (17) the same pattern follows from the contrast between *attract himself* and *attract* [a man like *himself*]. A moment's reflection shows that in cases like (17) and (18) nothing prohibits the result of substituting *him* for *himself*, so the lack of complementarity between *him* and *himself* in these contexts immediately follows from the system. These contrasts clearly show that the *obligation* to reflexive-mark is crucially restricted to arguments of a syntactic predicate. This restriction only applies to the obligation, though. A SELF anaphor can reflexive-mark a semantic predicate, as we will see in the discussion of (31).

ECM subjects as in (19) are also defined as syntactic arguments of the matrix verb, since they are assigned Case by it.

(19) a.   Lucie expects [herself to entertain herself]
     b.   *Lucie expects [myself to entertain myself]
     c.   *Lucie$_i$ expects [her$_i$ to entertain herself]

An anaphor in this position is not exempt, as shown in (19b), since it reflexive-marks the matrix verb, without being able to form a reflexive predicate. Technically, then, condition A is met in (19a) with no need for further elaboration, since the syntactic predicate of *expect* has two of its (syntactic) arguments coindexed.

A potential complication arises in cases where a SELF anaphor appears as the subject of a nonreflexive ECM-predicate, as in *Lucie expected* [*herself to finish the article*]. The question is why the downstairs predicate is not reflexive-marked, violating condition A. I will briefly discuss the issue in section 3.6.4. The issue will find a natural solution once we have the precise mechanism of reflexive-marking developed in chapter 6.

Exemption occurs in all contexts where *himself* is not an argument of a syntactic predicate.[10] A much-studied class of such cases is found with picture NPs.

For the CBT the grammaticality of (20) is governed by the canonical condition A, with an additional mechanism to explain why a pronoun is not excluded in this context.

(20) Lucie saw a picture of her(self).

In the framework of R&R the lack of complementarity with pronominals follows from condition B, with no further assumptions necessary. Since *her* and *Lucie* are not coarguments nothing prevents *Lucie* from binding *her*. However, in addition to the lack of complementarity with pronouns, such structures show all the properties of exempt anaphora. Ross (1970) has noted that a 1st-person anaphor can occur there freely, as in his (21a). Similarly, the 3rd-person anaphor is exempt from a local binding require-ment in (21b,c). Many other counterexamples to the syntactic view of picture-NP anaphora (like (21c) and (22a)) were cited by Jackendoff (1972).

(21) a. A picture of myself would be nice on that wall.
   b. Lucie thought that a picture of herself would be nice on that wall.
   c. The queen demands that books containing unflattering descriptions of herself will be burned.[11]

An important question is the interpretation exempt anaphors receive. If a SELF anaphor does not fall under the structural binding conditions, it is free to be interpreted by other available strategies. Since in exempt posi-tion they remain referentially dependent (due to the properties of SELF), one would not expect them to have the full freedom of pronominals. It can be shown that in certain positions, if not in all, they are interpreted as logophors (see section 1.8.2).

In its logophoric use an anaphor does not have to be c-commanded by its antecedent (Thráinsson 1991). This fact provides a good diagnostic for logophoricity. Such cases can be easily constructed with picture NPs, as in (22). More generally, an anaphor in NPs always allows the coreference, and not only the bound variable interpretation.[12] There is therefore no reason to attempt a separate account for (22).

(22) a. The picture of himself that John saw in the post office was ugly.
   b. Her pleasant smile gives most pictures of herself an air of confidence.

Under the present analysis, a SELF anaphor can be logophoric iff it does not reflexive-mark its syntactic predicate (otherwise condition A rules it out). This is obtained either when it is not an argument, or when it is an argument of a head that does not form a syntactic predicate (since in this case there is no syntactic predicate that it could reflexive-mark). I will as-sume that complements of the *picture* N are assigned a θ-role by it and are therefore syntactic arguments. Even if this is not so, the same anaphora facts are found with Ns that clearly assign a θ-role, such as *description* in (21c). Given the definition in (2), the Ns in all the examples above do not form a syntactic predicate, since they lack an external argument. Condition A applies to reflexive-marked syntactic predicates. Since no such predicate exists here, the condition is met (that is, it does not apply).

The subject condition, which was incorporated into the definition of governing category in the CBT, is incorporated here within the definition of syntactic predicates. This is how the difference traditionally assumed between (23a) and (23b) can be captured. When the subject is present, as in (23b), the N forms a syntactic predicate. Since one of its arguments is a SELF anaphor, condition A now applies to require that it be reflexive. But no two arguments of *picture* are coindexed, so the derivation is ruled out.[13]

(23) a.   Lucie liked [(a) picture of herself]
     b.   */?Lucie liked [your picture of herself]

Thus, we saw that condition A governs the split between the bound use of SELF anaphors and the "logophoric" use of SELF anaphors.

It may be helpful to state that R&R used the term *logophoric* in a broader sense than the original definition of Clements 1975, presented in section 1.8.2.2. This use coincides with the notion of exemption in Pollard and Sag 1992, 1994. Where necessary to avoid misunderstanding I will use the term *exempt anaphor* specifically for those instances of SELF anaphors that are neither reflexive markers nor clearly logophoric in the stricter sense.

That some cases do really involve logophoricity in a strict sense is well illustrated by the role of viewpoint in the following contrast, also from Pollard and Sag 1992:

(24) a.   John$_i$ was going to get even with Mary. That picture of himself$_i$ in the paper would really annoy her, as would the other stunts he had planned.
     b.   *Mary was quite taken aback by the publicity John$_i$ was receiving. That picture of himself$_i$ in the paper had really annoyed her, and there was not much she could do about it.

There is a clear difference in well-formedness between these two minidiscourses. Yet, structurally, the position of the anaphor *himself* is identical in both cases. The only relevant contrast is in the discourse status of the antecedent. In (24a) John's viewpoint is expressed, in (24b) Mary's. Hence, in (24b) *John* does not yield a proper discourse antecedent for *himself.*[14] Such facts illustrate that where syntax has nothing to say, discourse licensing comes in.[15]

Whether or not a SELF anaphor is exempt is purely determined by its structural position—the notion of a position being conceived irrespective of spell-out, to put it in minimalist terms, in order to capture the exemption effect of focalization discussed in R&R.[16]

Note that *being exempt* means *being in a syntactic environment that blocks the application of reflexive marking* and just that. The eventual interpretation of anaphors in exempt position will be determined by further properties of the environment (including discourse) in which they occur. Depending on the configuration it is in, an exempt anaphor can even be required to be bound, for instance, when discourse conditions for a free interpretation—logophoricity in the narrower sense—are not satisfied, and there is a potential binder.

As such the present analysis says nothing about the contrast between *de se* and *de re* interpretations (see Lewis 1979 and Chierchia 1989 for important discussion), although it is to be expected that differences in feature specification or in the way a dependency is established will contribute to determining whether a *de se* interpretation is obligatory.[17] This issue has been successfully taken up in Delfitto 2007 as well as in Delfitto and Fiorin 2007 and 2008.

Factors governing interpretation may be configurational conditions (c-command) or discourse properties, but also factors that are better understood in terms of the relation between the grammar and the processing system. The role of such factors is indicated by the sensitivity to the nature of interveners illustrated in (25) (the examples are from Pollard and Sag 1992, with some indexings added):

(25) a. $Bill_j$ remembered that Tom_i saw [a picture of $himself_{i/*j}$] in the post office

    b. $Bill_j$ remembered that the $Times_i$ had printed [a picture of $himself_{*i/?j}$] in the Sunday edition

    c. $Bill_j$ thought that $nothing_i$ could make [a picture of $himself_{*i/j}$ in the $Times$] acceptable to Sandy

As these examples indicate, *himself* must receive a sentential antecedent, but an intervening argument does or does not block a crossing dependency depending on whether it qualifies as a potential antecedent—note the striking contrast with the obligatory binding of *himself* when it is a syntactic argument of a predicate, as in *$Bill_j$ remembered that the $Times_i$ had printed $himself_{*i/*j}$ in the Sunday edition*, where there is no escape from "impossible" binding. This pattern follows if grammar just says *nothing* about which antecedent an anaphor in exempt position must take, but the human processor follows an economy principle to the effect that early binding of an open position is preferred—see chapter 4 for more discussion.

A further result of this take on condition A is that it eliminates the need for reconstruction to an intermediate position (Chomsky 1977; May 1977; Van Riemsdijk and Williams 1981; Higginbotham 1983; Barss 1986; Lebeaux 1988). Consider (26):

(26) a. Which picture of himself/herself does Max think that Lucie likes?

b. Max knows which pictures of himself/herself Lucie likes.

Since *himself* can have the value Max and *herself* in the same position can have the value *Lucie*, although neither *Max* nor *Lucie* c-commands *himself/herself*, the argument goes, it has to be the case that one of the options is for the anaphor to be bound in its base position. If not, *Lucie* is not in its local domain, or—in the case of *Max* as its antecedent—in the intermediate C-position in (26a) since otherwise the lower subject *Lucie* would block binding. However, independently the anaphor can choose any of the potential antecedents regardless of c-command and governing category in structures like (26), because its NP does not form a syntactic predicate, so it is not restricted by condition A. Thus, since the antecedent of *himself* in a picture noun need not be in a structurally defined binding domain at all, the facts in (26) by themselves do not prove reconstruction. What would be needed to show reconstruction are clear, categorical contrasts between (27a) and (27b), and between (27a) and (27c):

(27) a. John wondered whether Mary had burned that picture of herself.

b. John wondered whether that picture of herself had actually been burned by Mary.

c. John wondered whether Mary had burned that picture of himself.

Such contrasts, however, do not obtain. (See also Safir 1999 and 2004b for discussion.)

The contrast between (26) and (28) follows from the standard assumption (Sportiche 1988; Koopman and Sportiche 1991) that a subject is generated in the Spec of its predicate (VP, AP, etc.) and raises to the SpecTP position.

(28) a. How proud of *himself/herself$_1$ does Max think that Lucie$_1$ is
     b. Max knows how proud of *himself/herself$_1$ Lucie$_1$ is
     c. how [t$_1$ [proud of herself$_1$/*himself$_2$]]

In this case the internal structure of the moved AP contains the copy of
its moved subject (*Lucie*), as illustrated in (28c). *Proud* here, unlike the
NP cases, does form a syntactic predicate, since it contains a subject.
This predicate is reflexive-marked by the SELF anaphor; hence, it is
required by condition A to be reflexive. This requirement is met only if
the anaphor is coindexed with the subject copy, so only *herself* is allowed
here. The same would be true for VP-preposing, as illustrated in (29).

(29) [t$_1$ compromise herself$_1$/*himself$_2$] though Max$_2$ said that Lucie$_1$
     did, she is still terrific

This means that reconstruction is not needed to explain the distribution of
anaphors in these contexts. Similarly, anaphors in experiencing contexts
such as (30) pose problems no different than anaphors in any other context of logophoricity.[18]

(30) a. Jokes about herself amuse Lucie.
     b. Jokes about herself$_1$/her$_1$ amuse every philosopher$_1$

Note that in all cases discussed so far, the exempt anaphor is not in complementary distribution with a pronominal bound by the same antecedent. However, this is by no means a necessary state of affairs. Nothing
prevents a situation in which exemption is satisfied and condition B
nevertheless applies. (31b) is a case in point:

(31) a. The queen$_1$ invited both Max and herself$_1$ to our party
     b. *The queen$_1$ invited both Max and her$_1$ to our party

The anaphor in (31a) is in exempt position. However, in this environment
the logophor is nevertheless in complementary distribution with a pronoun, as shown by (31b). That this is so is a direct consequence of condition B. The expression sent off to the inference system is (32).

(32) the queen (λx (x invited Max & x invited x))

One of its conjuncts is the reflexive predicate *(x invited x)*, which violates
condition B since it is not reflexive-marked.[19]

   This analysis raises an obvious comparative question about the difference between English and Dutch (and other languages with SE anaphors). The judgments about exemption carry over from English to
Dutch for 1st- and 2nd-person pronominals, but not for 3rd-person *zich-*

zelf. For instance, in (33a) *zichzelf* can only have *de koningin* 'the queen' as its antecedent despite the fact that the reading is infelicitous. The intended reading requires the pronominal *hem* with or without *zelf.* In (33b) *de koningin* cannot be the antecedent of *zichzelf,* although that is the only felicitous interpretation. Again, a pronominal with or without *zelf* is required.

(33) a. Max₁ pochte dat de koningin Lucie en zichzelf*₁/hem₁(zelf)
voor een borrel had uitgenodigd
'Max boasted that the queen invited Lucie and himself for a
drink.'

b. De koningin₁ eist dat boeken met onflatteuze beschrijvingen van
zichzelf*₁/haarzelf₁ verbrand worden
'The queen demands that books containing unflattering
descriptions of herself be burned.'

The reason for this contrast resides in an independent factor, namely that *zichzelf* contains *zich*, which is φ-feature deficient. For this reason *zich* is subject to independent binding requirements. Although these requirements on φ-feature deficient elements are not absolute—witness logophoric *sig* in Icelandic discussed in chapter 1—in Dutch the conditions on exemption of *zich* are much harder to satisfy, and not at all in the examples given here. The way SE anaphors like *zich* are interpreted is discussed in chapter 5. From that discussion it will be clear that its interpretation mechanism has nothing to do with reflexive-marking as discussed here, hence environments exempting elements of the form ⟨pronominal-SELF⟩ will not exempt the SE part of ⟨SE-SELF⟩.

3.4 Semantic and Syntactic Predicates

One may wonder whether distinguishing between syntactic and semantic predicates does not carry a cost. Would it not be more parsimonious to entertain just one notion of predicate? This is a reasonable question at the macrolevel, if one entertains the idea that there is something like a grammatical module called "binding theory." However, in a theory that sets out to derive BT phenomena from the very way grammar operates at the microlevel, the question loses its relevance.

Reconsidering the contrast in (12), it is a matter of fact that *we voted for me* entails that the *vote-for* relation holds between each individual of the *we* set and *me.* Consequently, one of its entailments is *I (λx (x voted for x))*, whereas no such entailment holds in the case of *we elected me.* It is a matter of fact that the contrast in (13) correlates with a difference in entailment, and that the facts of (14) again show that it is entailment relations that are involved, not disjointness of reference. So any theory assuming that grammar feeds the inference system must assume that expressions of the relevant type exist.

Thus far, the ill-formedness of *Willem bewondert zich* 'William admires SE', repeated from (6), is captured by the same principle that also captures the degradedness of (12a), (13a), and (14), namely condition B operating on logical syntax predicates. The only consideration that counts, apart from the empirical contrasts discussed, is whether we need to introduce any specific stipulations to capture the contrasts. As we will see in chapter 6, no stipulations are needed. A general property of mental computations entails that expressions of the type $\lambda x \ (x \ P \ x)$ are to be excluded. Being general, it is free of cost, and could not possibly be kept from applying.

What about the notion of a syntactic predicate? Given the elimination of a binding-specific condition B, the question is not so much whether we need two notions of predicate, but what properties of predicates (note the difference) play a role in syntactic relations with SELF. As we will see in chapter 7, the relation between SELF and the predicate head is subject to syntactic conditions on movement, hence it is syntactic. Consequently, it cannot apply to the postsyntactic structures that are part of the inference system. Another difference between syntactic and semantic predicates as defined resides in the specific reference to the external argument in the definition of syntactic predicates. This is a residue of the subject as part of the definition of a governing category in the CBT, but still one might wonder about its conceptual justification. As will be discussed, in the end its role reduces to being a trigger for SELF movement. Thus, conditions A and B in (4), including their differences in application, will be ultimately derived from general properties of the grammatical system (broadly conceived, that is, including properties of representations for the inference system).

3.5   The Structure of SE Anaphors and SELF Anaphors

I will now specify my assumptions about structure and properties of SE anaphors and SELF anaphors. The canonical structure of DPs is as indicated in (34a) (Abney 1987). As Longobardi (1994, 2001) argues, D is the locus of referentiality, and its syntactic expression is raising of N to D as in (34b).

(34) a. [$_{DP}$ Det [$_{NP}$ ... N ...]][20]

    b. [$_{DP}$ [N [D]] [$_{NP}$ ... t$_N$ ...]]

Following the parallelism between pronouns and articles argued for by Postal (1970), I take pronominals to be in D. Bare pronominals may either originate as D-heads with an empty NP complement, as in (35a), or be raised into D from an N-position, as in (35b):[21]

(35) a. [$_{DP}$ [$_D$ PRON] [$_{NP}$ ... e ...]]

    b. [$_{DP}$ [PRON [D]] [$_{NP}$ ... t$_{PRON}$ ...]]

The structure in (35a) is in line with the analysis Déchaine and Wiltschko (2002) present for 1st- and 2nd-person pronominals in English. Their proposal is based on the fact that 1st- and 2nd-person plural pronominals may co-occur with a nonempty NP, as in *we linguists, you linguists,* and so on. In 3rd person this pattern does not carry over to all English dialects, nor do we find it in the singular, as they note, but there are dialects that realize it in 3rd-person plural, as in *them linguists.* Panagiotidis (2002) argues that the variation between 3rd-person pronominals on the one hand and 1st- and 2nd-person pronominals on the other resides in the relation between the D-position and the head of the N-projection. He argues that in 3rd-person pronominals, as in full DPs, N and D are related by N-to-D movement. If so, separate realization of N is ruled out. There would be much more to say about this issue, but I will adopt this proposal as the basis, leaving further issues of variation aside. So, (35b) represents the basic structure for 3rd-person pronominals in Germanic.

SE anaphors like Norwegian *seg,* Dutch *zich,* or Icelandic *sig* lack certain values for φ-features. This φ-feature deficiency is the property responsible for their defective nature.[22] While SE anaphors may have person features in many languages—but not, for instance, in Slavic—they always lack number and gender features.[23] (Comparing pronominals and anaphors with R-expressions, we may say that the referential properties of the former are determined only by their φ-features, whereas the referential properties of the latter are determined both by φ-features and lexical content.)

SE anaphors cannot take overt complements. In Dutch and other Germanic languages that have them, the counterpart of *wij taalkundigen* 'we linguists' with *zich* is completely impossible: **zich taalkundigen.* In fact, SE anaphors are highly restricted in their combinatory possibilities. They do not allow compounding, as in *het wij-gevoel* 'the we-feeling', but for no N can we find **de zich-N;* one can have *zijn oude ik* 'his old me', but not *zijn oude zich* 'his old SE'. In this respect SE anaphors are very much like 3rd-person pronominals. Ideally, such differences should follow from differences in feature content. One would expect that the possibility for compounding or modification depends on the availability of contentful features. As will be discussed in chapter 5, unlike 3rd person, 1st and 2nd person are indeed characterized by contentful features, which would explain these contrasts.

If SE anaphors are φ-feature deficient, the question comes up as to what consequences this has for their structure. Following up on Abney's proposal of a parallelism between the CP and DP structure, the internal articulation of the DP has received considerable attention. For instance, Ritter (1988, 1991) presented evidence for a functional Number head between the D- and the N-projection, as in (36a). Subsequent comparative research provided evidence for a number of further intermediate positions. Longobardi (2001) summarizes the state of the art in (36b), with a range of potential projections intervening between D and N, where each of the boldface positions indicates targets for N-movement for which independent evidence has been presented:

(36) a. [$_{DP}$ D [$_{NUMP}$ Num [$_{NP}$ ... N ...]]]
      b. [D [GenS [Num [**H1** [S-or [M1 **H2** [M2 **H3** [Arg **H4** [$_{NP}$ P [SO ... N]]$_{NP}$]]]]]]]]]

The explanatory "lexicon" Longobardi provides for (36) can be summarized as follows. D is the canonical D-position targeted by Romance proper names, among others. GenS is the construct-state genitive, and perhaps unmarked Romance possessive adjectives. Num is the base position for numerals, possibly to be collapsed with H1. H1 represents the target for Sardinian and Celtic Nouns. S-or, M1, M2, and Arg are Speaker (or Subject) oriented adjectives, Manner 1 and 2, and Argument adjectives respectively. H2 and H3 are the targets for common N's in most Romance varieties and Walloon, respectively. Note that these heads are specified on the basis of being positional targets, not because of their inherent content. H4 is the position of Scandinavian (and Bulgarian?— Longobardi's question mark) definite suffixes, and the target for N-raising in German, Greek, Slavic, and Scandinavian suffixed nouns. GenO is the position of the postnominal genitive, and P, S, and O are the base positions of Possessors and External and Internal arguments, respectively. N is the base position of the noun, and the NP-brackets indicate the phrase containing N and its arguments.

As Longobardi notes, N-movement does not provide direct evidence for more than one of these heads in each individual language. This indicates that some but not all features of the head of a nominal expression are represented in the functional structure. Lexical items must, therefore, have an internal feature structure, while a subset of those features find expression as a syntactic head in the functional structure. Hence, deficiency must be represented both internally and in the functional structure.

SE anaphors, as we saw, are not specified for number. This means that a number projection must either be absent, or minimally be inert. A reasonable assumption about the continuity of projection is that when a number projection is absent, there can be no D-projection either. There are various ways to formally implement this.[24] If we adopt this assumption, SE anaphors cannot be D's selecting a NumP. Rather they must instantiate a lower head in the left periphery of the DP. This difference between pronominals and SE anaphors will become important in our discussion of their ability to occur in the tail position of chains. I will be noncommittal about the precise nature of the head SE anaphors realize, as long as it is lower than Num (and hence lower than D). However, since in Germanic SE anaphors are marked for person, I will assume that their position is minimally as high as the position where Person is realized. For the sake of convenience, I will notate this position as Person (sometimes abbreviated as π). Hence, the structure of SE anaphors will be taken to be as in (37a).[25]

In the case of SELF anaphors, *SELF* is an N rather than a determiner, and it combines with a pronoun determiner as in (37b) or a SE anaphor, as in (37c).

(37) a. $[_{\pi P} SE_\pi [_{NP} \dots]]$
     b. $[_{DP} PRON_D [_{NP} self]]$
     c. $[_{\pi P} SE_\pi [_{NP} self]]$

As we saw, SELF anaphors have the property of being reflexive markers; briefly, they are *reflexivizers*. For an explanatory theory of binding it is important to determine how the property of *being a reflexivizer* can be derived from more basic lexical and grammatical properties. In chapter 6 we will see that SELF is a relational noun with semantic properties that contribute reflexivity to a predicate it is construed with. How it does so will be demonstrated in detail. For now I will instead focus on SE anaphors.

It is important to establish how precisely their deficiency determines the binding properties of SE anaphors. Any theory must account for the fact that certain contexts, such as Icelandic subjunctives, allow SE anaphors to remain free (as discussed in section 1.8.2.2 and chapter 8), whereas in other contexts they are obligatorily bound.

In the next section I discuss the nature of the difference between SE anaphors and pronominals in more detail, and explain why locally bound 3rd-person pronominals are ruled out in Dutch but not in Frisian.

3.6   An Independent Factor: Syntactic Chain Formation

3.6.1   Dutch versus Frisian
Although conditions A and B as formulated in R&R capture a substantial part of the binding facts, they leave an obvious gap in Dutch. As noted, Dutch has a three-way system, with a contrast not only between pronominals and anaphors, but within the class of anaphors also a contrast between SE anaphors and SELF anaphors. Recapitulating the facts, the gap will be noticeable. We saw that with verbs such as *schamen* 'be ashamed' and *wassen* 'wash' a SE anaphor is allowed, due to the fact that they are lexically reflexive, hence meet condition B without SELF-marking. Verbs such as *bewonderen* 'admire', *haten* 'hate', and so forth, are not lexically reflexive, and hence require *zichzelf* instead of *zich*:

(38) a. Willem$_1$ schaamt zich(??zelf)$_1$
         William shames SE
     b. Willem$_1$ wast   zich(zelf)$_1$
         William washes SE
     c. Willem$_1$ bewondert zichzelf$_1$/*zich$_1$
         William admires   SEself/SE

Thus, in Dutch conditions A and B regulate the distribution of SE anaphors versus SELF anaphors, and say nothing about the distribution of pronominals. True, a pronominal is ruled out in (39a) since it causes a violation of condition B, but nothing so far rules it out in (39b,c), since in both cases condition B is met:

(39) a. *Willem$_1$ bewondert hem$_1$
         William admires   him
     b. *Willem$_1$ schaamt hem$_1$
         William shames him
     c. *Willem$_1$ wast   hem$_1$
         William washes SE

The same holds true in the ECM case of (40):

(40) a. Willem$_1$ voelde [zich$_1$ wegglijden]
         William felt   SE   slip-away
     b. *Willem$_1$ voelde [hem$_1$ wegglijden]
         William felt   him   slip-away

In (40a) *Willem* binds *zich*. However, *Willem* and *zich* are not semantic coarguments, since the complement receiving the internal θ-role from *voelen* 'feel' is the clause *zich wegglijden*, not *zich* alone. Hence, condition B is satisfied, and the pronominal must be bad for some other reason.

As R&R show, the pronominal is indeed ruled out by an independent factor. In R&R's system this factor is represented as a general condition on A-chains. Two independent questions arise at this point: (i) Is such a condition independently needed? (ii) Can it be derived from other principles of grammar, or must it be stipulated as an independent principle?

The first question merits a clear yes, due to the very fact of the Dutch-Frisian contrast discussed earlier. As we saw, Frisian has a pronominal wherever Dutch has a SE anaphor. It has it in (7), repeated in (41a,b); it also has it in the ECM construction (41c) corresponding to (40):

(41) a. Willem$_1$ skammet him$_1$
         William shames   him
      b. Willem$_1$ wasket him$_1$
         William washes him
      c. Willem$_1$ fielde [him$_1$ fuortglieden]
         William felt   him   slip-away

There is no way of arguing that *him* is a SE anaphor in disguise; it has all the properties of a pronominal, and correspondingly, (41b,c)—without indices—are just ambiguous between a bound and a 3rd-party reading.

Since some parameter of the grammar must be able to be set independently of whatever pertains to reflexivity, a separate condition switched on in Dutch (and many other languages) and made inoperative in Frisian must be available. It is worth noting that this Dutch-Frisian contrast is not unique. In many current German dialects, *sich* is limited to accusative positions or even to just the direct object positions (Keller 1961). This is also true of Middle High German up to the fifteenth or sixteenth century (Keller 1978). In other positions one finds a pronominal. As will be discussed in more detail in chapter 8, in German locative and directional PPs, binding by the subject requires the anaphor *sich*, as in *Der Johann hat das Buch vor sich/*ihn gelegt* 'John has put the book before him', in contrast to English and Dutch. The claim is, then, that accounting for the ill-formedness of locally bound *hem* in Dutch in (39) and (40) in contrast to *zich*, requires no mechanism that is not needed independently for a range of other contrasts between anaphors and pronominals that do not fall under the reflexivity conditions and did not fall under any version of the CBT either. The question is, then, what the principle is, and is it separate, or can it be derived from more fundamental properties of the grammar? The preliminaries of an approach to this issue will be sketched in the following section.

3.6.2   Chains and the Chain Condition

Chain formation, however implemented precisely, is one of the basic ingredients by which the grammar can encode dependencies. As we saw in section 1.9, in current minimalist conceptions of grammar there are two types of operations involved in chain formation, movement/ dislocation (internal Merge) and agreement (technically Agree). It is this minimalist conception that provides the basis for the analysis to be presented in this book, as we will see in more detail in chapter 5. However, the approach used in R&R and minimalist conceptions are not unrelated. Hence, I will start with R&R's approach as a useful approximation.

In government-and-binding theory (Chomsky 1981) chains typically encode the dependencies resulting from movement, as in (42), where the source/tail position is empty. R&R propose that the coindexing involved in binding also creates chains, therefore allowing the tail position to be lexically realized. The intuitive basis for the idea that chain formation plays a role in anaphoric dependencies is the following empirical generalization: in the syntactic domain within which an NP can move—here represented by the NP-trace relation—an NP can bind an anaphor, but it cannot bind a pronoun:

(42) a. i. $Felix_1$ was fired t_1
         ii. $Felix_1$ behaved $himself_1$
         iii. *$Felix_1$ behaved him_1
     b. i. He_1 is believed [t_1 to be smart]
         ii. He_1 believes [$himself_1$ to be smart]
         iii. *He_1 believes [him_1 to be smart]
     c. i. $Felix_1$ was expected [t_1 to consider [$himself_1$ smart]]
         ii. $Felix_1$ expects [$himself_1$ to be considered [t_1 smart]]

The domain illustrated in (42) may be called the *A-chain domain* of a given NP. In a barriers-style syntax, an A-chain, under its broadest definition, is any sequence of coindexation that is headed by an A-position and that satisfies "antecedent government." That is, each coindexed link, except for the head of the chain, is c-commanded by another link, and there is no barrier between any two of the links.

For ease of reference I repeat the definition from R&R 1993, note 32 in (43):

(43) *Generalized chain definition*
$C = (\alpha_1, \ldots, \alpha_n)$ is a chain iff C is the maximal sequence such that
a. there is an index i such that for all j, $1 \leq j \leq n$, α_j carries that index, and
b. for all j, $1 \leq j < n$, α_j governs α_{j+1}.

The government clause (43b) expresses the requirement that chain links should be local. To see how it works, consider (44):

(44) a. Felix$_1$ [seems [t$_1$ to be sick]]
     b. Felix$_1$ seems'-I$_1$ [$_{VP}$ t'$_1$ [$_{IP}$ t$_1$ to be sick]]

For government (of clause 43b) to hold, there should be no barriers between the governor and the governee. In the framework of Chomsky 1986a, VP in for example (44a) is a barrier that can be canceled by movement of V to I, but V, or its LF trace, forms a minimality barrier, even when it moves to I at LF. Hence, the coindexation in (44a) cannot count as an A-chain without further assumptions. Chomsky argues that in A-chains across the VP, coindexation works via a link of V and I, as in (44b): the subject *Felix* is coindexed with I independently (because of agreement). Roughly, then, when V moves to I, it gets the same index. So in effect, the subject governs its trace via the coindexed V. As stated, the chain condition is a condition on representations, which does not differentiate between coindexings resulting from movement, and coindexings resulting from binding. (We will see in chapter 5 that such intervening heads will play a crucial role in our final implementation.)

In well-formed movement chains the element in head position has a richer morphosyntactic specification than the one in the source position. Typically, in A-movement the source position is not marked for Case, whereas the head position is. R&R propose that this is not so much definitional as in Chomsky 1986a, but rather a well-formedness requirement, as in (45):

(45) *General condition on A-chains*
A maximal A-chain $(\alpha_1, \ldots, \alpha_n)$ contains exactly one link—α_1— which is both +R and specified for structural Case.

The +R requirement stands for referential independence, which sets apart pronominals and R-expressions from anaphors (both of the SE type and the SELF type), as indicated in schema (9). Structural Case is the Case-licensed/checked by the functional system, typically—but not exclusively—nominative and accusative. Although as stated, +R seems a semantic property, R&R's leading idea is that +R status can be reduced to morphosyntactic feature composition. That is, an element is $+R$ iff it is fully specified for (relevant) ϕ-features. This is also expressed in the Feature Determinacy Thesis of chapter 1. In chapter 5 a fuller discussion of the notion of ϕ-feature specification will be given.

As R&R show, all that is needed to capture the Dutch-Frisian contrast is the general condition on A-chains in (45), coupled with an independent parameter reflecting a low-level difference in their Case systems. To see how, it suffices for the moment that Dutch *zich* lacks a specification for number (witness the fact that it can take singular and plural antecedents), whereas pronominals are specified for number.

Applying the chain condition to the structures in (46) and (47) we see that in all cases a chain $\langle Willem_1, zich(zelf)_1 \rangle$ is formed of which the head *Willem* is fully specified, but the tail *zich* is underspecified for ϕ-features.

(46) a. Willem$_1$ schaamt zich(??zelf)$_1$
       William shames   SE
     b. Willem$_1$ wast   zich(zelf)$_1$
       William washes SE

(47) Willem$_1$ bewondert zichzelf$_1$/*zich$_1$
     William admires   SEself/SE

The examples in (39), repeated here, all contain a chain $\langle Willem_1, hem_1 \rangle$. It is a chain by the definition of chain. But it violates the chain condition, since not only the head *Willem*, but also the tail *hem* are fully specified for ϕ-features and structural Case.

(39) a. *Willem$_1$ bewondert hem$_1$
        William admires   him
     b. *Willem$_1$ schaamt hem$_1$
        William shames him
     c. *Willem$_1$ wast   hem$_1$
        William washes SE

The same holds true for the chain $\langle Willem_1, hem_1 \rangle$ in (40), repeated here:

(40) a. Willem$_1$ voelde [zich$_1$ wegglijden]
        William felt   SE   slip-away
     b. *Willem$_1$ voelde [hem$_1$ wegglijden]
        William felt   him   slip-away

In Frisian the chain $\langle Willem_1, him_1 \rangle$ does not violate the chain condition given the definition as stated. This follows from a result on the Case system of Frisian reported in J. Hoekstra 1994. Hoekstra shows that Frisian has one pronominal paradigm that is not specified for structural Case (there is another that is, and in fact does give rise to condition B violations). These facts will be taken up again in chapter 8. For now it suffices to note that *him* can realize an entry that is not specified for structural Case, hence the chain condition is not violated. This contrast shows how a minor difference in morphosyntax between two languages may have a striking effect on binding possibilities.

In English the chain condition rules out locally bound *him*, as in Dutch. This is illustrated below:

(48) a. *Felix$_1$ behaves him$_1$
    b. *Felix$_1$ washes him$_1$
    c. *Felix$_1$ admires him$_1$

(49) a. *Felix$_1$ was expected [t$_1$ to consider [him$_1$ smart]]
    b. *Felix$_1$ expects [him$_1$ to be considered [t$_1$ smart]]

Note that of the examples given only (48c) violates condition B. In all the other cases the predicate is either lexically reflexive (48a,b), or no semantic reflexive predicate is formed at all (49a,b), hence only the chain condition is available to rule them out.

In all these cases replacing *him* by the anaphor *himself* yields a well-formed chain. Note that English has no SE anaphor; hence *himself* is the only option. Being an anaphor, *himself* is −R, hence the sentences in (50) meet the chain condition as understood so far.[26]

(50) a. Felix$_1$ washes himself$_1$
    b. Felix$_1$ was expected [t$_1$ to consider [himself$_1$ smart]]
    c. Felix$_1$ expects [himself$_1$ to be considered [t$_1$ smart]]

Of course, the role of Case raises further questions. Is it just a matter of deficiency or does structural Case play an independent role? In section 3.8 I provide some considerations in favor of the latter. But first I will complete my review of empirical issues.

3.6.3 Where Neither the Chain Condition nor Condition B Applies

According to the definitions in (2), an ECM subject is a syntactic argument of the matrix predicate but not a semantic argument. This is illustrated by the behavior of Dutch *zich* in (51):

(51) a. *Henk$_1$ overreedde zich$_1$ [PRO$_1$ te zingen]
      Henk persuaded SE [PRO to sing]

b. Henk$_1$ overreedde zichzelf$_1$ [PRO$_1$ te zingen]
  Henk persuaded himself [PRO to sing]
c. Henk$_1$ voelde [zich$_1$ wegglijden]
  Henk felt [SE slip-away]

In (51a,b) the anaphor is a syntactic and semantic argument of the matrix predicate, hence condition B requires it to be *zichzelf*. In (51c) it is a syntactic but not a semantic argument of the matrix predicate, hence it is realized as *zich*.[27]

Since *zich* is required by the chain condition one may wonder what happens if the chain condition is prevented from applying. This happens in the case of coordinated NPs as ECM subjects.

Chain formation establishes relations between syntactic arguments. As we know, coordinate NPs occupy one syntactic argument position; witness, for instance, the fact that in [*Lucie and him*]$_{pl}$ *are*$_{pl}$ *coming to the party* or its Dutch, Frisian, etc. counterparts, the verb takes plural rather than singular agreement. Consequently, the chain condition as given only applies to the coordinate NP as a whole, not to its members. So, in Dutch, we expect to find (52) acceptable, which it is:

(52) Henk$_1$ voelde [[Jan en hem$_1$] wegglijden]
  Henk felt [[John and him] slip-away]

If condition B does not apply, we would expect coordinate NPs with a "locally" bound pronominal to be acceptable with ECM subjects in English as well, regardless of the collective-distributive distinction. The contrast in (13), repeated here as (53), shows that this is indeed so.

(53) a. In the end John$_1$ convinced [Mary and him$_1$*(self)] [PRO to leave the country]
  b. In the end John$_1$ expected [[Mary and him$_1$(self)] to leave the country]

(54) a. */?We allow me [PRO to run for this job]
  b.   We expect [me to run for this job]

Similarly, no chain is involved in either case of (54) (since *we* and *me* are not coindexed). If *we* is interpreted distributively, then in (54a) a reflexive predicate is entailed *(λx (x allows x (x runs for the job)))* applying to *me*), which is ruled out, as unlicensed, by condition B. But in (54b) the entailed predicate is not reflexive *(λx (x expects (x run for the job)))* applying to *me*), so condition B allows it. Such facts seem impossible to capture in any theory that does not distinguish between the roles of predicates and syntactic chains in binding.

3.6.4 Chains and Hierarchy

As defined, conditions A and B do not refer to hierarchy. Consequently, for condition B, (55a) and (55b) are equally well formed (with V not a lexical reflexive):

(55) a. ... [NP [V SELF]]
     b. ... [SELF [V NP]]

In many environments and choices for NP (55b) will be ruled out for independent reasons, most notably by the chain condition.

More concretely, the binding conditions themselves cannot distinguish between (56a) and (56b). In both cases the *criticize* predicate is defined as reflexive-marked and as reflexive, so conditions A and B are equally met in both.

(56) a. Max heard [himself criticize himself]
     b. *Max heard [himself criticize him][28]

In (56a) the chain, headed by *Max*, contains appropriately only one +R element in its head position. But in (56b) the tail too contains, inappropriately, a +R NP, violating the chain condition.

As R&R show, however, it would in fact be wrong to incorporate a standard hierarchy into the binding conditions. That is, it can be demonstrated that condition A and B are insensitive to such a hierarchy. (But see chapter 7.) This is based on an examination of SE anaphors in Dutch. As we know, *zich* is prevented by condition B from being bound within its predicate, as in (57), but Everaert (1991) notes that it can be bound within its predicate in (58).

(57) a. *Jan besprak zich; [OK] Jan besprak zichzelf
         Jan reviewed SE   Jan reviewed himself
     b. *Jij   hoorde [Jan zich bespreken]
         you heard   [Jan SE   review]

(58) Jan hoorde [zichzelf zich bespreken]
     Jan heard   [himself SE   review]

This is precisely what conditions A and B predict. In (57), the *review* predicate is not reflexive-marked; hence condition B rules out reflexivity. In (58), however, the SELF anaphor reflexive-marks both the matrix predicate and the embedded predicate (which both also end up reflexive, satisfying condition A). Since the *review* predicate is reflexive-marked here, condition B is satisfied. Since *zichzelf* does not head a chain, but is only a link in a chain, the chain condition is observed as well. The full paradigm of this structure in Dutch comes out as follows:

(59) Jan$_1$ hoorde
    a. *[zich$_1$ zich$_1$ bespreken]
    b. [zich$_1$ zichzelf$_1$ bespreken]
    c. [zichzelf$_1$ zich$_1$ bespreken]
    d. ??[zichzelf$_1$ zichzelf$_1$ bespreken]
    e. *[zichzelf$_1$ hem$_1$ bespreken]

(59a) is ruled out by B, since the embedded predicate is reflexive, but there is no reflexive-marking SELF anaphor. (59c) (= (58)) and (59b) are indistinguishable, and they are both allowed. (59d) is allowed by the binding conditions, but it is highly marked, because of the redundant use of SELF-marking, in the same way that ??*Hij schaamt zichzelf* 'He shames himself' is disfavored. Like its English counterpart in (56b), (59e) is ungrammatical. However, with respect to the binding theory it is indistinguishable from (59c), so it is not condition B that rules out this sentence, but the chain condition alone. Building hierarchy requirements into the binding conditions themselves, would equally rule out both the bad (59e) and the good (59c).

This is the place to return briefly to the issue of ECM subjects of non-reflexive predicates brought up in section 3.3. Thus, consider again the relevant example:

(60) Lucie expected [herself to finish the article]

Applying condition A, *herself* correctly reflexive-marks the upstairs syntactic predicate of *expect*. It also reflexive-marks the downstairs predicate of *finish*. This is the wrong result, since this predicate is neither reflexive nor ill-formed. Yet, as (59) shows, the answer cannot be to simply eliminate the force of licensing reflexivity in the downstairs clause. R&R (note 49) present a technical solution that takes care of the problem. However, in chapter 7 I will show that one mechanism of reflexive-marking involves SELF movement. Since SELF can raise onto the matrix verb but not lower onto the verb in the complement, the asymmetry in (60) follows. It will be shown that the symmetry in (59b,c) will not be affected.

Another way to test the different scopes of the chain condition and the binding conditions is with conjoined or plural NP anaphora. In such cases, the pronoun does not form a chain with its antecedent, hence it can only be blocked by condition B. Relevant cases are the following:

(61) a. *I can't imagine you denouncing you or me.
    b. I can't imagine myself denouncing you or me.

(62) a. *?Did you ever hear [us praise me] in the past
    b. Did we ever hear [ourselves praise me] in the past

As in the Dutch example in (58), here we are examining anaphora in the embedded TP. In neither of these cases is a chain formed (since the relevant pronoun is embedded in an NP, in (61), or not even coindexed with its antecedent, in (62)). However, unlike the (a) cases, in the (b) cases the nonhierarchical condition B is satisfied, since the SELF reflexive-marks the embedded predicate. Even though the judgments are subtle, they favor the (b) cases over the (a) cases. If condition B were formulated to require the reflexive marker (the anaphor) to be the internal argument, the predicate in the (b) cases would not be reflexive-marked, and the sentences would be incorrectly ruled out.[29]

This overview of basic facts being completed, I will now continue with a discussion of condition B in NPs and PPs.

3.7   Condition B in N- and P-Predicates

3.7.1   N-Predicates

None of the NP-cases discussed so far pose any problem for condition B if a pronoun replaces the anaphor, as for example, in (63a). Since no arguments of N are coindexed in such cases, no reflexive semantic predicate is involved, and condition B is met. However, the contrast in (63)–(65) (discussed earlier by Jackendoff 1972, Chomsky 1986a, and Williams 1987) merits attention.

(63) a.   Lucie$_1$ saw a picture of her$_1$
      b.   *Lucie$_1$ took a picture of her$_1$

(64) a.   Max$_1$ heard a story about him$_1$
      b.   *Max$_1$ told a story about him$_1$

(65) *Lucie$_1$ performed an operation on her$_1$

Such cases illustrate that a syntactically unrealized θ-role of N may be present, affecting the anaphora options of the realized N-arguments. The lexical semantics of the verb entails that in (65), the agent of the verb must be identical to the agent of *operation*. Similarly, in (63b) and (64b) it is identical to the agent (producer) of *picture* or the teller of *story*. These N-roles produce a condition B effect inside the NP. In the case of *see* and *hear*, where the agents are not identified, no such effects are found.

Two lines of analysis of the structure of such NPs have been proposed: Chomsky (1986b) argues that a PRO-like element is present in the specifier of the DP of the starred cases above, as illustrated in (66) for (64b). (Abstracting away from the precise details of his analysis, we may assume that this PRO, which is always optionally present in NPs, is obligatorily required here, for the verb to assign its control feature.) In this case, any version of condition B will successfully block the coindexation inside the NP.

(66) *Max$_1$ told [PRO$_1$ story about him$_1$]

However, Williams (1982, 1985, 1987) argues convincingly that a PRO analysis for NPs is not feasible and, furthermore, that the apparent control effects also show up when the Spec position is filled, or when PRO is otherwise impossible. Instead, he proposes that the N agent role, which is not syntactically realized, is satisfied in the lexicon and gets some referential value, either from the context or by control. In the latter case, the value of, for example, *Lucie* in (65) is assigned directly to the agent position in the lexical grid of *operation*, rather than to an NP realizing this position syntactically. The same is true when the NP-Spec is lexically filled, as in (67).

(67) a. Max performed Lucie's operation.
     b. Yesterday's operation was successful.

In (67a) the agent of *operation* is controlled by *Max*, and in (67b) its value is supplied by the discourse. This line of analysis is further developed and defended by Grimshaw (1986, 1990). The precise nature of the operation is beyond the scope of this book. What is crucial, though, is that a position in the lexical grid may be valued and if so give rise to condition B effects.

The argument structure of N-predicates, thus, provides direct support for the distinction between syntactic and semantic predicates. Recall that condition B applies to semantic predicates. Hence, for this condition (unlike condition A), it is irrelevant whether all the arguments are realized syntactically. The value assigned to the agent role is an argument of the semantic predicate formed by the N. In (63b), (64b), and (65), the semantic predicate of N is reflexive regardless of whether the agent role is realized by PRO or is controlled directly, since in both cases, this role and the pronoun end up coindexed (with the same index as the controller of the N-role). Given that no SELF anaphor is present, this reflexive predicate is ruled out.[30] As indicated in section 3.2, we will come back to *picture* NPs in chapter 7.

3.7.2 P-Predicates

In sections 3.1 and 3.2, I noted that prepositions vary in whether they form their own predicate or not. In a standard three-place V-predicate, as in (68), P does not form its own predicate. It functions only as a role selector for the verb, and its NP-complement is just an argument of the V-predicate. Hence, no coindexation of any of the three arguments of the V-predicate is possible without reflexive-marking.

Whether or not a verb and a subcategorized preposition form a composite predicate together is subject to crosslinguistic variation depending on other parameters. In French, for instance, prepositions are known not to restructure with the verb, and in fact we will see in chapter 6 that this is reflected in their binding behavior.

In the case of locative and directional PPs, as in (69), the P, however, forms its own predicate. Hence, the NP-complement of P is an argument of P, rather than of the V. This is so regardless of whether the PP has been selected by the verb. In (69b) the verb selects for a location role—that is, the PP is its selected argument. But the NP-complement of P is not.

(68) a. Lucie$_1$ explained Max to *her$_1$/herself$_1$
    b. Lucie explained Max$_2$ to *him$_2$/himself$_2$
    c. Lucie$_1$ explained *her$_1$/herself$_1$ to Max

(69) a. Max$_1$ saw a ghost next to him$_1$/himself$_1$
    b. Max$_1$ put the book next to him$_1$/himself$_1$
    c. Max$_1$ pulled the cart toward him$_1$/himself$_1$

(70) a. *Lucie$_1$ said that I explained Max to herself$_1$
    b. Lucie$_1$ said that Max saw a ghost next to herself$_1$

This means that the binding conditions apply differently to the two types. In (68) they check the top V-predicate; in (69) they check only the P-predicate. Condition B thus rules out the coindexed pronouns in (68), since the coindexation renders the V-predicate reflexive. But this predicate is irrelevant for condition B in (69). Condition A allows a SELF anaphor in both cases, but again, in different ways. In (68) the anaphor is a reflexive marker of the verb *explain*. But in (69), the situation is analogous to the case of NPs: since there is no subject, there is no syntactic predicate, so the condition is automatically met (that is, it does not apply). This means that in (69), unlike (68), the anaphor should have logophoric properties. This is indeed the case: while the anaphor of (68a) cannot be long-distance bound, as in (70a), the locative anaphor can, as in (70b). The use of anaphors in (69) is much more marked than their use in (68). (See Hestvik 1991 for a survey of judgments.) Part of the reason is that in (68), the only grammatical choice is using the anaphor (since a choice of a pronoun violates condition B), whereas in (69), as far as syntax goes, both a pronoun and an anaphor are possible, hence other factors become relevant in the choice, specifically discourse factors. (The fact that where syntax does not bear on a choice, discourse effects become visible is a pervasive phenomenon in the division of labor between components of the language system.)

Consider next the following issue. While the pronominal argument of P can be freely coindexed with the external argument of the verb, in (69), or in the (a) cases of (71) and (72), it cannot be coindexed with the internal argument in (71b) and (72b).

(71) a. Max_1 rolled the carpet over him_1
b.   *Max rolled the $carpet_1$ over it_1

(72) a. Max_1 directed Lucie toward him_1
b.   *Max directed $Lucie_1$ toward her_1 (in the mirror)

As noted in R&R, one might consider a small-clause solution to this problem, assuming that the accusative argument is a subject of a PP small clause (as discussed and rejected in Chomsky 1981 and Koster 1985). Going over the discussion will be helpful for an understanding of the binding facts in PPs. Under the small-clause analysis, the sentences of (71) have the structure (73), which is analogous to the standard small clauses in (74). Prima facie, condition B applies in the same way to both structures. In (73b) and (74b) it encounters a reflexive predicate with no reflexive marking, and it rules it out. The parallel predicates in (73a) and (74a) are not reflexive, and hence, well formed. However, this parallelism breaks down in cases like (73c) and (74c). If these sentences have the same structure, then condition A should, incorrectly, rule out (73c) the way it rules out (74c). If P has a syntactic subject, it should form a syntactic predicate, which is subject to condition A, incorrectly enforcing reflexivity in (73c).

(73) a. Max_1 rolled [the $carpet_2$ over him_1]
b.   *Max rolled [the $carpet_2$ over it_2]
c. Max_1 rolled [the $carpet_2$ over $himself_1$]

(74) a. $Lucie_1$ heard [Max_2 praise her_1]
b.   *Lucie heard [Max_2 praise him_2]
c.   *$Lucie_1$ heard [Max_2 praise $herself_1$]

Note further that the generalization that governs condition B effects in locative PPs cannot be stated in purely structural terms. For example, it is not always the case that the pronoun cannot be coindexed with the verb's internal argument. In (75) it can. In other cases, the locative pronoun cannot be coindexed with the external argument of the verb, as in (76) (where there is also no potential subject to form a small clause). In such structures as well, the locative PP induces condition B effects in some cases (76a,b), but not in others (76c).

(75) Max praised/examined the carpet$_2$ underneath it$_2$

(76) a. *Max$_1$ stepped on him$_1$
  b. God is in   zichzelf$_1$/*zich$_1$
    God is inside itself$_1$/*it$_1$
    (Spinoza, pointed out by Jan Voskuil)
  c. Max$_1$ looked around him$_1$

The intuitive appeal of a small-clause analysis in the specific case of locatives and directional prepositions is that such P's appear to behave as two-place predicates—that is, as expressing a relation between two arguments. For example, a sentence like (73a) entails the carpet being over Max at some point. But, given that this analysis cannot solve the problem in (73), there has to be an alternative. What is in fact needed is the same mechanism already shown to be necessary for N-predicates. Locative and directional prepositions take, indeed, two θ-roles. But, along the lines of Williams's and Grimshaw's analysis of the control of N-roles discussed earlier, only one of these is realized syntactically, as the P-complement, while the other is satisfied in the lexicon and assigned a value by control. This role can be controlled either by an argument of the verb, or by the abstract EVENT argument (a suggestion by Teun Hoekstra, personal communication, 1991). Thus, in (71)–(73) the unrealized role of P is controlled by the verb's internal argument, yielding *over*, in (73a) as a relation holding between the carpet and Max. But in (75), the relation *underneath* holds between the carpet and the event of Max's praising or examining the carpet, which means that the unrealized role is controlled by the EVENT role. Similarly, in the intransitive case of (76a,b), the P-role is controlled by the subject, while in (76c), it is the event of looking that is the semantic argument of *around*. As was the case with NPs, control is largely determined by the semantics of the verb.

Thus, condition B works in predicative PPs just as it does in NPs: the value assigned to the syntactically unrealized role is a semantic argument of the predicate. Since condition B applies to semantic predicates, this argument is visible to it. If the assigned value has the same index as the second (syntactic) argument of P, P forms a reflexive predicate, which is licensed only if it is reflexive-marked. For example, in (76a) (*Max_1 stepped on him_1), the semantic predicate formed is on $\langle Max_1, him_1 \rangle$. This reflexive predicate is non-reflexive-marked, hence it is ruled out. (76b), (73b), and (72b) are filtered out in the same way. In all other sentences, no reflexive predicate is formed in the semantics, so condition B is met.[31]

Finally, I will discuss the problem in (77), which has been cited as indicating that the binding theory must incorporate a thematic hierarchy (e.g., Kiss 1991), or a functional hierarchy (Pollard and Sag 1992).

(77) a.   We talked with $Lucie_1$ about $herself_1$
      b. *We talked about $Lucie_1$ with $herself_1$

The contrast in (77) follows (as pointed out by Barbara Partee) if the with-PP is a θ-argument of the verb, but the about-PP is not (thus functioning as an adjunct). In this case, in (77a) the anaphor is logophoric, and it does not reflexive-mark the verb, but in (77b) it does. Hence, condition A requires that the predicate in (77b) be reflexive, which is not the case, since the coindexed Lucie is not a coargument. Indeed, the about-PP shows all other adjunct properties relevant to anaphora: a pronoun is not excluded, as in (78), and a first-person logophor is much easier in (79b) than in the argument position in (79a).

(78) We talked with $Lucie_1$ about her_1

(79) a. *Can you talk with myself about Lucie?
      b.   Can you talk with Lucie about myself?

Like any other independent preposition about will be relational. Under the assumption that the value of its first argument is controlled by the subject (certainly not by Lucie), in (78) condition B will not require reflexive marking internally to the PP either. However, if the complement of about is bound by the subject, reflexive marking is required as in (80):

(80) Max_1 talked with Lucie about $himself_1$

The contrast in (79) and (80) is repeated in Dutch:

(81) a. *Kun jij met mezelf over Lucie praten?
      b.   Kun jij met Lucie over mezelf praten?
      c. Max_1 sprak met Lucie over $zichzelf_1$/$hemzelf_1$/*hem_1

All this shows that the binding conditions A and B themselves do not contain any reference to either configurational or thematic hierarchy. Assuming a theory of semantic binding as discussed in chapter 1, we could say that the work of capturing anaphora is divided between at least four modules. The binding conditions are sensitive only to the reflexivizing function, taking care of matching it with predicate reflexivity. All other aspects of local anaphora, which have to do with the R-property, fall under a syntactic chain theory. The notion of binding itself pertains to semantics/logical syntax. Where neither chain theory nor issues of reflexivity are relevant, discourse conditions come into play.

3.8 Toward Explaining the Binding Conditions: Reflexivity and Chains

As we saw, binding phenomena as we know them result from the interaction of a number of different components of the grammar. These components include properties of predicates, narrow syntax, logical syntax, discourse, and economy principles. As indicated in the preview at the end of chapter 1, the notion of economy, the need to license reflexivity, and the ways of doing so will be discussed in chapters 4–6. This discussion of reflexivity straightforwardly builds on the results obtained so far. The relation between the chain condition and what can be encoded using the syntactic tools available in the MP merits some preliminary discussion.

R&R uses a purely representational framework (mainly for expository reasons). The syntactic component of the local binding conditions is represented by the chain condition, where chains are syntactic objects formed by c-command, coindexing, and the absence of barriers, along the lines reviewed. The previous chapter showed how the c-command requirement could be reconstructed in a minimalist approach. For reconstructing chain formation we have to understand how the MP encodes syntactic dependencies. For the moment it suffices to say that dependencies will have to established derivationally, on the basis of independently motivated morphosyntactic operations. Coindexing will be reduced to the dependency established by operations of checking/agree, along the lines indicated in section 1.1.9. These are realized in what Chomsky (2001, 2004) characterizes as *probe-goal* relationships. A detailed discussion follows in chapter 5. Note that the chain condition will not be lost. Rather, its results will be derived from more basic principles of grammatical computation, leaving it as a higher-order theorem (just as we aim to achieve for condition A).

The chain definition (43) is stated within the barriers framework (Chomsky 1986a). Let's now reconsider the chain condition, repeated here:

(82) *General condition on A-chains*
    A maximal A-chain $(\alpha_1, \ldots, \alpha_n)$ contains exactly one link—α_1—
    which is both +R and marked for structural Case.

The +R property is defined as (83):

(83) An NP is +R iff it carries a full specification for ϕ-features.

In the theory outlined the chain condition performs two roles: it captures
the distribution of pronominals versus SE anaphors and it captures the
hierarchical effects in local binding that do not follow from conditions
on reflexivity.[32]

   Let us first look at how the chain condition restricts the foot. The +R
property does not refer to Case, but the chain condition does. I mentioned that the source of the variation in local binding of 3rd-person pronominals resides in the Case system (with Hoekstra's specific evidence
that Frisian *him* is part of a paradigm without structural Case to be
reviewed in chapter 8). It would not do to say that in Frisian, the pronominal *him* in (84) can be −R, and bound by *Jan*, but can also be +R
and free.

(84) Jan$_i$ waske   him$_{i/j}$
    Jan washed him

So, the question is what precisely structural Case contributes. Consider
(85a), reflecting the situation in (84). The chain has a coindexed element
α_n in a potential foot position, where α_n would violate the chain condition
if it is +R, and yet the sequence $\alpha_1, \ldots, \alpha_{n-1} + \alpha_n$ is well formed with α_n
allowing a +R interpretation. Logically, there are two options: (i) α_n is
ambiguous; (ii) $\alpha_{n-1} + \alpha_n$ is not a chain link, despite allowing binding.[33]

(85) a. $\alpha_1, \ldots, \alpha_{n-1} \ldots$ (with $\alpha_1, \ldots, \alpha_{n-1}$ a chain)
    b. $\alpha_1, \ldots, \alpha_{n-1} + \alpha_n$

We have already rejected the first option, since it amounts to stipulating
the problem away. It is the second option that is interesting. In fact, it
brings to the fore a dynamic perspective on chain formation; chain formation requires more than just "coindexing" in a local configuration.
Bearing structural Case is, then, what appears to force the foot to enter
the chain. My view is that this happens since the structural Case enables
the verbal system to enter the chain formation process, and mediate
establishing a chain. Chomsky (2008) hypothesizes that dependencies between phrases are mediated by heads involved in a probe-goal relationship. It is the structural Case that establishes the relation.

In fact, the barriers framework already offers a precursor to this idea. To show this I will give a brief recapitulation of the barriers perspective on movement.

As stated in (43), the barriers framework requires that α_j governs α_{j+1} for pairs $\langle \alpha_j\ \alpha_{j+1} \rangle$ such that α_j, α_{j+1} form a chain link.[34] Thus a typical configuration for a chain link is given in (86):

(86) $\ldots \alpha \ldots [_\gamma \ldots \beta \ldots]$

Effectively, this means that chain members must be in a local relation. Whether the relation is sufficiently local is determined by the nature of what intervenes. So, whether α governs β is determined (i) by the c-command requirement, and (ii) by the nature of γ. Roughly, if γ is a maximal projection—DP, VP, CP, and so on—it will count as an intervener unless further conditions are met; for current purposes the details do not matter. Crucial to the barriers framework is a further condition, based on an even stronger conception of locality, illustrated on the basis of (87):

(87) $\ldots \alpha \ldots [_\gamma \delta \ldots \beta \ldots]$

Under this conception α does not govern β if there is a closer governor. So, the presence of δ will prevent α from governing β if δ is also in a relation with β that requires government. Specifically, if δ is a head that θ-marks β it will create such a minimality barrier.[35] Condition (87) is very strong and would effectively rule out all forms of movement out of the domain of a head, unless weakened. This weakening is effected by allowing the intervening head itself to become part of the chain, provided it bears the chain's index, as in (88):

(88) $\ldots \alpha_i \ldots [_\gamma \delta_i \ldots \beta_i \ldots]$

For instance, consider Chomsky's (1986a) discussion of the structure of passive *John was killed* as given in (89):

(89) John$_i$ [$_\alpha$ be-I]$_i$ [$_{VP'}$ t$_i$ [$_{VP}$ killed$_i$ ... t$_i$ ...]]

To obtain a licit chain between *John* and its trace *t*, John must not only have moved first to the left edge of the VP, indicated by the VP-peripheral trace, but the intervening heads must also be coindexed. This coindexing is effected by feature sharing, independently motivated as the agreement relation between *John* and the inflection, and the canonical dependency relation between inflection/auxiliary and verb. Effectively, then, in this framework each chain link must be licensed by feature sharing with the intervening head. It is easy to see that, conceptually, feature sharing survives in a system without indices, provided the feature sharing involves plain morphosyntactic features.[36]

Whereas the discussion of (88) involves movement chains, nothing essential changes if it is applied to generalized chains in the sense of the chain condition. Thus, here too a condition of feature sharing between α_n and the head intervening between α_{n-1} and α_n has to be observed, in order to avoid a minimality barrier. Such feature sharing shows up in the form of structural Case-licensing. This leads to the following revision of the chain condition that will be useful to complete the transition to a minimalist perspective:

(90) $C = (\alpha_1, \ldots, \alpha_n)$ is a chain iff C is the maximal sequence such that
    a. there is an index i such that for all j, $1 < j < n$, α_j carries that index, and
    b. for all j, $1 < j < n$, α_j governs α_{j+1}, where for any H such that $[\alpha_j [H \, \alpha_{j+1}]]$, there is a relation R such that $H \, R \, \alpha_{j+1}$, where R is a relation of feature sharing (including structural Case-checking).

The intuition behind (90) is easily transferable to minimalist theory. Elaborating on what I said earlier, in the MP checking structural Case exemplifies the most basic dependency, which is realized in a probe-goal relationship. The *goal* is an element that depends for a value on a c-commanding element in the structure, a *probe*. Crucial for entering a probe-goal relation is having an unvalued feature, which can be valued. So, in terms of (90) α_{j+1} can be a goal for the probe α_j only if α_{j+1} has an unvalued feature. If an argument requires structural Case, this makes it visible to a verbal head. If it is, it can enter further dependencies mediated by that head—for instance linking it up to the subject, via the inflectional system. The resulting feature sharing encodes the dependency in the syntax, as already indicated in (77) in chapter 1. Thus, giving a preview of what follows, the dependency in (91a) will not be encoded with indices as in (91b), but by sharing ϕ-feature bundles as in (91c):

(91) a. *Alice* voelde *zich* wegglijden.
       Alice felt   SE   slip-away
    b. Alice$_i$ voelde$_i$ zich$_i$ wegglijden
    c. Alice$_\phi$ voelde$_\phi$ zich$_\phi$ wegglijden

Thus, the ϕ-feature sharing between *Alice* and *voelde* is brought about by subject-verb agreement; the ϕ-feature sharing between *voelde* and *zich* is mediated by the structural Case relation.

The mechanisms and conditions on feature sharing will be discussed in detail in chapter 5.[37] But we can already see that this approach has consequences for the way the chain condition rules out (92) with a dependency between *Alice* and *haar*:

(92) Alice voelde haar wegglijden.
      Alice felt   her slip-away

First we have to exclude (93), with a φ-feature based dependency:

(93) *Alice$_\phi$ voelde$_\phi$ haar$_\phi$ wegglijden
       Alice felt   her   slip-away

Intuitively, we can see that (93) can be ruled out if deriving a φ-feature based dependency requires φ-feature deficiency of *zich*. That it does, and how will be shown in chapter 5. We will also have to exclude directly translating (92) into logical syntax as (94)—that is, as a binding dependency not mediated by a φ-feature dependency:

(94) Alice (λx (x voelde x wegglijden))
      Alice (λx (x felt   x slip-away))

We have to consider this option, since in syntax it is not marked whether *haar* is bound or free, but the bound reading must be ruled out. A way to do this is by comparing two derivations of (94): (i) a derivation of (94) from (91a), and (ii) a derivation from (92).

   In derivation (i), variable binding is derived from a structure in which the dependency is syntactically encoded (via φ-feature sharing as in (91c)); in derivation (ii), there is no encoding in the syntax. Applying the same logic as in Reinhart's Rule I, discussed in chapter 1, economy then rules out derivation (ii). This is the intuition that I will pursue. To make this work it is necessary to find a proper economy measure. This will be the subject of chapter 4.

   Given all this, a somewhat simplified analysis of Frisian goes as follows. As we saw, *him* in Frisian is part of a pronominal paradigm that is licensed by "inherent Case" instead of structural Case. Inherent Case is a subtype of selected/oblique Case.[38] Like much of the current literature (for instance, Chomsky 2008), I will refrain from discussing how inherent Case is licensed in detail. For current purposes all that is needed is that inherent Case is not checked via the inflectional system. If only structural Case is checked via the inflectional system, "no structural Case checking" effectively means "no chain."[39]

   Since *him* in (95) does not bear structural Case, and structural Case is essential for a chain link to be established, (95) does not violate the chain condition, even if *him* is fully specified for φ-features. Hence, bound *him* could not even be ruled out by competition with a SE anaphor even if the language had one, quod non.

(95) *Jan* waske *him*.

One of the important consequences of this result is given in (96):

(96) The Case system of a language is a crucial variable that has to be taken into account when addressing crosslinguistic variation in binding and patterns of diachronic change.[40]

The chain condition appears to pose a similar problem for 1st- and 2nd-person pronouns in general, since they can be locally bound in a great range of languages, as in German *ich wasche mich* 'I wash me', Dutch *jij wast je* 'you wash you', French *nous nous lavons* 'we wash us', and so on. The version of the chain condition in (90) does not resolve this. The analysis of 3rd-person pronominals in Frisian does not carry over to local binding of 1st- and 2nd-person pronominals. This is as it should be, since allowing local binding of 1st- and 2nd-person pronominals is a much more general property of languages. As will be shown in section 5.6, the local binding of 1st- and 2nd-person pronominals is a consequence of their semantics.

Finally, just as we find pronominals apparently in the foot position of a chain—but in fact they are not, as we saw—anaphors have been reported to be able to head chains (see Anagnostopoulou and Everaert 1999). Ideally, deriving the chain condition from more elementary properties of the system should also lead to a principled account of the conditions under which anaphors can head chains. And, in fact, as we will see in chapter 7, in the end nothing special needs to be said.

3.9 Conclusion

This chapter has laid the groundwork for an understanding of the design of the anaphoric system. It has disentangled the role of predicates and chains. Moreover, it has distinguished between the roles of semantic and syntactic predicates, presented a typology of anaphoric expressions distinguishing between pronominals, SE anaphors, and SELF anaphors, and showed how the specific feature composition of an anaphoric element determines its binding possibilities. In short, we went from the CBT toward a modular theory of binding.

Yet, important issues remain unresolved, although possible approaches to some of them have already been hinted at in the previous discussion. The main questions can be summarized as follows:

- What is the precise mechanism for chain formation in an index-free syntax, and how do conditions on chains follow from general principles?
- Why is there a condition B? That is, why must reflexivity be licensed? What precisely is the relation between lexical reflexive-marking and SELF-marking?
- Why is there a condition A? What precisely is the mechanism underlying reflexive-marking by SELF?

We have not yet discussed 1st- and 2nd-person pronominals. In the Germanic languages except English and in all the Romance languages, they can be freely locally bound where condition B does not apply. Is English special, and if so, why? These are the issues to be taken up in subsequent chapters.

4 Representing Anaphoric Dependencies: Issues of Economy

4.1 Introduction

Chapter 3 showed that a syntactic condition—the chain condition—rules out locally bound pronominals but not SE anaphors in environments where reflexivity condition B is satisfied. One of our goals is to derive the effects of the chain condition from independent properties of syntax. We had an informal discussion of how SE anaphors can enter a syntactic dependency with their antecedent by feature sharing. I indicated that 3rd-person pronominals are prevented from entering a feature chain since they are not ϕ-feature deficient. I will make this a bit more precise now, leaving details of the implementation to chapter 5. As discussed in the previous chapter, syntactic dependencies are being formed by ϕ-feature sharing. A way to implement this is by copying one bundle of ϕ-features into a ϕ-feature slot. Consider now what happens if the slot is not empty. If the ϕ-features present do not make an independent contribution to interpretation—for instance, if they are uninterpretable and are just there to drive the computation—it is easily to see that no problem should arise if they are overwritten. In fact, one of the features of the computational system in Chomsky 1995 and subsequent work is that uninterpretable features should be deleted before interpretation. Overwriting is a way to effect deletion. However, if the slot that is targeted contains features that make an independent contribution to the interpretation, they obviously should not be overwritten but should remain. In a nutshell, overwriting grammatical material (including features) should not affect interpretive options. This prohibition is reflected in a fundamental grammatical principle: the *principle of recoverability of deletion* (PRD).[1] The PRD as a condition on operations affecting features is discussed in Chomsky 1995. The way it restricts chain formation will be discussed in more detail in chapter 5. For now it suffices that the PRD prevents 3rd-person pronominals from entering a ϕ-feature chain.

However, from the fact that 3rd-person pronominals cannot enter a chain it does not yet follow that they cannot be locally bound. To see this, consider the contrast in (1):

(1) a. *Oscar* voelde *hem* wegglijden.
     Oscar felt   him slide-away
  b. *Oscar* voelde *zich* wegglijden.
     Oscar felt   SE slide-away

The puzzle it poses is that there is no reason to assume that (1a) involves a syntactic crash. True, *hem* cannot enter a chain with *Oscar*, but, as we saw, what should be made clear is how this prevents simply construing *hem* as a variable bound by *Oscar*, which would yield the same reading as (1b), shown in (2):

(2) Oscar (λx (x felt [x slide away]))

The relation between (1a) and (1b) is reminiscent of the relation between variable binding and coreference discussed in Reinhart 1983, 2006, and in Grodzinsky and Reinhart 1993, which I reviewed in section 1.10. Their proposal concerned the question of why in cases such as (1a), *hem* cannot be simply coreferent with *Oscar*. If coreference were available, this would bypass the canonical condition B (or what replaces it in the present approach). Covaluation, as we know, is not subject to the binding conditions.

Reinhart formulated the following interpretive condition:

(3) *Rule I: Intrasentential Coreference*
    NP A cannot corefer with NP B if replacing A with C, C a variable A-bound by B, yields an indistinguishable interpretation.

Applied to a sentence such as *Oscar hates him, Rule I compares the construal *Oscar hates him* & *him = Oscar* to the bound variable construal *Oscar λx (x hates x)*. Their interpretations are indistinguishable, hence only the latter is let through. In turn, the bound variable structure violates the canonical condition B, hence is ruled out. As a consequence, the sentence will end up being ruled out altogether under the intended interpretation, as is required. Put intuitively, Rule I states that the bound variable strategy takes precedence over the discourse strategy, even if its result is eventually rejected.

We find a similar situation in the case of (1a) and (1b) as sources for (2). The standard procedure for translating syntactic structures into logical syntax representations (see section 1.6.2) gives both (1a) and (1b) as possible sources for (2), yet the strategy based on (1b) as a source takes precedence. In (1b) the dependency is syntactically encoded, whereas in (1a) it is not. This contrast is represented in (4) (see Reuland 2001b):

(4) *Rule BV: Bound variable representation (general version)*
NP A cannot be A-bound by NP B if replacing A with C, C an NP such that B *R* C, yields an indistinguishable interface representation.

Here *R* is a syntactic relation encoding the dependency. As I indicated, the specific syntactic vehicle encoding the dependency is ϕ-feature sharing. As shown in Reuland 2001b, ϕ-feature sharing results in the formation of syntactic objects (CHAINS) that are equivalent to movement chains. The precise mechanism will be reviewed in chapter 5. Accordingly, the syntactic relation *R* can be identified as the relation of CHAIN formation, and the more general term "interface representation" can be replaced by the specific term "logical syntax" representation. So, (4) can be replaced by (5):

(5) *Rule BV: Bound variable representation (specific version)*
NP A cannot be A-bound by NP B if replacing A with C, C an NP such that B heads an A-CHAIN tailed by C, yields an indistinguishable logical syntax representation.[2]

Standard principles of interpretation lead from (1b) to (2), but also from (1a) to (2). (5) entails that *hem* in (1a) cannot be A-bound by *Oscar* due to the possibility for the alternative, *zich*, to enter a chain headed by *Oscar*. This is what had to be derived.

Together with Rule I, Rule BV expresses a hierarchy in the economy of encoding, which is given in (6):

(6) *Economy of encoding*
Narrow syntax < logical syntax (C-I interface) < discourse

The hierarchy in (6), however, gives rise to a nontrivial problem. As already pointed out in note 57 of chapter 1, Reinhart (2000, 2006) shows that one must be careful to avoid too simplistic an interpretation of economy. Consider for instance the following issue in that arises in VP-ellipsis:

(7) Max likes his mother and Felix does too.

This type of sentence allows both a strict reading, based on coreference, and a sloppy one, as indicated in (8a,b):

(8) a. Max λx ((x likes his mother & his=Max)) & Felix (λx (x likes his mother & his=Max))
b. Max (λx (x likes x's mother)) & Felix (λx (x likes x's mother))

Now, if the availability of the bound variable reading simply blocks coreference, it is puzzling how (8) can have both. As Reinhart discusses, one might attempt to save the coreference option by invoking the escape hatch of Rule I, repeated here:

(9) *Rule I: Intrasentential coreference*
    NP A cannot corefer with NP B if replacing A with C, C a variable A-bound by B, yields an indistinguishable interpretation.

That would require saying that the difference it makes for the interpretation in the second conjunct licenses the coreference option. But, as Reinhart notes, invoking this clause gives the wrong result for (10):

(10) a. He likes Max's mother and Felix does too. (he≠Max)
     b. Max praised him and Lucie did too. (him≠Max)

In both cases choosing the coreference option in the first conjunct leads to an interpretation of the second conjunct that is otherwise not available. It is indeed not available; Rule I must, therefore, apply to the conjuncts separately, which implies that the availability of the coreference in (7) and (8) becomes mysterious again. Reinhart, then, concludes that something is wrong with the economy-based interpretation of Rule I. As she puts it in Reinhart 2006, 183, "However, as plausible as the "least effort" approach seems, it is not clear to me that the human processor is indeed sensitive to this type of economy considerations." Instead she proposes the rationale in (11):

(11) *Against sneaking in*
    "If a certain interpretation is blocked by the computational system, you would not sneak in precisely the same interpretation for the given derivation, by using machinery available for the systems of use." (p. 185)

Reinhart (2006, 185) argues that this rationale follows from a broader economy principle: "minimize interpretive options." This principle prohibits applying a procedure that increases the number of interpretations associated with a given PF. Given this discussion, it is important to go carefully over the question of what aspects of mental computation could be reflected in an economy metric. Let's discuss, then, the rationales for economy.

4.2 The Nature of Economy: Its Rationales

Below I list a number of rationales for economy that have been proposed so far.

(12) *Possible rationales for economy*
   i. Demand on processing resources: close an open expression as soon as possible (Reinhart 1983)
   ii. Intrinsic (narrow syntax is automatic, blind)
   iii. Number of crossmodular steps (Reuland 2001b)
   iv. Temporal course of parsing (Friederici and Kotz 2003)
   v. Cooperation: "If a certain interpretation is blocked by the computational system, you would not sneak in precisely the same interpretation for the given derivation, by using machinery available for the systems of use." (Reinhart 2006, 185)

Reinhart (1983) proposed rationale (12i) in her original discussion of Rule I. In a conception where pronouns are essentially variables, expressions with free pronouns are open expressions that become closed only after the pronoun is valued (see also chapter 2). Variable binding entails closing an open expression immediately, whereas coreference allows closing the expression only after a further search through the discourse. Under the assumption that keeping an expression open requires keeping it in working memory, and that keeping material in working memory carries a cost, variable binding is less costly, hence preferred. Thus, expressions must indeed be closed as soon as possible.

Another possible rationale is (12ii), which holds that certain subsystems of the language system are intrinsically cheaper in their demand on processing resources than others. For instance, in the case of narrow syntax one could argue that many, if not all, of its operations are forced by triggering features. In operations such as Movement, Case-checking, or Agreement there is no choice. In the interpretation of *himself* in *John was standing below himself* we have no alternative but concocting an impossible situation in order to interpret it; the syntactic machinery is fully deterministic and leaves no options. Automatic, blind processes require little monitoring while they apply; you only have to worry about the outcome. This certainly is a possible rationale for why narrow syntax would be economical. Finding a binder for a variable is less constrained in logical syntax, hence more monitoring and attention are required, which would make it more costly. The same holds true a fortiori for the discourse system, which therefore would come out as costliest.

Reuland (2001b) proposes the rationale in (12iii) and uses the economy metric given in (13). This metric is based on the idea that a cost is associated with crossmodular operations—that is, with shifting from narrow syntax to logical syntax (in the C-I interface) and, again, with shifting from logical syntax to discourse.

(13) a. Discourse storage (values)

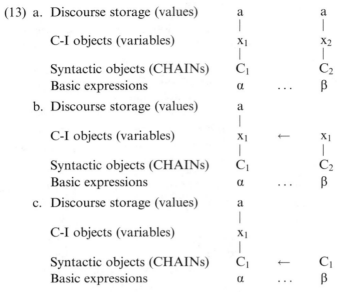

b. Discourse storage (values)

c. Discourse storage (values)

If you are doing something, switching to another type of task requires motivation, hence carries a cost. So, if you are carrying out a syntactic computation it is cheapest to keep doing so. If you are in the variable binding mode, it is costly to switch to discourse. This translates as a cost associated with crossmodular steps, which require starting to do something else. For example, going from two basic expressions such as *Oscar* and *hem* in (1) to a coreferential interpretation requires four crossmodular steps, from these to a BV interpretation, three, and interpreting them via syntactic chain formation requires only two crossmodular steps (not available for *Oscar* and *hem*, but available for *Oscar* and *zich*). The economy metric in (13) can be applied without taking grammar-external operations into consideration.

Work on the time course of natural language parsing by Friederici and Kotz (2003) provides yet a different rationale (12iv): irrespective of the intrinsic cost of steps or components of steps. It is obvious that in order to be able to even look for the value of an expression in discourse, the expression must be there in at least some rudimentary form. Variable binding relations require the representation of at least some basic syntactic hierarchy. Otherwise they are impossible to compute. Assigning a discourse value requires that at least the nature of the linguistic objects that would qualify to receive such a value is determined. Thus, the logic of interpretation imposes an intrinsic order on the type of processes that must be applied.[3]

Koornneef (2008) provides extensive discussion of the processing literature, showing that results in the literature such as those of Badecker and Straub (2002) that appear inconsistent with a temporal ordering as sketched are arguably lacking in temporal resolution. Moreover, Koornneef presents a range of experimental results that support the asymmetries underlying (6); Fiorin (2010) gives further supporting evidence. The question is, then, how to assess these different rationales. (Note that they all lead to the same ordering, and could in fact all be true.) To assess them we should distinguish between *preference* and *blocking*. By now there is a considerable amount of converging evidence from processing experiments of various kinds that a bound variable interpretation is more easily accessed than a coreferential interpretation. Burkhardt (2005) presents a range of processing experiments on English to this effect. Avrutin (2006) provides a general economy-driven perspective on the division of labor between syntactic and interpretive processes. Avrutin, Ruigendijk, and Vasić (2006), Vasić (2006), and Vasić, Avrutin, and Ruigendijk (2006) report systematic differences in the performance on strict versus sloppy readings by agrammatic aphasics, showing that they have considerable problems with strict readings. Koornneef (2008) reports eye-tracking experiments showing that even in contexts pragmatically biased for a strict reading the initial reading is the bound variable one, followed by a repair action. As a consequence, one must conclude that the human processor is indeed sensitive to the type of economy consideration discussed, even if one leaves open the precise source (as in (12i–iv); see Koornneef 2008 for more experiments and discussion).

Nevertheless, the problems noted by Reinhart for the VP-ellipsis case are real and should be resolved. This indicates that both types of considerations are correct. I will now show that a solution to the problem is found in combining the two approaches: "ranking procedures" and the "prohibition against sneaking in."

Note that even Reinhart's rationale does not escape from minimally making reference to the time course of interpretation. The process of determining whether a procedure increases the number of interpretations is defined with respect to a given PF as a starting point. (But of course, it is also compatible with stronger positions, as in (12ii) or (12iii).) On proper reflection there is another possible rationale for the prohibition to sneak in, which stays closer to the original intuition:

(14) The grammatical system does not consider alternatives for impossible derivations: Rejection by (one component of) the grammar is final.

From a processing perspective, (14) expresses the claim that entering an impossible derivation is equivalent to entering a "garden path," effectively a "garden hole" from which recovery is impossible. From a grammatical perspective, (14) subsumes the effects of a canceled derivation in the economy ranking in Chomsky's (1995) system.

Chomsky (1995) discusses cases where a set of alternatives contains a *canceled* derivation. A derivation is canceled if forming it would lead to an impossible syntactic object or violates the PRD. Such an impossible syntactic object is a chain with nonmatching—contradictory—features (i.e., a chain that is both 1st person and 3rd person). As he argues, such a canceled derivation still outcompetes the alternatives. Hence, neither the derivation with that chain nor its alternatives will be considered.

4.3   Competition in Brazilian Portuguese

There is an interesting set of facts in Brazilian Portuguese (BP) discussed by Menuzzi (1999) that support (14) as a rationale for the prohibition against "sneaking in" over a purely cooperative strategy of minimizing interpretive options.

BP has two ways of expressing the 1st-person plural pronominal: the expression *a gente* 'the people' and the canonical Romance pronoun *nós*. Its 1st-person interpretation notwithstanding, *a gente* is formally 3rd person, as indicated by verbal agreement. This shows that *nós* and *a gente* differ in ϕ-feature composition. Despite this fact, *nós* is a possible binder for *a gente* and vice versa. This indicates that for binding the semantic type prevails. The pattern is shown in (15):

(15) a. Nós achamos que o Paolo já viu a gente na TV.
        'We think that Paolo has already seen us on TV.'
     b. A gente acha que o Paolo já nos viu na TV.
        'We think that Paolo has already seen us on TV.'

This option also exists in a more local environment such as locative PPs:[4]

(16) a. Nós tínhamos visto uma cobra atrás de nós.
        'We had seen a snake behind us.'
     b. A gente tinha visto uma cobra atrás de nós.
        'We had seen a snake behind us.'
     c. A gente viu uma cobra atrás da gente.
        'We saw a snake behind us.'

In these environments, most importantly the one in (16), Dutch and English show no complementarity between pronominals and anaphors. This indicates it is an environment outside the domain of the chain condition. But in (17) a semantic match is not sufficient. The sentence is ruled out unless antecedent and pronominal match in ϕ-features:

(17) a. Nós deviamos nos preparar para o pior.
     'We must prepare ourselves for the worst.'
   b. *A gente devia nos preparar para o pior.
   c. A gente devia se preparar para o pior.
   d. *Nós deviamos se preparar para o pior.

A gente cannot bind *nos*, nor can *nos* bind the 3rd-person clitic *se*, which would be the proper bindee for a *gente*. (17) represents a narrower domain than (16). Here we have the domain of the chain condition. Clearly, a chain cannot be formed, since syntactic chains are based on ϕ-feature sharing.

Some principle should make it impossible for *a gente* to bind *nos*, bypassing the chain-forming mechanisms. Chomsky's notion of a canceled derivation gives this. Nonmatching features result in an ill-formed syntactic object. Thus the derivation must be canceled. Hence, the option in which *a gente* in (17b) simply semantically binds *nos*—which we know it can do in the other environments—is ruled out since it is in the set of alternatives for the canceled chain.

In this case it would be beside the point to speak of a strategy of minimizing interpretive options, since the result is no options. A better characterization is: *You are not allowed to bypass a narrow syntax prohibition by resorting to a "logical syntax" strategy.* This is precisely what (14) expresses.

The Brazilian Portuguese facts do in fact show three important things:

1. They provide independent evidence for competition between narrow syntax and logical syntax, along the lines discussed (as proposed in Reuland 2001b).
2. They show that a *rejection is final* rationale is preferable to a *cooperation* rationale.
3. They show once more how the syntactic microstructure down to the level of morphosyntactic features plays a crucial role in the conditions on binding.

4.4 A Synthesis: The Competition between *Hem* and *Zich* Revisited

In this section I argue that an economy hierarchy of components and the prohibition in (14) can indeed be combined, and in fact jointly enable us to return to the conservative position on economy sketched.

My position is that the intrinsic order in which operations become applicable determines a "starting point." (For present purposes it is immaterial whether this order of applicability is based on time course, economy counting crossmodular steps, intrinsic differences, or all of these.) Yet, it is not just a matter of intrinsic order. As soon as the operations of a particular module become available some principle must require them to apply and complete their work. If operations were not required to apply, the system could always wait for more information to become available before it moves on. As the eye-tracking results obtained by Koornneef show, this is not what happens. The processor first creates a variable binding reading, and only reverts to the contextually favored coreference reading after the relevant information has become available. But this regulating principle is in fact an economy condition with the same rationale as proposed in Reinhart 1983 and is therefore needed independently.

This economy-driven hierarchy of applicability is coupled with a generalized principle governing access. Thus the rationales I have covered can be summarized in (18), but note that these are not intended to replace the precise formulations we have, such as Reinhart's revised Rule I (Reinhart 2006), Rule BV, and so on:

(18) a. *Processing economy: Minimize unresolved dependencies*
- As soon as a process (of some component of the system) to resolve a dependency in an expression becomes applicable, it applies.
- Dissolving dependencies on the basis of subsequent information
  - carries a cost and
  - respects the integrity of grammatical objects.

   b. *Absolute economy: Rejection is final*
If the derivation of a particular interpretation of a certain expression in a given component of the language system violates a fundamental principle of grammar (feature coherence or PRD), this derivation is canceled. Hence access to subsequent components in the hierarchy to derive precisely the same interpretation for the given expression is prohibited.

The last bullet of (18a) reflects an asymmetry between anaphors and pronominals. Pronominals that have entered a BV dependency can be detached if subsequent information favors this, but after SE anaphors have entered a chain they cannot be detached, irrespective of any plausibility consideration. Yet, as we saw, one cannot say that they require a linguistic antecedent in general. The rationale is, then, that chain formation involves unification of their features with those of the other chain members. This unification cannot be reversed, since this would violate the integrity of a grammatical object.

To see how (18) works, consider again the *zich*/*hem* contrast in (19) and (20), discussed earlier:

(19) a. **Oscar* voelde *hem* wegglijden.
           Oscar felt   him slide-away
      b. *Oscar* voelde *zich* wegglijden.
           Oscar felt   SE   slide-away

(20) Oscar (λx (x felt [x slide away]))

Given (18), the competition between *zich* and *hem* is not direct (as in Reuland 2001b). It is indirect and is based on the following steps:

(21) i.   Forming an ⟨Oscar, zich⟩ chain is allowed, given the principles of chain formation stated above.
      ii. Forming an ⟨Oscar, hem⟩ chain is not allowed (because of the PRD).
      iii. Directly forming (20) from (19a) in logical syntax is blocked by (18).
      iv. Only ⟨Oscar, zich⟩ is left as a source for (20).

In this derivation, the ⟨*Oscar, hem*⟩ chain is independently ruled out, not just through comparison with the ⟨*Oscar, zich*⟩ chain. Forming the ⟨*Oscar, hem*⟩ chain would violate the PRD, which is a fundamental architectural principle. Hence, the derivation containing this chain is canceled, and the members in its set of alternatives are blocked. Although on a metalevel we can still say that one derivation is more economical than the other, this economy is not measured in a direct comparison between derivations. This is an important result. One of the issues with the analysis in Reuland 2001b is that it requires the comparison between derivations using different arrays of lexical items (different numerations in the Chomsky 1995 sense). The difference is minimal, namely one derivation involves *zich*, the other derivation involves *hem*, everything else being equal, and *zich* and *hem* are closely related items. Yet this makes the notion of economy that is appealed to transderivational, hence less restrictive than Chomsky's original conception. The conception of economy in (18b) is restrictive again. One derivation is ruled out, irrespective of whether there is an alternative. Hence, the analysis is now consistent with the conservative notion of economy of derivation (for more discussion, see the comparison of alternative approaches in chapter 9).[5]

English does not have a SE anaphor. Hence, a direct competition between encoding by chain formation and variable binding is lacking in English. It is important to note that the way I derive the effects of the original chain condition for SE anaphors does not carry over to complex anaphors like English *himself*. Rather, the conditions on *himself* follow from the process of reflexivization discussed in chapters 6 and 7. However, just as in the case of Dutch *hem*, the values of English *him* are governed by conditions on chains and economy. Absolute economy entails that in the domain of chain formation $DP\ V \ldots him \ldots$ cannot yield DP $(\lambda x\ (x\ V \ldots x \ldots))$, given that (DP, him) is an impossible chain. Absolute economy further entails that if chain formation, hence binding, is ruled out by Rule BV, DP and $him \ldots$ cannot be co-valued, unless binding and co-valuation do not lead to precisely the same interpretation, in accordance with Reinhart's Rule I.

The present approach has another important consequence. In a language system allowing locally bound (3rd-person) pronominals—as in Frisian—the absence of a competitor is not enough. If the pronominal could enter the chain—that is, if all conditions for chain formation were satisfied—and the resulting object violated the PRD, (18) would simply block any alternative using the same element. In the absence of a competitor this would entail ineffability.[6] Given this, what we expect is that locally bound pronominals are never an isolated phenomenon in a language. It always involves more than just the absence of a competitor.

Frisian presents a crucial case to illustrate this point. As discussed, a locally bound pronominal is licensed not via structural Case, but via inherent Case. This means the issue of forming a chain link does not arise; chain formation is not blocked due to a violation the ensuing chain would cause, but the conditions for chain formation are not met. Hence (18) does not come into play.

Consider, finally, the following issue. It is a recurrent question whether an approach to variable binding along the lines of (18) is sufficient to capture more complex patterns of variable binding. In recent literature we find a debate about a puzzle first noted in Dahl 1974. (See Roelofsen 2008 for useful discussion.) The question is how to derive the correct interpretive options in (22)—that is, what the possible values of *he* and *his* are in the italicized completion of the elided phrase:

(22) Max said that he called his mother. Bob did too. (= *Bob said that he called his mother*)
    a. ... Bob too said that Bob called Bob's mother.
    b. ... Bob too said that Max called Max's mother.

c. ... Bob too said that Bob called Max's mother.

d. ... Bob too said that Max called Bob's mother.

As Roelofsen puts it, the challenge is to account for the fact that (22a–c) are possible readings of the elided phrase, while (22d) is not. The fact has been discussed by a variety of authors, including Fiengo and May (1994), Heim (1998), Fox (1998, 1999), Safir (2004b), and Reinhart (2006). A recurrent property of accounts proposed for this pattern is that somehow local binding of *his* by *he* must be enforced. To this end Fox (1998) formulates rule H:

(23) *Rule H*
   A variable x cannot be bound by an antecedent a, if a more local antecedent b could bind x yielding an indistinguishable interpretation.

To obtain the illegitimate (22d), *Max* must have been able to bind *his* and corefer with *he* in the antecedent clause, as in (24):

(24) Max (λx (x said that he=Max called x's mother))

Rule H forbids that. With varying technical details, Safir (2004b) and Büring (2005) also explore the intuition that there is a locality restriction on binding. Reinhart (2006) argues that no special condition is needed in the system she developed, but Roelofsen shows that in the specific elaboration she presents, in fact not only is (22d) correctly blocked, but also, incorrectly, (22c). On the basis of this, Roelofsen argues that one should apply Reinhart's insight in a simpler and more intuitive way. He proposes the following formulation:

(25) *Rule S: A simpler interface rule*
   Interpretations that are ruled out by restrictions on binding cannot be sneaked in via other anaphoric mechanisms.

It is easily seen that (25) is just an instantiation of (18). Under this formulation neither (22d) nor (22c) is blocked. Roelofsen then argues for a separate locality condition to rule out (22d). The question is, then, whether one should keep pursuing a unified solution for VP-ellipsis, including Dahl's puzzle, or be content with a two-component solution. Initially, one might be inclined to reject a two-component solution, but the issue is really empirical: Do all the restrictions one has to account for indeed have the same status? In fact, I believe there is evidence that they do not. Canonical BT violations are categorical, and hard to impossible to obviate. However, the local binding requirement expressed by Rule H and its alternatives is quite sensitive to plausibility considerations. This is shown in the following example:

(26) Suppose John is a gambler; Bill does not like gambling himself but entrusts John with his capital.
    a. Dutch: Jan durfde niet toe te geven dat hij in Vegas zijn fortuin verspeeld had en Bill ook niet.
    b. English: John did not dare to admit that he lost his fortune in Vegas, and Bill didn't either.

In both English and Dutch the conjunct is fine with a J J J B J B interpretation. Since we have to construct an appropriate context to obtain this interpretation, and it is hard to impossible to get it in the case of (22), it seems safe to say that indeed some principle favoring local binding is active in language. However, its status must be that of a processing preference that is not grammatically encoded, and comparable to the preference for a sloppy interpretation over a strict interpretation in VP-ellipsis that has been demonstrated by psycholinguistic experimentation. My conclusion is, then, that the interplay between economy considerations and binding possibilities is best captured by a hierarchy of subsystems as expressed in (18).

4.5 Conclusions

In this chapter I have discussed a number of rationales for economy. I have presented converging evidence from a variety of sources that preferential factors—relative economy—play a role alongside an absolute economy principle: if a derivation violates a deep grammatical principle, bypassing it is not allowed. In short, *rejection is final.*

5   Binding by Chains: The Syntactic Encoding of Interpretive Dependencies

5.1   Introduction

This chapter continues the discussion of an index-free syntax for the binding of SE anaphors and pronominals. We will see why 1st- and 2nd-person pronominals behave differently from 3rd-person pronominals in binding. I discuss two specific technical implementations of chain formation. These implementations show that syntactic encoding of anaphoric dependencies is possible in different versions of current theory. Since over the years syntactic theory progresses, implementations change and will continue to do so. Hence, it is important to bring out that the core of the idea remains stable across different implementations. In this manner I hope to provide a perspective that is not too strictly time bound.

The proposal in a nutshell is that a chain must be formed between an anaphor and its antecedent if it can be formed. For independent reasons this will be possible for SE anaphors, but not in the same way for SELF anaphors, which will be discussed in the next chapter. A chain means that the tail is indistinguishable from the head of the chain. SE anaphors have unvalued φ-features, including unvalued number, which means that they can be made nondistinct from their antecedent and successfully form chains. 1st- and 2nd-person pronouns will also tail chains successfully, since 1st and 2nd person can be identified with their antecedents because of "indexical unmistakability." Third-person pronouns, however, cannot. Third-person pronominals have fully valued φ-features, including grammatical number, which prevents identification.

Much (though not all) of what I will be saying is relatively independent of specific implementations of syntactic theory. Irrespective of implementation, the chains formed to account for the pattern of anaphoric readings are a direct consequence of blind processes of feature checking/valuation, restricted by the PRD as discussed in the previous chapter, in tandem with the property of the C-I interface that it can only see objects that are terms in the sense of Chomsky 1995. In the case of binding, for example, this means that a feature bundle can only be read by the C-I interface if it corresponds in full to a syntactic term. Thus, although the features of SE anaphors form a subpart of the feature structure of a 3rd-person pronominal, the C-I interface cannot just read that part and leave the remainder uninterpreted. For instance, a plural feature on a pronoun, which blocks chain formation, cannot be left out of consideration for chain formation. When the antecedent is not a pronoun, but contains a common noun, the set expression of the common noun and the variable are different semantic objects, and I will assume that they are also represented as different objects syntactically, with the variable corresponding to the ϕ-feature bundle of the N.[1] So, effectively the chain is formed with the ϕ-feature bundle of the N. Similarly, I will be assuming that proper names also have a complex structure semantically and syntactically.[2]

In our discussion of chains so far, I related the difference between SE anaphors and pronominals to a difference in their ϕ-feature specification. SE anaphors can tail a chain since they are underspecified for some ϕ-features. Although intuitively simple, this idea needs attention in order to be made precise.

5.2 Underspecification

There is an extensive literature on underspecification, which it is impossible to do justice to here. To put the notion of underspecification in perspective, let me start with the following example.

In languages with rich morphology the number of different forms in (part of) a paradigm is often less than the number of distinctions the paradigm represents. For instance, Czech is a language with a rich Case system (seven Cases including vocative). In the feminine singular *a*-declension, these seven cases are distributed over six different forms.[3] In the feminine singular declension of adjectives ending in a nonpalatalized ("hard") consonant there are only four different forms for the seven Cases. But in the feminine singular declension of adjectives ending in a palatalized consonant, as in *posledni* 'last', there is only one form; for all cases these adjectives end in a long *-í*. In some sense, therefore, the morpheme *-i* appears to be underspecified.

In English we find such idiosyncrasies as well. For instance, the form *deer* serves both as singular and as plural. Similarly, the pronominal *he* in *he admired the deer* carries specifications for 3rd person, masculine, singular, and nominative. It contrasts with 1st- and 2nd-person pronouns, with 3rd-person singular feminine and neuter forms, with the plural form *they*, and with the object form *him*. *He* and its Dutch cognate *hij* would appear to be fully specified. In this, *he* differs from the neuter form *it* and its Dutch cognate form *het*. These do not distinguish a nominative form and an object form. In Dutch, the feminine singular weak pronominal *ze* is not formally different from the plural weak common gender pronominal *ze*. Here too, therefore, we have some form of underspecification. The type of underspecification illustrated here represents what is called *syncretism*.

Prima facie one could think that this is similar to what one finds in the SE anaphor *zich* in Dutch and its cognates in other Germanic languages. *Zich* does not care whether it has a masculine, feminine, neuter, singular, or plural antecedent. Since those factors generally do enter into the conditions on antecedency, it follows that *zich* must minimally be *nondistinct* from all these possible antecedents. That is, it cannot be fully specified for the values ⟨α gender, β number⟩. Yet there must be a difference. *Ze*, *het*, *it* cannot be locally bound, and *zich* can. *Ze*, *het*, *it* can be free, and *zich* cannot. We must, therefore, distinguish the type of underspecification in *deer*, *ze*, *poslední*, and so on from what obtains in *zich*. That is, *syncretism* must be distinguished from other ways in which values can be underspecified.

Baerman, Brown, and Corbett (2002) base the identification of *syncretism* on the comparison of the actual repertory of inflected forms in a language with an idealized underlying morphosyntactic paradigm.[4] For example, if verbs in a language are determined to bear the features "person" (with the values first, second, and third) and "number" (with values singular, dual, and plural), these multiply out into a paradigmatic grid with nine cells:

(1) *Paradigmatic grid* (Baerman, Brown, and Corbett 2002)

1sg	1du	1pl
2sg	2du	2pl
3sg	3du	3pl

Syncretism is, then, the correspondence of a single inflected word form to two or more morphosyntactic descriptions—that is, a single form occupies two or more cells in the underlying morphosyntactic paradigm. The values are underlyingly present, though.

Languages also differ in the paradigmatic distinctions they encode at all. Harley and Ritter (2002) propose a universal geometric analysis of crosslinguistic feature patterns. As they note, the absence of a contrast within the paradigmatic grid of one language (for instance, the absence of a formal contrast between 2du and 2pl for a certain verb class) must be distinguished from the overall absence of a contrast (for example, dual/plural) in a group of languages. If a contrast provided by Universal Grammar is systematically absent in a particular language, this is considered *conflation* rather than *syncretism*. A further instance of what may be seen as underspecification is *impoverishment* (Bonet 1991; Frampton 2002). Impoverishment occurs if a certain contrast is realized in one part of a paradigm and systematically absent in another. For instance, person contrasts are systematically absent in Dutch plural verb forms. This, then, represents impoverishment rather than conflation or syncretism.

Although these distinctions are important, neither impoverishment, nor conflation, nor syncretism captures what distinguishes *zich* from other cases of underspecification.[5] Logically, there is another option. If there is variation in the relation between forms and cells (syncretism) and in the number of cells (conflation and impoverishment), there must also be variation in whether the existing cells have content. This is the dimension of variation that provides the basis for the approach to features in Chomsky 2001 and subsequent work, as well as in Pesetsky and Torrego 2004a and 2004b. In their analysis features can also differ in being *valued* or *unvalued*. If an element is unvalued for certain features, the cells are there but lack content. Note that this account does not depend on particular assumptions about the representation of feature structures, either as more traditional feature clusters or as partial subtrees, as in the representations I adopted in section 3.5.

This notion of being unvalued makes precise the notion of underspecification in the chain condition.[6] That is, I will make the empirical assumption that SE anaphors such as *zich* are unvalued for number and gender. This in turn is what we need for the derivational notion of a feature chain.

5.3   Index-Free Binding

As discussed, minimalist theory dispenses with indices. This entails that each dependency that was stated with indices in preminimalist approaches must be reassessed. For binding theory this reassessment implied that the pie had to be cut differently, as discussed in section 1.9. The change from a Fiengo-and-May type of approach to a Reinhart-type approach—which had been shown to be preferable for independent reasons—is simply forced in the MP, like a strict separation between syntactic and semantic encodings.

In GB theory indices are crucial not only for binding but also for movement, because they mark the dependency between a moved element and its trace. In the MP, movement has been reduced to internal Merge: copying and merging, or remerging an element that has been merged/put into the structure in an earlier stage of the derivation. In this conception the role of indices to mark this dependency has been taken over by the identity relation inherent in *being a copy of*, or even stronger, by the conception of internal Merge. In this conception the result of internal Merge is that one element has two or more *occurrences* in a structure, where an occurrence of *a* in K is the full context of *a* in K (see the discussion in Chomsky 2000, 115).[7] Thus the use of indices as markers of identity in syntax has been taken over by identity as an intrinsic property of *a* in its different occurrences in an expression.[8]

Having eliminated indices from the syntax, Chomsky (1995) proposes that binding conditions must apply at the conceptual-intentional interface, where a purely semantic indexing procedure could in principle still be available. In the previous chapters we saw that this cannot be correct. Given the amount of microvariation and the presence of locality effects (see chapter 3), the conditions on binding cannot be accommodated at the C-I interface. Rather they must reflect a syntactic residue in binding.

We must, therefore, separate what is properly syntactic in binding from what takes place in the interpretive component. The minimalist architecture guides this endeavor, since it is unequivocal in what can be syntactic. Syntax allows for three types of operations: (i) Merge (external and internal); (ii) Match (in the form of check/Agree); and (iii) Delete (up to recoverability).

As discussed, *Merge* is the operation of building structure by combining more elementary objects. *Match* is a component of what is called *checking* in the earlier minimalist literature and subsequently *Agree*. It must be part of any computational system that can assess whether two occurrences of an object are occurrences of the same object. *Delete* is a component of feature checking and Agree.

A typical instance of Agree involves paired sets of features—for instance, in subject-verb agreement. To take an example from a more richly inflected language than English, in the Russian sentence *Sergey tancuet* 'Sergey dances' the subject *Sergey* is ⟨3rd person; singular⟩, and the inflected verb form *tancuet* is also ⟨3rd person; singular⟩. In nouns, person and number features are interpretable. In finite verb forms they are uninterpretable. There, they drive the computation that is needed to establish the subject-verb relation, which in turn is needed for the linking between arguments and semantic roles (see chapter 6 for further discussion of linking relations along the lines of Reinhart 2002 and Reinhart and Siloni 2005). The subject-verb relation is established on the basis of a match in features (this match may occasionally be incomplete, but I will ignore that for the moment).

In the framework of Chomsky 1995, all uninterpretable features, which are just there to drive the computation, must be used up for a syntactic structure to be ready for interpretation. This is the requirement of Full Interpretability. This is implemented by requiring that whenever an interpretable version of a feature—let's say 3rd person on a DP—is in a particular configuration with its uninterpretable counterpart, such as 3rd person on a finite verb, the latter is deleted.

Deletion is subject to a recoverability requirement. This is the PRD discussed in the previous chapter. Deletion may not result in loss of information; hence it always takes place under identity with a matching object. Thus, a 3rd-person feature on a subject may be used to delete an occurrence of the same person feature on the inflected verb, but not a 1st-person feature. (That it cannot was already demonstrated by the Brazilian Portuguese facts in the previous chapter.) This is the intuition behind the idea that the checking/agree relation is one of the means by which syntax expresses identity.

Logically, there are two ways the effect of deletion could be represented. One is to remove a particular occurrence of an element/feature from the structure, resulting in either an empty position/slot in a feature matrix or even the complete removal of the position. In either case, this original feature occurrence is entirely invisible for any subsequent step in the computation. Given the fact that in typical cases of checking, as in Case-checking on nouns or Agreement checking on finite inflection, the features remain visible for whatever determines morphological expression, this implementation can be discarded. The alternative is one in which the content of one occurrence of a feature is used to overwrite the content of another occurrence. In this case the slot/position remains and is visible to realization processes as required. One may think of various ways to implement this. As will be discussed in section 5.9, the implementation by Pesetsky and Torrego (2004a, 2004b) offers precisely what is needed, hence is the one I will ultimately adopt.

Importantly, all implementations based on *overwriting* (the content of) one occurrence with (the content of) another, *copying* a value, and so on, induce identity between the objects involved, just as the copying operation of internal Merge yields different occurrences of the same syntactic object. Pesetsky and Torrego make this effect explicit in distinguishing between occurrences of a feature and *instances*. If one occurrence of a feature is overwritten with the content of another occurrence, or if a value of one occurrence is copied onto another occurrence, these occurrences now represent instances of identical objects. Consequently, checking/agree also provides us with a representation of syntactic identity without indexing. Thus, the architecture of the Minimalist System enforces a demarcation between syntactic and semantic identity (or dependence).

One may perhaps wonder, is deletion licensed by recoverability under identity, or is identity forced by the recoverability needs of deletion? In fact both apply. As noted, the contribution of the PRD is that no information may be lost by the deletion/overwriting. So deletion of one or more features is only possible if the information they contained can be recovered. In the checking implementation to be discussed, it is the recovery itself that overwrites the previous occurrence and hence establishes identity. Recovery fails if information were to be lost, hence PRD acts like a filter. In the feature valuation implementation it is the overwriting that values an occurrence, hence establishes identity, with the PRD again acting as a filter. Intuitively, the slot whose values are overwritten must be interpretively empty. The same applies in a Frampton 2004–style remerge.[9]

What remains, then, is the task of precisely implementing the syntactic residue of binding—that is, the processes involved in binding that are subject to variation and locality, in a model allowing no more than (internal) Merge and Check/Agree. This entails that any strictly minimalist approach is committed to the Feature Determinacy Thesis, repeated from (15) in chapter 1.

(2) *Feature Determinacy Thesis*
    Syntactic binding of pronominal elements (including anaphors) in a
    particular environment is determined by their morphosyntactic
    features and the way these enter into the syntactic operations
    available in that environment.

In this chapter I first discuss an implementation in terms of checking, then show how it can be done in terms of Agree and feature valuation.

5.4 The Binding Requirement on Anaphors

It is generally taken for granted that anaphors (both SE anaphors and
SELF anaphors) have an intrinsic property that forces them to take a linguistic antecedent (the binding requirement of condition A). That is, they
are referentially defective.[10] The question is why this is so. A common
line of argument is that (3) holds (Bouchard 1984):

(3) In order for an argument α to be interpreted it must have a full
    specification for φ-features.

From a theoretical perspective, however, (3) is a stipulation. It cannot be
reduced to known properties of features, because the role lexical and formal features play is to constrain the interpretation of the elements carrying them. Thus, one should expect (4) to hold, rather than (3).

(4) If α has fewer φ-features than β, there are fewer constraints on the
    interpretation of α than on the interpretation of β.

So, a SE anaphor such as Icelandic *sig*, which carries only the feature
3rd person, should just have a broad range of application, namely to all
objects distinct from speaker and addressee. From this perspective, a general binding requirement on anaphors as commonly assumed, if true, is a
mystery. The question, then, is whether it is true.

As we have already seen (in section 1.8.2 for *sig* in Icelandic and in
chapter 3 for English *himself*), this is not in fact correct. Both *sig* and
himself allow for logophoric use, albeit under different conditions.

Within standard binding theory, this logophoric use of unbound anaphors is an exception that must be explained. For *himself* I described the
syntactic environment for exemption, and the role of discourse conditions
in chapter 3. In chapter 6 I will explain in more detail why exemption of
SELF anaphors occurs. For *sig*, two factors have been claimed to play a
role, namely the presence of subjunctive mood, and again discourse factors such as the availability of a discourse entity holding the perspective
of the sentence (e.g., Thráinsson 1991; Hellan 1988, 1991). Subjunctive
mood, however, is not a necessary condition. Crosslinguistically, only
the discourse factors appear constant. In other languages, logophoric interpretation of anaphors is also possible without subjunctive mood.[11]
From the perspective of standard binding theory this makes logophoricity
a rather puzzling phenomenon: if a discourse element is prominent
enough, this prominence can override a principle that otherwise should
lead to ungrammaticality. Such a role of interpretability goes against all
further known properties of the computational system. Thus, from this

perspective logophoric use of anaphors is not just an exception, but represents a real anomaly.

We thus have two anomalies: property (3), instead of the expected (4); and the availability of exemption/logophoricity. These warrant the following conclusion:

(5) There is no intrinsic property of anaphors that prohibits an unbound interpretation.

(5) is in line with (4). This does not imply that the choice of an element with low content such as a (logophoric) anaphor versus an element with higher content such as a pronoun is free. Rather, we expect the selection to be governed by accessibility conditions (Ariel 1990). That is, free anaphors, having a low descriptive content, can only be used for elements that are of the highest accessibility, in terms of discourse factors such as center of consciousness, point of view, and so forth. And this is what we find. Yet, it is not always the case that an unbound anaphor can be interpreted. In fact, there are many languages and environments where they never can be or are at least highly marked.

This is already a first step toward understanding. We started with two anomalies. These anomalies have been obviated. We are still left with a question, but it has shifted. Standard binding theory leads to the question of why, under certain conditions, logophoric interpretation is allowed. From the present perspective the question to ask is (6):

(6) Why, under certain conditions, is logophoric interpretation of anaphors blocked?

For *sig* this question is discussed in section 5.7. The approach I take exploits the economy principles discussed in chapter 4.

As we saw, an economy principle regulates the availability of coreference versus binding. Just as economy prohibits a coreference strategy if a bound variable strategy is available, I propose a rule (*Rule L*) regulating between a bound and a logophoric interpretation of elements like *sig*, and preferring the former when possible. Moreover, Rule L will be explained as a consequence of the economy principles discussed in the previous chapter. Rule L will be discussed in section 5.7. However, before I can do so, I must give a more precise analysis of the operations deriving the bound reading of SE anaphors.

5.5 Encoding Dependencies within C$_{HL}$

In this section I present a detailed discussion of which syntactic relation *R* distinguishes between anaphors and pronominals. It is based on the technical execution in Reuland 2001b, which uses the framework of Chomsky 1995, given certain specified changes that are independently justified.

Recall that my main goal is to show that a syntactic encoding of interpretive dependencies obeying the inclusiveness condition is in principle possible. I will therefore limit discussion as much as possible to environments and subcases needed for this goal. The basic idea is simple, as we saw in section 1.10 and chapter 3. It can be sketched on the basis of (7):

(7) DP   T   V   pronoun

      R1   R2   R3

R1–R3 are independently given syntactic dependencies. R1 stands for subject-verb agreement, R2 stands for the verb-tense dependency, and R3 for the structural Case dependency between a verb and its object. These dependencies can be composed. If and only if the pronoun is defective (a SE anaphor, or equivalent), composing R1, R2, and R3 yields a composite dependency (DP, SE) that carries over as an interpretive dependency at the C-I interface.[12]

The goal of the following discussion is to show that indeed the encoding of the syntactic residue of binding can be implemented in a well-defined and restrictive model of syntax without the use of indices. It qualifies as an existence proof. Since it was first presented (in fact for the first time in Reuland 1995, 1996), syntactic theory has made various advances, and no doubt it will continue to develop. Ideally, the conclusion that the syntactic residue of binding can be implemented without recourse to indices and the like should be stable. In support of the claim that it is, I provide further implementation in the framework of Pesetsky and Torrego 2004a, 2004b, in section 5.9. Readers more interested in the broad picture than in the technical details of the syntactic derivation can skip the following discussion and continue with section 5.6.

5.5.1 Dependencies in the Framework of Chomsky (1995)

Chomsky's (1995) approach limits the means available for expressing dependencies within C_{HL} to those in (8).

(8) i. The only ways to establish a dependency: Move/Attract and checking

     ii. The only way to force a dependency: checking grammatical features in a checking configuration

The antecedent-antecedee relation by itself does not provide a checking configuration (nor would it provide an *Agree* relation).[13] This precludes reinterpreting R&R-type chains directly as MP-type chains. However, we can do so indirectly.

We know independently that a subject DP enters into a dependency with the T-system (subject-verb agreement); an object DP enters into a dependency with the V-system (structural Case encodes a syntactic dependency between verb and object, which is marked on the verb by the discharge of the Case feature), and the T- and V-systems are related by a dependency as well (sharing a Tense feature). Note that these dependencies are real, and have to be taken into account by any theory. Within an MP-style system the dependencies involved are implemented by checking relations (by Agree within the framework of Chomsky 2001, 2004).

Chomsky (1995) states the following assumptions about lexical items and their features:

(9) *Lexical items and their features*
   i.   Lexical items are associated with a set of grammatical features (formal features).
        a. In the lexicon, lexical items are listed with inherent features (e.g., person and gender for N).
        b. Upon insertion into the numeration, optional features are added (e.g., number and Case for N; person and number for V).
   ii. Features come in two kinds: interpretable (e.g., number for N) and uninterpretable (e.g., Case for N, all φ-features for V).[14]
   iii. At the interface the uninterpretable features must be erased.
   iv. Movement is triggered by an attracting feature.
   v.   Covert movement moves formal features only.[15]
   vi. The features of a complement move at most as far as (the features of) its head.

In this system, agreement-type dependencies are encoded by feature movement, which is governed by attraction as in (10) (Chomsky 1995, 297):

(10) K *attracts* F if F is the closest feature that can enter into a checking relation with a sublabel of K.

There is no separate checking operation. Being in a checking relation just has the following immediate effects:

(11) a. A checked feature is deleted when possible.
     b. A deleted feature is erased when possible.

Intuitively, (11) expresses that checking takes place as soon as a checking configuration has been established. This is the driving force. The consequence of being in a checking relation is that as many features are deleted/erased as possible.[16] Since the deletion-versus-erasure distinction does not come up in my discussion, I will use the more canonical term *deletion*, keeping in mind that at the C-I interface such deleted features should effectively be made harmless as potential offenders of Full Interpretation. Note that this is achieved in Pesetsky and Torrego's valuation approach—to be discussed later—in a very natural way. Thus, *the core syntactic dependency is that between two "occurrences" of a feature, one being deleted (overwritten) by the other.* Syntactic dependencies between constituents are thus derivative of dependencies between features they contain.

With Chomsky, I assume that "possibility" in (11) is to be understood relative to other principles of UG. Specifically, a checked feature cannot delete if deletion contradicts the principle of recoverability of deletion (PRD), introduced in the previous chapter. As Chomsky points out, the principle of recoverability of deletion will not bar uninterpretable feature deletion. Effectively, being in a checking configuration entails deletion up to recoverability.

For reasons that will become clear below, we will have to allow dependencies based on occurrences of features that are both interpretable. Yet, Chomsky (1995) states that, as a consequence of the PRD, interpretable features cannot be deleted. If so, we must either find a significant relation between feature occurrences other than deletion, or else reject the claim that interpretable features can never be deleted (or overwritten). In Reuland 2001b I pursued the latter possibility, since, perhaps surprisingly, it is fully consistent with all relevant assumptions. I will retain it here.

Note that the claim that interpretable features cannot be deleted entirely depends on the PRD. Consequently, nothing bars deletion of an interpretable feature if no violation of the PRD results. As we will see, the PRD can in fact be met for certain interpretable features (though, crucially, not for all). Such features are not necessarily visible for attraction, since there is never a need for them to be deleted.

I will now show how the possibility of a syntactic encoding of interpretive dependencies between anaphors and antecedents can be derived. I will base my exposition on the structure in (12), discussed in the previous chapter.

(12) a. **Oscar* voelde *hem* wegglijden.
'Oscar felt him slide away.'
b. *Oscar* voelde *zich* wegglijden.

The relevant aspects of (12) are presented in (13)–(15) in the next section. Relations between target and source positions in movement are indicated by subscripts (for conventional reasons I will occasionally be using the term *trace* for the lower *copy*). In order for the implementation to be general we have to distinguish two cases. One is the case in which the relation between verb and inflection (V-to-T) is established in the overt syntax (yielding an Icelandic-type structure); the other is the case in which the V-to-T relation is established without a reflection in the overt structure—that is, by a covert operation, as in Dutch subordinate clauses. In all cases I will be abstracting away from operations such as "Verb Raising," V-second (movement of the Verb to the Complementizer position), and object scrambling, which I will be assuming is not Case driven. For uniformity of exposition I will be using a Dutch vocabulary even in Icelandic-type structures. Note that also in examples with covert V-to-T, any resemblance to actual Dutch sentence structures will be mostly superficial.

The exposition on the basis of a structure with overt V-to-T is the simplest. Therefore I will use that case as the basis for the discussion. After that I will discuss the case of covert V-to-T and show that the complications it involves do not affect the result obtained for overt V-movement.[17]

5.5.2 Overt V-to-T

When V-to-T is overt, (14) results from (13) by first adjoining *voelde* 'felt' to T and then moving *Oscar* to [Spec,TP]. For present purposes we may abstract away from the finer articulation of the V/T system into little v, AgrO, Asp, AgrS, T, and so on. It is immaterial, since, by assumption, the finite verb will end up in the highest position anyway. (Note that throughout, adjunction structures are represented by a label of the form $[_{x,x}]$.)

(13) $[_- [_T [\text{Oscar} [\text{voelde}_{+\text{fin}} [\text{zich T} [\text{wegglijden}_{-\text{fin}}]]]]]]$
Oscar felt$_{+\text{fin}}$ SE slide-away$_{-\text{fin}}$

(14) $[\text{Oscar} [[_{T,T} \text{voelde}_{+\text{fin}} \text{T}] [t_{\text{oscar}} [t_v [\text{zich T} [\text{wegglijden}_{-\text{fin}}]]]]]]$

Next, consider the effect of Case-checking by *zich*, assuming that Case-checking takes place in the covert syntax. As noted by Chomsky (1995, 304), the trace of the moved V is not a possible target for movement, hence the formal features of *zich* (FFz) must move higher up, adjoining to the matrix V/T complex.[18] The pair (FFz, *zich*) has the properties of an A-chain, since both positions are L-related, and FFz is nondistinct from an X-max (see Chomsky 1995, 270–276, for discussion).[19]

As discussed earlier, *zich* is characterized as 3rd person; in addition it may have a category feature, though we may stay uncommitted as to which (it cannot be D, given our discussion in section 3.5). It has no gender or number feature. The effect of movement is represented in (15), where FFz contains only a person feature:

(15) [Oscar [[$_{T,T}$ FFz [$_{T,T}$ voelde$_{+fin}$ T]] [t$_{oscar}$ [t$_{v}$ [zich T
 Oscar   felt$_{+fin}$ SE
   [wegglijden$_{-fin}$]]]]]]
   slide-away$_{-fin}$

We know independently that *Oscar*, having raised to [Spec,T], checked and deleted the verb's ϕ-features, since these are uninterpretable. This happened as soon as Oscar moved into [Spec,T]. The verb's features were visible to *Oscar* because they constitute a sublabel of T. One of the verb's features that was checked and deleted is the feature for 3rd person. Note now that FFz contains a 3rd-person feature as well. After adjunction of FFz to the V/T complex, the latter again contains a 3rd-person feature. Checking applies blindly. As discussed under (11), it is just the existence of a checking configuration, which is required for checking to obtain. The 3rd-person feature of *Oscar* will check any occurrence of 3rd person that it stands in a checking configuration with. Thus, the category and person features of *zich* will also be checked. Given (11), this leads to deletion of these features and the establishment of a formal dependency, provided no violation of the PRD ensues.

All this is independent of the mechanism used for deletion. Deletion of a feature Fα in DP$_1$ and recovery of Fα under identity with Fα in DP$_2$ is tantamount to treating Fα in DP$_1$ and Fα in DP$_2$ as copies, and in fact as occurrences of the same feature in the sense of the notion of an occurrence in Chomsky 2001, 29. Overwriting an occurrence of a feature by an occurrence of a counterpart of that feature is a way of implementing deletion, and straightforwardly captures the intuition we wish to express. So indeed, this checking-deletion mechanism is virtually equivalent to Agree, which copies feature values into feature matrices that are underspecified, and in fact returns to a much more traditional view of syntactic dependencies.

5.5.3 Checking *Zich's* Features

As stated, both features of *zich* (3rd person and Cat) are inherent (see the assumptions listed in (9). They are also interpretable. The question is, then, whether deleting them violates the PRD.

The conception behind the PRD is that deletion is possible provided a copy of the deleted element is retained that is interpretively equivalent. That is, no information may be lost. In the case of deletion of lexical elements this requirement can never be satisfied. If some lexical item LI has been twice selected in a numeration, both instances may be assigned different interpretations. Hence, trivially, one instance of LI cannot perform the role of two. However, by their very nature, formal features such as category and person features are interpretive constants. The contribution they make to interpretation is not contextually determined (for person features, at least within one reportive context) (this will be more extensively discussed in section 5.6). All occurrences of such features are therefore interchangeable. Thus, if we have a pair $\langle Fc, Fc \rangle$ and one member is used to delete the other, the remaining element can take over the role of the deleted one in full. In other words, different occurrences of such features are indeed just copies of one another. It appears, then, that nothing bars deletion of the features +Cat and 3rd person in FFz under identity with the person feature and relevant Cat-feature of *Oscar* (part of its extended projection lower than D).

If so, according to (11) these features will be deleted. However, given their contribution to interpretation they must be recovered. It is this recovery that expresses that there is a dependency between *Oscar* and FFz. Note that this is a real dependency enforced by (11) together with the PRD. Since Move/attract already created a dependency between FFz and *zich*, the result is a dependency between *Oscar* and *zich*. This dependency is mediated by FFz, and established by the checking of FFz's features by *Oscar*.

5.5.4 Linking

To be explicit about the relation between this formal dependency and the *chain* dependency formed by Move/attract, one may define a notion of a *Checking-chain*, abbreviated as *Chain*, formed by checking/deletion:

(16) *Chain definition*
    (α, β) form a Chain if (i) β's features have been (deleted by and) recovered from α, and (ii) (α, β) meets standard conditions on chains such as uniformity, c-command, and locality.[20]

(17) If (α, β) is a Chain, and both α and β are in A-positions, (α, β) is an
A-Chain.

Note that under this definition, not all pairs (α, β) such that one deletes
a feature of the other qualify as Chains. For reasons to be made clear
below, (16) singles out those cases where β's features are exhaustively
deleted (and recovered). However, since (16) is just a definition, no theoretical cost is involved. (I will leave open whether other significant relations can be encoded in a manner not meeting the definition of a Chain.
This is in principle possible, but need not concern us here.)[21] Note also
that there is no recovery without previous deletion, hence *deleted by* is redundant and can be omitted. Applying these definitions, the pair (*Oscar*,
FFz) in (15) can be said to form an A-Chain.

There is no significant difference between this case and the result of feature movement. The uniformity condition is met, as for the pair (FFz,
zich). C-command and locality are satisfied as well. The same reasoning
that makes (FFz, *zich*) an A-chain, makes (*Oscar*, FFz) an A-Chain.

A-Chains are similar to A-chains, since the objects they consist of have
the same syntactic types (DP, φ-feature bundles). Chains (uppercase) differ from chains in two respects: (i) Chains have been derived by checking instead of movement; (ii) in Chains the full DP c-commands a
head-adjoined φ-feature bundle, whereas chains either consist of a DP
and a copy (trace), or the head-adjoined φ-feature bundle c-commands
the DP.

Given this, the mechanism for chain-linking developed in Chomsky
and Lasnik 1993 provides a straightforward way of composing the relevant syntactic dependencies. Slightly adapting their definition, A-Chains
can be linked with A-chains, as in (18). Let's call these objects CHAINs.

(18) If (α_1, α_2) is a Chain and (β_1, β_2) is a chain and $\alpha_2 = \beta_1$, then
$(\alpha_1, \alpha_2/\beta_1, \beta_2)$ is a CHAIN.

If linking applies to the objects (α_1, α_2) and (β_1, β_2), the member to be
eliminated is α_2/β_1. The ensuing CHAIN is (19):

(19) (α_1, β_2)

In the next section I discuss how CHAINs compare to chains. Independent of the outcome of such a discussion, the present argument already
establishes an important result: *SE anaphors enter into a real dependency
with their antecedents within C_{HL}.* This gives us part of what is needed to
demonstrate that there is a syntactic relation that meets the conditions on
the relation *R* discussed in section 4.1.

Recall that we also have to derive the fact that pronominals cannot enter the same relation with an antecedent. In our preliminary discussions in chapters 3 and 4, we linked this prohibition to the fact that pronominals have a full specification for ϕ-features. Pronominals are specified for category, person, gender, and number. Category and person are interpretive constants. Hence overwriting them does not violate the PRD.

This leaves gender and number (and let's ignore gender for now). As will be argued in detail in the next section, *number* reflects a property that is not a constant. Hence overwriting it does violate the PRD. The question is, then, what happens in case some features can be deleted but others cannot.

For the sake of concreteness, consider (20), where binding of the pronominal *hen* by *de jongens* is not allowed:

(20) **De jongens* voelden *hen*   wegglijden.
       the boys   felt   them slide-away

Up to checking, the derivations are equivalent. The relevant structure is in (21), with FFh representing the formal features of *hen* in the T-system.

(21) [De jongens [[$_{T,T}$ FFh [$_{T,T}$ voelden$_{+fin}$ T]] [t$_{de\ jongens}$ [t$_V$ [hen T
       [wegglijden$_{-fin}$]]]]]]]

FFh contains category, person, gender, and number. The logic of the system is as follows: FFh contains number, which cannot be deleted, since deleting it would violate the PRD. Therefore, even if the subject is in a checking configuration with FFh, no deletion of (features of) FFh obtains. Therefore, no dependency is established between the subject and FFh, and consequently not between the subject and *them* in its English equivalent either. So, nothing more than conceiving of the PRD as a real, contentful principle is needed to derive the asymmetry between pronouns and anaphors with respect to syntactic binding.

5.5.5 Features and Feature Bundles

In comparing CHAINs to chains, let me further clarify my assumptions. In line with Pesetsky (2000), I am assuming that features are visible for attraction and so on, but that the objects to be interpreted are always full-feature bundles that have an independent status in the computational system. Within C_{HL} full ϕ-feature bundles (such as pronominals and SE anaphors) correspond to morphological objects. Furthermore, full ϕ-feature bundles, but not the individual ϕ-features, correspond to variables at the C-I interface. I will, therefore, make the assumption that only full φ-feature bundles can be manipulated by C_{HL} and may enter syntactic dependencies that can be interpreted. Consider, for instance, (20).[22] It was argued that no dependency between *de jongens* and *hen* can be formed since establishing a CHAIN would violate the PRD due to the nature of the number feature. Yet, *de jongens* and *hen* do share the features of category, person, and gender. From the assumption that interpretable dependencies can only be established between entire bundles of φ-features, it follows that no such dependency can be established between *de jongens* and *hen*, since identifying $φ_{de\ jongens}$ and $φ_{hen}$ violates the PRD and there are no identifiable linguistic objects in the structure corresponding to subparts of these bundles.[23] With *zich* instead of *hen* relevant conditions are met: $φ_{zich}$ corresponds to a linguistic object that as such can depend on $φ_{de\ jongens}$.

This brings us back to the discussion of the Chain definition in (16), repeated here:

(22) *Chain definition*

(α, β) form a Chain if (i) β's features have been (deleted by and) recovered from α, and (ii) (α, β) meets standard conditions on chains such as uniformity, c-command, and locality.

Reading β's features as all of β's features has the effect that bypassing, for instance, the number feature of β entails that the conditions for Chain formation are not met. Hence no interpretable syntactic dependency is established in that case.[24]

Coming back to our earlier discussion of the encoding of identity, note that a dependency based on deletion coupled with recovery—essentially overwriting—can easily be reconceptualized as *unification*, which comes very close to the ideas in Pesetsky and Torrego. As discussed, in their conception of chain formation, feature chains are formed on the basis of an Agree operation valuing unvalued features, turning different occurrences of features on different elements in the numeration into different instances of a feature within a feature chain.

(22) is sufficient to also eliminate another unwanted case of the general type illustrated in (23a), which would be instantiated by (23b):

(23) a. DP_1 V [$_γ$ SE F DP_2 V]

b. De held/*Ik hoorde [zich de soldaten verdedigen]
the hero/*I heard [SE the soldiers defend]

In (23) it is impossible for *zich* to take *de soldaten* as its "antecedent." If the matrix subject is feature-incompatible with *zich*, the sentence is ill-formed (as will be discussed in more detail below), if the matrix subject is compatible with *zich* it will serve as *zich*'s antecedent.

Note that in the counterpart of (23) with the positions of the arguments reversed, binding proceeds as one would expect:

(23') a. DP_1 V $[_\gamma DP_2$ F SE V]

b. De held/Ik hoorde [de soldaten zich verdedigen]
the hero/I heard [the soldiers SE defend]

In (23') the anaphor is obligatorily bound by *de soldaten*; a pronominal instead of SE is obligatorily free from *de soldaten*. Syntactic encoding of the anaphor-antecedent dependency should, therefore, be possible. Let's assume, then, as is standard, that the clausal complement of *horen* has a functional category as its head, and let's call it F. So, we have a functional projection F in γ such that F attracts the formal features of the lower verb and the formal features of its object, and such that it also has an EPP feature requiring the raising of the subject of γ to Spec,F. F does not check Case, hence for Case-checking the subject of γ will have to move to the V/T complex in the matrix clause.

Assume, then, that in (23) FF_{DP} moves up to F, hence enters into a checking configuration with SE, as in (23"a). The reverse case (23') is given in (23"b):

(23") a. *.... [zich [[$_{T,T}$ $FF_{de\ soldaten}$ [$_{T,T}$ FF_V F]] [t_{zich} de soldaten
SE   the soldiers

verdedigen]]]
defend

b. .... [de soldaten [[$_{T,T}$ FF_{zich} [$_{T,T}$ FF_V F]] [$t_{de\ soldaten}$ zich
verdedigen]]]

The difference between the good case and the bad case is that in the good case (23"b) the subject exhaustively deletes the formal features of the object on F, since the latter form a subset of the former; in the bad case (23"a) the subject cannot exhaustively delete the formal features of the object since it cannot delete the latter's number feature. Since exhaustive deletion is impossible here, given the formulation of (16), a Chain cannot be formed, hence no CHAIN and no interpretive dependency can be established in this manner.

5.5.6 CHAINs and Chains

Earlier I discussed how Chains and chains can be linked and form a CHAIN. The question is, then, how CHAINs relate to *chains*. Within chain theory as it is elaborated in the framework of Chomsky 1995, 2001, 2004, a reduction of CHAINs to chains requires careful scrutiny. If nouns (proper or common) are syntactically simplex, such a reduction is impossible. In this framework a chain can only be represented as a sequence (or set) of occurrences of some element α, where occurrences of α are identified in terms of their (differing) environments: an occurrence of α in K is the full context of α in K (see the discussion in Chomsky 2001, 29). It is clearly impossible for *zich* in (12) to be an occurrence of *Oscar* or vice versa. However, given the existence of agreement relations, be it between subject and verbal agreement, head noun and adjectives, and so on, the φ-feature content of a noun must be analyzable for C_{HL}. Assuming the same execution that enables one to identify occurrences of a Lexical Item α, abstracting away from differences in, for instance, Case, the anaphor *zich* and the φ-features of a DP to which it has become syntactically linked can be identified as occurrences of the same φ-feature bundle. Thus, CHAINs can indeed be reduced to chains.

Therefore, CHAIN formation resulting from checking and Move/attract indeed gives a precise reconstruction of the relation *R* in (4) in chapter 4, repeated as (24a), and leading to a more articulate version of Rule BV in (24b):

(24) a. *Rule BV: Bound variable representation (general version)*
NP A cannot be A-bound by NP B if replacing A with C, C an NP such that B *R* C, yields an indistinguishable interface representation.

 b. *Rule BV: Bound variable representation (specific version)*
NP A cannot be A-bound by NP B if replacing A with C, C an NP such that B heads an A-CHAIN tailed by C, yields an indistinguishable logical syntax representation.

In this form it can be reduced to the economy principles discussed in chapter 4. This being achieved, we will now continue our discussion with "covert" V-to-T.

5.5.7 Covert V-to-T

The only complication in case of covert V-to-T resides in the internal articulation of the T-system. With overt V-to-T, the formal features of the object will be attracted by V within the highest T-element, whatever the internal structure of the T-system, since the successive traces of V are invisible (assuming pied piping of the intermediate functional material).

In the case of covert V-to-T we may wish to make sure that the formal features of the object indeed end up high enough to be checked by the subject. Let's assume, then, that "V-to-T" is covert, and that there is an articulated T-system. Since qualitative differences between the elements in the functional structure can be abstracted away from, I will represent the T-system as T_1–T_n, where T_1 stands for the highest element (T) and T_n for the lowest element (perhaps light v). I assume that T_1 has a "strong" EPP feature, triggering overt movement of the subject, as indicated in (25).

(25) [Oscar [T_1–T_n [t_{oscar} [voelde$_{+fin}$ [zich T [wegglijden$_{-fin}$]]]]]]
     Oscar   felt$_{+fin}$ SE   slide-away$_{-fin}$

For reasons of exposition, *Oscar*'s (overt) movement to [Spec,T_1] has already been indicated in the structure, but note that there is only one cycle and movement of *Oscar* effectively follows the feature movement relating V to T. What can we say about the latter? It is clear that one would not want the verb to be able to skip intermediate positions such as v, Aspect, and so on. Allowing intermediate positions to be skipped would dissociate covert verb movement from overt verb movement. This would be unmotivated, since in fact, in overt and covert V-movement alike, all inflectional elements reflect different aspects of the verb, and are best viewed as together forming the extended V-projection in Grimshaw's sense.

Details of execution will depend on specific theoretical assumptions. If one may assume some principle like the head-movement contraint (HMC), the successive adjunction of V's formal features to intermediate positions on the way up to T_1 is enforced. However, as Chomsky (1995, 307) notes, its status as a general principle is dubious in the Minimalist Program. Alternatively, each of the intermediate inflectional elements must carry a "weak" feature triggering the required movement. For the sake of concreteness let's assume the latter: each T_i ($1 \geq i \geq n-1$) has a weak feature T_{i+1}, reflecting the fact that it selects T_{i+1}. So, covertly triggered by T_1–T_n's weak features, the matrix verb's formal features FFv, successively adjoining to the intermediate positions, end up adjoined to T_1.

The first step of covert V-movement will now adjoin FFv to T_n, to the left of t_{oscar}, as in (26).

(26) [Oscar [T_1 ... T_{n-1} [[$_{Tn,Tn}$ FFv T_n] [t_{oscar} [voelde$_{+fin}$ [zich T [wegglijden$_{-fin}$]]]]]]]]

We may assume that the Case of *zich* will be checked in the lowest T-position. If so, (27) will result (as discussed earlier, *zich* is characterized only as +Cat and 3rd person; FFz contains only a Cat-feature and a person feature):

(27) [Oscar [$T_1 \ldots T_{n-1}$ [[$_{Tn, Tn}$ FFz [$_{Tn, Tn}$ FFv T_n]] [$_{toscar}$ [voelde$_{+fin}$ [zich T [wegglijden$_{-fin}$]]]]]]]

In this position, FFz will not end up in a checking configuration with *Oscar*. However, by assumption, T_n is attracted by T_{n-1} and adjoins to it, and so on. To obtain a configuration in which FFz is checked by *Oscar*, movement of T_n has to carry FFz along. In fact, if some instance of T_n is to move, there are two candidates: either its minimal instantiation, T_n proper, or its maximal instantiation, [$_{Tn, Tn}$ FFz [$_{Tn, Tn}$ FFv T_n]], assuming that intermediate instantiations are invisible for Move. Even if otherwise allowed, moving the former would entail that FFv remains stranded, leaving the uninterpretable features of FFv unchecked. (Note that the economy argument against pied piping does not apply here, since all features involved are formal features.) The only possibility is that it is the largest instance of T_n that moves, moving along FFv and, as a consequence, also FFz. If so, all formal features within ⟨Tn, Tn⟩ will move along and end up adjoined to T_1, which for reasons of legibility I will simply represent as (28):

(28) [Oscar [[$_{T, T}$ FFz [$_{T, T}$ FFv T]] [$_{toscar}$ [voelde$_{+fin}$ [zich T [wegglijden$_{-fin}$]]]]]]

After adjunction of FFv to the highest element in the T complex the latter contains the φ-features of the finite verb as a sublabel, but also, as in the case of overt V-to-T, the 3rd-person feature of FFz. This configuration is similar to the one discussed earlier. Again, checking applies blindly as soon as a checking configuration obtains. Mediated by FFz a CHAIN will be formed between *Oscar* and *zich*, but not between *Oscar* and a pronominal. Thus, the results obtained for structures with overt V-movement carry over unchanged to structures with covert V-movement.[25]

Given economy as discussed in chapter 4, we know that if a pronominal cannot enter a chain because doing so it would violate the PRD, a binding strategy cannot bypass this prohibition. Hence a bound reading of *hem* in (12) or *hen* in (20) is ruled out. What remains at this point is to address the PRD in more detail. So we face the following question:

(29) What properties of a pronoun determine whether it can enter the tail of a chain and why?

5.6   Conditions on the Tail: What Blocks Chain Formation?

5.6.1   Recoverable Features

In this section I discuss the status of the different features that are involved in more detail, and show why one type of feature blocks the syntactic encoding of an interpretive dependency, whereas another does not.

Consider first *category*—for instance, in the form of a ⟨D-feature⟩ or an ⟨N-feature⟩. Category is often taken to be an interpretable feature, but in fact it is hard to see why. For example, saying that *every* is a determiner is shorthand for saying that *every* is an expression denoting a function from sets to sets of sets. Put differently, it is an expression *taking two sets as its arguments and returning 1 or 0 depending on the properties of the intersection between the two* (where the requirements on the intersection depend on the lexical content/specific instructions of the determiner —the subset relation for *every*, the intersection must be nonempty for *some*, etc.).

The italicized expression is shared between all (binary) determiners. That is, if we have a numeration with different determiners, each occurrence of the D-feature makes the same contribution to interpretation as another one: they are interchangeable, hence recoverable under deletion. Insofar as D-features are part of the syntactic makeup at all, they are purely formal. As a consequence, a D-feature on an item does not block chain formation. What about N or V? Again, it seems that these are formal rather than contentful features. Prima facie, one would say that *work* as a verbal form and *work* as a noun are distinguished by a feature ⟨+N⟩ and a feature ⟨+V⟩. If so, the feature would make a real contribution to interpretation. However, as argued in Baker 2003 and Vinokurova 2005, a distinction between basic nouns and basic verbs can be made at the conceptual level. For instance, Baker argues that nouns are characterized as satisfying the criterion of identity. They can be used in *same* contexts: *this tree is the same as that one*, and so forth. Vinokurova argues that basic verbs are intrinsically relational. A basic noun can be turned into a verb by a verbalizing affix, possibly null, affecting the argument structure of the element it operates on. The converse holds for basic verbs. If so, whether an element is a noun or a verb can be determined by inspection of the concept it represents. Again, the ⟨+N⟩ or ⟨+V⟩ feature is then nothing but shorthand for a formal property all nouns or all verbs share. So, if a chain is formed between *John* and *zich*, the occurrences of a ⟨+D⟩ or ⟨+N⟩ feature on each (they may well have both features) are guaranteed to make exactly the same contribution to interpretation, hence can be unified without a violation of the PRD (see Reuland 2010b for further discussion of the relation between lexical category and concept).

Consider *person features* next. There is an extensive literature on the interpretability of person features (for instance, Kratzer 1998, 2006; von Stechow 2003a, 2003b; Cable 2005; Heim 2005; and works cited there). Much of the most recent discussion centers on examples such as (30), from Kratzer 2006, attributed to Irene Heim. However, it is essentially the same issue as the cases of local binding given in (31) and (32):

(30) a. I am the only one around here who can take care of my children.
   b. Only you eat what you cook.

(31) a. Ik/Jij voelde mij/je wegglijden.
   'I/You felt myself/yourself slide away.'
   b. Wij/Jullie voelden ons/je wegglijden.
   'We/You felt ourselves/yourselves slide away.'

(32) a. Wij voelden ons wegglijden en jullie ook.
   'We felt ourselves slide away and you too.'
   b. Wij (λx (x voelden (x wegglijden))) & jullie (λx (x voelden (x wegglijden)))

As mentioned in chapters 1 and 3, in many languages including the Germanic languages except English and all the Romance languages, 1st- and 2nd-person pronominals can be freely locally bound in environments where condition B is satisfied.

So far, this was a puzzle for all versions of the binding theory. Generally, it was either ignored, or it was stipulated away by stating that 1st- and 2nd-person pronouns are ambiguous between being anaphors and pronominals. True as this may be in some sense, it still raises the question of why this would be so. One might entertain the possibility that with 1st- and 2nd-person pronouns there is never binding, but always coreference. However, this position is untenable since these pronouns allow variable binding, as demonstrated in (30) and (32) from Reuland 2001b. In fact, as we saw in the previous chapter, the facts of pronominal binding in Brazilian Portuguese (Menuzzi 1999) show that they must really be able to form syntactic chains.[26]

It is important to distinguish between *interpretability* as a property of a feature, and whether or not an occurrence needs to be independently interpreted in a particular environment. Clearly, the person feature is interpretable. But not every occurrence makes an independent contribution to interpretation. The reason why resides precisely in the interpretation person receives. For sake of perspicuity I will discuss person and number separately here. Crucially, *unification* of different occurrences of a feature in a syntactic chain is allowed just in case the PRD is not violated.

For example, unification is allowed in the case of 1st person, since all occurrences of a 1st-person pronoun in one reportive context are interpreted equivalently. In Reuland 2001b, following Benveniste 1966, this was expressed by the inherent feature specification of person in (33):

(33) i.   [+speaker, −addressee] → 1st person
     ii.   [−speaker, +addressee] → 2nd person
     iii. [−speaker, −addressee] → 3rd person

Let us elaborate on this analysis, by bringing the interpretation of these features into play. (33i) represents an instruction to relate a 1st-person pronoun to a particular individual in the coordinate system of the context of utterance. (33ii) does so for 2nd person. There are various ways to make this precise in semantic terms, as for instance in Schlenker 1999, 2003, 2005, or in Anand and Nevins's (2004) theory of context operators as adopted by Kratzer (2006).[27] The crucial property of all these approaches is that they ensure that all occurrences of a 1st-person personal pronoun in one reportive context receive dependent values, and similarly for 2nd-person personal pronouns.[28] Consequently, the syntactic features representing the notions of 1st- or 2nd-person pronoun in different occurrences of these pronouns in a numeration are interchangeable, and can be unified without violating the PRD. To put it more succinctly, *ik* and *mij* in (31a) can form a chain, since no options for interpretation get lost. The same intuition is also captured by more syntactic approaches such as Baker 2007, where all occurrences of 1st- (and 2nd-) person pronouns are bound by an operator in C. Thus, 1st- and 2nd-person features are compatible with forming 1st- and 2nd-person pronoun chains.

What about 3rd-person in SE anaphors? In languages such as Dutch they are clearly 3rd person in some relevant sense, since they cannot have a 1st- or 2nd-person antecedent. However, prima facie the value of *3rd person* appears to vary among occurrences of 3rd-person elements, since for instance different pronominals can be assigned different referents. To see how the 3rd-person property can be compatible with *zich* entering a chain, we should be careful in interpreting the notion 3rd. It cannot be an instruction to pick out a particular type of value. But, in fact, the correct interpretation is already given in (33iii), since it is interpretable as a negative requirement: pick out any value that is not 1st or 2nd. This is indeed a property that is constant for all 3rd-person elements and that can be unified as one instruction when *zich* enters a chain with an antecedent.

Person and category are the features *zich* has. Our discussion has shown that these features are indeed compatible with chain formation, assuming that the regulating principle is just the PRD.

5.6.2 A Nonrecoverable Property: Number

The question is, then, what blocks chain formation in the case of 3rd-person pronominals? There are two prima facie candidates in the feature system, namely gender and number. Gender cannot be the sole feature responsible. In all Germanic languages and many other language types, gender contrasts in pronouns are limited to the singular. If gender were the sole factor responsible one would expect that bound *him* in **John** *washes **him*** and its cognates is out, but bound *them* in **The girls** *are washing **them*** is well formed. There is no Germanic language where this is the case (in fact I do not know of any language that has this pattern, but for present purposes the Germanic case is enough). Instead let's concentrate on number.

As discussed, the PRD prohibits deletion/unification where identity of interpretation is not guaranteed. As a first go, I will show that grammatical number as found in 3rd person represents a feature that resists deletion.

It appears that number contributes to interpretation in a way other features do not. There is a clear contextually determined component in its interpretation.

Consider an example such as *The times were rough. Men were betraying men (and women were betraying women)*. Whereas features such as category, person, and gender have identical effects on the interpretation of the two occurrences of *men* and even the contributions of the set expressions of the two occurrences of *men* are identical, the two occurrences of *men* may, even must, pick out different sets of individuals, with potentially different cardinalities. Hence, some factor must cause the interpretation of the two occurrences of plural on *men* to differ.

In a similar vein, if we have different occurrences of plural in the numeration, as in *The men felt them slip away*, *the men* can easily refer to a plurality of three, and *them* to a plurality of five. There is no way in which identity in size between the *men* set and the *them* set is established prior to/independently of chain formation.

Context dependence can also be seen by comparing the respective contributions of plural in *I saw no men* with *I saw men*, or in *Mary was wearing pants yesterday* with *Mary was wearing dresses yesterday*. Similar cases can easily be constructed for the singular, as in *A lion is a mammal* versus *A lion caught a snake*.

There is a further difference between a category feature and plural. We were able to give a general formal characterization of the semantic properties of the D-class. That is, we considered an element like *every* with a particular semantics, and then let the D-feature reflect the properties of the class to which it belongs. Thus, the formal feature and the lexical semantics are represented separately. In the case of a plural feature of a morpheme we do not have this split: *the morpheme expressing plurality* appears to be all we have.

Consider again the role of number in 1st- and 2nd-person plurals. Here, the recoverability of person discussed in the previous section carries over to number, since it is intrinsically linked to the interpretation of person (what Reuland 2001b calls *inherent*). To see this, again consider (33), repeated here, and let [−speaker, −addressee] abbreviate as [other].

(33) i.   [+speaker, −addressee] → 1st person
     ii. [−speaker, +addressee] → 2nd person
     iii. [−speaker, −addressee] → 3rd person

Now, (i) is an inherent singular, but another possible feature combination [+speaker, +addressee] yields a plural: inclusive *we*. This is not "the plural of" *I*. Plurality is determined by the lexical feature composition, not grammatically marked. Exclusive *we* is [+speaker, +other]. Plurality follows from the lexical features and is not an optional grammatical feature.

Following Benveniste 1966, I assume that [−speaker, +addressee] is inherently singular, or unmarked for number. An inherently plural 2nd person can be specified as [+adressee, +[other]]. (Note that this specification is structured, hence no contradiction between positive and negative atomic feature values arises.) Thus, it is not only the person feature that receives a constant interpretation, but the combination person/number. Saying that number is inherent in 1st- and 2nd-person pronouns is equivalent to saying that person and number together are determined by the coordinates of the utterance.[29]

Number is not determined by the values [−speaker, −addressee] for 3rd person in (iii). Therefore, for 3rd-person pronouns number is an independent grammatical feature with the effect on interpretation sketched.

On the basis of these considerations there is no direct evidence for an independent role of gender features in blocking chain formation.[30]

Even from our present perspective, it need not be the case that the presence of a number-related morpheme in 3rd-person pronominals always blocks chain formation. For this, however, it is a prerequisite that its interpretation is not in the domain of number. This may be the case, for instance, if it does not participate in a number contrast. One may well argue that a formal singular marking of an element that is compatible with all number interpretations means that its contribution to interpretation is at the level of abstraction we discussed for category features.

This issue connects to a very interesting fact about number discovered by Gertjan Postma (2004). Postma conducted a careful investigation of a corpus of fifteenth-century law texts, covering a period of more than a century in an eastern Dutch dialect. As is well known, the current Dutch anaphor *zich* originated from German *sich* spreading into the Dutch language area. In the older texts no occurrences of *sich/zich* exist. Instead, as in contemporary Frisian, the 3rd-person pronominal may be bound in local contexts. However, what Postma found is that in these texts no number contrast obtains in local binding contexts. The same— morphologically singular—form is used both with singular and plural antecedents. As time moves on, *sich/zich* emerges in the texts. And as it emerges, this goes together with the development of a number contrast in the pronominal it supplants in reflexive contexts. Thus, we have an interesting type of support that grammatical number is a crucial factor in determining the status of a pronominal element with respect to local binding. I briefly return to this issue in discussing the status of locally bound pronominals in Frisian in chapter 8.

Returning to the difference between SE anaphors and 3rd-person pronominals, there is a property that SE anaphors but not 3rd-person pronominals share with 1st- and 2nd-person pronouns. I have noted that different occurrences of 1st-person pronouns have identical interpretations within one reportive context, and similarly for 2nd-person pronouns. Note now that the same restriction holds true for free/logophoric SE anaphors such as *sig* in Icelandic. No such restriction applies to standard pronominals. This contrast will come up again in our discussion in the next section.

5.6.3 A Further Perspective: The Role of D

In section 5.6.2 I compared the status of a D-feature with that of a number feature. In the case of the D-feature I argued that one could give a general formal characterization of the semantic properties of the class of items carrying it. In the case of a plural or singular feature of a morpheme I argued we cannot. If so, overwriting it immediately leads to a violation of the PRD. However, we have to take seriously the possibility that the actual state of affairs is a bit more complex.

Hence, let us pursue the possibility that there is a general, context-independent, instruction for the interpretation of plurals, whereas the differences between the pluralities denoted are independent of the feature plural, and similarly for the feature singular. So, the instruction for plural would be *pick out pluralities*, and the differences we identified then reduce to the fact that there are many different types of objects in the interpretation domain, with varying structures, that satisfy the requirement that they are pluralities. Such a theory of plurality is not trivial. One instance of nonuniformity is sufficient to guarantee a violation of the PRD under chain formation.[31] The existence of *pluralia tantum*, such as *pants*, *scissors*, and so forth already presents a very down-to-earth argument. The very existence of such items shows that there is a significant context-dependent component in the interpretation of plural morphology.

What about singular? Although prima facie less obvious than in the case of plurals, a unified, context-independent instruction for the interpretation of singulars is also lacking. In generic contexts the interpretation of a singular may be equivalent to that of a plural. Singulars may denote individuals or groups, or—in the case of mass nouns—they may have cumulative, nonquantized, reference. Again, semantically such uses of singular are different. Consequently, different occurrences of a +singular feature in the numeration cannot be used interchangeably without affecting the interpretive options. Therefore, chain formation involving *singular* would violate the PRD as well. But again a possible alternative is that the feature singular is interpreted just formally (pick *singularities*, whatever they may semantically be) with the variability of interpretation located elsewhere in the system.

The logic of the analysis, therefore, requires that we should consider the following options: (i) number is the essential factor in 3rd person (that is, there are no general context-independent characterizations of singular and plural); (ii) the relevance of number in 3rd person is only apparent; there is a more basic property of 3rd-person pronominals that manifests itself in number, and in a factor F that is the real reason the PRD blocks chain formation. F would then be the factor that underlies the fact that the interpretation of 3rd-person pronominals is not restricted (given a numeration with *n* 3rd-person pronominals, they may receive *n* different values). If so, F may ultimately be responsible for the inescapable context dependence of the interpretation of singular and plural expressions, for lexical DPs and pronominals alike.[32]

As discussed in section 3.5, Longobardi (1994, 2001) argues that the referential interpretation of DPs involves N-to-D movement, while Panagiotidis (2002) explicitly argues for N-to-D movement in 3rd-person pronominals. If so, N-to-D movement in pronominals is directly linked to their referential interpretation (abstracting away from their fate in a bound variable interpretation, which is—crucially—not syntactically encoded). Pursuing this line of thought, the variability of the interpretation of plurals and singulars is due not to the plural and singular morphemes themselves, but to the way they are interpreted in tandem with D. What is involved, then, is not the general category feature D, but the particular element residing in D when it has a pronominal complement: an element encoding definiteness, a generic operator, or any other operator determining the nature of the object the pronominal DP picks out. So, rather than number itself, it is this operator that violates the PRD in the case of chain formation. In terms of the structures in (35)–(37) in chapter 3, summarized in (34a), it is the D-head in which PRON is realized that contains the content blocking chain formation. It is this structure, then, that embodies the referential independence of 3rd-person pronominals.

(34) a. $[_{DP} [PRON [D]] [_{NumP} \ldots [_{PersP} \pi [_{NP} \ldots t_{PRON} \ldots]]]]$
b. $[_{PersP} [_{\pi} SE \pi] [_{NP} \ldots]]$

SE anaphors have the structure in (34b), as we saw. They have no D, hence lack N-to-D movement. This, then, is the reason they lack the freedom of interpretation we find in pronominals. Their highest projection is person, which is an interpretive constant in one reportive context, hence does not violate the PRD if overwritten. If they are not bound—see section 5.7—they receive their interpretation from the sentence's center as a last resort, and are therefore sensitive to perspective.

5.6.4 Definiteness and POSS Anaphors

There is an interesting correlation, to the best of my knowledge not noticed before, between the crosslinguistic distribution of POSS anaphors and definiteness. Many languages have possessive anaphors, as illustrated in (35) for Icelandic and Russian:

(35) a. Honum$_i$ líkar   bílinn sinn$_i$/*hans$_i$
       her$_{DAT}$ pleases car   SE's/her
       'She likes her car.'
    b. Nadya vidit svoj$_i$/*eë$_i$ avtomobil'
       Nadya sees SE's/her car

In (35) the anaphors are in complementary distribution with the bound pronouns. Binding of POSS anaphors—and hence the ensuing complementarity with pronominals (see the next section)—can be straightforwardly accounted for by general principles of chain formation. The POSS phrase is realized in the left periphery of the DP-projection, and hence in principle is accessible for chain formation with the verbal functional system, unless some other factor intervenes. Triggering factors may be the unvalued features of the POSS anaphor, and the fact that the Case-licensing of the DP takes place via the D-system. Chain formation via the extended verbal projection explains that POSS anaphors are subject oriented.

However, POSS anaphors give rise to the following question:

(36) Why do languages as varied as Icelandic, Romanian, Russian, and other Slavic languages have POSS anaphors, whereas Dutch, German, English, Italian,[33] or Modern Greek don't?

Of course, one can say that it is accidental that some languages have POSS anaphors and others do not. But it seems that more can be said if we look at definiteness marking. Although for a full picture more extensive research in crosslinguistic variation is needed, the following picture is at least suggestive:

(37) *Definiteness marking and POSS Anaphors*
    i. Icelandic, Norwegian, Swedish, Romanian, Russian, Czech, Polish, and so on have POSS anaphors, and they either have definiteness marking by postnominal affix/clitic or no obligatory definiteness marking at all.
    ii. Dutch, German, English, French, Italian, Modern Greek, and so forth have no POSS anaphors, and they mark definiteness by a prenominal article.

Reconsider now Longobardi's schema of the internal structure of DPs given in (36) in chapter 3 and repeated here:

(38) a. [DP D [NUMP Num [NP ... N ...]]]
    b. [D [GenS [Num [H1 [S-or [M1 **H2** [M2 **H3** [Arg **H4** [GenO [NP P [SO ... N]]NP]]]]]]]]]

P in this schema is the source position of the POSS phrase. Italian—which marks definiteness obligatorily by an article—shows that there is a position of the POSS expression between the D and Num positions:

(39) Gianni ama le sue due macchine.
  'Gianni loves his two cars.'

It seems reasonable to assume that the obligatory D-position marks an impenetrable domain (leaving open whether this is because it defines a phase domain, or whether it causes a minimality intervention). Hence, an element in the position of GenS cannot be attracted by an element outside the domain of D. In modern Dutch POSS phrases and articles are in complementary distribution. DPs like (40) are evidence that here too the D-position is to the left of the POSS phrase; the same holds true for German and so on:

(40) al zijn mooie auto's
  'all his beautiful cars'

It suffices to assume that the D-position is also present in cases without an overt article, as in (41):

(41) [$_{DP}$ Ø [zijn mooie   auto's]]
       his beautiful cars

If so, we have a straightforward explanation of the fact that Dutch, German, Italian, and so on do not have a POSS anaphor. If it were in the language, it could not be attracted, hence not form a chain. It is interesting to note that in languages like Italian, French, and Spanish, the form of the POSS pronoun is an immediate descendant of the Latin form *suus*, which is a POSS anaphor. So, the form survived, but its use changed due to the change in environment.[34]

  The following contrast between Hindi and Bangla, discussed in Mukherjee and Reuland 2009, provides interesting confirmation of the relevance of definiteness marking. Like the languages in (37i), Hindi has a dedicated POSS anaphor in complementary distribution with the POSS pronominal:

(42) *Possessive in Hindi-Urdu*
    a. ra:m$_i$ ne mohən$_j$ ko us-ki$_{*i/j/k}$ kita:b di:
       Ram-ERG Mohan-ACC 3GEN.FEM book give-PAST.FEM
       'Ram$_i$ gave his$_{*i/j}$ book to Mohan$_j$.'
    b. ra:m$_i$ ne mohən$_j$ ko əpn-i$_{i/*j/*k}$ kita:b di:
       Ram-ERG Mohan-ACC self-GEN.FEM book give-PAST.FEM
       'Ram$_i$ gave his$_{i/*j}$ book to Mohan$_j$.'

Bangla, however, has no dedicated POSS anaphor and uses the pronominal instead:

(43) *Possessive in Bangla*
   ram$_i$ mohon$_j$ ke   o-r/ta:-r$_{i/j/k}$ boi   di-l-o
   Ram Mohan-ACC 3N.GEN   book give-PAST.3N
   'Ram$_i$ gave his$_{i/j}$ book to Mohan$_j$.'

Hindi has no internal definiteness marking on the DP (only ACC case indicates definiteness on objects); Bangla obligatorily marks definiteness. So, the Hindi-Bangla contrast confirms the pattern in (37).[35]

This concludes the discussion of the relation between features and chain formation. The main result is that we have shown that the question in (29)—what properties of a pronoun (SE anaphor or pronominal) allow it to enter a syntactic chain—is answered by the independence of the contribution its features make to interpretation.

5.7 Binding versus Logophoricity

I now return to the question in (6) about binding and logophoricity, repeated here as (44):

(44) Why is logophoric interpretation of anaphors blocked under certain conditions?

Let's consider the logic behind this comparison in the light of our previous discussion. The logic of the original Rule I is that the coreference option is blocked when the BV option with the same interpretation is blocked. The logic of Rule BV is that resorting to variable binding is blocked if CHAIN formation is blocked. In the case of logophoric interpretation the logic is different. Whereas Rule I and Rule BV compare two derivations with the result held constant, (44) asks a much more standard question: Why is it that an element of a particular type in some environments ends up chain linked to an antecedent, whereas in other environments it does not? The mechanisms of chain linking developed so far are purely syntactic. Hence, the blocking mechanism should also be purely syntactic. Note that *logophoric use* means being used as a pronominal (though with restricted possibilities of interpretation). (See Thráinsson 1991, Reuland and Sigurjónsdóttir 1997, and section 8.5.5 for cases where the "logophor" is interpreted as a bound variable.) What should be blocking pronominal use is the possibility that the anaphor can be interpreted in some other way. What should be blocked is the canonical way for such an anaphor to be interpreted, namely by CHAIN formation. This yields the interpretive condition (45):

(45) *Rule L: Logophoric interpretation*
NP A can be used logophorically unless there is a B such that an
A-CHAIN $\langle B, A \rangle$ can be formed.

Rule L also reflects economy, but economy in Reinhart's original sense,
given under (12i) in chapter 4: "Close an open expression as soon as possible." Since chain formation leads to the closing of an expression and is
available early in the derivation of the interpretation, this route is taken
when possible.

Given the mechanism described, whenever a CHAIN can be formed it
will be formed. Thus, whenever SE can be hooked up as a CHAIN link,
this will block any other mode of interpretation. Conversely, we should
find logophoric interpretations of SE, if and only if a CHAIN-forming
mechanism is blocked. I will now go over two relevant cases.

5.7.1 Subjunctive

A common view about the relation between subjunctive and logophoricity is that subjunctive extends the domain in which an anaphor may be
bound (or signals that a last-resort interpretation must be assigned). In
the present view, however, there is only one role the subjunctive can
have: it should block, for purely syntactic reasons, CHAIN formation between anaphor and antecedent.

Let's consider how this follows. It has been shown that subjunctives
(of the Icelandic/Romance type) are licensed by an operator (Manzini
1993).[36] Assuming this to be a morphosyntactic property of subjunctive,
this licensing relation must be syntactically encoded. Within the present
framework, encoding involves (covert) movement of the formal features
of the V/I complex (using I for T in subjunctives).

Consider, then, the structure in (46), with *OP* being the relevant operator and the verb marked subjunctive, and with overt movement of V into
I as in Icelandic:

(46) OP $[_{\text{IP}}$ Oscar $[[_{\text{I,I}}$ FF$_{\text{sig}}$ $[_{\text{I,I}}$ V$_{\text{subj}}$ I$]]$ $[t_{\text{oscar}}$ $[t_{\text{v}}$ $[_{\text{IP}}$ sig$\ldots]]]]$

Suppose *OP* attracts the formal features of the subjunctive. This may
cause the full set of formal features in the V/I complex to move to *OP*.
The resulting structure will then be as in (47) (omitting details):

(47) $[_{\text{OP,OP}}$ $[_{\text{I,I}}$ FF$_{\text{sig}}$ $[_{\text{I,I}}$ FF$_{\text{vsubj}}$ I$]]_{\text{i}}$ OP$]$ $[_{\text{IP}}$ Oscar$_{\phi}$ $\ldots$ $[[\delta]$ Vsubj$_{\text{i}}]$ $\ldots$ sig$_{\phi}]$

Irrespective of certain details of the execution, CHAIN linking will
be blocked. Under a movement analysis all formal features have been

removed from the V/I position δ between *Oscar* and *sig*. Under a copying analysis the copy δ that the moved V/I left behind is frozen, hence inaccessible to linking. Under either analysis a CHAIN between DP and *sig* cannot be formed as a matter of principle. According to (45) this opens the way for a free "pronominal" interpretation of *sig*, which is sensitive to discourse factors. This is what I set out to explain.[37]

There is an alternative derivation, with feature movement applying only to FF_{vsubj}. Since subjunctive is morphologically encoded on the V, it is possible for just FF_{vsubj} to move to *OP*, leaving the other formal features in the position of the V/I complex behind. (Note that the argument requiring pied piping in (47) does not apply here, due to the direct relation between V_{subj} and *OP*.) If this route is taken, *sig* is able to enter a CHAIN with the subject, and a binding relation obtains. Hence, in this case, one expects to find the usual complementarity between *sig* and the pronominal *hann*. This expectation is borne out (Sigríður Sigurjónsdóttir, personal communication).[38]

This procedure makes use of a very special property of the syntactic environment. As discussed in chapter 3, English has logophoric use of *himself* in environments that are entirely independent of subjunctive. The specific mechanism will be discussed in the next chapter. One would expect the same to be true for other languages. It must be emphasized, however, that what should be expected to be universal is not any particular factor blocking a syntactic encoding of a binding relation, such as subjunctive. Rather, what blocks syntactic encoding should follow from the nature of each specific encoding device.

Note that the present approach has direct implications for the issue of whether "V2"-phenomena in Germanic (V/T to C) fall under the LF or PF part of the grammatical system. If V2 were to fall under the LF part of the grammar we would expect logophoric interpretation to abound in root clauses of V2 languages. It does not. On the contrary, in many of them, which lack subjunctive, there is hardly any logophoric interpretation of SE anaphors at all. Therefore, with Chomsky 1995 I will posit that V2 in Germanic is a PF phenomenon. In the absence of clear interpretive effects of V2, this position seems entirely straightforward.

5.7.2   Nonmatching Antecedents

To derive that logophoric *sig* only shows up in subjunctive clauses, we have to make sure that in other environments there will always be a

DP that is a potential CHAIN head for *sig*. So we should derive that a logophoric interpretation of SE will not arise if the subject of its clause just does not match in features, as for instance, in (48):

(48) *[Ik [[$_{T,T}$ FFz [$_{T,T}$ FFv T]] [t$_{ik}$ [voelde$_{+fin}$ [zich T [wegglijden$_{-fin}$]]]]]]
     I   felt   SE   slide-away

Assuming that the verb will be correctly marked for 1st person, *ik* will check the verb's features, deleting them as it should. But note that in the relation between *zich* and *ik* we seem to face a dilemma. Clearly, no well-formed CHAIN can be established, due to the feature mismatch between 1st-person *ik* and 3rd-person *zich*. However, if no CHAIN is established at all, we might expect a logophoric interpretation of *zich* to be possible, an incorrect result. This is then one more instance of a canceled derivation in the sense of Chomsky 1995, 309. As discussed in the previous chapter (section 4.2), a canceled derivation blocks any less optimal derivation (Chomsky 1995, 309). How, then, can a combination of checking and Move/attract lead to a canceled derivation in (48) without incorrectly ruling out a sentence such as *Ik voelde hem wegglijden* with *hem* instead of *zich*?

The answer follows from the properties of the different types of features involved. FF$_{zich}$ contains a D-feature and a person feature (3rd person). FF$_{hem}$ contains the same feature and in addition a number feature (singular). (It also has a gender feature that we need not discuss.) Although these are all interpretable, there is a contrast, as we have already seen. The D-feature and the person feature are interpretive constants; both contribute to the interpretation in a manner that is independent of their position in the numeration. All occurrences of such features are interchangeable (for person features, at least within one reportive context), which is why they can be shared, as required by the PRD when one occurrence is deleted.

This is not true of the number feature of the pronominal. Different occurrences in the numeration receive independent interpretations, hence the PRD prevents deletion. Therefore, in the *ik...zich* case there could have been a CHAIN if the features had matched (i.e., there is "almost" a CHAIN). In the *ik...hem* case there could not have been a CHAIN even if the features had matched. Hence, in the former case we have the effect of a canceled derivation, whereas in the latter case CHAIN formation is not even considered; there is no CHAIN, not even a canceled one.[39]

5.8 Maximality of Chains and Conditions on Chain Heads

5.8.1 The Issue

In this chapter we discussed the PRD as a condition on chain tails. Coupled with an intrinsic order of operations, the chain-forming mechanism entails that maximal chains will be formed. Given the mechanisms of C_{HL}, chain formation applies blindly, and if possible it cannot be bypassed. How far, then, can a chain be extended? One may assume that chain formation in general is sensitive to the locality conditions on grammatical operations. So, in principle the domain of feature chains will be coextensive with the domain of A-movement, as discussed in chapter 3. The chain condition also imposes a specific requirement on the head of the chain, namely that it must be +R and be marked for structural case. For ease of reference the definition of the +R property is repeated here:

(49) An NP is +R iff it carries a full specification for ϕ-features.

In chapter 3 we noted that the +R property has two sides. On the one hand it expresses a condition on morphosyntactic feature composition, and on the other it is intended to capture the semantic status of such elements as nonanaphors. As always, it is an empirical issue to what extent such a correspondence between two subsystems actually holds. Anagnostopoulou and Everaert (1999) show that Modern Greek has elements that are on the one hand anaphoric, and on the other can head chains as subjects of finite clauses. Amiridze (2006) shows the same for Georgian. As will be discussed in chapter 7, what sets these anaphors apart is that they are fully specified for ϕ-features. Hence, such facts just follow from the chain condition as formulated. But what happens if an element is not fully specified for ϕ-features?

5.8.2 SE as a Subject

It has always been a puzzle why, in Icelandic sentences with a VP-internal nominative argument, the latter cannot be an anaphor. This is so regardless of whether it has a logophoric or a bound variable interpretation. However, since, as I have argued, a SE anaphor is not required to have a binder, the same problem arises for nominative SE anaphors higher up in [Spec,TP]. We know independently that a possessive anaphor within a DP occupying a nominative position can be bound (Everaert 1990). Also, there is no general prohibition against anaphors in nominative position, as will be discussed in chapter 7 (Anagnostopoulou and Everaert 1999).

So, clearly some aspects of the specific relation between the SE anaphor and finite inflection are involved.

Suppose we have a nominative anaphor in the highest Spec-position, as in (50):

(50) [SE [T+V_{fin} [...]]]

This structure is ruled out, since SE, lacking number, will not be able to check and erase all uninterpretable features of V_{fin}. Hence, the possibility of a logophoric reading for SE will not arise.

Suppose we have a SE in nominative position in a construction with an expletive or a quirky subject, as in (51):

(51) [XP [T+V_{fin} [...SE_{nom}...]]]

The XP will in any case have checked T's EPP feature, which yields a dependency with the V/T complex. However, according to Taraldsen (1995, 310), quirky subjects never agree with the finite verb (for reasons that are not entirely clear but that need not concern us here); due to lack of features the same holds true for an expletive. Since other DPs in the position occupied here by SE may show agreement with the V/T complex, we find the following possibilities: (i) the V/T complex has a full set of φ-features (as in the case where a nominative DP would show full agreement). For convergence, SE must then check the φ-features (by covert movement); with SE failing to delete number, the derivation crashes as required. (ii) The V/T complex has a set of φ-features with default values (Chomsky (2001, 43) suggests that some unspecified reduction strategy may apply). If so, further deletion is not required, but we now obtain a mismatch between V/T's and SE's φ-features, the former being *reduced/impersonal* and the latter being *personal*. This results in a canceled derivation along the same lines as discussed in the previous subsection. Hence, neither a bound nor a logophoric interpretation is possible, and consequently, the structure comes out as ill-formed as required.[40]

In chapter 7 I will take up the issue again, and consider Greek and Georgian in more detail. This chapter will be concluded with a further perspective on the theory of encoding dependencies.

5.9 Agreeing to Bind

5.9.1 Background

As we saw, the notion of binding must be deconstructed into a C-I component expressing variable binding in general, and a syntactic component capturing locality (both as regards reflexivizing operations and as regards nonreflexivizing anaphors).[41]

To avoid duplicating (parts of) binding theory, C_{HL} should contain no statement specific to binding. Thus, the binding dependencies expressed in C_{HL} should be mechanical consequences of the basic mechanisms assumed to be part of it. The core question for binding theory in any of its specific implementations is *how to capture syntactic identity*. In our case the question became more specifically *how to do this without indices*. As is to be expected, the details of the grammatical mechanisms assumed will change over time as our knowledge of the system advances. It is, then, instructive to see what effects certain theoretical changes have had on our understanding of the mechanisms of syntactic binding.

The original chain condition from R&R that we started out with in chapter 3 has the advantage that it is simple. It has two disadvantages. One is theoretical, namely that the notion of an index it is based on is untenable. The other is empirical. Although the local binding of pronominals in Frisian could be accommodated on careful consideration, without leading to paradoxes with respect to the ±R property, the local binding of 1st- and 2nd-person pronominals could not, at least not without stipulating them to be ambiguous. These properties fell out, however, once we reconstructed chain formation in terms of checking operations and conditions on deletion.

Note that this is not to say that two nominal expressions receive the same interpretation if they have *the same specification for φ-features*. This is blatantly false, as is immediately seen in canonical cases like *John expects him to be on time*, where *John* and *him* have the same specification for φ-features, yet must have a different interpretation. Rather, two nominal expressions have an identical/dependent interpretation if they have *the same φ-features*, where sameness of φ-features arises from copying into/overwriting values. It is this implementation that has guided our discussion since chapter 1.[42] A particular implementation is presented in section 5.9.2. The discussion in that section is technical. Its aim is to show that such an implementation is possible. However, it can be skipped without problems by readers not interested in the technical details.

Chomsky (2001, 2004, 2008) proposes that syntactic derivation proceeds in chunks—phases—and that the triggers for movement are restricted to the phase heads and their immediate dependents: the complementizer system with its head C and T as its dependent and the verbal shell with the light verb v* as its head and V as its dependent. The phase heads are the probes. The probes look in their local c-command domain for goals to

Attract or Agree with. A goal can only "see" a goal that is active—that is, that has at least one feature that needs a value. Thus, the syntactic encoding mechanism reduces to *probe-goal relations*. The crucial change is that there are no syntactic dependencies except those mediated by a head. In the barriers system, as we saw, the local head had to be part of the chain in order to ensure proper government of a trace in its domain. In a sense the head's role was secondary in the system. The main dependency was between the elements in the source position and in the target. In the "On Phases" (OP) system, phase heads play a pivotal role. It is their properties that drive the computation. (This property was in fact already reflected in the role of heads mediating chain formation reviewed in the previous sections.)

In the CBT binding was just a relation between argument expressions, as was the chain condition in Reinhart and Reuland 1993. In our exposition here, pronominal binding in Frisian provided the first indication that a structural dependency on a mediating head can be relevant for the syntactic encoding of binding. In the checking-based system that we subsequently developed, the role of heads became crucial in mediating the encoding of binding, allowing us to dispense with indices, and at the same time the system allowed us to capture the behavior of 1st- and 2nd-person pronominals without stipulation.

As we will see, the pivotal role of phase heads in the OP system leads to the discovery of the fact that binding does not always require c-command between the argument expressions involved, but that c-command by a mediating head may be sufficient. This would be an anomaly under previous approaches, but follows from the role heads play in the OP system.

5.9.2 Implementation

In this section I will pursue a particular implementation based on the theory of Pesetsky and Torrego (2004a and 2004b; the latter is henceforth P&T)—specifically, their approach to feature valuation as feature sharing, and their analysis of structural Case as unvalued Tense.[43]

As we discussed, SE anaphors such as Dutch *zich*, Icelandic *sig*, and so on are not specified for the features number and gender. They are specified for person. In section 5.2 I discussed various types of underspecification and concluded that SE anaphors carry number and gender features that are unvalued. I will take this to be "unvalued in the sense of Chomsky 2001, 2008, and P&T."

Consider now sentences like (52), using ECM for a context where reflexivity condition B is satisfied.

(52) *Iedere professional* voelde [*zich*   aan de kant geschoven]
     every professional felt   himself to   the side pushed

The question is how *zich* is related to *iedere professional*. P&T's framework makes the following specific claims about feature values:

- Both interpretable and uninterpretable features come as valued and unvalued.
- Agree involves valuation and feature sharing → a feature chain with one valued instance is valued and every feature must end up with at least one interpretable instance.
- Structural nominative Case on the external argument DP (EA) is unvalued T.

Consider now the more abstract structure in (53):

(53) [Tns [EA [v* [V SE . . .]]]]

A Subject-v*-T-dependency is established by the following steps:

- Tns's unvalued interpretable T-feature probes and finds EA's uninterpretable and unvalued T-feature → Agree → link.
- Tns's unvalued T-feature probes again and finds v*'s valued uninterpretable T-feature → Agree → valuation of T on Tns and Subject.

Note that the Subject-verb dependency is encoded without depending on "ϕ-feature agreement." On the basis of these steps C_{HL} expresses a dependency between SE and its antecedent mechanically under the following conditions:

- SE anaphors have unvalued interpretable ϕ-features in addition to unvalued uninterpretable structural accusative Case.
- v*'s (object) EPP feature probes and finds SE as a goal → SE moves to the edge of v*.
- Tns has unvalued uninterpretable ϕ-features.
- Subject DP has valued interpretable ϕ-features.
- v* has unvalued uninterpretable ϕ-features.
- The Tns-v*-DP T-dependency established in (53) extends to a ϕ-feature dependency.
- In the configuration Tns [uϕ], SE [uϕ], EA [valϕ], v* [uϕ], Tns [uϕ] probes and finds SE [uϕ] → Agree → link.
- The remainder of the derivation follows with the proviso stated that the T-dependency extends to the full ϕ-feature dependency.

A ϕ-feature dependency should not be computed independently since we have Tns [uϕ], EA [vϕ], v* [uϕ] → Tns's first probing would be successful, leaving v* unlinked. As in the implementation based on checking, presented in section 5.5, the φ-feature dependency gets a free rider on the Case dependency. Thus structural Case sets the process in motion, since only structural Case is an independent syntactic trigger. The T-dependency extends to the full φ-feature dependency, since only full feature bundles correspond to morphosyntactic objects that can be interpreted. The dependencies are summarized in (54), with EA providing the required valued and interpretable instance of [φ]:[44]

(54) $[\text{Tns}_{u\phi} [\text{SE}_{u\phi} [\text{EA}_{val\phi} [v^*{}_{u\phi} [V (\text{SE}_{u\phi}) \dots]]]]]$

To interpret this syntactic dependency as a binding relation, the following assumption about the format of Lexical Items suffices, with p the instructions for pronunciation, g the instructions for grammatical computation, and i the instructions for interpretation:

(55) a. Format of Lexical Items: LI $= \{p, g, i\}$
      b. Format of SE $= \{p, g, u\phi\}$
      c. Valuing SE $\rightarrow \{p, g, \text{val } \phi_{EA}\}$

After valuing SE, the "instructions for interpretation" of SE are *the same as* for the φ-features of EA. That is, importing feature values from another expression is a copying relation representing identity along the lines discussed. This entails that the dependency will be interpreted as a binding relation.

5.9.3 An Empirical Consequence

If binding of SE anaphors is syntactically encoded as Agree, it is expected that the requirement that the binder c-command the bindee is derivative of the requirement that the SE anaphor be a target for a (c-commanding) probe. Thus, one should find cases where the bindee can be probed by a relevant head, but its eventual antecedent does not c-command it.[45] As pointed out in Chomsky 2008, this prediction can be tested by considering sentences with a nominative complement of an unaccusative or passive verb that has not raised to the [Spec,IP] position (due to the presence of an expletive in [Spec,IP]). Such sentences may contain a PP that must have been merged after the complement and is therefore higher in the structure than the latter. If this PP contains a "subject-oriented" reflexive (R), we have the configuration sketched in (56):

(56) EXPL *Tns* [[V DP_{NOM}] [$_{PP}$ P R ...]]

Here the probe *Tns* c-commands R, but DP_{NOM} does not. Unlike the CBT, the present approach predicts that c-command by *Tns* is sufficient to allow DP_{NOM} to bind R. As shown in (57), Norwegian and Icelandic provide precisely such configurations. Binding is indeed allowed in (57). Hence the prediction is borne out.[46]

(57) a. *Norwegian*
    Det *ble*   introdusert *en mann*_i for *seg*_iselv/*ham_iselv
    it   became introduced a   man   to   himself
  b. *Icelandic*
    það *kom*   *maður*_i með börnin   *sin*_i/*hans_i
    there arrived a-man with children SE

The further steps in the derivation carry over from the checking-based implementation discussed earlier in this chapter (section 5.5 and onward). As discussed in chapter 4, binding of the corresponding pronominal is blocked by economy. In section 5.6 I discussed what prohibits 3rd-person pronominals from entering a chain. There I concluded that the presence of D in tandem with grammatical number prohibits chain formation. Forming a syntactic chain implies forming one syntactic object from two (or more) others. Syntactic operations may not lead to loss of lexical information, as reflected in the PRD. This principle must still be taken to be operative in the current implementation, since a pronominal could carry an unvalued Case feature, hence be visible, yet must be prevented from entering the chain. But being a general principle, it carries no particular cost. It entails that if β enters a chain headed by α, β may not contain any feature f such that f in β could be interpreted differently from f in α. The contrast between 3rd-person pronominals and 1st- and 2nd-person pronominals that the implementations in sections 5.5 and 5.6 allowed us to make is preserved. Within one reportive context, uses of 1st- and 2nd-person pronominals with the same number specification are interchangeable; *us* cannot pick out different sets of individuals at different occurrences in such a context. Hence, forming ⟨*wij, ons*⟩ ('we', 'us') or ⟨*ik, mij*⟩ ('I', 'me') chains does not violate the PRD. One unvalued feature—for instance, structural Case—is sufficient to make a pronominal object visible as a goal, although nothing much hinges on this, given the fact that syntactically linked and unlinked occurrences of such pronominals will never enter an economy evaluation—except under the conditions realized in English ECM.

5.10 Conclusion

By way of a conclusion we can say that the elimination of indices provided the impetus to reintegrate the syntactic part of binding with the core properties of the grammar. The notion of syntactic identity can be reconstructed in terms of check/delete or Agree and value, both restricted by the general principle of recoverability of deletion.

This chapter has been relatively limited in terms of material discussed—though not in theoretical coverage—but I trust it is easy to see from an account like this one that small changes in feature composition or small changes in structure may have considerable impact on binding options. Thus, where macrovariation is observed, it is the details of the grammatical systems involved that matter for our understanding.

Having resolved how syntactic encoding takes place, I will continue in chapter 6 with the questions posed at the outset: Why does language have conditions A and B?

6   Deriving the Binding Conditions: Encoding and Sources of Invariance

6.1   Introduction

At the start of our enterprise, in section 1.2, I raised the issue of what the possible sources of invariance in natural language are. In section 1.5.1 I observed that one may expect the following sources of invariance if one considers natural language as a computational system:

- *Type 1* Necessary properties of computations, modulo a medium in which they take place
- *Type 2* Economy of computation, modulo resource types and restrictions
- *Type 3* General properties of computations specific to language

Such invariants complement the invariants from other sources, such as conceptual structure, conversational maxims, and other properties of human cognition. If linguistic computations can affect structure only through properties of elementary items such as (formal) features, there is little reason to expect that computational invariants show up as "exceptionless" macrouniversals of the GB type. Only to the extent that macroconstituents and their environments do not vary too much in terms of their feature composition, may one expect that invariants at the computational level can be observed at the macrolevel as good approximations and tendencies.

This way of looking at things leads to a different perspective on universals. The traditional perspective on linguistic universals only considers type 3 invariants. But properly considered, it is a real question where invariants come from. The overall computational system has only very general operations. Hence the only plausible source of type 3 invariants is the structure of the vocabulary items, the type of features they contain. This brings the possible source of specifically linguistic universals very close to what is already widely accepted as the locus of crosslinguistic variation, namely the feature composition of the functional system.

From this perspective, then, macrouniversals such as the canonical binding conditions A and B are just tips of the iceberg, where interactions of lower-level operations become visible. The task we set ourselves in the first chapter is to develop an explanatory theory of binding that derives the canonical binding conditions from general principles of computations and the specific feature makeup of pronominals and anaphors. Fulfilling this task requires carrying out a program that can be summarized as follows:

i.   Provide an independent definition of "binding"
ii. Investigate binding possibilities of elements in terms of
     a. Their intrinsic feature content (only features that are independently motivated, such as person, number, gender, etc., not +/− anaphor, +/− pronominal, etc.)
     b. Their internal structure (pronominal, additional morphemes)
     c. The interaction of these elements with the linguistic environment (semantic and syntactic) as it is driven by their features
iii. Explain whatever appears to be special about binding—including conditions A and B and other (near-)universals—in terms of independent properties of the grammar

The previous chapters provided the foundation. In the present chapter the program will be completed in the form of two specific proposals. To this end the results from the previous chapters must be brought together, so I will recapitulate what we have achieved so far.

As discussed in chapters 1 and 2, binding as such is an operation in logical syntax at the C-I interface. However, locality indicates that there is a syntactic residue in binding. Chapters 3–5 showed how syntactic dependencies needed for binding can be encoded in an index-free syntax. The chain condition—governing the choice between pronominals and anaphors—reflects a general economy principle favoring syntactic encoding of dependencies where possible. Logophoric interpretation of anaphors was shown to ensue where a syntactic process for interpreting a SE anaphor or SELF anaphor is blocked from applying.

We came across many empirical reasons for a modular approach to binding, separating conditions on reflexivity as a property of predicates from the effects of conditions on syntactic chain formation. In both areas crosslinguistic variation necessitates developing analyses at a much lower level of granularity than before. Finely grained properties of computations are needed to account for the many facts about anaphor binding (condition A) that have been uncovered in recent decades, such as the contrast between simplex anaphors (SE anaphors) and complex anaphors (for instance, Dutch *zich*, Norwegian *seg*, Icelandic *sig*, versus Dutch *zichzelf*, Norwegian *seg selv*, and Icelandic *sjalfan sig*, to mention a few cases in Germanic), the role of reflexive clitics in Romance or Slavic, verbal markings of reflexivity in languages as diverse as Georgian, Telugu, and Sakha, and so on. Equally important is the logophoric interpretation of free anaphoric forms in languages varying from English and Icelandic on the one hand, to Chinese and Japanese on the other side of the spectrum. Also, canonical condition B effects show an unexpected amount of crosslinguistic variation; see the overview in chapter 1.

One has no choice but to either accept a great variety of idiosyncratic variation or else deconstruct the macrouniversals of the CBT. To do so, rather than stipulating that an element is an anaphor or pronominal with concomitant binding properties, its behavior has to be explained in terms of its morphosyntactic feature composition, and the way the computational system makes these features interact with the linguistic environment. In chapter 5 I succeeded in doing so for SE anaphors versus 3rd-person pronominals, for 1st- and 2nd-person pronominals (accounting for their distribution in languages other than English, I should note), and for the logophoric use of SE anaphors in Icelandic. Similarly, the properties of complex anaphors should follow from the properties of their composite parts. Deriving how they do so is what I will set out to do here.

It may be not too difficult to conceive of languagelike systems that totally lack anything like binding as defined, or syntactic encoding of binding dependencies. But yet, perhaps it is harder than one might initially think. In any case, it should be clear that such systems will lack a considerable part of the expressive power of natural language as we know it.

It is far easier to conceive of languages that lack locality conditions on binding. As discussed at the beginning of chapter 1, here the puzzle is the other way around. Although it seems so natural that *Alice stopped her* cannot mean that *Alice stopped herself*—perhaps as natural as the fact that the sun rises every morning—it is equally puzzling. Why would this be the case? To avoid ambiguity? But given the context there was no ambiguity to begin with. And, anyway, why isn't ambiguity avoided in *Alice saw that the queen put the cake next to her*? To mention a different issue, it may seem natural that **The king hates herself* is ill-formed due to a feature mismatch, an agreement violation. But if so, why aren't sentences like *Alice was happy that the Hatter invited the cat and herself for tea* as ill-formed? I have already extensively discussed this fact, its implications for BT, and how it can be handled by our condition A. But formulating condition A as in chapter 3 is not equivalent to giving an answer to the question of why it holds. Of course, it is logically possible that there is no deep why—that these are just quirks of natural language and part of UG as they are (see, for instance, Chomsky 1980a, where it is suggested that the "specified subject condition" is part of UG and as such innate). In this chapter I will show that something more can be said.

In section 3.9 we ended with the following questions:

- What is the precise mechanism for chain formation in an index-free syntax, and how do conditions on chains follow from general principles?
- Why is there a condition B? That is, why must reflexivity be licensed? What precisely is the relation between lexical reflexive-marking and SELF-marking?
- Why is there a condition A? What precisely is the mechanism underlying reflexive-marking by SELF?

In chapters 4 and 5 I discussed question (i) and resolved it. Furthermore, I showed that the solution is theoretically robust since it carries over from one implementation to another. I reached a conclusion (section 5.9) that can be summarized as in (1):

(1) The results about the encoding of interpretive dependencies based on feature checking/deletion carry over to more parsimonious systems, where Agree-based relations fulfill the role of syntactically representing identity.

This provides the basis for addressing the questions in (ii) and (iii). These are the main issues to be discussed in the present chapter.

In section 6.2 I discuss and answer the first of our fundamental *why*-questions: *Why must reflexivity be licensed?* (That is, why is there a reflexivity condition B?) At that point we will move to the question of how reflexivity is licensed. In section 6.3 I will further elucidate the notion of binding. This section will specifically focus on reflexive-marking, lexical and otherwise. In section 6.4 I revisit the notion of binding and present an interim summary. Section 6.5 focuses on two scenarios for deriving the binding requirement on complex anaphors (condition A), one for SELF anaphors and the other for body-part reflexives. Here I will achieve my primary goal and show that under general empirical assumptions the binding requirements for SELF anaphors and body-part reflexives can be derived without recourse to any statement specific to binding. Section 6.6 discusses what conclusions our results permit us to draw for a typology of anaphoric expressions.

6.2 Deriving the Binding Conditions: Why Conditions A and B?

6.2.1 Why Is Reflexivity Marked?
In chapter 1 I noted that crosslinguistically binding of a direct object pronoun of a standard transitive verb by its local subject appears to be blocked, where *pronoun* stands for an expression solely consisting of φ-features (person, gender, number), thus for *hem* 'him', *zich*, etc., but not *zichzelf*. (Binding is indicated by italics.)

(2) a. *DP V Pronoun*
   b. **Jan* haat *zich*. (Dutch)
      John hates SE (where ⟨John, zich⟩ is a chain arising from chain composition)
   c. **Jan* hatet *him*. (Frisian)

This prohibition is pervasive, and the means languages employ to license reflexive predicates vary from reflexive clitics to doubling, from verbal affixes to body-part expressions. Languages that do not manifest this requirement are the exception rather than the rule (see our initial discussion in section 1.1). This phenomenon must reflect a deep property of natural language.[1]

Let's call reflexivization by one argument simply being bound by another as in (2b,c) "brute-force reflexivization" (BFR). Why is it ruled out? In this form, the prohibition is a good candidate for being a language invariant. This issue leads, then, to the initial question of chapter 1: What are the possible sources of language invariants? In the next section the discussion of the binding conditions will be carried out against the background of this general issue.

In our discussion I will address the status of the binding conditions within the overall structure of the grammar from the perspective sketched. I will argue that at least one principle of binding derives from a type 1 invariant, a property that holds of computations in general. (If it can be maintained, this thesis leads to many further questions about the computations our brain carries out in other domains, which would carry us beyond the scope of the present discussion, but should definitely be pursued in one form or another.)

6.2.2   Condition B and the IDI

In addressing the question of what is wrong with "brute-force reflexivization," I will show that the core cases of condition B as formulated in
chapter 3 can be derived from (3) as a general property of computational
systems:

(3) IDI = inability to distinguish indistinguishables

The IDI is not specific to binding, and in fact not specific to language. It
instantiates a general property of computations. In language this property
is also manifest in the Obligatory Contour Principle (for instance, Leben
1973), or the antilocality condition on movement (see Abels 2003). It
involves the inability of the computational system of human language to
handle identicals unless the linguistic environment allows them to be distinguished as different occurrences.[2] More specifically, the reason behind
the prohibition of BFR is the inability of the computational system to
distinguish between occurrences of identical variables in a domain where
neither order nor structure is defined.

Consider again the structure in (4a), and two of its instantiations:
Dutch (4b) and Frisian (4c), where *zich* is a SE anaphor and *him* a
pronominal.

(4) a. *DP V Pronoun*
     b. **Jan* haat *zich.* (Dutch)
         John hates SE
     c. **Jan* hatet *him.* (Frisian)

In Dutch the dependency between the SE anaphor and its binder is
encoded in the syntax; hence, the violation is straightforward: syntactically ⟨*Jan, zich*⟩ forms one chain, hence one argument. By assumption
V is a two-place predicate that has to assign different θ-roles to subject
and object. Hence, at the C-I interface it has to see two different grammatical objects to bear the θ-roles (θ-criterion). There is only one syntactic object, namely the chain ⟨*Jan, zich*⟩, and a violation ensues. In Dutch,
therefore, a θ-violation is there "before" the C-I interface.[3]

In Frisian, however, no syntactic chain is formed between *Jan* and *him*.
Yet licensing is required as well as in Dutch. This entails that the violation must arise at a different stage of the interpretation process. This tal-
lies with our discussion of condition B in chapter 3. There, we saw that
for a number of reasons (notably, distributivity effects), reflexivity condition B must apply to semantic predicates. In all the cases discussed there
is no syntactic chain between the arguments involved. The claim is that
these cases follow from the IDI alone.

Consider, then, (4c). As in the case of (4b), V is a two-place predicate that has to assign different θ-roles to subject and object. Hence, again two different grammatical objects are required to bear the θ-roles (θ-criterion), and up to the C-I interface there are. The next step, however, fails. Translating pronouns as variables together with the definition of binding yields

(5) DP (λx [x V x])

(5) contains two tokens of the variable x. The claim is that due to IDI the computational system cannot read them as two objects. Consider the process giving rise to (5) in more detail. Translating *DP V Pronoun* at the C-I interface involves the steps in (6):

(6) [$_{VP}$ x [$_{V'}$ V x]] → ([$_{VP}$ V "x x"]) → *[$_{VP}$ V x]
        1   2   3

The second step with the two tokens of x in "x x" is virtual (hence put in parentheses). Although the representation in (6:2) contains two tokens of the variable x, these instantiate one object.

This is just as in syntactic movement chains in the framework of Chomsky 1995 and subsequent work. In a passive such as (7), we also have two occurrences of one object, one copy in the complement position of V, the other in the specifier of TP.

(7) John was seen (John)

But in (6:2) the two occurrences of x cannot be distinguished; in (7) they can. A standard way of defining the notion of an occurrence is by the environments of the tokens involved: two tokens represent different occurrences iff they have different environments. As stated in Chomsky 1995, *An occurrence of x is the expression containing x minus x.* In (7) the two tokens do indeed represent different occurrences: ____ *was seen John* and *John was seen.* But in (6:2) they do not, as one can easily see by the following reasoning.

Two identical tokens can only be distinguished if they qualify as different occurrences in the sense given.

The tools for keeping track are order and hierarchy. Purely syntactic hierarchy is broken down by the interpretive procedures at the C-I interface (eliminating any structure that cannot be directly interpreted, specifically X'-level constituents that are not *terms*; see Chomsky 1995). In this sense, the C-I interface is entirely comparable to the PF interface, where syntactic hierarchy is also broken down in the transition to instructions for the motor system. Since hierarchy is not available, everything else being equal the two tokens of x in (6:2) could only be distinguished as different occurrences by their order. The question is, is there order in the relevant stage of derivation? It is important to maintain a distinction between properties of the computational system per se, and properties expressed by the systems involved in the realization of language. In this view syntax proper only expresses hierarchy, but no order. Order is imposed under realization by spell-out systems. In the absence of order, if hierarchy is lost, the computational system cannot distinguish between the two tokens of x in (6) on our mental "scratch paper." Thus, due to the IDI they are effectively collapsed as represented in (6:3).

However, by assumption, the arity of the verb *haten* 'hate' itself has not changed. Thematically, it is still a 2-place predicate, with two roles to assign ($\theta 1$ and $\theta 2$), but in (6) it "sees" only one argument.

This is illustrated in (6′): If the two arguments of a transitive verb such as *haten* 'hate' are bound by the same operator, they are identified.

(6′) a. Alice (λx [$_{haatte\,[\theta 1,\theta 2]}$ x x]) + zich
$$\downarrow$$
  b. Alice (λx [$_{haatte\,[\theta 1,\theta 2]}$ x]) + zich
$$?$$
$$\theta 1? \ \theta 2?$$

If the two internal variables are identified, there is an indeterminacy about how the two thematic roles are to be assigned. This leads to the ill-formedness. This is, then, what a licensing operation—reflexive-marking—has to remedy. This leads us to one important type of parameter in crosslinguistic variation. While (3) is universal, languages may vary in the means by which they license reflexivity.

This reasoning equally applies to languages like Frisian, and also to our ability to handle the entailments of *We voted for me* discussed in chapter 3. One of the entailments in that case is *I (λx (x voted for x))*, which is ruled out for precisely the same reason: our mental computations cannot keep the two tokens of x apart at the relevant level.

In the above discussion, the source of the grammatical problem is that IDI causes a mismatch, resulting in a θ-violation. However, given the logic of the problem the issue is more general. In general, the output of the computational system and what is read at the C-I interface should match, as is also expressed in the principle of Full Interpretation. Hence, any position specified by C_{HL} should be readable at the interface. As we will see at the end of this chapter, the case of English complex reflexives in semantically intransitive predicates falls under the same rationale.[4]

The issue is, then, how to obtain a reflexive interpretation while avoiding brute-force reflexivization. There are two options:

i. Make the argument structure compatible with this effect of IDI. This requires applying a lexical or syntactic reduction operation on the argument structure. That is, the *valence reduction* is independently licensed.

ii. Keep the two arguments formally distinct by *protecting a variable*.[5] This, as we will see, is the role of SELF elements, body parts, and so on.

The next section addresses these licensing strategies in turn.[6]

6.3 Licensing Reflexivity

The question is, then, what means natural language has to license valence reduction. It will be shown that no mechanisms and assumptions are needed that are specific to binding. Whatever is needed falls under a general theory of operations on argument structure.

For the discussion I will take lexical reflexivity as my starting point. This is an important component in any theory of reflexivization, which was left implicit in Reinhart and Reuland 1993. Note that it is not necessary that the property of being "lexically reflexive" stems from one source. As always, a particular phenomenon at the observational level may result from a number of different factors. The approach in R&R abstracted away from underlying mechanisms, but in the present chapter I will specifically address them.

The view on intrinsic reflexivization that underlies the approach in R&R is that it involves an operation on the verb's θ-grid, along the lines of Keenan 1988 and Chierchia 1989. Whether reflexive marking by a SELF anaphor is needed depends on the formal properties of the verb's argument structure as expressed on its grid.

A rather widespread alternative view is that the relevant factor is not in the argument structure, but rather involves the conceptual level, the semantic properties, or the pragmatics associated with the predicate.

For instance, König and Siemund (2000) argue that the relevant parameter is "self-directedness" versus "other-directedness." Self-directed verbs take a SE anaphor when reflexive; other-directed verbs take a SELF anaphor. In this view, then, when the reflexive use of a predicate is "unexpected" in some sense, an intensifier is needed to express it. However, this approach requires an independent characterization of other- and self-directedness. Many verbs that allow a SE anaphor do not fit into this conception. It is impossible to see why verbs like *verdedigen* 'defend', *branden* 'burn', and *ontwapenen* 'disarm', which allow a SE anaphor, would be more self-directed than a verb such as *bewonderen* 'admire' that does not. Moreover, the issue of why an intensifier would enforce binding remains unaddressed in this work.

Levinson (2000) discusses a possible derivation of conditions A and C from condition B, based on principles of pragmatic inference. I will limit myself to one important point. His starting point is the idea from Farmer and Harnish 1987, 557, that the core condition B pattern follows from a pragmatic Disjoint Reference Presumption (DRP) to the effect that "the arguments of a predicate are intended to be disjoint, unless marked otherwise." Levinson proposes that this presumption in turn can be reduced to stereotypes about the world: "The prototypical action—what is described by the prototypical transitive clause—is one agent acting upon some entity distinct from itself." Levinson's idea is, then, that any statement that deviates from the stereotypical norm should be marked: "Agents doing things to disjoint referents is the unmarked expectation, any deviation being marked either by formal or pragmatic means."[7] Interestingly, if we indeed took the data at their face value, this generalization would already be violated in Dutch and many other languages, from Russian to Sakha. It is precisely the class of agent-theme verbs that easily allow the simplex reflexive, as in de *soldaten verdedigden zich* 'the soldiers defended SE', *het kind brandde zich* 'the child burned SE', or *het leger ontwapende zich* 'the army disarmed SE'. It is the subject experiencer verbs, which definitely do not denote prototypical actions, that require the more explicit marking. As Levinson himself remarks, this DRP does not generalize to those environments where the anaphor is required in cases of noncoargument binding, as for instance in raising and ECM constructions. These are typically the cases that fall under the chain condition in my approach. A fundamental problem for the pragmatic approach is the fact that certain languages appear to mark very little, as will be discussed in more detail below. While Levinson adduces this as evidence of the variability of linguistic constraints, he can only do so at the cost of ascribing to speakers of such languages a different, in fact underdeveloped pragmatics. As we will see below, such languages do in fact fall squarely within the limits of expected variation.

Ken Safir, in a range of important works starting with Safir 1992 and culminating in his influential 2004a and 2004b publications, regards "implied noncoreference" as the key notion. The notion originated in

Safir's account for exemption effects (see Reinhart and Reuland 1989 for some discussion). The idea is that "similarity" or "dissimilarity" predicates, such as *equal/similar/identical to*, require their arguments to be distinct, at the risk of vacuity or contradiction. Clearly, in Dutch such predicates all take *zichzelf*, rather than *zich*. The same happens in Scandinavian languages; see Bergeton 2004, discussed below. Hence, it would initially seem plausible to extend the principle to capture the choice between SE anaphors and SELF anaphors in languages where the contrast exists. However, this idea cannot be extended to subject experiencer predicates (*admire*, *know*, etc.), whereas the approach to be presented in section 6.3.1 accounts for the full range of facts.[8]

Veraart (1996) presents an interesting array of facts from Dutch that may seem prima facie puzzling for the present approach. She argues on the basis of these facts that the core notions in reflexivity are *presupposed reflexivity* (always *zich*) versus *asserted reflexivity*, with either *zich* or *zichzelf*, depending on factors such as focus and stress, where in certain of its uses *zelf* is analyzed as an intensifier. But, again, properties of verbs such as *verdedigen* 'defend', *branden* 'burn', and *ontwapenen* 'disarm', do not lend themselves to an interpretation along the lines she discusses. More importantly, the facts she presents as problematic for Reinhart and Reuland 1993 are in fact easily accommodated once it is clear why reflexivity must be licensed and how it can be done. I will briefly come back to Veraart's facts in section 6.3.2. From her summary one can draw a very important conclusion, though, which cannot be sufficiently stressed: Properties of anaphors are determined by a great many interacting factors; an analysis based on one factor only is unlikely to give us the full picture.

Bergeton (2004) makes another attempt at an intrinsic semantic characterization, in terms of a contrast between *reflexive* (requires a SE anaphor), *antireflexive* (requires a SELF anaphor), and *neutral* (compatible with either). He again argues that the SELF of SELF anaphors is an intensifier, which is only necessary if the verb's semantics requires it— that is, if the verb is antireflexive. However, his definition of antireflexivity only applies to identity or similarity predicates (as in Safir 1992), and so on, but not to verbs such as *haten* 'hate' or *bewonderen* 'admire'. Consequently, Bergeton (2004, chap. 4) has to classify *haten*-type verbs as hidden neutral, which makes the theory unfalsifiable. Furthermore, there is no independent motivation why verbs with meanings such as *disarm*, *cut*, *burn*, or *hurt* should be characterized as neutral, although they allow both SE and SELF anaphors.[9] Finally, the role of SELF in enforcing binding remains as unclear as in the other approaches discussed.[10]

Interestingly, König and Siemund's original intuition that SELF is an intensifier is ultimately compatible with the analysis developed here, given a particular hypothesis as to what makes SELF an intensifier (see section 6.3.3). For the ensuing discussion I will take as my starting point the theory of operations on argument structure that was presented in Reinhart 2002.

As discussed in R&R 1993, Keenan (1988) and Chierchia (1989) developed theories of reflexivization as a process of valence reduction. Keenan (1988) and Van Benthem (1986) explicitly define the semantics of *self* as a function from binary relations to sets. In Keenan 1988 *self* is an operator that applies to a two-place predicate R (= a relation between atomic entities) and generates a one-place predicate over sets A of atomic entities, formalizing the interpretation of *themselves* in (8a), as in (8b):

(8) a. The girls admire themselves.

    b. REFL := $\lambda R.\ \lambda A.\ \forall x \in A\ [R\ (x, x)]$

Clearly, it is an empirical matter whether all reflexivizing processes in natural languages have the same semantic properties.[11] As we will see in section 6.4, certain languages may use structures with a different semantics to express reflexivity. (Given the logical semantics of the notion of reflexivity, this may seem paradoxical. The paradox will be resolved by making a principled distinction between structure and use.)[12]

The line of argument pursued here is that an operation similar to the one in (8b)—but crucially not involving the morpheme SELF or its kin—is in fact what underlies lexical reflexivization. This approach is further developed in Reinhart's work on thematic structure, as presented in Reinhart 2002 and subsequent publications. Reinhart's (2002) approach has been recently elaborated in a variety of works such as Siloni 2002, Reinhart and Siloni 2005, Marelj 2004, Papangeli 2004, and Vinokurova 2005, together developing a novel approach to thematic roles; the θ-*system*, the central system of concepts, henceforth TS. For ease of reference I will occasionally refer to these works together as the TS literature.

6.3.1 Operations on Argument Structure: The θ-System

It would lead me beyond the scope of this book to give a detailed exposition and justification of TS. Here I will limit myself to outlining its main properties. For discussion and justification I refer to the literature cited.

Its starting point is the following observation: In order for lexical entries to be linked to positions in the syntactic structures generated by the computational system (CS), some of their properties must be accessible to CS (for instance, transitivity, unaccusativity, unergativity, etc.). Yet, many properties of concepts are never relevant to linking or other processes of the syntactic computation. So whether some event is *fascinating* or *boring*, *threatening* or *appealing*, *fast* or *slow*, or shows other conceivable properties along such lines, they never show up in conditions on syntactic computations, however crucial such properties may be in other dimensions of language and its use. Hence what is needed is a principled theory of what properties of concepts are visible to the syntactic computation, a theory that captures the interface between the conceptual system and the computational system. This is, then, what TS provides.

Properties of abstract concepts need to be formally coded in order to be legible to CS.[13] TS, then, presents a system for formally encoding the information about abstract concepts the computational system—and the inference system—require. It has lexical entries (i.e., particular coded concepts), operations on entries, and merging instructions, specifying how a particular coded concept can be linked to the syntactic structure.

The information the computational system requires about a coded concept is presented in the form of *θ-roles*. All θ-roles are formally coded as clusters defined in terms of two binary features: [±c] (cause change), [±m] (mental state).

The feature +c indicates that the role is perceived as a sufficient condition in the sense of Shen 1985. The feature −c indicates that the argument is identified as not being the cause. If the c-feature is not represented, the causal status of the argument is (linguistically) undetermined (which does not imply that the argument cannot be a cause).

The +m feature reflects the mental state of the participant that is present in the relation 'motivate'. The +m feature entails animacy. A −m specification does not entail inanimacy, though. A cluster need not be specified for (all) features, allowing as a limiting case an unspecified cluster.[14]

The linguistic properties of Verbs (i.e., *n*-place predicates) are, then, encoded in terms of feature clusters visible to both the syntax and semantics. For instance, the verb *anger* as in *the mistake angered John* is encoded in such a way that the notion of causation is expressed on the first argument and the notion of mental involvement on the second argument, yielding ([+c], [−c+m]). The coding of a verb like *eat* as in *John ate an apple* must reflect that the first argument—being an agent—expresses both causation and mental involvement, and the second argument expresses neither, as in ([+c+m], [−c−m]). It is important to note that TS

presupposes an independent analysis of the semantic properties of a concept. The empirical claim is that what is readable to the CS coincides with
the results of this analysis in the c- and m-dimensions.

Reinhart proposes an explicit notation to generalize over feature clusters and their properties, which, for ease of reference, I give in (9):

(9) *Notation*
    [α] = Feature cluster α
    /α = Feature (and value) α (e.g., the feature /+m occurs in the
           clusters [+c+m], [−c+m], and [+m])
    [/α] = A cluster one of whose features is /α (e.g., [/−c] clusters are
           [−c+m], [−c−m], and [−c])
    [+] = A cluster all of whose features have the value +
    [−] = A cluster all of whose features have the value −

The characterization of a verb's thematic properties in terms of feature
clusters determines how it is linked to the syntactic structure. How this is
done, is made explicit in the following linking rules:

(10) *Marking procedures*
    Given an *n*-place verb-entry, $n > 1$,
    a. Mark a [−] cluster with index 2.[15]
    b. Mark a [+] cluster with index 1.
    c. If the entry includes both a [+] cluster and a fully specified
       [/α, /−c], mark the verb[16] with the ACC feature.[17]

(11) *Merging instructions*
    a. When nothing rules this out, merge an argument externally.[18]
    b. An argument realizing a cluster marked 2 merges internally; an
       argument with a cluster marked 1 merges externally.

A simple example of a transitive derivation is given in (12):

(12) *Transitive derivations*
    a. Max ate an apple.
    b. Base entry: *eat* ([+c+m], [−c−m])
    c. Marking: *eat*$_{\mathrm{acc}}$ ([+c+m]$_1$, [−c−m]$_2$)
    d. Merging: By (11b), ([+c+m]$_1$) merges externally, ([−c−m]$_2$)
                merges internally.

What makes the θ-system important for the discussion here is its thesis of
the *active lexicon*. This thesis provides a principled perspective on the
notion of lexical reflexivity that underlies the contrast between lexical
and syntactic reflexive-marking discussed in chapter 3. The notion of an

active lexicon acknowledges the existence of operations that take place on verbal concepts in the lexicon "before" their insertion into syntactic structure, thus making it possible to express the relatedness between verb forms by rules applying to their argument structure.

One of the core principles of TS is then the lexicon uniformity hypothesis (LUH):

(13) *Lexicon uniformity hypothesis*
Each verb concept corresponds to one lexical entry with one thematic structure. The various thematic forms of a given verb are derived by lexicon operations from one thematic structure.

Such lexical operations typically affect the arity of a verb concept. For instance, the unaccusative form in (14b) is related to the basic transitive form in (14a). (15a) is related to (15b), (16a) to (16b).

(14) a. Peter melted the ice.
b. The ice melted.

(15) a. Peter opened the door.
b. The door opened.

(16) a. The news worried *(John).
b. John worried (about the news).

There are three types of arity changing operations in TS: valence reduction, saturation, and entry-changing operations, which I will discuss in turn. These operations all apply on verbal concepts with feature clusters. The clusters may have to meet specific conditions. For instance, valence reduction can apply only in a two-(or more)-place entry one of whose roles is external (a [+] cluster). *Valence reduction* takes place in the form of reduction of the internal role or the external role. Internal role reduction is involved in lexical reflexivization. If the internal role is reduced, no internal argument can be projected. Typical examples are verbs such as English *wash* and *shave* and their cognates in other languages. As discussed in chapter 3, such verbs have to be listed in the lexicon with two entries, a true transitive entry—requiring SELF-marking if used reflexively—and an inherently reflexive entry—requiring no special marking. In the absence of further analysis, the postulation of such dual entries may prima facie look like a stipulation, even if there is independent empirical justification. In TS, however, their existence is predicted. If valence reduction is a linguistic operation, one expects the existence of both reduced and nonreduced entries. Note that if the internal argument position is reduced, this says nothing about the θ-role that would otherwise be assigned to the argument associated with that position. The semantic effect is that the θ-role that would otherwise go to the internal argument is bundled with the θ-role for the external argument. The latter then receives a composite θ-role.

Internal role reduction is illustrated in (17):

(17) *Internal reduction/bundling*
    a. $V_{acc}(\theta_1, \theta_2) \rightarrow R_s(V) (\theta_{1,2})$ (where $\theta_{1,2}$—also written as $[\theta_1 - \theta_2]$
       —stands for the bundling of θ_1 and θ_2)
    b. $R_s(V) (\theta_{1,2}) \leftrightarrow \theta_{1,2} (\lambda x (V (x, x)))$
    c. $shave_{acc}([+c+m]_1, [-c-m]_2)$: Lucie shaved him
    d. $R_s(shave) ([+c+m, -c-m]_1)$: Max shaved

The marking procedures mark transitive *shave* with the ACC feature. Yet, the reduced form *shaved* in *Max shaved* does not require a direct object, not even an expletive one. Case theory, therefore, implies that along with bundling/reduction, the case properties of *shave* are also affected. Internal role reduction, then, also eliminates the case requirement of the verb. Below I will present more discussion of this property and will show that it requires some qualification, but for the moment this will do.

I also illustrate external role reduction as it applies to the verbal concepts *open* and *worry*, although it will not play a significant role in our further discussion:

(18) *Expletivization: Reduction of an external [+c] role (semantically null function)*
    a. $V_{acc}(\theta_{1[+c]}, \theta_2) \rightarrow R_e V(\theta_2)$
    b. $R_e(V) (\theta_2) = V(\theta_2)$
    c. $open_{acc}([+c], [-c-m]) \rightarrow R_e(open)[-c-m]$
    d. $worry_{acc}([+c], [-c+m]) \rightarrow R_e(worry)[-c+m]$

Saturation involves "variable binding." A position in the argument structure of a lexical item is bound by an operator—for instance, the existential operator or a generic operator. Once saturation has applied to a position in the argument structure, the corresponding θ-role is unavailable for syntactic purposes, although it is still semantically active. A canonical example is passivization, where saturation existentially closes the external argument of a verb.

(19) a. $wash (\theta_1, \theta_2)$
    b. $\exists x (wash (x, \theta_2))$
      Max was washed $\leftrightarrow \exists x (x$ washed Max$)$

For completeness' sake, note that reduction and saturation are exclusive. Only one of them can apply to a lexical entry.

As we will see in more detail below, operations leading to bundling or saturation of θ-roles can take place not only in the lexicon but also in syntax. Such operations do not change concepts. They only change the way concepts are lexically and syntactically realized. In addition to operations that only affect the realization of a verbal concept relatively superficially, one can also conceive of lexical elements whose relatedness can only be expressed by rules that affect θ-clusters—and hence the conceptual structure underlying them—in a deeper way.

Role-changing operations are rules of the latter type.[19] Consider the relation between (20a) and (20b), or (21a) and (21b):

(20) a. The dog walked.
     b. Mary walked the dog.

(21) a. The horse jumped.
     b. The rider jumped the horse over the fence.

Whereas the dog in the *dog walked* is a sufficient causal condition, it is not in *Mary walked the dog*. One step in the derivation must be that of adding an agent, but in order to correctly represent the causal relationships in addition the original external role of *walk* should be decausativized. So, in changing the verbal concept of *walk* of (20a) into that of *walk* in (20b), two processes must apply: *decausativize* as in (22a) followed by *agentivize* as in (22b):

(22) *Lexical causativization*
     a. Decausativize: Change a $/+c$ feature to a $/-c$ feature.
         walk: ($[+c+m]$) $\rightarrow$ *walk*: ($[-c+m]$)
     b. Agentivize: Add an agent role.
         walk: ($[-c+m]$) $\rightarrow$ *walk*: ($[+c+m], [-c+m]$)

This type of process is different from the ones discussed earlier, not only since it adds a role, but also since one of the clusters undergoes a change in content: from $[+c+m]$ to $[-c+m]$. Note that such a change is not intrinsic to causativization processes by themselves. Notably, no such change is implied in syntactic causativization as in *Mary let the dog walk* or *Mary made the dog walk*.

This contrast between lexical and syntactic causativization reflects a fundamental difference between the two: *role-changing operations can only take place in the lexicon*. This general condition is stated in the lexicon interface guideline.

(23) *The Lexicon interface guideline*
The syntactic component cannot manipulate θ-grids: Elimination, modification, or addition of a θ-role are illicit in syntax.

As is argued in Reinhart 2002 and the subsequent TS literature, arity operations may apply in the lexicon or in the syntax. This is the lexicon-syntax parameter given in (24) (Reinhart and Siloni 2005):

(24) *The lex-syn parameter*
UG allows thematic arity operations to apply in the lexicon or in the syntax.

Clitic languages such as Romance and a number of Slavic languages have this parameter set to syntax. Dutch, English, and Scandinavian, but also Russian, have a lexicon setting. Given the general organization of the grammar, in which the lexicon feeds the syntax but not vice versa, it follows that in lexicon languages arity operation can feed lexical operations such as nominalization, but not in syntax languages. Given the lexicon interface guideline, arity operations on the syntax side cannot be role changing. Conversely, in a lexicon language an arity operation cannot affect a structure that only arises as the result of a syntactic operation.

Marelj (2004) offers extensive motivation for the lexicon-syntax parameter on the basis of crosslinguistic variation in middle formation, which provides an important set of diagnostics for the classification of a language as being a syntax or a lexicon language (the hypothesis is that the parameter is set uniformly for all operations on argument structure).[20] Here I will focus on reflexivization.

As noted, language such as Dutch and English are lexicon languages. Verbs allowing lexical reflexivization form a restricted class. In English, for instance we have (25a), but not (25b) or (25c):

(25) a. John shaved.
     b. *John defended.
     c. *John hated.

So, the process of (27) deriving the reduced *shave* from transitive *shave* should be prevented from applying to *defend* or *hate*. A first approximation is that the class of verb in English allowing reduction is that of grooming verbs; however, so far no characterization of this class in terms of a restriction on θ-clusters has been found. Consequently, for the moment this property has to be encoded as a lexical idiosyncrasy.

In Dutch the class of lexical reflexives should coincide with the *zich* class. The pattern is given in (26):

(26) a. Jan scheerde zich(zelf)/*scheerde.
　　　　'Jan shaved himself.'
　　b. Jan verdedigde zich(zelf)/*verdedigde.
　　　　'Jan defended himself.'
　　c. Jan haatte zich*(zelf)/*haatte.
　　　　'Jan hated himself.'

But, first of all, the question comes up of why we have *zich* at all. As briefly discussed at the beginning of this section, the contrast between English and Dutch indicates that the effect of reducing the internal argument on the verb's Case feature may differ. In Dutch, unlike in English, reduction leaves a residual Case. This Case residue is then checked by *zich*, which therefore effectively functions as an expletive rather than an argument here. In Dutch, as in English, reduction must be prevented from applying to *hate*-type verbs. As discussed in Reinhart and Siloni 2005, crosslinguistically the set of verbs in lexicon languages that allow bundling is limited to a subset of the set of agent-theme verbs. They leave open the nature of this restriction. Pending an explanation, in a lexicon language it is always possible to encode *whether or not bundling may apply* as a lexical property. However, more can be said.

Lemmen (2005) provides an extensive survey of Dutch verbs. The patterns she finds indicate that there is more regularity there than one might initially think. Although for an understanding of these patterns across all verb classes more research is needed, she shows that the Dutch agent-theme verbs that do not allow bundling reflect an independent lexical condition, namely *conceptual coherence*.

The factor coherence is illustrated on the basis of a verb like *aanrijden* 'crash into' (by car). A sentence like *John reed zich aan* 'John crashed into SE' is entirely unacceptable. Its unacceptability is of a different nature than the strangeness of *John reed zichzelf aan*. This difference reflects a linguistic contrast. The latter sentence involves *predicating identity* of the arguments, but, crucially, not bundling. It either denotes an impossible event—which is of course not to be blocked by linguistic means, because language is able to describe hallucinations and other impossible states of affairs, or it can be interpreted by assigning the anaphor a "proxy reading." A proxy reading is available for *zichzelf*, but not for *zich* (more on this type of interpretation will follow in section 6.5).

Why, then, can't the same happen in the *zich* case? The reason is that bundling is a lexical operation in Dutch and that applying it here would give rise to an impossible/incoherent concept. The claim is that although language has the means to express impossible events and situations, it cannot form incoherent concepts. Only the linguistic computation can combine elements in such a way that incoherence results. Thus, a lexicon operation is constrained by a *ban on incoherence*, but a syntax operation is not.[21]

This raises a new perspective on the source of the lexical restrictions on bundling. We can now say that all [+c+m], [−c−m] verbs—modulo the ban on incoherence—allow lexical bundling. It is striking that these are the maximally different θ-clusters. This can be interpreted as another reflex of IDI: *Easy bundling takes place where the feature specifications of the clusters are maximally distinct,* so bundling causes no interference between the values of the roles that are being bundled. Typical verbs that never allow lexical bundling are [+m], [−c−m] verbs like *hate*. The fact that these clusters are nondistinct on the c-value, then, is expected to cause interference when the clusters are being interpreted after bundling. So we have an explanation for one more puzzling fact that follows from the theory developed.

Just as Romance and Serbo-Croatian have syntactic middles (Marelj 2004), they also have a syntactic arity operation for reflexives. The trigger for the operation is the reflexive clitic (as in middles). The operation is defined as follows, slightly varying Reinhart and Siloni 2005, 404 (henceforth R&S):

(27) *Reflexivization in syntax*
   a. Case: Case is reduced by the appropriate morphology (such as the clitic *se*).
   b. Bundling: Operation (c) applies to unassigned θ-roles on merger of the argument for the external θ-role.
   c. $[\theta_i] [\theta_j] \rightarrow [\theta_i - \theta_j]$, where θ_i is an external θ-role

Systematic differences are predicted between reflexivization in lexicon languages and syntax languages (just like there are in middles).

To summarize: Lexical reflexivization is predicted to be lexically restricted, to be sensitive to the ban on incoherence, and to be able to feed lexical operations but unable to be fed by syntactic operations. Syntactic reflexivization is predicted to be productive and not sensitive to the ban on incoherence, and to be unable to feed lexical operations but able to be fed by syntactic operations.[22]

As R&S (2005, 409) show, there are reflexive nominalizations in lexicon languages (Hebrew *hitraxcut* 'self-washing') but not in syntax languages; agent nominals allow a reflexive interpretation in English (*Jean is an elegant dresser*), but not in French (*Jean est un excellent habillleur* is only possible as a dresser of others). And by and large the lexical restrictions found on reflexives with *zich* in Dutch are not matched by similar restrictions in syntax languages. For instance, in French, one finds all of the following:

(28) a. Jean se lave.
      'Jean washes himself.'
   b. Jean se défend.
      'Jean defends himself.'
   c. Jean s'aime. (R&S, 410)
      'Jean loves himself.'
   d. Jean se dessine. (R&S, 410)
      'Jean draws himself.'

As R&S (note 17) point out, not all syntax languages are as free as French in allowing reflexivization with experiencer verbs such as (28c). Greek and Serbo-Croatian, and also Italian, are more limited in this respect. I will come back to this issue when discussing German in chapter 8.

As already noted, TS goes against approaches that subsume all lexical operations under syntax such as distributive morphology (Halle and Marantz 1993; Marantz 1997 and subsequent work) and Borer's exo- and endoskeletal approach (Borer 2003, 2005). This line of work limits all computation involving lexical entries to syntax. Borer (personal communication) raises the question of whether it would not be preferable, both from a conceptual and from a methodological perspective, to have a system in which all operations on argument structure would be of the same kind and all applying in the same component. This issue is reminiscent of the question of whether it would not be more parsimonious to have no distinction between binding and coreference in order to establish anaphoric dependencies. Clearly, as we saw, there are empirical reasons to keep them apart. But also conceptually, their status is so different that the issue of parsimony cannot arise. A linguistic system without the means for coreference is just unthinkable, whereas a system without binding can easily be imagined.

In the paragraphs above we have seen a number of empirical reasons for a contrast between lexicon- and syntax-based arity operations. These follow naturally from the TS framework and seem hard to capture in a framework that does not allow such a distinction. The TS literature contains a number of further arguments to the effect that a distinction between presyntactic and syntactic operations must be made, including an important argument against the bare root theory by Vinokurova (2005) based on asymmetries in nominalization versus verbalization in Sakha (see also Reuland 2010b). Most importantly, Vinokurova's argument shows that there is a deep-rooted difference between verbal and nominal concepts that is independent of the syntactic combinatory system. If there are differences between concepts that are prior to the combinatory system, one may also expect there to be relations between concepts prior to the combinatory system. If so, their existence may be as unavoidable as the existence of coreference relations in the domain of anaphora. As we saw, in the domain of anaphora the combinatory system may create relations that seem prima facie overlapping with coreference, but are in fact different. Similarly, in the domain of argument structure the combinatory system may effect operations that are prima facie similar, but are in fact different from what the conceptual system allows. Marelj's lexical middles versus syntactic middles form a clear case in point.

From this perspective, then, the open issue is not so much whether syntactic and lexical operations on argument structure can be unified, but how to understand their division of labor. Since this issue is not directly relevant to the discussion of reflexivity, I leave it for future research.

I will now start discussing some existing patterns of crosslinguistic variation in anaphoric systems, trying to understand what is at stake, and occasionally touching on more fundamental issues as we proceed. As we will see, the issue of lexical versus syntactic reduction also arises within Germanic.

6.3.2 From Lexical Reflexivity to Structural Case and Pronouns in English

The TS approach to reflexivity leads to a dissociation between reflexivization and argument binding in a strict sense—this was already implicit in the disjunctive definition of reflexive marking in chapter 3. Cases in natural language where a predicate is interpreted reflexively without the presence of a corresponding argument anaphor abound. In English we have cases such as (29a), we have (29b) in Sakha (a Turkic language spoken in eastern Siberia; see Vinokurova 2005 for a detailed analysis), in Modern Greek we have (29c), and in Hebrew (29d), to mention just a few pertinent examples.

(29) a. The children washed.
   b. Gosha suu-n-ar. (Vinokurova 2005, 325)
      Gosha wash-REFL-PRES
   c. O Yanis pli-thi-k-e. (Papangeli 2004, 46)
      Yanis   wash-REFL-PERF-3SG
   d. Dan hitraxec. (Reinhart and Siloni 2005, 390)
      Dan washed (*hitpa'el* template)

In such cases a reflexive interpretation arises without an argument being bound. As we saw, in TS reflexivization can result from an operation of valence reduction on a two-place relation, leading to the formation of a composite θ-role, as for instance, in (30b). The internal argument is *reduced* (eliminated), hence the relation reduces to a property, and the θ-roles are bundled:[23]

(30) *Reduction of an internal role: Reflexivization*
    a. $V_{acc}(\theta_1, \theta_2) \rightarrow \underline{R_s(V)} \, (\theta_1 - \theta_2)$
    b. V[Agent]$_1$ [Theme]$_2$ → V[Agent - Theme]$_1$

Valence reduction also affects the Case-assigning properties of the predicate. TS proposes that languages vary as to whether valence reduction also eliminates the accusative (e.g., English, Hebrew), or leaves a Case residue that still has to be checked (e.g., Dutch, Frisian, Icelandic, Norwegian). The question is then how this is possible.

TS takes a componential approach to Case modeled on previous analyses of partitive case (Belletti 1988), and quirky Case in Icelandic (by various authors, including Andrews 1976 and Sigurðsson 1992).

Consider for illustration the following pair of structures, where V_{fin} requires a quirky subject, as in (31a). If the same clause is embedded as an infinitive under a control verb as in (31b), the "quirky argument" is realized as PRO. This indicates that the finite inflection of V_{fin} does not *assign/check* Case, but rather *licenses* it. This contrast between assigning/checking a case and licensing it is brought out, perhaps even more clearly, in ECM contexts. As indicated in (31c), a matrix ECM verb that standardly "assigns/checks" accusative, licenses not an accusative, but the quirky case in the downstairs clause:[24]

(31) a. ... V_{matr} [$_{CP}$ [DP$_Q$ V_{fin} ...]]
    b. ... V_{contr} [$_{CP}$ [DP$_Q$=PRO að [V_{inf} ...]]]
    c. ... V_{ECM} [DP$_Q$ að [V_{inf} ...]]

In fact, such a componential analysis of Case is implicit in any approach that assumes that checking of structural (accusative) Case never takes place in complement position (θ-position), but always requires movement into the functional domain (varying from AgrO to a specifier of little v). Specifically, then, I will assume that this general approach is correct: Accusative Case-checking involves two components: checking a case that more directly reflects θ-assignment—thematic accusative Case, akin to the quirky, verb-determined cases in (31), and a structural Case-licensing component associated with the functional structure of the verb—specifically v* and the T-system (as in Marantz 2000).

If valence reduction reduces the internal θ-role, this is tantamount to saying that no θ-role is linked to an object argument. Consequently, whatever element is in the object position, there is no thematic accusative case it can check.[25] However, if Case-checking has two components, it does not follow from the absence of thematic accusative that structural accusative is lacking. The claim is, then, that in a class of languages (including Dutch, Frisian, Icelandic, Norwegian), the structural accusative is still there and has to be checked. As we already saw, (32a) meaning (32b) is not possible in Dutch:

(32) a. Jan waste.
        'Jan washed (something else).'
     b. Jan waste zich.
        'Jan washed.'

This is the role of *zich* when merged in the complement position of a lexically reflexive verb in languages such as Dutch: checking and eliminating the structural Case residue.[26] For a language such as Hebrew the claim is that with the reduction of the internal argument, not only thematic Case, but also structural Case is reduced. As a consequence, in (29d) no object is present.

What about English? Reinhart (2002) and Reinhart and Siloni (2005) conclude that *wash* does not carry a structural Case feature (or induce it on its functional structure) when its valence has been reduced. This is the reason in (29a) no object is realized. If so, we have an immediate explanation for the fact that grooming verbs such as *wash* do not allow locally bound 1st- and 2nd-person object pronominals. The fact that the examples in (33a) are ill-formed is regularly cited as a problem for the reflexivity approach:

(33) a. *I washed me, *you washed you, *we washed us
     b. I washed, you washed, we washed
     c. I washed myself, you washed yourself, we washed ourselves

Prima facie, this might be against expectation, since, as discussed in chapter 5, 1st- and 2nd-person pronominals can be locally bound, and many languages show this. However, the English fact trivially follows, not from any particular property distinguishing English 1st- and 2nd-person pronouns from their counterparts in other languages, but from the fact that the reflexive entry has no case to assign, and an object cannot be licensed anyway. Hence, for the reflexive entry (33b) is the only option. The paradigm in (33c) arises by the use of a SELF anaphor with the transitive entry. I will come back to this issue in the next chapter and provide more extensive discussion.

Languages employ many different morphosyntactic means to bring about valence reduction or check the residual Case. The structure in (34) represents a general format for structures involving bundling of θ-roles. The verb V is accompanied by a morpheme (Morph, leaving open whether it is a bound or a free morpheme). Crosslinguistically, Morph ranges over a variety of forms, including clitics, verbal affixes such as -*n*- in Sakha, -*te* in Modern Greek, -*Kol* in Kannada (Lidz 1995), -*sk* in Icelandic, *sja* in Russian, *zich* in Dutch, and so on:[27]

(34) DP V(-)Morph → Refl

It is not a trivial matter to determine what each of these realizations of the morpheme contributes. As we should keep reminding ourselves, a language does not wear its analysis on its sleeve. As soon as one encounters a structure of this form, it requires detailed further investigation to determine what role the morpheme plays—whether it is just a residual Case-checker, is instrumental in encoding the reduction operation itself, or does some other related job. Clearly, any explanatory binding theory and typology of reflexives that goes with it should be able to capture the various options. What is important for now is that the θ-system provides us with a general and independently motivated theory of operations on argument structure, giving us a clear understanding of one of the two licensing strategies of reflexives.

The existence of two complementary licensing strategies is beautifully illustrated by the following paradigm in Georgian (from Amiridze 2006). One licensing strategy consists of marking reflexivity on the stem (here selecting the *i*-stem of the verb "to praise"). In that case the simplex anaphor *tav* is required. The alternative is selecting the *a*-form of the stem. In that case the complex anaphor *tav tavis* must be used:

(35) *Georgian* (Amiridze 2006)

a. *giorgi-m_i   tav-i_i*   *ø-i-k-o* (simplex + i)
   Giorgi-ERG self-NOM   3BNOM.SG-PRV-praise-
                                 3AERG.SG.AOR.INDIC

   'Giorgi praised himself.'

b. **giorgi-m_i   [tavis-i tav-i]_i*   *ø-i-k-o* (complex + i)
   Giorgi-ERG 3REFL.POSS.SG-NOM self-NOM 3BNOM.SG-PRV-praise-
                                        3AERG.SG.AOR.INDIC

   'Giorgi praised himself [not me, you or someone else].'

  c. *giorgi-m$_i$* *[tavis-i tav-i]$_i$*   *ø-a-k-o* **(complex + a)**
      Giorgi-ERG 3REFL.POSS.SG-NOM self-NOM 3BNOM.SG-PRV-praise-
                                        3AERG.SG.AOR.INDIC
      'Giorgi praised himself [not me, you or someone else].'

  d. **giorgi-m$_i$*   *tav-i$_i$*   *ø-a-k-o* **(simplex + a)**
      Giorgi-ERG self-NOM   3BNOM.SG-PRV-praise-
                                          3AERG.SG.AOR.INDIC
      'Giorgi praised himself.'

  e. *mam-iko-s$_i$*   *ø-u-xar-i-a,*   *rom* **(locality)**
      father-DIM-DAT 3BDAT.SG-PRV-be.glad-TS-3ANOM.SG that
      ana-ø$_j$ *[tavis tav-s]$_{*i//j}$*   *kargad*
      Ana-NOM 3REFL.POSS.SG self-DAT well
      ø-u-vl-i-s
      3BDAT.SG-PRV-take.care-TS-3ANOM.SG
      Daddy he.is.glad.of.it that Ana self's self well she.takes.care.of.
      her
      'Daddy is glad that Ana takes care of herself/*him well.'

With this type of paradigm in mind, let's now discuss option (ii) from p. 189.

6.3.3 Protecting a Variable

The option discussed in the previous section comes down to allowing the verb's θ-roles to be bundled as in (36), thereby matching formal and thematic arity.

(36) DP (λx [x V x)])   → DP (λx [V x)])
      V (θ$_1$, θ$_2$) →   V$_{Red}$ (θ$_1$ - θ$_2$)

The other way of creating a match between formal and thematic arity is to have a structure in which the occurrences of the variable tokens remain distinct. Any embedding of the second argument in a structure that is preserved under translation into logical syntax will do to keep the arguments distinct. I use the term *reflexive-licenser* (or briefly *licenser*) to refer to the morphological elements used to achieve this. This, I claim, is the role of SELF in Dutch *zichzelf*, etc. and the role of *tavis* in Georgian *tav tavis*, and so on.

    The general structure is illustrated in (37a) and (37b); *zelf*, then, is a particular instance of Morph.

(37) a. *DP* V *[Pronoun Morph]*
     b. DP (λx [V(x, [x M])])

Syntactically all that Morph needs to do is to create an embedding structure for x, such that formally the expression serving as the argument of V
is *[x M]* rather than *x*. Since IDI also applies at the C-I interface, M
should make some minimal contribution to interpretation. Otherwise it
would (i) violate the Full Interpretation requirement, and (ii) fail to protect *x* at the interface. However, this is all that is required. Any M can do
the job as long as it is compatible with the fact that ultimately (37a) is
used to express a reflexive relation. Thus, the choice and interpretation
of M are limited by conditions of use. So, M must be interpreted so as
to yield a function of x mapping it onto an object that can be a proxy
for x. Conditions on use restrict the admissible proxies. This is stated
in (38).

(38) DP (λx V(x, f(x)))
     Condition: $\|f(x)\|$ is sufficiently close to $\|x\|$ to stand proxy for $\|x\|$

The condition in (38) represents a requirement of FIT: *An encoding
should FIT conditions of use.*

(38) is the proper logical syntax representation of cases where Morph is
a Body part, a Focus marker, an Intensifier, and so forth. There is a class
of languages, varying from Caxur to Malayalam and Old Syriac, where
Morph is morphologically a double of the pronoun. Note that it is important to distinguish the various uses of Morph, and again to distinguish its
use from its historical development. For instance, König and Siemund
(see König and Siemund 2000, as well as Gast 2006 and the references
given there) have argued that the use of elements such as *self*, *zelf*, *selbst*,
etc., follows if they are understood as intensifiers.[28] As noted, in many of
their uses SELF elements do indeed act as intensifiers (or markers of contrastive focus). However, by itself this is not sufficient to account for their
distribution, nor to answer the question of why SELF elements are used
in reflexives, and may enforce reflexivization blindly and automatically.
Under the current approach their use as parts of complex reflexives is
explained by the fact that their presence in the structure protects the variable, and that semantically they are perfectly well suited to meet the condition in (38).

   Informally, SELF maps an individual on that individual's *self*, yielding
an inherently reflexive relation. A moment's reflection shows that this interpretation is quite in line with use as an intensifier. (I am very grateful
to Anne Zribi-Hertz (personal communication) for prompting me to
think about the relation between these uses of SELF.)

Elements expressing sameness do readily occur as intensifiers—witness French *même* and Russian *sam(yj)*—and *même* also occurs as a reflexivizer. This suggests that rather than the direction expressed in (39a), which appears to be the intuition underlying functionalist approaches, we have (39b):

(39) a. intensification → reflexivization
     b. identification → reflexivization
        identification → intensification

That is, expressing the identity between an individual and that individual's *self* is a way of expressing intensification. One and the same basic lexical property thus underlies both SELF's use as a reflexivizer and as an intensifier.

For Malayalam the doubling element appears to act as a Focus marker (Jayaseelan 1997); in other languages (Caxur, Old Syriac) the way Morph enters the semantics has yet to be investigated, but note that a relatively marginal contribution to the semantics suffices.[29] As Schladt (2000) mentions, a language such as Zande realizes the reflexive argument in a PP.[30] If V and P do not syntactically reanalyze, this is equally effective:

(40) DP (λx V(x, P(x)))
     where the θ-role $\theta_{2'}$ assigned by P is sufficiently close to the θ-role θ_2 that V would otherwise assign to its internal argument, so that $\theta_{2'}$ can stand proxy for θ_2.

Further variation on this theme is conceivable. Any verbal morpheme that introduces a structural asymmetry between the two arguments that is retained in logical syntax will have the same effect. Also processes like focalization may have this result. I will discuss one concrete example since it is illustrative of the care that is required in drawing conclusions from binding patterns.

Veraart (1996) makes the interesting observation that in certain Dutch double object constructions, focalization of either a subject or a verbal particle may license locally bound *zich* that is ruled out in the absence of focalization. To establish her point, Veraart compares the ill-formed expressions **Henk₁ wees mij aan zich₁ toe* 'Henk assigned me to SE' and **Henk₁ wees zich₁ aan mij toe* 'Henk assigned SE' (discussed as (15a) and (15c) in chapter 3) with their focused variants. These focused variants are **Henk₁** *wees mij aan zich₁ toe, niet* **Paul** 'Henk assigned me to SE, not Paul', *Henk₁ wees zich₁ aan mij* **toe** *in plaats van ons uit* **elkaar** *te houden* 'Henk assigned SE to me, instead of keeping us apart', and *Henk₁ wees*

*zich₁ aan **mij** toe, niet aan **Paul*** 'Henk assigned SE to me, not to Paul'.
She observes that these focused variants are entirely well-formed.[31] She
also notes that, quite surprisingly from her perspective, such effects of
focalization do not obtain with all predicates. With verbs such as *geven*
'give', *aanraden* 'advise', *aanbevelen* 'recommend' the result of focalizing
arguments or particles is not well formed. Veraart leaves this contrast
unresolved. However, on closer scrutiny one can observe a difference
in argument structure between the two types of verbs: in the case of
toewijzen 'assign' the predication relation in the V-shell between the two
internal arguments is syntactically (mediated by the head *toe*) and semantically transparent: *Henk* caused *zich* and *me* to form a pair. In the case of
geven 'give' the relation is syntactically opaque, and in the cases of verbs
like *aanraden* 'advise' and *aanbevelen* 'recommend', any shell structure
is both semantically and syntactically opaque. The claim is, then, that
with *toewijzen* focalization brings out a small-clause structure.[32] Consequently, like in the case of other clausal complements *zich* is licensed.
Clearly, focalization can only have this effect if the secondary predication
is visible to focalization and is preserved at the C-I interface—thus contrastive stress on *toe* or *me* does not just focalize these elements, but the
small-clause structure they are part of. Hence the contrast between verbs
like *toewijzen* with a transparent secondary predication, and verbs like
aanraden that lack it.

What the variations on the theme of (ii) have in common is that the
second argument is always bound by the subject in accordance with
the definition of binding in (41). So, the two strategies indeed reflect a fundamental split in their status with respect to binding strictly understood.

6.4 A Note on Binding and an Interim Summary

6.4.1 A Note on Binding

As I stated in chapter 1, the core notion of binding I am using is Reinhart's (41a). This definition of binding covers both local and nonlocal
binding, involving "pronominals" and "anaphors," as in (41b,c):

(41) a. *A-binding (logical-syntax-based definition)*
       α A-binds β iff α is the sister of a λ-predicate whose operator
       binds β.
    b. *No one* even asked *himself* **who** would be happy after **his**/*his*
       dream girl married **him**/*him*.
    c. No one (λx (x asked x [who (λy (y would be happy after x's
       dream girl married x))]))

It is from this logical syntax definition that we "reconstruct" binding relations between expressions in syntax. So, in (41c) *no one* binds *himself* since *no one* is the sister of the λ-predicate λx *(x asked x ...* whose operator binds the occurrence of the variable *x* into which *himself* has been translated. And similarly, *no one* also binds the other occurrences of x in (41c); and again, derivatively we can say that *no one* binds *his* and *him*. Note again that binding of *him* and *his* in these cases is not encoded in narrow syntax.

Any form of "syntactic" binding is derivative of this core notion. Note, that this definition by itself does not set apart "reflexive binding" from other instances of binding. The notion of binding itself "does not care." This is notwithstanding the fact that the interpretation of the forms that are generally referred to as "reflexives" may not always involve binding, for instance *John washed*. But it could also be doubted that *himself* in *John behaved himself*, represents a variable in logical syntax. If it does not, *John* does not bind *himself* in the sense indicated.[33]

As we saw in section 6.3, Keenan (1988) proposed that SELF is an operator on predicates that turns a transitive predicate into an intransitive one, as in (42b). Keenan assumes that SELF is a purely grammatical noun. As discussed above, SELF does have some lexical content, though. Insofar as it has, the effect on interpretation is represented in (42c). Keenan's (42b) is, then, a limiting case of (42c).

(42) a. The girls admire themselves.
   b. REFL:= $\lambda R.\ \lambda A.\ \forall x \in A\ [R\ (x, x)]$
   c. $REFL_{SELF}:= \lambda R.\ \lambda A.\ \forall x \in A\ [R\ (x, f_{SELF}\ (x))]$[34]

In both (42b) and (42c), the argument variables of R are bound by the ∀-operator, and "the girls" can be said to bind "themselves" only indirectly.[35] As we saw, both binding as an operation on argument structure and logical syntax binding are realized in natural language. As discussed, there are more cases where a predicate is interpreted reflexively without the presence of a corresponding argument anaphor, see (29), repeated here:

(29) a. The children washed.
   b. Gosha suu-n-ar. (Vinokurova 2005, 325)
      Gosha wash-REFL-PRES
   c. O Yanis pli-thi-k-e. (Papangeli 2004, 46)
      Yanis   wash-REFL-PERF-3SG
   d. Dan hitraxec. (Reinhart and Siloni 2005, 390)
      Dan washed (*hitpa'el* template)

In all these cases a reflexive interpretation arises without argument binding in any strict sense.

6.4.2 An Interim Summary

Lexical reflexivization is an operation of valence reduction on a two-place relation, leading to the formation of a complex θ-role, as in (43b). The internal argument is *reduced* (eliminated), hence the relation reduces to a property:

(43) *Reduction of an internal role: Reflexivization*
    a. $V_{acc}\ (\theta_1, \theta_2) \rightarrow \underline{R_s(V)}\ (\theta_1 - \theta_2)$
    b. $V[Agent]_1\ [Theme]_2 \rightarrow V[Agent - Theme]_1$

Reflexivization is parameterized in two respects:

- Languages vary as to whether valence reduction also eliminates the accusative (e.g., English, Hebrew), or leaves a Case residue that still has to be checked (e.g., Dutch, Frisian, Norwegian).
- Languages vary as to whether reflexivization applies in the lexicon or in the syntax.
  - Lexicon: $V[Agent]_1\ [Theme]_2 \rightarrow V[Agent - Theme]_1$
  - Syntax: Upon merge of an external argument, a stored unassigned θ-role must be discharged: $[\theta_i]_1 + [\theta_k]$.
  - Hebrew, English, and Dutch, among others have valence reduction in the lexicon; the element *zich* in *Jan wast zich* is only there to check the residual case left by the reduction operation.[36]
  - French, German, Italian, Serbo-Croatian, etc., have "bundling" in the syntax. "Reflexive clitics" such as *se*, *sich*, enforce the bundling operation.

The upshot is that we can have *"Reflexivity"* without *"binding."* Neither "reflexive" *zich*, nor the "reflexive" clitics occur here as "anaphors" that are bound in the relevant logical syntax sense.[37]

Like in the case of reflexives, the interpretation of reciprocals depends both on a nominal antecedent, and on the predicate they are arguments of. This can be illustrated by the examples in (44) (Dalrymple et al. 1994, 1998; Winter 2001). (Note that the following discussion only skirts the surface. An extensive and illuminating discussion of reciprocity is given in Dotlačil 2010; see also Dimitriadis 2000, 2008.)

Reciprocals in general allow a range of interpretations, two of which are illustrated in (44), with their contrast represented in (44ic) versus (44iic).

(44) i. a.   The girls know each other.
     b.   #... but Mary doesn't know Sue. (Strong Reciprocity)
     c.   Every girl knows every other girl.
 ii. a.   The girls are standing on each other.
     b.   ... but Mary is not standing on Sue.
     c.   #Every girl is standing on every other girl. (Inclusive
          Alternative Ordering (Dalrymple et al. 1994, 1998))

How are these dependencies represented? (45a) serves as a formalization
of Strong Reciprocity (SR) and (45b) for Inclusive Alternative Ordering
(IAO). The reciprocal marker is defined as an operator that applies to a
two-place predicate R (= a relation between atomic entities) and generates a one-place predicate over sets A of atomic entities:

(45) a. $SR = \lambda R.\ \lambda A.\ \forall x \in A\ \forall y \in A\ [x \neq y \rightarrow R\ (x, y)]$
     b. $IAO = \lambda R.\ \lambda A.\ \forall x \in A\ \exists y \in A\ [x \neq y \wedge (R\ (x, y) \vee R\ (y, x))]$

For the sake of concreteness we may assume that the dependency on the
predicate can be represented in terms of selection: which operator interpreting *each other* does the predicate select?[38] This part, therefore, does
not involve A-binding. What about the dependency between *each other*
and "its antecedent"?

   If we carefully consider (45) we see that (again) there is no logical syntax binding of *each other* by its "antecedent." What (45) expresses is that
just like in the case of certain types of reflexives, *each other* reduces the
internal argument, bundles the internal and external θ-roles, and imposes
a particular structure on the set that represents the value of the remaining
argument. Thus, after the operator has applied to the predicate P the result is (46).

(46) a. The girls $(\lambda A.\ \forall x \in A\ \forall y \in A\ [x \neq y \rightarrow P\ (x, y)])$ (SR)
     b. The girls $(\lambda A.\ \forall x \in A\ \exists y \in A\ [x \neq y \wedge (P\ (x, y) \vee P\ (y, x))])$ (IAO)

We have a configuration in which *the girls* is a sister to a λ-predicate, but
no variable corresponds to *each other*. There are variables on which the
subject and object θ-roles of the predicates are realized, but these are not
bound by *the girls*, but bound by the quantifiers that are syncategorematically introduced by the translation procedure. Thus, the dependency between *each other* and *the girls* is not represented as an A-binding relation
between the reciprocal expression and its antecedent. So, although there
is an interpretive dependency between *the girls* and *each other*, from the
perspective of the analysis sketched above it makes no sense to say that
the girls A-binds *each other*.

This is different for the analysis of reciprocity in Heim, Lasnik, and May 1991. This analysis is based on a compositional interpretation procedure in which *each* and *other* play distinguishable roles. In their analysis (47b) is the fully semantically determined Logical Form corresponding to (47a). *Each* is semantically defined as a distributor of the subject set. The relation of [$_{NP}$ [$_{NP}$ *the men$_1$*] *each$_2$*] to the trace e_2 is that of bound variable anaphora. *Other* has its range and contrast arguments supplied by the subject phrase. Simplifying, the bare essentials of the logical syntax structure can be given as in (47c), where *other* maps x onto a value of the subject set different from x.

(47) a. The men saw each other.
  b. [$_S$ [$_{NP}$ [$_{NP}$ the men$_1$] each$_2$] [$_S$ e_2 [$_{VP}$ [$_{NP}$ e_2 other(1)]$_3$ [$_{VP}$ saw e_3]]]]
  c. [$_{NP}$ [$_{NP}$ the men$_1$] each$_2$] (λx (saw (x, other (x))))

This analysis allows us to reconstruct a notion of binding as defined in (41). I will refrain from discussing semantic reasons for opting for the one or the other approach to reciprocity. But, note that in many cases a compositional analysis cannot be applied. For instance in sentences such as (48) there is neither a distributor, nor a "contrastor," yet the interpretation is reciprocal.

(48) a. The men met yesterday.
  b. Die Leute haben sich gestern getroffen.
    (same meaning)

It seems that "direct," noncompositional, assignment of a reciprocal interpretation as in (48) would most easily fit in with the proposal by Reinhart and Siloni (2005). They focus on cases without explicit reciprocalization. This type of reciprocalization operation is an operation on argument structure subject to the lexicon-syntax parameter; as they show, languages exhibit the same parameter setting for reciprocals as for reflexives. In Hebrew, Russian, and Hungarian reciprocals are formed in the lexicon, while in Romance languages, German and Serbo-Croatian they are formed in the syntax (see also Siloni 2008 for further arguments and discussion). The analysis further covers configurational restrictions on reciprocalization, for instance between reciprocal markers as direct arguments of predicates versus reciprocal markers as arguments within PPs. (See Gast and Haas 2008 for pertinent discussion of the restrictions on the reciprocal interpretation of *sich* in German.) However, for explicit reciprocals such as *each other* a compositional interpretation with *logical syntax binding* seems warranted. Thus, just like reflexivity, reciprocity may arise on the basis of

- A lexical operation
- A syntactic operator
- Explicit reciprocity marking

Furthermore, neither need involve binding in the canonical sense.

6.5 Deriving Condition A

As discussed in section 1.8.2, Faltz (1977) provides a broad overview of reflexive elements in the languages of the world. As we saw, Faltz's typology considers the nature of the reflexive elements, the origin of their composite parts, and the way they are morphosyntactically connected. Our discussion adds dimensions to this typology that are orthogonal to it. The upshot of the discussion so far is that the following dimension should be added to the typology of reflexives:

- ±operation on argument structure (valence reduction/bundling)

That is, some "reflexives" affect argument structure (either operating on the argument structure themselves, or taking care of a Case residue), others protect it (in ways that may vary).

There is another dimension of variation concerning *reflexive licensers* that is more striking from the perspective of the CBT. What I call here a reflexive licenser has among its instantiations anaphors in the CBT sense. And this brings us back to one of the main puzzles we started out with. Recall that by now we have a principled answer to the question of why in (49a) (varying the examples we started out with in chapter 1), *her* cannot get the value Alice, although in (49b) it can.

(49) a. *Alice* admired *her*.
     b. *Alice* saw that the cat was watching *her*.

It follows from IDI and the chain condition (together accounting for the fact that the two violations in (49a) make it worse than its Dutch counterpart *Alice bewonderde zich*, which only reflects the IDI. We also have a principled explanation of why something must be done to express the reading with *her* is (bound by) *Alice*, and that the complex *herself* is needed to do that job as in (50a).

(50) a. *Alice* admired *herself*.
     b. *Alice* expected the king to invite *herself* for a drink.

But it is not yet clear why (50b) is ill-formed. The *fact* that it is, is captured by reflexivity condition A (a reflexive-marked syntactic predicate is reflexive), but it is not yet clear *why* this condition holds. The question is, then, why *self* as a licenser of reflexivity when needed, also *enforces* reflexivity as in (50b), even if nothing appears to be gained by that, although in exempt environments nothing prevents a (locally) free interpretation, as we saw in chapter 3, exemplified in (51).

(51) *Alice* expected the king to invite [the White Rabbit and *herself*] for a drink.

This distinction between licensing and enforcing is a fundamental one. That it is needed even apart from exemption in English is shown by the fact that there are languages whose reflexive licensers do not enforce reflexivity—for instance, Malayalam, illustrated in (52) (Jayaseelan 1997):[39]

(52) a. raaman$_i$ tan-ne$_i$ *(tanne) sneehikunnu
         Raman SE-ACC self   loves
         'Raman loves him*(self).'
     b. raaman$_i$ wicaariccu [penkuttikal tan-ne$_i$ tanne sneehikkunnu
         Raman thought   girls   SE-ACC self love
         enna]
         COMP
         '*Raman* thought that the girls love *himself*.'
     c. *Raman$_i$ thought that the girls love himself$_i$

In this section I will address the following questions:

i.   What is the syntactic operation involved in reflexive-marking in English and how does exemption arise?
ii. What is the semantics of reflexive marking, and how can we unify the semantics of reflexive and exempt *himself*?
iii. What triggers reflexive marking?

6.5.1 The Syntax of Reflexive-Marking

Condition A as stated in chapter 3 just expresses a condition on interpretation, leaving open how reflexive-marking is brought about by SELF. To understand how it does so, we have to take into consideration both the semantics of SELF and its syntactic properties.

Let's assume, in line with earlier discussion that SELF anaphors have the structure in (53b) (for English, the structure will subsequently be refined), where *Pronoun* stands for either *him* or *zich* and *SELF (x)* in (53c) is a Higginbotham 1983–style representation of the set expression associated with SELF as a common noun head:

(53) a. himself/zichzelf

    b. [$_{DP}$ Pronoun [$_{NP}$ SELF]]

    c. [$_{DP}$ Pronoun [$_{NP}$ SELF (x)]]

However, SELF has a further property setting it apart from most common nouns. SELF is inherently relational: whereas a cat, dog, table, and so forth is not necessarily somebody's cat, dog, table, etc., a SELF is necessarily some individual's SELF. If one considers the elements in the set {x | SELF (x)}, they necessarily bear the *being-a-SELF-of* relation (briefly, the SELF-relation) to some individual. The expression SELF (x) must, therefore, be able to assign a semantic role expressing this. Hence, the pronoun in the external/POSS position receives the role of bearing the SELF relation, the variable *x* in the set expression bears the referential role in the sense of Zwarts 1992. Taking this one step further, one may argue that there is no ontological difference between an individual and that individual's SELF.

(54) [$_{DP}$ x [$_{NP}$ SELF$_{R1, R2}$ x]]

The above is just a very informal sketch. In section 6.5.2 I will present a precise picture based on the semantics of pronouns developed in Reuland and Winter 2009 (henceforth R&W).[40]

Although SELF as a noun has a semantically special status, we will see that an essential property of the structure in (54) also obtains in a range of expressions involved in reflexive marking in other languages. For the moment, however, we will restrict ourselves to SELF-type reflexives.

Given this preliminary sketch of how SELF's semantics internally encodes reflexivity, let us see know how it reflexive marks syntactic predicates. Reinhart and Reuland (1991) propose that the syntactic mechanism for reflexive-marking involves movement of SELF adjoining it to the nearest c-commanding predicate head, where locality follows from whatever underlies the head-movement constraint. For reason of space the mechanism was left implicit in Reinhart and Reuland 1993. There is prima facie evidence supporting a relation between SELF and a predicate head, give the prevalence of compounds like *self-hatred*, *self-destruction*, and so on, with a striking productivity in participial forms, not only in English but in a range of languages. Here I will elaborate this proposal.[41] As we will see below it allows us to reduce the contrast between exempt and nonexempt positions to independent properties of the grammatical system. A number of further properties will follow as well.

For reasons of exposition I will not discuss possible triggers for SELF movement at this point. These will be extensively discussed in section 6.5.3. Let us just assume for now that there is some property P that makes predicate heads attract SELF if possible. Note, that no property of the SELF-NP makes its interpretation dependent on attraction. Hence in logophoric contexts where SELF movement is not available, as we will see, in a suitable discourse environment no uninterpretability will result.

The SELF movement is illustrated in (55). In this configuration a *logical form* (LF)[42] representation of the form (55) can be derived by adjoining SELF to V by head to head movement—indicating its lower copy as (SELF). A partial LF of (55a), then, will be (55b), which yields the canonical binding configuration in (55c).

(55) a. Lucie adores herself.
      b.

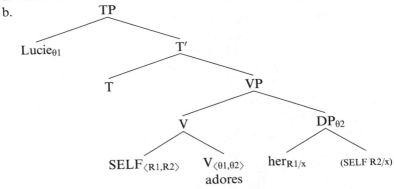

      c. Lucie (λx (x SELF-adores [x *([SELF x])*]))

Recall that the pronoun determiner in the SELF-DP must be cobound with the variable in the set expression of SELF. As discussed in more detail in section 6.5.3, the adjunction configuration is interpreted by intersection (Chomsky 2008). If so, the relation interpreting SELF-V will be the intersection of the SELF relation and the V relation, which is by necessity reflexive. If SELF would be semantically inert except for imposing reflexivity, (55c) would further reduce to (56) at the C-I interface, violating IDI.

(56) Lucie (λx (x adores x))

This is why the complexity of (55c) is essential. Crucial is that the reflexivizing function of SELF anaphors is obtained by their obligatory movement to V.

The immediate consequence of this movement analysis is that no special conditions are needed to express when SELF is an obligatory reflexive marker. The exempt positions discussed in chapter 3, such as coordinate structures, picture Noun phrases, *except* phrases, adjunct PPs, Focus phrases, and so on all share the property that head movement of SELF from its position as the NP-head onto the relevant predicate is blocked, as in (57):

(57) a. *Alice* expected the king to invite [Rabbit and *her*self] for a drink

b. *Alice* expected the king to invite [no one but *her*self] for a drink

c. *Alice* expected the king to read [stories about *her*self]

These constituents are all *islands* for head movement by independent constraints on movement, either general, such as the coordinate structure constraint, or specific to heads such as the head movement constraint.[43] So, the restrictions on SELF as a reflexive marker simply follow from movement theory, without any statement specific to binding.

Once adjoined to V, SELF will move along with V to any higher position, such as T. But this movement does not affect the interpretation of SELF, since a SELF that is attached to V is interpreted as reflexivizing this particular V. The locality of head movement therefore entails strict locality for SELF anaphors as reflexivizers.

If the SELF anaphor is in a configuration from which no movement can take place, the only consequence is that no predicate will be reflexive-marked. The interpretation of $\langle pronoun \rangle$ *self* will be identical to the interpretation of $\langle pronoun \rangle$ modulo the effect of *self*, which contributes a mapping of the denotation of the pronoun onto itself. This is the effect typically associated with *intensification*. Hence the analysis derives the connection between reflexivization and intensification directly from the semantics of SELF. The difference resides in how the SELF element interacts with the syntactic environment, in line with the analysis outlined in chapter 3.

So, in (58) covert adjunction of SELF to the predicate leads to the representation in (58b).

(58) a. DP ... [V] [$_{DP}$ PRON [SELF]]
     b. DP ... [$_{SELF}$ V] [$_{DP}$ PRON [SELF]]

The next question is, then, how *himself* is interpreted. Section 6.5.2 presents the formal semantic approach developed in R&W.

6.5.2 Reference by Proxy and the Functional Semantics of Pronominals

One of the well-known properties of reflexive pronouns is their ability to have "proxy readings." This is illustrated in (59) (Jackendoff 1992):

(59) (Upon a visit in a wax museum:) All of a sudden *Ringo* started undressing *himself*.

Himself in (59) can be interpreted as the "real" Ringo, but also as a statue of the Ringo denoted by the subject. In view of the previous discussion it is very tempting to reduce this proxy reading to the semantic contribution of *self*. However, as shown by Safir (2004a) in an illuminating discussion, such "proxy reference" can appear with all pronouns, not only with reflexives. Here we will pursue the implications of this fact for the combinatorics of anaphora and the reflexivizing element *self*/*zelf* in Dutch and English.

The analysis is based on Jacobson's (1999) variable-free semantics. R&W propose that

i. The context specifies a reflexive *proxy relation* that defines possible "proxies" for the entities referred to;
ii. Pronouns denote a particular type of function (*Skolem functions*; see (64) below) that take proxy relations as their argument;
iii. Elements like *self*/*zelf* are ordinary relational nouns, and their only special property is their ability to compose as lexical proxy relations with pronouns and binding operators.

As Jackendoff argues, proxy interpretations of reflexives in (59) must be related to a general property of language: the ability to refer to various "proxies" of an individual concept. In that respect, the reflexive in (59) is not different from nonanaphoric NPs, which can also refer to "noncanonical" proxies as in (60):

(60) Ringo/The man is made of stone, whereas Yoko/the woman is made of wax.

Jackendoff has argued that there is an asymmetry between NPs and anaphors in their ability to carry a proxy reading, and claims that in (61) we cannot have an interpretation where *Ringo* is the proxy and *himself* the person.

(61) *Ringo* fell on top of *him*self.

However, as discussed by R&W, it is possible to create contexts where such an interpretation is easily accessible. Consider a play where some actor plays a younger Ringo, and Ringo plays an older fan. It is no problem to interpret the sentence *Ringo stumbled and fell on top of himself* as true when the actor stumbled and fell on top of the real Ringo. Thus, the following generalization emerges:

(62) *Generalization*

The range of available proxies for a bound pronoun is the same range of proxies as for its antecedent.

Thus, while strict identity between the referents of a pronoun and its antecedent is not mandatory even under binding, identity of the *candidate proxy referents* for the two expressions is mandatory. This generalization reflects an important observation: *Also nonreflexive bound pronouns allow a proxy interpretation*. This is illustrated in (63):

(63) All of a sudden, every *pop icon* started taking off the shirt *he* was wearing.

In the wax-museum context of (59), sentence (63) has a bound reading where the pop icons took the shirts off their respective statues. To capture this effect, R&W propose that the context provides a reflexive proxy relation *PR*, describing the possible proxies $\lambda y.PR(x, y)$ of any entity x referred to. The reflexivity of *PR* guarantees availability of the standard, "strict identity," interpretation also in cases like (59) and (63). In (63) it is assumed that nonreflexive pronouns like *he*, instead of simply denoting the identity function on entities, as in Jacobson (1999), denote a *Skolem function*: a function from entities to entities that takes a relation as a parameter.[44] This parameter determines the range for each possible entity argument. Formally:

(64) A function f of type (ee) with a relational parameter PR is a *Skolem function* if for every entity x: $PR(x, f_{PR}(x))$ holds.

Note that when *PR* is assumed to be a reflexive relation, there is a Skolem function f such that f_{PR} is Jacobson's identity function. Sentence (63) is now analyzed as (63′):

(63′) $\forall x[pop\_icon(x) \rightarrow take\_off(x, \text{the shirt } \_f_{PR}(x) \_ was\_ wearing)]$

Thus, for every pop icon x, the Skolem function f picks up one of x's proxies, possibly x itself. Derivation of this analysis is straightforward within Jacobson's framework.

R&W's analysis of reflexive pronouns is based on decomposing the meaning of pronouns like English *himself* or Dutch *zichzelf*. First, *self* (*zelf*) is treated as a relational noun, denoting a proxy relation. This requirement amounts to assuming that *self* denotes a reflexive relation: an entity x can have more than one "self" in addition to x. A noun phrase like *Ringo's better self* is not substantially different from any other NP with a relational noun (e.g., *Ringo's better parent*), where the former NP may refer to one of Ringo's "better" proxies in the context of utterance. Also similarly to other relational nouns, *self* can semantically incorporate (Van Geenhoven and McNally 2005) with nominalized transitive verbs. For instance in (65):

(65) a. *self-hater* denotes the predicate $\lambda x.hate(x, \uparrow self(x))$
   (x is a self-hater if x hates the property (indicated by the
   $\uparrow$-operator) coupled with x's proxies)

   b. *parent-hater* denotes the predicate $\lambda x.hate(x, \uparrow parent(x))$
   (x is a parent-hater if x hates the property coupled with x's
   parents)

The only substantial difference we assume between *self* and other relational nouns is a syntactic one. The noun *self* is able to combine with Skolem functions denoted by nonreflexive pronouns independently of genitive case (i.e., *his self/himself* vs. *his parent/*him parent*). There are two ways this can occur:

1. *The unmarked option*—the noun *self* composes with the Skolem function through the binding mechanism. The noun *self* is covertly attached to the transitive predicate (as happens overtly in *self-hater*) and contributes a proxy relation to the nonreflexive pronoun through Jacobson's Z function[45] in its "proxied" version (66):

(66) $Z^{PR} = \lambda R.\lambda f.\lambda x.R(x, f_{PR}(x))$

In this version of the Z function, it provides the Skolem function f with its parameter.

The denotation of a VP like *undress himself* in (59) is obtained using the structure *self-undress him*, analyzed as follows:

(67) Z^{self} (**undress**) (**him**) $= Z^{self}$ (**undress**) $(f) = \lambda x.$ **undress**$(x, f_{self}(x))$
   $= \lambda x.x$ undressed one of x's *self* proxies (by definition of f as a
   Skolem function)

2. *A marked option*—the noun *self* composes with the Skolem function directly. This marked option can only occur in exempt positions as discussed in chapter 3 and the previous section, when incorporation with the predicate is syntactically blocked (e.g., *Max boasted that the queen invited [Lucie and himself] for a drink*). When formation of *self-V* is syntactically disallowed—in this case, because of the Coordinate Structure

Constraint as discussed, direct composition with the Skolem function leads to the analysis (68):

(68) $himself = f_{self}$ = a function mapping every entity x to one of its proxies in **self**(x)

Unlike the unmarked option, now there is no binding that is made necessary by *self*'s composition. As a result, the exempt reading of *himself* allows it to be interpreted as either bound or free, similarly to the non-reflexive pronoun *him*.

In Dutch, a critical difference between the reflexive pronouns *zich* and *zichzelf* is that *zich* does not allow a proxy reading (69a) (more precisely, it cannot be valued with a different element from the proxy set than its antecedent), whereas *zichzelf*, like English reflexives, does:

(69) a. Jan waste zich. ('Jan washed'—no proxy reading)
    b. Jan waste zichzelf. ('Jan washed himself'—proxy reading possible)[46]

This follows immediately from the account of this contrast in chapters 4 and 5. Bare *zich* forms one syntactic object (a chain) with the subject. Thus, the analysis of the intransitive usage of *waste* 'washed' in (69a) interprets the chain [*Jan,zich*] as (70):

(70) $f_{PR}(\textbf{jan})$ = one of Jan's proxies

This interpretation is indistinguishable from the "simple" denotation **jan** of the name *Jan*, given the generalization (62) that any referential NP can be interpreted as any member of the relative set of proxies. By contrast, in (69b), similarly to (59), the reflexive pronoun fills in a separate (object) argument position of a transitive verb (here, the transitive reading of *waste*). As a result, the analysis of (69b) is similar to the binding with the English sentence *Jan washed himself*.[47]

6.5.3 How SELF Movement Is Enforced

In informal terms, the analysis in the previous section says that SELF can either covertly move and attach to the verb, or—if movement is prohibited—compose with (the function denoted by) the pronoun.

But, saying that SELF can move, is not the same as explaining why it has to be there and why it has to move. Thus, to understand reflexivization it is important to distinguish the following two questions:

i. Why is a reflexive-licenser needed?
ii. If the licenser enforces a reflexive interpretation of the predicate, how does it do so?

The first question we did already effectively answer: Because of the IDI, either reduction of the argument structure or protection of the internal argument is required.

The second question has quite a few ramifications. The issue can be put more specifically as follows: From the morphosyntactic representation in (58a) it does not yet follow that *self* has to mark the predicate as reflexive. So, how is reflexivity enforced? True, given the semantics of *self* it will contribute to the predicate's interpretation in the specified manner if it attached to the predicate, but given the existence of an alternative interpretation in exempt position no semantic principle enforces either of the options.

Although most work within the Minimalist Program assumes that movement is in principle feature driven, it has been shown that it may also be driven by economy of interpretation.[48] These lines are not mutually exclusive. It is logically possible that the general mechanism is based on economy of interpretation, but that for some particular language it can be established that there is a syntactic trigger in the form of a feature. We will see that there are reasons to believe that this option is in fact realized.

Let us start our discussion with noting the well-known fact that not all licensers behave the same; for instance, whereas English *self* and Dutch *zelf* can incorporate, French *même* or Italian *stesso* do not allow incorporation. So we do not have *même-admiration* along the model of *self-admiration*. Thus, there are cross-linguistic differences between the way the licenser and the predicate interact that should find their way into typology.[49] Irrespective of the way specific licensers are to be analyzed, logic dictates that we have at least the following further typological dimension:

- ±(Covert) head movement[50]

But, even syntactic head movement does not by itself explain how reflexivity is enforced. In fact, this is one of the main problems any theory of binding has to address. In exploring possible accounts, I will use the following guiding principles:

- Assume only what is independently motivated.
- The properties of reflexive licensers should follow from minimal assumptions about their syntax and semantics.
- No special assumptions should be made about the computational and interpretive systems.

In the next sections I will be discussing two possible scenarios:

- A lexical semantics–based scenario
- An inalienable possession–based scenario

But first I will say a few words—from a syntactic perspective—about how the computational and interpretive systems interact, an issue that is relevant to both scenarios.

The combinatorial principles of natural language allow expressions to be combined in two ways. Within the framework of Chomsky 1981, these were referred to as *substitution* and *adjunction*, respectively. The former is typically reflected in predicate-argument relations, the latter in modification relations. Since substitution, as it was originally conceived, applied only to a subset of the relevant cases, in Chomsky (1995 and subsequent work) Merge was introduced as the basic combinatory principle. Merge comes in two forms: Set-merge and Pair-merge. Set-merge will reflect predicate-argument relations, Pair-merge yields adjunction structures, and is interpreted as modification. A canonical way of interpreting modification structures is by *intersection*. Thus, the expression *black cats* can be taken to denote the set of objects that are both black and cat.[51] Chomsky (2001) posits *interpretation by intersection* as the mechanism of choice for adjunction (pair-merge) in general. Intuitively, *self* applying to *x undress him* in (67) amounts to intersecting the *undress* relation with a reflexive proxy relation $x\ R\ f(x)$, yielding the undressing relation between x's and their proxies.

As often, the pretheoretical view does not precisely correspond to what one finds empirically. For instance, languages may allow the combination of verbs into verbal clusters (for instance, Dutch and German) by a mechanism of adjunction, yet one would be disinclined to call this a modification relation. Crucially, however, such verbal clusters are interpreted by a semantic composition mechanism that has intersection as one of its core ingredients. Similarly, expressions that are prima facie arguments are not always interpreted in that way. For instance, as discussed in De Hoop 1992, bare plural objects in Dutch (and other languages as well) are better interpreted by an incorporation mechanism than as independent arguments.

The syntactic mechanism expressing incorporation is head-adjunction (Baker 1996, 2001). This leads one to expect that again the interpretive mechanism is intersection, and indeed an expression as *boeken lezen* 'read books' in *Jan zal boeken lezen* 'John will read books' is readily interpreted as the intersection between reading events and events involving books. Although *interpretation by intersection* is an intuitively easy way to see the effect of SELF-marking, formally it has to be understood as in the previous section. Note that the assumption that head adjunction is available for argument licensing is nothing special. It is overtly available for all argument types in languages that are positively specified for the polysynthesis parameter (Baker 1996, 2001). Hence, we need assume no more than that a type of argument licensing that is overtly available in one class of languages is covertly available, at least for a subset of arguments, in another class.

In the next two sections I will discuss two possible derivations.

6.5.3.1 A Lexical Semantics–Based Scenario Consider again (58):

(58) a. DP...[V] [$_{DP}$ PRON [SELF]]
     b. DP...[$_{SELF}$ V] [$_{DP}$ PRON [SELF]]

We saw that *self* can attach to predicative stems. The question is: How can a reflexive interpretation of (58a) be enforced grammatically?

To answer this question and derive this enforcement the following empirical assumptions and steps suffice:

i. *Self* has minimal lexical content measured on the lexical-functional scale. It is a relational noun with the argument structure intrinsically denoting a reflexive relation, and purely functional (Z^{self} in (66) and (67)).
    Empirical assumption about the lexical semantics of self. That *self* has minimal lexical content is uncontroversial and reflected in the semantics assigned to it in (66) and (67). The specific semantics assigned has the status of a meaning postulate.

ii. Elements whose lexical content is under a certain threshold are −Ref(erential).[52]
    Empirical assumption about the relation between semantic properties and interpretation. The assumption itself appears to be widely shared, which does not entail that it does not raise further questions. From the perspective of grammaticalization theory it is quite natural that grammaticalized elements have reduced lexical content and lose their canonical role as arguments. However, ideally we should have a theory of threshold values, which we don't have at the moment. Note that we must assume that the −Ref property can be read off the lexical representation.

iii. The head of −Ref arguments (may) (covertly) head-adjoin/ incorporate to the predicate in order to saturate a thematic role.
Empirical assumption about argument licensing. As discussed, there are independent reasons to assume that *self* may incorporate/adjoin. As discussed in the introductory part to this section, based on the insights in Baker 1996, 2001, and De Hoop 1992, the possibility to interpret *self* by head adjunction is not a special fact about *self*, but follows from the general structure of the computational system. The question to what extent this head movement is enforced is discussed under (v) below. Note furthermore that this leaves open the question of how precisely the obligatory reflexive marking by elements such as French *même*, Russian *samyj*, and so on is captured. These have an independent use as identity predicates, which may well enable them to function as lexical reflexive markers. The precise mechanism will have to be left for future research.

iv. *Self* movement can only be to the nearest c-commanding predicate.
Follows from general theory of movement. Minimality is a fundamental property of (overt and covert) head movement. The result of the (covert) movement can be represented as in (71):

(71) a. ... [SELF $V_{\langle y, x \rangle}$] ... [Pron SELF]
b. ... $Z^{\textbf{self}}$ (V) (him SELF) = $\lambda x.$ V $(x, f_{\textbf{self}}(x))$

v. SELF movement (hence binding in the resulting configuration) is enforced for one of the following reasons:

a. Head movement is the only way to interpret −Ref arguments.

b. The intersection between *self* and the predicate it adjoins to is a reflexive relation. This effectively turns *self* into an operator on the argument structure of V, requiring that values for subject and object arguments are identical. *Self* is attracted by an operator feature on the verb.

c. Applying *self* to the predicate it adjoins to yields a reflexive proxy relation. This is a syntactic encoding of an interpretive dependency, which may then be preferred by economy. I will discuss the problems and merits of (a–c) below.

Consequences of steps so far together with a general property of the grammar. First, note that what we have here comes down to predicate composition resulting in a predicate meeting the joint interpretive requirements of each of the composed predicates. The effect of the semantics of *self* is that both arguments of the SELF-marked head will be cobound: λx (x, f_{self} (x)). Thus, composing *self* with the verb, the logical syntax representation of (72a) is (72b):

(72) a. DP V himself

　　　b. DP (λx (V (x, f_{SELF} (x))))

The interpretation of f_{SELF} (x) will be close enough to that of x for (72b) to FIT use as a reflexive, but arity is respected as required, since the two arguments of V are formally distinct in this representation.

Since we have three initially possible general mechanisms to enforce reflexive-marking, let's briefly discuss each.

Option (a) leaves open the question of how to interpret the occurrences of *self* in exempt position, since it assumes that the only means to interpret the SELF-DP is by movement, which is not in fact the case. In fact, we can discard it given the analysis given in 6.5.2.

Regarding option (b), in the analysis given in 6.5.2. *self* acts as an operator either on the V or on the pronoun. There is some further evidence that *self* as a verbal operator has independent semantic effects. As we will see in 6.5.3.2, *self* favors a distributive reading of the predicate it is an argument of. Interestingly, it cannot be felicitously combined with an explicit distributive operator such as *elk* 'each', as in *?de politici bewonderden elk zichzelf* 'the politicians admired each themselves', suggesting the involvement of a mechanism prohibiting *self* from duplicating *each*. A *Distr* position associated with the verb and attracting *self* would capture that. Yet, there would be no intrinsic requirement on *self* to be attracted. Hence, in exempt position the semantics of SELF as given would yield the intensifier reading as required.

Option (c) is the simplest possibility. It needs the fewest assumptions: given that adjunction of *self* yields the syntactic encoding of a binding dependency, this encoding is preferred by economy over other interpretive options (note that it is compatible with *self* effectively being an operator on the verb). Again, in exempt position the intensifier reading would obtain without further assumptions. However, it raises the question why obligatory SELF movement is restricted to SELF as an argument of a syntactic predicate as discussed in chapter 3. That is, if this economy condition were to apply to all predicates, the exemption observed in the domain of P- and N-heads (chapter 3) would be lost. This issue will be addressed in section 6.5.3.3.3.

Note that the two remaining mechanisms in (v) are both general. So, regardless of the eventual choice, we can conclude at this point that the obligatoriness of "binding" can be mechanically derived from general principles of grammar, without the obligatoriness itself being built into specific assumptions about the semantics of *self*.

6.5.3.2   The Inalienable Possession Model   Although many languages have reflexive markers that seem entirely functional encodings of a reflexive relation, a great many other languages use body-part reflexives as we noted.[53] In fact, as we know from Faltz and other typological studies, body-part strategies are among the most common reflexivization strategies that are around. As we will see, SELF reflexives end up as a limiting case of body-part reflexives. As a starting point, let's discuss the IP-model in more detail.

Pica (1987, 1991) suggested that "inalienable possession" (IP) constructions could provide a model for complex reflexives (see Helke 1973). Indeed, some typical IP constructions share "obligatoriness of binding" with reflexives. So, we have *John* craned *his* neck, *Everyone* craned *his* neck, but not **I craned his neck*. We have *John* extended *his* hand, *Everyone* extended *his* hand, but not **I extended his hand* (in the relevant sense). It seems, therefore, natural to ask whether the obligatoriness of binding in standard reflexives such as *John admired himself* could not have the same source. For instance, *self* could be analyzed as a body part, like *neck* or *hand*, and then trigger the same mechanism. Anagnostopoulou and Everaert (1999) and Everaert (2003) make the same suggestion. Let us then see what it requires to go through.

On the face of it, many cases of IP do indeed exhibit a binding requirement. However, we must be careful. Many of the most striking cases are idiomatic (to varying degrees); and the moment one has a verb that is not, the obligation disappears. Consider the related pairs in (73)–(75):

(73) a.   John raised his eyebrows.
     b.   *I raised his eyebrows.

(74) a.   John sprained his ankle.
     b.   *(?)I sprained his ankle.

(75) a.   During the fight, John twisted his ankle.
     b.   During the fight, I twisted his ankle.

In (73) it does not seem possible at all for the possessive *his* to be free, hence we have a clear binding obligation. *Sprain* does not (easily) allow it either (although a web search still gave me two instances of a free *his*), but *twist* does. Of course, one could say that in (75b) we do not have IP, but that would miss the point. The point is that with verbs as in (73) a non-IP reading is not allowed. This is crucial for the binding *obligation* (but see below for discussion whether IP is sufficient). So, the question is, how to formally distinguish the IP cases from the non-IP cases. If we cannot, the IP strategy is of no avail for an explanation.

Reconsidering (75) we see that there is a contrast between (75a) and (75b): under the IP reading *twist* lacks the agentive reading it has in the non-IP case. John is an experiencer rather than an agent in (75a) and in (74a). John did something, and as a result his ankle got twisted/sprained. Also, (75a) means that John sustained an injury, contrary to (75b).[54] So, in these cases the IP and the non-IP versions of the predicate are not strictly identical. This may help to identify proper IP cases.

However, there is a complication. Although in (75) the difference is easy to identify, in other cases it is more difficult to determine. Compare, for instance, (76a) and (76b):

(76) a. John proffered his hand.
     b. John proffered his bottle.

John is an agent in some sense in both cases. We do find a small difference, however. (76a) does not express a relation between "independent participants." In (76b) John performs a transaction on a bottle, whereas in (76a) John does not perform a transaction on a hand. More precisely, the transaction initiated by proffering can be completed in (76b) by taking the bottle, but not in (76a) (unless, of course, by severing the hand, but this gives us again the bottle case). We will keep this in mind as it may help us find an effective characterization of the distinction between the two cases.[55]

However, we have to be careful again about how far this gets us. So far, we focused on whether or not a particular POSS-NP construction was IP. But let's now consider cases where we can be sure we have an IP. For instance, in *his body*, *his hair*, *his eyes*, etc., the relation between POSS and NP is prototypically one of IP. However, it is not the case that in the structure DP V [$_{IP}$ Poss NP]], Poss is obligatorily bound by DP. This is illustrated by the examples in (77):

(77) a. John$_i$ hit his$_{i,j}$ knee (no bias)
     b. John$_i$ hated his$_{i,j}$ face (no bias)
     c. John$_i$ hated his$_{i,j}$ body (slight bias, but see the d-case)
     d. I hated his$_i$ body (fine)
     e. John$_i$ hated his$_j$ guts (somebody else)

These facts indicate that deriving the binding obligation of *complex anaphors* from an IP type strategy requires at least some additional assumption. Again, ideally, such an assumption should be independently motivated.

As we will see, it can be. The ingredients to carry out the derivation are available. Even with *proffering*, which was the least idiomatic of the cases discussed, we found a contrast between the IP and the non-IP case, involving the completion of the transaction. It reflects the intuition that in the IP case we do not have independent participants in a relation. Cutting things short, the inalienably possessed element is not referential in the way canonical arguments are.[56] If so, the following scenario applies, again leading to a derivation based on covert *adjunction/incorporation*.

As above, we take as our point of departure the structure in (58), repeated here as (78), but, for reasons of generality, replacing *self* with *body part* (BP):

(78) a. DP...[V] [$_{DP}$ PRON [BP]]
     b. DP...[$_{BP}$ V] [$_{DP}$ PRON [BP]]

For ease of reference we start at the same point as we did in the case of the lexical semantics scenario, indicating where we start diverging:

i.   *BP* has minimal lexical content.
     Empirical assumption about the lexical semantics of **BP**. At this point no specific assumption about the *BP*'s semantics is introduced yet.
ii. Elements whose semantic content is under a certain threshold are −Ref(erential).
     Empirical assumption about the relation between semantic properties and interpretation. Note again, that we must assume that the −Ref property can be read off the lexical representation.
iii. The head of −Ref arguments (may) (covertly) adjoin to the predicate (incorporate) in order to saturate a thematic role.
     Empirical assumption about argument licensing. No difference.
iv. BP-movement can only be to the nearest c-commanding predicate.
     Follows from the general theory of movement. Just a blind syntactic process is assumed, with no implications for interpretation except in what follows.
v.   *BP* is a relational noun.
     Empirical assumption about the lexical semantics of BP. Expressing an intrinsic relation is a property *self* shares with body-part expressions. Intuitively, what is used here is the fact that body-part nouns are intrinsically relational, like *self*. Conceptually, a body, head, etc., is always a body-of some individual. As is the case of SELF, *x* bears the referential role in the sense of Zwarts 1992. Thus, BP(x) in (79) defines the set expression, the set of objects that stand in the "body-of" relation to y.

(79) [$_{DP}$ PRON [$_{NP}$ BP $\langle$x, y$\rangle$]]

The inalienable possession interpretation of "body-of" is intrinsically represented in its lexical structure and hence in the relation it denotes. For sake of concreteness I will be assuming that in cases of "alienable" use of inalienably possessible elements (the "severed hand") a lexical reduction operation is involved of the type discussed in section 6.3.[57]

So, *hand*, *foot*, and so on have dual, but rule-related entries. Thus, the *body-of*-relation is restricted to pairs such that x is the inalienable body of y, excluding other types of "possession." Given the condition of FIT in (38) on the use of BP expressions as variable protectors, the value of x can stand proxy for the value of y.

vi. Binding obtains.

Consequence of previous steps. In line with the earlier discussion of SELF I will assume that the head of the BP is able to combine with Skolem functions denoted by nonreflexive pronoun in its POSS position (null or overt). As with *self* the BP head is covertly attached to the transitive predicate and contributes a proxy relation to the non-reflexive pronoun. The denotation of a VP like *V PronBP* is obtained using the structure *BP-V him*, analyzed just as in (67):

(80) $Z^{\mathbf{BP}}\,(\mathbf{V})\,(\mathbf{Pron}\;\mathrm{BP}) = Z^{\mathbf{BP}}\,(\mathbf{V})\,(f) = \lambda x.\,\mathbf{V}(x, f_{\mathbf{BP}}(x))$
   $= \lambda x.x$ V-ed one of x's *body's* proxies (by definition of f as a Skolem function)

As in the case of SELF we can informally say that the relation expressed by *BP* composes/intersects with the relation expressed by the verb that *BP* adjoins to.

vii. BP-movement (hence, binding) is enforced for one of the following reasons:

a. Head movement is the only way to interpret −Ref arguments.

b. The intersection between *BP* and the predicate it adjoins to is a reflexive relation. This effectively turns *BP* into an operator on the argument structure of V, requiring that values for subject and object arguments are identical. *BP* could, then, be attracted by a feature on the verb.

c. The intersection between *IP* and the predicate the BP adjoins to is a reflexive relation. This yields a syntactic encoding of an interpretive dependency, which is preferred by economy.

Consequence of previous steps. As in the case of *self*, the (a) option can be discarded (unless we find that BP reflexives are ill-formed in positions where *self* anaphors are simply exempt). The −Ref property is relevant in so far as it enables the head movement, not by enforcing it. The analysis effectively capitalizes on the intrinsically relational character of BP nouns. Like *self*, they can mediate in establishing the binding relation. They do appear to have more lexical content. This could in principle be reflected in restrictions on the admissible proxies. Although for languages such as Basque or Georgian no such restrictions have been reported, Muysken (1993) reports that in Papiamentu (a Creole spoken in the Netherlands Antilles) different types of verbs select for different forms.[58]

It is an open question whether option (b) of the discussion of SELF movement is applicable here. Prima facie it may seem unlikely that BPs are for instance, distributivity operators. However, one cannot exclude this without empirical investigation of semantic side effects of BP reflexives. Currently, such a project is underway. An answer will have to wait until the results of this project are available. As in the case of *self*, the c-option is the simplest, hence preferred, with the caveat mentioned, to which I turn in section 6.5.3.3.3.

Thus, if the BP allows for an interpretation as in (80), the IP model combines protection, the obligation of binding and a formal binding relation in logical syntax.

We went through two derivations of how a reflexivizer may enforce binding. Note that I introduced no assumption that is specific to binding. Both derivations rely on the same general claims about how the syntactic system deals with semantically light (−Ref) arguments, namely via adjunction/intersection. It relies on a general semantics for pronominals, and a particular proposal as to how the intrinsically relational chacter of SELF and BP nouns meshes with the semantics of the verb and a pronominal possessor. The two derivations only differ in a specific empirical assumption about the relevant property of the reflexivizer involved: (i) *self* as virtually only expressing a cobinding requirement; (ii) *BP* as also intrinsically expressing a dependency between its two arguments, but potentially still "tainted" and restricted by a lexical residue. Both conceptually and empirically the two models are extremely close.

6.5.3.3 Some Further Issues The most attractive position is that there is only one strategy, namely the IP strategy with *self* as a limiting case, as expressing a purely formal relation. I will come back to this issue in section 6.5.3.3.3. In any case, it is an empirical issue whether the IP model does indeed apply to BP-reflexives in all languages. Answering this question requires a thorough investigation of the crosslinguistic variation in reflexive binding. Currently we do not know precisely how pervasive the binding enforcement is. As we saw, Malayalam and Peranakan Javanese have been reported as languages possessing an anaphor without a binding enforcement. Cole et al. (2008) characterize *awake dheen* in Peranakan Javanese as a BP anaphor (which Malayalam *taan tanne* is arguably not). The range of BP-reflexive languages without a binding enforcement is not known at the moment, but it is entirely possible that there are more of such languages, and also that we simply have not yet asked the right questions about other languages that have not been sufficiently studied yet. In any case the fact that they exist raises the question of the factors involved in the variation. I will come back to this in section 6.5.3.3.3.

I will first discuss three further issues that bear on the generality of the IP model.

6.5.3.3.1 Statue Readings In both Dutch and English, *self*-anaphors allow the statue reading discussed in Jackendoff 1992. As discussed in section 6.5.2, Dutch simplex reflexives do not allow that reading, witness the contrast in (81) (from Reuland 2001b):

(81) "Madame Tussaud's" context: Consider the following situation:
Mary had gotten a statue at Madame Tussaud's. She walked in, looked in a mirror, and all of a sudden she became startled because:
a. Ze zag zich in een griezelige hoek staan.
   she saw SE in a creepy corner stand
b. Ze zag zichzelf in een griezelige hoek staan.
   she saw herself in a creepy corner stand
Favored interpretations: (a) *zich*=Mary: Mary saw herself;
(b) *zichzelf*=Mary's statue: Mary saw her statue.

The fact that English *himself* allows the statue interpretation and that Dutch *zichzelf* even prefers it, but that *zich* does not allow it follows from the semantics given in section 6.5.2. It would be important to study the crosslinguistic distribution of statue-readings and their covariation with reflexivization strategies.[59] This leads to another property SELF anaphors may have.

6.5.3.3.2 Distributivity In Dutch, reflexives with a plural antecedent show differences in distributivity. This is illustrated by the contrast in (82), using the verb *verdedigen* 'defend', which allows both a simplex and a complex reflexive. Suppose a group of soldiers has been given the assignment to hold a hill; subsequently the enemy attacks them. After the battle we can have a number of situations. For our purposes two are relevant: (i) the soldiers kept the hill, but at the cost of most of their lives; (ii) the soldiers lost the hill, they all stayed alive. In the first case one can properly say (82a), but not (82b). In the second case one can say either:

(82) a. De soldaten verdedigden zich   met succes.
         the soldiers defended   "them" successfully
     b. De soldaten verdedigden zichzelf   met succes.
         the soldiers defended   themselves successfully

What this shows is that *zichzelf* has a distributive reading (each of the soldiers must have defended himself successfully), whereas *zich* is collective. It is hard to see how this effect can be explained on the standard analyses of SELF anaphors. However, it fits if *zelf* is a distributor or allows a residual body-part interpretation (individuals may have bodies but collectives do not).

Again, it would be important to have a broader crosslinguistic investigation of the relation between the IP strategy and distributive versus collective interpretation. (It is interesting to note that Hara (2002) observes that the Japanese complex anaphor *zibun zisin* also gives rise to a distributive interpretation.)[60]

6.5.3.3.3 Toward a Final Simplification As we saw in chapter 3, the enforcement of reflexivization must be restricted to *syntactic predicates*, otherwise exemption in P- and N-predicates would be lost. Let us, then, reconsider the notion of a syntactic predicate. In (2) in chapter 3, the syntactic predicate of a head P was defined as follows:

(83) *Definition of syntactic predicate*
     The *syntactic predicate* formed of (a head) P is P, all its syntactic
     arguments, and an external argument of P (subject).
     The syntactic arguments of P are the projections assigned θ-role or
     Case by P.

Qualifying as a syntactic predicate crucially requires a subject, but no reference to syntactic category is made. Also raising verbs form syntactic predicates; hence the subject must be present, but need not receive its θ-role from the predicate head. So, what sets apart the subject is its obligatoriness. The syntactic predicate is a formally defined syntactic object. Note that descriptively, option (b) discussed above works fine. Attraction of the reflexivizing element can be annotated as a feature on the predicate, and in fact, at least for some uses, independent motivation as a *distr* feature can be given. So, one line of research would be to identify a general enough attracting feature, let's call it F_A. Ideally, then, such an attracting feature should be able to replace the subject part of the definition of syntactic predicate, or, optimally, the subject requirement and F_A could be reduced to each other. As we will see, in a discussion of *picture* NPs in the next chapter, not all "subjects" qualify, but only those that are arguments of a head with an event role. What these subject appear to share is that they are truly obligatory, independently of θ-requirements.

This indicates that the heads triggering attraction are those where the blind application of attraction is guaranteed to give a hit. In that case no independent attracting feature is needed: the formal configuration is effectively the "feature."

If so, economy of encoding is indeed the driving force: economy as a trigger for head movement will work if (i) the semantic properties of the predicate head to be adjoined are so impoverished that the encoding of the binding relation that is achieved is guaranteed to be FIT for use, and (ii) creating the configuration for reflexivization in a structure is guaranteed to work blindly.

Summarizing, then, the choice of Morph in (37), repeated here, is limited by conditions of FIT, restricting admissible Ms by what are admissible values of M(x). *F(x) should be fit for its role*:

(37) a. *DP* V [*Pronoun* Morph]
     b. DP (λx [V(x, [x M])])

(38) DP (λx V(x, f(x)))
     Condition: $\|f(x)\|$ is sufficiently close to $\|x\|$ to stand proxy for $\|x\|$

Under a strict economy approach, then, the same applies to adjunction of Morph to V (if it is not a verbal affix to begin with): Whether or not Morph will obligatorily adjoin to V will also be determined by a condition of FIT and Economy. Since Economy favours a blind syntactic encoding of an interpretive dependency if possible, adjunction of Morph onto V, deriving (84b) from (84a) is obligatory if the condition of (84c,d) is met, and the presence of a subject DP is guaranteed:

(84) a. *DP* V [*Pronoun* Morph]
     b. *DP* Morph-V [*Pronoun* (Morph)]
     c. FIT: $\|M\text{-}V\|$ can stand proxy for λx. V(x, x)
     d. Z^M (V) (**Pron** M) = Z^M (V) (*f*) = λx. V(x, $f_M(x)$) can stand proxy for λx. V(x, x)

Thus, the crucial condition is that $\|M\text{-}V\|$ be a relation that comes sufficiently close to the intended reflexive relation with *DP* binding *Pronoun*.

If so, this obviates the difference between the SELF strategy and the IP strategy as strategies that differ in any theoretically significant way.[61]

6.5.3.3.4 Another Type of Strategy Not all reflexive licensing need be based on the SELF or the IP model. For instance in a language that licenses reflexivity by doubling an anaphoric element, such as Caxur, the doubling is sufficient for protection, assuming that it has a semantic effect such as focalization, which stays visible in logical syntax. If one of the doubled elements enters into a feature dependency with an antecedent, as we find for instance with Caxur *wuž wuž*, where the second element has the local case and the first element the case of the antecedent, the process of feature sharing will be enough both to enforce a dependency, and to ensure it is local.[62]

So, any combination of complexity and feature deficiency leads to a local binding requirement. The local binding requirement per se is therefore independent of either the semantics of SELF or the semantics and structure of an IP expression. (See Spathas 2010 for some further discussion of differences in reflexivization strategies.)

In chapter 7 we will present an analysis of German *sich* that will show the same. As we will see, German *sich* arguably originates in the N-position and moves into the left periphery of its phrase, presumably Person/π. Thus it creates a doubling effect by movement into positions that are formally and interpretively distinct:

(85) $[_{\pi P} [_\pi$ sich$]$ $[_{NP} [_N$ (sich)$]]]]$

The two members of the chain have different categorial status, hence are distinguished at the interface. The binding requirement—including the cancellation if a feature mismatch ensues—follows from the same economy based mechanism as introduced for SE anaphors in general.

6.5.3.3.5 Summary of Complex Reflexives The analysis of complex reflexives of the SELF/IP type can be summarized in the following points:

i.   BP-head/SELF is a relational N.
ii. The semantic properties of BP/SELF impose strong restrictions on the choice of the value of one argument, in terms of the value of the other one, minimally as strong as the requirement that values of the internal argument can stand proxy for the values of the external argument (*x* and *the body/SELF of x*).
iii. Intuitively, intersecting the relation $R_{PRED} = \langle x, y \rangle$ with the relation $R_{IP} = \langle x, BP(x) \rangle$, yields the relation $R_r = \langle x, BP(x) \rangle$ as a subset of R. If BP(x) can stand proxy for x, $R_r = \langle x, BP(x) \rangle$ can in principle

stand proxy for a reflexive relation $R_{reflexive} = \langle x, x \rangle$. More precisely (86) holds:

(86) Z^M **(V) (Pron M)** $= Z^M$ **(V)** $(f) = \lambda x.\ V(x, f_M(x))$ standing proxy for $\lambda x.V(x, x)$

iv. Two general principles determine the obligatoriness of reflexive binding: a. FIT; b. Economy.

The alternative for doubling type languages is

i. Any process prohibiting identification of the copies at the interface creates a licensing configuration (Focus, categorical differentiation of copies).

ii. Feature deficiency leads to a local binding requirement.

The local binding requirement per se is therefore independent of either the semantics of SELF or the semantics and structure of an IP expression. Given this analysis, then, crosslinguistic (and intralanguage) variation in the obligation to reflexivize either involves syntactic factors (for instance factors enabling or prohibiting movement), or lexical factors preventing FIT.

6.6   Remaining Questions and Summary of Results

6.6.1   Revisiting Faltz's Typology

Faltz's original typology is based on the morphological status of the reflexive elements, the origin of their composite parts, and the way they are morphosyntactically connected. Our goal in this chapter has been to reveal a number of further dimensions that are relevant for the typology of reflexives (and anaphoric expressions more generally). We saw that any typology of anaphoric expressions should include the parameters discussed in chapter 3, and summarized below:

- $\pm$Reflexivizing function, $\pm$Referential independence

Clearly, the parameter $\pm$*Reflexivizing function* does not apply to all types of anaphoric elements. For instance, it does not apply to reciprocals. Although we did not discuss this here, the parameter $\pm$Referential independence does. One can certainly argue that *each... other* in *each of the men admired the other* stands to *each other* in *the men admired each other* as a pronominal to an anaphor. There is a sense in which expressions like *each other* depend on an antecedent for their interpretation just like reflexives as *himself*. What reflexives and reciprocals share is that at an abstract level both involve identifying the subject and the object set, and defining a restrictive relation over the result.

Thus conceived, both express some type of dependency between subject and object, but neither does necessarily involve binding in the sense defined in (41). Both, however, either involve a lexical operation reducing the arity of the predicate, or a syntactic bundling operation on θ-roles. Faltz's typology of reflexives must therefore be supplemented by dimensions reflecting properties of these processes:

- ±Operation on argument structure
  Lexicon versus syntax
  ±Case residue
    ±argumental "marker" (clitic, SE/PRON, Sakha -*n*)
- ±Chain formation (narrow syntax encoding versus logical syntax encoding)
  Factors:
    ±structural Case
    ±grammatical number
    person marking, etc.
- ±Reflexive licenser
  ±argumental (verbal/structural (oblique, PP)/argumental)
  ±enforcement
    ±movement/incorporation
      ±IP
        ±statue readings/*de se*
        ±distributivity

As we saw, ±*Operation on argument structure* applies to reciprocals as well. So a typology of reciprocals can to some extent be modeled on the typology of reflexives. Other properties of reflexives are independent of those of reciprocals. "Brute-force reciprocalization" does not appear to be possible due to the complexity of the operation semantically. But, we may also put it differently: any "protection" needed is already present in the operation itself. Could issues of chain formation play a role? In fact they do. Consider German in which *sich* is used with a predicate having reciprocal interpretation. Would one expect to find an alternative with a pronominal leading to the same interpretation? In Frisian, constructions with locally bound pronominals do not have a reciprocal interpretation (nor do Dutch *zich* constructions). However, given that *sich*'s role in German reciprocals is presumably that of checking a residual Case, it would be interesting to see whether one could have a language that is like Frisian in that it allows locally bound pronominals in the position of SE anaphors, but combines it with a reciprocal interpretation of the predicate. So we would have the equivalent of *die Leute haben sich geküsst*, but with a pronominal in the position of *sich*. This case is realized in Old English and shows that issues of chain formation also arise for reciprocals.[63]

6.6.2 The Notion "Anaphor": Its Theoretical Significance

Does the term *anaphor* have any theoretical significance, or is it merely a convenient label used to refer to a specific class of pronominals or pronounlike elements with certain ("defective") referential properties? The discussion in this chapter, coupled with the results of chapters 4 and 5, leaves no other conclusion than that the term *anaphor* as it was used in the CBT lacks theoretical significance. One could still use it as a convenient label used to refer to a class of pronominals or pronounlike elements with certain ("defective") referential properties. It is good to emphasize that this effectively puts an end to binding theory as we knew it.

There is a sense, however, in which the term *anaphor* can be resurrected, namely in terms of the process by which it receives its interpretation. One of the traditional diagnostics for *being an anaphor* as opposed to *being a pronominal* is that anaphors do not and pronominals do allow split antecedents. Despite the collapse of the anaphor-pronominal distinction in terms of inherent properties, we can nevertheless distinguish between the ways in which elements can receive an interpretation. One of the characteristics of syntactic chain formation is that chains are always uniquely headed. It is clear that the mechanisms for chain formation discussed in chapter 5 do not allow for multiply headed chains, hence don't allow split antecedents for SE anaphors. The same holds true for reflexivization. The definition of reflexive predicate as we gave it does not classify a predicate with two arguments providing the value of a third argument as reflexive, see (87):

(87) *John accidentally assigned Peter to themselves.[64]

Hence (87) is correctly marked as ill-formed due to a violation of condition A. So, the prohibition against split antecedents is a good diagnostic for particular types of anaphoric dependencies. Thus we can say that a particular element is *used as an anaphor* in a strict sense iff it is linked to its antecedent by a syntactic operation.

The ways elements are used to encode dependencies may be quite diverse, and depend not so much on their being "anaphors," but on the nitty-gritty details of their feature makeup, and the way these features interact with the grammatical environment. So, in actual fact, after an element has been classified as an anaphor the work only starts: Why it is an anaphor, and how can its properties be derived? This, surely, applies to reciprocals as well.

6.7 From Invariants to Variation: Masking

The present chapter makes a very strong claim: the need to license reflexivity is not just a quirk of the language system, but reflects a fundamental property of the computational system as it can run in the type of workspace we have. Consequently, it should be exceptionless and one would expect its effects to show up in every language. Nevertheless, an informal survey of languages whose anaphoric systems have been described shows a varying pattern. Of closely related language pairs such as Dutch and German, the former carries IDI effects on its sleeve, whereas German does not. In fact, the surface facts of German have been interpreted as problematic for R&R's reflexivity theory. German is one of the languages we will provide an in-depth discussion of in the next chapter. We will see that IDI effects do indeed show up under certain conditions, indicating they are real, and we will see why they are hidden under other conditions. Comparing well-behaved Dutch with closely related Frisian, typological surveys even list Frisian as a language without a systematic pronoun-anaphor contrast, incorrectly, as we have seen, but nevertheless food for thought.

Jumping to an entirely different area, guided by the excellent survey by Lust et al. (2000), we see again prima facie significant contrasts, from "well-behaved" Kannada (Dravidian) and Mizo (Tibeto-Burman) to Juang (Austro-Asiatic), where preliminary investigation hardly shows any systematic anaphor-pronoun contrast (Patnaik and Subbarao 2000). Japanese is a language that does not have transparent IDI effects, although careful investigation has shown they are there (Aikawa 1993; Hara 2002). Issues arise about certain Creole languages, about some Oceanic languages, as noted in chapter 1, and so on.

The question is, then, how to approach such variation? Accept that languages may be really different and that certain languages escape the effects, abandon the search for principled explanation altogether, or look for factors that *mask* the effects. It is my claim that much linguistic investigation—in the domain of anaphora, but potentially also outside—has been hampered by the fact that insufficient attention was given to the possibility of what I would like to call *masking*: the factor is there, but its effects are masked by a phenomenon or factor that is superimposed.

To see this, consider the following pattern in French discussed by Zribi-Hertz (1989) (see also Reuland 2006):

(88) a. *Jean* est fier   de *lui/lui-même.*
         Jean is proud of him/himself
    b. *Jean* est jaloux de **lui/lui-même.*
         Jean is jealous of him/himself
    c. *Jean* bavarde avec **lui/lui-même.*
         Jean mocks   (with) him/himself
    d. *Jean* parle de   *lui/lui-même.*
         Jean talks (of) him/himself

Configurationally (88a) and (88b) are identical, and the same holds for (88c) and (88d). If so, how can a pronominal be allowed in the one case, and not in the other? It has been argued, that such examples are a serious problem for a configurational approach to binding. They show that the selection of anaphors is sensitive to pragmatic conditions. For instance, how "expected" or "natural" is the reflexivity of the relation expressed by the predicate? It is, indeed, quite plausible that a pragmatic factor is involved in the paradigm of (88). The question is now, what this tells us about binding in general. To do so, other languages must be considered. It is striking, then, that in the corresponding Dutch paradigm the judgment is categorically that in all cases a complex anaphor is required.

(89) a. *Jan* is trots   op *zichzelf/*zich.*
         Jan is proud of himself
    b. *Jan* is jaloers op *zichzelf/*zich.*
         Jan is jealous of him/himself
    c. *Jan* spot   met   *zichzelf/*zich.*
         Jan mocks (with) him/himself
    d. *Jan* praat over *zichzelf/*zich.*
         Jan talks (of) him/himself

Here no influence of pragmatic factors can be observed. Clearly, that Dutch speakers have a different pragmatics is not a serious option. One should, therefore, look for a different factor. There is, in fact, an independent syntactic factor. The phenomenon only shows up in complement PPs. There is a difference between French and Dutch in the domain of PPs: Dutch has preposition stranding, but French does not. There must be a relation between P and the selecting predicate head that obtains in stranding languages like Dutch and not in French. Let's make the traditional assumption that this relation involves reanalysis. Thus, P reanalyzes with the selecting head in Dutch, not in French (following Kayne 1981). The effect of reanalysis must be represented in logical syntax. If so, in all cases of (89) we have (90) as a logical syntax representation:

(90) DP [V [P pro]] → ... [V-P] ... → DP (λx ([V-P] x x))

(90) contains a formally reflexive predicate which must be licensed, hence we find SELF in all cases, as required by our analysis. In French there is no V-P reanalysis, yielding (91):

(91) DP [V [P pro]] → DP (λx (V x [P x]))

(91) contains no formally reflexive predicate, hence no licensing is required. Therefore, it is indeed pragmatic factors that may determine whether a contrast marker like *même* is required. In brief:

(92) a. French: no syntactic V-P dependency → no licensing needed → pragmatic effects surface
    b. Dutch: syntactic V-P dependency → licensing required → pragmatic effects are masked

In a nutshell, we see how in one language a grammatical computation may cover an interpretive contrast that shows up in another.[65]

It is straightforward to construct potential further cases of masking. Consider the following option where properties that are independently shown to be possible are realized in a putative language. We know that (93) is a possible licenser of reflexivity in a language where null D's are licensed, but in such a language an element will not wear on its sleeve whether it is a simple or complex anaphor. But, of course, we can find out.

(93) [DP [D ø] [SE/SELF]

Suppose a language is like French in that bundling applies in the syntax, hence it is available for all predicates, and it combines this property with a Frisian Case system, where pronouns may be locally bound. It should be clear that such a language will show pervasive masking of the effects of IDI. In fact our theory predicts such languages to be possible (see Reuland 2009c for discussion).

Does it make a theory of anaphora unfalsifiable if the patterns it predicts do not surface in every language? In fact that's not so. All the properties working together to yield a particular pattern can be independently assessed, and the theory is falsified if properties predicted to be necessary for a particular pattern can be shown not to hold. Rather we have a situation that is quite common in science: every object or process must reflect the laws of nature, but not all of them are equally well suited to study them. The trajectories of the balls in a tennis match must surely obey the laws of motion, but if you want to study the laws of motion you better not start with watching a tennis match.

The same holds true for the study of the fundamental principles underlying binding and anaphora. We should take as the basis of our inquiries the languages where distinctions are visible. On the basis of the clues they provide us with we can profitably investigate languages with more puzzling systems, under the realization that in order to find out what they tell us an investigation of their fine structure is indispensable. I would like to end this discussion with some informative examples.

In his criticism of generative approaches to binding Levinson (2000, 334) notes that "the majority of Australian language would seem to lack anaphors. Instead, in many of these languages the reflexive meaning is indicated by a semantically general antipassive or detransitivized clause." From the current perspective, it is not at all surprising to find this. Apparently, such languages make use of operations on argument structure, which is one of the options our theory makes available. This makes it interesting to study the operations on argument structure they allow in more detail than has been done so far, but this would carry us beyond the scope of the present book.

In this connection Levinson discusses Guugu Yimithirr (p. 334). It has a special form for reflexives, but this form does not directly encode reflexivity, but only indicates directly that one argument is missing. As described, this may look "exotic." But in fact, this type of fact is no more exotic than forms like Dutch *De kinderen wasten zich* 'The kids were washing', which allows kids to be washing themselves as well as each other. In the framework of Reinhart and Siloni 2005, the lexical operation is argument reduction and bundling. The operation on the subject set can be either one of reflexivization or reciprocalization. The specific choice of the lexical items *themselves* or *each other* makes this explicit.

Another language Levinson (p. 336) reports on is Jiwarli. Jiwarli reflexives are indistinguishable from simple transitive clauses except, Levinson says, that the subject and object nominals are coreferential. Of course for a proper assessment one need to know what happens in the case of *love-hate* type verbs, otherwise the language needs not be more exotic than Frisian. Note furthermore that the claim involves coreferentiality. As we know, one must carefully distinguish between coreference/covaluation and binding. In fact, for a proper assessment the use of quantificational antecedents is always necessary. But let's assume that Jiwarli does indeed allow local binding of co-arguments throughout. If so, nothing more exotic need be involved than the case discussed above: a combination of Frisian (object arguments without structural Case) and French (free bundling).[66]

However, as the following case shows, even so, appearances can be deceptive (and I am very much indebted to Dagmar Schadler for drawing my attention to this fact). Next, Levinson discusses Fijian, and notes, quoting Dixon (1988), "In the third person, a verb with the transitive marker *-a* and without an explicit object is interpreted as having unmarked reference to a third-singular object which is not coreferential with the subject. If coreference or reflexivity is intended, a full object pronoun (e.g., *'ea*, third singular object) is required, and although this might be interpreted disjointedly, it encourages a coreferential reading" (p. 336):

(94) sa va'a-.dodonu-.ta'ini' 'ea   o   Mika
     ASP correct   3SG+OBJ ART Mike
     'Mike corrected himself.' or 'Mike corrected him.'

At a first glance, this goes against any reasonable expectation one might have given a structural binding theory: a pronominal facilitating a reflexive interpretation! However, a reassessment of the structure makes this pattern immediately fall out from the theory presented here. If Dixon's description is correct, Fiji allows null objects. Assuming that Fiji does not have a bundling operation applying to the verb *correct* (which makes it like English in this respect) assigning the interpretation *Mike λx (x corrected x)* to *Mike corrected $\emptyset_{pron}$* violates IDI. Hence it cannot receive the reflexive interpretation. The only way to obtain a reflexive interpretation is to protect the variable. Note that what is needed is just an element that contributes complexity. Using a pronominal element in that role is by no means unique crosslinguistically. We saw it already in Caxur and Malayalam. If so, the structure of (94) in the reflexive interpretation is in fact (94'):

(94') sa va'a-.dodonu-.ta'ini' [∅   'ea]   o   Mika
      ASP correct   3SG+OBJ 3SG+OBJ ART Mike
      'Mike corrected himself.'

The pronoun protects the variable, just like in the other cases discussed, and hence fully in line with what one would expect. The Fijian pattern, like the others, brings out clearly that one should not draw far-reaching conclusions from facts taken at their face value. Facts only show their significance on the basis of a careful analysis.[67]

6.8   Conclusions

Having arrived at the end of this chapter, I can say that I achieved my theoretical goals:

- In chapter 5 I showed in detail how SE anaphors can be syntactically related to their antecedents by Agree, at the same time yielding an unexpected perspective on c-command: the c-command requirement on syntactic binding can be reduced to probe-goal relations. The c-command requirement between anaphor and antecedent is just an epiphenomenon. It is not met where the probe has both the antecedent and the anaphor in its domain.
- In the present chapter I showed condition B to be a type 1 invariant, deriving it from the IDI as a general condition on computation.
- I showed condition A to be a type 2 invariant, deriving it from a general economy condition.

In the next two chapters we will explore the consequences of the approach developed.

In chapter 7 I discuss in detail the proposal that the relation between SELF and a predicate is one of movement, focusing the discussion on English and Dutch. Chapter 8 presents a case study of variation within Germanic.

7 Reflexive-Marking by SELF Movement: A Case Study

7.1 Introduction

In chapter 3 I presented the modular perspective on the anaphoric system developed in Reinhart and Reuland 1993. I disentangled the role of predicates and chains. I distinguished between the roles of semantic and syntactic predicates, presented a typology of anaphoric expressions differentiating between pronominals, SE anaphors, and SELF anaphors and showed how the specific feature composition of an anaphoric element determines its binding possibilities. Subsequently I moved from description to explanation. In chapters 4 and 5 I showed how binding relations can be syntactically encoded in an index-free syntax. We saw under what conditions it is possible for pronominals to be locally bound without stipulating that they are ambiguous between being pronominal and anaphoric. In chapter 6 I explained why reflexivity must be licensed, and discussed the nature of valence reduction, bundling and protection. Finally, I discussed the mechanism underlying reflexive-marking by SELF, distinguishing between the semantic operation providing its interpretation, and the syntactic process providing the relevant configuration. For English, as for Dutch and Scandinavian, we saw that the syntactic component of reflexive-marking by SELF anaphors involved covert SELF movement. In the present chapter I will discuss a number of consequences of SELF movement, focusing on English, but not exclusively so.

7.2 The Internal Structure of SELF Anaphors

The account given in the previous chapters abstracts away from the precise nature of the syntactic structure of *himself* and its cognates in other languages, or the details of the syntactic relation between the SELF element and the predicate. The basic form of the structure I have been positing for SELF anaphors is (1a), where X varies over D and π. In English this would be instantiated as (1b):

(1) a. [$_{XP}$ Pron/SE$_X$ [$_{NP}$ self]]
    b. [$_{DP}$ Pron$_D$ [$_{NP}$ self]]

Anagnostopoulou and Everaert (1999) (A&E) argue convincingly that there are significant crosslinguistic differences in the eventual realization. For instance, the anaphor *o eaftos tu* in Modern Greek, as they show, has the full syntactic structure of a POSS NP. Furthermore, as they argue, its head syntactically *incorporates* into V. For English *himself* they argue for a structure in which *him* and *self*, though syntactically merged separately as D and N respectively, undergo morphological merger at PF. The structure is given in (2a).

(2) a. [$_{DP}$ [$_{DP}$ [$_D$ [$_D$ him] [$_N$ self]$_i$] [$_{NP}$ e$_i$]]]
    b. [$_{\pi P}$ [$_\pi$ zich] [$_{NP}$ zelf]]
    c. [$_{XP}$ e [$_{NP}$ SELF]]

A&E argue that Dutch *zelf* in *zichzelf* is a focus marker. They propose a structure in which *zelf* is adjoined as a QP to a DP (a πP in our present terms) headed by *zich*. Syntactically, focus markers are quite diverse. Although the basic semantics assigned to *SELF* here fits in well with a role as a focalizing element, having focalizing properties is not incompatible with being in a head position. Since A&E did not present clear syntactic evidence for an adjunction position of SELF within the πP, I will stay with the structure in (2b), with *zelf* being an N-head. The syntactic differences between (1a) and (1b) are minor. (2a) and (2b) equally allow us to derive a covert adjunction structure with the required interpretive properties. Hence A&E's analysis of English only requires a minor further movement applying to the structure in (1b).[1]

What we find, therefore, is crosslinguistic variation in the specifics of implementation, while there is convergence in the overall structure. This is in fact what we expect to be the case. Language is based on general principles and strategies implemented on the basis of specific lexical items. These will vary in the details of their feature composition and hence their interaction with the environment. Meanwhile the more general patterns will be preserved. So, it is the structure of (1b) that will serve as the starting point for subsequent discussions.

As we saw in chapter 6, the complexity of the anaphoric expression plays a crucial role in the licensing of reflexivity. It then follows that (2c) may qualify as a SELF anaphor as well, provided it is in a language allowing the empty D to be licensed. In such a language, evidence for complexity may be more indirect than in languages with an overt D, but not necessarily less solid.

7.3 Further Consequences of SELF Movement

The movement approach to reflexive-marking by SELF introduced in the previous chapter raises three issues that do not come up in the theory of R&R 1993 as it is summarized in chapter 3, where reflexive-marking is simply a property of SELF that is realized in the environment specified in (3).

(3) A predicate (of P) is *reflexive-marked* iff either P is lexically reflexive or one of P's arguments is a SELF anaphor.

First and foremost, the movement approach to SELF raises the question of how reflexive-marking ensues when SELF is not c-commanded by the predicate head. To see this, reconsider example (59) of chapter 3, repeated as (4):

(4) Jan_1 hoorde
John heard
a. *$[zich_1 zich_1$ bespreken]
b. $[zich_1 zichzelf_1$ bespreken]
c. $[zichzelf_1 zich_1$ bespreken]
d. ??$[zichzelf_1 zichzelf_1$ bespreken]
e. *$[zichzelf_1 hem_1$ bespreken]
$pro_1 pro_2$ discuss

(4a) is ruled out by condition B, since the embedded predicate is reflexive, but there is no SELF anaphor to reflexive-mark it. (4d) is allowed by the binding conditions but is marked, because of the redundant use of SELF-marking. (4e) is ungrammatical due to a violation of the chain condition. The crucial cases are (4b) and (4c). (4b) is allowed since the predicate *bespreken* 'discuss' is both reflexive and reflexive-marked. This follows equally for movement and nonmovement. What about (4c)? Under the nonmovement implementation of condition A in chapter 3, *zichzelf* is a syntactic argument of both the matrix predicate *hoorde* 'heard' and the embedded predicate *bespreken*. Hence both are reflexive-marked, and correctly reflexive. If reflexive-marking requires movement, the question arises how reflexivity of the downstairs predicate is licensed, since it is not clear how SELF can move onto *bespreken*. This relates to another type of fact discussed in R&R 1993, 99:

(5) Max₁ heard [himself₁ criticize Lucie]

Here the SELF anaphor should mark the matrix predicate as reflexive, but it should also escape reflexive-marking the downstairs predicate, since the sentence is well formed despite the fact that *criticize* is not reflexive. R&R (1993) present a derivation in which the downstairs verb undergoes covert verb raising onto the matrix verb. In the structure resulting from movement of *criticize* onto *heard*, *himself* does not qualify as a subject for *criticize* given the definitions in chapter 3 (2), hence the predicate formed of *criticize* does not qualify as a syntactic predicate, and condition A does not apply. While this analysis derives the fact in (5), it requires a syntactic distinction between a verb and its trace that is incompatible with the current conception of movement as internal Merge.[2] Furthermore, it does not yet yield the correct result for (6), as discussed in R&R 1993, note 49:

(6) a. *Max₁ heard [Lucie criticize himself₁]
    b. *Max₁ criticize-heard [Lucie t himself₁]

(6) is to be ruled out by condition A, hence in this case moving *criticize* onto *heard* should not lead to an exemption. On the basis of this type of fact, it is proposed in R&R 1993, note 49, that eventhood may be a crucial factor, leading to the definition of syntactic predicate in (7):

(7) τ is the syntactic predicate of P iff
    a. τ consists of P and all its syntactic arguments, and
    b. either P has an e-role or P has a subject.
    The syntactic arguments of P are the projections assigned θ or Case by P and its external argument (subject).

Verbs have an e-role (whereas N's and P's do not). As a consequence, irrespective of whether *Lucie* in (6b) qualifies as a subject/external argument, *criticize* qualifies as a syntactic predicate, correctly ruling out (6b).

The assumption that reflexive marking by SELF is based on covert SELF movement avoids the problem of (4)–(6). The crucial factor in (4)–(6) is the asymmetry in c-command. In the cases where reflexive-marking should be enforced, the predicate head c-commands the SELF anaphor. Assuming that some property of the structure makes V attract SELF, SELF marking follows. (See chapter 6 for the relevant discussion.) In those cases where the result that the predicate is reflexive-marked gives the wrong result empirically, the SELF anaphor is in fact not c-commanded by the predicate head, hence it will not be attracted by the latter. (4c) and (5) together present one more instance of evidence that the *licensing* of reflexivity is dissociated from its *enforcement*. So, in (4c) *zichzelf* must be able to license reflexivity both upstairs and downstairs. Whereas in (4c) nothing goes wrong if one also takes SELF to enforce reflexivity downstairs, (5) shows that it does not do so. (The same applies to similar structures in Dutch.) This asymmetry is directly captured if enforcing reflexivity depends on SELF movement. Given the standard prohibition against lowering—whatever this follows from—SELF in (5) will not be able to move onto *criticize*, hence will not force it to be reflexive.

Two issues arise that need further discussion. One concerns the relation between the SELF anaphor and the verb in "SOV" languages. One might say that in Dutch the SELF anaphor c-commands the verb, rather than vice versa. However, Kaan (1992a, 1992b) and Zwart (1993, 1997) provide convincing evidence that in Dutch the surface configuration of direct object and verb is derived in line with Kayne's (1994) antisymmetry approach. In the position of first Merge we have a VO-structure in which V c-commands SELF as required.[3]

SELF anaphors in ECM subject position, as in (5), raise a further question. According to the definition of syntactic predicate in (2a) in chapter 3, *himself* reflexive-marks the upstairs syntactic predicate, which contains *Max* (external argument), *heard*, *himself* (by the Case clause of the definition), and *himself criticize Lucie* (by the θ-clause). This predicate indeed correctly comes out as reflexive (*Max* and *himself* are coindexed). However, if SELF movement results in a structure like (8), it is not clear how the reflexivizing property of SELF applies to the pair of arguments *Max*, *himself*, instead of to the pair *Max*, *himself criticize Lucie*.

(8) a. Max_1 heard [$himself_1$ criticize Lucie]

b.

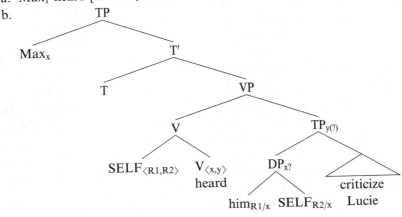

The latter option would yield an incorrect result, since in this case one really cannot bind the other, given their different types. But, one could argue, only the latter two are on the grid that is reflexivized by SELF. It is easy to see that technically this reasoning is not compelling. Given the way the notion of a syntactic predicate is defined, *Max* is a syntactic argument of *heard* both for reasons of θ and Case, *himself* is a syntactic argument for reasons of Case, and *himself criticize Lucie* is a syntactic argument for reasons of θ. The fact that *himself* reflexivizes the syntactic predicate of *heard* on the arguments *Max* and *himself* has as little bearing on the status of *himself criticize Lucie* as reflexive-marking has on *Bill* in the predicate *John introduced himself to Bill.* Hence, the principles as stated do indeed yield the correct result.

However, we will see that an analysis is available that is more transparent. The structure of (5)/(8) does not represent the fact that *Max* and *himself* are syntactic coarguments in terms of the configuration they are in. That they are, is only represented indirectly in terms of the Case dependency between the verb and *himself.* If we represent reflexive-marking by SELF configurationally, by SELF movement, it seems we run into a difficulty, as is sketched below.

Thematically, the internal argument of *heard* is just the TP. The TP contains the SELF anaphor, but if the effect of SELF movement is the identification of two positions on the verb's argument grid, it is impossible to represent this if *himself* is only indirectly related to a grid position on the predicate.

Hence, if reflexivization by SELF movement is to be represented configurationally, this forces a representation in which *himself* and *[himself₁ criticize Lucie]* have independent relations with the upstairs predicate. More precisely, the analysis requires that the ECM subject is external to the clause from which it originates at the level where the reflexivity requirement can be checked. That is, it has undergone raising.

The issue of subject-to-object raising has generated much debate since the 1970s (see Runner 2005 for an overview). Whereas Postal (1974) and others argued that the subject of an ECM clause has raised into the matrix clause, this went against some of the basic tenets of GB theory. However, within the minimalist framework there are no theoretical objections against the ECM subject moving into the matrix clause—for instance, into the V-domain for Case-checking purposes. Johnson (1991) presents a number of empirical arguments that the ECM subject moved out of its thematic position; consider examples like (9), where the ECM subject *Jerry* is separated from its clause by matrix material in the form of the particle *out*:

(9) She made Jerry$_i$ out [t$_i$ to be famous] (from Kayne 1985)

If ECM subjects are moved out, the ECM subject *himself* in (5) is indeed in a distinct argument position in the domain of the verb. Under the assumption that the Case-checking properties of a transitive verb are represented as properties of a specific segment of the lexical verb—for example, "little" *v*, or *v** (Chomsky 1995 and subsequent work)—the *syntactic predicate* in the sense of (2a) in chapter 3 is not just annotated in the structure, but configurationally represented (as is also made explicit in Chomsky 2008). If so, the relevant structure of (8a) is (10a) and that of (10b) (to use a *to*-infinitival) is (10c):

(10) a. Max$_1$ v*$_{heard}$ himself$_1$ [H$^0_{heard}$ [(himself$_1$) criticize Lucie]]
    b. Max expected himself to like Lucie.
    c. Max$_1$ v*$_{expected}$ himself$_1$ [H$^0_{expected}$ [(himself$_1$) to like Lucie]]

Here reflexive-marking applies to V/*v** and we can configurationally represent the reflexive character of V/*v**, without directly involving a position in the complement clause. Crucial in this analysis is that the accusative Case-assigning property of a verb is associated with an independent verbal grid position.[4] Thus, we make explicit one empirical assumption that was implicit in the disjunction (θ or structural Case) within the definition of syntactic predicate: the property of being able to assign/check structural Case is represented on the grid of a verbal predicate *as a position*. This is enough to obtain the dissociation between the relation between *himself* and the predicate and the complement TP and the predicate that is needed for SELF-marking to be defined configurationally.

If so, the syntactic predicate formed of *Max, heard, himself*, and *(himself) criticize Lucie* is not reflexive on the pair *Max, himself* just as the result of an arbitrary formal property of *himself*, but as a consequence of a standard syntactic operation that uses SELF's lexical properties (as I discussed in the previous chapter).

Given the approach developed in the previous chapters, the facts of (4)–(6) now follow without any additional assumptions.

7.4 The Definition of Syntactic Predicates: Which Property Attracts SELF?

As we have seen in the previous section, introducing reference to eventhood directly into the definition of syntactic predicate as in (7) is unnecessary to obtain an account of (4)–(6) and related facts.

However, whether or not reference to eventhood is necessary to capture these facts is orthogonal to the general issue of the role of eventhood.

R&R (1993, section 5) propose that the absence of an event role is what sets P and N predicates apart from V. The question is then how DPs and their subjects fare with respect to reflexivity and its marking. In most discussions of the CBT it is assumed that the subject of a DP creates a local domain for anaphor binding as in (23) in chapter 3, repeated here:

(11) a.   Lucie liked [(a) picture of herself]
     b. */?Lucie liked [your picture of herself]

As noted in chapter 3, the standard judgments have been called into question. A number of studies (Runner, Sussman, and Tanenhaus 2002, 2003; Keller and Asudeh 2001; Asudeh and Keller 2001; Jaeger 2004; Runner and Kaiser 2005) have experimentally investigated speakers' judgments with respect to Picture NPs containing possessors.[5] They have found robust evidence that reflexives are not limited to taking only the possessor as their antecedent; the subject of the containing sentence may also serve as the antecedent, as illustrated in (12). However, a pronoun in the same position is constrained to be disjoint from the possessor phrase, as indicated in (13) (both from Runner and Kaiser 2005).

(12) Ebenezer$_i$ saw Jacob$_j$'s picture of himself$_{j/i}$

(13) Ebenezer$_i$ saw Jacob$_j$'s picture of him$_{i/k/*j}$

Such facts are problematic for the definition of syntactic predicate based on the presence of an external argument, but would follow from the alternative presented by R&R (1993, note 49), repeated in (7), assuming that nouns such as *picture* do not have an e-role. Dropping the subject requirement, which is now superfluous, (7) can in fact be simplified to (14), eliminating the disjunction:

(14) τ is the syntactic predicate of P iff
     a. τ consists of P and all its syntactic arguments, and
     b. P has an e-role.
     The syntactic arguments of P are the projections assigned θ or Case by P[6] and its external argument (subject).

From this definition of syntactic predicate the full range of facts discussed follows.

    However, given that we no longer need the reference to the e-role to account for the ECM cases, let's also consider the option of reverting to the original definition with a subject requirement rather than an e-role, as in (14′):

(14′) τ is the syntactic predicate of P iff
    a. τ consists of P and all its syntactic arguments, and
    b. P has a subject.
    The syntactic arguments of P are the projections assigned θ or
    Case by P and its external argument (subject).

Which of the two represents the best way to go ultimately depends on the proper conception of a subject. It may well be that having an e-role and projecting an external argument position (subject) on the basis of an EPP feature—irrespective of whether there is a role to be assigned via that position, as in the case of raising verbs, and other verbs types minimally requiring an expletive—are two sides of the same coin. If so, verbs do, and nouns do not have subjects at all, and (14) and (14′) are equivalent.[7]

Having an e-role appears to be the more basic property, but the question is how this property is readable in the syntax. I will tentatively assume that it is realized syntactically as the property of requiring a subject. Hence for sake of concreteness I will propose—in line with the discussion in the previous chapter—that *having a subject* is the property that makes a predicate able to attract SELF, as (14′). The impossibility for *him* to be bound by *Jacob* in (13) needs no special discussion, since it immediately follows from the chain condition without any modification.

Note that whether all nouns lack an e-role is a matter of debate. However, as the discussion in Grimshaw 1990 shows, there are clear differences between nominals in their argument structure in relation to their eventivity (see Reuland 2010b for further discussion). Furthermore, the nominals Davies and Dubinsky (2003) classify as concrete (for instance, *book* as denoting an object versus *book* as denoting the result of a writing process) are also clearly noneventive. What we expect, then, is a correlation between not being eventive and allowing an interpretation of *himself* as exempt. Initial reports (Runner 2007; Davies and Dubinsky 2003) are in line with this expectation, although further research is still warranted.[8]

While these issues are general, it is the absence of SE anaphors in English that creates the conditions to observe them. Let's now return to a question discussed earlier, where English seems truly exceptional, the apparent inability for 1st- and 2nd-person pronominals to be locally bound.

7.5 Local Binding of 1st- and 2nd-Person Pronominals

The approach to local binding of 1st- and 2nd-person pronominals presented in chapter 5 is general in scope. It just predicts that 1st- and

2nd-person object pronominals may enter a chain with corresponding subject pronominals or be locally bound by them where no chain is formed (as in Frisian). Given this, the fact that English does not allow *I washed me, you washed you*, and so on may seem puzzling, and is often cited as a problem for R&R, as noted earlier.

In actual fact, this is a result that comes for free already under that approach. As we saw in the previous chapter, grooming verbs like *wash* have two related entries, one reflexive, the other transitive. The reflexive entry does not have a syntactic object, as in *I washed*; the transitive entry must, on the contrary, have a SELF anaphor as its object, as in *I washed myself*. Under any theory relating inherent reflexivity to a null realization of the object *I wash me* could not have been derived.

The following cases do merit discussion, though. One is the behavior of verbs like *behave*; the other concerns the binding of 1st- and 2nd-person pronouns as ECM subjects.

Alongside the use of *behave* in (15a) without an object argument we have (15b) where there is one (though it is nonthematic), but we do not have (15c):

(15) a.   We behaved.
    b.   We behaved ourselves.
    c.   *We behaved us.

Thematically, (15a) and (15b) are on a par. Both are semantically intransitive. One way of putting this is that the lexical operation of valence reduction, though it obligatorily reduces thematic accusative Case, may eliminate the structural accusative, but need not. Another way is to say that verbs in English can be thematically intransitive, but syntactically transitive. Note that regardless of one's pet theory, something special has to be said about verbs like *behave* and their kin. They are semantically intransitive, yet license structural accusative Case. Given that transitivity is reflected in the presence of v*, the simplest way is to stipulate that *behave* gives rise to a well-formed derivation both in a numeration with v* and in a numeration without one. Let us explore this idea.

Consider (15a). In this form the predicate has neither thematic nor structural Case. Hence, neither the object form *us* nor the object form *ourselves* could be licensed. Next consider the 1st-person plural form in (15b). By assumption, there is no thematic Case. However, there is structural Case. Therefore, by common assumptions we have *We* v*$_{behave}$ *us* V$_{behave}$ *(us)*, where *us* checks its Case with v*. This brings us back to the discussion in section 7.3, where we saw that transitivity is structurally represented. Irrespective of the details involved, the expression *we v* us* forms a *syntactic predicate* that is reflexive. If so, it must be reflexive-marked, as we saw in the previous chapter. Note that our reduction of condition B to IDI entails that it applies to all representations where expressions in the computation may fail to be distinguished. Although in this case we do not get a θ-violation, we do get a mismatch in the instructions for the interpretation of v*. Consequently, (15c) leads to a violation of IDI (condition B), and *ourselves* instead of *us* is required.

The same reasoning applies to ECM. As we saw in section 7.3, the structure of (16a) is (16b):

(16) a. Max expected himself to like Lucie.
  b. Max_1 $v^*_{expected}$ $himself_1$ $[H^0_{expected}$ $[(himself_1)$ to like Lucie]]

By the same token the structure of (17a) is (17b):

(17) a. I expected myself/*me to like Lucie.
  b. I_1 $v^*_{expected}$ me_1 $[H^0_{expected}$ $[(me_1)$ to like Lucie]]

Consequently, here too the v* heads a reflexive predicate that requires licensing along the lines discussed.

Why doesn't the same reasoning apply to Dutch—and related languages? That is, why is English special? In fact, English is special in another respect as well. Only in English does the T-system represent a full-fledged independent syntactic constituent. Consider the differences it shows under canonical tests such as VP-deletion, as opposed to the fusional character of the V-T system in the other languages under discussion, as illustrated by the contrast in (18):

(18) a. Alice saw the bottle and the cat did [VP ____] too
  b. *Alice zag de fles en de kat deed [VP ____] ook
  c. Alice zag de fles en de kat deed dat ook.
    Alice saw the bottle and the cat did that too

Only in English is there an independent realization of T taking a VP-complement.

Thus, only in English does the presence of structural accusative Case entail the presence of a syntactic category v* in the structure. Only in English, then, is there a syntactic predicate formed of v* to which conditions of reflexive licensing apply and that is not structurally coextensive with the predicate formed of V.[9]

We see, therefore, that a seemingly puzzling contrast between English and languages such as Dutch in the licensing of personal pronouns, follows from the way the fine structure of the grammar and binding interact.

On closer reflection, this should not be surprising. It has been noted all along that 1st- and 2nd-person pronominals can easily be found in "free dative" constructions like *I found me a book*.[10] So, the prohibition against local binding cannot be due to inherent properties of the pronominal anyway (a fact that has failed to be appreciated in the discussions so far, Conroy 2007 being a notable exception). Our analysis entails that English does not require a SELF anaphor wherever an argument can be licensed (i.e., can get Case) in exceptionally Case-marked complements in a way that does not involve moving into the matrix clause.

As shown in Reuland 1983, in ACC-*ing* constructions such as *Mary hated no one coming to the party*, the ACC of the subject is not licensed directly by the (functional projections of the) matrix verb, but indirectly via the -*ing*-head. The ACC subject cannot raise under passive; it does not allow wide scope. In brief, it stays put where it is.[11] If so, we now expect locally bound pronominals to be possible (note that due to the indirect nature of the Case-checking process, the chain condition is not violated). And this is what we find. A Google search gives a variety of examples as in (19):[12]

(19) a. I can see me having to pay his therapy bill for him when he's older.
   b. Do you recall you being invited and not wanting to go?
   c. He remembers him having to grow up the same way. He now understands what rich people are like.
   d. He does not recall him having to use a compass to get to the LP/OP site.[13]
   e. We see us having to pick up huge bills.
   f. They charged us for them having to clean the vent.

The same observation can be made for complements of *want*. The canonical analysis of *want*-type complements (e.g., Kayne 1981) is that they are headed by a null variant of *for*, which assigns or mediates Case. Again a Google search shows that examples of the type *I want me to VP*, and so on, are far from rare.[14]

Facts of this type have occasionally been noted, but they have so far escaped explanation. The fact that they are captured by the approach developed here is evidence that the way we relate the obligatoriness of SELF forms to their specific structural position is correct. Note that we do not expect these uses to be as frequent—or even as unmarked—as locally bound pronominals in the environments where we typically find them in Dutch and other languages. In those environments they do not face "competition" with PRO. In the English cases the pronominal reflects the effects of the "Avoid Pronoun Principle" (Chomsky 1981). (Whatever the explanation for this principle, and the precise status of PRO, descriptively it appears to hold quite widely.) Hence we will only expect the pronominal to show up felicitously under conditions where the Avoid Pronoun Principle is obviated. For us, the important point is, then, that unexpectedly for the standard accounts, locally bound pronouns do show up in English in the environments discussed.

This concludes the discussion of local binding in English. I will now turn to a final issue in the conditions on chains: What elements can head a chain?

7.6 Maximality of Chains and Conditions on Chain Heads

7.6.1 The Issue

Chapter 5 provided extensive discussion of the PRD as a condition on chain tails. Given the mechanisms of C_{HL} chain formation applies blindly, and if possible, it cannot be bypassed. This entails that the chains to be formed are always maximal. How far, then, can a chain be extended? Chain formation as a process is sensitive to the general locality conditions on grammatical operations. The chain condition as formulated by R&R also imposed a specific requirement on the head of the chain, namely that it must be +R. For the sake of simplicity I will couch the discussion in the terms of R&R. For ease of reference the definition of the +R property is repeated here:

(20) An NP is +R iff it carries a full specification for ϕ-features.

In chapter 3 I noted that the +R property has two sides. On the one hand it expresses a condition on morphosyntactic feature composition, and on the other it is intended to capture the semantic status of such elements as nonanaphors. As always, it is an empirical issue to what extent such a correspondence between two subsystems actually holds. As discussed earlier, Anagnostopoulou and Everaert (1999) show that Modern Greek has elements that are on the one hand anaphoric, and on the other can head chains. Amiridze (2006) shows the same for Georgian. However, as we will see, these facts are fully compatible with the chain condition as we elaborated it, since in both cases the anaphoric element is fully specified for ϕ-features.

In chapter 5 I discussed the fact that in Icelandic nominative anaphors of the SE and SE-SELF type are excluded, despite the fact that there are nominative positions where they could be bound. There it was shown that this property follows without stipulation, given the fact that the nominative element must check the uninterpretable φ-features of the V-T complex, which, being deficient, SE cannot do. Given this logic the +R-requirement on chain heads should fully reduce to their relation to the agreement system. If an anaphor has the φ-features to check the uninterpretable φ-features of the V-T complex, requirements of narrow syntax will be satisfied, and it will get the interpretation that the interpretive component assigns.

In the next section I will consider Greek and Georgian in more detail.

7.6.2   Nominative Complex Anaphors

The question is how to handle the part of the chain condition that requires a chain to be headed by a +R element. In R&R 1993, section 6.2.2, it was noted that this assumption is problematic since it rules out logophors as chain heads. Logophors may head a chain, and some of them are both morphosyntactically and interpretively −R in that system. In R&R 1993, section 6.2.2, it was therefore proposed that the chain condition does not apply to single-member chains. This proposal works for English, since logophoric *himself* does not occur as a syntactic argument of a verb, and hence does not undergo "raising." However, it is problematic for languages such as Icelandic where logophoric *sig* can occur in argument position—for instance, as the exceptionally Case-marked subject of an unaccusative—and where it does head a nontrivial chain. This makes a general solution limiting them to one-member chains impossible to maintain. Consequently, we will have to reassess the conditions on the head of the chain, and more specifically the status of subject anaphors.

For the purpose of this discussion I will limit myself to SE anaphors and SELF anaphors, where SELF anaphors are understood as complex anaphors that obligatorily reflexivize the predicate they are arguments of. That is, they show the canonical behavior of anaphors in some of the environments in which they occur. Note that it is not guaranteed that they show this behavior in other environments. So, in addressing this issue we have to distinguish the following questions: Can a particular form occur in a position where it would be a chain head—for example, in a specifier position of a *finite* TP? If not, why not? And if it can, how will it be interpreted?

My general approach will be based on the methodology adopted throughout this book. Conditions on chain heads require the same type of recourse to the microstructure of the grammar as conditions on chain tails. Consequently, there is no reason to expect that macronotions such as *anaphor* provide for the level of detail needed for explanation. (This also puts natural limits on the number of cases we can go through.) Hence we will have to go over the options on a case-by-case basis.

Consider first the case of SE anaphors. For the syntactic encoding of the dependency on their antecedent, they have a free ride on processes of chain formation. The first question is, then, why a SE anaphor cannot occur in the position indicated in (21):

(21) C . . . T . . . C [SE T_{Agr} . . .]

This is a case we already considered in chapter 5, but for a broader perspective let us briefly review some of the relevant literature on this subject. Rizzi (1990a) and Woolford (1999) proposed the condition in (22) to cover this case:

(22) *The anaphor-agreement effect*
      Anaphors do not occur in syntactic positions construed with agreement.

Everaert (2001) gives an extensive discussion of this effect and points out a number of theoretical and empirical problems. From the present perspective the major problem with (22) is that it falls short of being an explanation. It relies on a notion of anaphor that itself lacks theoretical status. Its theoretical motivation requires a technology that is no longer available to us. But, as Everaert points out, there are also many empirical problems given the existence of subject anaphors in a variety of languages.

As we saw in chapter 5, the impossibility of the configuration in (21) follows directly from the current view on agreement features in T. Agreement features on T are uninterpretable features that must be checked and deleted before the structure is handed over to the interpretive system (given the Principle of Full Interpretation). In the canonical case such as *the white rabbit was running along*, the subject *the rabbit* deletes the uninterpretable agreement features on the finite form *was*. However, this can only work if the subject is fully specified for the relevant features. A SE anaphor is underspecified. Hence, if it occurs as a subject, the uninterpretable features on T for which SE has no match will be left and will yield a crash at the C-I interface. Note that this analysis generalizes over all cases where the SE anaphor stands in an agreement relation with finite T, including Icelandic constructions with quirky Case subjects where the anaphor "long distance" agrees with T from a position in the VP. This is illustrated in (23), from Everaert 1990:

(23) *Honum$_i$ finnst sig$_i$ veikur
     him$_{DAT}$ finds SE$_{NOM}$ sick
     'He considers himself sick.'

As Everaert (2001) argues, such an account works straightforwardly
for all SE anaphors construed with agreement. Moreover, as Everaert
observes, it immediately derives the result noted in the literature on the
anaphor-agreement effect, that in languages lacking agreement (such as
Chinese and Japanese) there is no prohibition against anaphors in subject
position. All this requires no principle that is specific to binding at all.

What about potentially intermediate cases, as in (24)? Could SE head a
chain in the position indicated in (24)?

(24) C ... T ... [C$_1$ [DP T$_{Agr1}$ ... V$_1$ SE ...]]

Given that SE is part of the C$_1$-T$_1$-V$_1$-chain by virtue of the relations it
independently and unavoidably enters, it cannot head a chain by virtue
of necessity. As we will see in more detail in chapter 8, in OV languages
the chain SE can only be extended as far as the C-system of the first full
clause—infinitive or finite—containing it. In all cases a SE anaphor construed with nonmatching AGR will lead to a crash. This checking part of
the account applies irrespective of whether SE is used anaphorically or
logophorically. What about the possibility of SE to head a chain in logophoric contexts? As we saw in chapter 5, logophoric *sig* in Icelandic must
be licensed by a subjunctive. The syntactic role of the subjunctive is that
of blocking the formation of a chain between *sig* and T$_{Agr}$. This frees the
anaphor from the requirement to be construed with its local antecedent.
For its interpretation discourse conditions prevail, much like in the case
of English SELF when it is prevented from reflexivizing the predicate.

The same factor disallowing simplex anaphors as subjects of finite
clauses will also rule out all complex anaphors that fail to carry the features required for checking, such as Dutch *zichzelf*, Norwegian *seg zelv*,
and Icelandic *sjálfan sig*. However, there is nothing intrinsic in anaphors
that makes them incompatible with such features, so one may expect
crosslinguistic variation to show up.

As already noted at the beginning of this part of our discussion, there is
indeed a range of languages that allow anaphors in (finite) subject position. Here, I will limit discussion to two. Anagnostopoulou and Everaert
(1999) (A&E) present a discussion of subject anaphors in Modern Greek.
Amiridze (2006) covers binding in Georgian, including object camou-
flage and anaphors in subject position. Everaert (2001) synthesizes these
issues.

Greek and Georgian are illustrated in (25) (from A&E) and (26) (from Amiridze 2006 and Amiridze and Everaert 2000 respectively).[15]

(25) a. O Jannis$_i$ ton$_i$ agapai ton eafto tu$_i$
       the John$_{NOM}$ CL$_{ACC}$ loves   himself$_{ACC}$
       'John loves himself.'

   b. [O   eaftos tu]$_i$ tu$_i$ aresi   [tu   Petru]$_i$
      the$_{NOM}$ self$_{NOM}$ his$_{GEN}$ CL$_{DAT}$ like$_{3SG}$ the$_{DAT}$ Peter$_{DAT}$
      'Peter pleases himself.'

(26) a. prezidentma$_i$ Ø-i-xsn-a   [tavisi   tavi]$_i$
       president$_{ERG}$ him-i-saved-he head's$_{NOM}$ head$_{NOM}$
       'The president saved himself.'

   b. [tavisma   tavma]$_i$ Ø-i-xsn-a   prezidenti$_i$
      head's$_{ERG}$ head$_{ERG}$ him-i-saved-he president$_{NOM}$
      Lit.: 'Himself saved the president.'
      'His own positive/*negative personal properties, and/or his past achievements/*failures, etc. saved the president.'

Let us first consider the Greek case. To begin, A&E show that *o eaftos tu* clearly is a "complex anaphor." As shown in (25a), *ton eafto tu* licenses a reflexive predicate just like its English or Dutch counterparts, but as is seen in (25b), unlike these it can occur in subject position. The question is how surprising this is. It is surprising from the perspective of any principle such as (22) that is couched in terms of a macronotion like *anaphor*. However, if one considers the feature composition and internal structure of *ton eafto tu*, it is not. As A&E show, it has the full internal and external structure of a POSS NP. The article that heads it is fully specified for φ-features; it has accusative Case in object position and nominative in subject position. Hence no failure-checking uninterpretable T features will arise. As a consequence, there is no syntactic prohibition against it showing up in subject position. The question is whether the configuration in (25b) predicts a condition B or C violation—as it would, incorrectly, in the CBT. A&E show that, due to the internal structure of the anaphor, any element that would be coindexed with the antecedent—in an index-based framework—does not c-command it; hence no binding between the phrases *tu Petru* and *o eaftos tu* as such obtains. As they note, there are some interpretive restrictions on its occurrence. For independent reasons *o eaftos tu* does not allow a logophoric interpretation. Consequently, it can only appear in a configuration where it is able to license reflexivity. A&E argue that the head noun *eaftos* is semantically weak, and can therefore only be interpreted by incorporation (Baker 1988).

Consequently, they predict that *o eaftos tu* is solely possible in derived subject positions—with incorporation taking place from a position of first Merge—which they show is borne out, witness the contrast between (25b) and (27):

(27) *[O   eaftos$_i$ tu]   ton antopathi ton Petro$_i$
     [the self   his]$_{NOM}$ CL disliked   the Petros$_{ACC}$
     'Himself disliked Petros.'

Thus, Modern Greek provides an interesting further illustration of the role syntactic microstructure plays in binding. (See also Spathas 2010.)

Georgian provides another example. Georgian has two anaphoric forms, a simplex anaphor *tav*, and a complex anaphor *tav tavis* modeled on a POSS construction, lit. 'his head'. In chapter 6 I discussed the nature of the contrast between the two in the context of another issue. (26a) illustrates the canonical use of the complex anaphor as a reflexivizer, and as such it just shows the standard properties of a reflexive anaphor (see Amiridze 2006 for discussion). In (26b) it shows up in the subject position. It is fully specified for the features involved in agreement. Hence, again, conditions on feature checking are met, and no syntactic factor prevents it from occurring in this position. (As Amiridze observes, its simplex counterpart is not fully specified and is excluded from the subject position, as one would expect.) As its Modern Greek counterpart, *tav tavis* does not allow for a logophoric interpretation.[16] And again this leads to a restriction on its interpretation. As indicated in the gloss of (26b), *himself saved the president* does not simply mean that *he himself saved the president* or something similar. Rather, as Amiridze notes, the proper interpretation of the subject anaphor in finite clauses is always inanimate. What is found is a *properties of* or *image of* interpretation. Thus, in (26b) it is the (positive) *properties* of the president that saved him. Given this, there is no chain condition violation in any of the implementations of chains we have, nor is there a condition C violation. As Amiridze notes, the interpretation assigned to the anaphor is effectively a function of the interpretation of the antecedent. Thus the relevant structure of (26b) in logical syntax would be captured by (28):

(28) the president (λx (f(x) [saved x]))

Here the f of $f(x)$ is pragmatically chosen in such a way that $\|f(x)\|$ may stand proxy for x, along the lines discussed in chapter 6.[17]

So far, we have seen that SE anaphors as finite subjects are disallowed since they lead to a crash at the C-I interface. Where complex anaphors— or perhaps also simplex anaphoric elements that do not qualify as SE anaphors by our definition—are sufficiently specified for φ-features, syntax allows them as finite subjects, although their semantics may impose independent restrictions. Where they are φ-feature-deficient the same reasoning applies as in the case of SE anaphors. How, then, about English *himself*? Where SELF cannot reflexive-mark a predicate—where it is not a syntactic argument of the predicate—an exempt/logophoric interpretation is assigned. If it is a syntactic argument of a predicate—including the ECM subject of a clausal complement—it will obligatorily reflexive-mark its predicate, hence will not be in the head position of its chain. The remaining question is why *himself* is excluded from the subject position of finite clauses. Reuland and Reinhart 1995 argued that *himself* is −R since it is not in a Case opposition—*there is no heself* with which it contrasts. A&E note that this has the air of circularity, since the absence of a Case contrast is what one might wish to explain. They then give a number of arguments indicating that *himself* may indeed qualify as −R for independent reasons.

Be this as it may, it is worth pointing out that a simple answer may be possible. As things have been developing in our discussions, the chain condition as originally stated, turned out to be a descriptive generalization that we want to derive from independent mechanisms. The account of the tail end of the chain was no longer couched in terms of −R or +R. The reason SE anaphors cannot be nominative and head a chain does not refer to the −R property either. Rather it is just their feature composition that counts. Hence, in the case of *himself* as a subject, two questions must be distinguished: (i) Why can't we have *himself was running late*, other than in the substantivized reading; and (ii) Why don't we have *heself was running late*?

The first question has the trivial answer that *himself* is not nominative and the structure has no redeeming features like the coordination in *me and him were running to the party* that make up for that. Why is there no *heself*? Given the fact that nothing prevents anaphoric forms from occurring as subjects, the reason should be morphosyntactic, rather than strictly in the domain of binding.[18] As we saw, A&E claim that the element *himself* is an expression where both members are equally prominent (with the further structure given in (2a)). For a putative element *heself*, this leads to a lethal ambiguity if agreement is to apply. This ambiguity is for the worse, since both components trigger a different kind of agreement, as A&E indicate, citing evidence from Joseph 1979.[19] If so, one expects to find an expression in this position that does have a built-in asymmetry. Such an expression is *he himself*, which is the form we find.

7.7 Summary and Conclusions

In this chapter I explored a number of consequences of the proposal that reflexive-marking by SELF has two components: licensing by the complexity of the SELF anaphor and enforcing reflexivity by SELF movement. We saw that the asymmetry in ECM (upstairs enforcing and licensing, downstairs licensing only) immediately follows. I discussed the fact that SELF anaphors in picture NPs need not be locally bound, and I reassessed the definition of "syntactic predicate" as the property attracting SELF. SELF movement was shown to fit in with the raising analysis of exceptional Case-marking in English and to explain why in English 1st- and 2nd-person ECM subjects show up as SELF anaphors when locally bound. We have seen that there is no intrinsic property of 1st- and 2nd-person pronouns that forbids local binding in English. Finally, I discussed SELF anaphors in subject position/SpecTP. We saw that there cannot be a general prohibition against their occurrence in SpecTP. Rather, whether or not they are allowed depends on their fine structure, and to what extent their ϕ-features are able to check the ϕ-features of the finite verb.

We arrived at a simple account of the fact that *himself* cannot be the subject of a finite clause in English. It is based on a fairly shallow property of *himself*, but in view of the fact that subject anaphors do occur in a variety of languages, this is a bonus for our analysis rather than a problem. This is all the more true since the other canonical anaphor, the reciprocal *each other*, so easily enters the subject position of finite clauses in a variety of English dialects. In the next chapter we will continue our discussion with an analysis of the variation of anaphoric systems in Germanic, and see how further puzzling variations in anaphoric systems follow from simple differences in structure.

8 Variation in Anaphoric Systems within Germanic

8.1 Introduction

A systematic study of patterns of crosslinguistic variation in any domain requires a theory that tells one what to look for, that provides clues as to what type of variation to expect. It also requires languages that have been described in the detail that is necessary. Over the last few years many anaphoric systems in languages over the world have been described and analyzed in some detail. Studies with an impressive global coverage include Huang 2000 and Safir 2004a. Lust et al. (2000) present a typology of anaphoric dependencies in a smaller, but typologically diverse, range of languages. Yet, as we will see in this chapter it is details of analysis that one may not expect to find represented in surveylike studies, which are needed for a proper understanding of the processes involved. Such details are often scarce, and not available in a systematic manner. Hence, in this chapter I will focus on a group of languages that have been studied in sufficient depth.

Such a group is Germanic. As was discussed in section 1.8.2, there is considerable variation in the anaphoric systems of the Germanic languages. One fact turned out to be highly significant for a proper perspective on binding, namely the fact that in Frisian 3rd-person pronominals can be locally bound. In retrospect, one may wonder why local binding of pronominals was not considered significant much earlier (Burzio 1991 being a notable exception), since local binding of 1st- and 2nd-person pronominals is a wide spread phenomenon. Possibly, this is due to the fact that 1st- and 2nd-person pronominals were considered to be different anyway, as in fact was borne out by our discussion in the previous chapters. In the following sections I will present a detailed analysis of a number of contrasts in the binding of anaphors and pronominals within Germanic.

In the course of this study a number of factors in variation have already been discussed. We came across variation in local binding of 3rd-person pronominals (roughly, Frisian versus the more general pattern). We have already seen how this pattern can in principle be reduced to properties of the Case system. The details of the argument had to wait. In section 8.2 I will go over the facts in detail.

We found variation in local binding of 1st- and 2nd-person pronominals (English versus the pattern in other languages). In the previous chapter we saw how this variation can be reduced to independent differences in the syntactic structure correlated with structural Case.

Some languages allow logophoric interpretation of SE anaphors (Icelandic as we already saw, and Faroese as will be briefly discussed below). In chapter 5 we saw how the locus of this variation resides in the behavior of the (finite) verb as a subjunctive operator. An extensive discussion of logophoricity in Icelandic will be presented in section 8.5.

Further types of variation that warrant discussion include the variation in the manifestation of complexity in reflexive markers (German, possibly Swedish). As briefly indicated in chapter 6, elements that are prima facie SE anaphors may in fact show morphosyntactic complexity. In section 8.3 I will extensively discuss the case of German. Differences in anaphoric systems (three-way as in Dutch, and four-way in Scandinavian) represent a second type of variation. These will briefly come up in section 8.4.2, where they will be shown to follow from the analysis of POSS phrases in chapter 5, modulo a simple grammatical contrast. A third type of variation includes differences in the binding domains of SE anaphors across the Germanic languages. These differences form the main subject of our discussion in section 8.4.3. I will start now with the discussion of Frisian. For the sake of convenience, binding relations will be annotated by indices.

8.2 Local Binding of Pronouns in Frisian

The basic facts of Frisian were already briefly mentioned in sections 1.3, 1.8, 3.2, and 5.6.2.

Like English, Frisian has a two-member anaphoric system in 3rd person; there is an anaphor *himsels* and a pronominal *him*. However, unlike Dutch and English, Frisian has locally bound 3rd-person pronominals. The generalization is that wherever Dutch allows the SE anaphor *zich*, Frisian allows a bound pronominal. The paradigm is illustrated in (1)–(3).

(1) a. Willem$_i$ skammet him$_i$
    William shames   him
  b. Willem$_i$ wasket him$_i$
    William washes him

These are lexically reflexive verbs. Verbs that are not lexically reflexive pattern as one would expect, and must be SELF-marked, in accordance with condition B:

(2) Willem$_i$ bewûnderet himsels$_i$/*him$_i$
    William admires   himself/him

In terms of the lexicon-syntax parameter discussed in chapter 6, Frisian, like Dutch, qualifies as a lexicon language. The classes of verbs requiring SELF-marking by and large coincide in Dutch and Frisian.

    Locative PPs behave as in Dutch and English in allowing bound pronominals (see the discussion in chapter 3):

(3) Klaas$_i$ treau   de karre foar   him$_i$ út
    Klaas pushed the cart   before him out

As subjects of ECM constructions, Frisian has bound pronominals alongside SELF anaphors, as illustrated in (4) and (5).

(4) Jan$_i$ seach [him$_i$/himsels$_i$ yn 'e film de partij winnen]
    Jan saw   [him/himself in the film the match win]

(5) Jan$_i$ fielde [him$_i$/himsels$_i$ fuortglieden]
    Jan felt   him   slip-away

Thus, with respect to conditions A and B, Frisian behaves just like Dutch. However, as discussed in chapter 3, in Dutch the sentences with pronominals corresponding to those in (1), (4), and (5) are ruled out by the chain condition.

    In our discussion of chain formation and economy in chapters 4 and 5 I further analyzed the source of chain condition effects. We saw that a feature chain cannot be formed between a pronominal and its antecedent, since this would violate the PRD. We further saw that chain formation results from a blind syntactic process. Our interpretation of economy entails that a violation is final, as is the case with locally bound pronominals in Dutch, or local binding of *a gente* by *nos* (or vice versa) in Brazilian Portuguese. A chain condition violation can only be avoided if the conditions for chain formation are not met. The absence of an alternative anaphoric element is not sufficient to license local binding of a pronominal.[1] The crucial property setting Frisian apart is, then, that the

conditions for a chain link to be formed are not met, since object pronominals can be licensed without structural Case. This claim is based on
findings by Jarich Hoekstra (1994), which I will now review.

The key to the discussion is the fact that two pronominals, namely the
3rd person singular feminine and the 3rd-person plural (common gender)
have two object forms: both may be realized as *har* as well as *se* (the plural pronominal has the form *harren* as well, but for all purposes it behaves
just like *har*). (Despite appearances, *se* is a pronominal and not to be confused with a SE anaphor or the French clitic *se*.) Often, these forms are
used interchangeably. This is illustrated in (6) and (7).

(6) Jan   hat har   juster   sjoen.
    John has her/them yesterday seen

(7) Jan   hat se   juster   sjoen.
    John has her/them yesterday seen

However, unlike *har*, *se* may not be locally bound.

(8) a. Marie$_i$ wasket harsels$_i$/har$_i$/*se$_i$
       Mary   washes herself/her/her
    b. De bern$_i$ waskje harsels$_i$/har$_i$/*se$_i$
       the children wash   themselves/them/them
    c. Marie$_i$ skammet har$_i$/*se$_i$
       Mary   shames   her/her
    d. De bern$_i$ skamje har$_i$/*se$_i$
       the children shame them/them

The ungrammaticality of the sentences with bound *se* shows that, for *se*,
the chain condition works in Frisian as it does in Dutch. Hoekstra shows
that *har* and *se* differ in Case. He establishes this point on the basis of a
variety of contexts, but I will just summarize his considerations. One significant context is the so-called free dative construction.

Frisian has a *free dative* construction—that is, a clause may contain an
object DP expressing some kind of indirect involvement in the eventuality
denoted. This DP is licensed independently of any specific lexical property of the predicate of the clause, as illustrated in (9).[2]

(9) a. Hy hat my in soad dronken.
       he has me much   drunk
    b. De blommen wiene harren ferwile.
       the flowers   were them   wilted
    c. Jim balte harren te lûd.
       you shout them   too loud

  d. De kjitten steane har yn'e   tún.
     the weeds stand her in the garden

In this context *har* may not be replaced by *se* either, as shown in (10).

(10) a. *De blommen wiene se   ferwile.
        the flowers   were them wilted
     b. *Jim balte se   te   lûd.
        you shout them too loud
     c. *De kjitten steane se   yn'e   tún.
        the weeds stand her in the garden

As the name reflects, in many languages allowing such objects, they are marked by dative Case (as, for instance, in German). In line with this, Hoekstra proposes that a Case distinction also underlies the contrast between (9) and (10). Further evidence for the role of Case is that *se* is barred from locative PPs, as illustrated in (11). Pronominal arguments of adjectives also require the *har*-form, as in (12).

(11) Ik seach wat   bewegen efter   har/*se.
     I saw something move   behind her/her

(12) Harren/*Se tige tagedien,   diene wy alles   om   harren te
     them/them very attached-to did   we everything in-order them   to
     skewielen.
     assist

Hoekstra concludes that the difference between *se* and *har* is that *se* requires structural Case, whereas *har* does not, but is licensed with inherent Case. I will adopt this conclusion. I will be assuming that this distinction carries over to the masculine and neuter members of the pronominal paradigm where two object forms are not distinguished. (That is, they exhibit *syncretism* along the lines discussed in section 5.2.) The claim that Frisian has an option for licensing case that is not available in Dutch is supported by the very fact that Frisian has "free datives," as we saw. Dutch does not. So whereas Frisian has (13a), its Dutch counterpart is impossible, regardless of whether a pronominal or a SE anaphor is used.

(13) *Free dative*
     a. Jehannes hat him in moaie   wein kocht.
        Johannes has him a beautiful car bought
        'Johannes bought a beautiful car for himself.'
     b. *Johannes heeft zich/hem een mooie auto gekocht.
        'Johannes bought a beautiful car for himself.'

Given what we know about thematic structure, this contrast cannot be encoded as a difference in thematic licensing; linking it to variation in the case system is the only available option.

As discussed earlier, I assume that structural Case is Case that is licensed by the agreement/Tense system (Chomsky 1992) and subsequent work on Case, such as Marantz 2000a). Specifically, I assume that it is uninterpretable Tense in line with Pesetsky and Torrego 2004a and 2004b. Inherent Case is, then, Case that is licensed under selection by a lexical projection or purely configurationally, as in the case of free datives and ECM subjects, which are both not selected by the licensing verb. I will remain uncommitted about the precise way inherent Case is licensed. The crucial point is merely that inherent Case is not linked to the T-system.[3] The difference between Dutch and Frisian can be summarized as in (14) and (15):

(14) *Dutch*

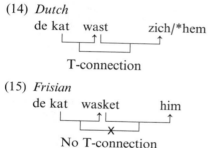

Since only structural Case is checked via the inflectional system, "no structural Case-checking" means "no chain." Thus, from the economy perspective developed in chapters 4 and 5, *him* in (15) is not a possible goal for the probes in the $v*/T$ system. Hence, there is no direct competition between derivations with a pronoun that has structural Case and a pronoun that has inherent Case. So, the derivation with inherent Case cannot be blocked by the fact that the derivation with the structural Case variant is canceled.[4]

The effects of Case may be subtle, though. Languages need not always use the "universally" cheapest possible strategy to encode dependencies. They are restricted to the cheapest available option in their grammar. If a language lacks a SE anaphor, local binding can take place without chain formation under the conditions sketched. However, assuming that economy does exert some diachronic pressure, one may expect such a system to be unstable, and move (in the long run) toward a system with a SE anaphor that allows syntactic encoding (assuming some form of grammaticalization to be active). Let's briefly consider two potential cases.

Suppose we have a language that lost most, or even all, morphological distinctions within the structural system and the formal distinctions within the inherent Case system without losing the difference between the two modes of Case-licensing per se. That is, we have Case syncretism in the sense discussed above. If so, little of any consequence should follow. An element α may appear in direct object position in a form that is homophonous with the form it assumes in a position of inherent Case-licensing, but nevertheless one will see competition effects on α as a direct object, if α as a pronominal has a SE competitor.

However, consider the following slight twist in the licensing: α is also licensed by the inherent strategy when it appears in direct object position. If so, we can say that α is not marked (=lacks a cell) for structural Case (uninterpretable Tense). But this implies that α cannot be probed by the v*/T system and chain formation is not available as an encoding strategy for α's dependency in that language. Therefore, there is no potential competition between α as SE or α as a pronominal. Recall that the competition is not between SE anaphors and pronominals as such, but between encoding in syntax proper or beyond. So, diachronically there would be no pressure on such a system to develop a SE anaphor if it lacked one, or to retain it if it had one. The latter option describes the situation in Frisian.[5]

8.3   German *Sich*

While Frisian is different from other (Germanic) languages in allowing locally bound 3rd-person pronouns, German is remarkable in two other respects:

i. It allows the anaphor *sich* where Dutch and other Germanic languages require (a cognate of) *zichzelf*.
ii. In locative PPs, where Dutch allows either *zich* or *hem*, German only allows *sich*.

I will now discuss these issues in turn.

8.3.1   German *Sich* and Reflexivity

As we saw in section 1.8.2, most Germanic languages show a distribution of SELF versus SELF-less forms as predicted by the approach outlined in chapter 3. Only German seems to go against this pattern, because in non-dative positions (see R&R 1993 for a discussion of datives) it allows the anaphor *sich*, where the other languages have complex forms such as *himself*, *zichzelf*, or *himsels*, as illustrated in (16)–(19). Prima facie, *sich* is a

SE anaphor. Hence the question arises how this is compatible with the claim that reflexivity must be licensed. It is therefore necessary to make a precise assessment of the status of *sich*. For ease of exposition I will focus on the contrast between Dutch and German.

Dutch

(16) Max$_i$ haat zich*(zelf)$_i$
     'Max$_i$ hates himself$_i$.'

(17) Max$_i$ praat over zich*(zelf)$_i$
     'Max$_i$ speaks about himself$_i$.'

German

(18) Max$_i$ hasst sich$_i$
     'Max$_i$ hates himself$_i$.'

(19) Max$_i$ spricht über sich$_i$
     'Max$_i$ speaks about himself$_i$.'

Given the present approach, there are two positions to be explored:

(20) a. *Sich* is not what it appears to be.
     b. The relation between *sich* and the verb is different in German.

As we will see, both positions are in fact correct.

Taking the first position first, we discussed the contrast between SE anaphors and SELF anaphors in chapter 3. As a first approximation, it was stated that SE anaphors are simplex and SELF anaphors are complex. In section 3.5 we proposed that SE anaphors have the structure in (21a), where the NP complement is just empty and that SELF anaphors have the structures in (21b,c):

(21) a. [$_{\pi P}$ SE$_\pi$ [$_{NP}$ ...]]
     b. [$_{DP}$ Pron$_D$ [$_{NP}$ self]]
     c. [$_{\pi P}$ SE$_\pi$ [$_{NP}$ self]]

In chapter 6 we saw that morphosyntactic complexity is necessary for reflexive licensing. However, it does not follow that the Pron/SE part in D has to be overt. Thus, assuming that the ø-element can be licensed, nothing prohibits a structure of the form (22a) or (22b) from qualifying as a SELF anaphor:

(22) a. [$_{DP}$ ø [$_{NP}$ SELF]]
     b. [$_{\pi P}$ ø [$_{NP}$ SELF]]

The same applies to (23a), with SE in the head position. But, in fact, complexity can also be expressed by N-movement in the sense of Longobardi

1994, 1996, as in (23b), where some features of D or π attract SE. The two members of the chain have different categorial status, hence will be distinguished at the interface (see the discussion of the role of complexity in chapter 6).

(23) a. $[_{D/\pi P}\ \emptyset\ [_{NP}\ SE]]$
     b. $[_{D/\pi P}\ SE\ [_{NP}\ (SE)]]$

So, again, expressions do not wear their analysis on their sleeves. If we find an expression that is prima facie simplex, it has to be assessed whether it actually is. The question is, then, whether we can find evidence bearing on the structure of German *sich*. And in fact its stress pattern shows that in some of its uses *sich* must have more structure than meets the eye.

In both Dutch and German the head of the N-projection bears the main stress of the NP: *deze luie dikke KAT* 'this lazy fat cat', *diese faule dicke KATZE* 'this lazy fat cat'. (Stress is indicated by capitalization.) Dutch anaphors conform to this pattern. In (24a,b) the internal stress of the NP is on *zelf*, but in (24c), where we have a SE anaphor, and the head position is empty, the stress cannot be on the—empty—head, nor can it be on *zich*. Consequently, the anaphor is without stress. The same holds true of the *zich* in locative PPs where the stress ends up on the P-head (see also chapter 3, note 31).

(24) a. Max$_i$ haat zichZELF$_i$
         Max$_i$ hates himself$_i$
     b. Max$_i$ praat over zichZELF$_i$
         Max$_i$ speaks about himself$_i$
     c. Max$_i$ gedraagt zich$_i$/*ZICH$_i$
         Max$_i$ behaves SE$_i$/SE$_i$
     d. Max$_i$ legt het boek achter zich$_i$/*ZICH$_i$
         Max$_i$ puts the book behind SE$_i$/SE$_i$

As observed in Everaert 1986, *zich* also fails to undergo topicalization. This restriction also applies where the verb is prima facie transitive. Thus in (25), only the SELF form can be topicalized.

(25) Zichzelf/*Zich wast Max.
     'Himself$_i$ Max$_i$ washes.'

German *sich* bears stress in some, and is unstressed in other positions (e.g., Everaert 1986). The crucial fact is now, that the positions in which *sich* may bear stress coincide with the positions in which Dutch has *zich-zelf*. In positions where *sich* may not bear stress, Dutch has *zich*.[6]

(26) a. Max$_i$ hasst SICH$_i$
   'Max$_i$ hates himself$_i$.'
   b. Max$_i$ spricht über SICH$_i$
   'Max$_i$ speaks about himself$_i$.'
   c. Max$_i$ benimmt sich$_i$/*SICH$_i$ (gut)
   'Max$_i$ behaves himself$_i$ (well).'
   d. Max$_i$ legt das Buch hinter sich$_i$/*SICH$_i$[7]
   'Max$_i$ puts the book behind himself$_i$.'

As is the case with Dutch *zich*, unstressable *sich* cannot be topicalized (Everaert 1986):

(27) *Sich benimmt Max gut.
  himself behaves Max well

Variations in stress are significant indicators of differences in structure given a theory of phrasal stress along the lines of Cinque 1993. In this theory phrasal stress is *determined* by the syntactic structure; conversely, the stress pattern that obtains must reflect the syntactic structure. Unstressable *sich* can indeed be assumed to originate in a peripheral π-position with an empty—or no—NP complement. Stressable *sich* must originate in the N-position. This means that stressed *sich* minimally reflects the complexity of (23a).

The idea that German *sich* in fact has a dual structure has received independent support in work by Gast and Haas (2008). They investigate the conditions under which *sich* contributes to a reciprocal interpretation of the predicate it is an argument of. They show that two uses of *sich* must be distinguished, *sich* as a clitic and *sich* with full pronominal structure, including the capacity to bear stress, appear in PPs, and so on. Reciprocal interpretation can only be realized in the presence of clitic *sich*. (28a) is a particularly illustrative example which contrasts with (28b) (Gast and Haas 2008, (22)):

(28) a. SICH konnten die Spieler nicht leiden, aber sie mochten den
   SICH could the players not bear but they liked the
   Trainer.
   coach
   'The players couldn't bear themselves/*each other, but they liked the coach.'
   b. Die Spieler konnten sich nicht leiden ...
   'The players could not bear themselves/each other ...'

In (28a) the *sich* is fronted—and stressed. Although a reading in which the players did not like each other while they do like the coach is pragmatically not only conceivable but even preferred to the reflexive reading, this reading is not available, as they note. So, the grammatical restriction on the reciprocal interpretation of tonic *sich* is robust. Moreover, *sich* cannot have the reciprocal meaning either if it is coordinated with another noun phrase (Gast and Haas 2008, (23)), again a use where it is in nonclitic position.

(29) Erst lobten die Spieler SICH und dann die GEGNER.
      first praised the players SICH and then the opponents
      'The players first praised themselves/*each other and then their
      opponents.'

What remains is how to choose between (23a) and (23b). The question is under what conditions an empty D-position may be licensed. It has been noted that there is a correlation between the nature of the Case system and the licensing of empty determiners (Saddy 1987). That is, in languages with rich Case systems, articles can often be omitted, suggesting that an empty D can be licensed by a "strong" enough Case. Although German has a far richer Case system than Dutch, it does not generally license empty determiners. Consequently, the alternative in (23b), with *sich*-to-D-movement is more consistent with the properties of German. The fact that *sich* bears stress in its derived position follows from the fact that feature-driven movement retains the original stress (see Slioussar 2007, 91–95, for discussion). Thus, the stressability of *sich* reflects the syntactic complexity of the DP it heads.

The binding requirement—including the cancellation if a feature mismatch ensues—follows from the same economy-based mechanism as introduced for SE anaphors in general. The upshot is, then, that the distinction between SE and the SELF anaphors is just expressed a bit more indirectly in German than in Dutch, namely in the stress pattern, rather than directly in the overt morphological complexity of the form.

This brings us to the second position indicated in (20b): What Gast and Haas show is that in some of its uses *sich* is a clitic in German. This ties in with an observation about a difference between German and Dutch that relates to the analysis of middles in Reinhart's θ-system, as discussed in chapter 6. German has *sich* in an environment where it is typically lacking in standard Dutch, as illustrated in (30):

(30) *Middle*
      a. Das Buch verkauft sich gut.
         'The book sells well.'
      b. Het boek verkoopt (*zich) goed.
         'The book sells well.'

Following the approach in Marelj 2004, this contrast indicates that in middle formation German is a syntax language in the sense of the TS, whereas Dutch is a lexicon language. If so, the difference between Dutch and German in the formation of middles reflects a more deeply seated contrast in the way operations on argument structure take place. That is, German is also a syntax language in the domain of reflexivization. Consequently, we now expect productivity of reduction/clitic reflexivization, much as in other syntax languages.

However, two properties would remain unaccounted for if this were all there is to say: the fact that *sich* is also able to license reflexivity in PPs, and the fact that German shows no restrictions on *sich*-reflexivization of verbs with experiencer subjects. As to the first property, note that clitic languages do not allow cliticization from positions in PPs. For instance, in French PPs we find the pronominal *lui/lui même*, in Italian PPs we find either tonic *sè* or *se stesso* (Napoli 1979; Reuland 1990b), and the same pattern obtains in Serbo-Croatian. The fact that *sich* in PPs does not allow the reciprocal interpretation indicates that in PPs it indeed cannot mark an arity operation. This leads to the conclusion that *sich* in German can indeed be used both as a clitic and, when it is tonic, as a reflexivizer, along the lines discussed in chapter 6.

The second property relates to a broader issue of crosslinguistic variation. As noted in chapter 6, not only lexicon languages such as Dutch and English (and also Sakha; see Vinokurova 2005) but also syntax languages, such as Modern Greek, Serbo-Croatian, and Italian have restrictions on bundling with subject experiencer verbs. For instance, (31)–(33) are difficult to impossible on the intended reflexive readings:

(31) *Modern Greek*
     *O Yannis jnorizete. (Papangeli 2004)
     'Yannis knows himself.'

(32) *Serbo-Croatian*
     On se voli ≠ he loves himself (Marijana Marelj, personal communication)

(33) *Italian*
     *?Gianni si   odia. (Pino Longobardi, personal communication)
     Gianni CL hates

Instead a full reflexive is required. From this perspective, the fact that German so easily allows (34) is in need of an explanation:

(34) Der Johann hasst sich. (Fully well-formed)

Given what has been established about German *sich* so far, this fact immediately follows: nonclitic *sich* reflexive-marks the predicate *hassen* just like any other SELF anaphor does.[8]

8.3.2 Case and Case Distinctions

In chapter 3 it was noted that Dutch and English locative and directional PPs show no complementarity between bound pronouns and anaphors. So, in Dutch we have both *Jan$_i$ zag een slang naast zich$_i$* 'John saw a snake next to him' and *Jan$_i$ zag een slang naast hem$_i$* (same meaning). Modern High German requires *sich* in such cases. This is illustrated in (35):

(35) a.   Claus$_i$ sah eine Schlange neben sich$_i$
    b.   *Claus$_i$ sah eine Schlange neben ihm$_i$
        'Claus saw a snake next to him.'
    c.   Claudia$_i$ setzte die Pflanze hinter sich$_i$
    d.   *Claudia$_i$ setzte die Pflanze hinter ihr$_i$/sie$_i$
        'Claudia put the plant behind her.'

In this section we will see that the contrast immediately follows if Case plays the role in chain formation sketched above. That is, structural Case makes it possible for a chain to be formed and hence for the chain condition in the form we derived it to apply.

As noted earlier, German differs from the other West Germanic languages in that it expresses morphological Case distinctions. These Case distinctions not only distinguish arguments of the verb (e.g., direct versus indirect object), but they also show up in locative and directional PPs, and so on. In PPs the Case of the NP (accusative, dative, or genitive) is not only determined by the preposition, but it also reflects whether the PP expresses location or direction, as illustrated in (36).

(36) a. Manuela tanzte *im*   Zimmer (herum).
      Manuela danced in-DAT-the room (location)
    b. Manuela tanzte *ins*   Zimmer (hinein).
      Manuela danced into-ACC-the room (direction)

Note that for the contrasts in (36) to follow from the chain condition, there must be a chain headed by the subject, with the DP of the locative in the tail. As we saw in our earlier discussions of the chain condition, in order for there to be a chain between *Claus* and *sich* their relation has to be mediated by real relations with the verb (*sah*) and the head of the PP (*neben*). The issue hinges on whether the P counts as an intervener for a verbal head probing for the complement of P, and if it is, whether P—or rather a head in the functional domain of P—can attract the complement, bringing it within range of the relevant V-head. At this point I would like to cut the technical details short, and simply note what (36) shows: the Case of P's complement is not just determined by P. The Case that marks location versus direction is determined by V and P jointly, which minimally requires that there is a real grammatical relation between V and the complement of P.

Pursuing the analysis of Case introduced earlier, the following position seems warranted (see the discussion in Reinhart and Siloni 2005). Where VP-internal arguments are concerned, the verb always checks the thematic Case. Thus, a full PP checks the thematic Case of the verb—if it is linked to a θ-role—but the preposition checks the Case feature of the DP. The pattern in (36) shows that German has morphological Case—checked by P—that must be licensed by V. If so, the Case on the complement of P has a structural component related to the V-system. This is what makes *sich/ihn* enter the chain headed by *Claus*, leading to a violation of the chain condition for the pronominal *ihn*.

In Frisian, Case-checking with and within the PP establishes no Case connection between V and the complement of P. There is no Case contrast and no structural Case component forcing the complement of P to enter a chain with V. Frisian is, then, simply the opposite of German. There is no SE anaphor in PPs, only a pronominal.

Dutch is intermediate, as we saw, and allows both. Again, the question is why? A simple way to accommodate the case of Dutch is in the form of a low-level stipulation, saying that the Dutch Case system optionally allows P to license its argument by inherent Case. Concretely, in a sentence like *Alice zette het flesje naast **haar*** 'Alice put the bottle next to her', there is a numeration (where *naast* checks inherent Case) in which the conditions for *haar* entering the chain are not met; hence, the derivation with *Alice* binding *haar* is not canceled. This would reduce the contrast to a simple parameter. However, the behavior of complement PPs raises a further issue.

The core question involves the relation between P and V. In Dutch, Verb-Preposition combinations as in *Alice vertrouwde op zich*(zelf)* 'Alice put trust in herself' form the composite head of a semantic predicate. In French, they don't (see section 6.7). The question is how this formal dependency—"reanalysis"—between V and P is encoded. As is well-known, an independent difference between French and Dutch is that Dutch allows a restricted form of preposition stranding (see Van

Riemsdijk 1978, and also Koopman 2000), whereas French does not. Preposition stranding is also based on a formal dependency between verb and preposition, and, as discussed in section 6.7, I assume that both formal dependencies are in fact the same. At that point I left open how this dependency is formally encoded.

Specifically, one may assume that prepositions in English, Dutch, German, and Scandinavian are deficient in their Case-checking properties. This allows for V (or a functional element of the V-system) to probe for P and establish an Agree relation. Hence, when a SE anaphor is probed by P for Case, it enters a syntactic dependency with the V-T system and ends up bound. However, a pronominal in this position will also be probed for by P and invoke the PRD; hence, the derivation with binding will be canceled.

Kayne (1981) proposed that reanalysis is blocked if P and V do not assign Case in the same manner. In present terms that would mean that they do not both check the same type of Case. If so, the assumption that the noncomplementarity resides in the option of structural versus inherent Case would entail optionality of complex anaphors in complement PPs (such as *Alice vertrouwde op zich*(zelf)* 'Alice put trust in herself'), just as in French. This is not the case, however, as we saw.

Hence, we must look for a factor that induces an intervention effect in chain formation, is specific to Dutch (and Frisian), and is independently motivated.

There is, in fact, such an independent factor. Dutch PPs allow extraction of P's complement only via a designated specifier position as an escape hatch (the +R-position; see Van Riemsdijk 1978). This position agrees with the P in a Place feature. The restriction in Dutch is that only formally locative pronominals can be extracted—so-called +R words such as *waar* 'where', *daar* 'there', and *hier* 'here'. Despite their locative form, their interpretation is that of an argument (in principle inanimate, but colloquially animate interpretations are also allowed). In Scandinavian there is no such restriction.

This contrast allows the following explanation. In order for V-P reanalysis to obtain, the verb has to target a feature of P. If it targets the Case feature of P, we have the derivation discussed so far. And this is indeed the situation that obtains in German and in Scandinavian, where only anaphors can be bound by the local subject, not pronominals.

However, in Dutch also P's Place property is encoded as a morphosyntactic feature and is therefore a possible goal. If V targets the Place feature of P, the conditions for a pronominal (not carrying the Place

Chapter 8

feature) to enter the chain are not met, since the pronominal is Case-licensed, not Place-licensed. If so, no cancellation results, and binding is possible. This is precisely what had to be derived. Since we have reanalysis either by Case or by Place, the French-Dutch contrast in complement PPs still follows.

This derivation makes the prediction that a +R "pronoun" (such as *er* 'it', *daar* 'that', *hier* 'this') in a locative PP cannot be bound by the local subject. This prediction is indeed borne out. Consider the sentence **het gezelschap** *legde de papieren naast* **zich** 'the gathering put the papers next to it'. This sentence is fine. But in **het gezelschap** *legde de papieren er naast* 'the gathering put the papers there next to', the interpretation where *er* is *het gezelschap* 'the gathering' is sharply ungrammatical, although the sentence is fine if *er* is interpreted as a table, and so on. And under nonlocal conditions *het gezelschap* is fine as a value for *er*.

Thus, the absence of complementarity between bound *hem/haar* and *zich* observed in Dutch follows from the option for V to target the Place feature. Despite the lack of complementarity with *haar*, *zich* in these cases cannot remain free. This is due to Rule L introduced in chapter 5. As discussed in section 5.7, *zich* must be interpreted via the syntactic route if there is a derivation making that possible. In the present case there is such a derivation, namely the derivation where V and P enter a formal dependency via P's Case feature. Hence, that is the route that must be taken.

This is a somewhat roundabout way for an economy measure to work. However, it is precisely this property that explains a finding by Burkhardt 2005. Burkhardt investigated the way *zich* in locative and directional PPs is processed, using a cross-modal lexical decision task. She found increased reaction times for sentences with non-coargument *zich* as compared to coargument *zich*, indicating that the former requires more processing resources.

The complex anaphor *zichzelf* raises another interesting issue. We find *zichzelf* in complement PPs, owing to the effects of IDI. But unlike its counterpart in Scandinavian, *zichzelf* can be bound by a nonsubject, like *Marie* in *per ongeluk wees Jan* **Marie** *aan* **zichzelf** *toe* 'accidentally John assigned Mary to herself'. The question then is why *zich* in *zichzelf* escapes the effect of Rule L, which properly considered not only blocks logophoric interpretation if a chain can be formed, but could be expected to block nonsubject antecedents as well. Interestingly, in cases like these, there is no complementarity between SE-*zelf* and Pron-*zelf*. Replacing *zichzelf* by *haarzelf* with binding by *Marie* is also fine.

This fact, then, follows on the same footing as the noncomplementarity between *zich* and pronominals in the non-coargument cases discussed above. If the verb targets the Place feature of the preposition to establish a dependency, this frees *zich* from the obligation to enter a chain and allows a pronominal in Pron-*zelf* to be bound without violating the PRD. Nevertheless, *zich* will not be freed for construal as a logophor, since *zelf* enforces local binding as discussed in chapter 6. (The fact that binding is encoded by *zelf* under all available options explains the difference between the coargument cases and the non-coargument cases Burkhardt found.)

8.3.3 Concluding the Discussion of Case and Chains

In this section I have surveyed variation in local binding in West Germanic. The survey led us from locally bound 3rd-person pronominals in Frisian to the interpretation of German *sich* in environments where Dutch and other Germanic languages require a SELF anaphor, and to PPs where German requires *sich*, while other Germanic languages allow a bound pronominal as well. In section 7.5 I discussed the use of SELF forms in English—specifically in 1st and 2nd person—where other Germanic languages have a simplex form.

In all these cases we were able to account for the variation in terms of crosslinguistic differences that are entirely independent of binding. No differences in opacity factors or other parameters in the definition of binding domains were postulated. The conditions on reflexivity could be uniformly maintained, like the conditions on chain formation. All that is needed to explain the otherwise puzzling variation in the distribution of simplex anaphors versus pronominals in the West Germanic languages is independent differences in some low-level properties of the Case systems, the extent to which the verbal functional structure is fusional (English versus other Germanic languages), and the difference in internal syntactic structure that is reflected in the contrast between clitic and tonic forms of German *sich*.

Clearly, there is more crosslinguistic variation than could be discussed here. Dutch dialects, for example, use anaphoric strategies that are based on *z'n eigen* "his own," rather than a SELF form. The precise properties and distribution of *z'n eigen* definitely merit a careful study that would lead us beyond the scope of this book (see Barbiers and Bennis 2003 for many interesting facts; see also Barbiers et al. 2005).

In many current German dialects, *sich* is limited to accusative positions or even to just the direct object positions (Keller 1961). This is also true of Middle High German up to the fifteenth or sixteenth century (Keller 1978). The German pattern of variation falls well within the scope of our approach, if in such dialects all accusatives are structural and all datives are inherent.

Older stages of English appear to lack a special anaphor altogether (see Keenan 2000 for an overview and a specific interpretation of the facts, and Van Gelderen 2000 for a careful study of subsequent historical developments). The question is, then, how the Old English facts tie in with our present approach. Although space is lacking for an extensive discussion, two remarks can be made. It is noteworthy that Keenan observes that in the initial period investigated the accusative pronominal *hine* is replaced by the dative *him*. If dative is an inherent rather than a structural Case, this makes the relevant stage of Old English surprisingly much like Frisian. Van Gelderen provides an extensive analysis of the Old English Case system and the changes it went through. She shows convincingly that at the Old English stage even the formal accusative was inherent rather than structural (among other data, given the absence of canonical passives in Old English). That is, these OE patterns are consistent with the conditions on chain formation as discussed. As the Case system changes the binding patterns develop toward the modern system. What about condition B? In this respect one may note that all the cases of locally bound *him* discussed by Keenan would be perfectly acceptable in Modern Frisian.[9] Sentences of the form *x hates him*, *x admires him*, etc. that would require *himsels* in Frisian are lacking among the examples, though. This leaves us with two options that we would require further evidence to decide. OE could be like Frisian and Modern English in being a lexicon language. If so, one would expect to find that locally bound pronoun with such verbs co-occur with some material contributing complexity.[10] Alternatively, OE could allow bundling in the syntax, just like German or French. Again, this would lead to predications that can in principle be tested, if the material allows us to.

This leads to a more general issue that deserves to be stressed. What I have developed in the present book is not just a theory. Rather it is also a proposal for a method of how to go about investigating binding phenomena. The present approach is committed to the view that BT principles should reflect general properties of the computational system of human language, and the design of the language faculty in general. Crosslinguistic variation is then to be captured by investigating how these general principles interact with the fine structure of the elements that constitute the material for the computations.[11]

In the next section the same general method will be applied to the variation in nonlocal binding possibilities that obtain among the Germanic languages.

8.4 Long-Distance Anaphors in Germanic

8.4.1 Introduction

As was discussed in chapters 1 and 3, the CBT is based on a two-way distinction between *pronominals* and *anaphors*.[12] Crosslinguistically, this two-way distinction between anaphors and pronominals as it is found in English is the exception rather than the rule. As we saw, many Germanic languages have a contrast between simplex anaphors, such as Icelandic *sig*, Norwegian *seg*, Dutch *zich*, and so forth, and complex anaphors of the general form ⟨*pron*⟩ *SELF*, where *pron* stands for a pronominal or simplex anaphor, which gives rise to three-way and four-way contrasts, not even counting anaphoric possessives. It took some time for systematic studies to emerge that assessed the theoretical implications of these observations. The previous section provided some coverage of variation in the local domain and of the factors involved. There is also considerable variation in the binding possibilities beyond the local domain, however.

The earliest attempt I know of to systematically address the questions posed by the Germanic languages as a group is by Everaert (1986), who developed an approach to binding based on chain theory in a barriers-type framework, and who explains crosslinguistic differences in binding domains on the basis of independent structural differences between languages. In fact, the way he approached the issue is fully in line with the methodology adopted here. Subsequently, Manzini and Wexler (1987) developed a theory of parameterization of binding domains based on lexical differences between anaphors. Hellan (1988) proposed that binding involves the interaction between two types of conditions: containment conditions that are purely structural (such as c-command) and connectedness conditions that require a particular substantive relation between the anaphor and its antecedent, such as predication command (the anaphor is contained in a constituent predicated of the antecedent), or perspective command, which requires that the antecedent qualify as a perspective holder. (The latter type of condition is a typical indicator of logophoricity.)

One result of these works is that a distinction was discovered between *local anaphors*, which must be bound in their governing category, and *long-distance anaphors*, which are exempt from condition A of the

CBT.[13] A second result is that the contrast between simplex and complex anaphors reflects properties of argument structure (as shown by Everaert (1986) and Hellan (1988), and elaborated in chapter 3). A third result (Hellan 1988) is that the binding properties of complex anaphors result from contributions of both components.

The differences found by Thráinsson (1976a, 1976b, 1991), Maling (1984, 1986), Anderson (1986), and Hellan (1991) between long-distance binding into finite clauses (indicative or subjunctive) and long-distance binding into infinitival clauses showed that a further distinction exists. Only long-distance binding into infinitival clauses reflects structural binding. The other occurrences of long-distance anaphors are logophoric (as discussed in Clements 1975 and Sells 1987). As such, their distribution is much freer and they are governed by discourse, rather than by purely structural factors. This will be taken up in the discussion of logophoricity in Icelandic in the end of the present chapter. Below I will summarize some of the basic facts about the major Germanic languages, before once more addressing the nature of the pattern they present.[14]

8.4.2 Anaphors across Germanic Languages

English, as we saw, has a two-way distinction between anaphors and pronominals. It does not have SE anaphors. All its anaphors (*myself, yourself, himself, ourselves, yourselves, themselves*) are formally SELF anaphors. They are either locally bound in accordance with canonical condition A, or are exempt. If so they may end up being bound by a non-local antecedent or receive a logophoric interpretation if no binder is available. There is no "intermediate" syntactic binding domain. A limited number of lexically reflexive predicates (mostly verbs of grooming, such as *wash*) allow the absence of an overt object where other languages require an overt anaphor. This is a manifestation of the interplay between binding and properties of argument structure, as we discussed in detail in chapters 3 and 6.

Icelandic has a four-way distinction resulting from the fact that the SELF element *sjalfan* combines both with the third person SE anaphor *sig* and with the elements in the pronominal paradigm (*hann*, etc.). In addition, Icelandic has a possessive 3rd-person anaphor *sin*. The anaphors *sig* and *sjalfan sig* must be bound by a subject, like the possessive anaphor. When the antecedent is not a subject, *hann sjalfan*, and so on is used instead of *sjalfan sig*, and the corresponding pronominal form instead of *sig* or *sin*. In 1st and 2nd person the standard pronominal form is used throughout, with *sjalfan* where a complex anaphor is required.

Sjalfan sig must be locally bound (i.e., it reflexive-marks the predicate it is an argument of; see Sigurjónsdóttir 1992 and subsequent work). *Sig* can be long-distance bound or interpreted logophorically. Icelandic freely allows violations of the Specified Subject Condition (SSC) with binding into infinitives and DPs. Long-distance binding of *sig* may cross a number of clausal boundaries, as illustrated in (37) where *Jón* is a possible binder for *sér*:

(37) Jón$_i$ sagði [Maríu$_j$ hafa$_{(inf.)}$ látið [mig þvo$_{(inf.)}$ sér$_{i,j}$]]
     John said   Mary   have   made me wash   SE
     'John said that Mary had made me wash him.'

Logophoric interpretation is possible only for an anaphor in the domain of a subjunctive, and which appears in a *reportive context*. For logophoric interpretation the antecedent need not c-command the anaphor. In fact, the antecedent need not be linguistically expressed at all, as we already saw in example (69b) in chapter 1.

Faroese, as it is described by Barnes (1986), has a three-way distinction. The SELF element *sjálvan* combines with the 3rd-person SE anaphor *seg* forming a complex anaphor *seg sjálvan*. In addition, Faroese has a pronominal paradigm and a possessive anaphor *sín*. Combining a 3rd-person pronominal with *sjálvan* appears to give an emphatic pronominal rather than an anaphor. The distribution of simplex and complex anaphors in local binding contexts is largely determined by properties of the predicate and appears to essentially follow the pattern found for Dutch. The complex anaphor is exclusively local. As Barnes (1986) notes, some speakers may allow a stressed variant of the simplex anaphor, and others colloquially even an unstressed one, where the majority requires a complex anaphor. Faeroese freely allows SSC violations with binding into infinitival clauses and DPs as in (38):[15]

(38) a. Pætur$_i$ sá   Mikkjalsa$_j$ bílæt   av sær$_{i/j}$/sær sjálvum$_j$/hunum$_o$
        Pætur saw Mikkjal's   picture of SE/SE-SELF/him
     b. Jógvan$_i$ bað   meg$_j$ PRO$_j$ raka   sær$_i$/honum$_{i/o}$
        Jógvan asked me   (to) shave SE/him

The antecedent of a SE anaphor must be the subject of a predicate containing the SE anaphor. Thus, for instance, the indirect object of a subject-control verb is not a possible antecedent for an anaphor in its complement:

(39) Eg$_i$ lovaði   Jógvan$_j$ PRO$_i$ at raka honum$_j$/*sær$_j$
     I   promised Jógvan   to shave him/SE

Faroese also allows a free SE anaphor in finite complements subject to restrictions that are similar to the conditions on logophoricity in Icelandic.

(40) Jógvan segði, at   Mortan hevði verið glaður, um Guðrun hevði
     Jógvan said   that Mortan would be   happy if   Guðrun had
     kyst   seg.
     kissed SE

The majority of speakers allows both *Mortan* and *Jógvan* as antecedents for *seg* in (40). Objects, as *Jógvan* in *Eg fortaldi Jógvan . . .* ("I told J.") appear not to be possible antecedents. Barnes reports a relatively sharp blocking effect if intervening subjects do not have the same specification for person. So (41) is a variant of (40), in which the nearest subject is first person and the result is ill-formed:

(41) *Jógvan$_i$ segði, at   tú   hevði verið glaður, um eg hevði kyst   seg$_i$
     Jógvan said   that you would be   happy if   I   had   kissed SE

Such a contrast has not been reported for Icelandic. Given the impoverished verbal morphology of Faroese (number contrasts but no person contrasts) as compared to Icelandic this contrast is consistent with extant accounts of the *blocking effect* if number and person are checked separately (Huang and Tang 1991; see also Sevcenco 2006 for an overview). Note, that the double intervention is not crucial; two-clause sentences with only the higher subject matching in features are also bad. However, if in (41) the nearest subject *eg* is replaced by *Guðrun*, and the mismatching subject is in a higher clause, the reading with *seg* dependent on *Jógvan* becomes considerably better. I will leave this fact for further investigation.

   Barnes mentions that this long-distance antecedency relation in Faroese is almost exclusively found in the complements of verbs corresponding to English *say, believe, want, learn (information), feel, intend.* These are typically verbs of the sort licensing logophoricity in other languages, inducing a *reportive context.* As in Icelandic, the antecedent need not c-command the anaphor as in (42), or be linguistically expressed.

(42) Vón hennara$_i$ var at   sær$_i$ fór   at dáma tann nýggja
     hope her   was that SE   was-going to like   the   new
     prestin
     minister

What makes Faroese particularly interesting is that, in contrast to Icelandic, it does not have an overt distinction between indicative and subjunctive. That subjunctive is not a necessary condition for licensing logophoricity is not new by itself. Many other languages (such as Chinese and Japanese, and also English) have logophoricity without a (relevant) subjunctive. The interesting question is what sets the Faroese inflectional system apart from that of the mainland Scandinavian languages (and other Germanic languages) where logophoricity (at least involving *seg*-type anaphors) does not occur. Although determining possible microfactors in this difference would require a detailed investigation that goes beyond the scope of the present book, there is an interesting factor at the macro-level. Faroese subordinate clauses allow both V_{fin} *Adv* order and *Adv* V_{fin} order, indicating overt raising of the finite verb to T. In allowing overt raising it sides with Icelandic and contrasts with Mainland Scandinavian languages. As we saw in chapter 5, a crucial factor in the licensing of logophors in subjunctive contexts in Icelandic is the covert movement from V/T to C of a subjunctive operator. Independently of the details of such movement, it can only be licit if the head bearing the operator is high enough to be attracted or alternatively—if subjunctive is a matter of selection—if it is in a position high enough to be selected for. If so, the assumption that Faroese preserved subjunctive in some covert form, could account for the facts, and would not be empirically vacuous.[16]

Mainland Scandinavian (Danish, Norwegian, Swedish), like Icelandic, has a four-way distinction (for discussion, see, among others Vikner 1984, 1985; Hellan 1980, 1988; Hestvik 1991, 1992). The SELF element *selv* combines both with the 3rd-person SE anaphor *seg* and with the elements in the pronominal paradigm (*ham*, etc.). In addition, these languages have a possessive anaphor *sin*. The Norwegian anaphoric system may serve as a model for the system of mainland Scandinavian languages in general, since the systems are very similar. The main difference among the mainland Scandinavian languages is reported to be that Swedish *själv* differs from *selv* in not being obligatory in a case like *Johan föraktade sig* 'John despised himself' as it is in Norwegian (Hellan 1988, 97n10), but see Schadler 2009. The anaphors *seg* and *seg selv* must be bound by the subject of a predicate containing the anaphor. The same holds true of the possessive anaphor. When the antecedent is not a subject, *ham selv*, and so on is used instead of *seg selv*, and the corresponding pronominal form instead of *seg* or *sin*. As in Icelandic, in 1st- and 2nd-person the pronominal forms are used, with *selv* where a complex anaphor is required.

Given our discussion of POSS reflexives in section 5.6.4, little more needs to be said about the reasons behind the distribution of SE-*selv* and *Pron-selv*. In Scandinavian the left-peripheral position in the DP is accessible for chain formation. This holds true for the POSS position in "lexical" DPs, and also for the peripheral position in DPs headed by SELF, as in $[_{\pi P}\ SE_{\pi}\ [_{NP}\ self]]$. Hence the complementarity between *seg selv* and *ham selv* follows from the same principles as the complementarity between *sin* and *hanns*: the latter cannot enter a chain with T-system and subject without violating the chain condition, the former will always enter a chain with the subject via the T-system if possible (see the discussion of Rule L in chapter 5).

Unlike Icelandic, Norwegian does not have a systematic use of *seg* as a logophor. This correlates with the absence of subjunctive in Norwegian (but see the discussion of Faroese). As in Icelandic, X-*selv* is local, and bare *seg* allows long-distance binding. The following example illustrates long-distance binding in Norwegian (from Hellan 1991, 30).

(43) Jon$_i$ bad oss forsøke å få deg til å snakke pent om   seg$_i$
　　 Jon asked us (to) try to get you to talk   nicely about SE
　　 'Jon asked us to try to get you to talk nicely about him.'

For both possessive and nonpossessive forms the upward bound on the binding domain is the minimal tensed S (Hellan 1991, 31), in accordance with Chomsky's (1973) Tensed-S Condition. This is illustrated by the ill-formedness of (44):

(44) *Jon$_i$ var ikke klar   over at   vi hadde snakket om   seg$_i$
　　 Jon was not aware over that we had   talked about SE
　　 'Jon was not aware that we had talked about him.'

One of the intriguing questions in the theory of binding is what factors are involved in the limitations on long-distance binding in languages such as Dutch and German as compared to Norwegian and other Scandinavian languages.

Dutch, as we already saw, distinguishes between pronominals (1st- and 2nd-person singular and plural, 3rd-person singular masculine, feminine, and neuter, 3rd-person plural common gender), *SE anaphors* and *SELF anaphors*. The SE anaphor *zich* only occurs in 3rd person (no singular/plural contrast). In environments where *zich* would be used for 3rd person, 1st and 2nd person are realized by a canonical pronominal form. Although, in general, complementarity between pronouns and anaphors holds, as in other languages, it should be noted that local binding of 3rd-person feminine singular *haar*, and to some extent also 3rd-person plural common gender *hun* is not as bad as one might expect on the basis of the canonical condition B. Interestingly, these forms are also used in positions of nonstructural Case-licensing, namely as POSS phrases. This suggests that they can be licensed in a manner that allows them to escape from entering a chain, just like we saw in Frisian and certain German dialects (see Baauw 2002 for a discussion of the feature structure of Dutch pronouns from an acquisitional perspective). Binding of the SELF anaphor *zichzelf* and its 1st- and 2nd-person counterparts is strictly local.

The behavior of *zich* and *zichzelf* is covered by the principles introduced so far; see specifically the discussion in section 8.3.2.

Pron-zelf occurs in a wider range of positions than *zich* or *zichzelf* (see Koster 1985 for relevant discussion). For instance, Dutch *zich* is impossible in positions corresponding to those of exempt anaphors in English; *zichzelf* in such positions must have its antecedent in the local domain, as in (45). *Hemzelf* is possible in such positions with a long-distance reading, as it is in picture NPs. In such positions its interpretation shows logophoric characteristics:

(45) a. Max_i telde vijf toeristen in de kamer behalve $*zich_i/zichzelf_i/$
       $*hem_i/hemzelf_i$
       'Max counted five tourists in the room apart from himself.'

   b. De $koningin_i$ eist dat boeken die onflatteuze beschrijvingen van
      $haar_i/haarzelf_i/*zich_i/*zichzelf_i$ bevatten worden verbrand
      'The queen demands that books containing unflattering
      descriptions of herself will be burned.'

Logophoric interpretation of 1st- and 2nd-person SELF anaphors is available under similar conditions as in English.

Long-distance binding of *zich* is possible, but it is more restricted than long-distance binding of Icelandic *sig* and Norwegian *seg*. *Zich* in *te*-infinitives (corresponding to *to*-infinitives) cannot be bound from the outside, as in (46), whereas *zich* in causative or perception verb complements can, as in (47) (see Everaert 1986).

(46) Ik hoor dat Jan_i Piet gevraagd heeft een boek voor
      I hear that Jan Piet asked   has a   book for
      $zich_{*i}/hem_i$ mee te brengen
      SE/him   along to bring
      'I hear that Jan_i has asked Piet to bring a book for him_i.'

(47) Jan_i hoorde Marie een lied voor $zich_i/hem_i$ fluiten
      Jan heard Marie a   song for SE/him   whistle
      'Jan heard Marie whistle a song for him.'

This latitude is restricted to *zich* in PPs. In the following cases with *zich* in direct object position only local binding is possible (in (48a) both readings are pragmatically okay; in (48b) where the local reading is pragmatically disfavored, the nonlocal reading is still impossible):

(48) a. Jan$_i$ voelde Marie$_j$ zich$_{*i/j}$/zichzelf$_{*i/j}$ verdedigen
        John felt   Mary   SE/SE-SELF   defend
        'John felt Mary defend herself.'

    b. Jan$_i$ hoorde Marie$_j$ zich$_{*i/?j}$/zichzelf$_{*i/j}$ verwensen
        John heard   Mary   SE/SE-SELF   curse
        'John heard Mary curse herself.'

With causative ECM constructions, judgments about object (relative to the lower verb) *zich* are essentially the same:

(49) Jan$_i$ liet Marie$_j$ zich$_{*i/j}$/zichzelf$_{*i/j}$ wassen
     John let Mary   SE/SE-SELF   wash
     'John let Mary wash herself.'

Indirect object *zich*, does, however, allow a nonlocal reading:

(50) Jan$_i$ liet Marie$_j$ zich$_{i/?j}$/zichzelf$_{*i/j}$ een boek brengen
     John let Mary   SE/SE-SELF   a   book bring
     'John let Mary bring herself a book.'
     'John let Mary bring him a book.'

Note that in some of these cases, replacing *zich* with a pronominal is less than well formed under the intended interpretation:

(51) a. Jan$_i$ voelde Marie$_j$ hem$_{?i}$ verdedigen
        John felt   Mary   him   defend
        'John felt Mary defend him.'

    b. Jan$_i$ hoorde Marie$_j$ hem$_{?i}$ verwensen
        John heard   Mary   him   curse
        'John heard Mary curse him.'

With causative ECM constructions, judgments about embedded object *hem* become sharper when the predicate is an intrinsic reflexive, as illustrated by the contrast between (52a) and (52b):

(52) a. Jan$_i$ liet Marie$_j$ hem$_{*i}$ wassen
        John let Mary   him   wash
        'John let Mary wash him.'

    b. Jan$_i$ liet Marie$_j$ hem$_{?i}$ verdedigen
        John let Mary   him   defend
        'John let Mary defend him.'

Embedded indirect object *hem* is fine, though:

(53) Jan$_i$ liet Marie$_j$ hem$_i$ een boek brengen
    John let Mary him a   book bring
    'John let Mary bring him a book.'

These issues tie in with the general role of *zich*, as either an argument anaphor or an element inserted to check the residual structural Case left by reduction, along the lines discussed in chapter 6. I will come back to this later in this chapter.

German distinguishes between pronominals (1st- and 2nd-person singular and plural, 3rd-person singular masculine, feminine, and neuter, 3rd-person plural common gender), and the anaphor *sich*, which only occurs in 3rd person (no singular/plural contrast) and that superficially resembles a SE anaphor. In the type of environments that require the anaphor for 3rd person, 1st and 2nd person are realized by a canonical pronominal form. There is an anaphoric form *sich selbst*, which superficially resembles a SELF anaphor. In 1st and 2nd person it is realized as the corresponding pronominal with *selbst*. Antecedents for these forms need not be strictly local. The theoretical implications of this are difficult to assess, given the fact that *selbst* occurs as a focalizing particle and focalization generally contributes to exemption (see chapter 3).[17] As discussed in the previous section, *sich* occurs both as a clitic and as a tonic anaphor. And because German is a syntax language, the form *sich* can be used in most positions where Dutch has *zichzelf*.

Interestingly, in positions corresponding to those of exempt anaphors in English *sich selbst* or *ihn selbst* are preferred, as in (54):[18]

(54) Max$_i$ zählte fünf Touristen im Zimmer ausser *sich$_i$/sich selbst$_i$/
    *ihm$_i$/ihm selbst$_i$
    'Max counted five tourists in the room apart from himself.'

A logophoric interpretation of *sich* and *sich selbst* with nonlocal antecedents is impossible in German. It is possible to have *sich* in a true expletive construction, though, as in (55):

(55) Es hat sich   ausgekuschelt.
    it has SICH out-schmoozed
    'Schmoozing is over now.'

A logophoric interpretation of 1st- and 2nd-person *selbst* forms is available under similar conditions as for the corresponding SELF anaphors in Dutch and English.

Long-distance binding of *sich* is possible, but, like in Dutch, it is more limited than long-distance binding of Icelandic *sig* and Norwegian *seg*. *Sich* in *zu*-infinitives (corresponding to *to*-infinitives) cannot be bound from the outside, as in (56) and (57), whereas, to a certain extent, *sich* in causative or perception verb complements can, as in (58).

(56) Hans$_i$ befahl   Peter [(PRO) ihn$_i$/*sich$_i$/*sich$_i$ selbst jeden Tag zu
     Hans ordered Peter   him/*SE/*SE-   SELF every day to
     rasieren]
     shave
     'Hans ordered Peter to shave him every day.'

(57) Ich hörte, dass Johann$_i$ Peter gebeten hat ein Buch für *sich$_i$/ihn$_i$
     I   heard that John   Peter asked   has a   book for SE
     mitzunehmen
     to-bring
     'I heard that John$_i$ has asked Peter to bring a book for him$_i$.'

(58) Johann$_i$ hörte Maria ein Lied für sich$_{\%i}$/ihn$_i$ pfeifen
     John   heard Mary a   song for SE/him   whistle
     'John heard Mary whistle a song for him.'

Apparently there is variation in the acceptance of the *sich*-variant in (58), indicated by the %-sign before the subscript. Insofar as there is such latitude in ECM, it is limited to *sich* in PPs. In the following cases, with *sich* in direct object position, binding is only local. Note that in (59a) both readings are pragmatically okay; in (59b), where the local reading is pragmatically less plausible, the nonlocal reading is still impossible.

(59) a. Johann$_i$ fühlte Maria$_j$ sich$_{*i/j}$/sich selbst$_{*i/j}$ verteidigen
        John   felt   Mary   SE/SE-SELF   defend
        'John felt Mary defend herself.'
     b. Johann$_i$ hörte Maria$_j$ sich$_{*i/j}$/sich selbst$_{*i/j}$ verwünschen
        John   heard Mary   SE/SE-SELF   curse
        'John heard Mary curse herself.'

With causative ECM constructions, judgments about object *sich* are essentially the same (note that a main clause reading of the pronoun is unobjectionable, unlike in Dutch):

(60) Karl$_i$ liess Paul$_j$ sich$_{*i/j}$/ihn$_{i/*j}$/ihn selbst$_{i/j}$ rasieren
     Karl let Paul   SE/him/him self   shave
     'Karl let Paul shave him.'

Indirect object *sich* does not allow a nonlocal reading either:[19]

(61) Karl$_i$ liess Paul$_j$ sich$_{*i/j}$/ihm$_{i/*j}$ ein Buch besorgen
     Karl let Paul   SE/him   a   book bring
     'Karl let Paul bring him a book.'

Gunkel (2003) reports the following variation. Whereas adjunct PPs equally allow both the anaphor and the pronominal in ECM, as in (62), there is a difference between two types of complement PPs in (63) and (64).[20]

(62) Karl$_i$ liess mich neben sich$_i$/ihm$_i$ schlafen
    Karl let me next-to SE/him sleep
    'Karl let me sleep next to him.'

(63) a. Karl$_i$ liess uns nur ungern über ??sich$_i$/ihn$_i$ schimpfen
       Karl let us only unwillingly at SE/him scold
       'Karl let us scold him only unwillingly.'
   b. Karl$_i$ liess mich an ?sich$_i$/ihn$_i$ einen Brief schreiben
       Karl let me to SE/him a letter write
       'Karl let me write a letter to him.'

(64) Er$_i$ liess mich mit sich$_i$/ihm$_i$ spielen
    he let me with SE/him play
    'He let me play with him.'

From the perspective of our discussion of long-distance anaphora it is important that German exhibits the same type of restrictions in this domain as Dutch and is quite unlike the Scandinavian languages.

Frisian and Yiddish are to be mentioned only for sake of completeness in this connection. Since Frisian lacks a SE anaphor and the forms used instead are truly pronominal, the question of long-distance binding of anaphors does not arise. Long-distance binding of pronominals is, of course, possible throughout.

In exempt positions, the form *pronominal-SELF* has the full range of logophoric possibilities as its counterpart in English and Dutch. For the purpose of the discussion of long-distance anaphors in Germanic it can, henceforth, be ignored.

Yiddish has a simplex anaphor *zikh*, which as in many Slavic languages is used for all persons, and a complex form *zick aleyn*, which in its use appears to be closer to German *sich selbst* than to Scandinavian *seg selv*.[21] A thorough analysis of Yiddish anaphora appears to be lacking. The literature (for instance, Weinreich 1971, 100–101) provides no indication that Yiddish has any long-distance or logophoric use of *zick* or *zick aleyn*.

8.4.3 Capturing the Variation in Binding Domains

As described in the previous section, there is considerable variation within Germanic in the domains in which SE anaphors must be bound. As we saw, SE anaphors may allow their antecedent in a position beyond the governing category as computed in the CBT, but languages differ in how far. Since much of the discussion in the literature of long-distance anaphora is couched in preminimalist terms, I will summarize some of the previous analyses in their own terms and also point out some of the problems they faced, before presenting my analysis.

The pattern of variation I just summarized has been taken to suggest that there are at least three possible (nonlocal) binding domains across languages. Systematic attempts to account for the variation observed include parameterized versions of the binding theory, with binding-theory specific parameters, as proposed in Koster 1985 and Manzini and Wexler 1987, and a chain-based analysis in which the variation follows from chain formation interacting with independent structural differences as proposed in Everaert 1986. Manzini and Wexler, for example, hypothesized that the governing category may vary across languages and anaphor types in terms of an opacity factor. The notion of an opacity factor generalizes the role of the subject in the canonical formulation of the binding theory.

(65) a. b is a governing category for a iff b is the minimal category containing a, a governor of a and F (F an opacity factor).
     b. Possible values of F include: (i) (accessible) SUBJECT, (ii) Agr, (iii) Tense, (iv) indicative Tense, (v) Root Tense.

Descriptively, this approach gives a good approximation. However, it leaves open by what principles the set of possible values of F can be restricted (otherwise predicting too many possible domains). Moreover, it treats the dependencies in all domains on a par, not distinguishing between logophoric dependencies and structural binding.

Everaert (1986) summarized the variation in the binding of SE-anaphors we observed in terms of the following three domains:

(66) i.   Small clauses (causatives and complements of perception verbs)
     ii.   Nonfinite clauses (including both *to*-infinitives and small clauses)
     iii. Nonindicative clauses (including subjunctive tensed clauses and nonfinite clauses)

Since the third domain involves logophoricity, variation in structural binding domains appears to be limited to just domains (i) and (ii). Moreover, we saw that in Dutch and German the possibility of long-distance binding does not extend to anaphors in the object position of the embedded verb. So, the two relevant domains can be characterized as follows:

(67) i. Small clauses (causatives and complements of perception verbs, except for the object argument of the lower verb)

ii. Nonfinite clauses (including both *to*-infinitives and small clauses)

Everaert, followed by Reinhart and Reuland (1991), observes that the choice between (i) and (ii) is linked to an independent syntactic factor: (i) is found in the Germanic OV languages Dutch and German, and (ii) in the Scandinavian VO languages.

There are a variety of proposals in the literature to capture the subject orientation and nonlocality of SE anaphors. Most of them explore the idea in Lebeaux 1983 and Chomsky 1986b that restrictions on binding correlate with restrictions on movement. (See Pica 1985, 1987; Battistella 1987; Huang and Tang 1991; Cole, Hermon, and Sung 1990; and Hestvik 1991, 1992.)

That SE anaphors move has been argued to follow from the fact that they are underspecified for ϕ-features. Bouchard (1984) argued that in order to be interpreted an argument requires a full specification of ϕ-features. From that perspective, being underspecified, SE anaphors must acquire ϕ-features in the course of the derivation. This requirement can be met by association with an element carrying them.

Following up on this, a possible line was, then, to analyze the association of SE with a source for ϕ-features as an instance of X^0 (head) movement (assuming that SE is a head in, for instance, the D-position). The set of available sources is restricted: Since heads can only move to head positions, the SE anaphor can only receive the necessary features from another head. Verbs will not do (nor will prepositions, etc.), since they do not contain ϕ-features. A c-commanding DP will not do either, since it is a maximal projection. The only element that meets the requirements that it c-commands the anaphor, is in head position, and carries ϕ-features is AGR.[22] For sake of concreteness, (68) gives the rule as it was stated in Reinhart and Reuland 1991, 302:

(68) SE heads adjoin to AGR at LF.

Since AGR is always coindexed with the subject and SE anaphors always link to AGR, it follows that SE anaphors, in their grammatical (nonlogophoric) use are subject oriented.[23]

As we will see, the approach in this form raises a number of issues. I will discuss them in turn.

8.4.3.1 "LF Movement" of SE and Relativized Minimality Everaert (1986) formulated a representational theory of anaphoric dependencies where proper binding requires that the coindexing between anaphor and antecedent creates a licit chain-type object. The anaphor must be properly governed by the index of its antecedent. This, in turn, requires a barriers style licensing of indices by a sequence of governing heads (see the discussion of NP-raising in Chomsky 1986a, as it was recapitulated in our discussion of chains in chapter 3).

(69) $DP_i [_z \ldots Z_i [_Y \ldots Y_i [_X \ldots X_i \ldots SE_i]]]$

Lebeaux (1983) and, subsequently, Chomsky (1986b), in an endeavor to subsume binding theory under movement theory, developed an approach to binding involving covert movement (*LF Movement*). Near the end of the 1980s it was found that movement obeys the relativized minimality condition (Rizzi 1990b). If SE movement instantiates head movement, it follows from any implementation of relativized minimality that subjects are not interveners. In principle this could yield an extension of the binding domain beyond the minimal governing category. However, the framework of Chomsky 1986a puts severe limitations on head-to-head movement. The movement "passing through H" sketched in (70a) is always illicit since the intermediate trace violates the ECP (as discussed in, for instance, Baker 1988), apart from the question of whether H would be a minimality barrier, as we discussed. "Long" head movement skipping H as in (70b) is also ruled out—it is equally ruled out in current theories based on probe-goal relationships, with H effectively intervening.[24]

(70) a. $*[_b a_i b] \ldots [_H t_i H] \ldots t_i$
      b. $*[_b a_i b] \ldots H \ldots t_i$

It has been argued that long movement is allowed if H is not a head of the same type—that is, not an intervener in the sense of relativized minimality (Roberts 1991). However, if (70b) is taken as the general model, it is predicted that SE always links to the nearest source of φ-features, namely the local AGR. Since the actual binder may be higher up, one must either assume a dissociation between *being a binder* and *being a source for φ-features* or assume that binding is a by-product of attracting a larger constituent than just the anaphor. The former option underlies approaches modeled after Chinese (see Battistella 1987; Huang and Tang 1991; Cole, Hermon, and Sung 1990; and Huang and Liu 2000).

Reinhart and Reuland (1991) model the LF-domain extension of anaphors on the overt formation of complex predicates in verb raising languages like Dutch. This comes down to claiming that such anaphor movement uses massive covert pied piping. SE first adjoins to its governing verb.[25] From there, V moves to T, taking SE along.[26] The V/T complex thus formed may then move up further to a higher V, yielding a new V/T complex, then to yet a higher T, and so on, until SE with the V/T complex arrives at a position where SE associates with AGR. For an object control complement the structure is illustrated in (71). AGR is represented by the index on T; the SE anaphor is, then, eventually bound by the subject of the matrix clause, as, for example, in Norwegian (72) and (73).

(71)

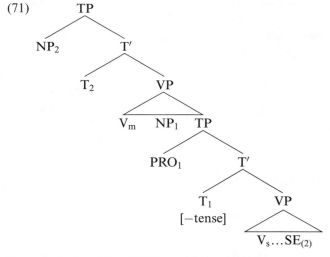

Recapitulating: First $V_sSE_{(2)}$ is formed. Subsequently, $V_sSE_{(2)}$ moves to T_1 merging in that position, then $SE_{(2)}/V_s/T_1$ moves up to V_m, and finally, $SE_{(2)}/V_s/T_1/V_m/$ moves up to T_2. Here the SE-bearing Verb merges with T_2, and SE may pick up the latter's ϕ-features. Interpretability only requires that SE gets its features at some point, but is insensitive to whether this happens when the verb merges with the lower T_1, with the higher T_2 or even with some higher up T. Thus, in both (72) and (73) the anaphor will be able to be bound by the highest subject as required:

(72) Jon$_j$ bad   oss snakke om   seg$_j$
     Jon$_j$ asked us (to) talk about SE$_j$

(73) Jon$_i$ bad   oss forsøke å få deg til å snakke pent   om   seg$_i$
     Jon asked us (to) try to get you to   talk   nicely about SE

Since finite clauses are opaque for "Verb raising" and similar head-to-head movements it follows that the upper bound for the binding of a SE anaphor is the first finite clause containing it (thus, this type of binding observes the "Tensed-S Condition").

From the perspective of current theory this implementation raises a number of questions. For instance, triggering such generalized verb raising requires an interpretation-driven distribution of attracting features, which is problematic. However, from this conception it is a small step toward an implementation in the feature-checking/valuation approach presented in chapter 5. This is what I set out to do now. As a first step, I will discuss the word-order contrasts in Germanic.

8.4.3.2 The OV-VO Contrast

As we saw, reporting an observation by Everaert (1986), in Dutch and German *zich/sich* in *to*-infinitives cannot be bound from the outside, as illustrated in the Dutch example (74), whereas in causative or perception verb complements they can, as in (75). In Scandinavian languages binding is possible into both types of clauses as we saw in the previous section.

(74) Ik hoor dat Jan$_i$ Piet gevraagd heeft een boek voor zich$_{*i}$ mee te
     I   hear that Jan Piet asked   has a   book for SE   PRT to
     brengen
     bring
     'I hear that Jan$_i$ has asked Piet to bring a book for him.'

(75) Jan$_i$ hoorde Marie een lied   voor zich$_i$/hem$_i$ fluiten
     Jan heard   Marie a   song for SE/him   whistle
     'Jan heard Marie whistle a song for him.'

As noted, Everaert (1986) relates this to the OV-VO contrast. He proposed that the OV-VO contrast leads to a difference in the configuration involving binder, matrix verb and bindee. This difference is due to the position of attachment of the infinitival clause in OV-VO languages (using a framework in which the base position of the infinitival clause is to the left of the verb in OV languages, and to its right in VO languages).

Reinhart and Reuland (1991) implemented this idea. Although this implementation will have to be revised in the end, I will briefly discuss it, since some of its insights will be retained. The embedded clause originates to the left of the verb, and is subsequently extraposed, leaving the trace indicated by t$_{CP}$ in (76a) (using the then standard idea of rightward extraposition). If the extraposed *te*-clause moves to the right of the finite verb in Dutch (as discussed in Reuland 1990a, there is no possibility of attachment between V and T), the lowest available attachment site is that of adjunction to TP; thus, the clause must end up higher than the finite verb, as indicated in (76a), omitting details. The anaphor *zich* and any verb within $CP_{infinitive}$ it attaches to are not c-commanded by the higher V-T complex (e.g., *heeft* in (76a)). Hence, they cannot form a chain headed by a higher T/AGR using the procedure illustrated in (71). This makes it impossible for *zich* to be interpreted.

In Scandinavian, being VO, the complement clause stays in the VP (possibly after VP-adjunction) and is c-commanded by T, so the necessary chain can be formed. This is illustrated in (76b):

(76) a.

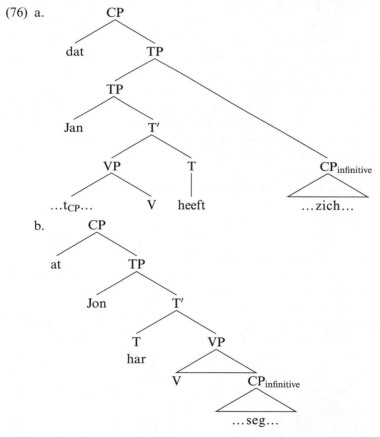

The general structure of this account is thus based on the idea that the OV structure creates a discontinuity in any chain-type dependency between anaphor and antecedent that is mediated by the governing verb of the constituent containing the anaphor. As such, it is independent of the specific mechanism for chain formation assumed.

This particular implementation depends on the assumption that there is rightward movement/extraposition of *te*-infinitives. As is well known, this assumption is incompatible with most versions of current syntactic theory.[27]

However, Everaert's insight that the OV structure creates a discontinuity prohibiting the establishment of the relevant dependency is not dependent on this particular implementation. In the next section it will be shown that it can also be implemented in theories without extraposition.

The other contrast between the OV and the VO languages concerns the impossibility of LD binding of direct object *zich/sich* in Dutch and German (and indirect object *sich* in German) even in small clauses. Everaert (1986) discusses this fact as well (see also Reis 1976). He notes that overt verb raising applies in Dutch and German, but not in the Scandinavian languages. On the basis of this fact Everaert proposes that the contrast can be reduced to a difference between full verbs and verb traces as licensers of anaphors. Under the current copy theory of movement such a distinction cannot be maintained. Our perspective on the role of *zich* as checking residual structural Case makes it possible to pursue an alternative. This we will do in the end of the next section.

8.4.4 Discussion from Current Perspectives: Long-Distance Binding and Minimalism

The general line that SE anaphors move in order to acquire φ-features is problematic from a minimalist perspective, in so far as it is based on a self-serving movement of the anaphor that is not triggered by an independent requirement of feature checking. As we saw, this problem can be circumvented by assuming a composite movement in which the anaphor associates with a verbal projection for Case-checking, and the verbal projection moves further for independent reasons. Yet, providing such motivation is still a nontrivial task.

Let's therefore pursue this a bit further. For ease of exposition I will give a short summary of the mechanisms in chapter 5. As we saw, there is a derivational procedure that mechanically captures the syntactic component of binding.

The informal sketch is repeated in (77), with R1 standing for the syntactic relation that holds between subject and finite verb (Agreement, Nominative Case), R2 for the relation between the elements of the verbal complex (Tense, Agreement, Main Verb) and R3 for structural accusative Case-checking:

(77) DP   T   V   SE
      └────┘└────┘└────┘
         R1   R2   R3

The dependencies these relations reflect can be composed. Composing R1, R2, and R3 yields a composite dependency (DP, SE) based on a feature chain. Hence, the following parameter should enter a typology of interpretive dependencies:

- ±syntactically encoded

In this approach, feature specifications determine what elements can be linked up to a chain. Note, that it is no longer necessary assume covert movement of SE along with the verb if it is the Case-checking relation between SE and the verbal system itself that determines the dependency between the two. It suffices that it is encoded on the verb or its functional structure that checking has taken place, and that this information is preserved when the verb moves, or, more generally, when it enters a dependency with a c-commanding head. So, chain formation is a by-product of independently existing dependencies, and anaphor binding results from this chain formation.

We must, then, consider what further relevant dependencies there are in order to account for anaphor binding across clauses. Prime candidates are C-T dependencies. (For the moment I abstract away from the fine structure of the left periphery; see Rizzi 1997.) We know independently from the work on tense interpretation that T is dependent on C or a c-commanding higher T, and that C's are also dependent on c-commanding higher C's. Much of this evidence comes from sequence of tense (SOT) phenomena, beginning with Enç's influential 1987 article. (I will not review this literature here. Much relevant work can be found in Guéron and Lecarme 2004 and references cited there. An extensive overview and a detailed analysis are presented in Khomitsevich 2008; see also Reuland and Avrutin 2005 and 2010 and Khomitsevitch and Reuland 2007.) I will furthermore adopt the proposal that a close dependency exists between clausemate T and C, as discussed in Chomsky 2005.

As we saw, binding of SE anaphors is sensitive to the OV/VO contrast. And in fact this very variation shows that at least part of the computations for their interpretation is carried out within *narrow syntax* in the Chomsky 1995 sense. Although we can be sure that a syntactic factor is involved, this does not entail that all of the computation is carried out in syntax. As always, the facts do not wear their analysis on their sleeves.

But in the remainder of this section I will sketch how a syntactic dependency between SE anaphor and its antecedent involving the mechanism of (77) can be established—and more specifically, show how an SOV structure blocks such a dependency. I will leave aside the precise specification of the triggers, though.

If chain formation between a SE anaphor and matrix T_{AGR} (and subsequently the antecedent) is based on composing dependencies along the lines indicated in (77), clearly no chain can be formed unless mediated by the matrix verb. The relevant configuration in Norwegian is given in (76b), repeated here, making explicit some of the structure in the downstairs clause:

(78)

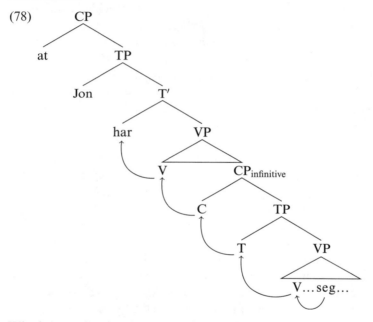

Whether one has head movement, or chain composition as a model, in all implementations a route including all intermediate heads is required. As we will see, this requirement cannot be met in the "extraposition" configurations of OV languages.

What most current approaches to the phrase structure of Germanic SOV languages have in common is that an "extraposed" clause is in fact assumed to have been left behind in a low position by movements depleting the original verb phrase from verb and nominal arguments, where the latter material actually moves higher in the structure. There are two types of approaches. One in which the VP gets depleted by a combination of head movement and XP-movement, the other in which there is only XP-movement; cases where prima facie only V is moved, are analyzed as involving moving a remnant VP (as for instance in Koopman and Szabolcsi 2000). For reasons of space it will not do to go into the details of the various analyses. It is enough that they all present converging evidence for the following structural pattern (for ease of exposition I am using traces and X'-notation with some unspecified labels in the representations; no theoretical status should be attributed to these notations):

(79) In an SOV structure there is at least one step in which a phrase containing the verb that originated as a sister to the complement clause, moves up to a position to the left of its inflection—if more than the verb is moved, the CP-complement has left the verb phrase before movement takes place.

The configuration, based on (76a), is given in (80):

(80)

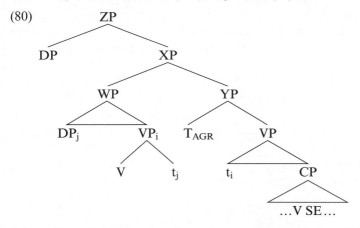

It is easily seen that moving the verb (or a constituent containing it) from the sister position of the infinitival clause (indicated by t_i), crossing T_{AGR}, disrupts the possibility to form a DP, T_{AGR}, V, ... SE chain. Assume that a dependency (checking relation, or agreement) holds between DP and T_{AGR}. The next link in the dependency cannot be V, since it moved across. It cannot be t_i either, since being the tail of the V-constituent that crossed T_{AGR} it is inert (Chomsky 2004). Hence, t_i cannot participate in the formation of the dependency. Other options are equally unavailable, hence forming the dependency is blocked, and SE in the lower clause cannot be syntactically linked to the matrix DP.[28] In the Scandinavian SVO languages the verb stays to the right of inflection, hence lower than the latter. Since there is no crossing, nothing prohibits the matrix V from mediating in establishing a chain relation between SE and the matrix T_{AGR} and subsequently the subject, as illustrated in (81):

(81)

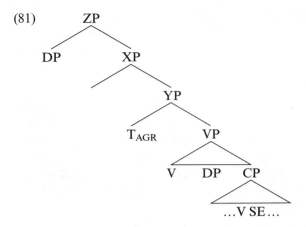

Precisely because in small clauses and bare infinitivals in Dutch and German, no "extraposition" structures obtain, binding into these constructions is possible, except when some other process interferes—such as the role of *zich/sich* as a Case checker and marker of an arity operation, as discussed below.[29]

The discussion so far leaves open two questions: (i) Why can SE anaphors in Scandinavian "skip" one or more intervening PRO-subjects? Why isn't the first available antecedent simply selected, and the derivation canceled, if this leads to a feature mismatch? And (ii) Why is there no complementarity between nonlocally bound SE anaphors and pronominals? The property of (i) was already illustrated in (73). I repeat the example here as (82) with structure added:

(82) $[_{S0}$ $\varnothing_{C0}$ $[Jon_i$ T_0 bad_{V0} oss $[_{S1}$ $\varnothing_{C1}$ $[PRO$ T_1 $forsøke_{V1}$ $[_{S2}$ $å_{C2}$
         Jon   asked us   PRO   (to) try   for
PRO T_2 $få_{V2}$ deg $[_{S3}$ til_{C3} PRO T_3 å $snakke_{V3}$ pent om $seg_i]]]]]]$
PRO   get you   to   PRO   to talk   nicely about SE
'Jon asked us to try to get you to talk nicely about him.'

This structure is to be compared with the Dutch examples in (83):

(83) a. *$[_{\varnothing C0}$ Jan_i T_0 heeft ons $gevraagd_{V0}$ $[_{S1}$ om_{C1} $[PRO$ T_1 aardig
            Jan   has us asked   for   PRO   nicely
      over $zich_i$ te praten]]]
      about SE   to talk

    b. $George_i$ heeft $Tony_j$ gesmeekt om PRO_j niemand tegen
       George has   Tony implored for PRO nobody against
       $zich_{j/*i}$ in opstand te laten komen
       SE   in uprising to let   come
       'George implored Tony to let nobody rise against him.'

(83a) illustrates on the basis of an example parallel to—but simpler than—(82) that LD binding is impossible in Dutch. (83b) illustrates that the local PRO acts as an antecedent.

Deriving the effect of the OV-VO contrast on long-distance binding requires that in both Dutch and Norwegian the syntactic route must be chosen for the binding of SE anaphors. If a SE anaphor could be simply bound by any c-commanding antecedent, the crosslinguistic contrast would be lost, since in Dutch a remote subject c-commands *zich* as well and is not a licit binder. Hence, I will indeed make that assumption.

The answer to these two questions lies in the properties of the C-T system in nonfinite clauses and the way it differs from the C-T system in finite clauses. In a finite clause the C-T system is valued syntactically, and φ-features, including person, are represented as low as on T (the verbal agreement). Hence, when the local finite T is merged to the structure containing the V-SE chain, the chain is extended and SE is immediately valued (for perspicuity's sake I omit the light verb v* from the representations). This leads to a cancellation as discussed in chapters 4 and 5 if the feature values of SE and the subject are incompatible, or if PRD is violated. Hence, we find complementarity between the pronominal and the SE anaphor.

In control structures, the C-T system is defective. Specifically, nonfinite T is not specified for φ-features (with Chomsky (2008), I assume no special specifier-head agreement relation). Consequently, when, as in (82), a T_3-V_3-SE chain is formed, it does not immediately lead to valuing SE, nor can it lead to a cancellation due to a feature mismatch. Subsequent merger of further defective T and C projections does not change that.

Let's now examine the factors determining the way the dependency between a SE anaphor and its antecedent in control structures is established. The key factor is the structure of the C-system (Force system) in the left periphery of the clause. There is good reason to assume that the C-system is in fact richly structured (for evidence and discussion see Haegeman 1984, Rizzi 1997, Bianchi 2000 and 2001, Sigurðsson 2004, Baker 2007, and others). Within the C-system, minimally Force, Tense, and φ-features must be realized. The T-system must minimally allow encoding of Tense and φ-features (Agreement).

A further factor is control. An elaborate theory of control is presented in Landau 2003, 2006, and 2008.[30] Since a detailed discussion of control would go beyond the scope of this book, I will abstract away from the precise mechanisms of control.

Instead, I will focus on those properties of the system that are relatively independent of specific implementations and show how they help explain the puzzling facts.

First of all, let us note that every major system in the verb's extended projection ($v*$, T, and C) carries both Tense features and ϕ-features (valued or unvalued, interpretable or uninterpretable). Consequently, dependencies can be established along both dimensions. This causes an indeterminacy in the formation of dependencies. It is this indeterminacy that makes it possible to encode the dependency between *Jon* and *seg* in (82), skipping the intervening PRO's.

Rizzi (1997), for instance, posits that finiteness is represented in the C-system as Fin, the lowest functional head above the T-system. Bianchi (2000, 2001) adopts this proposal and posits that Fin has the value +fin in finite clauses, and −fin in control clauses. Specifically, she proposes that −fin Fin (henceforth Fin^{-fin}) mediates in transmitting the value of the controller to PRO.

Sigurðsson (2004) and Baker (2007) propose that person features are encoded in the C-system. From this perspective, the crucial difference between finite and nonfinite clauses is that in finite clauses one person is privileged, and represented low in the functional structure as T_{AGR}. In nonfinite clauses no person has a privileged status.

I now present the outlines of an implementation based on the following minimal assumptions: (i) in nonfinite clauses the C-system contains Fin^{-fin}, and minimally one other member—let's call it C^T (as we saw, the current consensus is that there are many more, but for my purpose, the existence of just one such member suffices); (ii) Fin^{-fin} and C^T are equidistant with respect to the T-system below and with respect to the V-system in the matrix clause.[31]

It is the choice between Fin^{-fin} and C^T that creates the crucial indeterminacy. To see this, consider the T_3-V_3-SE chain. At the point where Fin is merged, the controller has not yet been merged. Therefore, whatever the precise way control is syntactically encoded, at the point where Fin is merged, control cannot contribute to the valuation of SE. Hence, at that point economy (Rule L) cannot enforce a local dependency.

If so, when the T_3-V_3-SE chain is linked to the C_3-system, economy entails no preference for which member of the C-system it is linked to. Specifically, both Fin^{-fin}_3 and C^T_3 are admissible as targets. We now have the following options: (i) The T_3-V_3-SE chain is linked to Fin^{-fin}_3. If the eventual controller, once merged, has the value 3rd person, we have binding. If it has a different value, there is a feature mismatch and the derivation is canceled. (ii) The T_3-V_3-SE chain is linked to $C^T{}_3$, which does not transmit control. Therefore, after a controller is merged, this does not lead to valuing SE. This is what allows skipping a matching controller—as, for instance, in the variant of (82) that obtains if we replace *deg* in S_2 by a 3rd-person expression such as *Anders*.

If $C^T{}_3$ is taken as a target, the chain can be continued upward via the next higher V (V_2), it can link to T_2, and so on. For any subsequent infinitival clause the same reasoning applies, and there is no limit to the number of times extension can take place. (Recall that a finite clause has a privileged person that is marked on T's φ-features, below the point of indeterminacy. Owing to this property of T, economy (Rule L) requires V_3-SE to establish a φ-feature chain, and skipping Fin^{+fin} to link up to $C^T{}_3$ is not an option.)

Consider finally the issue of complementarity between a bound pronominal and SE. In S_3, the chain formation process up to T is deterministic. Irrespective of the eventual choice and merger of the controller, a PRO-T_3-V_3-SE chain is possible. Hence, local binding of the pronominal by PRO is blocked since PRON is in a configuration to form a *PRO*-T_3-V_3-*PRON* chain, which is canceled in accordance with the principles discussed. However, in the domain beyond T_3 the process forming the dependency is not deterministic. We should consider two cases. The first case is one in which T_3-V_3-PRON links to $C^T{}_3$, as in

- $[_{S1} \varnothing_{C1} [\boldsymbol{DP} \, \mathbf{T_1} \, \mathbf{V_1} \, \underline{oss} \, [_{S2} \, \mathbf{C^T{}_2} \, Fin^{-fin}{}_2 \, [\text{PRO} \, \mathbf{T_2} \, \mathbf{V_2} \, \underline{deg} \, [_{S3} \, \mathbf{C^T{}_3} \, Fin^{-fin}{}_3 \, [\text{PRO} \, \mathbf{T_3} \, \mathbf{V_3} \, ^{OK}seg/^{CANC}ham]]]]]]$.

The C^T linking is represented in boldface; the relevant control relations are represented by underlining; and the dependency relation that is encoded is represented by italics. In this case complementarity holds. When DP in S_1 is subsequently merged, the PRON is in a configuration where it could have been chain-linked to the DP via the C^T systems and T_1. Hence, this derivation is canceled, and semantic binding is blocked.

The second case is the alternative in which T_3-V_3-PRON links to $Fin^{-fin}{}_3$, which does mediate control, and values the PRO in S_3, as in

- $[_{S1} \varnothing_{C1} [\boldsymbol{DP} \, \mathbf{T_1} \, \mathbf{V_1} \, \underline{oss} \, [_{S2} \, \mathbf{C^T{}_2} \, Fin^{-fin}{}_2 \, [\text{PRO} \, \mathbf{T_2} \, \mathbf{V_2} \, \underline{deg} \, [_{S3} \, \mathbf{C^T{}_3} \, \mathbf{Fin^{-fin}{}_3} \, [\text{PRO} \, \mathbf{T_3} \, \mathbf{V_3} \, ham]]]]]]$.

Here again the control relations are represented by underlining, the link of T_3-V_3-PRON to $Fin^{-fin}{}_3$ is represented in boldface, and the C^T dependency plays no role. The $Fin^{-fin}{}_3$-T_3-V_3-PRON chain is not upward extended (this is the route in which a SE in the position of PRON would be forced to be locally bound). Consequently, PRON in S_3 is not in a configuration where it could have been chain-linked to the subject of S_2 or S_1. Hence, the issue of cancellation does not arise. The subject of S_2 or S_1 may, therefore, semantically bind PRON in S_3. The same applies to binding by subjects in yet higher clauses.

In short, there is an asymmetry between pronominals and SE anaphors. For the SE anaphor the possibility of finding a licit encoding of the dependency counts, because of economy. What counts for the pronominal is the existence of a licit way to avoid the encoding configuration. It is this asymmetry that underlies the observed noncomplementarity. (In this respect the present case is similar to noncomplementarity in PPs.)

For Dutch/German, the system works as follows. Again consider (83), repeated here.

(83) a. *$[\varnothing_{C0}$ Jan$_i$ T_0 heeft ons gevraagd$_{V0}$ [$_{S1}$ om$_{C1}$ [PRO T_1 aardig
         Jan   has   us asked   for   PRO   nicely
         over   zich$_i$ te praten]]]
         about SE   to talk

    b. George$_i$ heeft *Tony*$_j$ gesmeekt om *PRO*$_j$ niemand tegen
       George has   Tony implored for PRO nobody against
       zich$_{j/*i}$ in opstand te laten komen
       SE   in uprising to let   come
       'George implored Tony to let nobody rise against him.'

I assume that the C-system has the same structure as in Scandinavian, specifically including a Fin head and a C^T head. There are the following options for (83a): *Ons* as a 1st-person controller of Fin in S_1 leads to a feature clash/cancellation because of the mismatch with *zich*'s 3rd-person feature if the T_1-V_1-SE chain links up to Fin. If the chain links up to C^T, no valuation obtains. In Scandinavian this is the option that leads to extension. In Dutch/German, however, a grammatical operation derives the "extraposition" configuration of (80), which does not allow the syntactic V-C link connecting clauses.

Consequently, when in (83a) the C^T_1-T_1-V_1-SE chain is formed, this chain cannot be extended to include matrix C-T-V. Bypassing syntax by having the matrix subject *Jan* just semantically bind *zich* at the C-I interface is disallowed by economy (the rejection due to the disrupted chain link is final). Thus, the only options are a cancellation by feature mismatch, as in (83a), or local binding by PRO with a 3rd-person controller, as in (83b).

This explains the contrast between the perception verb complements illustrated in (75) and *te*-infinitives. In the perception verb cases, there is no disruption of the chain and hence the dependency can be syntactically encoded.[32]

This approach has an interesting consequence. The PPs in (83) are direct complements of the verb. Let's consider noncomplement PPs, such as locative or directional (LD) PPs, but also PP's in picture NP's. As discussed in section 8.3.2, *zich* in LD PPs is only forced to enter a local binding relation, since Rule L requires taking the syntactic route. However, in *te*-infinitivals the syntactic route is blocked. This accounts for the cases discussed so far, where the syntactic route is the only option, since the blocked derivation may not be bypassed. However, consider the configuration where a locally bound pronoun is licensed (the "Place" version of the P-V dependency). Everything else being equal, assume we have *zich* in that position. This time Rule L does not come into play. The syntactic route is not available, hence cannot be considered. Therefore, variable binding by a long-distance antecedent should become an option. And, as we see in (84a), it does. Here, *Alice* is a possible binder of *zich*. The same holds true of picture NP's. In (84b), *Alice* is also available as a binder of *zich*.

(84) a. *Alice* had **mij** gevraagd [**PRO** het flesje naast   *zich* neer te
        Alice had me asked   (PRO) the bottle next-to SE   down to
        zetten]
        put
        'Alice had asked me to put the bottle next to her.'
    b. *Alice* had **mij** gevraagd [**PRO** een foto   van *zich* mee te
        Alice had me asked   (PRO) a   picture of SE   along to
        brengen]
        bring
        'Alice had asked me (PRO) to bring along a picture of her.'

To my ear such cases are considerably better than (83a).

In a nutshell, in these cases the prohibition against bypassing syntax in valuing *zich* does not apply. Hence, semantic binding of *zich* is available. This result concludes our discussion of the effects of the OV-VO contrast on long-distance binding and brings us to the last issues to be discussed in this section.

8.4.5 Long-Distance Binding of Direct Object SE
The pattern in Dutch illustrated in (85) poses an intriguing problem. (85) shows that there is a contrast between the binding possibility of SE in PPs and in direct object position.

(85) a. Jan$_i$ hoorde [zich$_i$ zingen]
      Jan$_i$ heard [SE$_i$ sing]
      'Jan heard himself sing.'

   b. *Jan$_i$ hoorde [jou zich$_i$ becritiseren]
      Jan$_i$ heard [you SE$_i$ criticize]
      'Jan$_i$ heard you criticize him$_i$.'

   c. Jan$_i$ hoorde [jou tegen   zich$_i$ argumenteren]
      Jan$_i$ heard [you against SE$_i$ argue]
      'Jan$_i$ heard you argue against him$_i$.'

Prima facie, such a contrast is unexpected. Their counterparts in Scandinavian are well formed. However, as we will see, there is an independent factor that is responsible for the contrast. Recall that we assume a componential analysis of accusative Case. Accusative Case has a structural and a thematic component, which can be checked independent of each other. As we discussed in chapter 6, *zich* has the property of checking residual structural case, where thematic case is absent. Suppose now that *zich* can only check structural Case, and is unable to check thematic Case. If so, the pattern follows. In (85a), where *zich* is the subject of the embedded clause, the latter (TP) is the thematic argument of the matrix verb *hoorde* 'heard', and, thus, checks the thematic component of the accusative Case. The subject of TP, *zich*, only needs to check the structural component of this Case, which it can do. Hence the structure is well formed. The impossibility of binding in (85b) follows from the same assumptions. In (85b) *zich* occurs as the direct complement of the lower verb; hence it is the only element that could possibly check both the thematic and the structural accusative components of the verb. Since due to its deficiency it cannot check the thematic component, the derivation crashes. Finally, consider what blocks the case with *wassen* 'wash', instead of *becritiseren* 'criticize', as in (86):

(86) *Jan$_i$ voelde [jou zich$_i$ wassen]
    Jan$_i$ felt   [you SE$_i$ wash]
    'Jan$_i$ felt you wash him$_i$.'

Here we have two options. *Wassen* 'wash' is either the transitive or the reduced entry. In the former case, things are just like (85b). Consider then the latter option. Since the entry is lexically reflexive any construal in which the subject is *jou* and the "object" is interpreted as Jan is incoherent. Thus, the facts follow immediately from the analysis given. So, why wouldn't *zich* be able to check thematic Case? Note, that there are independent differences between pronominals and SELF anaphors on the one hand and *zich* on the other. For instance, *zich* cannot bear stress, as we saw.[33] So, we could simply stipulate as a lexical property that *zich* cannot check thematic Case. However, it seems that we can come a little further. In our discussion of German *sich* we noted that stress goes to the N-head. Suppose, then, that in order to be able to bear stress an N-projection is necessary. Pronominals, then, reflect N-to-D movement (Longobardi 1994, 1996), with a full-fledged N-projection, whereas *zich*'s position of first merge is in the periphery (π), and no N-projection is generated. The final step is then the empirical assumption that only N-heads project a full argument that can check thematic Case. The claim that Dutch *zich* is structurally weaker than other pronouns is supported by the following fact: *zich* may occur higher in the functional structure than pronominals. This is illustrated by contrasts like the one in (87), where the well-formed (87a) comes from a Web search:

(87) a. Ook bij de Nomads zijn er   een aantal 'regels' die voor
        also with the Nomads are there a   number rules   that for
        iedereen gelden en   waarvan we dan ook verwachten dat
        everyone hold   and whereof we then also expect   that
        zich iedereen eraan   houdt.
        SE   everyone thereto adheres
        'The Nomads as well have a number of "rules" that hold for
        everyone and that everyone is expected to adhere to.'
     b. Ook voor de voorzitter zijn er   een aantal 'regels' waarop
        also for the chair   are there a   number rules   whereon
        iedereen moet toezien en   waarvan we dan ook verwachten
        everyone must watch   and whereof we then also expect
        dat *iedereen hem | ??**hem iedereen*** eraan   houdt.
        that everyone him | him everyone thereto holds
        (constructed and minimally modified to make *hem* pragmatically
        felicitous)
        'The chair as well is subject to a number of "rules" that
        everyone must watch, and we also expect that everyone makes
        him adhere to.'

Øystein Nilsen (personal communication) informs me that such sentences are entirely ill-formed in Norwegian:

(88) a. *I gamle dager føyde   seg   alle etter reglene.
           in old   days obeyed REFL all after rules-the
     b. [OK]I gamle dager føyde alle seg etter reglene.

The ill-formedness of (88a) indicates that *seg* in Norwegian is stronger than *zich*. But then *seg* is able to project a full argument, and has the option of receiving thematic Case. Hence Norwegian allows the counterparts of (85b) and (86) with the SE anaphor as a direct object. Thus the contrast between Dutch and Norwegian in long-distance binding of object SE follows from an independent difference between *seg* and *zich*.

Binding of *zich* in the PP in (85c) follows from the principles outlined in section 8.3.2, section 8.4.2, and subsequent sections.[34]

As noted, German shows the same pattern as Dutch. This is expected under the present analysis. *Sich* in object position either marks reduction, yielding a reflexive entry, which trivially allows no possibility for nonlocal binding, or is tonic, hence a reflexive-marker of the downstairs predicate, and no nonlocal binding is possible either. In PPs, either *sich* is tonic and licenses reflexivity, or it projects the same structure as its Dutch counterpart *zich* and is interpreted in the same manner.

I conclude this chapter with a discussion of logophoricity in Icelandic.[35]

8.5 Logophoricity: Icelandic Logophoric Anaphora

8.5.1 Introduction

As outlined in Thráinsson (1976a),[36] *sig* in Icelandic may take a long-distance antecedent, when the clause that contains *sig* is infinitive or subjunctive (i.e., the antecedent may be beyond the nearest c-commanding subject), in violation of condition A of the binding theory. However, if *sig* is contained in an indicative clause, it can only be bound by the local antecedent. This is exemplified in (89).[37]

(89) a. Jón$_j$ skipaði Pétri$_i$ [að PRO$_i$ raka$_{infinitive}$ sig$_{i,j,*k}$ á   hverjum
        Jon ordered Peter to   shave   SIG   PRT every
        degi]
        day

    b. Jón$_j$ segir [að Pétur$_i$ raki$_{subjunctive}$ sig$_{i,j,*k}$ á   hverjum degi]
        Jon says that Peter   shaves   SIG   PRT every   day

    c. Jón$_j$ veit   [að Pétur$_i$ rakar$_{indicative}$ sig$_{i,*j,*k}$ á   hverjum degi]
        Jon knows that Peter   shaves   SIG   PRT every   day

The proposals in the literature to account for the long distance use of *sig* in sentences like (89a) and (89b) can be divided into two groups. One group assumes a unified binding analysis of long distance *sig* in subjunctives and infinitives. One of these analyses is Anderson's (1986) "tense-agreement" account of Icelandic anaphora. Anderson postulates an "anaphoric domain" in which *sig* has to be bound by a "superordinate subject."[38] Infinitive complements always constitute an anaphoric domain whereas in subjunctives an anaphoric domain is established when a rule of "Tense-Agreement" that copies the tense of the matrix clause onto the subjunctive complement has applied. It follows that *sig* can take a long-distance antecedent out of infinitives and subjunctives, given that an anaphoric domain has been established in subjunctives. Thus, the same account, stated in terms of an anaphoric domain, is given for long-distance *sig* in infinitives and subjunctives.[39] Also, both the Parameterized Binding Theory, developed in Wexler and Manzini 1987,[40] and the head movement analysis of anaphors, proposed in Pica 1985 and 1987,[41] treat long distance *sig* in subjunctives and infinitives in a parallel fashion. Within the Wexler and Manzini (1987) Parameterized Binding Theory, the governing category for *sig* is determined by [+indicative mood], and thus the antecedent possibilities for *sig* should be the same out of infinitives and subjunctives. Similarly, Pica (1987) proposes that *sig* undergoes head movement out of infinitives and subjunctives at the level of Logical Form, again predicting parallel antecedent possibilities on the two conditions.

The other approach to long-distance anaphora in Icelandic maintains that the long distance use of *sig* out of subjunctives is ruled by discourse factors rather than syntactic principles. Thráinsson (1976a, 1990, 1991), Maling (1984), Sells (1987), Sigurðsson (1990), and Sigurjónsdóttir (1992) observe that the antecedent possibilities of long-distance *sig* in subjunctives are not constrained by structural conditions such as c-command but rather by discourse factors such as perspective or point of view. Also, as pointed out by Thráinsson (1976a, 1990), the presence of a subjunctive complement is not enough to license long distance use of *sig*. Thus, only a certain type of subjunctives allow *sig* to take a long distance antecedent, in particular, subjunctives that imply "a report from the higher subject's 'point of view'" (Thráinsson, 1976a, 229). Subjunctives that state a fact about the matrix subject and do not convey the higher subjects perspective or point of view, on the other hand, do not allow *sig* to be coindexed with the matrix subject. Thus, the long-distance use of *sig* is not uniquely determined by the presence of a subjunctive complement. Rather, it seems as if discourse information can only be accessed if there is a subjunctive. If it can, it still has to be of the "right kind."

Hagège (1974) and Clements (1975) subsume the use of long distance *sig* in subjunctives under logophoricity. This idea was further pursued in Maling (1984). A semantic characteristic of logophoric pronouns is that they are used in "reportive contexts" to refer back to an individual (other than the speaker-narrator) whose speech, thought, feeling, or point of view is reported on in the sentence (from Maling 1984, 211, 231). As discussed most extensively by Sigurðsson (1990), this more or less sums up the semantic properties of *sig* when it takes a long distance antecedent out of subjunctives.

These two approaches to long-distance anaphora in Icelandic make different predictions regarding the antecedent possibilities of *sig*. According to the first approach, long distance *sig* should be subject to the same constraints in subjunctive and infinitive clauses—that is, structural conditions such as c-command and discourse factors should play the same role in both domains. The second approach predicts that long distance *sig* in subjunctives and infinitives is governed by different factors. Whereas discourse factors should be relevant for the logophor *sig* in subjunctives, such factors should not play a role in the infinitive case where the interpretation of *sig* should only be constrained by structural principles. Such a difference between infinitival and subjunctive domains does not by itself exclude the possibility that strictly grammatical factors play a role. For instance, it could be that some grammatical factor associated with subjunctives, but not with infinitives, entails that logophoric interpretation is in principle admissible, whereas discourse factors determine whether the ensuing interpretation is well formed. This possibility will be discussed later. Until then the two approaches will be discussed at a more general level.

In the literature, the focus of research has been the subjunctive domain and how it differs from the indicative. Much less attention has been paid to the infinitive case and until now the different tests for discourse versus syntactic principles have not been applied systematically to the two domains. This calls for a more detailed analysis of the mechanisms governing *sig* in subjunctives and infinitives, and it will be attempted to give the relevant data for each case.

8.5.2 Subjunctives

It is a well-known fact that long-distance *sig* in subjunctives in Icelandic can take as its antecedent a non-c-commanding DP. Thus, as first observed by Maling (1984), the DP *Jón* can serve as the antecedent for *sig* in sentences like (90), although it does not c-command the anaphor.

(90) a. [DP Skoðun Jóns$_i$] er [að   sig$_{i, acc}$ vanti$_{subj}$ hæfileika][42]
          opinion Jon's is that SIG   lacks   talents
      'Jon's opinion is that he lacks talents.' (see Maling 1984, 222)

b. [$_{DP}$ Álit Jóns$_i$]$_j$ virðist [t$_j$ vera [að ég hati$_{subj}$ sig$_i$]]
   belief Jon's seems be that I hate SIG
   'Jon's belief seems to be that I hate him.'

c. Björn sagði Pétri frá [$_{DP}$ ósk Jóns$_i$] um [að Ari sýndi$_{subj}$
   Björn told Peter about wish Jon's about that Ari showed
   sér$_i$ virdingu]^{43}
   SIG respect
   'Björn told Peter about Jon's wish that Ari showed him respect.'

Furthermore, *sig* in subjunctives can refer to a non-c-commanding matrix object, as illustrated in (91).

(91) ?Jón$_i$ er masókisti. Þad gledur Jón$_i$ [að ég muni$_{(subj.)}$ lemja sig$_i$
   Jon is a-masochist it pleases Jon that I will hit SIG
   í hausinn med spýtu á morgun]
   in the-head with a-stick tomorrow
   (cf. Sigurjónsdóttir 1992, 95)

These sentences show that the antecedent possibilities of *sig* in the long distance subjunctive case are not constrained by a c-command requirement. (There may be some ill-understood variation among speakers. Sigurðsson (1990) presents another case showing the same point.) By comparing these sentences to the ones in (92), we see that the antecedent-anaphor relations are discourse dependent. The antecedent of *sig* must be the person (distinct from the speaker-narrator) whose perspective or point of view is reported in the sentence.

(92) a. *[$_{DP}$ Skoðun Jóns$_i$] fær mig til að halda [að sig$_{i, acc}$ vanti$_{subj}$
      opinion Jon's leads me to to believe that SIG lacks
      hæfileika]
      talents
      'Jon's opinion leads me to believe that he lacks talents.' (cf. Maling 1984, 222)

   b. *[$_{DP}$ Vinur Jóns$_i$] telur [að ég hati$_{subj}$ sig$_i$]
      friend Jon's believes that I hate SIG
      'Jon's friend believes that I hate him.'

   c. *Þetta vandamál$_i$ krafðist þess [að við hugsuðum$_{subj}$
      this problem demanded it that we thought
      stödugt um sig$_i$]
      constantly about SIG
      'This problem demanded that we constantly thought about it.'
      (cf. Sigurðsson 1990, 335)

In the ill-formed sentences in (92), the coindexed DP bears the same structural relation to *sig* as in the well-formed sentences in (90). The difference between these two sets of sentences is that in (90), *Jón* is the person (distinct from the speaker) whose opinion, belief, or wish is reported in the sentences. In (92a,b), on the other hand, the sentences are not reported from *Jón*'s point of view; rather it is the 1st person pronoun *me* in (92a) and the DP *Jon's friend* in (92b) which carry the perspective of these sentences. This analysis is further supported by the example in (92c), which shows that an inanimate DP, which cannot possibly be a perspective holder, cannot serve as the antecedent for *sig* in subjunctives.[44]

Also, it has been noted in the literature (Maling 1984, 232; Sigurðsson, 1990, 336) that passives in Icelandic do not in general allow their subject to serve as a long-distance antecedent for *sig* in the cases considered. If *sig* in embedded subjunctives is ruled by discourse factors, the derived subject of a passive should not be able to serve as an antecedent for *sig*, since a derived subject does not carry the perspective or point of view of the sentence. This is illustrated in (93).

(93) a. Jón$_i$ sagði Pétri$_j$ [að   ég elskaði$_{subj}$ sig$_{i, *j}$]
        Jon told   Peter that I loved   SIG
    b. Pétri$_j$ var sagt (af Jóni$_i$) [að   ég elskaði$_{subj}$ sig$_{*i, *j}$]
        Peter was told (by Jon)   that I loved   SIG

In (93a) *sig* takes the perspective holding subject *Jón* as its antecedent, but in the passive sentence in (93b) where neither *Jón* nor *Pétur* bear the perspective of the sentence, *sig* cannot refer to the c-commanding subject nor to the object of the *by*-phrase.[45]

The minimal pair in (94), reported in Sells (1987, 451), is further evidence that the antecedent possibilities of *sig* in subjunctives are determined by discourse factors.

(94) a. Barnið$_i$ lét ekki í ljós [að   það   hefði$_{subj}$ verið hugsað vel
        the-child put not in light that there had   been thought well
        um   sig$_i$]
        about SIG
        'The child didn't reveal that she had been taken good care of.'
    b. *Barnið$_i$ bar þess ekki merki [að   það   hefði$_{subj}$ verið hugsað
        the-child bore it   not signs that there had   been thought
        vel um   sig$_i$]
        well about SIG
        'The child didn't look as if she had been taken good care of.'

The difference in grammaticality between (94a) and (94b) can be attributed to the fact that in the (a) sentence, the report is made from the child's point of view—that is, it is the child, and not the speaker, who did not reveal that he/she had been taken good care of, whereas in the (b) sentence, it is the speaker who reports that the child did not look as if he or she had been taken good care of. Hence, *sig* in subjunctives demands an antecedent that bears the perspective or point of view of the sentence and whether or not this DP c-commands the anaphor is irrelevant.

8.5.3 Infinitives

This contrasts with what we find in infinitives. Here the derived subject of a passive is a possible antecedent for *sig*, even if it is not a perspective holder. That c-command is sufficient is witnessed by the examples in (95) and (96).

(95) Jón$_i$ sagði [Maríu$_j$ hafa$_{inf}$ látið [mig þvo$_{inf}$ sér$_{i,j}$]]
Jon said Mary have made me wash SIG
'Jon said that Mary had made me wash him/her.'

(96) María$_j$ var sögð (af Jóni$_i$) [t$_j$ hafa$_{inf}$ látið [mig þvo$_{(inf.)}$ sér$_{j,*i}$]]
Mary was said (by Jon) have made me wash SIG
'Mary was said (by Jon) to have made me wash her/*him.'

As exemplified in (96), *sig* in an infinitive complement can take the subject of a passive sentence as an antecedent, although this subject does not carry the perspective or point of view of the sentence. This shows that only c-command determines the antecedent possibilities of *sig* in infinitives.[46]

There are some further facts worth noting although they would not be conclusive by themselves. For instance, *sig* in infinitives can only take a matrix subject and not a matrix object as an antecedent (cf. Thráinsson 1979, 1991; Sigurjónsdóttir 1992). This is illustrated in (97).

(97) a. Jón$_i$ skipaði mér$_j$ [að PRO$_j$ lemja$_{inf}$ sig$_i$]
Jon ordered me to hit SIG
b. *Eg$_j$ hótaði Jóni$_i$ [að PRO$_j$ lemja$_{inf}$ sig$_i$]
I threatened Jon to hit SIG

Note, that the contrast between (97a) and (97b) could follow from the difference in perspective these sentences might be argued to show. But given that perspective is not operative as shown by (96), the difference in c-command is enough to account for the contrast.[47] The sentences in (98) are also interesting in this connection. These sentences contain a propositional attitude noun, with a possible perspective holder, that does not c-command *sig*. These sentences are ruled out:[48]

(98) a. *[$_{DP}$ Skoðun Jóns$_i$]$_j$ virðist [t$_j$ vera$_{inf}$ hættuleg   fyrir sig$_i$]
           opinion Jon's   seems   be   dangerous for   SIG
           'Jon's opinion seems to be dangerous for him.'

    b. *[$_{DP}$ Ósk Jóns$_i$]$_j$ er líkleg til [t$_j$ að hafa$_{inf}$ slæmar afleidingar
           wish Jon's   is likely to   to have bad   consequences
       fyrir sig$_i$]
       for   SIG
       'Jon's wish is likely to have bad consequences for him.'

    c. *[$_{DP}$ Álit   Jóns$_i$]$_j$ er sagt [t$_j$ hæfa$_{inf}$ sér$_i$ vel]
           belief Jon's   is said   suit   SIG well
           'Jon's belief is said to suit him well.'

But, as pointed out by an anonymous reviewer, this fact is not decisive, since unlike what we see in (90), the complement clause is not interpreted as in the scope of the attitude noun. So, ideally one should test structures of the form (99):

(99) Jon's wish is for SIG to have talent

However, as Sigga Sigurjónsdóttir (personal communication) informed me, a structure such as (99) or any other structure with the required properties does not exist in Icelandic.

This leaves us with the contrast between the ill-formed (93b) and the well-formed (96). This contrast is enough to prove the point.

8.5.4 Summary of the Facts

There are consistent differences between the conditions on long distance antecedents for *sig* in subjunctive and infinitive complement clauses. *sig* in subjunctives is constrained by discourse factors; in particular, the antecedent of *sig* has to be the person (other than the speaker-narrator) whose perspective or point of view is presented in the sentence, and whether or not this antecedent c-commands *sig* is irrelevant.

The antecedent possibilites of *sig* in infinitives, on the other hand, are uniquely governed by the structural condition of c-command. Absence of perspective is not relevant.

If the mechanisms governing *sig* in subjunctives and infinitives were of same type, as proposed by Anderson (1986), Wexler and Manzini (1987), and Pica (1985, 1987), among others, this difference would be unexpected. It appears that the Icelandic data is only consistent with analyses that differentiate between the mechanisms governing long distance *sig* in subjunctives and infinitives.

8.5.5 The Interpretation of *Sig*: Binding versus Coreference

Since Reinhart's work on anaphoric relations it has been established that syntactic binding requires c-command (see Reinhart 1983 for detailed discussion of the properties of the c-command relation). One might, of course, entertain the possibility that, nevertheless, syntactic binding of some sort is involved in cases such as (90), since variable binding appears to allow violations of c-command (as in *every boy's mother loves him*) (see chapter 2).[49]

However, as discussed in Thráinsson 1991, 60, the strict/sloppy identity ambiguity typically associated with pronouns also shows up with *sig* in the long distance subjunctive case and is sensitive to differences in c-command. (100) shows the strict/sloppy ambiguity:

(100) Jón$_i$ telur   [að prófessorinn muni fella$_{subj}$ sig$_i$ á prófinu] og
      Jon believes that the-professor will fail   SIG on the-test and
      Ari$_j$ telur   það líka
      Ari believes that too
      a. =Ari believes that the professor will fail Ari on the test.
      b. =Ari believes that the professor will fail Jon on the test.

Where *sig* in subjunctive contexts is not c-commanded by its long-distance antecedent, the sloppy reading is much harder to obtain. This is illustrated in (101):

(101) Skoðun Jóns$_i$ er [að sig$_i$ vanti hæfileika] og það er skoðun
      opinion Jon's is that SIG lacks talents   and that is opinion
      Péturs$_j$ líka
      Peter's too
      'Jon's opinion is that he lacks talents and that is Peter's opinion too.'
      a. ??Peter's opinion is that Peter lacks talents.
      b. =Peter's opinion is that Jon lacks talents.

This is evidence, that the relation between *Jón* and *sig* in a subjunctive context such as (101) must be one of co-reference, rather than syntactic binding. The conclusion is strengthened by the fact noted in section 8.2.2 that *sig* may occur, and be interpreted, without a linguistic antecedent:

(102) María var alltaf svo andstyggileg. Þegar Ólafur$_j$ kæmi segði hún
        sér$_{i/*j}$ áreiðanlega að fara. (Thráinsson 1991)
        'Mary was always so nasty. When Olaf would come, she would
        certainly tell himself [the person whose thoughts are being
        presented—not Olaf] to leave.'

In such cases *sig* must be able to get its interpretation just like pronominals do. If in subjunctive contexts *sig* and its antecedent may be related,
not by binding, but, by coreference, this is at variance with the canonical
view of anaphors (Bouchard 1984; Reinhart and Reuland 1991) requiring
the underspecified element to obtain its missing ϕ-features, directly or
indirectly, from its antecedent in the syntax by chain formation of some
sort. It would still be possible to develop a theory in which *sig* acquires
its ϕ-features from a covert source, for instance a null operator. If one
allows *sig* is to pick up its ϕ-features from a discourse antecedent in
(102) one must be careful not to make the theory of syntactic relations
vacuous. Construing a contentful analysis along these lines is a nontrivial
matter, to say the least.

   The other, more straightforward, interpretation is that there is no intrinsic necessity for anaphors to be syntactically linked to an antecedent
in order to be interpreted. This is, therefore, the position I have adopted
here.

8.5.6   Conclusions and Open Issues

Consistent differences are found between the conditions on long-distance
antecedents for *sig* in subjunctive and infinitive complement clauses. The
interpretation of *sig* in subjunctives is constrained by discourse factors;
the interpretation of *sig* in infinitives involves a structural relation with
its antecedent. Ideally, these differences should follow from a general
theory about the interplay between structural conditions and discourse
factors, and about the nature of logophoric interpretation.

   As argued in chapter 5, the role of the subjunctive in Icelandic is that
of blocking a syntactic connection between *sig* and it antecedent. This
reflects a general pattern. Napoli (1979) observes that Italian *sè/si* can
only have a long-distance antecedent in positions where it cannot cliticize.
In Reuland 1990b, I show that cliticization leads to the syntactic encoding
of an interpretive dependency. In English, as we have seen, *himself* can
have a logophoric interpretation in positions where establishing a syntactic dependency by head movement of SELF to the verb would be
blocked. What is observed in these languages appears to be governed by

a regularity: *Free reflexives are syntactically licensed not by what is the case, but by what is blocked.* True, these are just a few among the many languages of the world. The challenge is therefore to find out to what extent this pattern shows up elsewhere as well. This, however, has to be a task for future research.

8.6 Summary and Conclusions

In this chapter we discussed three patterns of crosslinguistic variation in Germanic: (i) variation in the local binding of 3rd-person pronominals; (ii) variation in long-distance binding of SE anaphors, and (iii) licensing of logophoric *sig* in Icelandic.

Given the theory of chain formation developed in the previous chapters, the variation in local binding of pronominals—from objects in Frisian to propositional objects in German—was shown to follow from small differences in the licensing of structural versus inherent Case: we find SE anaphors in environments of structural Case, and locally bound pronominals in environments of inherent Case.

Differences in the binding of SE anaphors between Scandinavian and the West Germanic OV languages were shown to follow from the fact that the OV configuration blocks chain formation.

The restriction on long-distance binding of SE anaphors in object position in Dutch, but not in Norwegian was shown to follow from an independent difference in internal structure.

The patterns found and the explanations given show three important points:

i. Variation in binding domains can be accounted for without specific reference to binding or anaphora.
ii. Conditions on binding are intricately connected with the fine structure of the grammar. Understanding the binding patterns in a language requires an in-depth understanding of its grammar as a whole.
iii. There are fundamental differences between the nature of the dependency in long-distance binding, and that involved in logophoric interpretation.

9   Discussion, Summary, and Conclusions

9.1   Introduction

In the previous chapters we saw that an explanatory theory of anaphoric dependencies requires a distinction between encoding within C_{HL}, encoding at the C-I interface, and encoding in the discourse system. It was argued that the types of encoding are governed by an economy hierarchy. Whereas the modes of encoding at the C-I interface and the discourse system were taken to be standard, a specific proposal was presented as to how the syntactic residue of binding is encoded in an index-free syntax. This proposal derives the chain condition effects from one of the basic properties of the computational system, namely the mechanism of morphosyntactic feature checking, coupled with the notion of copying/overwriting as the locus of identity in syntax. The main focus of the discussion of chain condition effects was on the role of SE anaphors versus pronominals. Moreover, a proposal was developed as to why natural language has SELF anaphors and other complex anaphors, in addition to SE anaphors and pronominals. It was shown that a distinction must be made between the binding requirement on SELF anaphors and their role as licensers of reflexive predicates, and detailed discussion was provided on how both can be derived from basic mechanisms of linguistic computation, as set out in chapter 1.

This chapter brings the discussion to a close. In section 9.2, I compare a number of alternative mechanisms for syntactic encoding of anaphoric dependencies that have been proposed in the recent literature. In section 9.3, I summarize the overall results.

9.2 How to Encode Anaphoric Dependencies: Theoretical and Crosslinguistic Variation

In recent years, a number of proposals have been presented to encode anaphoric dependencies by strictly syntactic mechanisms, in the spirit of the Minimalist Program. Here I will consider four such proposals, namely in Kayne 2002, Zwart 2002, and Boeckx, Hornstein, and Nunes 2007, which elaborates earlier ideas in Hornstein 2000, as well as a recent proposal in Hicks 2009. In addition I will briefly comment on Safir 2004a and 2004b. In evaluating these proposals it is important to include an assessment of how well they can be expected to cover the type of variation among anaphoric systems that exists. For the sake of concreteness I will take as a reference point the pattern of variation found within the group of Germanic languages. I will then take up the question of how the present framework accounts for such facts. A small subset of cases (section 1.1) should suffice:

i. Types of anaphoric expressions
    - English has a two-way system (complex anaphors versus pronominals).
    - Frisian has a two-way system, but in a different way, with complex anaphors versus pronominals, allowing locally bound 3rd-person pronouns where other Germanic languages have SE anaphors.
    - Standard German shows a two-way system (*sich* versus pronominals) but differs from Dutch in only allowing *sich* in PPs.
    - Dutch has a three-way system: pronominals such as *hem* 'him', SE anaphors such as *zich* 'himself', complex anaphors (SELF anaphors) such as *zichzelf* 'himself'.
    - Icelandic (and Norwegian with the other mainland Scandinavian languages) has a four-way system: pronominals, SE anaphors, SE SELF, and pronominal SELF.
    - In all these languages, prima facie except for English, 1st- and 2nd-person pronouns can be locally bound.
ii. Differences in "binding domains"
    - Dutch and German: binding of SE anaphors out of causative and perception verb complements, not out of *to*-infinitives.
    - Scandinavian languages: binding out of all nonfinite clauses (including *to*-infinitives) is allowed.
iii. English and Icelandic (and Faroese): exempt SELF anaphors and logophoric SE anaphors, respectively.

iv. Many languages have poss anaphors, others do not.

v. Some languages allow subject anaphors, others do not.

vi. Some languages allow local binding of names, others do not.

9.2.1 Kayne 2002

9.2.1.1 Summary Kayne explores the idea that the quintessential syntactic mechanism for encoding dependencies of all kinds is movement. This means that not only anaphor binding, but also variable binding in general and even coreference are encoded by movement. It is only in the case of mistaken or doubtful identity that coreference is not syntactically encoded. In Kayne's system a sentence such as (1) is derived as in (2):

(1) John thinks he's smart.

(2) a. thinks [John he] is smart →

    b. John$_i$ thinks [t$_i$ he] is smart

That is, the coreferent pair ⟨John, he⟩ is base generated as one constituent with the binder as the specifier of the bindee. The dependency remains configurationally represented after movement by the trace of John. Kayne proposes that the same mechanism also applies in the case of crosssentential anaphora, as illustrated in (3) and (4).

(3) John is famous. He's smart, too.

(4) John is famous, and [(John) he]'s smart, too.

Note that this analysis assumes that movement into a θ-position is licit, in line with work by Hornstein and others. The question, then, is why there is a condition B. Why are (5) and (6) not derivable in parallel fashion to (1), starting from (7) with movement of the double *John* to subject θ-position?

(5) *John thinks highly of him.

(6) *John considers him intelligent.

(7) ____ thinks highly of [John him]

Kayne posits that *John* must pass through an intermediate A-bar position in moving from within the doubling constituent up to the position in which it gets its θ-role. He suggests that the required intermediate position is available in (1) but not in (5) or (6). The question why condition B effects exist would then become the question why such successive cyclicity holds. More specifically, Kayne proposes that the crucial intermediate step is actually movement of the doubling constituent itself. The analysis is based on the following assumptions:

- Unstressed pronouns must invariably move.
- A pronoun heading a doubling constituent—for example, the *he* of [*John he*]—in moving, pied-pipes the whole doubling constituent → the crucial intermediate step is in effect induced by properties of pronouns.
- The nature of the position where [*John he*] moves to is left open, except for the following claims:
  i. There is no appropriate licensing position for the pronoun within VP or between VP and the subject θ-position. →
  ii. The pronoun (hence the doubling constituent) must move to a position above the subject θ-position (i.e., outside the thematic part of the structure).

Given this, the impossibility of binding/coreference in (8) is derived as follows:

(8) John praises him.

There must be a "doubling constituent" [*John him*] that originates in the object θ-position. (i) and (ii) together entail that [*John him*] must raise to a position above the subject θ-position. This in turn entails *John* will get no θ-role (and the subject θ-role will remain unassigned). Consequently, (8) is impossible in the intended reading. Why, then, is *John praises himself* or *John considers himself intelligent* well formed under the intended reading? What is the role of *self*? Kayne proposes that *self* makes available an intermediate position for the pronoun that is not available in the absence of *self*. This is illustrated in (9):

(9) ____ thinks highly of D0 [John-he] ('s) self

The reasoning is as follows:

- Spec,DP counts as an intermediate pronoun position to which [*John he*] can raise prior to *John* raising to the subject θ-position of *think*.
- The presence of the noun *self* licenses a possessive-type DP structure one of whose Specs fulfills the pronoun's need, so that [*John he*] has no need to raise to a position above the θ-position of *think*.

As Kayne acknowledges, though, the locality of SELF anaphors does not follow from this account. Extending his account to languages with richer anaphoric systems, Kayne also includes a discussion of SE anaphors. He argues that these are doubled by a distributive operator, as in (10):

(10) Gianni ha *DB* parlato di sé

Here *DB* is the abstract (and degenerate) *each*. Kayne attributes the locality conditions on *sé* to the relation between *DB* and *sé*. In addition there is a relation between *DB* and the antecedent, here *Gianni*, since a "floating" distributor must be c-commanded by its "antecedent."

9.2.1.2 Discussion   The proposal to capture dependencies by movement is in fact one of the few options available in a minimalist framework, as we saw. However, in its current state it faces a number of major problems that seem difficult to overcome.

First of all, there are a number of conceptual problems. The proposal claims to eliminate free coreference, but it remains unresolved what blocks it where no dependency is encoded. That is, in many languages pronominals mark in no way whatsoever whether they are bound or free. In Dutch, for instance, even a weak pronoun can be assigned a discourse referent that has not been mentioned in the preceding context. It is perfectly natural to say, thinking about Jan: *Ik denk niet dattie komt* 'I don't think he$_{weak}$ will come'. If *ie* can get the value Jan in this case directly from the discourse, then the same mechanism should in principle be available in *Jan denkt niet dattie komt* 'John doesn't think he$_{weak}$ will come' as well. So what remains is only a claim about variable binding (unless, of course, the theory is complemented with a Rule I–type principle ruling out coreference where variable binding is available). Another problem is that the nature of the relation between the moved element and the pronoun remains unspecified. Do we have coindexing between *John* and *he* in *[John he]*? Is it a semantic mechanism that assigns *John* and *he* the same value in this configuration? If so, where is it stated, and how? It appears to require specific statements about pronouns that are not related to their feature structure. In this respect it does not succeed in eliminating binding-specific statements from the grammar. Consider also the following case:

(11)   John thought that he would be able to convince Bill that he should be allowed to bring all his assets with him to the new country he was planning to spend the time that would remain him in.

Under the reading where *John* is coreferential with all the pronouns all these relations should be preencoded in the occurrence of *him* in *remain him*. Effectively the system requires unlimited look-ahead to provide a source for sentences—and also texts—with *n* coreferential pronouns. In view of the fact that it is impossible to get rid of (co-) reference anyway, the gain appears moot. Moreover, obliterating the contrast between binding and coreference makes it hard to account for the canonical Heim cases with a contrast between referential and quantificational antecedents where it directly matters.

A theoretical issue requiring attention is that the system must allow movement from syntactic islands, since binding is free into constituents such as adjuncts and members of coordinate structures that are solid islands for movement. One might think that the binding configuration could be treated as a resumptive structure, since a pronominal is present. However, without further stipulation this is not enough, since the gap does not coincide with the pronoun, but with its sister; hence one would expect a double pronoun if resumption is operative.

The proposal also faces an array of empirical problems. It is impossible to see how it would capture the difference between exempt and non-exempt *himself* in English (short of postulating lexical ambiguity), non-complementarity between pronominals and anaphors, disjointness effects that do not coincide with canonical condition B, locally bound pronominals (either 3rd, or 1st and 2nd person), and so on. In general, it is hard to see how it can provide the tools for capturing crosslinguistic variation. One final remark: its analysis of SE anaphors depends on a distribution operator. However, as we saw in chapter 6, it is SELF anaphors, rather than SE anaphors, that are distributive.

9.2.2   Zwart 2002

9.2.2.1   Summary   Zwart's analysis is much in the spirit of Kayne 2002. The main differences are listed below: (i) All pronouns and anaphors originate syntactically as a general "unspecified" pronoun. (ii) Although the dependency between pronoun and antecedent is represented in an *[antecedent he]* configuration as in Kayne's system, it is in addition made explicit by the feature [+coreferent] that is added syncategorematically. (iii) The precise shape of anaphoric elements (pronoun, SELF anaphor, SE anaphor, etc.) is determined by spell-out rules.

9.2.2.2   Discussion   Zwart's analysis inherits the problems of Kayne's approach. Unlike Kayne's procedure, it specifies the relation between the antecedent and the anaphoric element. However, the way it does so—by adding feature [+coreferent]—goes against the inclusiveness condition. By the use of spell-out rules it has a tool for expressing crosslinguistic variation. These spell-out rules are language specific, essentially expressing that in language A a certain combination of morphosyntactic features is realized as a SE anaphor, in language B as a SELF anaphor, and in language C as a pronominal. As a descriptive tool this can work, but it is hard to see how it allows us to capture crosslinguistic variation in a principled way.

9.2.3 Boeckx, Hornstein, and Nunes 2007

9.2.3.1 Summary Like Kayne and Zwart's proposals, the proposal by Boeckxs, Hornstein, and Nunes (henceforth BHN) uses movement as the mechanism for expressing anaphoric dependencies. However, unlike Kayne and Zwart, BHN limit themselves to anaphors, in fact SELF anaphors. They express no claim that all binding or coreference relations are to be captured by a syntactic mechanism (see Hornstein 2004).

They base their proposal that anaphor binding involves movement on one intriguing type of fact. Utilizing analyses by Lee (2003) and Mortensen (2003), they argue that there are in fact two languages, namely San Lucas Quiavini Zapotec (SLQZ) and Hmong, that wear a movement analysis on their sleeves.

SLQZ and Hmong allow reflexive constructions such as the following:

(12) *SLQZ* (Lee 2003)
    a. R-yu'làaa'z-ëng   la'anng.
       HAB-like-3SG.PROX 3SG.PROX
       'She/He likes her/him-self.'
    b. R-yu'làaa'z Gye'eihlly Gye'eihlly.
       HAB-like   Mike   Mike
       'Mike likes himself.'

(13) *Hmong* (Mortensen 2003)
    a. Nwg yeej   qhuas nwg.
       3SG   always praise 3SG
       'He always praises himself.'
    b. Pov yeej   qhuas Pov.
       Pao always praise Pao
       'Pao always praises himself.'

Both (12) and (13) are apparent violations of conditions B and C. In SLQZ and Hmong, they claim, such violation is permitted provided one has pronoun/pronoun or Name/Name pairs: the *Identical Antecedent Requirement*. This, they argue, immediately follows if such pairs arise from movement. Thus, antecedent anaphor and control relations are instances of movement understood as the composite of Copy and Merge (p. 3). With Kayne they share the theoretical assumption that movement into θ-position is allowed. Taking this idea as their starting point, they turn to SELF anaphors in English. Their main question is, naturally, why local binding in English requires a SELF anaphor, leading to the question of what SELF does, and why the pronominal is blocked. They argue that in English SELF is needed to license movement of the object into the subject position: movement is blocked unless SELF is there to check Case. The relevant structure is (14):

(14) [TP John [T′ T [vP John [VP likes John-self]]]]

They claim that morphemes like -*self* are not "anaphoric" in nature; they simply knock out a Case feature that would prevent a (local) movement to a θ-position from taking place. One may wonder why we find *himself* in English, instead of simply ∅-self. They argue that the pronoun arises as the spell-out of a copy. They assume that in principle only one copy of a movement chain is spelled out. This is an effect of Kayne's (1994) Linear Correspondence Axiom (LCA), which states that phrase structure completely determines linear order. Thus, order is not stipulated as an independent dimension of representation, but there is an algorithm that derives linear order given a particular statement of hierarchical relations.

The question is then what this algorithm operates on: elements as they appear in the numeration, or copies. If copies are the elements that the algorithm looks at, nothing interesting follows. The three copies of *John* in (14) are then simply different elements the LCA operates on. However, they argue, if the LCA algorithm operates on the item *John* as it appears in the numeration, it cannot be consistently linearized. Specifically, it is incoherent for the same element to both precede and follow the verb *like*. Since linearization is a PF property, consistency can be maintained if only one copy is spelled out: ∅-elements are not ordered. Thus, to use a simple example, *John was hit (John)* can be consistently linearized just in case the lower copy of John has a null realization.

This entails that copies that for some reason do not interfere with linearization will in principle be able to surface overtly. More specifically, they claim that if a terminal hides inside a word—is morphologically fused—it is not subject to the LCA. But only those terminals can be fused that satisfy morphological requirements of one another. Morphological complex elements cannot be fused. Hence it would be impossible to get *the man praised the man self*, since in order to be realized, the lower copy of *the man* must be able to fuse, which it cannot do because of its complexity.

The next question is, then, why we do not get *John praised* John *self*. This, they claim, is due to the affixal properties of *self*. *Self* is an affix that requires an element to attach to, but it can only attach to pronouns. Hence, *him* is inserted as a last resort, leading to *John praised himself* as empirically required. This analysis raises the question of why a derivation with SELF is needed for a well-formed result. That is, why can't *John praised him* be interpreted with *John* binding *him*? Like Reuland (2001b), BHN argue that this follows from economy. Syntactic encoding is preferred over other modes of expressing dependencies. However, as they note, comparison of derivations in the Chomsky 1995 model is limited to derivations with the same numeration. Thus they argue that economy comparison of derivations applies to numerations without functional material.[1]

How does this analysis carry over to SLQZ and Hmong? BHN argue that these languages have a null SELF, with the general properties of English SELF. The difference is that it allows fusion of the null SELF both with pronominals and with proper names.

9.2.3.2 Discussion   The general idea that binding phenomena should, as much as possible, be captured by independently motivated properties of the computational system is important and entirely in line with the proposal developed here. As always, it is the details that count in the end. As can be seen, for BHN's analysis to work it requires many language-specific stipulations that detract from the elegance of their starting point. The reason resides in an arbitrary limitation on the linguistic mechanisms they consider.

In their introduction BHN argue against a modular approach to binding saying that "Occam urges that modularity *internal* to the Faculty of Language is, *ceteris paribus*, to be avoided. In effect, unless one has very strong empirical reasons for multiplying relations and grammatical operations, one should not do so. In the best case, there should be exactly *one* way of coupling disparate elements" (p. 2). However, to evaluate this statement it should be clear what is meant by "Faculty of Language." What is the Faculty of language? Narrow syntax (NS)? The full computational system (NS + Semantics (SEM)) in Chomsky 2005? NS + SEM + IS (the interpretation system)? The canonical minimalist schema minimally offers three, perhaps four modules (not counting PF): NS, the C-I interface, the interpretive system (language of thought), and depending on one's position with respect to distributive morphology, the lexicon.

Even as regards NS, BHN appear to entertain the a priori assumption that Move is the "best" or only minimalist possibility. However, irrespective of the details, natural language does have matching operations, either in the form of checking as in Chomsky 1995, or in the form of Agree or valuation. This property cannot be completely reduced to Move, since even if one has feature movement, some form of checking/matching must take place. Hence, an approach reducing syntactic binding to basic syntactic operations should consider Agree-type relations in addition to movement and its kin.

If A-movement is the only way to encode local binding dependencies it is impossible to make sense of the crosslinguistic variation we discussed. Neither SE anaphors as in Dutch, Scandinavian, or German, nor locally bound pronominals as in Frisian lend themselves to analysis along the lines of BHN.[2] As a small detail, note that Dutch *zich* is never a resumptive pronoun, which makes it impossible to extend the analysis of English *himself* to Dutch *zichzelf*. From a crosslinguistic perspective, the existence of complex anaphors that are needed for local binding, but that do not enforce local binding, is unaccounted for in BHN's analysis. Of course, this is not to say that it cannot be extended to cover a wider range of empirical facts, but it is hard to see how it can acquire the empirical coverage of the account presented here.[3]

The question is, then, whether the facts of SLQZ and Hmong really warrant the conclusions BHN draw. In fact, the pattern these languages show is not at all surprising from the perspective so far presented in this book. What is needed to yield the *pronoun verb pronoun* pattern is just the general availability of an operation of reduction/bundling on the argument structure of verbs, as discussed in section 6.3.1, with obligatory checking of the Case residue.[4] The main puzzle is why proper names are allowed. I will limit discussion to a brief sketch of an answer based on processes available in UG. One possible operation is bundling, as we have seen. If it is available, the object and subject occurrences must be able to form one argument syntactically or semantically (the choice is not important for the present sketch). The question is, then, how strange a phenomenon chain formation or local binding of proper names really is.

As discussed in chapter 5, in Dutch and many other languages 1st- and 2nd-person pronouns can form chains with local antecedents. This is so because their interpretation is constant in one reportive context, and hence the features of different occurrences of such pronominals are interchangeable (if deletion is assumed, it does not violate the PRD). Proper names (and some other nouns, varying from *mother* and *father* and their cognates to designations of functions such as doctor, vicar, etc.) may be used as forms of address, a property they share with 2nd-person pronouns. Interestingly, such nominals may also be used with the function of 2nd-person pronouns. To what extent they can is clearly subject to crosslinguistic variation. For instance, the sentences of (15) are completely normal forms of address in Frisian (with 3rd-person verb agreement); (15a–c) are in fact preferred over the form with the pronominal. In Dutch, as in English, they are absolutely weird, though.

(15) a. Wol   dominy d'r   efkes   ynkomme?
        wishes vicar   there for-a-moment in-come
     b. Dokter kin syn tas wol efkes   delsette.
        doctor may his bag PRT for-a-moment down-put
     c. Mem   moat Mem   har tas net ferjitte.
        Mother should Mother 's   bag not forget
     d. Wol   Jan hjoed meiite?
        wishes Jan today (to) eat-with (us)

What this shows is that it is not at all exotic for certain noun types, including proper names, to acquire the semantic properties of 2nd person. It is just a simple step from the pattern in (15) to acquire full 2nd-person properties, including the property of allowing local binding. If so, whatever mechanism allows for local binding of 1st- and 2nd-person pronouns—and specifically the proposal put forward in chapter 5—also allows it in SLQZ and Hmong, given a slight extension of the microvariation independently observed.

9.2.4   Safir 2004a and 2004b

Both Safir 2004a and 2004b (especially the former) present a comprehensive theory of anaphoric relations covering an impressive range of crosslinguistic variation. Safir's main theoretical claims are that indices are to be eliminated as incompatible with minimalist principles; their role is taken over by the notion of a dependency, which is seen as an irreducible property of the linguistic system. The core principle of his theory of anaphoric dependencies is *competition.* Where two potentially anaphoric forms compete, economy selects the least (or sometimes the most) specified form. Safir's main claim can be summarized as follows: A theory based on the notion of a dependency as a primitive can cover the ground of theories based on coindexing, and—if supplemented with the notion of competition—with substantially increased empirical coverage. I present an extensive assessment in Reuland 2009b, and as I note there, this empirical claim is indeed substantiated, which makes the book very valuable. Safir's empirical coverage sets an important mark, and in this respect achieves much more than the other competitors. For lack of space I will not present a detailed comparison of our theories here. I will limit myself to noting two theoretical differences. Safir takes the notion of syntactic dependency as a primitive, whereas my proposal aims at further reducing it. Safir's notion of competition is essentially competition between anaphoric forms in a dependency, whereas in the present approach competion and economy involve derivations. An important difference in our results is that Safir's main principles (summarized in Reuland 2009b) are all specific to binding. My goal in this book is to eliminate all principles specific to binding, hence, as should be clear by now, only the definition of binding itself is specific to binding.

9.2.5 Hicks 2009

Although not as comprehensive as Safir's works, Hicks's book discusses far more material than the other alternatives I have summarized. It provides a very good overview of the issues that come up in a minimalist approach to binding, and explicitly motivates a particular implementation in terms of the Agree relation. In relying on Agree it is similar to Reuland 2005a. Again, space limitations prevent me from giving an extensive overview. An important difference between our approaches is that Hicks postulates a special semanticosyntactic feature VAR that is unvalued in anaphors such as *himself* and that gets valued by Agree. In the present approach such a special feature is unnecessary. Similarly, the properties of Dutch *zich* are encoded in a special feature REFLEXIVE, again a type of feature that is unnecessary in the present approach. In general the set of language facts discussed by Hicks is a subset of the facts discussed here. Hicks analyzes English *himself* and Dutch *zichzelf* as morphosyntactically simplex.[5] This makes it hard to see how his analysis can be extended in a principled way to all the simplex-complex contrasts that obtain in natural languages. Moreover, his analysis does not shed light on the question of why so many languages use general operations of valence reduction in the domain of reflexivity.

As it is, Hicks has to stipulate the contrast between bound and exempt (logophoric) anaphors in English as a lexical contrast (without indicating how their differences in distribution can be accounted for). As a final point, Hicks proposes to derive condition B on the basis of an economy account. He attempts to avoid competition between derivations with different numerations. Anaphors have an unvalued VAR feature and pronominals enter the derivation with a valued VAR feature. Features are directly valued upon Merge. He assumes a principle of Maximize Featural Economy. In a structure such as *$Mary_i$ hates her_i* this principle will be violated. As he puts it, "Maximize Featural Economy will be violated, since the dependency could have been more economically established by Agree valuing the VAR feature" (p. 208). Yet this phrasing shows that there is still a reference to the alternative numeration. However, this may not be a matter of principle. I could see ways of incorporating an intuition along the lines of *rejection is final* into Hicks's system. But that would require a thorough reassessment of his feature system, which it is not feasible to attempt here.

9.3   Overview and Summary of Results

In this section I will briefly outline the main results of the individual chapters. I will do so on the basis of a diagram similar to the one in (104) of chapter 1, presenting the overall course of the argumentation and relating it to crucial factors in the development of the approach.

(16) *Structure of the argumentation*

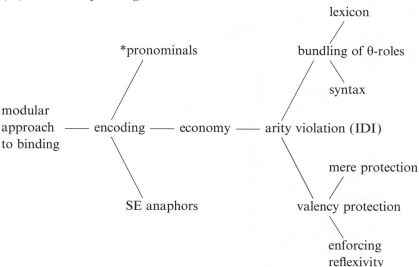

In chapter 1 I formulate the main question guiding the research reported in this book: What are the possible sources of linguistic universals? Anaphoric dependencies are presented as the empirical domain for this investigation.

Chapter 2 addresses the role of c-command in binding. It shows how the requirement follows from compositionality of semantic interpretation given the definition of binding in (i):

(i) *A-binding*
  α A-binds β iff α is the sister of a λ-predicate whose operator binds β.

(i) applies to pronouns on the assumption in (ii):

(ii) Pure ϕ-feature bundles can be translated as variables in logical
  syntax.

Chapter 2 further shows how the fact that SELF anaphors reflexive-mark a predicate enables us to explain the way POSS phrases and other adjuncts may license variable binding but not anaphor binding.

Chapter 3 outlines a modular approach to binding, teasing apart properties of predicates and syntactic chains, coupled with a typology of anaphoric expressions. It shows that reflexivity must be licensed (lexically or by reflexive-marking by a SELF anaphor), and that whether a SELF anaphor enforces reflexivity is sensitive to the syntactic configuration.

Chapter 4 discusses the role of economy in grammar. It provides evidence for a relative economy hierarchy that can be summarized as syntax < semantics < discourse. This hierarchy governs preferential patterns as in (iiia). It is supplemented by the absolute condition in (iiib).

(iii) *Economy*
  a. Processing economy: minimize unresolved dependencies.
    syntax < logical syntax < discourse
  b. Absolute economy: rejection is final.

A derivation that would violate a deep principle of grammar cannot be bypassed. Thus, (iiib) reflects the effect of a canceled derivation in the sense of Chomsky 1995. It explains why 3rd-person pronominals cannot be locally bound in an environment in which the preconditions for chain formation are satisfied.

Chapter 5 shows how anaphoric dependencies—specifically, dependencies of SE anaphors and pronominals—are encoded. A syntactic encoding process is presented that is blind, purely feature driven, and creates feature chains:

(iv) Check/agree → feature chains (binding of SE anaphors)

It dispenses with syntactic indices because of (v):

(v) Copying/Overwriting of feature values encodes identity.

Feature chain formation is restricted by the condition in (vi) as a fundamental principle of grammar:

(vi) *Principle of recoverability of deletions*
Overwriting may not lead to loss of information.

(vi) entails that the formation of feature chains can apply to SE anaphors, but *not to 3rd-person pronouns*. It can apply to 1st- and 2nd-person pronouns, though, which explains the pervasive differences between these 1st- and 2nd-person pronouns on the one hand and 3rd-person pronouns on the other.

Chapter 6 resolves the questions of why reflexivity must be licensed, and why reflexivity is enforced even if this leads to ill-formedness. Reflexive predicates require special licensing since "brute-force" reflexivization (the formation of a reflexive predicate without licensing) does not preserve the arity of a predicate. This reflects a type 1 invariant. It follows from a general property of computations modulo the space in which they take place: the inability to distinguish indistinguishables (=IDI).

The linguistic computation cannot distinguish between identical variables given the properties of the space (no order, no syntactic hierarchy) in which it must take place. If two variables corresponding to arguments of a transitive predicate cannot be distinguished, this leads to a violation of conditions on thematic role assignment: a role will stay unassigned.

This leads to two options: (a) apply a procedure of bundling θ-roles; (b) protect the variables by creating an environment allowing them to be distinguished. This is sketched in (vii):

(vii) IDI → a. An operation on argument structure with bundling of θ-roles
b. Protection

Bundling of θ-roles, which may go together with valence reduction, is captured by the theory of argument structure (the θ-system) developed by Reinhart, Siloni, Marelj, and others. Protection requires a structure that is preserved in the semantics. This can be done by creating a configuration that is preserved or by creating a semantic object that is sufficiently similar to the antecedent to enable it to stand proxy for it, and sufficiently different to escape the consequences of IDI. The computational system puts no constraints on the protection mechanisms other than these. Hence languages are allowed to vary in the means employed, and they actually do.

A specific strategy is the formation of head reflexives, where the pronominal element ends up as the specifier of a lexical head. The requirement that the semantic object created must be sufficiently similar to the antecedent to be able to stand proxy for it entails that the head performing this role must be semantically weak. Depending on the semantic properties of the head the obligation to reflexive-mark may follow from a general economy principle to the effect that syntactic encoding applies blindly when possible (a type 2 invariant). Or it can follow from specific semantic properties it has, requiring it to be interpreted as an operator on the verb (a general requirement that features that can be interpreted must be interpreted can also be argued to be a type 2 invariant: economy requires that an instruction that can be applied, must be applied). The obligation to reflexive-mark can also reflect a requirement on semantically weak argument expressions that they can only be interpreted by incorporation (a type 3 invariant). Yet, as we saw, other strategies are also possible, and in fact employed, that do not depend on the IP/SELF model. Reflexive-marking by SELF involves the following operation:

(viii) Internal Merge (covert head movement of SELF in the case of
        SELF anaphors)

SELF movement involves the following triggers:

(ix) *Triggers of SELF movement*
      a. Formal: economy
      b. Substantive: SELF *is* a verbal operator, hence attracted by V.

Finally, its effect rests on the following postulate about the meaning of SELF:

(x) *SELF (like body parts in general)*
      Inherently relational (elements in the set $\{x \mid SELF(x)\}$ necessarily
      bear the *being-a-SELF-of* relation to some individual, hence can
      stand proxy for that individual)

Only (i) is specific to binding; none of the other factors are.

Chapter 7 explores the consequences of the movement approach to SELF-marking. It addresses the status of picture-NPs in English and provides an explanation for why English requires SELF anaphors in 1st- and 2nd-person objects of lexically reflexive verbs, in contrast to other Germanic and Romance languages. It shows that this is a consequence of properties of this particular syntactic environment. In other environments such pronominals can be locally bound as in other languages. The last section discusses crosslinguistic variation in subject anaphors, and shows how it can be explained in terms of their φ-feature composition.

Chapter 8 shows how Case plays a crucial role in chain formation, and how differences in Case systems underlie differences in the local binding properties of pronominals and SE anaphors. Domain differences in long-distance binding of SE anaphors in OV versus VO languages are shown to follow from general conditions on chain formation, again without any further stipulations. Finally, the chapter shows how the difference between syntactic encoding– and discourse-based strategies is manifested in the contrast between the bound and logophoric interpretation of *sig* in Icelandic.

9.4 General Conclusions

Given these results, what are our answers to the questions we started with? Why do we have the pattern in (17), and why that in (18)?

(17) a. *_Alice_ admired _her_.
     b. _Alice_ saw that the cat was watching _her_.

(18) a. _Alice_ admired _herself_.
     b. *_Alice_ expected the king to invite _herself_ for a drink.

The impossibility of (17a) follows from IDI, the principle of recoverability of deletion, and economy in the form of *rejection is final*. The impossibility of (18b) follows from SELF movement and from the locality of head movement, again coupled with *rejection is final*.

Thus, we have achieved our objective. I have explained the core instances of the CBT—conditions A and B as macroprinciples specific to binding—from the basic fabric of the language system. In addition, I derived the crosslinguistic variation from the interaction between universal principles of grammatical computations with superficial parameters of encoding.

Turning around a saying by our former national soccer hero Johan Cruyff—*ellek nadeel hebse foordeel* 'every disadvantage has its advantage'—we can say *every advantage has its disadvantage*. Doing away with macrouniversals of the condition A and B type means a lot of work for linguists and no easy solutions. If binding facts follow from the fine structure of the grammar, an isolated binding fact of a language can be puzzling, but its significance for grammatical theory can no longer be assessed without an in-depth analysis. One might say that this makes it harder to falsify a particular theory of binding, hence our explanatory advance leads to a practical disadvantage. However, not surprisingly, this can be turned around again. Given the way binding theory is embedded in the grammar, many more facts outside binding can potentially falsify a particular proposal. So this disadvantage has its advantage after all.

The role of economy in the explanations offered and the crosslinguistic differences in the selection of certain formal means of encoding have a certain optimality-theoretic flavor. However, unlike in standard optimality theory, in the present system the economy principles and their ranking are universal. It is the variation in the functional system that determines which encoding strategies are available for particular pronominal elements. The competition obtains between particular encoding strategies at the microlevel.[6]

Different grammatical systems may represent alternative "engineering solutions" to problems that the interaction between cognitive systems poses. One may find local optima in creating a balance between competing mechanisms. But importantly, there is no general notion of optimality to be applied to grammatical systems. And most crucially, there is no evolution of grammatical systems toward "better" solutions to engineering problems.

It is crucial to see that we did not develop a theory of the observed diversity, nor do I believe that a general theory of linguistic diversity is possible at all. The best we can do is a theory about the limits of diversity. Just as we cannot have a linguistic theory of why the same object is called *table* in English and *stol* in Russian, we cannot have a linguistic theory of why Caxur and German have doubling strategies—be it rather different in detail—and Dutch and Japanese do not. What we could in principle have a theory of is what the limits are on the crosslinguistic variation in lexical, and specifically, functional inventory; and of the variation in strategies that are compatible with the resources the functional and lexical inventory of a language makes available. These issues, however, are still very much unresolved. Two further questions emerge from this view:

i.   Why is a particular strategy selected over another?
ii. Why is the selection of strategies in each language so limited?

The first question definitely leads us beyond what we can reasonably be expected to find systematic answers for. It seems to me that we cannot eliminate historical accident and development from our understanding of how languages come to be the way they are. The second question could in principle be amenable to investigation. A metagrammatical economy principle of the type "if you have one working solution don't go to the trouble of developing another one" would do. In fact, it could even result from an acquisition strategy: if you have already acquired a strategy as a solution to a problem, you don't bother to acquire another one. This would bias against the transmission of systems with more than one strategy for resolving a problem.

By uncovering the microstructure of linguistic computations, it becomes possible to raise and answer questions of linguistic universals in a principled way. It helps us to investigate how the structure of language is represented in the brain, to link linguistic to neurocognitive processes, to uncover the restrictions on the hypothesis space that makes language learnable, and to shed light on the nature of the evolutionary event that led to language as we know it. More specific discussion of these issues would lead us beyond the scope of this book. I reviewed some of the relevant work in the domain of processing in chapter 4 (for instance, Koornneef 2008). Some discussion of language from an evolutionary perspective—partly in response to the Hauser, Chomsky, and Fitch versus Pinker and Jackendoff (2005a, 2005b) debate—can be found in Reuland 2009a and 2010a.

Our results emphasize the strictly modular design of the language system. The interpretation process is all about the division of labor between four subsystems: the lexicon, morphosyntax, logical syntax, and discourse (in fact, phonology as a fifth system if we consider the role of stress). These systems show a partial overlap in the dependencies they may encode, precisely because they are so independent. Only economy governs their interaction. A crucial design property of the interface of the computational system with the interpretation system is that the interface allows expressions to be interpreted in terms of other expressions.

We have seen that the highly complex patterns of crosslinguistic variation in the domain of anaphoric relations reflect the interaction between very simple principles of computation and interpretation, general principles of economy, and properties of the computational space that may not be specific to language, together with general properties of the linguistic objects these computations apply to—the feature structure of predicates (θ-features) and of anaphoric expressions (φ-features). The crosslinguistic diversity follows, in line with current assumptions, from differences in settings within the functional system, reflected in simple yes-no patterns: X does or does not attract Y, hence a dependency can or cannot be established in a particular subsystem.

Thus, all complexity in language derives from very simple operations and principles. This brings us back to Alice and the Queen, where we started. In the end, what looked so simple has become simple again, but now through understanding.

Notes

Chapter 1

1. There is a related puzzle illustrated in (i):

(i) a. *Alice* was surprised how fast *she* was growing.
   b. *She was surprised how fast *Alice* was growing.

The question is why *she* in (ib) cannot get the value Alice. This fact is captured by condition C of the canonical binding theory (Chomsky 1981), given in (6C).

2. As pointed out in Reuland 2001a and 2001c, it is crucial to distinguish between frameworks and theories, although in practice these terms are often used interchangeably. Theories answer particular questions about reality by stating laws, establishing generalizations, representing interconnections, and so on. Theories—like the binding theory from Chomsky 1981 discussed below or the theory proposed in this book—may be false or hold up against the evidence obtained so far; they may be the best we have in the absence of alternatives and may be replaced as soon as a more convincing answer becomes available. Frameworks (e.g., the principles-and-parameters framework as a whole; see also the notion of paradigm in Kuhn 1996) are characterized by general concerns, types of questions to be explained, types of theoretical vocabulary, and basic operations. Frameworks as such are not true or false. Rather they are fruitful (or not), insofar as they facilitate the development of theories that answer the questions the framework allows to be put on the agenda and systematically addressed. A framework has heuristic power if it stimulates those using it to find interesting new facts and generalizations, uncover interesting new relations between phenomena, and develop theories leading to new insights.

3. In some of the linguistic literature the term *anaphor* is used for any expression that refers to an individual previously mentioned. So, under that use *the idiot* in *George decided to attack. The idiot thought he could fool everyone.* is an anaphor. The same would be true of *After Tony had fooled his country, the idiot even fooled himself.* In such cases an expression like *the idiot* is called an *epithet*. Here I will follow the standard usage in the generative literature and reserve the term *anaphor* for "specialized" anaphors. So, *the idiot* is not an anaphor, although it is used here as an epithet that is anaphoric to Tony.

4. I occasionally use the term *pronoun* as an umbrella term for both anaphors and pronominals but mostly I use *pronoun* and *pronominal* interchangeably.

5. The term *referential expression* has become customary in the syntactic literature, although it covers a range of expressions that are not referential in the semantic sense, such as *no cat*, and so on. In line with current usage, I will utilize the term *R-expression* for this syntactic notion.

6. Much of the literature uses the term *reflexive* as interchangeable with the term *anaphor*. As we will see in the next section, not all anaphors need to be bound in a local domain. I will reserve the term *reflexive* for anaphors that make a predicate reflexive.

7. As is often the case, a notion such as complexity raises its own questions. Kayne (2000, 2003) argues that Romance pronouns such as *me/te/se*, *moi/toi/soi*, and *mon/ton/son* are in some sense complex, since they minimally contain a separate person marker *m- /t- /s-*. What is needed, for complexity in the relevant sense, as we will see in detail in chapter 6, is syntactic complexity preserved in the semantic structure, minimally a pronoun in the left periphery of an extended nominal projection. For this the morphological complexity Kayne describes is not enough; however, these forms could still be complex because of other factors. I come back to this in chapter 6, where I discuss the role of complexity. I am grateful to Ken Safir (personal communication) for bringing this issue up.

8. As is customary, the notation $x*(y)$ indicates that the expression is ungrammatical unless y is present; $x(*y)$ indicates that the expression is ungrammatical if y is present.

9. For instance, work by Zurif and by Grodzinsky on agrammatism (Zurif 1978; Grodzinsky 1982, 1986, and subsequent work) and Wexler's work on specific language impairment (e.g., Rice and Wexler 1996; Wexler 2002).

10. See Frazier and Fodor 1978 as well as Frazier and Rayner 1982 for some very early work, and later, for instance, Pritchett 1992 or Phillips 1996, just to mention a few examples from the extensive literature.

11. This schema is neutral about the "size" of lexical elements: whether they are minimal size *morphemes*—only stems such as *bear* and affixes such as the plural affix *-s*—or whole constructions in the sense of Jackendoff 2002, as, for instance, *kick the bucket*.

12. If the essence of the linguistic combinatorics does indeed need no more than this, a close relation between the language faculty and mathematics, as suggested by Chomsky—most recently in Chomsky 2008—looks quite plausible indeed. Note that a system ensuing from very simple operations need not be "simple" in expressive power, as just a moment's reflection on the basic operations of mathematics and its expressive power shows (Kleene 1971).

13. See Reuland 2001a and 2001c for a response to criticisms of this notion of perfection in Lappin, Levine, and Johnson 2000, and see Reuland 2005c for discussion of this notion of perfection in an evolutionary context.

14. Pretheoretically, these are the positions associated with grammatical functions, such as subject, object, and so on. I will refrain from discussing how this is

reflected in current theories of Case assignment or Case-checking. The intuitive concept of "dual use" also covers the option that the C-I interface can read the PF for *what* directly, with an interpretation that would make the system crash on ** What did you think that Mary fixed the bike* but not on *What did you think that Mary fixed*, provided that interpretation does reflect the proper answers to the question (supplying a value for x such that *Mary fixed x*).

15. A connectionist attempt as in Ellefson and Christiansen 2000 fails at an elementary level (see Reuland 2008b for a brief discussion).

16. This is close to the notion of recursion underlying the definition of natural number:

(i) 1 is a natural number.
   If n is a natural number, its successor n+1 is a natural number.
   These are all the natural numbers.

So, we have an instruction that applies to its own output: if you want to create a natural number, take something that is a natural number and add 1 to it. More generally we can say: *Recursion is the calling of an instruction while that instruction is being carried out.*

17. Types 1 and 2 correspond to what Chomsky (2005) refers to as *third factors*.

18. In the case of a physical system such as language, the notion of space is indeed some physical space, but the space requirement also applies to abstract computational systems such as the Turing machine (named after the British mathematician Alan Turing (1912–1954) who described it), which represents a precise definition of what is computable.

19. Safir (2004a, 182) argues against theories that, as he says, put too much burden "on the morphological properties internal to an anaphor to predict its full distribution. I [=Safir, EJR] shall refer to theories of this type as *rigid internalist* approaches, because they propose that establishing a form's inner nature should directly predict its distribution." Thus formulated, such rigid internalist positions do not take the interaction with the linguistic environment into account, hence, as I stated in Reuland 2009b, theories of the type advanced here are not rigidly internalist. As Safir informs me, what he had in mind as the crucial property is whether or not a theory allows competition in his sense, which I am happy to hereby acknowledge.

20. Informally speaking, saying that some property must be licensed means that an expression cannot have this property just by itself. Some other operation must take place to make the result well formed.

21. Schladt mentions four languages that he claims do not require special marking. Among the languages he mentions is Frisian. Heine and Miyashita (2008) mention São Tomè Creole, Harway, Frisian, and Old English. For Frisian this is mistaken, as I show in section 1.8.2 and more extensively in chapters 5 and 8. The case of Frisian is very important from a methodological perspective, since it shows that reliable conclusions require a very fine-grained analysis of the grammatical system. In a slightly different vein this is also shown by binding in High German (see chapter 8). The patterns found in Old English are not significantly

different from Frisian in relevant respects. Van Gelderen (2000) presents a detailed analysis of Old English, supporting this parallel. See chapter 8 for more discussion.

22. There may well be principles that regulate admissible combinations. I just assume that no cost is associated with ruling a particular combination in, only with ruling it out. Note that we have to distinguish between strictly morphosyntactic restrictions, functional restrictions, and accidental crosslinguistic differences in the selection of feature combinations. Assuming that pronominal elements are used to refer to entities, given some specific assumption about the contribution certain features make to interpretation, certain feature combinations may fail to pick out any useful set of individuals, hence will not be lexicalized. The relevant point in the text, however, is that there is no a priori reason why a language that has the φ-features [α person] [β number] [τ gender] should not contain an element only marked for [α person] and a category feature, like Dutch *zich*. Similarly, there is no reason why a language would not contain an element that has only category features, and beyond that neither person nor number nor gender, like the Russian reflexive *seb'a*.

23. See Faltz 1977. Section 1.8 presents some examples.

24. It is important to see that this position is entirely compatible with the "internalist view" of reference defended in Hinzen 2007. Nothing requires that the objects we identify are really "out there" as objects. There are many good reasons—found, for instance, in quantum physics—for thinking that what we perceive has little resemblance to what is there. But on proper reflection it is easy to see that we do not need quantum physics to tell us that, since the facts of reference are as clear in fact as in fiction. Note that this internalist view of reference does not entail that we are only dealing with mental constructs. The fact that we have only incomplete, mostly misleading knowledge of what is out there, does not prevent what is there from affecting us.

25. Even if a system only had intransitive sentences, the option of coreference would still obtain cross-sententially (thanks to Alexis Dimitriadis (personal communication) for raising this point).

26. As Alexis Dimitriadis (personal communication) notes, α is also required to have the right—argumental—type.

27. Thus, λx *(x likes the garden)* is a function from individuals (such as Alice) to propositions.

28. In line with Reinhart 2006, 171, we may specify the following procedure for relating syntactic derivations to logical syntax representations: Move the subject *Alice* from its argument position, adjoining it higher up in the structure (by quantifier raising or QR in the sense of May 1977), substitute a variable for its trace in the original position, and prefix the minimal category containing the subject and the pronominal to be bound with λx. If the variable translating *her* and the variable resulting from QR are chosen identically—which is just an option, but not enforced, since *her* may refer to someone else—both will be bound by the prefixed λ-operator and end up being A-bound as defined by the original argument in its adjoined position. Thus, we have the following derivation: Alice likes her

cat → Alice [$_{TP}$ t [$_{VP}$ likes [x's cat]]] → Alice [$_{TP}$ λx [$_{TP}$ x [$_{VP}$ likes [x's cat]]]]. It is important to see that this logical "machinery" is nothing more than what is needed to make the notion of linguistic binding precise. Note that this is one implementation. In Heim and Kratzer 1998, no QR is involved.

29. In preminimalist versions of the theory where movement gave rise to traces, the instruction was to *restore* the moved element into its trace position for binding purposes. Hence the terms *reconstruction* and *reconstruction effect* in some of the literature.

30. See Koopman and Sportiche 1982 for an alternative explanation.

31. Note that in the approach to dislocation in Chomsky 1981 and in particular as elaborated in Aoun 1986 and subsequent work, dislocation was subsumed under a generalized binding theory. The idea was that the phonologically null categories (traces) left by dislocation had the status of anaphors, hence had to be bound. However, this crucially relied on a theoretical approach to the null categories resulting from dislocation that has now been abandoned.

32. Barker and Shan (2007) provide an analysis of donkey anaphora in a paper called "Donkey Anaphora Is Simply Binding." As interesting as their analysis is, their paper makes clear that what donkey anaphora needs is not *simply* binding. What it involves goes beyond binding as defined in (28), if only because it is not subject to a c-command requirement. This book focuses on dependencies that do not need that extra machinery.

33. This informal sketch closely matches the standard assignment function interpreting variable binding. Take the instruction for interpreting the dependency between *every boy* and *that boy* in (39), and compare it to (i) and (ii):

(i) For some language L, interpretation domain D, and interpretation function I_L for L, if g is an assignment function, g[d/x] is the assignment function g' defined by g'(x) = d and g'(y) = g(y) if y ≠ x.

(ii) For L, D, I_L, and an expression E of L,
$|\text{Every } x.E|^{D, I, g} = 1$ if $|E|^{D, I, g[d/x]} = 1$ for all d ∈ D
$= 0$ otherwise

It has been proposed that expressions like *that N* be treated as containing a variable (Noguchi 1997). This brings them under the scope of (i) and (ii) (assuming the necessary formal adjustments), with the ensuing overgeneration discussed in the text.

34. For instance, one may wonder why *every student* is allowed to act as a binder for *he*, although it does not c-command it. As Reuland and Avrutin show, the crucial difference is that *he* is an expression solely consisting of φ-features. In a nutshell, this allows a dependency to be formed between *every student* and *he* that is syntactically encoded via the Tense/Agreement system of the main clause in a manner not available to *that student*. Since the dependency is established prior to movement, quantifier movement of *every student* does not lead to a weak crossover violation in (44) but does in (46).

35. Alexis Dimitriadis (personal communication) has pointed out to me that there are also dependencies as in *every sports fan frequents the local bar* that could

be seen as involving a hidden indexical (=variable), hence as involving binding. Whether they in fact do is an empirical matter. Prima facie it seems to me that their binding pattern sides with demonstratives rather than pure pronouns. I will leave discussion to another occasion.

36. Thanks to Ken Safir for the examples.

37. Note that (copies of) argument expressions can also occur in nonargument position, as in the case of topicalization. Also note that in the case of adverbial modifiers such as *during the concert*, *the concert* is still in an A-position, namely as an argument of *during*.

38. This does not imply that R-expressions cannot be used anaphorically, or that in some cases an anaphoric use cannot be strongly preferred; see note 3.

39. See note 3.

40. Apart from other problems with the notion of an index to be discussed below, English also presents an empirical problem for (49) (thanks to Ken Safir for the great example).

(i) In some societies everyone feels they have the right to vote, but in ant colonies no one does.

Clearly, *everyone* binds *they*, yet they differ in syntactic number. This is not exceptional. As we will also see in section 4.3, binding dependencies require semantic rather than strictly syntactic nondistinctness.

41. For the sake of concreteness, we will say that a is nondistinct from b if there is no feature F such that a carries a different value for F than b.

42. Covert operations are operations that affect the interpretation of a sentence but do not manifest themselves in its form. We saw this illustrated with the operation of scope assignment to *every building* in section 1.6.2. In certain versions of the theory a special level of the grammar, *logical form* (not to be confused with *logical syntax* as we are using it), was thought to be involved. In our current version, the only property that sets them apart is the copy selected for spell-out.

43. Intuitively, proper government reflected the idea that the content of the trace had to be recoverable (identified). Formulated within the framework of Chomsky 1986a, the trace was required to be either governed by a member of a lexical category, notably V, or antecedent-governed. Failing this it violated the empty category principle (ECP). In current theory government is not a basic concept; the same holds for ECP. Rather the aim of current theory is to explain any effects attributed to government and ECP by more fundamental properties of the grammar. Since ECP plays no role in current BT discussions, I will not discuss it any further.

44. A canonical example of a parasitic gap construction is (i), first studied in Engdahl 1983:

(i) Which articles$_i$ did you file t$_i$ after reading ec$_i$

Here *which articles* appears to be linked to both the object position of *file* and the object position of *reading*, although conditions on movement forbid the movement of *which book* from the latter position. The *ec* in the object position of *reading* gives rise to a paradox in the Chomsky 1981 conception of empty categories, leading to its abandonment in the end.

45. Although clitics in Romance may share with SE anaphors such as Dutch *zich* a φ-feature deficiency, their clitichood may entail properties that do not necessarily obtain for *zich* and its cognates. Hence, they are not SE anaphors in the present sense, although they may share some of the properties of SE anaphors.

46. I elaborate on this idea in chapter 6.

47. Faltz analyzes English *himself* as an adjunct reflexive as well, with SELF the adjunct. This view is also adopted in Solà 1994 and Jayaseelan 1997. See Helke 1973 for a different view. Here, I will side with Helke's view that *self* is the head, although in fact not too much is at stake here. At least in 1st and 2nd person formally the structure is more that of a head reflexive with a POSS pronoun than that of an adjunct reflexive.

48. The exceptions in English were noted earlier by Ross (1970), Cantrall (1974), and Kuno (see, for a summary, Kuno 1987).

49. Languages for which this phenomenon has been described in some depth include Icelandic, English, Italian, Japanese, and Mandarin Chinese.

50. That is, "renvoyant au discours" (pertaining to the discourse event).

51. *Yĕ*'s nonhigh tone, represented by the grave accent, distinguishes it from the nonlogophoric strong form *ye*, which bears high tone. The logophoric pronoun is also distinct from a reflexive; in Ewe these are formed by affixing a genitive form of a pronoun to the noun *d̦okui* 'self', and, according to Clements, behave much like their English counterparts.

52. This may well be a reflection of the fact that logophoricity occurs in reportive contexts since the complementizer *be* is a "grammaticalized" form of the verb *bè* 'say'. In fact, as Sells (1987) notes, there is a common tendency for the verb 'say' to develop into a complementizer.

53. The logophoric forms *yè* (singular) and *yèwo* (plural) each allow both 3rd- and 2nd-person antecedents. In many languages with indirect reflexives this is impossible.

54. There are reasons to believe that the role of subjunctive in Icelandic is less idiosyncratic than Clements implies. In general it is necessary to distinguish between conditions facilitating a logophoric interpretation, and the conditions determining the interpretation that is actually obtained. For instance, Cole, Hermon, and Lee (2001) discuss the variation between two Chinese "dialects" in Hong Kong, showing that the syntactic conditions under which logophoric interpretation obtains are identical, but that the discourse conditions vary. In chapters 5 and 8 I will come back to the licensing conditions on the logophoric interpretation of Icelandic *sig*.

55. There is no language in which *the idiot* in (i) assumes a different form depending on whether it is covalued with *Tony* or with *George*.

(i) After Tony had met George the idiot declared war.

56. In terms of Chomsky 1995 I am assuming that C_{HL} in toto obeys inclusiveness. Chomsky 2005 presents a more explicit picture of the part of the linguistic system connecting the PF and the C-I interfaces in which "narrow syntax" obeys inclusiveness, but part of the computations leading up to the C-I interface do not. Under the assumption that in any case the interface must be "active," I will retain my assumption that C_{HL} obeys inclusiveness in toto, and that computations that look into the atomic elements of the morphosyntactic vocabulary are part of the interface. Note that this position does not entail that the operations entering into the computations before and beyond the C-I interface are all vastly different. In fact, one may hope they are not. Ideally, then, the only divide between pre- and post-C-I interface operations is the divide caused by the very application of "translation" operations translating the outcome of C_{HL} into expressions over a different vocabulary (including variables, operators, etc.), a type of operation that by its very nature violates inclusiveness, unless variables and operators can also be reconstructed as morphosyntactic objects (for some tentative discussion, see Reuland forthcoming).

57. An approach using guises either has to stipulate that (83) is ill-formed if *Bill* and *him* refer to the same guise of some entity, or else has to derive this from whatever difference in fate befalls the *one guise twice* option as compared to the *two guises once* option. Reinhart (2000, 2006) discusses a number of problems arising with Rule I as formulated, and shows how they can be obviated given certain modifications, including adopting the definition of binding presented in (28). She argues that what underlies Rule I is a cooperation strategy. Reinhart gives the following intuitive statement of a general principle that could be involved: "If a certain interpretation is blocked by the computational system, you would not sneak in precisely the same interpretation for the given derivation, by using machinery available for the systems of use" (p. 185). I return to this issue in chapter 4.

58. Note that children perform well on tasks involving a quantified antecedent as in (i), correctly rejecting a bound reading:

(i) *Every bear$_i$ tickles him$_i$

In this case coreference does not enter the picture, since *every bear* is not a referring expression, as we saw in section 1.6.1. Note that Wexler and Chien (1985) developed an account of the delayed condition B effect based on a pragmatic principle P, which also regulates the choice between binding and coreference. Their proposal is that children's bad performance on condition B is due to the fact that they acquire this principle late in the language-acquisition process.

59. Heim (1998) and Thornton and Wexler (1999) elaborate an alternative to the *bound variable/coreference* contrast based on the notion of a *guise*. Under this approach *Bill* and *him* in the second clause of (83) are not strictly speaking interpreted as the same semantic object, but as different "guises"—that is, different ways to represent the same individual (where the assignment of guises is governed by pragmatic considerations). Assuming that condition B is sensitive to difference in guise, *Bill adores him too* does not violate condition B, since *Bill* and *him* are not interpreted strictly identically. The choice between approaches based on core-

ference or on guises is orthogonal to our present concerns. In a guise-based approach one still needs a principle to tell why different guises are required, and when, precisely, this requirement obtains. Hence, all the relevant lines of the present argument are preserved. (See Baauw and Delfitto 1999 for a discussion of various implications of a guise-based approach.)

60. Structural Case is the Case licensed/checked by the functional system, typically—but not exclusively—nominative and accusative.

Chapter 2

1. One could think about a possible rationale in the following way. In order for two elements to be combinable, they must have a matching property, expressing a functor-argument relation—for instance, that of a Case assigner versus a Case receiver, an Agreement assigner versus an Agreement receiver, and so on. An element may have more than one property for which it requires a match. If some matching requirements are still unsatisfied, for example of the head β contained in β' in (3b), this is visible on β'. If α and β' are to be combinable, α will have to satisfy a requirement of β'. It appears that functor-type expressions do not satisfy requirements of functor-type expressions, and argument expressions do not satisfy requirements of argument expressions. A functor-type expression can only become an argument of another functor if all its requirements are satisfied. For instance, only a VP with all matching requirements met (fully saturated) can be licensed as an argument of a Tense head, and so on. If so, relevant matching requirements will only be visible on the current root, hence yielding the extension condition.

2. Of course, this is quite close to Kayne's intuition. The intuitive idea can be illustrated on the basis of (i).

(i) a c-commands b iff a is a sister to a category γ containing b.
   a. Schematically: $[[_\tau \text{ a c}] \quad [_\gamma \ldots \text{b} \ldots]]$
   b. Schematically: $[[_{\langle a, a \rangle} \text{ a c}] \, [_\gamma \ldots \text{b} \ldots]]$

(ia) is the standard case: τ contains constituents a and c, but only τ qualifies as the sister of γ. Hence when γ is translated as a λ-expression, only τ is visible as an argument of that expression. (ib) is the case where c has been *adjoined* to a. Adjunction means that c is not contained in the category a, only in a *segment* of a. Following Chomsky 1995, adjunction ("pair-merge") is notated by labeling the node containing a and c by an order pair: $\langle a, a \rangle$. Since c is not capped by a full category, it qualifies as a sister of γ (just as the full category a—both segments together—does). When γ is translated as a λ-expression, either c or the full a can be fed in as an argument. So, binding by an element in adjoined position (or specifier position thus understood) is straightforwardly accommodated.

3. Following a suggestion by an anonymous reviewer, I changed the original experiencer verb *disappointed* to the verb *tired* to create a better minimal pair.

4. Reuland (1998) provides some discussion of variability in judgments of inverse linking and factors that bear on it. I will not review this here, since it does not affect the thrust of the analysis.

Chapter 3

1. "Logical syntax" offers a more specific definition than the original wording "at the relevant semantic level" in R&R.

2. Henceforth I will use the terms *condition A* and *condition B* for the conditions as defined here. To avoid confusion, I will henceforth refer to the conditions A and B in the form they have in the CBT as *canonical condition A* and *canonical condition B*.

3. Criticisms by Veraart (1996) and Bergeton (2004) will be taken up in chapter 6 and shown to be mistaken.

4. Anagnostopoulou and Everaert (1999) show how in Modern Greek the SELF anaphor *eaftos tu* can occur in subject position as the head of a chain, and, as they argue, represents the combination of the +R and the SELF property. I come back to this issue in chapter 6.

5. The complexity can either be directly represented in their morphological makeup, as in the case of the SELF anaphors discussed, or it can be "hidden" in the syntactic structure, as will be discussed in chapter 6.

6. Chomsky (1981) observed that the grammaticality of sentences like (11a) was problematic for condition B as formulated there. Although both *him* and *himself* are possible in locative PPs, there may be a difference in interpretation. For instance, Strahan (2006) notes that in Australian English in *John put the book before himself* the book should be close enough to touch. With *him* it can be anywhere in front of John.

7. I refer the reader to Safir 2004b for discussion of a range of further interesting facts about the role of distributivity versus collectivity in coargument dependencies (although we differ in our conclusions and analysis; see Reuland 2009b for more discussion).

8. For reasons of economy, double reflexive marking is avoided unless there is discourse justification.

9. Veraart (1996) argues that there are problems with the interpretation of this example, since focalization subject or indirect object improves (15a,c). I will come back to this interesting observation in chapter 6, where it will be shown to follow from the precise way reflexive-marking works.

10. This notion of exemption is purely structural. To my knowledge not a single semantic or discourse reason has been offered for why we would find contrasts as in (17) or (18). Note, however, that if an anaphor is exempt from a binding obligation it still can be bound, but once a binding obligation has been obviated other factors come into play and determine preferential binding patterns. Hence the favored binder may well turn out to be the local binder that is not obliged to bind. (Thanks to Ken Safir for stimulating me to bring this out more clearly.)

11. Note that, although (21b) could have fallen under the accessibility clause of the CBT, violating the i-within-i condition (see section 1.7.2), in the case of (21c) that is much less straightforward. In any case, that is not a solution that is available in the theory as it developed since Chomsky 1995. Exemption in object position could not have been accommodated anyway, though.

12. As evidence that a logophor need not be a bound variable, consider (i).

(i) Only Lucie buys pictures of herself.

The anaphor in (i) is logophoric. It is easy to see an ambiguity here between the bound and the referential interpretation (Lucie is the only person who buys pictures of Lucie, though perhaps buying one's own pictures is true of everybody).

13. It should be noted, though, that the judgments on *picture* NPs are more variable than one would initially expect. In chapter 7 we will come back to this issue with a discussion of *picture* NPs based on recent research by Asudeh, Keller, Runner, and others, including a note on event nominals.

14. Williams (1994, 104) takes issue with R&R's approach. He claims—I quote— that "the fundamental problem with R&R's [=Reinhart and Reuland 1993, EJR] account is that there is nothing in the account intermediate between lexical and logophoric anaphora. In Dutch, for example, *zichzelf* does seem to hold roughly of co-arguments.... However, not only is *zich* not a discourse-level anaphor, it in fact has rather tight locality restrictions, something like English *himself*—a property R&R's account will entirely miss." He continues: "What is needed...is something intermediate between coargument and discourse level." Regrettably, Williams's remarks on R&R's analysis of *zich* are based on a misunderstanding. Reinhart and Reuland (1991) contains extensive discussion of the interpretation of *zich*, with a precise analysis of the way its locality properties are derived, giving indeed a domain that can be characterized as "intermediate." (This analysis is explicitly referred to and adopted in R&R, 659.) In chapters 4 and 5 I will take up the mechanisms for the interpretation of *zich* again. Concerning "intermediacy" in the analysis of English *himself*, *himself* is not a SE anaphor such as Dutch *zich*, nor does it contain one like Dutch *zichzelf*, and its properties are quite different from either. Hence, indeed, there is no syntactically determined intermediate domain for English *himself*. Once exempt, the interaction between general conditions on interpretability (binding, discourse) will determine the range of its possible antecedents, as we saw in the text.

As to the analysis of *each other*, it is indeed true that in view of the well-formedness of (i) (repeated from R&R, note 7), the ill-formedness of Williams's (ii) may be surprising:

(i) The arguments that John and Mary presented were the basis for each other's articles.

(ii) *John and Mary think that Bill wants pictures of each other to be in the post office.

However, two things must be separated: (i) the proper characterization of exempt positions, and (ii) characterizing the interpretations available for elements in exempt position. R&R claimed to do no more than (i). As regards the contrast between (i) and (ii), the issue is what principles determine whether a potential antecedent for a reciprocal in exempt position is, in fact, an admissible antecedent. Structurally, the positions in (i) and (ii) are different, at least. And insofar as the interpretation of reciprocals makes use of movement of one of the subparts of *each other*, a contrast between (i) and (ii) (where *each other* is contained in a subject) is not unexpected. In any case, available analyses of reciprocal interpretation make use of very different mechanisms than I will be proposing for reflexives. This holds true both for Heim, Lasnik, and May's (1991) approach and for the analysis offered by Dotlačil and Nilsen (2009) and Dotlačil (2010).

15. There is a pervasive claim in the literature—for instance, by Heinat (2005) and Hicks (2009)—that the problem exempt anaphors pose for the CBT could be resolved by postulating the existence of two distinct lexical elements: $himself_1$, which is an anaphor, and $himself_2$, which is a logophor. It is trivial to see, however, that in such a theory one would have to prevent $himself_2$ from being introduced in the environments that do not lead to exemption as characterized here. So, to avoid overgeneration, in a sentence like *John was excited that the queen invited himself for tea, himself should be prevented from being $himself_2$. Therefore the conditions on the insertion of $himself_2$ would have to recapitulate condition A, with no empirical gain, but only explanatory loss.

16. Condition A allows a SELF anaphor to be used logophorically just in case it does not occupy an argument position of a predicate, since in this case it does not reflexive-mark the predicate (though what counts as a predicate will be further specified). The study of discourse anaphors has observed two distinct uses. The use that was originally labeled *logophoric* (starting with Clements 1975) is the point-of-view use. The other is the use of discourse anaphors as focus, which has been labeled *emphatic* (see Kuno 1987; Zribi-Hertz 1989). As focus, a free SELF anaphor can occur even in an argument position. Such examples are harder to find and are more marked; some are given in (i).

(i) a. This letter was addressed only to myself.
    b. Why should the state always take precedence over myself?
    c. "Bismarck's impulsiveness has, as so often, rebounded against himself." (quoted in Zribi-Hertz 1989)
    d. Himself$_i$ [Bismarck's impulsiveness has, as so often, rebounded against e$_i$]

That focus anaphors are exempt from condition A, follows directly, if we assume that the focus expression undergoes covert movement. In this case, the active copies of the anaphors in (i) are no longer in argument positions. Hence, they do not reflexive-mark the verbs, so condition A does not require the predicate to be reflexive. The precise mechanism will become clear in chapter 6, where the syntactic mechanism of reflexive-marking is explained.

17. These notions are illustrated by the well-known contrast in (i) between the interpretations (ib) and (ic), discussed by Kaplan (1989). Pavarotti may have a belief that is adequately captured by (ia). But he may or may not be aware that it is his own pants that are on fire.

(i) a. Pavarotti believes his pants are on fire.
    b. My pants are on fire!
    c. That guy's pants are on fire.

Chierchia (1989) examines the distinction between long-distance reflexives and pronouns in Italian in this connection. He observes that there is a contrast between (iia) and (iib).

(ii) a. Pavarotti crede   che i   **propri** pantaloni siano in fiamme. Ma non si
         Pavarotti believes that the self   pants   are   in flames but not CL
         e' accorto che i   pantaloni sono i   propri.
         realize   that the pants   are   the own
         'Pavarotti believes that self's pants are on fire, but he hasn't realized that
         the pants are his own.'
      b. Pavarotti crede   che i   **suoi** pantaloni siano in fiamme. Ma non si
         Pavarotti believes that the his pants   are   in flame but not CL
         e' accorto che i   pantaloni sono i   propri.
         realize   that the pants   are   the own
         'Pavarotti believes that his pants are on fire, but he hasn't realized that
         the pants are his own.'

The sentence in (ia) has the air of a contradiction, whereas (ib) where the personal
pronoun *suoi* is substituted for *proprio* does not. The use of the long-distance reflexive *proprio* requires that Pavarotti realize that it is his own pants that are on
fire—that is, proprio is *necessarily de se*. Such a requirement does not hold for
the personal pronoun *suo*.

18. These contexts still raise an issue with respect to variable binding. Though the
logophor in, say, (30a) need not be a bound variable, it can be, as illustrated in
(30b) with a quantified antecedent (and as can be further checked in ellipsis contexts). Similarly, in (26) the anaphor could also be a bound variable, as can be
shown by substituting a quantified NP for *Max* or *Lucie*. In this respect, there is
no difference between logophors and pronouns in such contexts. Both can serve as
bound variables, as illustrated for the experiencing context in (30b). Generally,
variable binding requires that the antecedent c-command the variable at some
stage of the derivation. The present analysis sheds no new light on the question
of where (i.e., at which stage of the derivation) this requirement must be met (see
Reinhart 1987 for a proposal in preminimalist terms).

19. This issue was originally pointed out by Hans Kamp (personal communication).

20. One may assume a logical syntax structure as in (i), with the determiner binding the variable of the set expression (Higginbotham 1983).

(i) $[_{DP} Det_i [_{NP} \ldots N(x_i) \ldots]$

Here and elsewhere I will assume that logical syntax variables translate morphosyntactic ϕ-feature bundles. However, we need not go into this for now.

21. See Neeleman and Szendrői 2007 for an alternative view.

22. For the sake of clarity, this is not to say that all anaphors are ϕ-feature deficient. English *himself* would fail this. But, of course, *himself* is not a SE anaphor
to start with, and its dependence is encoded in the semantic and syntactic properties of SELF.

23. This may serve as a defining characteristic of SE anaphors. Some languages
have simplex forms that appear to be referentially restricted without lacking
marking for number. For instance, Telugu *tanu* is marked for number (Lust et al.
2000 and Mukkerji 1999; see also Koring 2005). Hence it does not qualify as a SE
anaphor as defined above. If so, the FDT (chapter 1, (15)) predicts that it is less

dependent on a binder than Dutch *zich*. This is borne out. Further research is required for a precise assessment of its feature makeup and the way its features interact with its environment.

24. The precise mechanism does not concern us here. One may think of Cinque 1999–style functional sequences in the left periphery of nominal projections, as in the verbal projection, with a cutoff point and order stipulated or derived by semantic requirements (see Nilsen 2003) or selection relations. For instance, if D selects a NumP, the absence of a NumP requires the absence of D. Alexis Dimitriadis (personal communication) notes that a rigid version of selection raises the question of how verbs can be so flexible in their selection that they ignore the difference between, let's say, DPs and πP. This is related to an observation by Dominique Sportiche (2001) that verbs do not select for a type of D in their arguments, but only for properties of the conceptual structure of the N. In Sportiche's analysis selection requires sisterhood, and, as he argues, the functional structure of N is indeed merged later than the verb. This raises a great number of important issues, but discussion would lead us too far afield at this moment.

25. Déchaine and Wiltschko (2002) do not discuss SE anaphors. They do discuss reflexive clitics such as French *se* and suggest that these are pure ϕ-feature bundles without further internal structure. Their analysis too would entail that *zich* is not a full DP, but realizes a lower projection. In their analysis the full DP-projection has the structure in (i). However, since *zich* is ϕ-feature deficient it cannot realize ϕ—assuming that ϕ stands for the full set of ϕ-features—but must realize a still lower position, as indicated in the text.

(i) $[_{DP}$ D $[_{\phi P}$ ϕ $[_{NP} \ldots N \ldots]]]$

26. A comment on the $-$R status of *himself* seems warranted. Observationally it is clear that *himself* in all of its uses is $-$R, since it cannot be used deictically. In the case of Dutch *zich* $-$R status has a clear morpholexical correlate: it is demonstrably underspecified for ϕ-features. Since the *him* of *himself* is fully specified for ϕ-features, the source of its referential dependence must reside elsewhere. In chapter 6 I will present a semantics of SELF that makes this precise. In chapter 7 I show that the morphosyntactic composition of *himself* causes its impossibility in chain-initial positions.

27. There is some variation between predicates. Some verbs (*horen* 'hear') are sometimes claimed to prefer *zichzelf*. A relevant factor appears to be how strongly they favor interpretation as indirect or direct perception (with the latter preferring *zichzelf*). In chapter 7 I discuss a structural correlate of this distinction.

28. I use the ECM case for illustration. The same pattern is shown by finite clauses as in (i):

(i) a.   Max said that [he$_1$ criticized himself$_1$]
    b. *Max said that [himself$_1$ criticized him$_1$]

However, here *himself* is excluded for an independent reason. I take up this issue in chapter 7.

29. In (i) *herself* might be argued to head a chain in violation of the chain condition.

(i) Mary$_1$ admires no one but herself$_1$

Herself in this case is certainly an independent argument, not part of a chain headed by *Mary*. R&R provide a technical solution that need not concern us here. In chapter 6 a derivational perspective on SELF-marking and a precise semantics of SELF are presented from which the status of exempt anaphors immediately follows.

30. Where the two approaches may differ empirically is in the case of condition A. If a syntactic PRO-subject is obligatory in the control cases, a logophor would be excluded, since the definition of a syntactic predicate would be met. For example, (iia), with the structure (iib), should be worse than (i), which also allows the no-PRO structure, since only in (iib) is a syntactic predicate formed. If the agent role is controlled lexically, as in Williams's approach, then (i) and (ii) are indistinguishable syntactically (in both, no syntactic predicate is formed for the N), so they should be equally allowable by condition A.

(i) Max was glad that Lucie saw [a picture of himself]

(ii) a. Max was glad that Lucie took a picture of himself.
      b. Max was glad that Lucie$_1$ took [PRO$_1$ picture of himself]

The judgments appear to favor Williams's approach.

31. The view that anaphors such as Dutch *zichzelf* are reflexivizers and involve coargumenthood is occasionally challenged. Veraart (1996), for instance, states that sentences such as (i) are problematic for this view:

(i) Jan sprak namens zichzelf.
    'John spoke on behalf of himself.'

As she argues, *namens zichzelf* is a sentential adverbial modifier, hence *zichzelf* and *Jan* cannot be coarguments, and the ill-formedness of **Jan$_i$ sprak namens hem$_i$* shows that *zichzelf* cannot be a logophor here. (Note that, as discussed in section 3.2, *zichzelf* is unlikely to be a logophor in any case.) However, this argument misses the point, since, as discussed, PPs can have an argument structure with a controlled subject. Under the assumption that the PP *namens zichzelf* has a two-place argument structure [*x namens y*], with *x* controlled by *Jan*, the problem dissolves, since in (i) we now have a reflexive semantic predicate [*x namens x*] that must be reflexive-marked. Veraart also claims that the *zich* in locative and directional PPs is in fact a "hidden" *zichzelf*:

(ii) Max legde het boek naast zich.
     'Max put the book next to him.'

According to Veraart, we have *zich* instead of *zichzelf* due to a phonological rule deleting *zelf* in a PP with a stressed preposition. Apart from the problems this raises from a crosslinguistic perspective (languages like English, Frisian, etc., have a pronoun here; would it also result from SELF deletion?), a rule like SELF deletion is awkward from a theoretical perspective, and moreover unnecessary to capture the correlation. The correlation between stress on P and the presence of *zich* simply follows from the fact that *zich*, not being in the head position of the NP, cannot be stressed, and that therefore the stress on the PP can only be realized if shifted onto the P.

32. The chain condition as envisaged was not specific to binding. As shown in R&R 1993, notes 32, 33, 42, 43, in the representational framework as adopted there, the chain condition regulates all chains, irrespective of whether they arise by coindexing or movement. So the criticism in Safir 2004a that the chain condition lacks independent motivation is not justified given the theoretical context in which it was proposed.

33. Note that it is not enough to say that that there cannot be a chain without coindexing; the question is what would allow a putative −R element to have an independent index.

34. For ease of reference I quote the original definitions from Chomsky 1986a, 8:

(i) α governs β iff α m-commands β and every barrier for β dominates α.

(ii) α c-commands β iff α does not dominate β and every γ that dominates α dominates β.
Where γ is restricted to maximal projections..., α m-commands β.

35. Note that the intuition behind this is still relevant. This conception of a minimality barrier is effectively carried over into the Minimalist Program in the form of intervention effects on probe-goal relationships.

36. As Chomsky notes, θ-government is not enough, since it would open the way for "superraising." Similarly, a Case that is only configurationally licensed is not enough.

37. In the theory of valuation outlined in Chomsky 2001, 2004, as well as in Pesetsky and Torrego 2004a, 2004b, having unvalued features is what makes an element visible for syntactic computation. Unvalued features are valued by the Agree operation (subject to the standard conditions on chain formation of c-command and locality) with an element that is valued for these features. So, with *zich* being unvalued for number and gender, Agree will specify it for these features. Thus, entering a chain and becoming valued is the result of an elementary, blind grammatical process.

38. The traditional distinction between casus recti and casus obliqui roughly corresponds to the distinction between *structural* and *inherent* Case as the terms are used here. With respect to earlier versions of syntactic theory, the characteristic of inherent Case is that the element licensing the inherent Case of α must be the same element that assigns a θ-role to α.

39. Note that "no chain" does not entail "no binding." It only entails "no encoding of the binding relation in narrow syntax." This distinction is crucial for evaluating this approach when applied to other languages. No language carries its analysis on its sleeve. The existence of a binding relation between α and β, where β is fully specified for φ-features, only bears on the chain condition if there are relations R_i such that $\alpha \cdot R_1 \cdot R_2 \cdot R_3 \ldots R_n \cdot \beta$ (where · stands for the composition operation).

40. See Van Gelderen 2000 for an illuminating discussion of the relationship between Case and reflexives in the history of English.

Chapter 4

1. See, for instance, discussions in the 1960s against deriving expressions with null objects such as *John ate*, from *John ate an apple* (Katz and Postal 1964).

2. For current purposes the simple version will do. Compare the full version: T may not translate an expression E′ in SEM′ with syntactically independent NPs A′ and B′ into an expression E in SEM in which A is A-bound by B, if there is an expression E″ resulting from replacing A′ in E′ with C′, C′ an NP such that B′ heads an A-CHAIN tailed by C′, and T also translates E″ into E.

3. Friederici and Kotz (2003) present a time-course model that relates differences in the stages of the interpretation procedure to differences in ERP signature and in some cases to differences in the fMRI signal. Discussion here would lead us beyond the scope of this work. The interested reader is referred to the works cited.

4. Menuzzi does not give the *Nós ... a gente* pattern in PPs, but a Google search also instantiates this pattern.

5. No derivations need to be compared with numerations containing different elements. It is not necessary, either, to limit numerations to lexical elements, as in Boeckx, Hornstein, and Nunes 2007.

6. As we will see, in some cases, local ineffability is indeed what a language system can deal with. If so, a very different mode of expression may be used as an alternative.

Chapter 5

1. This assumption is not always made explicit in the literature, but should in fact not be controversial since Higginbotham 1983.

2. I am very much indebted to Alexis Dimitriadis and Ken Safir for their help in formulating a simple summary.

3. Dative Case and prepositional Case are represented by one form; in fact in no singular nominal declension are they distinguished, but in the plural they systematically are.

4. Their general instruction for generating the morphosyntactic paradigm is as follows: (i) for any language, establish the morphosyntactic features (e.g., number) and their values (e.g., singular, plural) that are correlated with some distinct inflectional behavior; (ii) for each distinct word class within a language, establish which morphosyntactic features are in operation; and (iii) project all the logically possible feature-value combinations to produce the underlying morphosyntactic paradigm.

5. Note that these issues notwithstanding, the chain condition as stated in chapter 3 technically works for *it*, as for *him*, ruling out local binding. The distribution of pronominal forms and of overt versus null arguments in English warrants that English has a rudimentary Case system. That is, minimally it must have structural Case, which participates in the syntactic computations involving argument linking, as in Chomsky 1981 and subsequent work. Thus, *deer* in *deer are running*

around is marked for structural Case, checked/assigned by the Tense/agreement system, and *the deer* in *I admired the deer* is marked for structural Case checked/ assigned by the Tense/Agreement/V-system. A pronominal such as English *he* in *he admired the deer* is specified as 3rd person, masculine, singular, and nominative (=structural) Case. Its neuter counterpart *it* is also fully specified, namely as 3rd person, neuter, and singular. It shows a number contrast with *they*, just as *he* does. Like any English DP it will be marked for structural Case if it is in subject or object position. Thus, *it* meets the requirements of being +R in the sense of the chain condition—that is, it cannot tail a chain. The issues raised come up only if one sets out to derive the chain condition from more fundamental principles, as I will be doing here.

6. This is independent of whether we think of features as defining a grid in a paradigm (which appears to be the assumption in the morphological literature cited), or as separate heads in an extended nominal projection along the lines sketched as in section 3.5, which is presupposed in Pesetsky and Torrego's implementation. Note that also for the latter, bundles of features are a significant unit in the system, which can be represented as partial subtrees.

7. Note that in versions of minimalist grammars that use numerations, there is a use of the term *index* to mark the number of occurrences of a lexical item in the numeration—for instance, the numeration that will yield *the girl hit the ball* contains two occurrences of *the*. These have different indices, or alternatively, *the* will have the index 2 to represent that there are two *the*'s in the numeration. This use as a computational device has to be distinguished from the use of indices in the canonical binding theory.

8. In fact, as one element relating to two different syntactic environments in the approach in Frampton 2004.

9. Thanks to Alexis Dimitriadis (personal communication) for urging me to clarify this issue.

10. To my knowledge, virtually all of the current linguistic literature (including Reinhart and Reuland 1991, 1993) takes this position.

11. The possibility of logophoric interpretation may depend on real-world knowledge, such as whether the envisaged discourse antecedent is alive or dead, as is the case in Chinese (C.-T. James Huang, personal communication).

12. Note that conceptually little changes if one considers prepositional complements:

Whether a syntactic dependency between the pronoun and the DP can be formed depends on the nature of the relation between P and V. If the dependency between V and P is syntactically expressed, for instance by covert movement, and assuming there is also a syntactic relation between P and the pronoun (such as by checking), composition can take place. If either condition is not met, no syntactic dependency between the pronoun and the subject DP can be formed.

13. Heinat (2005) proposes that agree-type relations can be directly established between maximal projections, but offers no convincing evidence for this claim.

14. The dichotomy between interpretable and uninterpretable features has sparked considerable conceptual controversy. The reason why is unclear. To say that there are uninterpretable features that must be erased at the C-I interface says no more than that there are features that represent triggers for certain computations that have semantic effects, but do not embody these semantic effects themselves. As instructions they must be followed, and all such triggers for instructions must be used up.

15. To avoid possible misunderstandings I should point out that covert movement as understood in Reuland 2001b is simply feature movement without pied piping of lexical material, and takes place in one cycle with all other checking-driven movement. Therefore, this gives a type of covert movement that is "pre-spell-out." (Note that this says nothing about QR, which I do not assume is feature driven (see Reinhart 2006), hence post-spell-out.) The "weak" versus "strong" property of attracting features is then just the property of attracting feature bundles versus requiring pied piping.

16. The deletion-versus-erasure question raises many issues that are not immediately relevant to the present discussion. It arises from the somewhat paradoxical situation that uninterpretatable features embody instructions for the morphology (Case, Agreement morphemes), hence must be visible there, yet they do not represent possible instructions for the interpretive system and therefore must, for reasons of Full Interpretation, be invisible there. The problem resolves in the system of Pesetsky and Torrego 2004a and 2004b, where interpretability is a condition on feature chains, instead of individual occurrences of features.

17. There has been extensive discussion of the nature of Dutch clause structure, or of SOV structure in general (see, for instance, Zwart 1997 and Koopman and Szabolcsi 2000). An underlying SVO structure is entirely compatible with a syntactic encoding of the dependencies studied here. For more, see chapter 7.

18. Note that Chomsky 1995 must assume generalized pied piping of the verb and any functional material it picks up on the way up. If the verb were allowed to excorporate, intermediate functional material would still constitute a potential target for other movements, contrary to what must be assumed. At this point I leave open how, precisely, pied piping of intermediate functional projections takes place.

19. An anonymous reviewer of Reuland 2001b expresses the concern that the features of the object moving up as high as T for checking purposes may cause a mixup in checking of subject versus object features. Chomsky (1995, 370ff.) contains extensive discussion as to how such a mixup is avoided. I will limit myself to referring to that discussion.

20. In accordance with Chomsky 1995.

21. Thanks to Tanya Reinhart for helpful discussion.

22. This might seem to go against the view of lexical items in distributive morphology. In fact, one may stay uncommitted with respect to the morphology-

syntax interface. What is required, though, is that at the C-I interface expressions are maximized. That is, although variables exist that only reflect category and person (such as SE anaphors), translation of a configuration with category, person, and number may not leave the number feature stranded.

23. Thanks to an anonymous reviewer of Reuland 2001b for raising this issue.

24. It follows that not all feature checking leads to a configuration satisfying the definition of a Chain. For instance, a DP checking its Case will in general not enter a Chain with its checker. Since the canonical cases of Move/attract discussed in current literature only involve partial checking, there will be no unwanted interaction with other instances of chain formation.

25. For binding in PPs this implementation works as follows. We have to distinguish between complement PPs and noncomplement PPs (locative and directional PPs). In the former case binding yields a reflexive predicate. Hence condition B applies, requiring a SELF anaphor, as discussed in chapter 3. In locative and directional PPs we have a SE anaphor or a pronominal.

For all PPs we have to specify the relation between P and its complement, and the relation between P and V. As in the case of the relation between V and its complement, one may assume that the Case relation between P and its complement is visible on P. In the specific implementation considered here, this is expressed by FFz (or FFh) adjoining to P.

If there is a formal dependency between P and V (as when V determines the Case of P's complement), this is expressed by P's formal features (FFp) adjoining to V. Given that FFz/FFh have adjoined to P, these will move along; they are also visible as part of the formal feature structure adjoined to V. This yields the by-now-familiar type of configuration (e.g., (15)). FFz (or FFh) are realized on V's extended projection, and the conditions for Chain and CHAIN formation are met (and only the case with FFz will survive the PRD and cancellation).

If there is no Case dependency between V and P, there is no movement of the subtree [FFh [FFp]]. Assume this is an option in Dutch (details and crosslinguistic variation will be discussed in section 8.3.2). If this assumption is correct, the structural conditions for chain formation are not met. Under this option, then, the absence of complementarity between bound *hem* and *zich* follows. Despite the lack of complementarity with *hem, zich* in these cases is not free. This is due to Rule L (see also section 5.7), which requires *zich* to enter a dependency with an antecedent via the syntactic route if possible.

26. Déchaine and Wiltschko (2002) make the interesting observation that in (i) a bound variable interpretation is absent:

(i) I think that the police saw me and Mary does too.
    =a. I think that the police saw me and Mary thinks that the police saw me too.
    ≠b. I think that the police saw me and Mary thinks that the police saw her too.

They observe that French does allow the bound variable reading. To my mind Dutch sides with English in this case. This indicates that the bound variable reading is available in the domain of chain formation, but not beyond.

27. Note that the intuition behind (33i) is entirely consistent with the possibility that the coordinate systeem may be shifted as in Schlenker's discussion of Amharic (see, for example, Schlenker 1999), where a 1st-person pronominal may receive the value of a local source as in *John said that I am sick* where *I = John*. See Khomitsevich 2008 for extensive discussion of related phenomena.

28. Of course, one may wonder what happens in famous cases like *I dreamt that I was BB and that I kissed me.* Any analysis should capture that at some level of abstraction, there is a continuity between the referents of the pronouns. In fact, such continuity is the basis of the whole joke. Such referents are connected by a proxy relation, as elaborated in Reuland and Winter 2009. See also the discussion of proxy relations in chapter 6.

29. See also the discussion in Kratzer 2006 of plurality and groups.

30. It is noteworthy, though, that in many languages gender contrasts in pronouns are restricted to the singular. A possible speculation is that singular number is semantically less complex than plural, leaving space for the expression of one additional variable.

31. Winter (2001), for instance, shows that there is a systematic ambiguity in the interpretation of plural noun phrases, reflecting a very different semantics, which by itself is sufficient to make the point. Consider, for instance, (i) and (ii), discussed by Winter:

(i) All the committees reached a decision together last week.

(ii) Every committee reached a decision together last week.

(i) has two readings reflecting an ambiguity in the meaning of plural nouns. On one reading, (i) and (ii) are synonymous. Under this reading *all* and *every* have the same meaning and the plural noun has the meaning of the corresponding singular. On the second reading of (i), the committees meet with each other. Under this reading the plural denotes a set of sets of committees (see also Schwarzschild 2001 for discussion).

32. I am grateful to an anonymous reviewer for a comment that made me pursue this option.

33. Italian *proprio* does not qualify as a POSS anaphor in the relevant sense. Its use is not obligatory and it can be combined with a possessive pronominal, as in *sui propri figli* 'their own children'. So, in fact, it is an expression of the same type as English *own*.

34. Note that the claim is not that *all*, etc. by themselves are interveners. In that case we would expect that in Norwegian and other Scandinavian languages, where the same order is available, the choice of the POSS anaphor *sin* versus the pronominal genitive *hanns* would be influenced by the presence or absence of *al* 'all' or its cognates. Rather, the argument is that the D-position is there, and that due to its properties it defines an opaque domain in languages that obligatorily marks definiteness in this position.

35. As striking as the correlation is, the precise execution merits attention. Unlike the languages in (37ii), Bangla has no definite article but marks definiteness by

a classifier showing up in postnominal position. The question is, then, why Bangla does not go with the Scandinavian languages that also marks definiteness postnominally.

Bangla DP structure is investigated in Bhattacharya 1998. As he shows, the classifier originates in prenominal position, and in fact in a position higher than the base position of the POSS element. This is in line with the schema in (38b). The POSS element moves to its final position for Case reasons. The contrast between Bangla and Scandinavian must reside in the properties of the position where definiteness is marked. One can think of the following scenarios that should be investigated before final conclusions can be drawn. (i) Bangla has an empty operator in the position of D inheriting its properties from the classifier, whereas in Scandinavian the definiteness marking stays low. (ii) In Bangla the position where the POSS phrase is realized is an A'-position (making it immune to entering an A-chain); in Scandinavian the surface position is an A-position. (iii) In Bangla the classifier projects a specifier for the POSS to move through (where it picks up the definiteness marker) and the Scandinavian suffix does not.

36. Manzini's analysis does not apply to the German subjunctive, which is not operator licensed. Consequently, one need not expect the subjunctive to license logophors in German.

37. The derivations are perhaps complex, so it may be useful to go over them carefully. For instance, in a discussion of the Minimalist Program, Graf (2007) addresses the argument given here as it appears in Reuland 2001b. He claims that the assumptions about the CHAIN-formation process that make the subjunctive block CHAIN formation in (47), are impossible to reconcile with the assumptions needed to allow it in (i):

(i) Who$_i$ did he$_j$ ask himself$_j$ [(who)$_i$ has killed SE$_i$]

Graf argues that if moving V$_{subj}$ creates a problem in (47), so should moving *who* in (i) create a problem there. Note, however, that as defined, the CHAIN-formation algorithm operates on C/chains as syntactic objects. In (i) Chains/chains are formed between SE and *has*, between *has* and *who*, and also between *who* in C and *who* as a subj. Thus we must assess how CHAIN composition as in Reuland 2001b, 43–44, applies to the Chains (*who*, *has*), (*has*, SE) (*who*$_C$, *who*$_{subj}$). In fact CHAIN composition can apply to the Chains (*who*, *has*) and (*has*, SE), yielding a CHAIN between *who* and SE. The timing ensures that this CHAIN can be computed irrespective of the further fate of *who* (although, since linking applies to C/chains, it is in fact fine for *who* to move).

In (47), however, three C/chains are relevant for the computation: (*Oscar*, V$_{subj}$), (Op, V$_{subj}$), and (V$_{subj}$, *sig*). The chain (Op, V$_{subj}$) is on the path between *Oscar* and *sig*. What was left implicit in the exposition of Reuland 2001b (but was taken to be obvious given that CHAINS are a generalization of Chains and chains) is that in order for chain composition/linking to be possible for any Chains A and B, the tail of A must command the head of B, and that for any term in the composition, all Chains it is part of must be considered. Another way of putting this is that C/chains are syntactic objects. You cannot carry out the composition using only part of an object, just as only a whole chain—not merely its foot—causes intervention effects. Or to put it differently, for composition to be possible, *Oscar* should have entered into a relation with *Op*. But, even irrespective of content, this would have been structurally impossible since *Op* c-commands *Oscar* rather than vice versa.

38. I am indebted to Tanya Reinhart (personal communication) for bringing this case to my attention.

39. This discussion can be made more precise along the following lines. Following Chomsky 1995, 309, let us distinguish between a checking configuration and a checking relation. For the motivation for this distinction I refer the reader to the original discussion in Chomsky 1995. Suppose K attracts F, which raises to form $\{H(K), \{F,K\}\}$. Each feature of FF[F] including F is in the checking domain of each sublabel f of K. At this point, (i) will be taken to hold:

(i) Feature F′ of FF[F] is in a *checking configuration* with f; and F′ is in a *checking relation* with f, if, furthermore, F′ and f match.

Consider now the difference between (i) *Ik (FF$_{zich}$) voelde zich*... and (ii) **Ik (FF$_{hem}$) voelde hem*.... (Note, incidentally, that FF$_{zich/hem}$ and FF$_V$, despite being sublabels of the I-complex, are different feature bundles, and hence may have a different fate.) According to Chomsky's assumptions we have a checking configuration in (i), but no checking relation, *although there could have been one if the features had matched*. (The italicized condition is precisely what characterizes when a derivation is canceled.) In (ii) there is a checking configuration; there is no checking relation, *and (on our assumptions) there could not have been one even if the features had matched*. As expressed by the clause in (ii), since the existence of a checking relation would violate a fundamental principle of grammar, namely the PRD, the option of checking is not considered. There is no CHAIN, not even a canceled one.

An anonymous reviewer of Reuland 2001b raised the question of why the derivation *must* be canceled because of feature mismatch between *ik* and *zich* in the environment of chain formation, since there is no feature in (48) that is left dangling whose checking remains unsatisfied. All we need is the preference for syntactic encoding expressed in Rule L and Rule BV coupled with a strictly derivational view of syntactic and interpretive processes. Assume a bottom-up procedure for the formation and interpretation of syntactic objects in which all decisions are made as soon as possible. Given a sentence with a pronoun (SE anaphor or pronominal), Rule L says first to link it up as a CHAIN tail. The question is what makes (i)...1st SUBJ SE different from (ii)...1st IND SE and the latter, in turn, different from (iii)...1st IND PRON. In cases (i) and (iii) there can be no CHAIN for general reasons. Hence an alternative procedure can be started. In case (ii) there could have been a well-formed CHAIN if the features had matched. But instead there is a feature mismatch in precisely the sense discussed by Chomsky: interpreting SE by forming a CHAIN link fails since it gives rise to an illegitimate syntactic object. Therefore, we are not allowed to pursue a less optimal alternative by assigning it an interpretation by nonsyntactic means. That is, *blocking the syntactic part within C$_{HL}$ of an interpretive procedure is final*. This consequence can immediately be understood in terms of limiting computational space, if not within C$_{HL}$ proper, then within the broader system of linguistic computations.

40. As is well known, Chinese *ziji* and Japanese *zibun* may appear in the subject position of finite clauses. This is entirely consistent with the analysis developed here, since there do not seem to be independent reasons to assume that such languages have an agreement system with φ-features that have to be deleted for convergence.

41. The main ideas of this section were published in Reuland 2005a, a squib (with the same title) for Henk van Riemsdijk.

42. This effect of copying is regrettably missed in the otherwise very careful discussion of Hicks 2009, 112. Nor did Hicks take into account that the present implementation is part of a more comprehensive theory. His criticisms, consequently, miss the point. For instance, as is made explicit in Reuland 2001b, pronominal binding is not syntactically encoded. Similarly, English complex anaphors are interpreted by SELF movement onto the predicate, departing from R&R 93.

43. In this discussion I clarify a number of issues brought up in Hicks 2009.

44. As Hicks (2009) rightly points out, this derivation assumes a second specifier. My implementation here is in line with Chomsky 1995 and subsequent work, where such an Edge position (reflecting Object shift) is also postulated for *wh*-movement from object position. Note that in Dutch and Scandinavian this edge position is independently needed for Object shift. In Dutch it is anyway necessary to allow for a position of *zich* higher than the subject (see chapter 8).

45. I am grateful to Noam Chomsky (personal communication) for bringing this consequence to my attention.

46. Thanks to Øystein Nilsen, Halldór Sigurðsson, and Sigríður Sigurjónsdóttir (personal communication) for providing me with these facts.

Chapter 6

1. As already noted, it has been claimed that there are exceptions. In at least one case the claim has been based on a misanalysis (Frisian), in another case the facts seem prima facie inconclusive (Old English) but are in fact not exceptional at all. In view of the pervasiveness of the phenomenon, from Oceanic languages to creoles, should be investigated with the utmost care. Note that only an in-depth analysis of such a language can establish whether it is a real counterexample or only an apparent one, potentially involving a licensing factor that is less easily observed. Reflexivity in Japanese is case in point. *Zibun* can sometimes have a local antecedent, whereas at other occasions *zibun-zisin* is required if the antecedent is local. Aikawa (1993) shows that *zibun-zisin* is required when the predicate is not inherently reflexive, and the antecedent is quantificational, concluding that where *zibun*'s antecedent is local it is interpreted by coreference, rather than by binding. Hara (2002) takes the issue further, addressing a number of theoretical and empirical problems Aikawa's account left open, resolving them on the basis of a detailed analysis of the feature composition of *zibun* and the distribution of null pronouns. Space limitations prevent a further discussion at this point. Instead, I refer the reader to these works. However, I

wish to point out that the issue reflects a methodological point I wish to stress. A proper understanding of the binding patterns in a language requires an in-depth analysis. Analyses staying at a macrolevel are unlikely to add much to our insight.

2. It may well be part of the larger family of distinctness requirements, as discussed in Richards 2006.

3. I am grateful to Denis Delfitto and an anonymous reviewer for urging me to clarify this.

4. Recall the issue. Chomsky (1995 and subsequent work) assumes that transitive verbs are complex, with an articulation into [EXT v* [INT V (INT)]]. As we will see, this complexity may be syntactically realized, but only in languages like English. Since a separate v* is only projected for syntactic reasons, the structure will not be preserved at the C-I interface, unless licensed by a SELF anaphor. Hence, their particular distribution in English follows, as will be discussed in detail later. Languages like Dutch are fusional in their extended V-projection. Hence, the issue does not arise. That is, the presence of accusative Case is compatible with the absence of a syntactically articulated v*. A fortiori, there is no reason to assume that v* can be instrumental in arity-preservation.

5. Prima facie the intuition behind IDI may seem similar to the nonredundancy principle proposed in Schlenker 2005. Schlenker proposes a semantic reinterpretation of the binding theory, specifically condition B. It involves a condition preventing any individual—or description of an individual—from appearing twice in the sequence of evaluation used for the semantic interpretation of an expression. The proposal developed here is essentially syntactic, in the sense that it involves the workings of the computational system. Schlenker's proposal is ambitious, but irrespective of its potential in accounting for condition C effects and phenomena such as weak and strong crossover, it is bound to fail for the phenomena that form the subject of this book. As Schlenker himself notes, the proposal does not address issues of cross-linguistic variation. This, however, is not accidental. Since, as I have shown throughout this book, there is an irreducibly syntactic component to binding, reduction to semantics is impossible in principle, at least without redundantly importing the necessary syntactic notions into the semantics. Space prevents me from including the extensive discussion of Schlenker's proposal it certainly merits. Let me therefore limit myself to pointing out a number of crucial issues I cannot see how it could possibly be extended to: local binding of 3rd-person pronominals in Frisian and German dialects, local binding of 1st- and 2nd-person pronominals (as is pervasive), the fact that complex anaphors preserve, rather than reduce valence, the contrast between SE anaphors and SELF anaphors (pace Schlenker's reference to the criticisms in Bergeton 2004, since these are easily seen to miss the point; see for instance note 60), and many other facts discussed in this book. Not only does an exclusively semantic approach to binding offer no hope for the understanding of such facts, the very foundation of Schlenker's approach to condition B presents a problem. To allow "exceptional coreference" as in cases like *I know what Mary and Oscar have in common. Mary admires him and Oscar admires him too*, Schlenker has to resort to a guise-based approach. As I already observed in Reuland 2001b, notes 10, 11, invoking guises only shifts the problem. Also Schlenker notes that there are problems in his

approach. Unlike him I am not optimistic about principled ways to solve them in the end.

6. From a broader perspective, there is a third way to express that two arguments of a predicate receive the same value, namely by avoiding binding as defined and use covaluation instead. But, since this option does not involve binding proper it does not enter into the analysis to be developed below.

7. This quote is followed by a reference to Reinhart and Reuland 1993 for a "similar presumption." However, I am not aware of any presumption of this kind in our work.

8. I am indebted to Ken Safir (personal communication) for the following straw variant of a pragmatic approach. "Suppose that X *loves* Y is uttered and the listener knows who X is but not who Y is. Suppose a name/description is not used for Y. What would provide the listener with the most unmistakable information about Y? Information that Y could be anyone other than X, but someone in particular, or information that Y can be none other than X? The strongest possible information is the latter. This pragmatic fact does not explain anything about locality, but it does say why marking identity with a special form is more likely than marking nonidentity with a special form." Note, however, that such an approach predicts that the choice between an anaphor and a pronominal should be highly influenced by the discourse environment. But it is not. As we saw in the beginning of chapter 1, when in the first paragraphs of *Alice's Adventures in Wonderland* Alice is falling down the rabbit hole, it is clear that the only person she would think of stopping, or who she found falling, can be Alice. Yet the pronominal *her* is not possible. *Herself* is clearly required.

9. Bergeton's approach makes more predictions that fail in a fundamental way. Consider, for instance, expressions such as "to talk to someone about oneself." These require a SELF anaphor in Danish and in Dutch. Yet, the predicate they contain is not antireflexive as defined. Crucially, the French equivalent *Jean parle de lui* does not require *même* (Zribi-Hertz 1989), which is entirely surprising under such an account (see section 6.4 for discussion and an explanation). Next note that a sentence such as (i) is fine, hence his notion of intentionality is irrelevant as well.

(i) Hij verwondde zich met opzet.
   he hurt   SE intentionally

Also note, that with SELF classified as just an intensifier, the binding requirement on elements such as X-SELF has to come from the X. With complex anaphors such as *seg selv* or *zichzelf* this could in principle work, but it leaves unexplained the binding requirement of Frisian *himsels*, or even Danish *ham selv*. In short, Bergeton's approach does not provide a viable alternative. His other criticisms of Reinhart and Reuland 1993 do not fare better. A detailed discussion would lead us too far afield.

10. Occasionally one finds misunderstandings in the literature due to misinterpretation of the data. For instance, the verb *zien* 'see' requires a SELF anaphor in cases such as (i):

(i) Max zag zichzelf/*zich.
   'Max saw himself.'

However, in cases like (ii), *zelf* is optional:

(ii) Max zag zich(zelf) in de spiegel.
   'Max saw himself in the mirror.'

The question is why. Does it reflect factors like presence or absence of contrast, expectations, or other pragmatic factors, thus casting doubt on the present approach? Actually, the fact that *zelf* is required in (i) and not in (ii) is a direct consequence of the theory. In (ii) the structure contains a secondary predication; *zich in de spiegel* is a small clause. Hence we have a configuration where the grid of the predicate—*zien*—is not reflexive, hence reflexive marking is not required.

11. Note, incidentally, that the argument variables of R are bound by the ∀-operator, and there is no sense in which "the girls" binds "themselves." Anna Volkova (personal communication) notes that the Russian (i) has two interpretations:

(i) Девочки восхищаются   собой.
   girls   enthuse-themselves (about) themselves
   'The girls admire themselves.'

In addition to the distributive interpretation expressed by (8b), Russian also allows a collective interpretation, not expressed by (8b). This ties in with our subsequent discussion of the effects of Dutch *zelf* as favoring distributive interpretation. This is typically a property by which one would expect reflexivizers to differ.

12. Note that the semantic perspective on binding sketched does not by itself preclude annotating certain dependencies in the syntax, for instance by coindexing. That is, we could define the interpretation of the coindexing in (i) as (8b):

(i) The girls$_i$ admire themselves$_i$

Consequently, nothing precludes defining the syntactic predicate in (i) as reflexive, in terms of the coindexing between its arguments, and consistent with its interpretation.

13. Prima facie it would seem that the conceptual structure—as such not visible to the CS—has a similar status as the *encyclopedia* in approaches such as distributive morphology or DM (Marantz 1997; Borer 2003, 2005). It seems that there is one important difference, though. Concepts in TS do not just represent facts about the world, but reflect mental principles underlying the way we organize and conceptualize the world. Thus conceived, the conceptual system in TS is in one dimension more restrictive, in another dimension more comprehensive than the encyclopedia in DM.

14. The two binary features define nine feature clusters.

1. [+c+m]   Agent
2. [+c−m]   Instrument
3. [−c+m]   Experiencer
4. [−c−m]   Theme

5. [+c]   Cause
6. [−c]   Recipient Goal/Benefactor
7. [−m]   Subject Matter/Source
8. [+m]   Sentient
9. [−]   Arb in Middles

15. Using the annotation of Williams 1981.

16. Note again that it is immaterial whether structural accusative Case is here as a basic property of such verbs, or is encoded by requiring the presence of an appropriate segment of a verb in the form of "little v," which then represents the case requirement.

17. As noted in Marelj 2004, the generalization in (10c) straightforwardly captures the fact—discussed in Pesetsky 1982—that verbs like *ask* and *wonder* differ in their Case properties, witness the contrast between *John asked the time* and **John wondered the time*. As Marelj shows, *ask* is encoded as ([+c+m], [−c−m]), *wonder* as ([+m], [−m]). Hence *ask* meets the requirement for assigning ACC, *wonder* does not.

18. The notion of external merge is neutral to the issue how precisely the notion of externality is syntactically realized.

19. I use *role changing* rather than *entry changing*, as in Reinhart 2002 and subsequent work, since strictly speaking valence reduction and saturation do change the lexical entry, but they do not change the content of clusters and the roles these represent.

20. For instance, whereas middles in lexicon languages cannot be coerced to receive an episodic interpretation, in syntax languages the corresponding forms can, witness the contrast between (ia,b) and (ii) (Marelj 2004, 233–236).

(i) a.   This dress buttons.
     b.   *This dress is buttoning today.

(ii) Tristram Šendi   se (upravo)   čita.
     Tristram Shandy SE (at the moment) reads
     '(At the moment), Tristram Shandy is being read.'

In the lexicon languages only verbs with a [/+c] role on their grid are visible to the lexicon middle formation operation. The contrasts in (iiia–c) show that such a restriction does not apply in SC, French, or Italian. Just like [/+c] verbs, [/+m] verbs, such as *love*, *hate*, *see* form felicitous middles in these languages.

(iii) a. i.   Dobra deca se lako vole.
          ii.   *Nice children love easily.
      b. i.   Les ennemis cruels se détestent facilement.
          ii.   *Cruel enemies hate easily.
      c. i.   La luce gialla ha il vantaggio di vedersi bene anche nella nebia più
                fitta. (Cinque 1988)
          ii.   *Yellow lights have the advantage of seeing even in the thickest of
                fog.

The syntax lexicon parameter also accounts for the contrast in ECM constructions between French and SC on the one hand and English and Dutch on the
other.

(iv) a. Ces maisons peuvent se croire belles   facilement seulement avec
        these houses can   SE think beautiful easily   only   with
        beaucoup de bonne volonté.
        lots   of good will
     b. Nerazradjena ideja se teško   smatra dobrom.
        unworked   idea SE with difficulty consider good
        'It is difficult to consider an idea that is not worked out good.'

(v) a. *John considers stupid easily.
    b. *Dergelijke ideeën beschouwen gemakkelijk als niet goed
        such   ideas consider   easily   as not sufficiently
        uitgewerkt.
        worked-out

21. This summary is based on Lemmen's tables, her discussion of individual
verbs, and my own assessment that a number of complex [+c+m], [−c−m]-
verbs that Lemmen does not offer an explanation for, are in fact blocked by
incoherence.

22. Ken Safir (personal communication) wonders whether allowing such operations to apply either in syntax or the lexicon should not be considered problematic
as a violation of the strong minimalist thesis. First of all, irrespective of the theory
adopted, the contrast between French and other languages as described must be
accommodated. So every theory must contain a parameter relating constraints
on middle formation, productivity of a reflexivization operation, and restrictions
on feeding other lexical processes. Second, what does the contrast amount to?
Nothing more than to saying this: a language such as French has an underspecified clitic *se* that upon being merged in the structure has the property that it can
satisfy an ACC Case requirement of the verb without saturating a θ-role, leaving
the latter to be assigned to the external argument. These are purely lexical properties that do not involve the workings of C_{HL} proper.

   In fact, Marelj and Reuland (2010) derive the contrast between French and
Dutch from the fact that French is a clitic language and Dutch is not. *Se* is a
clitic—that is, simultaneously an X^0 and an XP—whereas Dutch *zich* is only an
XP. For reasons discussed in the cited paper, the X^0/XP status of *se* allows the
external argument to acquire both the internal theme role and the external agent
role in the syntax by movement. The XP status of *zich* blocks the movement
option in Dutch. For details, see Marelj and Reuland 2010.

23. Reinhart (2002) uses the term *reduction*, thus focusing on the fact that the
syntactic valency of the predicate is reduced. Reinhart and Siloni (2005) use
the term *bundling*, focusing on the fact that the θ-role of the grid position that is
reduced does not disappear, but is bundled with that of the remaining grid position. Henceforth I will mostly be using the term *bundling*, but still use *reduction*
where that focus is more appropriate.

24. This property is illustrated in (i)–(iii) from Schütze 1993:

(i) Mér líkar við hann.
    I(D) like   him(N)

(ii) María telur   mér/*mig   líka við hann.
     Mary believes me(D)/*me(A) to-like him(N) (Thráinsson 1979, 352)

(iii) Mér   er talið   líka við hann.
      me(D) is believed to-like him(N) (Thráinsson, cited in Schütze 1993)

25. Note that there is a distinction between thematic Case, which is directly associated with the thematic structure of a verb, and inherent Case. So-called free
datives such as *my* in Frisian *it reint my te folle* 'it rains me too much' crucially
express a much looser connection between *my* and the predication than in indirect
objects, and also looser than in *it rains too much for me*. Frisian *my* does not bear
a role in the predicate's argument structure. Yet it has Case. This is what typically
instantiates inherent Case.

26. Note, that nothing I say here is incompatible with the definitions of reflexive
predicate introduced in chapter 3. The fact that a SE anaphor like *zich* is in some
sense dependent on its antecedent can be syntactically annotated by coindexing,
allowing one to define a syntactic notion of reflexivity if useful. Also, nothing prevents it from entering a syntactic dependency with its antecedent along the lines of
chapter 3. Thus, syntactically, *zich* can still be considered bound.

27. It is also possible that both options can be unified.

28. See, for a related argument, Veraart 1996 and Bergeton 2004. It is often
observed that in Dutch, Danish, and so on, SELF can be independently used as a
focus marker, as in *Ik zag de man zelf* 'I saw the man himself'. Clearly, if SELF
can be combined with any DP one may expect that it also combines with (argumental) *zich*, forming a transparent *zich zelf*. Although it is occasionally suggested
that this is problematic for the approach presented here, it is easily seen that it is
not, since *zelf* induces the very complexity that is needed for protection.

29. In the case of Caxur, Ekkehard König and Volker Gast (personal communication) remark that the reflexive may well be a focus marker, just like in
Malayalam. This notwithstanding, the form of the reflexive is that of a duplicated
pronominal $wuž_{Case1}$ $wuž_{Case2}$, where Case 1 is the case of the antecedent, and
Case 2 the local case (Toldova 1996).

30. Note the following example from Zande:

(i) Mì-ímí tì-rὲ.
    I-kill on-me
    'I kill myself.'

31. Note that at the start of her discussion Veraart states that Reinhart and Reuland's grammaticality judgments are incorrect. However later it becomes clear
that she shares the judgments on the text cases, but that focalization changes the
status of the examples. As always, proper procedure is then to investigate the
source of that effect instead of "abandoning" the theory.

32. I leave open whether a verb like *toewijzen* is ambiguous in structure, where focalization yields the text result relative to the structure it affects, or whether focalization results in this particalar articulation of the structure.

33. But note, that *logical syntax* is not *semantics*. Hence, it is conceivable that logical syntax contains expressions with variables that have only syntactic status. In fact, this could be so under the most straightforward interpretation of the results of object shift in English ECM.

34. It may be helpful to clarify a terminological issue around the notion of being *intransitive*. From a type-logical perspective any argument merged with a transitive predicate yields an intransitive predicate. So any argument is a potential arity reducer. From the canonical syntactic perspective, (in)transitivity is a property of heads. So, there is a distinction between an expression saturating an argument position of a predicate and an operator on a transitive head, yielding an intransitive head—that is, a head only requiring one additional argument in order to yield a proposition. However, even in the latter case two states of affairs must be distinguished: (i) an operator that changes the arity of the lexical entry (i.e., eliminates a θ-role or bundles two θ-roles), and (ii) an operator that respects the arity (i.e., does not affect the thematic organization but only enforces cobinding, which still gives a predicate that is intransitive in the sense of requiring only one further argument to yield a proposition). Ultimately, this comes down to the question touched on in the previous note of whether there is more to lexical structure than logical semantics.

35. Note that the semantic perspective on binding sketched does not by itself preclude annotating certain dependencies in the syntax—for instance, by coindexing. That is, we could define the interpretation of the coindexing in (i) as (42b):

(i) The girls$_i$ admire themselves$_i$

Consequently, nothing precludes defining the syntactic predicate in (i) as reflexive, in terms of the coindexing between its arguments, and consistent with its interpretation.

36. Note that from this perspective, *zich* is a marker of reflexivity only in a very special sense. It witnesses that a reflexivization operation has taken place, but, as discussed above, it does not itself reflexivize a predicate.

37. Again the fact that they are in some sense dependent on their antecedents can be syntactically annotated by coindexing, allowing one to define a syntactic notion of reflexivity if useful.

38. As Alexis Dimitriadis (personal communication) points out, the selection may in fact depend on more than just the verb. For instance, *the children gave each other presents* has weak reciprocity, but *the children gave each other measles* has intermediate alternative reciprocity, since each child can get measles only once. Discussion of such facts would lead us beyond the scope of this book. But note that they are in line with the general point I am making.

39. Cole et al. (2008) discuss the anaphor *awake dheen* in *Peranakan Javanese* which has similar properties.

40. Reinhart and Reuland (1991) propose a semantics that differs from the semantics proposed here. They analyze SELF as an identity predicate (identifying x and y: λx. λy. (x=y)). This semantics was also adopted in Reuland 2001b. The semantics to be developed here has a number of advantages, notably the fact that it naturally accounts for the range of available proxy readings. However, none of the syntactic arguments is affected by this change.

41. The idea that SELF is a relational noun is originally due to Pica (1987, 1991).

42. I use the term LF for the representations that result from applying all and only the syntactic operations, including covert movement (i.e., movement after spell-out), feature movement, agreement operations, and so on, but no operations that would violate inclusiveness, such as translating pronominal elements into variables. The variables in the structure are part of the lexical grid of—predicative—lexical items that are inserted. LFs are thus syntactic representations. It is an empirical issue whether there is covert movement. It may well be the case that patterns that some of the literature captures in terns of covert movement, and other "LF-operations," for one part reduce to relations that can be expressed by feature movement and/or agree as discussed, and for another part to nonsyntactic interpretive mechanisms (see, for instance, Reinhart 2006 for discussion). If covert movement does not exist, LF by definition coincides with the structure that is handed over to both the PF and CI interfaces. Note that once more that LF is to be distinguished from *logical syntax*.

43. For current purposes it is irrelevant to what extent these conditions can be further reduced.

44. See Partee, Ter Meulen, and Wall 1993 for more discussion and illustration of skolem functions.

45. It would lead us too far to discuss the general ideas and merits of Jacobson's approach. Informally the Z-function expresses a binding requirement in the following way. Consider *John loves his mother*. Under the bound reading this is equivalent to the relation between John and the function that, once applied to John, delivers John's mother as a value. More formally, *John Z-loves f_{mother}* yields *John loves f_{mother} (John)*, which yields in turn that John loves John's mother. *John loves himself* is then equivalent to *John Z-loves f_{SELF}*, which in turn is interpreted as John loves the value of the SELF function applied to John.

46. See section 6.5.3.3.1 for further discussion of the facts.

47. Coming back to the discussion of the French clitics *se*, *Jean se lave* does allow a "proxy reading" for the object. See note 59 for further information. From the present perspective, this indicates that the relation between *Jean* and *se* is not that of an A-chain (see note 22).

48. See Reinhart 1998. To avoid issues of terminology, nothing hinges on the term movement. It suffices that we have a dependency that is subject to the same constraints that obtain in dislocation-type dependencies.

49. This is what puts limits on the explanatory potential of too coarsely grained analyses, be they formulated in GB-style coindexing terms, general discourse properties, or statistical patterns.

50. Note that to say that *a* has undergone *covert movement* to a position *b* expresses nothing more than that *a* is interpreted as if it is in the position *b*, and that, moreover, the path between *a* and *b* obeys standard conditions on movement paths.

51. Putting aside here the more complex cases such as non-intersective adjectives.

52. Note, that this −Ref property is to be distinguished from the −R property that characterizes SE anaphors and reflexives as such, although in the case of reflexives I seek to reduce their −R property to the −Ref property. As Ekkerhard König and Volker Gast (personal communication) pointed out, my use of the term *referentiality* in this connection is rather loose. So, perhaps ±Ref is better understood as the ability to project an independent argument. Nevertheless, since all terminological alternatives seem quite cumbersome, I propose to retain the abbreviation ±Ref.

53. With many thanks to Martin Everaert for making me think about this option during a LOT summer course we taught together a couple of years ago.

54. As pointed out by Alexis Dimitriadis (personal communication).

55. The following facts provide independent reasons for a binding obligation in the case of IP. Passivized IP's are quite awkward, as the sample in (i) illustrates:

(i) a. John sprained his ankle *→ his ankle was sprained by John
 b. John twisted his ankle *→ his ankle was twisted by John (-IP OK)
 c. John raised his eyebrows *→ his eyebrows were raised by John
 d. John proffered his hand *→ his hand was proffered by John (-IP OK)

This pattern can be understood as follows. Binding requires c-command. *John* does not c-command *his*, making binding impossible. But the alternative construal on the basis of coreference that is available in non-IP construction is unavailable, precisely because IP requires binding. Hence, there is no solution that meets all requirements and ungrammaticality ensues.

This restriction is not limited to English. Dutch, which allows impersonal passives with unergative 1-place predicates (*er werd gedanst* 'there was danced') is as restrictive as English in the case of IP constructions:

(ii) a. ??Zijn hand werd door Jan   uitgestoken.
       his hand was by   John extended
 b. *Zijn enkel werd door Jan   verdraaid.
       his ankle was by   John twisted
 c. *Zijn ogen werden door Jan   uitgestoken.
       his eyes were by   John put-out

56. I realize that such a use of the notion of referentiality glosses over a number of problems. I assume that for present purposes the intuition is clear enough.

57. Although some caution is in order since TS is conceived as a theory of operations on verbal concepts.

58. For instance, in cases where the self is purely mental or figurative the form *su mes* must be used. In cases that are purely "corporeal" the form *su kurpa* is obligatory, whereas other verbs admit both.

59. I am very grateful to Anne Zribi-Hertz (personal communication) for bringing up the issues discussed in this note. She provides the following French translations for the examples in (81):

(81′) [Tournant les yeux vers un miroir, Marie sursaute car:]
   Looking into a mirror, Marie is startled when
   a. Elle s'aperçoit debout dans la pénombre.
      'She sees herself standing in the shadows.'
   b. Elle s'aperçoit elle-même debout dans la pénombre.
      'She sees herSELF standing in the shadows.'

As she observes (examples renumbered), "In (81′a) we have a simplex SE-V form,
and in (81′b) SE is doubled by a MEME strong pronoun, which triggers an intensive reading ('centrality' effect, in König's sense). But I also have similar intuitions
wrt. the 'identity' relation as those described by ER for Dutch: in (81′a) my first
interpretation would be 'real Marie', whereas in (81′b) my first interpretation
would be 'statue Marie'. [Upon second thought, however, I would say that both
examples allow both readings.] I think I actually have the same intuitions wrt.
English (81″) (same context).

(81″) a. She saw herself standing in the shadow!
      b. She saw herSELF standing in the shadow!

Here too my spontaneous readings would be real-Mary in (a) and statue-Mary in
(b), although upon second thought (and provided an adequate discourse context
justifying focus structure) both readings seem available in both examples."

   It seems to me that these observations are in line with the main thrust of
the analysis I am proposing. That the statue-reading is not the only reading of the
complex reflexive follows from the analysis in the main text: being able to stand
proxy for has identity as a limiting case. That French and English are more liberal
than Dutch is in its interpretation of the SE anaphor, follows from the fact that
neither the clitic *se*, nor the anaphor *herself*, has the syntactic status of a SE anaphor. In the latter case this is obvious; for the analysis of *se*, see Reinhart and
Siloni 2005, Siloni 2008, and Marelj and Reuland 2010. Crucial is that, unlike
zich, *se* need not enter an A-chain with an antecedent.

   As Zribi-Hertz further notes, "In both French (81′) and English (81″) the
'bodypart' analysis which is considered for 'zelf' by ER is clearly unavailable
since neither F *même* nor focal stress may reasonably be analysed as bodyparts.
So the parallel intuitions wrt. the 'identity' relation in (81), (81′) and (81″) might
be evidence against the assumption that the 'identity' contrast between (81a) and
(81b) in Dutch are due to the bodypart nature of 'zelf'."

   This is an important remark, and I am quoting it in full since it enables me to
stress some crucial points. First of all, according to (38) the minimal requirement
on the protecting element is that it yields an f(x) that can stand proxy for x. As
long as focal stress and *même* can do that, the conditions of (38) are met, and the
possibility of a statue reading follows. Second, strange as this prima facie may
seem, it is conceivable that the BP strategy successfully applies to an element that
is not a body part. In fact, the empirical question is whether it is an identity statement in the meaning of SELF, or other intensifying elements based on identity

statements (*même*, *sam*), that is crucially involved, or whether just having a relational character is sufficient (assuming that bleaching the meaning of body-part expressions essentially reduces them to being relational).

60. Bergeton (2004) argues against a possible connection between SELF anaphors and distributivity, saying that "the sentence in (91b) [=(i) EJR] clearly falsifies the claim that the complex reflexive *sig selv* must have a distributive reading, thus refuting the alleged direct link between distributivity and intensification of reflexives:

(i) Soldaterne forsvarede sig   selv, men overladte civil befolkningen til
    soldiers-the defended   REFL self but left   civil population   to
    fjenden.
    enemy-the
    'The soldiers defended themselves but left the civilians to the enemy.'"

I fail to see the argument here. Note that the type of sentence is ill-suited to base any argument on since there is no well-formedness judgment involved. Apparently Bergeton feels that a "collective interpretation" of the elided DP in the second conjunct blocks a "distributive interpretation" of *the soldiers* in the first conjunct. However, there is no reason to expect this to be true, especially since SELF operates on the predicate. Thus, in general, there is nothing wrong with structures as in (ii) or vice versa as shown in (iii):

(ii) [DP λx ((x P_{distr} . . .))] Con [(DP) λx ((x P_{Coll} . . .))]

(iii) The three men had hurt themselves but lifted five pianos.

61. This line may well answer an issue raised by Anne Zribi-Hertz (personal communication). She feels that inalienable possession and locality restrictions are quite independent from each other, especially in so far as inalienable possession is an ingredient of metonymy. The analysis here focuses on formal conditions that may be met by some, but not necessarily by all IP constructions. In fact, if the last section is on the right track we have formal operations that kick in whenever their conditions for applying are met. The formal operations themselves are simply ingredients of the computational system. When they kick in is determined by general economy conditions.

62. This is illustrated in (i), from Toldova 1996:

(i) Rasulu-k'le žu-k'le-ža-r   wuž   Glaže.
    Rasul-AFF   self-AFF-EMPH-H self-NOM sees

Here, *žu-k'le-ža-r wuž* is a complex reflexive of which the first part *žu-k'le-ža-r* agrees in Case (AFF) with the antecedent *Rasulu-k'le*, and the second part *wuž* carries the local Case (NOM). The spelling and glosses are as given by Toldova.

63. This is independent of the fact that reciprocal interpretation may involve other instances of chain formation, as in the case of *long distance reciprocals* such as *The boys think that they like each other*=[each boy$_j$]$_i$ thinks that he$_i$ likes the other boys$_j$. See Dimitriadis 2000 for discussion.

64. Note, that replacing the anaphor by a pronominal only rescues the sentence under a collective interpretation, since otherwise a condition B violation ensues.

65. Whereas Dutch argument PPs instantiate a typical case of masking, in Dutch ECM one sees the opposite. Veraart (1996) shows that in Dutch ECM constructions additional factors may yield a preference for either *zich* or *zichzelf*. This is not surprising. Condition B entails that *zich* is allowed. However, as discussed in chapter 3, if *zich* is allowed only economy bars *zichzelf*. So we expect to find *zichzelf* in such environments if for some other reason *zich* is dispreferred. For instance, *zich* cannot bear stress, as we have seen. Consequently, in any construction where contrastive stress is assigned we expect to find *zichzelf*. This is what Veraart's discussion shows.

66. Peter Austin (2001), who studied the language, reports that regrettably, the last fluent speaker of the language died in 1986.

67. The same applies to Levinson's discussion of Chamorro. Chung (1989) provides a rather detailed and insightful analysis of Chamorro. Levinson dismisses Chung's analysis on the basis of a superficial assessment. For reasons of space I will have to postpone a discussion of Chamorro anaphora until another occasion.

Chapter 7

1. It is conceivable that in the end, covert adjunction will have to be reanalyzed as a result of interpretation working in tandem with Merge—interpretive Merge (IM) as discussed in chapter 2. However, at this point I see no way to implement this in such a manner that the results from the movement analysis are preserved. I will not attempt to pursue this here.

2. If verb movement leaves a verb copy downstairs, it appears that there is no way to avoid applying the definition of syntactic predicate to this copy, with the incorrect empirical results.

3. This could raise a further question about the nature of SELF movement—that is, why the derived position of the SELF anaphor is spelled-out, and the "derived position" of SELF is not. This touches on issues concerning the nature of covert movement, specifically the covert movement of SELF, that would lead me beyond the scope of this book. This issue would be resolved if, as suggested above, covert movement reflects a process of semantic interpretation taking place in tandem with Merge.

4. Note that the question of whether transitivity is marked by a separate head, in the form of v^* is orthogonal to current debates concerning the relation between conceptual and lexical-syntactic structure. Roughly sketched, distributive morphology (DM; see Halle and Marantz 1993, Marantz 1997, and Borer 2003) contends that conceptual structure—the encyclopedia—is entirely independent of the lexicosyntactic encoding. Little *n*, *v*, *a*, is what makes a concept a noun, verb, or adjective; the functional head v^* is what makes a verbal projection transitive. Siloni (2002) and Vinokurova (2005) show that there are many problems with this view. Being a basic verb, a basic noun, a basic adjective, are properties inherent in the concept. As we will see in the next section, Reinhart (2002) and subsequent literature show that properties such as being transitive, being able to license accusative Case, and so on can be read off the conceptual structure, hence are

not induced by syntactically adding a v*, etc. In this theory, θ-roles are encoded as feature clusters. Certain combinations of feature clusters cause a verb to be marked as an accusative Case assigner, or require an argument to be merged externally. The theory does not make explicit how *being able to license ACC*, or *being linked to an external argument*, is syntactically represented. This is what I wish to do here. The text proposal represents the position that externality may be configurationally represented, as for instance in English. If a verbal concept is such that one of its roles must be realized on an external argument, syntax may do so, by projecting a v*. If a verbal concept is such that its internal argument receives ACC, this can be syntactically realized as a property of the v*. Essentially, this allows us to adopt certain specific proposals as they have been developed in the context of the Minimalist Program and DM, without adopting DM's particular view on the interface with the conceptual system.

5. The experimental methods they used include magnitude estimation and eye-tracking. See the sources cited for description of the experiments.

6. Or dependent on P for Case and θ, to use a more neutral formulation.

7. Higginbotham (1983) argues that the POSS phrase in DPs does not bear a θ-role assigned by the head noun—which in many instances would require raising—but rather an R-role associated with the possessive morphology. This R-role represents a general aboutness relation, which can, but need not, be interpreted as one of the unsaturated θ-roles of the head noun (unless there is an obligation to do so intrinsically to the semantics, as in the case of SELF discussed above). This process is not syntactic. Furthermore, NPs do not have expletive POSS phrases as would be expected if there were some last-resort requirement for a "subject" position to be filled.

If the POSS phrase does not receive its θ-role from the N, not even by a raising mechanism, it does not qualify as an argument of N, nor as a subject in whatever sense. Note that complex event nominals do not carry a subject requirement (Grimshaw 1990). From the present perspective this can mean that they never carry an e-role the way verbs do (but see Larson 1995), or that they always allow a construal as lacking an e-role. Suppose we assume the latter. If so, they are in principle ambiguous. The uncertainty we find reported in the literature could then stem from an indeterminacy as to how to construe the POSS phrase: (i) as not receiving its θ-role from the grid of the head noun, reflecting a construal without an e-role, or (ii) receiving its θ-role from the grid of the head noun as its subject, in which it reflects the presence of an e-role in the N, the N heads a syntactic predicate, and a local binding requirement ensues. More research is needed in order to sort out the possible interdependencies. See also the facts reported by Runner (2007), discussed in the next note.

8. Runner (2007) also discusses the following pattern:

(i) a. !/?Jill found Matt's article about herself.
     b. !/?Martina looked for Michael's book about herself.
     c. !/?Marissa hates Brandon's picture of herself.

(ii) a. *Jill found Matt's fear of herself surprising.
     b. *Joanna was irritated by Mark's pride in herself.

As Runner observes, the type of nominal easily allowing nonlocal binding of *himself* corresponds to what Davies and Dubinsky (2003) classify as concrete nominals, lacking an e-role. The same contrast shows up in the difference in binding potential between the two readings in (iii):

(iii) a. !/?Joe$_i$ destroyed Harry's book about himself$_i$ (concrete)
      b. ?/*Joe$_i$ wrote Harry's book about himself$_i$ (result)
          'Joe wrote the book about himself that Harry owns.'

This is further evidence that it is indeed the presence or absense of an e-role in the noun that determines whether or not its POSS phrase qualifies as a real subject and SELF is attracted, in accordance with (14'). This ties in with a question raised by Ken Safir (personal communication). Safir observes that there is a contrast between (iva) and (ivb):

(iv) a. *The destruction of herself would bother Mary.
     b. The destruction of her character would bother Mary.

(iva) is "not possible even under the most favourable discourse conditions," but (ivb) is entirely fine. *Destruction* in (iva) is clearly eventive. Along the lines discussed in the text, either the e-role is sufficient by itself to create a syntactic predicate, or it entails the presence of a subject (PRO). PRO is either arbitrary, hence incompatible with a reflexive interpretation, or controlled by Mary. In the latter case the sentence is pragmatically odd, given conflicting presuppositions on whether Mary has control over what is happening to her. That (ivb) is fine follows from the fact that coreference is freely available, and the presence of an e-role in *destruction* is irrelevant. Ken Safir (personal communication) also brings up the following contrast:

(v) a. John's investigation of himself lasted three weeks, after which he said he was exonerated.
    b. Cheney claimed that the ongoing investigation of himself would damage the party.

Safir suspects that (b) is less acceptable for most speakers, unless Cheney is talking about an investigation that he has undertaken of himself, suggesting a controlled subject.

9. It is interesting to note that in Dutch ECM predicates—which are limited to causative and perception verbs—do favor a SELF anaphor in the case of direct perception. It is reasonable to assume that in such cases the ECM subject has undergone raising (scrambling) into the matrix clause.

10. This so-called personal dative (PD) has been discussed by Webelhuth and Dannenberg (2006) and Conroy (2007). As they note, its use is widespread in Appalachian English and Southern American English and is not limited to 1st and 2nd person (*she$_i$ got her$_i$ a pair of shoes*). Conroy shows that there are important differences between the regular reflexive and the PD. For example, one has (i), but not (ii):

(i) She$_i$ loves her$_i$ some beans

(ii) *She$_i$ loves herself$_i$ some beans

Furthermore, the PD cannot be passivized and does not imply transfer of possession. The impossibility to passivize indicates that there is no structural Case relation between PD and the verb. This entails that there is no chain, hence no chain violation. The contrast between (i) and (ii) indicates that the PD is not a thematic argument of the predicate, hence no reflexive predicate is formed and no licensing needed. Consequently the parameter involved in the variation is independent of binding theory. What is at stake in whether a dialect allows the PD is whether an argument in the position of the PD can be licensed within the inherent Case system.

11. Note that as already discussed in Reuland 1983, the *-ing* affix may also be used to form a present participle, which can be employed as an adjectival modifier. This use shows up in perception verb complements, enabling a simple small-clause construction. Thus a sentence such as (ia) has the structure in (ib), which allows a passive as in (ic), on the same footing as the passive in (id):

(i) a. I saw George leaving the building.
    b. I saw [SC George [AP leaving the building]]
    c. George was seen [SC George [AP leaving the building]]
    d. George was seen [SC George [AP drunk]]

12. Search conducted October 8, 2006, 9 p.m., schema "pron * pron having to."

13. 1st-person singular and plural abound. For some reason, 3rd-person plural is very rare. For 3rd-person singular, examples with a PP were more frequent:

(i) He complained about him having to take a dump.

(ii) He blamed me for him having to make several trips to the ATM.

14. Google searches of structures like *we behaved us* give surprisingly few results. Interestingly, ECM structures show more instances of locally bound personal pronouns. This would follow if the same licensing strategy that is available for the personal datives is also marginally available in ECM, somewhat along the lines that must be the case in Frisian (see the next chapter).

15. See also Rákosi 2007 for an interesting analysis of subject anaphors in Hungarian. The simplex anaphor *maga* cannot be a subject; the complex *önmaga* can.

16. For this I can offer no explanation. A more extensive investigation of logophoric use of anaphoric forms would be required. For now I can only speculate that it could be related to the POSS structure of the expression, or to specific lexical properties of the head noun.

17. Amiridze adds the observation that the class of verbs allowing subject reflexives not only includes object experiencer verbs, but also transitive verbs with an affected theme argument. She notes further that the reciprocal *ertmanet* also occurs in subject position. Although prima facie this may seem puzzling, since *ertmanet* seems to give rise to a fairly straightforward reciprocal interpretation, and not a "properties of" interpretation, this is less puzzling than it may seem, since as discussed in chapter 6 a reciprocal canonically involves an f(x) interpretation (informally: pick out another individual from the set than the one under consideration).

18. What does follow from the mechanisms underlying binding, is that subject anaphors will be interpreted in special ways, as in Modern Greek and Georgian. In this respect the situation with subject anaphors is much like that with exempt anaphors in English: syntax says that a particular process cannot apply; if so the interpretive system takes over and assigns the interpretation it can. Thus, one may expect to find idiosyncrasies based on lexical differences, as for instance in the presence or absence of a *properties of* reading.

19. In (i)—a "nurselike" *we* sentence—the pronominal part of the SELF anaphor agrees in number with the syntactic antecedent; the *self* part agrees according to sense:

(i) We seem a bit displeased with ourself/*ourselves/*yourself, don't we?

Chapter 8

1. In this, my approach differs from Safir 2004a, where blocking always requires comparison with a possible derivation. See the discussion in chapter 4.

2. This characterization is what one finds as a common denominator in more traditional literature. The free dative is also called *indirect dative*. Traditional grammar distinguishes a number of subtypes, such as *ethical dative, possessive dative,* or *dativus commodi* and *incommodi* for objects undergoing beneficial versus harmful effects. However, for present purposes what is relevant is that they all share the indirect relation with the predicate.

3. The text difference is the only difference needed. As discussed in section 6.3.1, the marking procedure for lexical entries delivers verbs marked with the ACC feature. In Dutch, a residual ACC feature must be checked by an "expletive" pronominal element (*zich*). In this respect, Frisian is taken to be just like Dutch. In Frisian, the ACC feature is checked by the pronominal *him*. The only respect in which Frisian is stipulated to be different is in the way this ACC relates to the T-system. Just as a preposition has a Case that can be checked by an element that does not bear uninterpretable Tense, so V's ACC can be checked by such an element. All further properties follow.

4. It is important to note that being weak or strong in the classification of Cardinaletti and Starke (1996) has no bearing on this.

5. So, the loss of the SE anaphor in the early stages of Old English is expected to be related to changes in the Case system. Eighteenth-century Frisian provides a slightly different instantiation of this mechanism. Historical sources show that with the spread of *sich/zich* over the territory of the Netherlands, it also reached Frisia. However, unlike what happened in Dutch, in Frisian it did not catch on, disappearing from the language in later sources. This is a puzzle for any economy based analysis—such as Safir 2004b—that limits economy considerations to the feature composition of individual forms. However, it immediately follows from an analysis like the present one in which economy involves the interaction between feature composition and environment. In the absence of structural case in the relevant position, there is no economy advantage of SE over the pronominal, hence no reason for it to be adopted into the language. I thank Arjen Versloot

(personal communication) of the Fryske Akademy for bringing this fact to my attention.

6. I am grateful to Martin Everaert, Hans den Besten, and Jan Koster for bringing these facts, and the significance of the stress patterns, to my attention.

7. A reviewer of Reuland and Reinhart 1995 remarked that stressed *sich* in locative PPs is not always bad. For instance, in (i) it is completely well formed:

(i) Hinter/Neben wen   hat er das Buch gelegt? Hinter/Neben SICH.
    behind/next-to whom has he the book put   behind/next-to himself

This in fact supports the parallelism between Dutch *zichzelf* and stressed *sich*, since the Dutch equivalent of (i) allows *zichzelf*, but not *zich*.

8. Unlike Italian, French allows bundling with verbs such as *hair* 'hate' without problems. A simple google search gives a great many instances of *on se hait, il se hait*, etc. Also recall the fact that French *se* allows proxy readings, see chapter 6, notes 22, 47, and 59. Note, furthermore, that French allows an object reflexive together with the clitic, as in *il se hait lui-même*. The facts follow if the clitic in fact goes with a null object in cases where it appears to occur alone.

9. One exception being a form of *cyssan* "kiss," with a plural subject and an object pronominal in a reciprocal interpretation. Since Frisian, like Dutch, lacks lexical reciprocalization this fact reduces to an independent property.

10. Note that the question is in fact not so much whether we would find a SELF anaphor in such environments, but whether or not OE would employ other resources (for instance, modifiers) in order to license reflexivity with such predicates.

11. This entails that easy explanations are not guaranteed. For instance, Heinat (2005) argues that Swedish allows simplex anaphors in a much wider variety of contexts than Danish or Norwegian. The pattern he sketches is reminiscent of that found in German. Schadler (2009) presents a detailed study of the relevant environments in Swedish, and shows that in coargument cases it in fact patterns like Norwegian (with some idiomatic lexical differences). The main difference is in PPs, for which she presents an independent explanation.

12. This section presents an approach to long distance binding in Germanic whose outlines were earlier discussed in Reuland 2005e. That text in turn was an elaboration of a section in Reinhart and Reuland 1991. I would like to thank Patrick Brandt, Martin Everaert, and two anonymous reviewers for their very helpful comments on that version. The usual disclaimers apply.

13. One of the earliest GB accounts of the contrast between local and long-distance binding is Giorgi 1984, which is mainly based on Italian.

14. I will put aside reciprocals, since their analysis does not contribute to the main issues to be discussed.

15. The subscript *0* indicates that the pronominal is free.

16. As pointed out by Halldór Sigurðsson (personal communication), there are also Icelandic speakers who accept logophoric reflexives in indicative environments provided the indicative can be interpreted as having perspective semantics. This suggests the same approach as given here for Faroese.

17. Nonlocal antecedents of *selbst*-forms are illustrated in (i) and (ii), provided by an anonymous reviewer:

(i) Ich möchte nicht dass Hans für jemand anderen arbeitet. *Ich möchte dass er für mich selbst* arbeitet.
'I do not want John to work for somebody else. I want him to work for myself.'

(ii) Hans will nicht, dass ich für jemand anders arbeite. Deshalb lässt er mich nur für sich selbst arbeiten.
'Hans does not want me to work for somebody else. Therefore he lets me work only for himself.'

Note that in these cases the *selbst*-form is heavily focused. For an explanation of the role of focus in exemption, see R&R and section 6.3.3. As the reviewer points out, *selbst* combines with 3rd-person pronouns as well, but there is no reason to treat such forms as anaphors.

18. See, among others, Everaert 1986, Reis 1976, and Gunkel 2003 for discussion of the German facts. I would like to thank Patrick Brandt (personal communication) for help with the data.

19. Some speakers marginally allow this reading, however. An anonymous reviewer points out that there is one type of exception to this locality pattern. It involves ECM constructions in which the embedded verb is nonagentive, as illustrated in (i):

(i) a. ?Hans$_1$ sah sich$_1$/*ihm$_1$ den Gegner   unterliegen
       Hans saw SE/him$_{DAT}$ the opponent$_{ACC}$ underlie
       'Hans saw that the opponent was being defeated by him.'
    b. Sie$_1$ liess sich$_1$/*ihr$_1$ die Sonne ins   Gesicht scheinen
       she let SE/her   the sun   in-the face   shine
       'She let the sun shine in her face.'

As the reviewer notes, there is extensive discussion of these data in the literature with disagreement on their grammaticality (see among others Reis 1976; Grewendorf 1983, 1989; and Gunkel 2003).

20. Gunkel (2003) attributes the difference to the semantic status of the prepositions involved. Notice, however, that some further factors may have to be controlled for in order to obtain the full picture. Patrick Brandt (personal communication) reports that if *nur ungern* is omitted from (63a) the contrast gets much sharper as in (i), and similarly if one has the DP-PP order as in (ii):

(i) Karl$_i$ liess uns über *sich$_i$/ihn$_i$ schimpfen
    Karl let us at   SE/him   scold
    'Karl let us scold him.'

(ii) Karl$_i$ liess mich ein Päckchen zu ??sich$_i$/zu ihm$_i$ schicken
     Karl let me   a   package to SE/him   send
     'Karl let me send a package to him.'

Further research will hopefully shed more light on these contrasts.

21. I am very much indebted to Sten Vikner (personal communication) and Beatrice Santorini (personal communication) for their help in clarifying the status of Yiddish.

22. With Borer 1989, one may assume that both infinitival and finite INFL are associated with AGR, which is anaphoric in the former case. Anaphoric AGR bears φ-features just like finite AGR, hence, it is equally suitable as a "host" supplying these features to the SE anaphor. To allow subjects of small clauses as antecedents of SE anaphors we have to assume that small clauses carry AGR too. Much of the current literature makes this assumption, although direct empirical arguments like those for anaphoric AGR in infinitival clauses are lacking.

23. It is interesting to note, that this family of movement approaches is already closer to the minimalist conception of binding, even if in their implementation most use indices.

24. Note that in this analysis SE movement is an instantiation of canonical head-movement. Although it may be tempting to equate SE movement with clitic movement of some sort, clitic movement seems to be freer (see Kayne 1990 for discussion), and, may well be a different phenomenon. (It certainly involves different conditions, also witness the fact that languages may have SE anaphors without having true clitics.)

25. This has no effect on the verb's interpretation, since SE is neither a reflexivizer, nor a clitic which satisfies a grid position lexically; it just leaves the relevant thematic position unsaturated until it is bound.

26. For the sake of consistency I am replacing their I by T.

27. As noted by an anonymous reviewer, another problem appears to be posed by the fact that at least German CP-infinitives (zu-infinitives) need not be extraposed. Yet, also in these structures long binding from outside the zu-infinitive is prohibited, as illustrated in (i):

(i) dass Hans$_i$ uns$_j$ [$_{CP}$ PRO$_j$ ihm$_i$/*sich$_i$ ein Buch mitzubringen] bat
    that Hans us   him   a   book bring   asked

A reasonable assumption is that the CP in (i) is not in its position of first merge, but rather moved there from a position as the complement of bat.

28. If a SE anaphor does not need to acquire φ-features in order to be interpreted, one may wonder why the subject DP does not simply end up binding the downstairs SE anaphor, irrespective of the fact that no chain can be formed. It follows from the discussion on economy in chapter 5 that this is impossible. The interpretive system cannot license an outcome that a fundamental syntactic principle prevents.

29. I will refrain from discussing Yiddish here, since analyses in sufficient depth are not yet available.

30. Landau develops a theory of control that is based on Agree relations between light v (for object control) or T (for subject control) in the matrix clause with C or T in the complement clause, leading to valuing PRO. (See also Teomiro García 2005.) Targeting T results in exhaustive control; if C is targeted, the effect is partial control. It would be an important undertaking to integrate Landau's

approach to control with the present proposals for the syntactic encoding of non-local binding. Doing so will have to wait for another occasion, though.

31. The notion of order may be a way to resolve the issue of how extensive the C-system in the left periphery is (Rizzi 1997 and subsequent work versus Chomsky 2004 and 2008). It seems natural to assume that configurationally all unordered functional heads in a domain collapse into one position.

32. It is important to see that the impossibility of chain extension only blocks types of dependencies that are formed by morphosyntactic feature sharing. There are Tense dependencies, including Sequence of Tense phenomena, in OV languages just as there are in VO languages. However these are not affected, just like variable binding is not affected.

33. Except in some idioms, such as *op zich is dit waar* 'as such this is true'.

34. One may wonder what this entails for SE anaphors in real adjuncts, as in *John lives in Fryslân*. Since real adjuncts do not allow pronouns, or, alternatively, have their own pronominal paradigm, the issue does not arise. Witness the impossibility of (i) and (ii) under that type of construal:

(i) *John lives in it. (where *it* = *Fryslân*)

(ii) *John woont erin. (where *er* = *Fryslân*)

35. Material in the next section was published in Reuland and Sigurjónsdóttir 1997 and in Reuland 2005d. I am very grateful to Sigríður Sigurjónsdóttir for the work we were able to do together, and to Halldór Sigurðsson, Sigríður Sigurjónsdóttir, and an anonymous reviewer for their helpful comments on the 2005 version.

36. See also Thráinsson 1979, 1990, 1991; Maling 1984, 1986; Anderson 1986; Rögnvaldsson 1986; Sells 1987; Sigurðsson 1990; Sigurjónsdóttir 1992; among others.

37. One may abstract away from the two different verb classes which have different effects on the interpretation of *sig*. With one class of verbs, like the verb *raka* "shave" exemplified in (1), *sig* can take either a local or a long distance antecedent in the infinitive and subjunctive domain, whereas with the other class of verbs, *sig* can only refer to the long distance antecedent. These facts will not be discussed since the class of verbs only affects the interpretation of *sig* in the local domain which is not the domain that concerns us here. These lexical effects in Icelandic (first noted by Thráinsson) are described by Hyams and Sigurjónsdóttir (1990), Sigurjónsdóttir (1992), and Sigurjónsdóttir and Hyams (1992). Similar lexical effects have been discussed by Everaert (1986) and Reinhart and Reuland (1989, 1991, 1993) for Dutch and by Hellan (1988) for Norwegian.

38. Anderson (1986, 76) gives the following definition of an anaphoric domain: "The ANAPHORIC DOMAIN of A is the minimal S or NP containing A, a governor of A, and a subject of either tensed S or NP which c-commands A."

39. Anderson's proposal accounts for the fact that in embedded infinitives in Icelandic, *sig*, but (normally) not the pronouns, can take the matrix subject as its antecedent, whereas both *sig* and the pronouns can refer to the matrix subject in subjunctives. The obligatoriness of *sig* in this domain in infinitives follows from

Anderson's analysis since an infinitive and its matrix clause always constitute an anaphoric domain. The rule of Tense-Agreement, on the other hand, optionally applies to the subjunctive clause, and hence either an anaphoric domain is established and *sig* refers to the matrix subject or there is no anaphoric domain in which case a pronoun is used to refer to the long-distance antecedent. An alternative analysis for these facts is proposed in Sigurjónsdóttir (1992).

40. See also, Manzini and Wexler 1987, Johnson 1984, Koster 1984, and Yang 1984.

41. See also Lebeaux 1983, 1985, and Chomsky 1986b.

42. Note that *sig* in Icelandic cannot license agreement (see Everaert 1990 and the discussion in section 5.8.2). Hence, *sig* can occur in subject position only with those verbs that have a nonnominative "subject" (i.e., with the so-called quirky case verbs in Icelandic). The verb *vanta* 'to lack, need' that appears in example (90a) is one of these verbs and takes an accusative subject. Quirky subjects in Icelandic have been discussed in a number of publications; see, for example, Andrews 1976; Thráinsson 1979; Bernódusson 1982; Zaenen, Maling, and Thráinsson 1985; and Sigurðsson 1989, 1992.

43. Note that there are two DPs in this sentence whose perspective or point of view are being reported (i.e., *Jón* and *Björn*). Hence, *sig* could also take *Björn* as its antecedent.

44. Objects are generally not the perspective holding DP of a sentence, and hence, they do rarely qualify as antecedents for the logophor *sig* (see Sigurðsson 1990, 334).

45. As observed by Sigurðsson (1990, note 22), the exceptions to this generalization show that the passive as such does not block long distance coreference of *sig*. Thus, as illustrated in (i), the derived subject of a passive (*honum* 'him' in this case) can serve as an antecedent for *sig* in subjunctives, given that it carries the perspective or point of view of the sentence. As pointed out by Sigurðsson: "made x to believe" implies "x believes."

(i) Honum$_{i\ (dat.)}$ var talin trú   um   [að   sig$_{i\ (acc.)}$ vantaði$_{(subj.)}$ hæfileika]
    him   was made belief about   that SIG   lacked   talents
    'He was made to believe that he lacked talents.' (cf. Maling 1984, note 28)

46. As Halldór Sigurðsson (personal communication) points out, under the copy theory of movement some of the infinitival cases discussed here fall under a clause-internal scenario. For the argument it suffices that moving the envisaged antecedent into the higher clause does not add any possibilities not present in its position of first merge.
    He also points out that to his ear (i) is only slightly less natural than (90a):

(i) Krafa   Jóns$_i$ til okkar$_j$ um   [að PRO$_j$ styða   sig$_i$ við   þessar
    demand Jon's to us   about to   support SIG under these
    aðstæður]   er skiljanleg
    circumstances is understandable
    'Jon's demand that we support him under these circumstances is understandable.'

Nevertheless, there is a contrast, as we would expect. Note, that the infinitival clause in this case is a complement to the head noun *krafa* 'demand'. Hence it depends on ill-understood details of the internal structure of the DP whether or not *Jóns* c-commands *sig*.

Sigurðsson also notes that the sentences in (ii) are not as good as their counterparts in (95) and (96) (in contrast to what is reported in Reuland and Sigurjónsdóttir 1997):

(ii) a. ??Jón$_i$ sagði [þetta vandamál$_j$ hafa$_{inf}$ neytt okkur$_k$ til [að PRO$_k$ leysa$_{inf}$ sig$_j$]]
   Jon said this problem have forced us to to solve
   SIG
   'Jon said this problem has forced us to solve it.'

   b. ??Þetta vandamál$_j$ var sagt [t$_j$ hafa$_{(inf.)}$ neytt okkur$_k$ til [að PRO$_k$ leysa$_{inf}$ sig$_j$]]
   this problem was said have forced us to to solve
   SIG
   'This problem was said to have forced us to solve it.'

The sentences in (iii) are perfect, however:

(iii) a. Jón sagði [þetta vandamál$_i$ hafa minnt á sig$_i$]
    Jon said this problem have reminded of SIG
   b. Þetta vandamál$_i$ var sagt [t$_i$ hafa minnt á sig$_i$]
    this problem was said have reminded of SIG

Although (95) and (96) suffice to prove the main point in the argumentation, one may wonder what causes the contrast between (ii) and (iii). One possibility is that there is an independent difference in lexical semantics between *remind* and *force*, making the latter less easily compatible with an inanimate subject. Alternatively, it could be the case that LD-bound *sig* favors an animate antecedent. I will tentatively go for the first possibility—keeping in mind the option that the contrast has a deeper cause.

47. I am making the standard assumption here that in (97b) *hótaði* is first merged with its theme object *Jón*. Subsequently, the subordinate clause is merged.

48. These and other nonattributed examples are from Reuland and Sigurjónsdóttir (1997).

49. Recall that even in these cases appearances are deceptive, since binding is only allowed under the reading where *every boy* also scopes over *mother*, which is compatible with an adjunction structure, such that under a definition of c-command that reflects the segment-category distinction *every boy* does c-command *him*.

Chapter 9

1. Reuland 2001b addresses the same issue. There it is argued that the comparison may involve different items if their feature sets are in a subset relation. Thus *hem* and *zich* can be compared since *zich* contains a subset of *hem*'s features.

2. Norbert Hornstein (personal communication) notes that this analysis, indeed, does not extend to *zich*-type anaphors, for which he sees no solution in the system he proposes. From my perspective this is one more indication that the restriction to movement is not warranted.

3. A small comment on note 30 where BHN take issue with the analysis of exempt anaphors in R&R 1993. They discuss (i) (their (68)). Here *himself* is in an exempt/logophoric position, yet the reflexive is obligatory. They argue that this shows that SELF must be able to raise, despite the fact that it is inside a coordinate structure. However, that there is no complementarity is independent of raising, but follows from RR's condition B: one of the instantiations of the *praise* relation is reflexive, which must be licensed.

(i) *John* praised Mary and *himself*.

Note that lexical operations can only affect the status of full syntactic arguments, not selectively one conjunct (e.g., Dutch does not allow SE anaphors in coordinations).

4. Of course, showing that SLQZ and Hmong do indeed have such bundling processes, and how they are restricted, requires a more extensive investigation than has been carried out so far.

5. In fact, Hicks still postulates a structural difference between *zich* and *zichzelf* that is not too different from the structures I am assuming, but decides not to use it (p. 223).

6. This contrasts with the macrocomparison one finds in a typical optimality-theoretic approach such as Fischer 2004, in which the binding conditions are represented in the form of separate stipulations, unconnected to the structure of the grammar.

References

Abels, Klaus. 2003. Successive Cyclicity, Anti-locality, and Adposition Stranding. Doctoral dissertation, University of Connecticut, Storrs.

Abney, Steven. 1987. The English Noun Phrase in Its Sentential Aspect. Doctoral dissertation, MIT.

Aikawa, Takako. 1993. Reflexivity in Japanese and LF-Analysis of Zibun Binding. Doctoral dissertation, Ohio State University.

Amiridze, Nino. 2006. *Reflexivization Strategies in Georgian*. Utrecht: LOT International Dissertation Series.

Amiridze, Nino, and Martin Everaert. 2000. On subject anaphora in Georgian. Paper presented at the tenth Caucasian Colloquium, Munich, August 2–5.

Anagnostopoulou, Elena, and Martin Everaert. 1999. Towards a more complete typology of anaphoric expressions. *Linguistic Inquiry* 30(1), 97–118.

Anand, Pranav, and Andrew Nevins. 2004. Shifty operators in changing contexts. In Robert B. Young, ed., *Proceedings of SALT XIV*. Ithaca, NY: Cornell University, CLC Publications.

Anderson, Stephen. 1986. The typology of anaphoric dependencies: Icelandic (and other) reflexives. In Lars Hellan and Kirsti Koch Christensen, eds., *Topics in Scandinavian Syntax*, 65–88. Dordrecht: Kluwer.

Anderson, Stephen, and Paul Kiparsky, eds. 1973. *A Festschrift for Morris Halle*. New York: Holt, Rinehart and Winston.

Andrews, Avery. 1976. The VP complement analysis in Modern Icelandic. *NELS* 6, 1–21. Amherst: GLSA, University of Massachusetts.

Aoun, Joseph. 1986. *Generalized Binding*. Dordrecht: Foris.

Arbib, Michael A. 2005. From monkey-like action recognition to human language: An evolutionary framework for neurolinguistics. *Behavioral and Brain Sciences* 28, 105–167. Text distributed by BBS for peer commentary.

Ariel, Mira. 1990. *Accessing Noun-Phrase Antecedents*. London: Croom Helm.

Asudeh, Ash, and Frank Keller. 2001. Experimental evidence for a predication-based binding theory. In *Papers from the Thirty-Seventh Meeting of the Chicago Linguistic Society*, 1–14. Chicago: Chicago Linguistic Society.

Austin, Peter. 2001. Word order in a free word order language: The case of Jiwarli. In Jane Simpson, David Nash, Mary Laughren, Peter Austin, and Barry Alpher, eds., *Forty Years On: Ken Hale and Australian Languages*, 205–323. Canberra: Pacific Linguistics.

Avrutin, Sergey. 2006. Weak syntax. In Y. Grodzinsky and K. Amunts, eds., *Broca's Region*, 49–62. Oxford: Oxford University Press.

Avrutin, Sergey, Esther Ruigendijk, and Nada Vasić. 2006. Reference assignment: Using language breakdown to choose between theoretical approaches. *Brain and Language* 96(3), 302–317.

Baauw, Sergio. 2002. *Grammatical Features and the Acquisition of Reference: A Comparative Study of Dutch and Spanish*. New York: Routledge.

Baauw, Sergio, and Denis Delfitto. 1999. Coreference and language acquisition. In Denis Delfitto, Jan Schroten, and Henriëtte de Swart, eds., *Recherches de Linguistique Française et Romane d'Utrecht* (Utrecht Studies in Romance Linguistics) *XVIII*. Utrecht University.

Baddeley, Alan D. 2007. *Working Memory, Thought and Action*. Oxford: Oxford University Press.

Badecker, William, and Kathleen Straub. 2002. The processing role of structural constraints on the interpretation of pronouns and anaphors. *Journal of Experimental Psychology: Learning, Memory, and Cognition* 28, 748–769.

Baerman, Matthew, Dunstan Brown, and Greville Corbett. 2002. *The Surrey Syncretisms Database*. http://www.smg.surrey.ac.uk/syncretism/index.aspx.

Baker, Mark. 1988. *Incorporation: A Theory of Grammatical Function Changing*. Chicago: University of Chicago Press.

Baker, Mark. 1996. *The Polysynthesis Parameter*. Oxford: Oxford University Press.

Baker, Mark. 2001. *The Atoms of Language: The Mind's Hidden Rules of Grammar*. New York: Basic Books.

Baker, Mark. 2003. *Lexical categories: Verbs, nouns, and adjectives*. Cambridge: Cambridge University Press.

Baker, Mark. 2007. *The Syntax of Agreement and Concord*. Cambridge: Cambridge University Press.

Barbiers, Sjef, and Hans Bennis. 2003. Reflexives in dialects of Dutch. In Jan Koster and Henk van Riemsdijk, eds., *Germania et alia: A linguistic Webschrift for Hans den Besten*. http://odur.let.rug.nl/~koster/DenBesten/contents.htm.

Barbiers, Sjef, Hans Bennis, Gunther De Vogelaer, Magda Devos, and Margreet van der Ham. 2005. *Syntactic Atlas of the Dutch Dialects, Volume 1: Pronouns, Agreement and Dependencies*. Amsterdam: Amsterdam University Press.

Barker, Chris, and Chung-Chieh Shan. 2007. Donkey anaphora is simply binding. Ms., draft 2523, Rutgers University, August 6.

Barnes, Michael. 1986. Reflexivisation in Faroese. *Arkiv för Nordisk Filologi* 101, 95–126.

Barss, Andrew. 1986. Chains and Anaphoric Dependence. Doctoral dissertation, MIT.

Battistella, Ed. 1987. Chinese reflexivization. Paper presented at the Second Harbin Conference on Generative Grammar, Heilongjiang University, Harbin, People's Republic of China; ms., University of Alabama at Birmingham.

Belletti, Adriana. 1988. The case of unaccusatives. *Linguistic Inquiry* 19, 1–34.

Benthem, Johan van. 1986. *Essays in Logical Semantics*. Dordrecht: Reidel.

Benveniste, Emile. 1966. *Problèmes de linguistique générale*. Paris: Gallimard.

Bergeton, Uffe. 2004. The Independence of Binding and Intensification. Doctoral dissertation, University of Southern California.

Bernódusson, H. 1982. Opersónulegar setningar. Master's thesis, University of Iceland, Reykjavík.

Bhattacharya, Tanmoy. 1998. DP-internal NP movement. In John Harris and Corinne Iten, eds., *UCL Working Papers in Linguistics 10*. London: University College London.

Bianchi, Valentina. 2000. Finiteness and nominative Case licensing. *Quaderni del Laboratorio di Linguistica 1 (nuova serie)*, 145–168. Pisa: Scuola Normale Superiore.

Bianchi, Valentina. 2001. On finiteness as logophoric anchoring. In Jacqueline Guéron, and Liliane Tasmowski, eds., *Temps et point de vue/Tense and Point of View*, 213–246. Université Paris X—Nanterre.

Bloomfield, Leonard. 1927. A set of postulates for the science of language. *Language* 2, 153–164.

Boeckx, Cedric, Norbert Hornstein, and Jairo Nunes. 2007. Overt copies in reflexive and control structures: A movement analysis. In A. Conroy, C. Jing, C. Nakao, and E. Takahashi, eds., *University of Maryland Working Papers in Linguistics 15*, 1–46. College Park, MD: UMWPiL.

Bonato, Roberto. 2006. An Integrated Computational Approach to Binding Theory. Doctoral dissertation, Università degli Studi di Verona.

Bonet, Eulàlia. 1991. Morphology after Syntax: Pronominal Clitics in Romance. Doctoral dissertation, MIT. Distributed by MITWPL, Department of Linguistics and Philosophy, MIT.

Borer, Hagit. 1989. Anaphoric AGR. In Osvaldo Jaeggli and Kenneth Safir, eds., *The Null Subject Parameter*, 69–109. Dordrecht: Kluwer.

Borer, Hagit. 2003. Exo-skeletal vs. endo-skeletal explanation. In John Moore and Maria Polinsky, eds., *The Nature of Explanation in Linguistic Theory*. Stanford, CA, and Chicago: CSLI Publications and University of Chicago Press.

Borer, Hagit. 2005. *Structuring Sense*. 2 vols. Oxford: Oxford University Press.

Bouchard, Denis. 1984. *On the Content of Empty Categories*. Dordrecht: Foris.

Brody, Michael. 1984. On the complementary distribution of empty categories. Paper presented at GLOW, University College London.

Büring, Daniel. 2005. *Binding Theory*. Cambridge: Cambridge University Press.

Burkhardt, Petra. 2005. *The Syntax-Discourse Interface: Representing and Interpreting Dependency.* Amsterdam/Philadelphia: John Benjamins.

Burzio, Luigi. 1991. The morphological basis of anaphora. *Journal of Linguistics* 27(1), 1–60.

Cable, Seth. 2005. Binding local pronouns without semantically empty features. Ms., Department of Linguistics, MIT.

Cantrall, William. 1974. *Viewpoint, Reflexives and the Nature of Noun Phrases.* The Hague: Mouton.

Cardinaletti, Anna, and Michal Starke. 1996. Deficient pronouns: A view from Germanic. A study in the unified description of Germanic and Romance. In Höskuldur Thráinsson, Samuel Epstein, and Steve Peter, eds., *Studies in Comparative Germanic Syntax*, vol. 2, 21–66. Dordrecht: Kluwer.

Carroll, Lewis (Charles Lutwidge Dodgson). 1865. *Alice's Adventures in Wonderland.* London: Macmillan.

Carroll, Lewis (Charles Lutwidge Dodgson). 1872. *Through the Looking-Glass, and What Alice Found There.* London: Macmillan.

Chien, Yu-Chin, and Kenneth Wexler. 1991. Children's knowledge of locality conditions in binding as evidence for the modularity of syntax and pragmatics. *Language Acquisition* 1, 225–295.

Chierchia, Gennaro. 1989. Anaphora and attitudes *de se*. In Renate Bartsch, Johan van Benthem, and Peter van Emde Boas, eds., *Language in Context*. Dordrecht: Foris.

Chierchia, Gennaro. 1995. *Dynamics of Meaning, Anaphora, Presupposition, and the Theory of Grammar.* Chicago: University of Chicago Press.

Chomsky, Noam. 1973. Conditions on transformations. In Stephen R. Anderson and Paul Kiparsky, eds., *A Festschrift for Morris Halle*. New York: Holt, Rinehart and Winston.

Chomsky, Noam. 1977. On WH-movement. In Peter Culicover, Thomas Wasow, and Adrian Akmajian, eds., *Formal Syntax*, 71–132. New York: Academic Press.

Chomsky, Noam. 1980a. On binding. *Linguistic Inquiry* 11, 1–46.

Chomsky, Noam. 1980b. On cognitive structures and their development: A reply to Piaget. In Massimo Piattelli-Palmarini, ed., *Language and Learning: The Debate between Jean Piaget and Noam Chomsky*. Cambridge, MA: Harvard University Press.

Chomsky, Noam. 1981. *Lectures on Government and Binding.* Dordrecht: Foris.

Chomsky, Noam. 1982. *Some Concepts and Consequences of the Theory of Government and Binding.* Cambridge, MA: MIT Press.

Chomsky, Noam. 1986a. *Barriers.* Cambridge, MA: MIT Press.

Chomsky, Noam. 1986b. *Knowledge of Language: Its Nature, Origin, and Use.* New York: Praeger.

Chomsky, Noam. 1992. A minimalist program for linguistic theory. MIT Occasional Papers in Linguistics 1. Cambridge, MA: MITWPL, Department of Linguistics and Philosophy, MIT.

Chomsky, Noam. 1995. *The Minimalist Program.* Cambridge, MA: MIT Press.

Chomsky, Noam. 2000. Minimalist inquiries: The framework. In Roger Martin, David Michaels, and Juan Uriagereka, eds., *Step by Step: Essays on Minimalist Syntax in Honor of Howard Lasnik*, 89–157. Cambridge, MA: MIT Press.

Chomsky, Noam. 2001. Derivation by phase. In Michael Kenstowicz, ed., *Ken Hale: A Life in Language.* Cambridge, MA: MIT Press.

Chomsky, Noam. 2004. Beyond explanatory adequacy. In Adriana Belletti, ed., *Structures and Beyond: The Cartography of Syntactic Structure, Vol. 3.* Oxford: Oxford University Press.

Chomsky, Noam. 2005. Three factors in language design. *Linguistic Inquiry* 36(1), 1–22.

Chomsky, Noam. 2008. On phases. In Carlos Otero and Maria Luisa Zubizarreta, eds., *Foundational Issues in Linguistic Theory: Essays in Honor of Jean-Roger Vergnaud*, 133–166. Cambridge, MA: MIT Press.

Chomsky, Noam, and Howard Lasnik. 1993. The theory of principles and parameters. In Joachim Jacobs, Arnim von Stechow, Wolfgang Sternefeld, and Theo Vennemann, eds., *Syntax: An International Handbook of Contemporary Research*, 506–569. Berlin: Mouton de Gruyter.

Chung, Sandra. 1989. On the notion "null anaphor" in Chamorro. In Osvaldo Jaeggli and Ken Safir, eds., *The Null Subject Parameter.* Dordrecht: Kluwer.

Cinque, Guglielmo. 1988. On *si* constructions and the theory of *arb*. *Linguistic Inquiry* 19, 521–582.

Cinque, Guglielmo. 1993. A null theory of phrase and compound stress. *Linguistic Inquiry* 24, 239–298.

Cinque, Guglielmo. 1999. *Adverbs and Functional Heads: A Cross-Linguistic Perspective.* Oxford: Oxford University Press.

Clements, G. N. 1975. The logophoric pronoun in Ewe: Its role in discourse. *Journal of West African Languages* 10, 141–177.

Cole, Peter, Gabriella Hermon, and Cher-Leng Lee. 2001. Grammatical and discourse conditions on long distance reflexives in two Chinese dialects. In Peter Cole, Gabriella Hermon, and C.-T. James Huang, eds., *Long-Distance Reflexives.* Syntax and Semantics 33. San Diego: Academic Press.

Cole, Peter, Gabriella Hermon, and Li-May Sung. 1990. Principles and parameters of long-distance reflexives. *Linguistic Inquiry* 21, 1–23.

Cole, Peter, Gabriella Hermon, Yassir Tjung, Chang-Yong Sim, and Chonghyuk Kim. 2008. A binding theory exempt anaphor. In Ekkehard König and Volker Gast, eds., *Reciprocals and Reflexives: Theoretical and Typological Explorations*, 77–591. Berlin: Mouton.

Conroy, Stacey. 2007. I'm going to do me a talk on Personal Datives…but not really. Syntax Lunch Talk, February 21.

Dahl, Östen. 1974. How to open a sentence: Abstraction in natural language. *Logical Grammar Reports 12.* University of Gothenburg.

Dalrymple, Mary, M. Kanazawa, Y. Kim, Sam Mchombo, and Stanley Peters. 1998. Reciprocal expressions and the concept of reciprocity. *Linguistics and Philosophy* 21, 159–210.

Dalrymple, Mary, M. Kanazawa, Sam Mchombo, and Stanley Peters. 1994. What do reciprocals mean? In *Proceedings of Semantics and Linguistic Theory, SALT4*, University of Rochester.

Davies, William, and Stanley Dubinsky. 2003. On extraction from NPs. *Natural Language and Linguistic Theory* 21, 1–37.

Deacon, Terrence. 1997. *The Symbolic Species: The Co-evolution of Language and the Brain*. New York: W.W. Norton.

Déchaine, Rose-Marie, and Martina Wiltschko. 2002. Decomposing pronouns. *Linguistic Inquiry* 33(3), 409–442.

Delfitto, Denis. 2007. A case study in grammar, meaning and linguistic diversity: The nature of person features. In *Proceedings of the Annual Meeting of the Società Italiana di Glottologia—Scuola Normale Superiore Pisa*. Rome: Il Calamo.

Delfitto, Denis, and Gaetano Fiorin. 2007. Person features and pronominal anaphora. Ms., University of Verona. (To appear in *Linguistic Inquiry*.)

Delfitto, Denis, and Gaetano Fiorin. 2008. Towards an extension of *de se/de re* ambiguities: Person features and reflexivization. *Lingue e Linguaggio*, 25–46.

Dimitriadis, Alexis. 2000. Beyond Identity: Topics in Pronominal and Reciprocal Anaphora. Doctoral dissertation, University of Pennsylvania.

Dimitriadis, Alexis. 2008. Irreducible symmetry in reciprocal constructions. In Ekkehard König and Volker Gast, eds., *Reciprocals and Reflexives: Theoretical and Typological Explorations*, 375–411. Berlin: Mouton.

Dixon, R. M. W. 1988. *A Grammar of Boumaa Fijian*. Chicago: University of Chicago Press. Oxford: Oxford University Press.

Dotlačil, Jakub. 2010. *Anaphora and Distributivity: A Study of Same, Different, Reciprocals, and the Others*. Utrecht: LOT International Dissertation Series.

Dotlačil, Jakub, and Øystein Nilsen. 2009. A null-theory of long-distance reciprocity in English. In *Proceedings of NELS 2008*, Amherst: GLSA, University of Massachusetts.

Ellefson, M. R., and M. H. Christiansen. 2000. Subjacency constraints without Universal Grammar: Evidence from artificial language learning and connectionist modeling. In L. R. Gleitman and A. K. Joshi, eds., *The Proceedings of the 22nd Annual Conference of the Cognitive Science Society*, 645–650. Mahwah, NJ: Erlbaum.

Enç, Mürvet. 1987. Anchoring conditions for tense. *Linguistic Inquiry* 18, 633–657.

Engdahl, Elisabet. 1983. Parasitic gaps. *Linguistics and Philosophy* 6(1), 5–34.

Epstein, Samuel. 1994–1995. The derivation of syntactic relations. Ms., Harvard University.

Epstein, Samuel. 1999. Un-principled syntax and the derivation of syntactic relations. In S. Epstein and N. Hornstein, eds., *Working Minimalism*. Cambridge, MA: MIT Press.

Evans, Gareth. 1980. Pronouns. *Linguistic Inquiry* 11, 337–362.

Everaert, Martin. 1984. Icelandic long reflexivization and tense connectedness. *Trondheim Working Papers in Scandinavian Syntax* 12.

Everaert, Martin. 1986. *The Syntax of Reflexivization*. Dordrecht: Foris.

Everaert, Martin. 1990. Nominative anaphors in Icelandic: Morphology or syntax? In W. Abraham, W. Kosmeijer, and E. J. Reuland, eds., *Issues in Germanic Syntax*, 277–307. Berlin: Mouton de Gruyter.

Everaert, Martin. 1991. Contextual determination of the anaphor/pronominal distinction. In Jan Koster and Eric Reuland, eds., *Long-Distance Anaphora*, 77–118. Cambridge: Cambridge University Press.

Everaert, Martin. 2001. Paradigmatic restrictions on anaphors. In K. Meegerdoomian and L. A. Bar-el, eds., *WCCFL 20 Proceedings*, 178–191. Somerville, MA: Cascadilla Press.

Everaert, Martin. 2003. Reflexives in discourse. In Jan Koster and Henk van Riemsdijk, eds., *Germania et Alia: A Linguistic Webschrift for Hans den Besten*. http://odur.let.rug.nl/~koster/DenBesten.

Everaert, Martin, and Henk van Riemsdijk, eds. 2005. *The Blackwell Companion to Syntax*. 5 vols. Oxford: Blackwell.

Faltz, Leonard. 1977. Reflexivization: A Study in Universal Syntax. Doctoral dissertation, University of California at Berkeley. Distributed by University Microfilms International, Ann Arbor, MI, and London.

Farmer, Ann, and Robert Harnish. 1987. Communicative reference with pronouns. In J. Verschueren and M. Berucelli, eds., *The Pragmatic Perspective*, 547–565. Amsterdam: Benjamins.

Fiengo, Robert, and Robert May. 1990. Anaphora and ellipsis. Ms., CUNY and University of California, Irvine.

Fiengo, Robert, and Robert May. 1994. *Indices and Identity*. Cambridge, MA: MIT Press.

Fiorin, Gaetano. 2010. *Meaning and Dyslexia: A Study on Pronouns, Aspect, and Quantification*. Utrecht: LOT International Dissertation Series.

Fischer, Silke. 2004. Optimal binding. *Natural Language & Linguistic Theory* 22(3), 481–526.

Fox, Danny. 1993. Chain and binding: A modification of Reinhart and Reuland's "Reflexivity." Ms., MIT.

Fox, Danny. 1998. Locality in variable binding. In Pilar Barbosa, Danny Fox, Paul Hagstrom, Martha McGinnis, and David Pesetsky, eds., *Is the Best Good Enough?*, 129–157. Cambridge, MA: MIT Press.

Fox, Danny. 1999. *Economy and Semantic Interpretation*. Cambridge, MA: MIT Press.

Frampton, John. 2002. Syncretism, impoverishment, and the structure of person features. In Mary Andronis, Erin Debenport, Anne Pycha, and Keiko Yoshimura, eds., *CLS 38: Papers from the 38th Annual Meeting of the Chicago Linguistics Society*, 207–223. Chicago: University of Chicago, Chicago Linguistic Society.

Frampton, John. 2004. Copies, traces, occurrences, and all that evidence from Bulgarian multiple wh-phenomena. Ms., version 2, Northeastern University, September.

Frampton, John, and Sam Gutmann. 2000. Agreement is feature sharing. Ms., version 2, Northeastern University, August 14.

Frazier, Lyn, and Janet Fodor. 1978. The sausage machine: A new two-stage parsing model. *Cognition* 6, 291–325.

Frazier, Lyn, and Keith Rayner. 1982. Making and correcting errors during sentence comprehension: Eye movements in the analysis of structurally ambiguous sentences. *Cognitive Psychology* 14, 178–210.

Friederici, Angela. 2002. Towards a neural basis of auditory sentence processing. *Trends in Cognitive Sciences* 6(2), 78–84.

Friederici, Angela, and Sonja Kotz. 2003. The brain basis of syntactic processes: Functional imaging and lesion studies. *NeuroImage* 20, 8–17.

Gast, Volker. 2006. *The Grammar of Identity*. London: Routledge.

Gast, Volker, and Florian Haas. 2008. Reflexive and reciprocal readings of anaphors in German and other European languages. In Ekkehard König and Volker Gast, eds., *Reciprocals and Reflexives: Theoretical and Typological Explorations*. Berlin: Mouton.

Geenhoven, Veerle van, and Louise McNally. 2005. On the property analysis of opaque complements. *Lingua* 115, 885–914.

Gelderen, Elly van. 2000. *A History of English Reflexive Pronouns: Person, Self, and Interpretability*. Amsterdam: Benjamins.

Giorgi, Alessandra. 1984. Towards a theory of long distance anaphors: A GB approach. *Linguistic Review* 3, 307–359.

Graf, Thomas. 2007. From Vagueness to Disaster: On the Intricacies of Feature Checking. Diplomarbeit, Universität Wien.

Greenberg, Joseph. 1963. Some universals of grammar with particular reference to the order of meaningful elements. In Joseph Greenberg, ed., *Universals of Language*. Cambridge, MA: MIT Press.

Grewendorf, Günther. 1983. Reflexivierung in deutschen A.c.I.-konstruktionen— Kein transformations-grammatisches Dilemma mehr. In Werner Abraham, ed., *Groninger Arbeiten zur Germanistische Linguistik* 23, 120–196. Groningen: Germanistisch Instituut.

Grewendorf, Günther. 1989. *Ergativity in German*. Dordrecht: Foris.

Grimshaw, Jane. 1986. Nouns, arguments, and adjuncts. Ms., Brandeis University.

Grimshaw, Jane. 1990. *Argument Structure*. Cambridge, MA: MIT Press.

Grimshaw, Jane. 1991. Extended projections. Ms., Brandeis University.

Grodzinsky, Yosef. 1982. Syntactic representations in agrammatism: Evidence from Hebrew. Paper presented at the Academy of Aphasia, Mohonk, NY.

Grodzinsky, Yosef. 1986. Language deficits and the theory of syntax. *Brain and Language* 27, 135–159.

Grodzinsky, Yosef. 1990. *Theoretical Perspectives on Language Deficits*. Cambridge, MA: MIT Press.

Grodzinsky, Yosef, and Tanya Reinhart. 1993. The innateness of binding and coreference. *Linguistic Inquiry* 24, 69–101.

Guéron, Jacqueline, and Jacqueline Lecarme, eds. 2004. *The Syntax of Time*. Cambridge, MA: MIT.

Gunkel, Lutz. 2003. Reflexivierung in AcI-Konstruktionen. In Lutz Gunkel, Gereon Müller, and Gisela Zifonun, eds., *Arbeiten zur Reflexivierung*, 115–133. Linguistische Arbeiten 481. Tübingen: Niemeyer.

Gunkel, Lutz, Gereon Müller, and Gisela Zifonun. 2003. *Arbeiten zur Reflexivierung*. Linguistische Arbeiten 481. Tübingen: Niemeyer.

Haegeman, Liliane. 1984. Complementiser agreement, extraction and pro-drop in West Flemish. In Hagit Borer, ed., *Clitics and Syntactic Theory*. Syntax and Semantics 18. Orlando, FL: Academic Press.

Hagège, Claude. 1974. Les pronoms logophoriques. *Bulletin de la Société de Linguistique de Paris* 69, 287–310.

Halle, Morris, and Alec Marantz. 1993. Distributed Morphology and the pieces of inflection. In Kenneth Hale and Samuel Jay Keyser, eds., *The View from Building 20*, 111–176. Cambridge, MA: MIT Press.

Hara, Takaaki. 2002. *Anaphoric Dependencies in Japanese*. Utrecht: LOT International Dissertation Series.

Harley, Heidi, and Elizabeth Ritter. 2002. Person and number in pronouns: A feature geometric analysis. *Language* 78, 482–526.

Hauser, Marc D., Noam Chomsky, and W. Tecumseh Fitch. 2002. The faculty of language: What is it, who has it, and how did it evolve? *Science* 298, 1569–1579.

Heim, Irene. 1982. The Semantics of Definite and Indefinite Noun Phrases. Doctoral dissertation, University of Massachusetts, Amherst. (Published in 1989 by Garland, New York.)

Heim, Irene. 1998. Anaphora and semantic interpretation: A reinterpretation of Reinhart's approach. In Uli Sauerland and Orin Percus, eds., *The Interpretive Tract*, 205–246. MIT Working Papers in Linguistics 25. Cambridge, MA: MIT, MIT Working Papers in Linguistics.

Heim, Irene. 2005. Features on bound pronouns: Semantics or syntax? Ms., MIT.

Heim, Irene, and Angelika Kratzer. 1998. *Semantics in Generative Grammar*. Malden, MA: Blackwell.

Heim, Irene, Howard Lasnik, and Robert May. 1991. Reciprocity and plurality. *Linguistic Inquiry* 22(1), 63–103.

Heinat, Fredrick. 2005. Probes, Pronouns, and Binding in the Minimalist Program. Doctoral dissertation, Lund University.

Heine, Bernd, and Hiroyuki Miyashita. 2008. The intersection between reflexives and reciprocals: A grammaticalization perspective. In Ekkehard König and Volker Gast, eds., *Reciprocals and Reflexives: Theoretical and Typological Explorations*, 169–225. Berlin: Mouton.

Helke, Michael. 1973. On reflexives in English. *Linguistics* 106, 5–23.

Hellan, Lars. 1980. On anaphora in Norwegian. In Jody Kreiman and Almerindo Ojeda, eds., *Papers from the Parasession on Pronouns and Anaphora*. Chicago: Chicago Linguistic Society.

Hellan, Lars. 1988. *Anaphora in Norwegian and the Theory of Grammar*. Dordrecht: Foris.

Hellan, Lars. 1991. Containment and connectedness anaphors. In Jan Koster and Eric Reuland, eds., *Long-Distance Anaphora*, 27–48. Cambridge: Cambridge University Press.

Hestvik, Arild. 1991. Subjectless binding domains. *Natural Language & Linguistic Theory* 9(3), 455–496.

Hestvik, Arild. 1992. LF-movement of pronouns and antisubject orientation. *Linguistic Inquiry* 23(4), 557–594.

Heycock, Caroline. 1995. Asymmetries in reconstruction. *Linguistic Inquiry* 26, 547–570.

Hicks, Glyn. 2009. *The Derivation of Anaphoric Relations*. Amsterdam: Benjamins.

Higginbotham, James. 1983. Logical form, binding and nominals. *Linguistic Inquiry* 14, 395–420.

Hinzen, Wolfram. 2007. *An Essay on Naming and Truth*. Oxford: Oxford University Press.

Hoekstra, Jarich. 1994. Pronouns and Case: On the distribution of Frisian *harren* and *se* 'them'. *Leuvense Bijdragen* 83, 47–65.

Hoekstra, Teun. 1991. Small clauses everywhere. Ms., University of Leiden.

Hoop, Helen de. 1992. Case Configuration and Noun Phrase Interpretation. Doctoral dissertation, Groningen University.

Hornstein, Norbert. 1995. *Logical Form: From GB to Minimalism*. Oxford: Blackwell.

Hornstein, Norbert. 2000. *Move! A Minimalist Theory of Construal*. Oxford: Blackwell.

Hornstein, Norbert. 2004. Pronouns in a minimalist setting. Paper presented at the Workshop on the Copy Theory on the PF side. Utrecht, December 14–15, 2004.

Huang, C.-T. James. 1982. Logical Relations in Chinese and the Theory of Grammar. Doctoral dissertation, MIT.

Huang, C.-T. James. 1993. Reconstruction and the structure of VP: Some theoretical consequences. *Linguistic Inquiry* 24, 103–138.

Huang, C.-T. James, and C.-S. Luther Liu. 2000. Logophoricity, attitudes, and *ziji* at the interface. In Peter Cole, Gabriella Hermon, and C.-T. James Huang, eds., *Long-Distance Reflexives*, 141–192. Syntax and Semantics 33. New York: Academic Press.

Huang, C.-T. James, and C.-C. Jane Tang. 1991. The local nature of the long distance reflexive in Chinese. In Jan Koster and Eric Reuland, eds., *Long-Distance Anaphora*, 263–282. Cambridge: Cambridge University Press.

Huang, Yan. 2000. *Anaphora: A Cross-Linguistic Study*. Oxford: Oxford University Press.

Hyams, Nina, and Sigríður Sigurjónsdóttir. 1990. The development of "long distance anaphora": Cross-linguistic comparison with special reference to Icelandic. *Language Acquisition* 1, 57–93.

Jackendoff, Ray. 1972. *Semantic Interpretation in Generative Grammar*. Cambridge, MA: MIT Press.

Jackendoff, Ray. 1992. Mme. Tussaud meets the binding theory. *Natural Language & Linguistic Theory* 10, 1–33.

Jackendoff, Ray. 2002. *Foundations of Language*. Oxford: Oxford University Press.

Jacobs, Roderick A., and Peter S. Rosenbaum, eds. 1970. *Readings in English Transformational Grammar*. Waltham, MA: Ginn.

Jacobson, Pauline. 1999. Towards a variable-free semantics. *Linguistics and Philosophy* 22, 117–184.

Jaeger, T. Florian. 2004. Binding in picture NPs revisited: Evidence for a semantic principle of extended argument-hood. In M. Butt and T. H. King, eds., *Proceedings of the LFG04 Conference*, 268–288. Stanford, CA: CSLI Publications.

Jayaseelan, K. A. 1997. Anaphors as pronouns. *Studia Linguistica* 51(2), 186–234.

Johnson, Kyle. 1984. Some notes on subjunctive clauses and binding in Icelandic. *MIT Working Papers in Linguistics* 6, 102–137.

Johnson, Kyle. 1991. Object positions. *Natural Language & Linguistic Theory* 9, 577–636.

Jong, Jelly J. de. 1996. The Case of Bound Pronouns in Peripheral Romance. Doctoral dissertation, Groningen University.

Joseph, Brian. 1979. On the agreement of reflexive forms in English. *Linguistics* 17, 519–523.

Kaan, Edith. 1992a. A Minimalist Approach to Extraposition. Master's thesis, University of Groningen.

Kaan, Edith. 1992b. A minimalist approach to extraposition of CP and Verb (Projection) Raising. In D. Gilbers and S. Looyenga, eds., *Yearbook of the Research Group for Linguistic Theory and Knowledge Representation: Language Cognition* 2, 169–179. Groningen: University of Groningen.

Kamp, Hans, and Uwe Reyle. 1993. *From Discourse to Logic*. Dordrecht: Kluwer.

Kaplan, David. 1989. Demonstratives. In J. Almog, H. Wettstein, and J. Perry, eds., *Themes from Kaplan*, 581–563. Oxford: Oxford University Press.

Katz, Jerrold J., and Paul Postal. 1964. *An Integrated Theory of Linguistic Descriptions*. Cambridge, MA: MIT Press.

Kayne, Richard. 1981. On certain differences between French and English. *Linguistic Inquiry* 12, 349–371.

Kayne, Richard. 1985. Principles of particle constructions. In Jacqueline Guéron, Hans-Georg Obenauer, and Jean-Yves Pollock, eds., *Grammatical Representation*, 111–140. Dordrecht: Foris.

Kayne, Richard. 1990. Romance clitics and PRO. In *NELS 20*. Amherst: GLSA, University of Massachusetts.

Kayne, Richard. 1994. *The Antisymmetry of Syntax*. Cambridge, MA: MIT Press.

Kayne, Richard. 2000. *Parameters and Universals*. New York: Oxford University Press.

Kayne, Richard. 2002. Pronouns and their antecedents. In Samuel Epstein and Daniel Seely, eds., *Derivation and Explanation in the Minimalist Program*, 133–167. Malden, MA: Blackwell.

Kayne, Richard. 2003. Person morphemes and reflexives in Italian, French and related languages. In C. Tortora, ed., *The Syntax of Italian Dialects*, 102–136. New York: Oxford University Press.

Keenan, Edward. 1971. Names, quantifiers and a solution to the sloppy identity problem. *Papers in Linguistics* 4(2).

Keenan, Edward. 1988. On semantics and the binding theory. In John Hawkins, ed., *Explaining Language Universals*. Oxford: Blackwell.

Keenan, Edward. 2000. An historical explanation of some binding theoretic facts in English. Ms., UCLA; presented at the UCSD conference Explanation in Linguistics, 1999.

Keenan, Edward, and Bernard Comrie. 1977. Noun phrase accessibility and Universal Grammar. *Linguistic Inquiry* 8, 63–99.

Keller, F., and A. Asudeh. 2001. Constraints on linguistic coreference: Structural vs. pragmatic factors. In Johanna D. Moore and Keith Stenning, eds., *Proceedings of the 23rd Annual Conference of the Cognitive Science Society*, 483–488. Mahwah, NJ: Erlbaum.

Keller, R. E. 1961. *German Dialects: Phonology and Morphology*. Manchester: Manchester University Press.

Keller, R. E. 1978. *The German Language*. London: Faber and Faber.

Khomitsevich, Olga. 2008. *Dependencies across Phases: From Sequence of Tense to Restrictions on Movement*. Utrecht: LOT International Dissertation Series.

Khomitsevich, Olga, and Eric Reuland. 2007. On the encoding of temporal dependencies. In Peter Kosta and Lilia Schürcks, eds., *Linguistic Investigations into Formal Description of Slavic Languages*, 227–245. Berlin: Peter Lang.

Kimball, John. 1973. Seven principles of surface structure parsing in natural language. *Cognition* 2(1), 15–47.

Kiss, Katalin É. 1991. The primacy condition of anaphora and pronominal variable binding. In Jan Koster and Eric J. Reuland, eds., *Long-Distance Anaphora*, 245–263. Cambridge: Cambridge University Press.

Kleene, Stephen C. 1971. *Introduction to Metamathematics*. 6th ed. Groningen: Wolters Noordhoff.

König, Ekkehard, and Peter Siemund. 2000. Intensifiers and reflexives: A typological perspective. In Zygmunt Frajzyngier and Traci Curl, eds., *Reflexives: Forms and Functions*. Amsterdam: Benjamins.

Koopman, Hilda. 2000. Prepositions, postpositions, circumpositions, and particles. In *The Syntax of Specifiers and Heads*, collected essays of Hilda J. Koopman, 204–260. London: Routledge.

Koopman, Hilda, and Dominique Sportiche. 1982. Variables and the Bijection Principle. *Linguistic Review* 2, 139–160.

Koopman, Hilda, and Dominique Sportiche. 1991. The position of subjects. *Lingua* 85, 211–258.

Koopman, Hilda, and Anna Szabolcsi. 2000. *Verbal Complexes*. Cambridge, MA: MIT Press.

Koornneef, Arnout. 2008. *Eye-Catching Anaphora*. Utrecht: LOT International Dissertation Series.

Koring, Loes. 2005. Binding in het Telugu en het Hmar. BA thesis, Utrecht University.

Koster, Jan. 1984. On binding and control. *Linguistic Inquiry* 15, 417–459.

Koster, Jan. 1985. Reflexives in Dutch. In Jacqueline Guéron, Hans-Georg Obenauer, and Jean-Yves Pollock, eds., *Grammatical Representation*, 141–168. Dordrecht: Foris.

Koster, Jan, and Eric J. Reuland, eds. 1991. *Long-Distance Anaphora*. Cambridge: Cambridge University Press.

Kratzer, Angelika. 1998. More structural analogies between pronouns and tenses. In Devon Strolovich and Aaron Lawson, eds., *Proceedings of SALT 8*. Ithaca, NY: Cornell University, CLC Publications.

Kratzer, Angelika. 2006. Minimal pronouns. Ms., University of Massachusetts, Amherst.

Kuhn, Thomas. 1996. *The Structure of Scientific Revolutions*. 3rd ed. Chicago: University of Chicago Press.

Kuno, Susumu. 1972. Functional sentence perspective: A case study from Japanese and English. *Linguistic Inquiry* 3, 269–320.

Kuno, Susumu. 1975. Three perspectives in the functional approach to syntax. In *Proceedings of the Chicago Linguistic Society, Parasession on Functionalism*, 276–336. Chicago: University of Chicago, Chicago Linguistic Society.

Kuno, Susumu. 1987. *Functional Syntax: Anaphora, Discourse, and Empathy*. Chicago: University of Chicago Press.

Landau, Idan. 2003. Movement out of control. *Linguistic Inquiry* 34(3), 471–498.

Landau, Idan. 2006. Severing the distribution of PRO and Case. *Syntax* 9(2), 153–170.

Landau, Idan. 2008. Two routes of control: Evidence from case transmission in Russian. *Natural Language & Linguistic Theory* 26, 877–924.

Landman, Fred. 2000. *Events and Plurality: The Jerusalem Lectures.* Dordrecht: Kluwer.

Langacker, Ronald W. 1987. *Foundations of Cognitive Grammar, Volume 1: Theoretical Prerequisites.* Stanford, CA: Stanford University Press.

Langacker, Ronald W. 1991. *Foundations of Cognitive Grammar, Volume 2: Descriptive Application.* Stanford, CA: Stanford University Press.

Lappin, Shalom, Robert Levine, and David Johnson. 2000. The structure of unscientific revolutions. *Natural Language & Linguistic Theory* 18, 665–671.

Larson, Richard. 1995. Olga is a beautiful dancer. Paper presented at the Linguistic Society of America meetings, New Orleans, LA.

Lasnik, Howard. 1989. *Essays on Anaphora.* Dordrecht: Kluwer.

Lebeaux, David. 1983. A distributional difference between reciprocals and reflexives. *Linguistic Inquiry* 14, 723–730.

Lebeaux, David. 1985. Locality and anaphoric binding. *Linguistic Review* 4, 343–363.

Lebeaux, David. 1988. Language Acquisition and the Form of the Grammar. Doctoral dissertation, University of Massachusetts, Amherst.

Leben, William. 1973. Suprasegmental Phonology. Doctoral dissertation, MIT. Distributed by Indiana University Linguistics Club.

Lee, Felicia. 2003. Anaphoric R-expressions as bound variables. *Syntax* 6, 84–114.

Lemmen, Hanneke. 2005. To Bundle or Not to Bundle? Researching Verbs in Dutch on Reflexivization. Master's thesis, Utrecht University.

Lenneberg, Eric. 1967. *Biological Foundations of Language.* New York: John Wiley.

Levinson, Stephen. 2000. *Presumptive Meanings.* Cambridge, MA: MIT Press.

Lewis, David. 1979. Attitudes *de dicto* and *de se. Philosophical Review* 88, 513–543.

Lidz, Jeffrey. 1995. Morphological reflexive marking: Evidence from Kannada. *Linguistic Inquiry* 26(4), 705–710.

Longobardi, Giuseppe. 1994. Reference and proper names: A theory of N-movement in syntax and logical form. *Linguistic Inquiry* 25, 609–665.

Longobardi, Giuseppe. 1996. The syntax of N-raising: A minimalist theory. *OTS Working Papers* 1996, 1–151. Utrecht: UiL OTS, Utrecht University.

Longobardi, Giuseppe. 2001. The structure of DP's. In Mark Baltin and Chris Collins, eds., *The Handbook of Contemporary Syntactic Theory*, 562–603. Oxford: Blackwell.

Lust, Barbara, Kashi Wali, James Gair, and K. V. Subbarao, eds. 2000. *Lexical Anaphors and Pronouns in Selected South Asian Languages: A Principled Typology*. Berlin: Mouton de Gruyter.

Maling, Joan. 1982. Non-clause-bounded reflexives in Icelandic. In Thorstein Fretheim and Lars Hellan, eds., *Papers from the Sixth Scandinavian Conference of Linguistics*, 90–107. Trondheim: Tapir.

Maling, Joan. 1984. Non-clause-bounded reflexives in Modern Icelandic. *Linguistics and Philosophy* 7, 211–241.

Maling, Joan. 1986. Clause bounded reflexives in Modern Icelandic. In Lars Hellan and Kirsti Koch Christensen, eds., *Topics in Scandinavian Syntax*, 53–63. Dordrecht: Kluwer.

Manzini, Maria Rita. 1993. The subjunctive. In *Paris 8 Working Papers*, vol. 1. Paris: Université Paris 8.

Manzini, Maria Rita, and Kenneth Wexler. 1987. Parameters, binding theory, and learnability. *Linguistic Inquiry* 18, 413–444.

Marantz, Alec. 1997. No escape from syntax: Don't try morphological analysis in the privacy of your own lexicon. In Alexis Dimitriadis, Laura Siegel, Clarissa Surek-Clark, and Alexander Williams, eds., *Proceedings of the 21st Annual Penn Linguistics Colloquium*, 201–225. Pennsylvania Working Papers in Linguistics 4.2. Philadelphia: University of Pennsylvania, Penn Linguistics Club.

Marantz, Alec. 2000a. Case and licensing. In Eric Reuland, ed., *Arguments and Case: Explaining Burzio's Generalization*. Amsterdam: Benjamins.

Marantz, Alec. 2000b. Lecture notes, MIT.

Marelj, Marijana. 2004. *Middles and Argument Structure across Languages*. Utrecht: LOT International Dissertation Series.

Marelj, Marijana, and Eric Reuland. 2010. Deriving reflexives—Deriving the lexicon-syntax parameter. Ms., Utrecht Institute of Linguistics OTS, Utrecht University.

May, Robert. 1977. The Grammar of Quantification. Doctoral dissertation, MIT.

Menuzzi, Sergio. 1999. *Binding Theory and Pronominal Anaphora in Brazilian Portuguese*. HIL dissertation, Leyden. LOT International Dissertation Series 30. The Hague: Holland Academic Graphics.

Mitkov, Ruslan. 2002. *Anaphora Resolution*. New York: Longman.

Mortensen, David. 2003. Two kinds of variable elements in Hmong anaphora. Ms., University of California, Berkeley.

Moyse-Faurie, Claire. 2008. Constructions expressing middle, reflexive and reciprocal situations in some Oceanic languages. In Ekkehard König and Volker Gast, eds., *Reciprocals and Reflexives: Theoretical and Typological Explorations*, 105–168. Berlin: Mouton.

Mukherjee, Aparna, and Eric Reuland. 2009. Binding possessives in Hindi vis-à-vis Bangla. Paper presented at the Universals and the Typology of Reflexives Workshop 1, Utrecht, February 2–3.

Mukkerji, N. S. 1999. Long-Distance Binding in Telugu & Hmar. MPhil dissertation, University of Delhi.

Muysken, Pieter. 1993. Reflexes of Ibero-Romance reflexive clitic + verb combinations in Papiamentu: Thematic grids and grammatical relations. In Francis Byrne and Donald Winford, eds., *Focus and Grammatical Relations in Creole Languages*, 285–301. Amsterdam: Benjamins.

Napoli, Donna-Jo. 1979. Reflexivization across clause boundaries in Italian. *Journal of Linguistics* 15, 1–2.

Neeleman, Ad, and Kriszta Szendrői. 2007. Radical pro drop and the morphology of pronouns. *Linguistic Inquiry* 38, 671–714.

Nilsen, Øystein. 2003. *Eliminating Positions*. Utrecht: LOT International Dissertation Series.

Noguchi, Tohru. 1997. Two types of pronouns and variable binding. *Language* 73, 770–797.

Nunes, Jairo. 2004. *Linearization of Chains and Sideward Movement*. Cambridge, MA: MIT Press.

Panagiotidis, Phoevos. 2002. *Pronouns, Clitics and Empty Nouns: "Pronominality" and Licensing in Syntax*. Amsterdam: Benjamins.

Papangeli, Dimitra. 2004. *The Morphosyntax of Argument Realization: Greek Argument Structure and the Lexicon-Syntax Interface*. Utrecht: LOT International Dissertation Series.

Partee, Barbara, and Emmon Bach. 1981. Quantification, pronouns, and VP-anaphora. In *Formal Methods in the Study of Language*. Amsterdam: Mathematisch Centrum, Amsterdam University. Also in Jeroen Groenendijk, Theo Janssen, and Martin Stokhof, eds., *Truth, Interpretation and Information: Selected Papers from the Third Amsterdam Colloquium*. Dordrecht: Foris, 1984.

Partee, Barbara, Alice ter Meulen, and Robert E. Wall. 1993. *Mathematical Methods in Linguistics*. Dordrecht: Kluwer.

Patnaik, M., and K. V. Subbarao. 2000. An initial note on lexical anaphors and pronouns in Juang. In Lust et al., eds., 2000.

Pesetsky, David. 1982. Paths and Categories. Doctoral dissertation, MIT.

Pesetsky, David. 2000. *Phrasal movement and its kin*. Cambridge, MA: MIT Press.

Pesetsky, David, and Esther Torrego. 2001. T-to-C movement: Causes and consequences. In Michael Kenstowicz, ed., *Ken Hale: A Life in Language*, 355–426. Cambridge, MA: MIT Press.

Pesetsky, David, and Esther Torrego. 2004a. The syntax of valuation and the interpretability of features. Ms., MIT and University of Massachusetts Boston. http://web.mit.edu/linguistics/www/pesetsky/Pesetsky_Torrego_Agree_paper.pdf.

Pesetsky, David, and Esther Torrego. 2004b. Tense, Case, and the nature of syntactic categories. In Jacqueline Guéron and Jacqueline Lecarme, eds., *The Syntax of Time*. Cambridge, MA: MIT Press.

Phillips, Colin. 1996. Order and Structure. Doctoral dissertation, MIT. Distributed by MITWPL, Department of Linguistics and Philosophy, MIT.

Pica, Pierre. 1985. Subject, tense and truth: Towards a modular approach to binding. In Jacqueline Guéron, Hans-Georg Obenauer, and Jean-Yves Pollock, eds., *Grammatical Representation*, 259–291. Dordrecht: Foris.

Pica, Pierre. 1987. On the nature of the reflexivization cycle. In *NELS 17*, 483–499. Amherst: GLSA, University of Massachusetts.

Pica, Pierre. 1991. On the interaction between antecedent-government and binding: The case of long-distance reflexivization. In Jan Koster and Eric Reuland, eds., *Long-distance Anaphora*, 119–135. Cambridge: Cambridge University Press.

Pinker, Steven, and Ray Jackendoff. 2005a. The faculty of language: What's special about it? *Cognition* 95(2), 201–236.

Pinker, Steven, and Ray Jackendoff. 2005b. The nature of the language faculty and its implications for evolution of language. *Cognition* 97, 211–225.

Pollard, Carl, and Ivan Sag. 1992. Anaphors in English and the scope of the binding theory. *Linguistic Inquiry* 23, 261–305.

Pollard, Carl, and Ivan Sag. 1994. *Head Driven Phrase Structure Grammar*. Stanford, CA, and Chicago: CSLI Publications and University of Chicago Press.

Postal, Paul. 1970. On so-called "pronouns" in English. In David Reibel and Sanford Schane, eds., *Modern Studies in English*, 201–224. Englewood Cliffs, NJ: Prentice Hall.

Postal, Paul M. 1974. *On Raising*. Cambridge, MA: MIT Press.

Postma, Gertjan. 2004. Structurele tendensen in de opkomst van het reflexief pronomen 'zich' in het 15de-eeuwse Drenthe en de Theorie van Reflexiviteit. *Nederlandse Taalkunde* 9(2), 144–168.

Pritchett, Brad. 1992. *Grammatical Competence and Parsing Performance*. Chicago: University of Chicago Press.

Rákosi, György. 2007. *Dative Experiencer Predicates in Hungarian*. Utrecht: LOT International Dissertation Series.

Reinhart, Tanya. 1976. The Syntactic Domain of Anaphora. Doctoral dissertation, MIT.

Reinhart, Tanya. 1983. *Anaphora and Semantic Interpretation*. London: Croom Helm.

Reinhart, Tanya. 1987. Specifiers and operator binding. In Eric Reuland and Alice ter Meulen, eds., *The Representation of (In)definiteness*, 130–167. Cambridge, MA: MIT Press.

Reinhart, Tanya. 1998. *Wh-in-situ* in the framework of the Minimalist Program. *Natural Language Semantics* 6, 29–56.

Reinhart, Tanya. 2000. Strategies of anaphora resolution. In Hans Bennis, Martin Everaert, and Eric Reuland, eds., *Interface Strategies*, 295–324. Amsterdam: Royal Netherlands Academy of Arts and Sciences.

Reinhart, Tanya. 2002. The theta system: An overview. In W. Sternefeld, ed., *Theoretical Linguistics* 28, 229–290. Berlin: Mouton.

Reinhart, Tanya. 2006. *Interface Strategies: Reference Set Computation.* Cambridge, MA: MIT Press.

Reinhart, Tanya, and Eric Reuland. 1989. Anaphoric territories. Ms., Tel Aviv University and Groningen University. (Also in Werner Abraham, ed., *Groninger Arbeiten zur germanistischen Linguistik* 34. Groningen: Groningen University, 1991.)

Reinhart, Tanya, and Eric Reuland. 1991. Anaphors and logophors: An argument structure perspective. In Jan Koster and Eric Reuland, eds., *Long Distance Anaphora*, 283–321. Cambridge: Cambridge University Press.

Reinhart, Tanya, and Eric Reuland. 1993. Reflexivity. *Linguistic Inquiry* 24, 657–720.

Reinhart, Tanya, and Tal Siloni. 2005. The lexicon-syntax parameter: Reflexivization and other arity operations. *Linguistic Inquiry* 36, 389–436.

Reis, Marga. 1976. Reflexivierung in deutschen A.c.I.-konstruktionen, Ein transformations grammatisches Dilemma. *Papiere zur Linguistik* 9, 5–82.

Reuland, Eric. 1981. On extraposition of complement clauses. In Victoria Burke and James Pustejovsky, eds., *NELS 11*, 296–318. Amherst, MA: GLSA, University of Massachusetts.

Reuland, Eric. 1983. Governing -*ing*. *Linguistic Inquiry* 14(1), 101–136.

Reuland, Eric. 1990a. Head movement and the relation between morphology and syntax. In A. Jongman and A. Lahiri, eds., *Yearbook of Morphology*, 129–161. Dordrecht: Foris.

Reuland, Eric. 1990b. Reflexives and beyond: Non-local anaphora in Italian revisited. In Joan Mascaró and Marina Nespor, eds., *Grammar in Progress*, 351–362. Dordrecht: Foris.

Reuland, Eric. 1995. Primitives of binding. Abstract in *GLOW Newsletter* 1995. Paper presented at GLOW 18, Tromsø, Norway.

Reuland, Eric. 1996. Pronouns and features. In Kiyomi Kusumo, ed., *Proceedings of NELS 26, Harvard University and MIT*, 319–333. Amherst: GLSA, University of Massachusetts.

Reuland, Eric. 1998. Structural conditions on chains and binding. In *NELS 28*, 341–356. Amherst: GLSA, University of Massachusetts.

Reuland, Eric. 2000. Anaphors, logophors, and binding. In Peter Cole, Gabriella Hermon, and C.-T. James Huang, eds., *Long-Distance Reflexives*, 343–370. Syntax and Semantics 33. San Diego: Academic Press.

Reuland, Eric. 2001a. Confusion compounded. *Natural Language & Linguistic Theory* 19(4), 879–885.

Reuland, Eric. 2001b. Primitives of binding. *Linguistic Inquiry* 32(3), 439–492.

Reuland, Eric. 2001c. Revolution, discovery, and an elementary principle of logic. *Natural Language & Linguistic Theory* 18(4), 843–848.

Reuland, Eric. 2005a. Agreeing to bind. In Hans Broekhuis, Norbert Corver, Riny Huybregts, Ursula Kleinhenz, and Jan Koster, eds., *Organizing Grammar: Linguistic Studies in Honor of Henk van Riemsdijk*. Berlin: Walter de Gruyter.

Reuland, Eric. 2005b. Binding conditions: How are they derived? In Stefan Müller, ed., *Proceedings of the HPSG05 Conference Department of Informatics, University of Lisbon*. Stanford, CA: CSLI Publications. http://csli-publications .stanford.edu/.

Reuland, Eric. 2005c. On the evolution and genesis of language: The force of imagination. *Lingue e Linguaggio* 1, 81–110.

Reuland, Eric. 2005d. Icelandic logophoric anaphora. In Martin Everaert and Henk van Riemsdijk, eds., *The Blackwell Companion to Syntax*. Oxford: Blackwell.

Reuland, Eric. 2005e. Long distance anaphors in Germanic languages. In Martin Everaert and Henk van Riemsdijk, eds., *The Blackwell Companion to Syntax*. Oxford: Blackwell.

Reuland, Eric. 2006. Gradedness: Interpretive dependencies and beyond. In Gisbert Fanselow, ed., *Gradience*. Oxford: Oxford University Press.

Reuland, Eric. 2008a. Anaphoric dependencies: How are they encoded? Towards a derivation-based typology. In Ekkehard König and Volker Gast, eds., *Reciprocals and Reflexives: Cross-Linguistic and Theoretical Explorations*, 502–559. Berlin: Mouton de Gruyter.

Reuland, Eric. 2008b. On language and evolution: Why neoadaptationism fails. Commentary in *Behavioral and Brain Sciences* 31(5), 531–532.

Reuland, Eric. 2009a. Language, symbolization and beyond. In Rudie Botha and Chris Knight, eds., *The Prehistory of Language*. Oxford: Oxford University Press.

Reuland, Eric. 2009b. The syntax of anaphora (review). *Language* 85(1), 231–237.

Reuland, Eric. 2009c. *Taal en regels: Door eenvoud tot inzicht*. Inaugural lecture, Faculty of Humanities, Utrecht University.

Reuland, Eric. 2010a. Imagination, planning, and working memory: The emergence of language. In Frederick Coolidge and Thomas Wynn, eds., *Working Memory: Beyond Language and Symbolism*. Supplement to *Current Anthropology* 51(S1), S98–S110.

Reuland, Eric. 2010b. What's nominal in nominalizations. In Jaklin Kornfilt and John Whitman, eds., Special issue of *Lingua*. (Paper presented in 2006.)

Reuland, Eric. Forthcoming. Binding, locality and sources of invariance. In Balázs Surányi, ed., *Proceedings of the Conference on Minimalist Approaches to Syntactic Locality*. 26–28 August 2009, Budapest.

Reuland, Eric, and Sergey Avrutin. 2005. Binding and beyond: Issues in backward anaphora. In Antonio Branco, Tony McEnery, and Ruslan Mitkov, eds., *Anaphora Processing: Linguistic, Cognitive and Computational Modelling*, 139–163. Amsterdam: Benjamins.

Reuland, Eric, and Sergey Avrutin. 2010. Interpretive dependencies: The case of backward anaphora. *Linguistic Analysis* 34(3–4), 271–315.

Reuland, Eric J., and Jan Koster. 1991. Long-distance anaphora: An overview. In Jan Koster and Eric J. Reuland, eds., *Long-Distance Anaphora*, 1–26. Cambridge: Cambridge University Press.

Reuland, Eric, and Tanya Reinhart. 1995. Pronouns, anaphors and Case. In Hubert Haider, Susan Olsen, and Sten Vikner, eds., *Studies in Comparative Germanic Syntax*, 241–269. Dordrecht: Kluwer.

Reuland, Eric, and Sigríður Sigurjónsdóttir. 1997. Long distance binding in Icelandic: Syntax or discourse? In Hans Bennis, Pierre Pica, and Johan Rooryck, eds., *Atomism in Binding*, 323–334. Dordrecht: Foris.

Reuland, Eric, and Yoad Winter. 2009. Binding without identity: Towards a unified semantics for bound and exempt anaphors. In Sobha Devi, António Branco, and Ruslan Mitkov, eds., *Anaphora Processing and Applications*. Berlin: Springer.

Rice, Mabel, and Kenneth Wexler. 1996. Toward tense as a clinical marker for specific language impairment in English-speaking children. *Journal of Speech and Hearing Research* 39, 1239–1257.

Richards, Norvin. 2006. A distinctness condition on linearization. Ms., MIT, October.

Riemsdijk, Henk van. 1978. *A Case Study in Syntactic Markedness: The Binding Nature of Prepositional Phrases*. Dordrecht: Foris.

Riemsdijk, Henk van, and Edwin Williams. 1981. NP-structure. *Linguistic Review* 1, 171–217.

Ritter, Elizabeth. 1988. A head-movement approach to construct-state noun phrases. *Linguistics* 26, 909–929.

Ritter, Elizabeth. 1991. Functional categories in noun phrases: Evidence from Modern Hebrew. In Susan Rothstein, ed., *Perspectives on Phrase Structure*, 37–62. Syntax and Semantics 25. San Diego: Academic Press.

Rizzi, Luigi. 1990a. On the anaphor-agreement effect. *Rivista di Linguistica* 2, 27–42.

Rizzi, Luigi. 1990b. *Relativized Minimality*. Cambridge, MA: MIT Press.

Rizzi, Luigi. 1994. Some notes on linguistic theory and language development: The Case of root infinitives. *Language Acquisition* 4, 371–393.

Rizzi, Luigi. 1997. The fine structure of the left periphery. In Liliane Haegeman, ed., *Elements of Grammar*. Dordrecht: Kluwer.

Roberts, Ian. 1991. Head-government and the local nature of head-movement. Paper presented at GLOW 14, abstract in *GLOW Newsletter* 26, Foris.

Roelofsen, Floris. 2008. Anaphora Resolved. Doctoral dissertation. Institute for Logic, Language, and Computation, University of Amsterdam, The Netherlands.

Rögnvaldsson, Eiríkur. 1986. Some comments on reflexivization in Icelandic. In Lars Hellan and Kirsti Koch Christensen, eds., *Topics in Scandinavian Syntax*, 89–102. Dordrecht: Reidel.

Ross, John R. 1967. Constraints on Variables in Syntax. Doctoral dissertation, MIT.

Ross, John R. 1970. On declarative sentences. In Roderick A. Jacobs and Peter S. Rosenbaum, eds., *Readings in English Transformational Grammar*. Waltham, MA: Ginn.

Runner, Jeffrey T. 2005. The accusative plus infinitive construction in English. In Martin Everaert and Henk van Riemsdijk, eds., *The Blackwell Companion to Syntax*. Oxford: Blackwell.

Runner, Jeffrey T. 2007. Freeing possessed NPs from binding theory. In L. Wolter and J. Thorson, eds., *University of Rochester Working Papers in the Language Sciences, 3(1)*, 57–90. Rochester, NY: University of Rochester.

Runner, Jeffrey T., and Elsi Kaiser. 2005. Binding in picture noun phrases: Implications for binding theory. In Stefan Müller, ed., *Proceedings of the HPSG05 Conference*. Department of Informatics, University of Lisbon. Stanford, CA: CSLI Publications. http://csli-publications.stanford.edu/.

Runner, Jeffrey T., Rachel S. Sussman, and Michael K. Tanenhaus. 2002. Logophors in possessed picture noun phrases. In Line Mikkelsen and Chris Potts, eds., *WCCFL 21 Proceedings*, 401–414. Somerville, MA: Cascadilla Press.

Runner, Jeffrey T., Rachel S. Sussman, and Michael K. Tanenhaus. 2003. Assignment of reference to reflexives and pronouns in picture noun phrases: Evidence from eye movements. *Cognition* 89, B1–B13.

Saddy, Doug. 1987. On the notion maximal projection. In J. McDonough and B. Plunkett, eds., *NELS 16*, 539–550. Amherst: GLSA, University of Massachusetts.

Safir, Kenneth. 1992. Implied non-coreference and the pattern of anaphora. *Linguistics and Philosophy* 15, 1–52.

Safir, Kenneth. 1996. Derivation, representation, and resumption: The domain of weak crossover. *Linguistic Inquiry* 27, 313–339.

Safir, Kenneth. 1999. Vehicle change and reconstruction in A′-chains. *Linguistic Inquiry* 30, 587–620.

Safir, Kenneth. 2004a. *The Syntax of Anaphora*. Oxford: Oxford University Press.

Safir, Kenneth. 2004b. *The Syntax of (In)dependence*. Cambridge, MA: MIT Press.

Schadler, Dagmar. 2009. The anaphoric system in Swedish in comparison to Dutch and German. In Sobha Devi, António Branco, and Ruslan Mitkov, eds., *Proceedings of the 7th Discourse Anaphora and Anaphor Resolution Colloquium*, 73–81. Chennai: AU-KBC Research Centre.

Schladt, Mathias. 2000. The typology and grammaticalization of reflexives. In Zygmunt Frajzyngier and Traci Curl, eds., *Reflexives: Forms and Functions*, 125–153. Amsterdam: Benjamins.

Schlenker, Philippe. 1999. Propositional Attitudes and Indexicality: A Crosscategorial Approach. Doctoral dissertation, MIT.

Schlenker, Philippe. 2003. A plea for monsters. *Linguistics and Philosophy* 26, 29–120.

Schlenker, Philippe. 2005. Non-redundancy: Towards a semantic reinterpretation of binding theory. *Natural Language Semantics* 13(1), 1–92.

Schütze, Carson T. 1993. Towards a minimalist account of quirky case and licensing in Icelandic. In Colin Phillips, ed., *Papers on Case and Agreement* II, 321–375. Cambridge, MA: MITWPL, Department of Linguistics and Philosophy, MIT.

Schwarzschild, Roger. 2001. Review of "Flexible boolean semantics. Coordination, plurality and scope in natural language," by Yoad Winter. *Glot International* 5(4), 141–149.

Sells, Peter. 1987. Aspects of logophoricity. *Linguistic Inquiry* 18, 445–479.

Sevcenco, Anca. 2006. *Terms of Binding*. Doctoral dissertation. LOT International Dissertation Series. Utrecht: UiL OTS.

Shen, Yeshayahu. 1985. The Structure of Action in the Short Narrative Text. Doctoral dissertation, Tel Aviv University.

Sigurðsson, Halldór Ármann. 1989. Verbal Syntax and Case in Icelandic. Doctoral dissertation, University of Lund, Sweden.

Sigurðsson, Halldór Ármann. 1990. Long distance reflexives and moods in Icelandic. In Joan Maling and Annie Zaenen, eds., *Modern Icelandic Syntax*, 309–346. New York: Academic Press.

Sigurðsson, Halldór Ármann. 1992. The case of quirky subjects. *Working Papers in Scandinavian Syntax* 49, 1–26.

Sigurðsson, Halldór Ármann. 2004. The syntax of Person, Tense, and speech features. *Italian Journal of Linguistics/Rivista di Linguistica* 16(1), 219–251.

Sigurjónsdóttir, Sigríður. 1992. Binding in Icelandic: Evidence from Language Acquisition. Doctoral dissertation, University of California, Los Angeles.

Sigurjónsdóttir, Sigríður, and Nina Hyams. 1992. Reflexivization and logophoricity: Evidence from the acquisition of Icelandic. *Language Acquisition* 2, 359–413.

Siloni, Tal. 2002. Active lexicon. *Theoretical Linguistics* 28, 383–400.

Siloni, Tal. 2008. The syntax of reciprocal verbs: An overview. In Ekkehard König and Volker Gast, eds., *Reciprocals and Reflexives: Theoretical and Typological Explorations*, 451–499. Berlin: Mouton.

Slioussar, Natalia. 2007. *Grammar and Information Structure: A Study with Reference to Russian*. Utrecht: LOT International Dissertation Series.

Solà, Jaume. 1994. A uniform analysis for SELF elements. Ms., University of Groningen.

Spathas, Giorgos. 2010. *Focus on Anaphora*. Utrecht: LOT International Dissertation Series.

Sportiche, Dominique. 1988. A theory of floating quantifiers and its corollaries for constituent structure. *Linguistic Inquiry* 19, 425–449.

Sportiche, Dominique. 2001. Movement types and triggers. Paper presented at Tools in Linguistic Theory (TiLT), Utrecht 2001. Ms., Department of Linguistics, UCLA.

Stechow, Arnim von. 2003a. Feature deletion under semantic binding. In Shigeto Kawahara and Makoto Kadowaki, eds., *Proceedings of the Thirty-Third Annual Meeting of the North East Linguistic Society*. Amherst: GLSA, University of Massachusetts.

Stechow, Arnim von. 2003b. Postscript to feature deletion under semantic binding. Ms., Eberhard-Karls-Universität, Tübingen. http://www2.sfs.uni-tuebingen.de/~arnim10/Aufsaetze/vonstech.pdf.

Strahan, Tania E. 2006. Beer, doonas, books and blankets: Contrasting reflexives and pronouns in locative PPs in Australian English. ALS Online Proceedings. http://www.als.asn.au/proceedings/als2005/strahan-beer.pdf.

Szabolcsi, Anna. 1983. The possessor that ran away from home. *Linguistic Review* 3, 89–102.

Taraldsen, Tarald. 1995. On agreement and nominative objects in Icelandic. In Hubert Haider, Susan Olsen, and Sten Vikner, eds., *Studies in Comparative Germanic Syntax*, 307–327. Dordrecht: Kluwer.

Teomiro García, Ivan. 2005. Control and Syntactic Chains: The Timing of PRO. Master's thesis, University of Utrecht.

Thornton, Rosalind, and Kenneth Wexler. 1999. *Principle B, VP Ellipsis, and Interpretation in Child Grammar.* Cambridge, MA: MIT Press.

Thráinsson, Höskuldur. 1976a. Reflexives and subjunctives in Icelandic. In *NELS* 6, 225–239. Amherst: GLSA, University of Massachusetts.

Thráinsson, Höskuldur. 1976b. Some arguments against the interpretive theory of pronouns and reflexives. In Jorge Hankamer and Judith Aissen, eds., *Harvard Studies in Syntax and Semantics*, 573–624. Cambridge, MA: Harvard University.

Thráinsson, Höskuldur. 1979. *On Complementation in Icelandic.* New York: Garland.

Thráinsson, Höskuldur. 1990. A semantic reflexive in Icelandic. In Joan Maling and Annie Zaenen, eds., *Modern Icelandic Syntax*, 289–307. New York: Academic Press.

Thráinsson, Höskuldur. 1991. Long distance reflexives and the typology of NPs. In Jan Koster and Eric Reuland, eds., *Long-Distance Anaphora*, 49–75. Cambridge: Cambridge University Press.

Toldova, Svetlana. 1996. Materialy k voprosu o povedenii mestoimenija *wuž* v caxskom dialekte caxurskogo jazyka. Ms., Moscow.

Tomasello, Michael. 2003. *Constructing a Language.* Cambridge, MA: Harvard University Press.

Ullman, Michael. 2004. Contributions of brain memory circuits to language: The declarative/procedural model. *Cognition* 92, 231–270.

Vasić, Nada. 2006. *Pronoun Comprehension in Agrammatic Aphasia: The Structure and Use of Linguistic Knowledge.* Dissertation, Utrecht University. Utrecht: LOT International Dissertation Series.

Vasić, Nada, Sergey Avrutin, and Esther Ruigendijk. 2006. Interpretation of pronouns in VP ellipsis constructions in Dutch Broca's and Wernicke's aphasia. *Brain and Language* 6(2), 191–206.

Veraart, Fleur. 1996. On the Distribution of Dutch Reflexives. Master's thesis, MIT.

Vikner, Sten. 1984. Anaphors in Danish as Compared to English Seen from the Point of View of the Government-Binding Theory. Master's thesis, University of London.

Vikner, Sten. 1985. Parameters of binder and of binding category in Danish. *Working Papers in Scandinavian Syntax* 23. Trondheim: University of Trondheim.

Vinokurova, Nadezhda. 2005. *Lexical Categories and Argument Structure: A Study with Reference to Sakha*. Utrecht: LOT International Dissertation Series.

Walker, Marilyn, Aravind Joshi, and Ellen Prince, eds. 1998. *Centering Theory in Discourse*. Oxford: Clarendon Press.

Webelhuth, Gert, and Clare Dannenberg. 2006. Southern American personal datives: The theoretical significance of dialectal variation. *American Speech* 81(1), 31–55.

Weinreich, Uriel. 1971. *College Yiddish*. 5th ed. New York: YIVO Institute for Jewish Research.

Wexler, Kenneth. 2002. Lenneberg's dream: Learning, normal language development and specific language impairment. In J. Schaeffer and Y. Levy, eds., *Language Competence across Populations: Toward a Definition of Specific Language Impairment*. Mahwah, NJ: Erlbaum.

Wexler, Kenneth, and Yu-Chin Chien. 1985. The development of lexical anaphors and pronouns. In *Papers and Reports on Child Language Development* 24. Stanford, CA: Stanford University.

Wexler, Kenneth, and Peter Culicover. 1980. *Formal Principles of Language Acquisition*. Cambridge, MA: MIT Press.

Wexler, Kenneth, and Maria Rita Manzini. 1987. Parameters and learnability in binding theory. In Thomas Roeper and Edwin Williams, eds., *Parameter Setting*, 41–76. Dordrecht: Reidel.

Williams, Edwin. 1981. Argument structure and morphology. *Linguistic Review* 1, 81–114.

Williams, Edwin. 1982. The NP cycle. *Linguistic Inquiry* 13, 227–295.

Williams, Edwin. 1985. PRO and subject of NP. *Natural Language & Linguistic Theory* 3, 297–315.

Williams, Edwin. 1987. Implicit arguments, the binding theory and control. *Natural Language & Linguistic Theory* 5, 151–180.

Williams, Edwin. 1994. *Thematic Structure in Syntax*. Cambridge, MA: MIT Press.

Winter, Yoad. 2001. *Flexibility Principles in Boolean Semantics: The Interpretation of Coordination, Plurality, and Scope in Natural Language*. Cambridge, MA: MIT Press.

Winter, Yoad. 2001. Plural predication and the Strongest Meaning Hypothesis. *Journal of Semantics* 18, 333–365.

Woolford, Ellen. 1999. More on the anaphor agreement effect. *Linguistic Inquiry* 30, 257–287.

Yang, Dong-Wee. 1984. The extended binding theory of anaphors. *Theoretical Linguistic Research* 1, 195–218.

Zaenen, Annie, Joan Maling, and Höskuldur Thráinsson. 1985. Case and grammatical functions: The Icelandic passive. *Natural Language & Linguistic Theory* 3, 441–483.

Zribi-Hertz, Anne. 1989. A-type binding and narrative point of view. *Language* 65(4), 695–727.

Zribi-Hertz, Anne. 2008. From intensive to reflexive: The prosodic factor. In Ekkehard König and Volker Gast, eds., *Reciprocals and Reflexives: Cross-Linguistic and Theoretical Explorations*, 591–631. Berlin: Mouton de Gruyter.

Zurif, Edgar. 1978. Language and the brain. In Morris Halle, Joan Bresnan, and George Miller, eds., *Linguistic Theory and Psychological Reality*. Cambridge, MA: MIT Press.

Zwart, C. Jan-Wouter. 1993. Dutch Syntax: A Minimalist Approach. Doctoral dissertation, University of Groningen.

Zwart, C. Jan-Wouter. 1997. *Morphosyntax of Verb Movement*. Dordrecht: Kluwer.

Zwart, C. Jan-Wouter. 2002. Issues relating to a derivational theory of binding. In Samuel Epstein and Daniel Seely, eds., *Derivation and Explanation in the Minimalist Program*, 269–294. Malden, MA: Blackwell.

Zwarts, Joost. 1992. X′ Syntax–X′ Semantics: On the Interpretation of Lexical and Functional Heads. Doctoral dissertation, Utrecht University.

Author Index

Abels, Klaus, 186
Abney, Steven, 96, 98
Aikawa, Takako, 240, 368n1
Amiridze, Nino, 173, 205, 259, 262–264, 383n17
Anagnostopoulou, Elena, 120, 173, 228, 248, 259, 262–263, 265, 354n4
Anand, Pranav, 161
Anderson, Stephen, 52, 286, 314, 320, 388n36, 388nn38–39
Andrews, Avery, 203, 389n42
Arbib, Michael A., 25
Ariel, Mira, 26, 145
Aoun, Joseph, 349n31
Asudeh, Ash, 254, 355n13
Austin, Peter, 380n66
Avrutin, Sergey, 36, 129, 303, 349n34

Baauw, Sergio, 291, 353n59
Baddeley, Alan, 16
Badecker, William, 129
Baerman, Matthew, 139
Baker, Mark, 9, 159, 161, 224–226, 263, 298, 307–308
Barbiers, Sjef, 283
Barker, Chris, 349n32
Barnes, Michael, 287–288
Barss, Andrew, 93
Battistella, Ed, 297–298
Belletti, Adriana, 203
Bennis, Hans, 283
Benthem, Johan van, 192
Benveniste, Emile, 161, 163
Bergeton, Uffe, 191, 354n3, 369n5, 370n9, 374n28, 379n60

Bernódusson, H., 389n42
Bhattacharya, Tanmoy, 366n35
Bianchi, Valentina, 307–308
Boeckx, Cedric, 326, 331, 333–334, 361n5
Bonet, Eulàlia, 140
Borer, Hagit, 201, 371n13, 380n4, 387n22
Bouchard, Denis, 144
Brandt, Patrick, 385n12, 386n18
Brody, Michael, 46
Brown, Dunstan, 139
Büring, Daniel, 135
Burkhardt, Petra, 129, 282
Burzio, Luigi, 267

Cable, Seth, 160
Cantrall, William, 44, 351n48
Cardinaletti, Anna, 384n4
Chien, Yu-Chin, 28, 352n58
Chierchia, Gennaro, 28, 72, 79, 92, 189, 192, 356n17
Chomsky, Noam, 3–6, 8–9, 11–15, 17–20, 29, 38–43, 46, 55, 59–60, 69–71, 77, 80, 86, 93, 102–103, 131, 133, 138, 140–142, 146–150, 152, 156–157, 171–172, 174–175, 178, 184, 217, 224, 253, 259, 272, 290, 297–298, 303, 305, 307, 333–334, 338, 343, 345nn1–2, 346n12, 347n17, 349n31, 350n43, 351n44, 352n56, 353n2, 354n6, 354n11, 360n34, 360nn36–37, 361n5, 363n18, 363nn19–20, 367n39, 368nn44–45, 369n4, 388n31, 389n41

Christiansen, Morten, 347n15
Chung, Sandra, 380n67
Cinque, Guglielmo, 9, 276, 358n24, 372n20
Clements, G. N. (Nick), 48, 51–52, 91, 286, 315, 351n51, 351n54, 356n16
Cole, Peter, 233, 297–298, 351n54, 375n39
Comrie, Bernard, 9
Conroy, Stacey, 258, 382n10
Corbett, Greville, 139
Culicover, Peter, 5

Dahl, Östen, 134–135
Dalrymple, Mary, 211–212
Dannenberg, Clare, 382n10
Davies, William, 382n7
Deacon, Terrence, 25
Déchaine, Rose-Marie, 97, 358n25, 364n26
Delfitto, Denis, 92, 353n39
Dimitriadis, Alexis, 211, 348nn25–26, 349n35, 361n2, 362n9, 375n38, 377n54, 379n63
Dixon, R. M. W., 244
Dotlačil, Jakub, 211, 356n14
Dubinsky, Stanley, 382n7

Ellefson, Michelle R., 347n15
Enç Mürvet, 303
Engdahl, Elisabeth, 350n44
Epstein, Samuel, 71
Evans, Gareth, 28, 36
Everaert, Martin, 9, 47–49, 84, 107, 120, 173, 228, 248, 259, 261–263, 265, 275–276, 285–286, 291, 296–298, 300, 302, 354n4, 377n53, 385n6, 386n18, 388n37, 389n42

Faltz, Leonard, 9, 49, 85, 214, 228, 237, 238, 348n23
Farmer, Ann, 190
Fiengo, Robert, 28, 53–55, 86, 135, 141
Fiorin, Gaetano, 92, 129
Fischer, Silke, 391n6
Fitch, W. Tecumseh, 17, 29, 343

Fodor, Janet, 346n10
Fox, Danny, 135
Frampton, John, 55–56, 140, 143, 362n8
Frazier, Lyn, 346n10
Friederici, Angela, 127–128, 361n3

García, Teomiro, 387n30
Gast, Volker, 207, 213, 276–277, 374n29, 377n52
Geenhoven, Veerle van, 221
Gelderen, Elly van, 284, 348n21, 360n40
Giorgi, Alessandra, 385n13
Graf, Thomas, 366n37
Greenberg, Joseph, 19
Grewendorf, Günther, 386n19
Grimshaw, Jane, 110, 113, 255, 381n7
Grodzinsky, Yosef, 20, 28, 57–58, 60, 124, 346n9
Guéron, Jacqueline, 303
Gunkel, Lutz, 295, 386nn18–20
Gutmann, Sam, 56

Haas, Florian, 213, 276–277
Haegeman, Liliane, 307
Hagège, Claude, 50–51, 315
Halle, Morris, 201, 380n4
Hara, Takaaki, 36, 234, 240
Harley, Heidi, 140
Harnish, Robert, 190
Hauser, Marc D., 17, 29
Heim, Irene, 28, 35, 61, 135, 160, 213, 330, 343n29, 349n28, 352n59, 356n14
Heine, Bernd, 23, 347n21
Helke, Michael, 228, 351n47
Hellan, Lars, 48, 52, 84, 144, 285–286, 289–290, 388n37
Hermon, Gabriella, 297–298, 351n54
Hestvik, Arild, 111, 289, 297
Hicks, Glyn, 326, 336–337, 356n15, 368nn42–44
Higginbotham, James, 93, 215, 357n20
Hinzen, Wolfram, 348n24
Hoekstra, Jarich, 105, 115, 270–271
Hoekstra, Teun, 113
Hoop, Helen de, 224, 226

Hornstein, Norbert, 46, 77, 326–327, 331, 333–334, 361n5, 391n2
Huang, C.-T. James, 288, 297–298, 362n11
Huang, Yan, 42, 267
Hyams, Nina, 388n37

Jackendoff, Ray, 90, 109, 219, 233, 343, 346n11
Jacobson, Pauline, 34, 219–220, 346n45
Jaeger, T. Florian, 254
Jayaseelan, K. A., 49, 208, 215, 351n47
Johnson, David, 346n13
Johnson, Kyle, 252, 389n40
Jong, Jelly J. de, 70
Joseph, Brian, 265
Joshi, Aravind, 4

Kaan, Edith, 251
Kaiser, Elsi, 254
Kamp, Hans, 357n19
Kaplan, David, 356n17
Katz, Jerrold J., 361n1
Kayne, Richard, 30, 58, 75, 77, 79, 242, 251, 253, 258, 281, 326–332, 346n7, 353n2, 387n24
Keenan, Edward, 9, 28, 79, 189, 192, 210, 284
Keller, Frank, 254, 355n13
Keller, R. E., 48, 101, 283, 284
Khomitsevich, Olga, 303, 365n27
Kimball, John, 72
Kiss, Katalin E., 114
Kleene, Stephen C., 346n12
König, Ekkehard, 189, 192, 207, 374n29, 377n52, 378n59
Koopman, Hilda, 93, 281, 305, 349n30, 363n17
Koornneef, Arnout, 20, 129, 132, 343
Koring, Loes, 357n23
Koster, Jan, 112, 291, 296, 385n6
Kotz, Sonja, 127–128, 361n3
Kratzer, Angelika, 35, 160–161, 349n28
Kuhn, Thomas, 345n2
Kuno, Susumu, 44, 351n48

Landau, Idan, 46, 307, 387n30
Landman, Fred, 37
Lappin, Shalom, 346n13
Larson, Richard, 381n7
Lasnik, Howard, 86, 152, 213, 356n14
Lebeaux, David, 43, 297–298, 389n41
Leben, William, 186
Lecarme, Jacqueline, 303
Lee, Cher-Leng, 351n54
Lee, Felicia, 331
Lemmen, Hanneke, 199, 373n21
Lenneberg, Eric, 9
Levine, Robert, 346n13
Levinson, Stephen, 27, 190, 243–244, 380n67
Lidz, Jeffrey, 205
Liu, C.-S. Luther, 298
Longobardi, Giuseppe, 96, 98, 166–167, 274, 278, 313
Lust, Barbara, 240, 267, 357n23

Maling, Joan, 48, 52, 286, 315–318, 388n36, 389n42, 389n45
Manzini, Maria Rita, 179, 285, 296, 315, 320, 366n36, 389n40
Marantz, Alec, 10, 201, 203, 272, 371n13, 380n4
Marelj, Marijana, 192, 198, 200, 202, 279, 339, 372n17, 372n20, 373n22, 378n59
May, Robert, 28, 53–55, 86, 135, 141, 348n28, 356n14
McNally, Louise, 221
Menuzzi, Sergio, 70, 130, 160, 361n4
Meulen, Alice ter, 376n44
Mitkov, Ruslan, 4
Miyashita, Hiroyuki, 23, 347n21
Mortensen, David, 331
Moyse-Faurie, Claire, 23
Mukherjee, Aparna, 168
Mukkerji, N. S., 357n23
Muysken, Pieter, 232

Napoli, Donna-Jo, 278, 322
Neeleman, Ad, 357n21
Nevins, Andrew, 161
Nilsen, Øystein, 313, 356n14

Noguchi, Tohru, 348n33
Nunes, Jairo, 15, 326, 331, 333–334, 361n5

Panagiotidis, Phoevos, 97, 166
Papangeli, Dimitra, 192, 202, 210, 278
Partee, Barbara, 114, 376n44
Patnaik, M., 240
Pesetsky, David, 140, 142–143, 146, 148, 153–154, 176, 177, 272, 360n37, 362n6, 363n16, 372n17
Phillips, Colin, 346n10
Pica, Pierre, 228, 376n41
Pinker, Steven, 343
Pollard, Carl, 88, 91–92, 114
Postal, Paul, 44, 97, 252, 361n1
Postma, Gertjan, 164
Prince, Ellen, 4
Pritchett, Brad, 346n10

Rákosi, György, 383n15
Rayner, Keith, 346n10
Reinhart, Tanya, 20, 28, 30–31, 33, 37, 54–55, 57–58, 60–64, 67, 70–72, 79–85, 88, 90–92, 100–104, 107–108, 112, 115, 119, 124–127, 129, 132, 134–135, 141–142, 147, 170, 176, 189, 191–192, 194, 198–202, 204, 210, 213, 216, 243, 240, 247, 250–251, 254, 259–260, 265, 273, 277, 280, 297–298, 300, 321–322, 339, 348n28, 352n57, 354n1, 355n14, 357n18, 359n29, 360n32, 362n10, 363n15, 363n21, 367n38, 368n42, 370n7, 370n9, 372n19, 373n23, 374n31, 376n40, 376n48, 378n59, 380n4, 385n7, 385n12, 388n37, 391n3
Reis, Marga, 302, 386nn18–19
Reuland, Eric, 16, 20, 29, 36, 62–64, 71, 79–84, 88, 90–92, 100–104, 107–108, 112, 115, 125, 127, 131, 133, 146–148, 160–161, 163, 168–169, 176, 189, 191–192, 201, 216, 219–220, 233, 240–242, 247, 250–251, 254–255, 258–260, 265, 273,

278, 297–298, 300, 303, 322, 333, 335–336, 343, 345n2, 346n13, 347n15, 347n19, 349n34, 352n56, 354n1, 355n14, 359n29, 360n32, 362n10, 363n15, 363n19, 364n23, 365n28, 366n37, 367n39, 368nn41–42, 369n5, 370nn7–8, 373n22, 376n40, 378n59, 383n11, 385n7, 385n12, 388n35, 388n37, 390n46, 390n48, 390n1, 391n3
Rice, Mabel, 346n9
Richards, Norvin, 369n2
Riemsdijk, Henk van, 9, 93, 281, 368n41
Ritter, Elizabeth, 98, 140
Rizzi, Luigi, 9, 261, 298, 303, 307–308, 388n31
Roberts, Ian, 298
Roelofsen, Floris, 134–135
Rögnvaldsson, Eiríkur, 388n36
Ross, John R., 17, 351n48
Ruigendijk, Esther, 129
Runner, Jeffrey T., 252, 254–255, 355n13, 381nn7–8

Saddy, Doug, 277
Safir, Kenneth, 74, 79, 93, 135, 190–191, 219, 267, 326, 335–336, 346n7, 347n19, 350n36, 350n40, 354n7, 360n32, 361n2, 370n8, 373n22, 382n8, 384n1, 384n5
Sag, Ivan, 88, 91–92, 114
Schadler, Dagmar, 289, 385n11
Schladt, Mathias, 22–23, 208, 347n21
Schlenker, Philippe, 161, 365n27, 369n5
Schütze, Carson T., 374n24
Schwarzschild, Roger, 365n31
Sells, Peter, 52, 286, 315, 318, 351n52, 388n36
Sevcenco, Anca, 288
Shan, Chung-Chieh, 349n32
Shen, Yeshayahu, 193
Siemund, Peter, 189, 192, 207
Sigurjónsdóttir, Sigríður, 52, 169, 171, 287, 315, 317, 319–320, 368n46, 388n35, 388n36, 388n37, 390n48

Sigurðsson, Halldór Ármann, 52, 203, 307–308, 315–318, 368n46, 385n16, 388nn35–36, 389n42, 389nn44–46
Siloni, Tal, 67, 85, 142, 192, 198–202, 204, 210, 213, 243, 280, 339, 373n23, 378n59, 380n4
Slioussar, Natalia, 277
Solà, Jaume, 351n47
Spathas, Giorgos, 236, 264
Sportiche, Dominique, 93, 349n30, 358n24
Starke, Michal, 384n4
Stechow, Arnim von, 160
Strahan, Tania E., 354n6
Straub, Kathleen, 129
Subbarao, K. V., 240
Sung, Li-May, 297–298
Sussman, Rachel S., 254
Szabolcsi, Anna, 77, 363n17
Szendröi, Kriszta, 357n21

Tanenhaus, Michael K., 254
Tang, C.-C. Jane, 288, 297–298
Taraldsen, Tarald, 174
Thornton, Rosalind, 352n59
Thráinsson, Höskuldur, 48, 50, 52, 90, 144, 169, 286, 314–315, 319, 321–322, 374n24, 388nn36–37, 389n42
Toldova, Svetlana, 374n29
Tomasello, Michael, 27
Torrego, Esther, 140, 142–143, 146, 148, 154, 176, 177, 272, 360n37, 362n6, 363n16

Ullman, Michael, 16

Vasić, Nada, 20, 129
Veraart, Fleur, 191, 208–209, 354n3, 354n9, 359n31, 374n28, 374n31, 380n65
Vikner, Sten, 84, 289
Vinokurova, Nadezhda, 159, 192, 201–202, 210, 278, 380n4

Walker, Marilyn, 4
Wall, Robert, 376n44
Webelhuth, Gert, 382n10

Weinreich, Uriel, 295
Wexler, Kenneth, 5, 9, 28, 285, 296, 315, 320, 346n9, 352nn58–59, 389n40
Williams, Edwin, 93, 109–110, 113, 355n14, 359n30, 372n15
Wiltschko, Martina, 97, 358n25, 364n26
Winter, Yoad, 79, 211, 216, 219–220, 365n28, 365n31
Woolford, Ellen, 261

Yang, Dong-Wee, 389n40

Zaenen, Annie, 389n42
Zribi-Hertz, Anne, 88, 207, 241, 356n16, 370n9, 378n59, 379n61
Zurif, Edgar, 346n9
Zwart, C. Jan-Wouter, 251, 326, 330–331, 363n17
Zwarts, Joost, 216, 230

Subject Index

A-binding, 30–35, 37, 42, 46, 58, 60–62, 69, 72, 80, 209, 212, 338
A-bound, 45, 57, 124–126, 156
Accessibility, 26–27, 41, 145
  conditions, 145
  theory, 26
Accusative, 101, 103, 112, 203, 263, 279, 283–284, 312
  structural, 68, 177, 203–204, 256–257, 302 (see also Case structural)
  thematic, 203–204, 256 (see also Case thematic)
A-chain, 63, 101–104, 116, 150, 152
A-Chain, 152
A-CHAIN, 125, 156, 170
Adjunct, 21, 49, 62, 77–78, 80, 114, 330, 338
  island condition, 21
  PP, 218, 295
Adjunction, 77, 149, 157–158, 217–218, 224, 227, 230, 232, 235, 248, 301. See also Intersection; Pair-merge; Substitution
  head, 224–226
Against sneaking in, 126, 129–130. See also Minimize interpretive options
Agree, 12–13, 18, 25, 56, 66, 102, 115, 141–143, 146–147, 150, 154, 176–178, 180, 184, 245, 281, 334, 336–338
Agreement, 12–13, 25, 41, 52, 102–103, 106, 117, 127, 130, 142, 147, 156, 174, 184, 260–262, 264–265, 272, 302, 305, 307, 335
  specifier-head, 307

subject-verb, 13, 18, 41, 118, 141, 146–147, 156
tense-, 314–315
Ambiguity, 183, 265, 321, 330
  avoid, 3, 183
Anaphor, 2, 4–8, 22, 24, 38–46, 50–52, 59–60, 65, 67, 74, 79–81, 83, 87–94, 100–103, 105, 109, 111, 114, 120, 143–145, 148, 153, 155, 164, 167, 169, 170, 173, 175, 182, 190–191, 199, 202, 210–211, 214, 231, 233, 237, 239–241, 243, 245, 248, 260–266, 268, 273, 275, 281, 284–289, 293, 295–299, 301–302, 315–317, 319, 322, 331, 336, 345n3. See also Complex anaphor; Simplex anaphor
-agreement effect, 261–262
binding, 56, 74, 79, 183, 254, 303, 327, 331, 338
exempt, 63, 90–92, 94, 291, 293. See also Exempt position; Exemption
in subject/nominative position, 43, 173, 262
local, 115. See also Locality
long distance, 43, 48, 285–286, 295, 315–316. See also Long-distance binding
pronominal/pronoun and, 3, 21–22, 24, 35, 37–38, 40, 42–43, 48, 54, 58, 81, 97, 100–101, 112, 130, 132, 145, 160, 182–183, 209, 267, 279, 285, 330
subject/nominative, 68, 174, 259–262, 264, 266, 327, 341

Anaphora, 66, 81, 108–109, 115, 202, 203, 219, 240, 242–243, 295, 314, 325, 327
donkey, 35
resolution, 4, 27
Anaphoric dependencies, 19, 27–28, 52, 68, 102, 239, 267, 298, 325, 335, 337–338
encoding of, 14, 49, 54, 60, 65, 137, 325, 326
Anaphoric relations, 27–28, 39, 225, 321, 343
Anaphoric system, 47, 49, 83, 120, 202, 240, 247, 266–268, 289, 326, 328
Antecedent, 3, 5–7, 28–29, 33–35, 38, 40–44, 47–48, 50–52, 54, 56, 64–67, 72, 81, 83, 90–93, 95, 102, 108–109, 112, 131–132, 135, 137–139, 144, 146, 148, 152–155, 161–162, 169–170, 177–178, 211–212, 220, 222, 236–237, 239, 245, 254, 261, 263–264, 269, 285–289, 291, 293, 296, 298, 301, 304, 306–307, 314–322, 329–331, 339
discourse, 91, 322
local, 5, 67, 262, 286, 311, 334
long distance, 311, 314–316, 318, 321–322. See also Long-distance binding
plural, 39, 104, 138, 164, 233
quantificational, 28–29, 38, 244, 330
split, 37, 239
A-position, 15, 32–33, 38, 102, 152
A′-position, 15, 32–33
Argument structure, 67, 110, 159, 189, 195–196, 202, 209, 214, 223, 225–226, 231, 255, 286
operation on, 25, 66–67, 85, 189, 192, 198, 201–202, 205, 210, 214, 238, 339, 342, 378
Arity, 188, 195, 206, 227, 238, 337, 339
operation, 195, 198, 200–201, 278, 306. See also Argument structure
Assignment function, 35–36
Asymmetry, 72, 80, 108, 132, 153, 208, 219, 250–251, 265–266, 310

Attraction, 46–47, 148, 153, 217, 234–235
Australian, 243
Avoid Pronoun Principle, 259

Bangla, 168–169
Barrier, 63, 102–103, 115, 117
minimality, 103, 117–118, 298
-style, 102, 298
Barriers framework/system, 115, 117, 176, 285
Basque, 49, 232
Binding. See A-binding; logical syntax binding; variable binding
Binding conditions, 6–7, 19, 22, 40, 69, 81, 88, 90, 107–108, 111, 114–115, 124, 141, 181–182, 185, 249
Body-part (BP), 23, 49, 85, 185, 189, 207, 228, 230–234, 236, 340
noun, 7, 24, 230, 232. See also Inalienable Possession
reflexive, 35, 67, 184–185, 228, 232–233. See also Complex anaphor
Bound variable, 56–57, 72, 90, 124, 126, 129, 145, 166, 169, 173. See also Rule VB; Variable binding
Brazilian Portuguese, 130–131, 269
Brute-force reflexivization, 185–186, 189, 339. See also Locally bound pronoun
Bundling, 196–197, 199, 200, 205, 211, 214, 238, 242–244, 247, 278, 284, 334, 337, 339. See also θ-system

Canonical binding theory (CBT), 3, 6–8, 19, 20, 22, 24–25, 35, 38, 42–50, 53–56, 59–61, 63, 69, 74, 79, 81, 88–89, 91, 96, 101, 120, 176, 178, 183, 214, 239, 254, 263, 285–286, 296, 341
problems for, 8, 48, 50, 88
puzzling for, 7, 74, 79
Case
-checking, 25, 88, 118–119, 127, 142, 149, 155, 203–204, 252–253, 258, 272, 280, 281, 302–303
residue, 199, 203–204, 211, 214, 334

structural, 63–64, 103–105, 116, 118–
119, 134, 146–147, 173, 176, 178–
179, 202, 204, 244, 253, 256, 268,
270–273, 279–280, 284, 293, 302,
312, 323. *See also* Accusative
system, 14, 64, 70, 104, 116, 120, 138,
242, 268, 272–273, 277, 280, 283–
284, 341
thematic, 203–204, 256, 280, 312–
313
Category, 12, 17, 29, 39, 70, 77, 79,
150–151, 153–155, 159–160, 162,
234, 257
feature, 24, 150, 163–164, 166
Causative, 7, 291–292, 294, 296–297,
300, 326
Causativization, 197
Caxur, 207–208, 236, 244, 342
CBT. *See* Canonical binding theory
C-command, 29, 32–33, 40–41, 52–54,
60–63, 66, 70–71, 74, 76–77, 90, 93,
102, 115, 151–152, 154, 175–176,
178, 216, 226, 230, 245, 249–251,
264, 285, 287, 297, 301, 303, 307,
314–321, 329, 338. *See also*
Sisterhood
exception to, 75
requirement, 29, 58–59, 61, 63, 71,
74, 80, 117, 245, 317
Chain (lower case), 15, 63–65, 78, 81,
99, 102–104, 107–109, 115–121,
123–125, 130–134, 137–138, 140,
147, 151–156, 158–159, 161–162,
189, 173, 179, 184–186, 222, 236,
238–239, 247, 256, 259–260, 262,
264–265, 269, 272, 275, 279–280,
282–283, 285, 290–291, 296, 298,
201, 304–305, 307–311, 334, 341
condition, 63–64, 102–108, 115–116,
118–120, 123, 131, 134, 140, 173,
175–176, 182, 191, 214, 249, 255,
258–260, 264–265, 269–270, 279–
280, 290, 325
feature, 25, 123, 154, 177, 303, 338–
339
formation, 65, 71, 100, 102, 106,
115–116, 121, 123, 128, 132–134,
137–138, 154, 159, 162–167, 169,

175–176, 179, 183–184, 238–239,
259, 261, 269, 272, 273, 279, 281,
283–284, 290, 296, 301, 303, 304,
309, 322–323, 338, 341
link, 117, 119, 134, 270, 310
linking, 152, 169
movement, 103, 118, 187, 332
syntactic, 63–65, 115, 128, 160–161,
169, 186, 239, 338
Chain (upper case), 151–152, 154–155
CHAIN, 125, 128, 152–156, 158, 169–
172
formation, 156, 169–170, 172
linking, 170
Check(ing), 18, 65, 137, 141–158, 172.
See also Agree; Case-checking;
Checking relation; Feature sharing
Checking-chain. *See* Chain (upper
case)
Checking relation, 147–148, 305
Chinese, 7, 43, 52, 183, 262, 289, 298
C-I (conceptual-intentional) interface,
11–12, 14, 56, 61, 64, 69–70, 125,
127, 138, 141, 146, 148, 153, 182,
186–188, 207, 209, 217, 261, 264,
310, 325, 333
Cognitive system, 4, 5, 9, 14, 17, 18,
60, 342
human, 4, 11
Coindexed, 39–41, 53–54, 62, 82, 87,
89–91, 94, 102–103, 106, 109–114,
116–117, 251, 263, 297, 315, 317
Coindexing, 39–41, 53–55, 64, 102,
104, 115–117, 298, 329, 335
Collective reading, 30, 234
Combinatory system, 202
Comparing derivations/Competition,
58, 119–120, 130–131, 133–134,
259, 273, 335–336, 342
Complement, 70, 78, 85, 90, 97, 101,
108, 114, 147, 155, 166, 178, 181,
209, 253–254, 257–258, 265, 280–
281, 287–288, 291, 294–297, 299,
300–301, 305, 307, 310–312, 315,
319–320, 322, 326
NP, 97, 111, 274, 276
position, 187, 203–204
PP, 241, 280–282, 295

Complementarity, 171, 290, 307, 309–310
lack/absence of, 43–44, 89, 90, 282
no/non-, 43, 130, 279, 281–283, 305
Complementary distribution, 6, 94, 167–168
Complex anaphor, 7–8, 22, 24, 32, 35, 46–47, 49, 83, 85, 134, 183, 184, 205, 229, 234, 241–242, 260, 262–264, 281–282, 285–287, 289, 325–326, 334
Complex reflexive, 49, 188, 207, 228, 233, 236. See also Complex anaphor
Compositional, 69, 72
Computational system, 10, 12–13, 19–21, 30, 35, 53, 60, 67, 123, 126–127, 141, 144, 153, 181, 183, 186–188, 193, 226, 240, 325, 333
of human language (CHL). 11, 21, 55, 186, 284. See also Narrow syntax
Conceptual system, 5, 11, 13, 193, 202
Condition A (CBT), 6, 22, 41, 44–45, 58, 81, 87–88
Condition A (Reflexivity), 21, 62, 67, 82–83, 87–91, 93, 107–108, 110–112, 115, 121, 144, 183–184, 214–215, 245, 249–250, 285–286, 314, 341
Condition B (CBT), 6, 8, 19–22, 41, 44–45, 48, 57, 86
Condition B (Reflexivity), 57, 62, 67, 81–83, 85–90, 94, 96, 100–101, 105–114, 121, 123–124, 160, 176, 183, 184, 186, 190, 245, 249, 257, 263, 269, 284, 290, 327, 330, 336
Condition C, 6–7, 32, 264
Conflation, 140
Control, 45, 86, 110, 113, 203, 287, 299, 307–310, 331
Cooperation, 26, 127
Cooperative strategy, 130
Copy, 15, 16, 32–33, 42–43, 55–56, 79, 94, 123, 141, 143, 149, 151, 153, 171, 176, 178, 187, 217, 326, 332, 338

-based approach, 55
and Merge, 141, 332
theory of movement, 302
Coreference, 23, 25–30, 34–35, 37, 44, 56–59, 90, 124–127, 132, 145, 160, 169, 201–202, 243–244, 321–322, 327–331. See also Covaluation
accidental, 54, 58
intended, 53
intrasentential, 57, 124, 126
Covaluation, 35, 53, 124, 243. See also Coreference
Covert movement, 43, 68, 78, 147, 170, 174, 226, 289
V-to-T, 149, 156–157
Creole, 23, 232, 240
Crosslinguistic variation, 9, 13, 37, 59, 68, 111, 120, 167, 182–183, 188, 198, 232, 248, 262, 267, 283, 323, 326, 330–331, 334–335, 341–342
C-system, 262, 307–308, 310
C-T system, 307

Dahl's puzzle, 135
Danish, 8, 47, 84, 289
Dative, 258, 270–273, 279, 284
Definiteness, 65, 166–169
Delayed condition B effect, 58
Deletion, up to recoverability, 148. See also Principle of recoverability of deletion
Dependency. See Anaphoric dependencies, Interpretative dependencies
Derivation, canceled, 130–132, 172, 174, 272, 281, 306, 309, 338
D-feature, 159, 163–164, 172
Directional PP, 85, 101, 111, 113, 279, 311
Direct object, 14–15, 48, 101, 185, 196, 251, 273, 283, 291, 294, 302, 311, 314
Discourse, 16, 26–27, 35, 51, 58, 61, 64, 91–92, 110, 112, 115, 124–125, 127–128, 144, 217, 262, 286, 315–317, 325, 329, 338, 341, 343
antecedent, 92, 322

factors, 52, 112, 144–145, 171, 315–
316, 318, 320, 322
principles of interpretation, 81
referent, 26–28, 59
storage, 56, 128
Disjoint reference, 86
presumption (DRP), 190
Dislocation, 21, 32, 35, 45, 55, 70,
102
property, 14
Distributed morphology (DM), 201,
333
Distributive
operator, 227, 328
reading, 30, 227, 234
Distributivity, 186, 232–233, 238
Division of labor, 30, 58, 60–61, 112,
129, 202, 343
Double object constructions, 208
Double of the pronoun, 207, 330
Doubling, 23, 185, 208, 236–237, 327–
328, 342
Downstairs predicate, 89, 108, 249–
250, 314. See also Embedded
predicate
Dutch, 7–8, 22, 24, 39–40, 47–49, 62,
64–65, 70, 77, 81, 83, 85, 94–95, 97,
100–101, 104–107, 109, 114, 120,
130, 134, 136, 139–140, 149, 161,
164, 167–168, 176, 183, 185, 186–
187, 190–191, 198–199, 201, 203–
206, 208, 211, 214, 219–220, 222–
224, 233, 238, 240–243, 245, 247–
248, 251, 257–258, 262–263, 268–
283, 285, 287, 290–291, 293–297,
299–300, 302, 306–307, 310–311,
313–314, 326, 329, 334–336, 342

ECM, 63, 87, 89, 100–101, 176, 179,
190, 203, 252, 254, 257, 266, 269,
292, 294
subject, 68–69, 105–106, 108, 251–
253, 256, 265–266, 269, 272
Economy, 20, 60, 64–67, 73–74, 78,
115, 119, 123, 125–126, 129–134,
136, 145, 158, 170, 179, 181, 223,
226–227, 231, 235, 237, 245, 269,

272, 277, 283, 308–310, 333, 335–
338, 340–341, 343
absolute, 132, 134, 338. See also
Rejection is final
encoding of, 64, 125
hierarchy, 61, 64, 131–132, 325
metric, 126–128
principles, 25, 28, 61, 64, 93, 115,
126, 136, 145, 156, 182, 342
rationales for, 126–127, 136
Elided phrase, 134–135. See also VP-
ellipsis
Embedded clause, 52, 300, 312
Embedded predicate, 107–109, 249
Emphasis, 49. See also Focus
Encoded, syntactically, 56, 66, 71, 119,
125, 166, 170, 178, 247, 303, 308,
311, 327
Encoding of anaphoric dependencies,
14, 49, 60, 65, 137, 325–326
Enforce/Enforcing dependency, 67,
151, 236, 308
English, 2, 3, 7–9, 13, 22, 25, 35, 41,
44, 46, 48, 50, 52, 68, 81, 84–85, 94,
97, 101, 105–106, 108, 127, 129,
134, 136, 138, 141, 145, 153, 160,
167, 171, 179, 183, 188, 195, 198–
200, 202, 204, 211, 215–216, 219,
220, 222–223, 233, 244–245, 247–
248, 255–260, 262–263, 265–266,
268–269, 278–279, 281, 283–286,
288–289, 291, 293, 295, 322, 326,
330, 332, 335–336, 340, 342
EPP feature, 155, 157, 174, 177, 255
E-role, 250, 254–255. See also Event
role
Eventhood, 250, 253
Event role, 113. See also E-role
Evolution of language/language
evolution, 17, 25, 29, 343
Ewe, 51–52
Exceptional Case Marking. See ECM
Exempt anaphor. See Anaphor exempt
Exemption, 46, 81–82, 89, 91, 94–95,
144–145, 191, 215, 234, 250, 293
Exempt position, 92–94, 218, 221, 223,
227, 295

Exhaustively delete, 152, 155
Expletive, 174, 178, 196, 199, 255

Faroese, 47, 48, 268, 287–290, 326
FDT. *See* Feature determinacy thesis
Feature
  attracting, 147, 235, 300
  binary, 44, 193
  bundle, 56, 138, 153, 178
  category. *See* Category feature
  cluster, 140, 193–195
  composition, 8, 22, 24, 38–39, 104,
    120, 163, 173, 180–183, 247–248,
    259, 263, 265
  content, 58, 65, 98, 156
  content, intrinsic, 46, 182
  deficiency, 65, 97, 119, 236–237
  deficient, 64–65, 95, 98, 123, 265
  determinacy thesis (FDT), 22, 24, 60,
    104, 143
  formal, 147, 150–151, 153, 155–158,
    163, 170
  mismatch, 50, 62, 89, 172, 174, 184,
    236, 306–308, 310
  movement, 147, 157, 171, 334
  φ, 6, 22, 24, 32, 35–37, 39, 56, 63–64,
    72, 95, 97–98, 104, 116, 118–120,
    123, 125, 130–131, 137–138, 144,
    147, 150, 152–154, 156, 158, 173–
    175, 177–178, 259–260, 263, 265–
    266, 297–299, 302, 307–309, 322,
    338, 341, 343
  sharing, 64, 117–119, 123, 177, 236
Fijian/Fiji, 7, 244
Focalization, 92, 208–209, 236, 293
Focus, 34, 50, 191, 207–208, 218, 237,
  248
Free variable, 31, 76
French, 8, 47, 70, 111, 120, 168, 200–
  201, 208, 211, 223, 226, 241–242,
  244, 270, 278, 280–282, 284
Frisian, 8, 14, 19, 48, 63–64, 70, 81,
  83–85, 100–101, 104–106, 116, 119–
  120, 134, 164, 175–176, 185–186,
  188, 203–204, 211, 238, 240, 242–
  244, 256, 267–273, 280–281, 283–
  284, 291, 295, 323, 326, 334–335

Full Interpretation, 188, 207, 261
Full specification for φ-features, 116,
  144, 153, 173, 259, 297
Functional system, 11, 13–14, 66, 103,
  167, 182, 342–343

Gender, 6–7, 12, 24, 39–40, 47, 64, 83,
  97, 139–140, 147, 153–154, 162–
  163, 172, 176, 182, 185, 270, 290,
  293
Georgian, 7, 173–174, 183, 205–206,
  232, 259, 260, 262–264
German, 7–8, 48–49, 68, 70, 98, 101,
  120, 164, 167–168, 201, 211, 213,
  224, 236, 238, 240, 268, 271, 273–
  281, 283–284, 290–291, 293, 295–
  297, 300, 302, 304, 310, 313–314,
  323, 326, 334, 342
Germanic, 7, 46–49, 68, 70, 97, 99,
  121, 139, 162, 171, 183, 202, 245,
  267–268, 273, 280, 283, 285–286,
  289, 295, 297, 300, 323, 326
Goal, 118, 175–177, 179, 272, 281. *See
  also* Probe-goal relationship
Governing category, 40–42, 45, 48, 91,
  93, 96, 285, 296, 298, 315
Government, 70, 102–103, 117, 176
Grammar, independent property of,
  49, 58
Grammatical features, 6, 38, 146–147,
  163. *See also* Features formal
Grammaticalization, 225
Greek, 98, 167, 173–174, 201–202,
  205, 248, 259–260, 262–264, 278
Grooming verb, 198, 204, 256, 286
Guugu Yimithirr, 243

Head
  movement, 217–218, 223, 226, 231,
    235, 298, 304, 315, 322, 340–341
  movement constraint, 21, 157, 216,
    218
  position, 103, 107, 248, 265, 274–275,
    297
Hebrew, 49, 200, 202–204, 211, 213
Hindi, 168–169
Hmong, 331, 333–335

Icelandic, 8, 24, 40, 43, 47–48, 50, 52,
    65, 68, 81, 95, 97, 99, 144, 149, 164,
    166–167, 170, 173, 176, 179, 183,
    203–205, 259–262, 268, 285–291,
    293, 314–316, 318, 320–323, 326,
    341. *See also* Long distance binding;
    Logophor
Identical Antecedent Requirement,
    331
Identicals, problems handling, 66–67.
    See also IDI
Identity, 13, 39, 56, 141–143, 150–151,
    154, 159, 162, 175, 178, 180, 184,
    191, 199, 208, 220, 226, 321, 325,
    327, 338
function, 220
relation, 141
syntactic, 143, 175, 180
IDI. *See* Inability to distinguish
    indistinguishables
Impoverishment, 140
Inability to distinguish indistinguish-
    ables (IDI), 67–68, 186–189, 200,
    207, 214, 217, 223, 240, 242, 244–
    245, 257, 282, 337, 339, 341
Inalienable possession, 39, 224, 228,
    231
–based model, 228
Inclusiveness, 55, 69, 70, 81, 146, 330
Incorporation, 221, 224, 230, 238,
    263–264. *See also* Head movement
Index, 39, 41, 43, 53–56, 60, 62, 69,
    81–82, 86, 101, 103, 110, 113, 117–
    118, 140–141, 146, 175–176, 179,
    194, 263, 268, 298–299, 335, 338
-free, 65, 121, 137, 140, 182, 184, 247,
    325
set, 86
Indexing, 39, 42–43, 92, 141, 143
Indirect object, 279, 287, 292, 294,
    302
Indirect reflexive, 50–51. *See also*
    Exempt anaphor, Logophor
Indistinguishable interpretation, 57,
    124, 126, 135. *See also* Rule I
Inference system, 5, 30–31, 34, 58, 86,
    94, 96, 193

Infinitival, 52, 253, 286, 300, 305–306,
    309, 311, 316
Inflection, 41, 117, 142, 149, 157, 174,
    203, 305
Inflectional system, 118–119, 272, 289
Inherent case, 119, 272–273, 280, 323.
    See also Quirky case
Inherently relational, 216, 340
Instance, 143, 151, 154, 228. *See also*
    Occurrence
Intensification, 208, 218
Intensifier, 49, 85, 189–192, 207–208,
    227
Interface representation, 125, 156
Intermediate position, 93, 98, 157,
    327–328
Internal argument, 89, 109, 112–113,
    195–196, 199, 203–204, 208, 211–
    212, 223, 236, 252
Internal merge, 43, 102, 141, 143, 250,
    340
Internal structure, 73, 94, 156, 167,
    182, 247, 263, 323
Interpretability, 142, 144, 160, 217,
    299
Interpretation by intersection, 224–
    225
Interpretation procedure, composi-
    tional, 61, 69, 72, 76, 80
Interpretative dependencies, 25, 28, 30,
    34–35, 38, 66, 71, 138, 146, 155,
    159, 184, 212, 235, 303, 322
Interpretive component, 55, 141, 260
Interpretive merge (IM), 72
Intersection, 159, 217, 224–226, 231–
    232
Intervening head, 103, 117–118, 298.
    See also Head movement constraint
Intervening subject, 288, 306
Intrasentential Coreference, 57, 124,
    126. *See also* Rule I
Invariance. *See* Sources of invariance
Inverse linking, 75, 77–78
Irish, 49–50
Italian, 45, 47, 70, 167–169, 201, 211,
    223, 278, 322
i-within-i condition, 41

Japanese, 7, 183, 234, 240, 262, 289, 342
Jiwarli, 243–244

Kannada, 205, 240
Keep the arguments distinct, 189, 206. *See also* Protection

λ-operator, 31, 62, 81
λ-predicate, 31, 58, 62, 72, 209–210, 212, 338
Language design, 29, 284, 343
Language faculty, 9, 284, 333
Last resort, 14, 166, 170, 333
Latin, 50, 168
Left periphery, 55, 99, 167, 236, 303, 307
Lexical
bundling, 200. *See also* Bundling
entry, 11, 192–193, 195, 197, 201
grid, 110. *See also* θ-grid
item, 17–18, 35, 37, 55, 64, 88, 99, 133, 147, 151, 156, 178, 196, 243, 248
reflexivization, 85, 192, 195, 198, 200, 211. *See also* Reflexivization
semantics–based scenario, 225
Lexically reflexive, 63, 82, 84, 100, 105, 189, 249, 269, 286, 312, 340
Lexicon, 11–13, 15, 60, 62, 66–67, 71, 88, 98, 110, 113, 145, 195, 197–201, 211, 213, 238, 269, 333, 337, 343
active, 194
interface guideline, 198
language, 269, 278, 284. *See also* Lexicon-syntax parameter; θ-system
uniformity hypothesis, 195
Lexicon-syntax parameter, 198, 213, 269. *See also* Theta-System
LF. *See* Logical Form
License/Licensing reflexive predicate, 23, 52, 185, 263, 325
Licensing reflexivity, 23, 67, 82, 84, 108, 115, 121, 184, 188–189, 191, 205, 215, 236, 240, 242, 247–248, 251, 263, 274, 278, 314, 338–339. *See also* Reflexive licenser

Linear Correspondence Axiom (LCA), 332
Local binding of 3rd person pronominals, 8, 14, 65, 84, 90, 100, 116, 268, 290, 323. *See also* Locally bound pronominal/pronoun
Local domain, 6, 8, 40, 59, 93, 254, 285, 291
Locality, 20, 40, 70, 117, 135, 141, 143, 151–152, 154, 175, 182, 206, 216, 218, 328, 341
conditions, 6, 17, 20, 40, 58, 69–70, 135, 173, 183, 259
Locally bound pronominal/pronoun, 8, 48, 84, 106, 123, 134, 164, 238–239, 242, 258, 284, 311, 323
Locative PP, 43, 85, 101, 111–113, 130, 269, 271, 273, 275, 279, 282, 311
Logical form (LF), 55, 103, 171, 213, 217, 298, 315
Logical syntax, 31, 34, 37, 58, 60–61, 64, 70, 81–82, 86, 96, 115, 119, 125, 127, 131, 133, 156, 182, 206–208, 210–211, 213, 226, 232, 236, 238, 242, 264, 338, 343
Logical syntax binding, 31, 69, 210, 213
Logophor, 51–52, 90, 94, 169, 260, 283, 289–290
Logophoric, 91, 112, 114, 145, 164, 174, 217, 260, 262, 286–287, 295–296, 314, 326, 336
interpretation, 65, 144–145, 169–172, 174, 182–183, 263–265, 268, 282, 286–287, 291, 293, 316, 322–323, 341
pronoun, 51–52, 315
sig, 171, 260, 262, 316
use, 90–91, 144–145, 169–171, 183, 295
Logophoricity, 68, 90–92, 94, 144–145, 268, 285–286, 288–289, 296, 314–315
Long-distance anaphora, 48, 295, 315–316. *See also* Logophor
Long-distance binding, 52, 286–287, 290–291, 293, 295–296, 302, 307, 311, 314, 323, 341

into infinitival clauses, 52, 286–287, 291, 293, 311, 314–315
Long distance *sig*, 52, 287, 291, 293, 314–318, 320–321

Macrolevel, 21, 95, 181
Macrouniversal, 19, 21, 181–183, 341
Madame Tussaud's context, 233. *See also* Proxy reading; Statue reading
Malayalam, 49, 52, 67, 207–208, 215, 233, 244
Marking procedures, 194, 196
Masking, 38, 68, 240–242
Match, 141
Matrix predicate, 105–107, 249–250
Maximal chain, 63, 103, 116, 173, 259
Merge, 12–18, 69–71, 80, 141, 224. *See also* Internal Merge; Interpretive Merge, Pair merge, Set merge
Microstructure, 10, 131, 260, 264, 343
Middles, 200, 202, 277–278
Minimalist program (MP), 8, 10, 12, 55, 60, 69, 115, 118, 141, 147, 157, 223, 326
Minimality barrier, 103, 117–118, 298
Minimize interpretive options, 126
Minimize unresolved dependencies, 132, 338
Modular approach, 24, 55, 66, 81, 182, 333, 337–338
Morph, 205–208, 235. *See also* Protection
Morphosyntactic, 55, 61, 70, 82, 85, 103, 115, 139, 170, 178, 205, 214, 223, 237, 260, 265, 268, 274
feature, 22, 25, 59–60, 118, 131, 143, 330

Narrow syntax, 11, 35, 61, 64, 115, 125, 127, 131, 210, 238, 260, 303, 333
Natural language, 3, 5, 9–10, 14, 17–19, 23–24, 26, 73, 128, 181, 183–185, 189, 219, 224, 334
expression, 13, 27, 30, 55
Nominalization, 198, 200–201

Nominative, 103, 139, 173–174, 177–178, 259–260, 263, 265, 302
Norwegian, 8, 47, 97, 167, 179, 183, 204, 211, 262, 285, 289–291, 293, 299, 304, 307, 313–314, 323, 326
N-position, 97, 276
N-predicate, 109–110, 113, 234
N-to-D movement, 97, 166, 313
Number, 6–7, 12, 24, 39–41, 47, 64–65, 83, 97–99, 104, 137, 139, 140, 142, 147, 150, 153–155, 161–166, 172, 174, 176, 179, 182, 185, 238, 288
Numeration, 133, 147, 151, 154, 159, 161, 165, 172, 256, 280, 332–333, 336–337

Occurrence, 141–143, 148, 150–151, 156, 160–161, 164–165, 172, 179, 186–188, 206, 210, 263
Oceanic, 23, 240
Old English, 8, 239, 284
Opacity factor, 283, 296
Open expression, closure of, 57, 127, 170. *See also* λ-operator
Operation on argument structure, 25, 66–67, 85, 189, 192, 198, 201, 202, 205, 210, 213–214, 238, 243, 278, 339
Overt V-to-T, 149, 156, 158
Overwritten/Overwriting, 64, 123, 142–143, 148, 150, 153–154, 164, 166, 175, 325, 338–339
OV-VO contrast, 300, 307, 311

Pair-merge, 224. *See also* Adjunction
Parsimonious system, 59, 184
Parsimony, 10, 12, 22, 26, 30, 34, 55, 60, 201
Parsing, 127–128
Peranakan Javanese, 67, 233
Person, 6–7, 12, 24, 39–41, 64, 99, 140, 142, 147, 150–151, 153–154, 160–163, 166, 172, 176, 182, 185, 236, 238, 288, 307–308
1st, 47, 65, 90, 130, 161, 163–164, 172, 256, 310, 318

Person (*cont.*)
  2nd, 8, 40, 44, 47, 65, 68, 94, 97–98,
    120–121, 137, 139, 160–161, 163–
    164, 175, 179, 183, 204, 255, –256,
    258, 266–268, 283, 286, 289–291,
    293, 326, 330, 334–335, 339–340
  3rd, 8, 14, 19, 40, 47–48, 64–66, 83,
    84, 90, 94, 97–98, 100, 116, 120,
    123–124, 130–131, 134, 137–139,
    142, 144, 150–151, 158, 161–166,
    172, 179, 183, 267–268, 270, 273,
    283, 286–287, 289–290, 293, 308–
    309, 310, 323, 326, 335, 338–339
φ-feature. *See* Feature
φ-feature deficient, 64, 95, 98, 123,
  265. *See also* Underspecified for
  φ-features; Feature
Phonetic form (PF), 11–14, 126, 129,
  171, 187, 248, 332–333
Picture noun/NP, 44, 89, 93, 110, 218,
  235, 254, 266, 291, 311, 340
Pied piping, 156, 158, 171, 299
Plural antecedent, 39, 104, 139, 164,
  233
Plurality, 162–163, 165
Point of view, 51–52, 145, 315–320
Possessive anaphor, 47, 65, 166–168,
  173, 287, 289, 327
P-predicate, 109–111
Pragmatic, 3, 20, 27, 52, 75, 129, 189,
  190, 241–242, 264, 276, 292, 294,
  313
PRD. *See* Principle of recoverability
  of deletion
Predicate (P)
  reflexive, 23, 52, 62, 83–84, 86, 90,
    94, 105–106, 108, 110, 113–114,
    185, 239, 242, 257, 263, 286, 326,
    339
  semantic, 62, 82–83, 89, 95, 110,
    114
  syntactic, 62, 82–83, 85, 89–91, 93–
    94, 95–96, 111, 114, 120, 227, 234–
    235, 247, 250–255, 257, 266
  three-place, 87, 110
  two-place, 113, 186–187, 192, 203,
    211–212
Preposition stranding, 241, 280–281

Principle of recoverability of deletion
  (PRD), 65–66, 123, 130, 132–134,
  137, 142–143, 148, 150–151, 153–
  154, 158, 160–162, 166, 172–173,
  179, 180, 259, 269, 281, 283, 307,
  334, 339
Probe, 118, 175, 177–178, 245, 272,
  281
Probe-goal relationships, 115–116,
  118, 176, 245, 298
Processing resources, 58, 127, 282
Pronominal, 3–8, 22, 24–25, 27–28,
  32, 36–47, 58–59, 64, 66, 70–71, 79,
  84, 90, 101, 104–105, 120, 132, 153,
  161, 166, 172, 186, 219, 237, 239,
  244, 247, 281–282, 310, 313, 323,
  329–335, 337, 346n4. *See also*
  Anaphor and pronominal/pronoun;
  Locally bound pronominal/
  pronoun; Pronoun
Pronoun, 3, 8, 22, 24, 35–38, 56, 58,
  88–89, 97, 102, 108, 111, 127, 138,
  146, 158, 162, 169, 185–187, 207,
  215–220, 227, 257, 268, 272, 313,
  321, 328–335, 346n4. *See also*
  Anaphor and pronominal/pronoun;
  Locally bound pronominal/
  pronoun; Logophoric pronoun;
  Pronominal
Proper names, 38, 98, 138, 333–335
Protecting a variable, 189, 206
Protection, 66–68, 223, 232, 236, 238,
  247, 337, 339
Proxies, 66, 207, 219–222, 224, 231–
  232
Proxy, to stand, 207–208, 231, 235–
  237, 264, 339–340
Proxy reading, 199, 219, 222

Quantificational antecedents, 28–29,
  38, 244, 330
Quantifier raising (QR), 74, 76, 78
Quirky Case, 203, 261

Reanalysis, 242, 280–281
Reciprocal, 211–213, 237–240, 243,
  266, 277–278
Reciprocalization, 213, 238, 243

Reciprocity, 23, 211–214
Reconstruction, 42, 76, 93–94, 156
Recursion, 17, 29
Reduction, internal role, 195–196, 203–204, 211
Referential independence, 84, 103, 166, 237
Referentially defective, 39, 144
Reflexive, 38, 44, 62, 79–82, 89, 164, 178, 198, 200–201, 205, 210, 214, 219, 228, 237–238, 323, 336, 346n6. *See also* Lexically reflexive; Predicate reflexive; Reflexivity
  clitic, 47, 84, 183, 185, 200, 211
  marked, 62, 82–83, 86, 89, 91, 94, 107, 109, 114, 214, 218, 249–250
  marker, 62, 83, 85, 87, 91, 99, 109, 218, 226, 228, 268, 314
  marking, 62, 82, 87–89, 92, 95, 108, 111–112, 114, 121, 184, 189, 194, 202, 215–216, 226–227, 247, 249–250, 252–253, 266, 338, 340
  licenser, 206, 214–215, 222–223
Reflexivity
  enforce/enforcing, 82, 215, 223, 251, 266, 337–339. *See also* Reflexive-marked; Reflexive marking
  licensing, 108, 189, 215, 236, 242, 248, 251, 266, 274, 339. *See also* Reflexive licenser
Reflexivization, 68, 79–80, 85, 88, 134, 185, 189, 192, 195, 198, 200–201, 203, 207–208, 211, 218, 228, 233–235, 243, 252, 278, 339
Reflexivizing function, 82, 237
Rejection is final, 131–132, 136, 337–338, 341
Relational noun, 99, 219–221, 225, 230
Relation R, 118, 125, 145, 152, 156
Relativized minimality, 298
Remerging, 56, 141
Reportive context, 51, 65, 151, 161, 164, 166, 172, 179, 287–288, 315, 334
Residual Case, 199, 205, 211, 238
R-expression, 5, 6, 32, 38–41, 44–45, 64, 97, 103, 346n5
Role-changing operations, 197

Romance, 47, 70, 98, 121, 130, 160, 170, 183, 198, 200, 213, 340
Rule BV, 125, 132, 134, 156, 169
Rule H, 135
Rule I, 57–58, 60, 119, 124–127, 132, 134, 169
Rule L, 145, 170, 282, 290, 308–309, 311
Rule S, 135
Russian, 8, 40, 84, 141, 166–167, 190, 198, 205, 208, 214, 226, 343

Sakha, 7, 183, 190, 201–202, 205, 238, 278
San Lucas Quiavini Zapotec (SLQZ), 331, 333–335
Saturation, 195–197
Scandinavian, 7, 47, 68, 81, 98, 198, 247, 268, 281–282, 289, 295, 297, 300–302, 306, 310, 323, 326, 334
  mainlaind, 48, 289, 326
SE
  anaphor, 7–8, 47, 65–66, 68, 83–85, 88, 95–101, 105–107, 116, 120, 123, 132, 134, 137–140, 144–146, 152–153, 161, 164, 166, 169, 171, 173–174, 176–178, 182–183, 186, 189–191, 236, 239, 245, 247, 255, 260–262, 264–265, 268, 270–275, 277, 280–281, 286–289. *See also* Simplex anaphor
  as subject/in nominative, 173–174
SELF
  anaphor, 46–49, 62, 68, 82, 84–85, 87–92, 94, 96, 99–100, 107–108, 110–111, 120, 137, 144, 182, 184–185, 189, 191, 204, 215, 217, 218, 233–234, 247–252, 256, 258, 260, 266, 269, 274, 277, 279, 283, 291, 293, 312, 325–326, 328, 330–332, 338, 340. *See also* Complex anaphor
  individual's, 207, 216
  marking, 62, 68, 86, 108, 121, 184, 195, 225, 250, 253, 269, 340. *See also* Reflexive marking
Semantic argument, 105–106, 113
Semantic predicate. *See* Predicate semantic

Semantic role, 15, 40, 45, 142, 216. *See also* θ-role

Serbo-Croatian, 200–201, 211, 213, 278

Set merge, 80, 224

Simplex anaphor, 7–8, 22–24, 46, 49, 64–65, 83, 183, 262, 264, 283, 285, 287, 295

Simplex reflexive, 22, 190. *See also* Simplex anaphor

Sisterhood, 58, 72

Skolem function, 219–222, 231

Slavic, 40, 97–98, 167, 183, 198, 295

Sloppy reading, 34, 56, 125, 129, 136, 321. *See also* VP-ellipsis

Small clause, 112–113

Source position, 15, 32, 42, 103, 167, 176

Sources of Invariance, 6, 19–20, 60, 67, 181. *See also* Crosslinguistic variation

type 1, 20–21, 67, 181, 185, 245, 339

type 2, 20–21, 67, 181, 245, 340

type 3, 20–21, 181, 340

Spanish, 70, 168

Specified Subject Condition, 40, 184, 287

Split antecedent. *See* Antecedent split

Statue reading, 233, 238. *See also* Proxy reading

Stress, theory of phrasal, 276

Strict reading, 34, 56, 125, 129, 136, 321. *See also* VP-ellipsis

Subject anaphor, 68, 260–262, 264, 266, 327, 341

Subject experiencer verb, 190, 278

Subject-to-object raising, 252

Subjunctive, 52, 99, 144, 170–171, 262, 268, 286–287, 289–290, 296, 314–322. *See also* Logophor

Substitution, 224

Swedish, 47, 167, 268, 289

Syncretism, 139–140, 271, 273

Syntactically encoded, 56, 66, 71, 119, 125, 166, 170, 178, 247, 308, 311, 327

Syntactic argument, 62, 82, 88–90, 92, 106, 234, 249–250, 252, 254–255, 260, 265

Syntactic islands, 69, 330

Syntactic predicate. *See* Predicate syntactic

Syntactic residue of binding, 58, 70, 141, 143, 146, 182, 325

Syntax language, 278, 293. *See also* Lexicon-syntax parameter; θ-system

T-feature, 177

Thematic hierarchy, 114

Theta-role. *See* θ-role

Theta system (TS). *See* θ-system

θ-criterion, 186–187

θ-grid, 189, 198

θ-role, 76, 82–83, 88–91, 101, 109, 113, 186–187, 193, 196–198, 203–204, 206, 208, 211–212, 234, 238, 280, 327–328, 338–339

θ-system, 192–195, 198, 201, 205, 277, 340

T-system, 147, 153, 156–157, 203, 257, 290, 307–308

Underspecified for φ-features, 47, 104, 138, 297, 322. *See also* φ-feature deficient

Unification, 133, 154, 161–162

Uniformity, 13–14, 149, 151–152, 154, 195

Uninterpretable, 123, 142, 147–148, 150, 158, 174, 177, 260, 261, 263, 272–273, 308

Universal, 19–24, 59, 171, 181, 171, 337–343. *See also* Macrouniversal

Unvalued, 118, 137, 140, 154, 157, 176–177, 179, 308, 336

Variable binding, 28, 34, 54, 55, 69, 71, 74, 79, 119, 124, 127–128, 132, 134, 160, 169, 174, 196, 311, 321, 327, 329–330, 338

Variable, bound, 56–57, 72, 90, 124–126, 129, 145, 156, 166, 169, 173

Variable-free semantics, 34, 219

Verb. *See also* Predicate
  agent-theme, 190, 199
  admire/hate/love type, 84, 191, 199,
    243
  grooming. *See* Grooming verb
  perception, 291, 294, 296–297, 300,
    310, 326
  shame type, 84, 100
  wash type, 84, 100
VP-ellipsis, 34, 56, 125, 130, 135. *See
  also* Sloppy reading; Strict reading
V-to-T, 149, 156–158

Working memory, 127
Workspace, 13, 20, 71

Yiddish, 295

Z function, 221. *See also* Variable-free
  semantics

Linguistic Inquiry Monographs

Samuel Jay Keyser, general editor

1. *Word Formation in Generative Grammar*, Mark Aronoff
2. *X̄ Syntax: A Study of Phrase Structure*, Ray Jackendoff
3. *Recent Transformational Studies in European Languages*, Samuel Jay Keyser, editor
4. *Studies in Abstract Phonology*, Edmund Gussmann
5. *An Encyclopedia of AUX: A Study of Cross-Linguistic Equivalence*, Susan Steele
6. *Some Concepts and Consequences of the Theory of Government and Binding*, Noam Chomsky
7. *The Syntax of Words*, Elisabeth O. Selkirk
8. *Syllable Structure and Stress in Spanish: A Nonlinear Analysis*, James W. Harris
9. *CV Phonology: A Generative Theory of the Syllable*, George N. Clements and Samuel Jay Keyser
10. *On the Nature of Grammatical Relations*, Alec P. Marantz
11. *A Grammar of Anaphora*, Joseph Aoun
12. *Logical Form: Its Structure and Derivation*, Robert May
13. *Barriers*, Noam Chomsky
14. *On the Definition of Word*, Anna-Maria Di Sciullo and Edwin Williams
15. *Japanese Tone Structure*, Janet Pierrehumbert and Mary E. Beckman
16. *Relativized Minimality*, Luigi Rizzi
17. *Types of Ā-Dependencies*, Guglielmo Cinque
18. *Argument Structure*, Jane Grimshaw
19. *Locality: A Theory and Some of Its Empirical Consequences*, Maria Rita Manzini
20. *Indefinites*, Molly Diesing
21. *Syntax of Scope*, Joseph Aoun and Yen-hui Audrey Li
22. *Morphology by Itself: Stems and Inflectional Classes*, Mark Aronoff
23. *Thematic Structure in Syntax*, Edwin Williams
24. *Indices and Identity*, Robert Fiengo and Robert May
25. *The Antisymmetry of Syntax*, Richard S. Kayne
26. *Unaccusativity: At the Syntax–Lexical Semantics Interface*, Beth Levin and Malka Rappaport Hovav
27. *Lexico-Logical Form: A Radically Minimalist Theory*, Michael Brody
28. *The Architecture of the Language Faculty*, Ray Jackendoff
29. *Local Economy*, Chris Collins
30. *Surface Structure and Interpretation*, Mark Steedman

31. *Elementary Operations and Optimal Derivations*, Hisatsugu Kitahara

32. *The Syntax of Nonfinite Complementation: An Economy Approach*, Željko Bošković

33. *Prosody, Focus, and Word Order*, Maria Luisa Zubizarreta

34. *The Dependencies of Objects*, Esther Torrego

35. *Economy and Semantic Interpretation*, Danny Fox

36. *What Counts: Focus and Quantification*, Elena Herburger

37. *Phrasal Movement and Its Kin*, David Pesetsky

38. *Dynamic Antisymmetry*, Andrea Moro

39. *Prolegomenon to a Theory of Argument Structure*, Ken Hale and Samuel Jay Keyser

40. *Essays on the Representational and Derivational Nature of Grammar: The Diversity of* Wh-*Constructions*, Joseph Aoun and Yen-hui Audrey Li

41. *Japanese Morphophonemics: Markedness and Word Structure*, Junko Ito and Armin Mester

42. *Restriction and Saturation*, Sandra Chung and William A. Ladusaw

43. *Linearization of Chains and Sideward Movement*, Jairo Nunes

44. *The Syntax of (In)dependence*, Ken Safir

45. *Interface Strategies: Optimal and Costly Computations*, Tanya Reinhart

46. *Asymmetry in Morphology*, Anna Maria Di Sciullo

47. *Relators and Linkers: The Syntax of Predication, Predicate Inversion, and Copulas*, Marcel den Dikken

48. *On the Syntactic Composition of Manner and Motion*, Maria Luisa Zubizarreta and Eunjeong Oh

49. *Introducing Arguments*, Liina Pylkkänen

50. *Where Does Binding Theory Apply?*, David Lebeaux

51. *Locality in Minimalist Syntax*, Thomas S. Stroik

52. *Distributed Reduplication*, John Frampton

53. *The Locative Syntax of Experiencers*, Idan Landau

54. *Why Agree? Why Move?: Unifying Agreement-Based and Discourse-Configurational Languages*, Shigeru Miyagawa

55. *Locality in Vowel Harmony*, Andrew Nevins

56. *Uttering Trees*, Norvin Richards

57. *The Syntax of Adjectives*, Guglielmo Cinque

58. *Arguments as Relations*, John Bowers

59. *Agreement and Head Movement*, Ian Roberts

60. *Localism versus Globalism in Morphology and Phonology*, David Embick

61. *Edge-Based Clausal Syntax*, Paul M. Postal

62. *Provocative Syntax*, Phil Branigan

63. *Anaphora and Language Design*, Eric Reuland